Everything Irish

Ireland

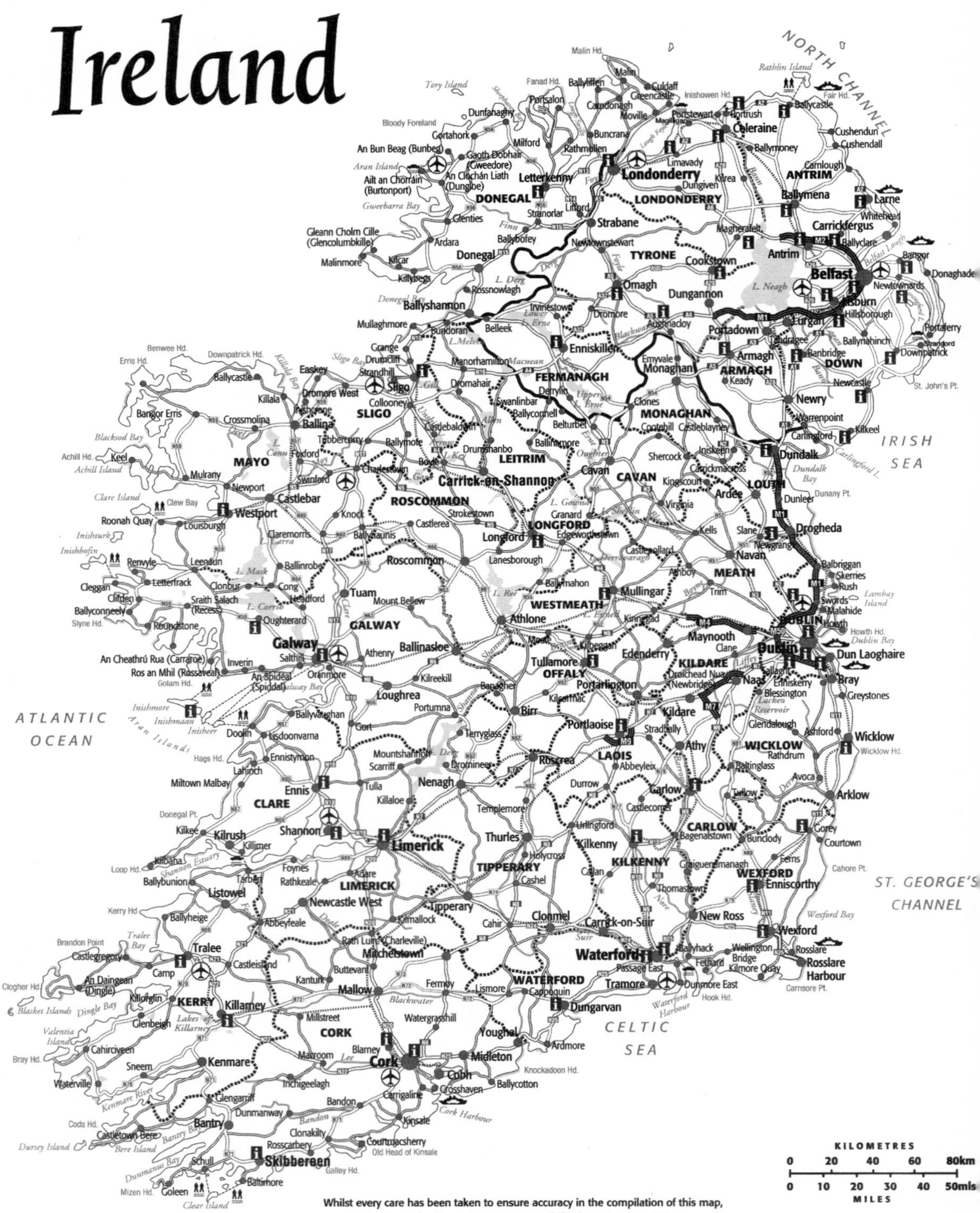

Whilst every care has been taken to ensure accuracy in the compilation of this map, Tourism Ireland cannot accept responsibility for errors or omissions

Everything Irish

The History, Literature, Art, Music, People and Places of Ireland from A–Z

edited by

Lelia Ruckenstein and James A. O'Malley

Mercier Press
Douglas Village, Cork
www.mercierpress.ie

Trade enquiries to
Columba Mercier Distribution,
55a Spruce Avenue, Stillorgan Industrial Park, Blackrock, Co. Dublin

First published in 2003 by Ballantine Books, USA

1 85635 449 0

10 9 8 7 6 5 4 3 2 1
A CIP record for this book is available from the British Library

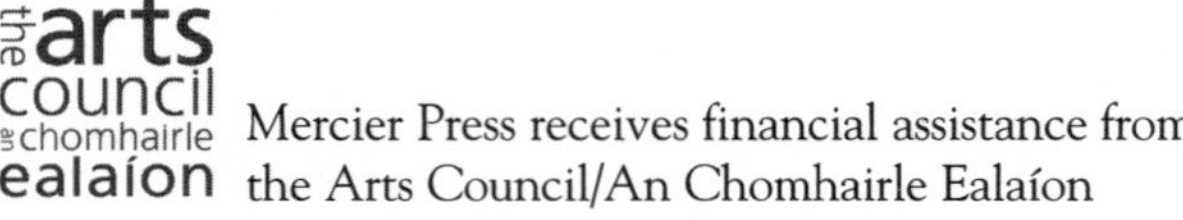

Mercier Press receives financial assistance from the Arts Council/An Chomhairle Ealaíon

Printed in Ireland by ColourBooks Ltd.

General Editorial Advisor
Lawrence J. McCaffrey

Editorial Consultant for Literature
José Lanters

Contributors

John Allen (J.A.) Deputy music critic for the *Irish Times*; lecturer, broadcaster and writer on opera

Linda D. Almeida (L.D.A.) Adjunct Professor, New York University

Bernadette Andreosso (B.A.) Head of the Economics Department, University of Limerick

Stephen Andrew Ball (S.A.B.) Archivist at the National Library of Ireland, Manuscripts Department

Frank Biletz (F.B.) Lecturer in History, Loyola University of Chicago

Sighle Breathnach-Lynch (S.B-L.) Curator of Irish paintings, National Gallery of Ireland, Dublin

Terence Brown (T.B.) Professor of Literature, Trinity College, Dublin

Robert Burns (R.B.) Professor of History, Emeritus, University of Notre Dame

Michael P. Cahill (M.P.C.) Ph.D., University of Chicago; Adjunct Professor, University of St Mary of the Lake, Illinois

Tony Canavan (T.C.) Co-founder of *History Ireland*; Parliamentary Reporter at Oireachtas Éireann (the Irish Parliament)

Tony Clayton-Lea (T.C.-L.) Writer on popular music

Caitriona Clear (C.C.) Lecturer in History, National University of Ireland, Galway

Eileen Connolly (E.C.) Lecturer in Politics, Dublin City University

Mary Cosgrove (M.C.) Lecturer in Art History, Queens University, Belfast

Thomas Oliver Coughlan (T.O.C.) Solicitor and Lecturer at National University of Ireland, Cork

John Cronin (J.C.) Researcher in history and civilisation, European University Institute in Florence

Troy D. Davis (T.D.) Assistant Professor of History, Stephen F. Austin State University, Texas

Ciaran Deane (C.D.) Editor and author of *The Guinness Book of Irish Facts & Feats*

Breandán Delap (B.D.) Editor of the Irish language magazine, *Foinse*

Michael Dervan (M.D.)-classical music critic for the *Irish Times*

Paul Dillon (P.D.) Ph.D. History, National University of Ireland, Dublin

Donal A. Dineen (D.A.D.) Dean, Kemmy Business School, University of Limerick

John Doyle (J.D.) Director of the Centre for International Studies, Dublin City University

Ryan Dye (R.D.) Assistant Professor of History, St Ambrose University, Davenport, Iowa

Patrick J. Egan (P.E.) Head of the History Department, Riversdale Community College, Dublin

Co-Contributors
Patricia M. Deane (P.M.D.), Science Department, Riversdale Community College
Marie T. Denny (M.T.D.), History Department, Riversdale Community College
Patrick Nulty (P.N.), History Department, Riversdale Community College
Toyah O'Connell (T.OCon.), History Department, Riversdale Community College

Michael Ellison (M.E.) Journalist for the *Guardian*

Tyler Farrell (T.F.) Lecturer in English, University of Wisconsin, Milwaukee

Thomas Gilbert (T.G.) Writer

Dermot Gilleece (D.G.) Sports writer for the *Irish Times*

Brian Griffin (B.G.) Professor of History, Bath Spa University College, UK

Thomas E. Hachey (T.E.H.) Executive director of the Center for Irish Studies, Boston College

Peter Harbison (P.H.) Archaeologist, writer; former editor of *Ireland of the Welcomes*

Cheryl Herr (C.H.) Professor of English, University of Iowa

Patrick Hicks (P.J.H.) Assistant Professor of English, Augustana College, Sioux Falls, South Dakota

John Horgan (J.H.) Professor of Journalism, Dublin City University

Nainsí Houston (N.H.) Assistant Professor of English, Irish Studies Program, Creighton University, Omaha, Nebraska

Elmer Kennedy-Andrews (E.K-A.) Head of the English Department, University of Ulster at Coleraine

Andrew Kincaid (A.K.) Assistant Professor of English, University of Wisconsin, Milwaukee

José Lanters (J.C.E.L.) Professor of English, Co-Director, Center for Celtic Studies, University of Wisconsin, Milwaukee

Pádraig Lenihan (P.L.) Lecturer in History, University of Limerick

Colm Lennon (C.L.) Senior Lecturer in History, St Patrick's College, Maynooth

James Liddy (J.L.) Poet and Professor of English, University of Wisconsin, Milwaukee

Hugh Linehan (H.L.) Entertainment editor, the *Irish Times*

Michael Liston (M.L.) Chairman of the Department of Logic, University of Wisconsin, Milwaukee

Ailfrid MacLochlainn (A.ML.) Former Director of the National Library in Dublin and the National University of Ireland, Galway Libraries

P. J. Mathews (P.J.M.) Lecturer in English, St Patrick's College (DCU), Dublin

Alan Matthews (A.M.) Head of the Economics Department, Trinity College, Dublin

Lawrence W. McBride (L.MB.) Professor of History, Illinois State University

Lawrence McCaffrey (L.J.MC.) Professor of History, Emeritus, Loyola University of Chicago

John P. McCarthy (J.P.MC.) Professor of History and Director, Institute of Irish Studies at Fordham University, New York

Jim McDonnell (J.McD.) Professor of English, Carleton College, Northfield, Minnesota

Joe McDowell (J.MD.) Assistant Professor of English, Augustana College, Rock Island, Illinois

Kathleen McInerney (K.MI.) Assistant Professor of English, Chicago State University

Eileen McMahon (E.McM.) Assistant Professor of History, Lewis University, Romeoville, Illinois

Elizabeth S. Meloy (E.S.M.) Ph.D. Candidate in History Department, Brown University

Seán Moran (S.M.) Sports writer for the *Irish Times*

Eileen Morgan (E.M.) Assistant Professor of English, State University of New York–Oneonta

Marc E. Mullholland (M.M.) Lecturer in History, St Catherine's College, Oxford University

John A. Murphy (J.A.M.) Professor of History, Emeritus, National University of Ireland, Cork

Shakir M. Mustafa (S.M.M.) Assistant Professor of English, Boston University

George O'Brien (G.OB.) Professor of English, Georgetown University

Brian O'Connor (B.OC.) Sports writer for the *Irish Times*

Thomas H. O'Connor (T.H.OC.) University Historian, Boston College

Ruan O'Donnell (R.OD.) Lecturer in History, University of Limerick

Nollaig Ó Gadhra (N.ÓG.) Journalist, historian and writer

Daithi Ó hOgain (D.Oh.) Head of the Department of Irish Folklore, National University of Ireland, Dublin

James A. O'Malley (J.OM.) Writer, editor

Fionan Ó Muircheartaigh (F.OM.) Chief economic advisor of Enterprise Ireland

Gearóid Ó Tuathaigh (G.OT.) Professor of History, National University of Ireland, Galway

Jim Patterson (J.P.) Assistant Professor of History, Centenary College, New Jersey

Jody Allen Randolph (J.AR.) Poetry critic

Lelia Ruckenstein (L.R.) Writer, editor

Michael Seaver (M.S.) Director of Kinetic Reflex Dance publishing house; dance critic for the *Irish Times*

Andrew Shields (A.S.) Tutor in History, University of New South Wales, Australia

Frank Shouldice (F.S.) Writer; journalist for the *Irish Voice* and RTÉ

David Sprouls (D.S.) Director of Admissions, New York School of Interior Design

Mary S. Thompson (M.S.T.) Lecturer in English, St Patrick's College (DCU), Dublin

Alan Titley (A.T.) Head of the Irish Department, St Patrick's College (DCU), Dublin

Paul A. Townend (P.A.T.) Assistant Professor of British and Irish History, University of North Carolina at Wilmington

Gearóidín Uí Laighléis (G.U.L.) Lecturer in Irish, St Patrick's College (DCU), Dublin

Fintan Vallely (F.V.) Lecturer in traditional Irish music, Dundalk Institute of Technology, County Louth; editor of *The Companion to Irish Traditional Music*

Gordon M. Weiner (G.M.W.) Professor of History and Jewish Studies, Emeritus, Arizona State University

Kevin Whelan (K.W.) Director of Notre Dame Centre of Irish Studies, Dublin

Timothy White (T.W.) Professor of Political Science, Xavier University, Cincinnati

Sabine Wichert (S.W.) Senior Lecturer in History, Queens University, Belfast

Everything Irish

Glossary and terms

Dáil Éireann – Irish parliament

INLA – Irish National Liberation Army

IRA – Irish Republican Army

MP – member of parliament

Oireachtas – legislature

Príomh-Aire – chief minister

RIC – Royal Irish Constabulary

RUC – Royal Ulster Constabulary

Seanad Éireann – senate

Tánaiste – deputy prime minister

Taoiseach – prime minister

TD – *Teachta Dála* – member of parliament

UDA – Ulster Defence Association

UDR – Ulster Defence Regiment

UVF – Ulster Volunteer Force

A

Abbey Theatre, the. Ireland's national theatre. Considered one of the most prestigious theatre companies in the world, the Abbey is one of the important institutions to emerge from the *Irish Revival of the late nineteenth century. In 1899, Lady *Gregory, W. B. *Yeats and others created the Irish Literary Theatre, which became known as the Abbey Theatre in 1904. As a writers' theatre, its main objective was to encourage the staging of Irish plays for Irish audiences at a time when *theatre in Ireland was dominated by the offerings of British touring companies. The Abbey also aimed to uphold the highest artistic principles and to provide an alternative to the melodrama and vaudeville of the commercial theatres. Early on, the movement produced a crop of talented playwrights, including Yeats, Lady Gregory, J. M. *Synge and Seán *O'Casey, whose contribution to world drama has been widely acknowledged. The Abbey's initial success was considerably enhanced by the acting talents of Frank and Willie *Fay. Some of the early productions became embroiled in the politics of the day, causing disturbances in the theatre. Most notoriously, J. M. Synge's *Playboy of the Western* World (1907) and Seán O'Casey's *The Plough and the Stars* (1926) caused riots because of their iconoclastic attacks on idealised cultural nationalism. Destroyed by fire in 1951, the theatre was redeveloped to include a smaller auditorium (the *Peacock) and reopened in 1966. Although criticised for its conservatism at times, the Abbey continues to be the most important institution in Irish theatre. In 1990, the Abbey triumphed with a production of Brian *Friel's *Dancing at Lughnasa*, which toured to great acclaim in London and New York. The best of contemporary playwrights continue to work at the Abbey, including Marina *Carr, Conor *McPherson and Eugene O'Brien. P.J.M.

Adams, Gerry (1948–). Politician, president of *Sinn Féin (1983–present), Member of Parliament for West *Belfast. Gerry Adams was born on 6 October 1948, into a working-class *republican family in West Belfast. Educated in local *Catholic schools, Adams joined the republican movement in 1964. When Sinn Féin split in 1969/70, he sided with the Provisional wing and became active in the *Northern Ireland Civil Rights Association (NICRA) campaign. By early 1970, he was suspected of playing a leading role in the Ballymurphy unit of the Provisional *IRA in Belfast. He is credited with devising the 'economic targets' bombing campaign. In 1972, Adams was interned without trial, but briefly released to participate in secret peace talks with the British government. The talks failed, but Adams reputedly became adjutant for Belfast and important in the 'middle leadership' of the IRA. He was interned again in 1973–76 and 1978 and was officially charged with membership in the IRA but was never convicted.

As a northern leadership of the IRA emerged in the late 1970s, Adams pressed for its political wing, Sinn Féin, to be more involved in electoral politics in *Northern Ireland. He consolidated his leadership role as Sinn Féin vice president during the republican prisoners' *hunger strikes of 1981 and in 1983 he became president of Sinn Féin.

A member of the United Kingdom parliament since 1983 (except for 1992–97 when

Gerry Adams

*SDLP (Social Democratic and Labour Party) representative Dr Joe Hendron defeated him), Adams has refused to take his seat at Westminster in keeping with party policy.

Following talks with SDLP leader John *Hume (started in 1988) and overtures to the British and Irish governments, Adams helped to secure an IRA cease-fire in August 1994, which lasted until February 1996. In September 1997, after the declaration of a second IRA cease-fire in July of that year, Adams and his negotiating team joined multi-party talks to end the conflict. The resulting Belfast (or *Good Friday) Agreement, April 1998, fell well short of republican objectives, but Adams hoped it could be used as a base for further negotiations and campaigned vigorously for its acceptance. In May 1998, 95% of the people in the *Republic and 71% of those in Northern Ireland accepted the agreement. In June 1998, Adams won a seat in the new Northern Ireland assembly. He led Sinn Féin to an electoral peak of 21.7% in the Westminster election in the summer of 2001, narrowly overtaking the SDLP as Northern Ireland's largest *nationalist party. In the autumn of 2001, he helped to secure an IRA decommissioning of part of its arsenal and, early in 2002, spoke openly of the need to secure the consent of a majority of the people of Northern Ireland for a united Ireland. Although he has largely been successful in unifying the republican movement behind the *peace process, Adams has not been able to prevent splits in the IRA, though they have been limited in significance. His immediate ambition, it seems, is to make Sinn Féin the largest nationalist party in Northern Ireland and a more significant force in the Republic, as well. M.M.

Aer Lingus. Ireland's national airline. In April 1936, Aer Lingus Teoranta, which comprised one six-seat aircraft, was registered as a private airline by the Irish government. Having provided the vital *Dublin to Liverpool air link during the Second World War, Aer Lingus greatly expanded its fleet and services over the next two decades. Routes to numerous British and European cities were opened between 1945 and 1960 and services from Dublin and Shannon to *New York, *Boston and *Chicago were inaugurated between 1958 and 1966. In 2000, Aer Lingus operated a fleet of 38 aircraft carrying close to seven million passengers and made a profit of €79.9 million. As a consequence of the events of 11 September 2001, the airline lost 50 million dollars in 2001. Aer Lingus adapted to the worldwide fall in demand for air travel by restructuring and reducing its workforce by one-third. S.A.B.

agriculture. Ireland's *economy has traditionally been based on agriculture. Sixty-four percent of the land of Ireland (17 million acres) is used for agriculture, with forestry accounting for a further 9.4% in 2001. Ireland's maritime climate, with high rainfall and relatively low summer but high winter temperatures, is suitable for grass growing and animal production, but makes growing crops difficult. The percentage of grassland (80%) is the highest of any *European Union (EU) country. Therefore, agricultural production is dominated by livestock, with beef, dairy products and sheep meat accounting for about three-quarters of overall production. Minor commodities include grain, sugarbeet, potatoes, pigs and poultry. Around two-thirds of total production is exported and access to lucrative export markets has always been a government priority.

Some of the earliest farming settlements in Europe, circa 3000 BC, were discovered at the *Céide Fields in County *Mayo. The *Celts who arrived about 300 BC introduced the *brehon system of tribal land tenure, which survived up to the time of *Elizabeth I, much longer than elsewhere in Europe, where crop production favoured the individual possession of land. The arrival of the *Normans in the twelfth century had no long-term impact on agricultural practices or structures. However, the *plantations in the sixteenth and seventeenth centuries rudely disrupted the old order. Not only was tribal tenure replaced by the feudal system, but ownership of land passed completely into the hands of the old *Anglo-Irish families or the new English and Scottish settlers. By the end of the eighteenth century, about 95% of Ireland's land was owned by settlers (who constituted less than 0.5% of the population), many of them absentee *landlords.

During the nineteenth century, livestock became firmly established as the preferred mode of farming because it was more profitable than tillage. A numerous tenantry, once an asset, now became a liability, leading to a sharp increase in *emigration. The *Land Act of 1885 introduced a voluntary purchase scheme to enable tenants to own their land. Land purchase was subsequently made compulsory in the first Land Act passed by the *Free State government in 1923. The owner-occupied family farm became the fundamental unit of agricultural production.

In the first five decades of independence, the Land Commission enforced a programme of land purchase and redistribution to maximise the number of families working the land. However, technological progress in farming, together with rising incomes outside of agriculture, has increased the minimum size for farm viability. While the number of family farms has declined steadily from 398,000 in 1900 to 144,000 in 1999, average farm size has increased from 31.4 acres to 72.4 acres. With the growth of non-agricultural employment in rural areas, part-time farming has become common. It is now estimated that on 45% of farms, either the farmer and/or his or her spouse has an off-farm job.

Agriculture, traditionally the backbone of the economy, is becoming less important as Ireland's economic structure diversifies. In 1922, the agricultural sector in the Irish Free State accounted for about one-third of gross domestic product, just over half of total employment and almost three-quarters of merchandise exports. By 2001, agriculture's share of national output had fallen to just over 3%, while its share of national employment was 6.5%.

Farmers reacted to their declining importance by lobbying hard for protection and support. They enthusiastically supported Ireland's membership in the European Economic Community (as the *EU was then called) in 1973 not only because it guaranteed market access to the high-priced EU market, but, more significantly, because the cost of supporting farm prices was transferred from the Irish to the much larger EU budget through the operation of the EU's Common Agricultural Policy (CAP).

However, the CAP itself became subject to pressures for reform on budgetary grounds. Milk quotas were introduced in 1984 and in 1992, on the proposal of Agricultural Commissioner Ray MacSharry, support prices were reduced for some commodities while farmers were compensated through increased direct payments. Direct payments now account for 57% of farmers' total income and this will rise in the next few years.

Agriculture has had both negative and positive environmental impacts. Fertiliser run-off contributes to the eutrophication of waterways and rising nitrate levels in groundwater. Silage effluent spillages have been responsible for killing fish. Agriculture in Ireland contributes one-third of total greenhouse gas emissions of all EU countries. On the other hand, agriculture has shaped the natural environment and produced much of Ireland's breathtaking landscape. Integrating environmental considerations into agricultural policy is a major challenge for the industry in the new millennium. Whether agriculture's future lies in being a competitive producer of food or a supplier of amenities and environmental goods is now the key question for debate. A.M.

Ahern, Bertie (1951–). Politician, *Taoiseach, leader of *Fianna Fáil. Born in *Dublin, Ahern worked as an accountant before becoming a full-time public representative. Member of the *Dáil since 1977, he was minister for labour (1987–91) and minister for finance (1991–1994). Leader of Fianna Fáil since 1994, Ahern became Taoiseach in 1997. He developed a reputation as an excellent constituency worker early in his career and soon became the dominant politician in his inner-city Dublin community. He came to national prominence as minister for labour as a negotiator and mediator in labour disputes. Ahern played a major role in the development of the model of social partnership between the government and the main national interest groups, which has become the dominant policy model in Ireland since 1987 and which is credited with the rapid growth in the Irish *economy since then. He has established excellent relations with the Irish *trade union movement. His political skills were used by Fianna Fáil as they negotiated their first coalition government agreement in 1989 and also in the peace talks leading to the *Good Friday Agreement signed in *Belfast on 10 April 1998. In May 2002, Ahern led Fianna Fáil to a major victory (81 seats) in a general election. J.D.

Aiken, Frank (1898–1983). Politician, government minister, *IRA leader. Born in County *Armagh, Aiken joined the Irish *Volunteers in 1913 and was an IRA commander during the *War of Independence. Opponent of the *Anglo-Irish Treaty of 1921, he succeeded Liam Lynch as chief of staff of the IRA in April 1923, after Lynch was shot by *Free State troops. He immediately sought an end to the *Irish Civil War, which officially ceased in May 1923. Aiken was a founding member of *Fianna Fáil and served under Éamon *de Valera and Seán *Lemass, most notably as minister for defence in 1932–45, finance 1945–48, and foreign affairs 1951–54, and again in 1957–69. P.E.

aisling. A common motif in *Celtic mythology that takes its name from the Gaelic word for a dream or a vision. From the eighteenth century onward the word was associated with a form of allegorical poetry – most commonly practised in *Munster – in which a beautiful woman (Ireland) bemoans being forsaken by her husband in the aftermath of the Jacobean wars. The poems often ended on a positive note with hope of French, Spanish or papal deliverance from British rule. B.D.

Allgood, Molly (1887–1952). Actress, stage name Máire O'Neill. Born in *Dublin, Molly was sent to an orphanage, along with her sister Sara *Allgood, after their father's death, and subsequently apprenticed to a dressmaker. In 1905, she joined the *Abbey Theatre Company, where, with Sara and the *Fay brothers, she developed the understated Abbey style of acting. Also in 1905, Molly became engaged to J. M. *Synge, who died four years later. She played Pegeen Mike in Synge's *The Playboy of the Western World* (1907); the play caused riots in Dublin, but subsequent performances in London were a personal triumph. In 1911, she married George Herbert Mair and continued her successful acting career in England. After Mair's death in 1926, she married an Abbey actor, Arthur Sinclair. With him and her sister Sara, she appeared many times in plays by Seán *O'Casey. Her later years were troubled by divorce and financial problems. J.C.E.L.

Allgood, Sara (1883–1950). Actress. Born in *Dublin, Sara and her sister Molly *Allgood were raised in an orphanage. In the first years of the century, Sara acted in plays performed by Maud *Gonne's women's *nationalist group, Inghinidhe na hÉireann (Daughters of Ireland). The stage manager of these plays, William *Fay, invited her to join the National Theatre Society in 1903. Sara acted in *Yeats' *The King's Threshold* (1903) and played Maurya in *Synge's *Riders to the Sea* (1904). With her sister Molly and the Fay brothers, she was instrumental in developing the *Abbey Theatre's acting style. Her interpretation of Maurya, modelled on her own grandmother, was praised for its naturalness and intensity of emotion. On the opening night of the Abbey Theatre in 1904, she played Mrs Fallon in Lady *Gregory's *Spreading the News*. She joined John Hartley Manner's touring company in 1915 and married another actor, Gerald Henson, while on tour in Australia. He and their son died of influenza in 1918. Allgood returned to the Abbey in 1920 and gave memorable performances as Juno in Seán *O'Casey's *Juno and the Paycock* and as Bessie Burgess in the London production of *The Plough and the Stars*. After an American tour she settled in Hollywood in 1940, but her transition to film acting was not successful. She died in poverty. J.C.E.L.

Alliance Party of Northern Ireland (APNI). Political party. The APNI, a moderate, cross-community party, was formed in April 1970 by activists who had campaigned for *unionist Prime Minister Captain Terence *O'Neill in the February 1969 'Crossroads' election. Though in favour of the union with Britain, the party advocates a united community within *Northern Ireland. Largely middle-class in composition, it draws support from both *Catholics and *Protestants – the only significant party to do so. Currently aligned with the Liberal Democrat Party in Britain, the APNI, while supporting union with Britain, would accept formal links with the *Republic of Ireland. The party appears to be in long-term decline, because moderates and liberals are joining mainstream unionist parties. M.M.

Allingham, William (1824–89). Poet. Allingham was born in Ballyshannon, County *Donegal. While working as a customs officer, he frequently visited London, where he befriended many writers, including Leigh Hunt, Carlyle, the Brownings, Tennyson and members of the Pre-Raphaelite circle. Rossetti and Millais illustrated his poetry collection *Day and Night Songs* (1854). Allingham retired to London in 1870, where he became the editor of *Fraser's Magazine*. His poetry was inspired by philosophical, social and psychological ideas. He also published an anthology of ballads and wrote poems about the fairy world, which profoundly influenced the young W. B. *Yeats. His most ambitious work was *Laurence Bloomfield in Ireland* (1864), a long narrative poem addressing the tensions between *landlords and tenants. J.C.E.L.

Altan. Traditional *music band. Altan was formed in 1983 by fiddler and singer Mairéad Ní Mhaonaigh of Gweedore and her husband, flute player Frankie Kennedy (1955–94). Rooted in the repertoire and style of County *Donegal, the unique, thorough integrity of Altan's many albums has made considerable impact not only in Ireland, but in folk music circles in Europe and in the United States. F.V.

American Civil War, the (1861–65). The most violent and traumatic episode in US history, resulting in some 620,000 deaths. This conflict is considered the defining moment of the American Republic, ensuring the survival of the Union and the abolition of slavery. Having predominantly settled in the urban centres of the north, Irish immigrants played an important, if often exaggerated, part in the Union victory. Nearly 150,000 of the over two million troops who served in the Federal armies, were of Irish origin. Included in these ranks was the famous Irish Brigade, commanded by the *Young Irelander Thomas Francis *Meagher. This unit consisted of three regiments recruited from *New York City's Irish population, including the celebrated 'Fighting 69th', which lost more than half its men in a heroic charge at the Battle of Antietam.

However, Irish enlistment rates were below those of other immigrant groups and native-born Americans. Most likely, this was because of the antagonism of *Catholic immigrants (who mainly supported the peace faction of the Democratic Party) toward the nativist Republican Party and its pro-war, anti-slavery platform. Irish fear of competition at the bottom of the socio-economic ladder fuelled a series of anti-black 'draft riots', the most infamous of which occurred in New York City in 1863. Immigrants from Ireland also contributed to the Confederate side. For example, Irish dock workers from New Orleans were a major component of the 'Louisiana Tigers', while John *Mitchel, the Young Ireland radical, was an ardent supporter of the South. The war, although disruptive of *Fenian fund-raising efforts in the United States, ultimately provided a number of hardened veterans for the *nationalist cause. Most prominently, Union Captain T. J. Kelly became the leader of the Fenian Brotherhood and led the 1867 rising. J.P.

American Revolution, the (American War of Independence) (1775–83). The rebellion of 13 British North American colonies caused by resentment over taxation and the absence of parliamentary representation. Despite a number of early setbacks, the colonists (significantly aided by France from 1778) won important victories at Saratoga in 1777 and Yorktown in 1781, culminating in the independence and the foundation of the United States in 1783. Irish *immigrants and Irish Americans, particularly *Ulster Presbyterians who constituted the largest white, non-English ethnic group in the colonies, played a central role in the Revolution. As much as one-third of the Continental army was of Irish descent, including 26 general officers. General Richard Montgomery, a Dublin native, commanded the American forces that invaded Canada in 1775. Continental army Major General John Sullivan waged a devastating campaign against the Iroquois (British allies). Sullivan was the son of Limerick-born James Sullivan, the former governor of Massachusetts. Another son of Irish immigrants, Henry Knox, served as Washington's head of artillery. After the war, Knox became the army's commander in chief and then secretary of war of the new republic. John Barry, a Wexford native, is credited as founder of the American navy. Timothy Murphy (a generation removed from Ireland) was believed to be the best shot in the Continental army. From a distance, he successfully killed two ranking British officers, thereby contributing to the American victory at Saratoga.

The Revolution deeply affected Ireland, where many Irish 'patriots' clearly recognised common grievances with the American colonists. Irish reformers headed by Henry *Grattan and backed by the *Volunteer movement (local units nominally raised to defend Ireland while much of its regular garrison was engaged abroad) took advantage of the imperial crisis to extract important economic and political concessions (free trade 1779 and legislative independence 1782) from the British government. J.P.

An Claidheamh Soluis (1899–1930). The newspaper of the *Gaelic League. Its title means 'The Sword of Light'. The newspaper was extremely influential both culturally and politically, particularly up to the establishment of the *Irish Free State in 1922. Its more famous editors included Eoin *MacNeill and Patrick *Pearse. The newspaper had a bilingual policy of developing and supporting debate and literature in both Irish and English. A.T.

Ancient Order of Hibernians (AOH). *Catholic, *nationalist benevolent society. The Ancient Order of Hibernians was formed in *New York in 1836. In Ireland, its origins are unclear, but its roots were in the late-eighteenth-century secret peasant societies such as the *Defenders and Ribbonmen, which were formed as Catholic reaction to the *Orange Order. The AOH, which remains exclusively Catholic and male, adopted freemason-style rituals and regalia. After the *Famine, the AOH became one of the strongest Irish movements in America. Its purpose was to defend the Irish Catholic community, and it was prominent in New York during anti-Irish riots in the 1840s and 1850s, and the Orange riots of the 1870s. The order was active in Irish American politics and raised money for nationalist movements in Ireland. Its association with the Molly Maguires, a secret society among Irish miners in the Pennsylvania coal fields in the 1870s, was the subject of press hysteria, but the connection seems to have been exaggerated.

During the 1880s, *Clan na Gael dominated the American organisation. In 1878, the American AOH opened membership to those of Irish descent. The Irish organisation, which had become more formally organised and publicly active from the 1870s, split in the 1880s, but reunited at the turn of the century as the Ancient Order of Hibernians (Board of Erin). From the 1880s, the AOH became increasingly more important in Ireland, mainly in *Ulster. After the lifting of a clerical ban (as a 'secret society') in 1904, the order spread to other parts of Ireland and AOH halls in many Irish towns date from these years.

The Belfast nationalist Joseph Devlin was the order's national president in Ireland from 1905 to 1934. Under Devlin, the AOH expanded as a political network. Membership grew from 10,000 in 1905 to 60,000 in 1909, mainly in Ulster and the neighbouring counties, as the AOH worked alongside the parliamentary nationalist movement. The renewed prospect of *home rule also prompted constitutional nationalists to join the AOH. The *Irish Parliamentary Party, led by John *Redmond, needed it as a branch network to replace its declining grass-roots organisation, the United Irish League (UIL).

Because of its narrow sectarianism and its association with machine politics and jobbery, the AOH was much despised by *Sinn Féin, by some nationalist leaders, including the land agitator and MP William *O'Brien, and by *socialists like James *Connolly and James *Larkin. In *Northern Ireland, the order was closely associated with the *Nationalist Party until the 1970s. Although the AOH survives in Ireland, it has declined in recent decades and is now politically insignificant. In America it remains widely organised, but mostly middle-class and conservative. The AOH has been at the centre of controversy since the early 1990s for excluding the Irish Lesbian and Gay Organisation from the New York St Patrick's Day parade. P.D.

Andrews, John Millar (1871–1956). Prime minister of *Northern Ireland, 1940–43. Born in County *Antrim, into a business family, Andrews was MP for County *Down, 1921–29, and for Mid-Down from 1929. He was minister for labour in the Northern Ireland cabinet, 1921–37, and minister for finance, 1937–40. He served briefly as *Stormont prime minister from 1940 to 1943. His most significant achievement was to negotiate an agreement with the British exchequer to maintain the equivalent British welfare services in Northern Ireland. Failure to mobilise effectively for war led to his replacement by Basil *Brooke. He died in 1956. M.M.

Anglo-Irish, the. At its simplest level, this term denotes people, born or living in Ireland, who are of English ancestry. Traditionally, the English presence in Ireland is dated from 1170, when Dermot *MacMurrough, the deposed king of *Leinster, invited *Anglo-Norman Lord Richard fitz Gilbert (*Strongbow) to help him regain his throne. This invitation opened a veritable Pandora's box, which ultimately led to English domination of Ireland.

The Anglo-Saxon presence in Ireland is, actually, the result of a highly complex process. Both Strongbow and his overlord, *Henry II, the first King of England to claim sovereignty in Ireland, were in fact Normans. These descendants of the *Vikings had subjugated England from their French Duchy in 1066 and until the fourteenth century they remained a French-speaking ruling-class in their newly acquired kingdom of England. In Ireland, Norman lords came to dominate the *Pale (an area around Dublin) and were scattered throughout much of the rest of the country where, over time, they often intermarried with the families of Gaelic chieftains, creating a hybrid culture that was often more Irish than Norman. This process of assimilation was so alarming to the English authorities that the Anglo-Norman-dominated Irish *parliament passed the notorious Statute of *Kilkenny (1366). The statute, although ultimately doomed to failure, was a direct attempt to preserve English law, customs and culture within the Anglo-Norman colony in Ireland. Some of its clauses banned intermarriage between English settlers and Gaelic natives and the use of the *Irish language and dress.

Historically, many of the most powerful and influential Irish families, like the Butlers and Fitzgeralds – to name only two – were descended from these so-called Anglo-Normans. With the Protestant *Reformation and *Henry VIII's establishment of a formal kingship over Ireland in the 1530s and 1540s, a new nomenclature emerged to distinguish between old, usually Catholic, families of Norman and Saxon origin and new Protestant officials and settlers from England. Thus, the respective names Old English and New English were born. The Catholic Old English sided with their Gaelic co-religionists in the *Rebellion of 1641 and the ensuing Confederate War (1641–53). After the *Cromwellian Settlement of the 1650s, the Old English ceased to be distinguished from the Gaels and both became simply Catholic. In turn, the New English, joined by a sizable influx of Protestant settlers, became known as the Anglo-Irish. This latter nomenclature is most commonly used to denote the tiny minority (the so-called Protestant Ascendancy) drawn from the established Protestant *Church of Ireland, who owned some 90% of the land and dominated Ireland economically, politically and socially in the eighteenth, nineteenth and early twentieth centuries. Yet, it is important to remember that there were also tens of thousands of Anglo-Irish farmers, merchants and artisans (totalling some 10% of the population) in the south of Ireland by 1700.

The Anglo-Irish have traditionally played a disproportionate cultural role in Irish society, particularly in the realm of *literature in English. For example, Jonathan *Swift (author of *Gulliver's Travels*), the Protestant dean of *St Patrick's cathedral in Dublin, was the most prominent Irish writer of the eighteenth century. More significantly, many of the writers involved in the *Irish Revival (c.1890–1910) were Anglo-Irish. Included in this movement, which centred on the *Abbey

Theatre in Dublin, were such internationally renowned playwrights and authors as W. B. *Yeats, Lady *Gregory, J. M. *Synge and, less directly, George Bernard *Shaw. Ironically, the Anglophone writers of the Irish Revival, who were reacting against a perceived English cultural imperialism, were themselves often dismissed as 'West Britons' by members of the contemporaneous *Gaelic Revival who advocated a purely Irish language literature.

Some of Ireland's greatest *nationalist leaders and politicians have been Anglo-Irish, such as Henry *Grattan, Wolfe *Tone, Robert *Emmet, Isaac *Butt, Charles Stewart *Parnell and Erskine *Childers, to name a few. With the disestablishment of the *Church of Ireland (1869), land reform (1881, 1903) and, finally, independence (1922), the Anglo-Irish gradually shrank to the roughly 4% of the population of the *Republic that they are today and the term is rarely used in a modern context. J.P.

Anglo-Irish Agreement (1985). Agreement between the Irish and British governments, signed at Hillsborough, County *Down, on 15 November 1985. Since the failure of *Sunningdale's Council of Ireland in 1973, British policy in Ireland had concentrated on security and finding common ground for an internal settlement. *Unionists preferred direct rule from London to any form of power-sharing, and the influence of constitutional *nationalism waned in the absence of any real progress. Following the *hunger strikes of 1981, nationalist supporters began to desert the *Social Democratic and Labour Party (SDLP) in favour of *Sinn Féin's sterner *republicanism. Both the *Fine Gael–Labour coalition in *Dublin and *Margaret Thatcher's Conservative government in London were seriously concerned that Sinn Féin would become the majority voice of the *Catholic nationalist community. In 1985, the Anglo-Irish Agreement committed both governments to the principle that *Northern Ireland's constitutional status would not change without the consent of a majority of its people. The agreement also gave a consultative role to the government of the *Republic of Ireland in the administration of *Northern Ireland.

There was some disappointment on both sides. The Irish government found its influence to be strictly secondary to Britain's perceptions of stable administration. The British were disappointed at the poor level of co-operation between the north and south on security. Republicans generally rejected the agreement but were impressed by Britain's willingness to defy unionist objections. Unionists, for their part, were frightened by the prospect of deals over their heads and began to organise resistance to joint authority. Sinn Féin's electoral advance was checked temporarily, while loyalist paramilitaries saw an incentive to act. Nevertheless, the agreement moved both republicans and loyalists toward sowing the seeds of peace. M.M.

Anglo-Irish Treaty (1921). Agreement ending the *War of Independence. In a meeting on 8 July 1921, Éamon *de Valera and General Macready, the commander in chief of British forces in Ireland, agreed to end the *Anglo-Irish War. The truce came into effect on Monday 11 July 1921. De Valera arrived in London the following day to meet with British Prime Minister *Lloyd George, but initial negotiations failed to secure an agreement.

On 29 September, Lloyd George suggested that Irish delegates come to a conference in London with a view to determine 'how the association of Ireland with the British Commonwealth may be reconciled with Irish national aspirations'.

De Valera sent a delegation representing *Dáil Éireann, consisting of chief negotiators Arthur *Griffith, Michael *Collins and Robert *Barton and legal advisors Éamonn Duggan and George Gavan Duffy. Erskine *Childers also attended as non-voting secretary. The delegates had the power to sign any agreement, but they were also confusingly told to report back to Dublin before signing anything. In what some have seen as a controversial move – that has been open to many interpretations – de Valera decided not to attend, arguing that his presence was needed in Dublin to gather support for any agreement. Some historians have argued that he did not want to take the blame in the event of a compromise solution.

Negotiations opened in London on 11 October 1921, with the British delegation led by Prime Minister Lloyd George, Winston *Churchill, Austin Chamberlain and Lord Birkenhead. The Irish delegation had been instructed to seek recognition for the thirty-two county Irish *Republic, which had been created by the first *Dáil in January 1919. If this failed, the delegates were told to give up some independence in return for the preservation of unity. De Valera also argued for some degree of 'external association' between a united Ireland and Britain, whereby Ireland would not actually be part of the British empire, but would be closely affiliated with it.

The British, on the other hand, were adamant that Ireland should remain part of the *Commonwealth and that the demands of the *Ulster unionists be satisfied. Given these divergent positions, talks on political sovereignty and unity remained divisive, while matters such as trade, defence and national debt were quickly resolved.

On 2 November, Arthur Griffith, the leader of the Irish delegation, agreed that Ireland would remain part of the Commonwealth in return for Lloyd George's promise to persuade Ulster unionists to accept Irish unity. His efforts failed and on 8 November, as an alternative solution, Lloyd George offered to establish a *Boundary Commission that would redefine the *Northern Ireland border. The British continued to reject the idea of 'external association' and insisted that Ireland remain part of the British empire. Griffith reluctantly accepted the proposal and at the end of November returned to Dublin with a final draft of proposals for a treaty. On 3 December, the Dáil rejected the proposals and instructed Griffith to renegotiate, without giving him specific guidelines.

Back in London, Griffith brought up the question of *partition again, but Lloyd George pointed out that they had already agreed to a Boundary Commission. He did, however, modify the *oath of allegiance and agreed that the Free State should be free to impose its own tariffs. Griffith wanted to bring these new terms back to Dublin, but Lloyd George gave him an ultimatum – they either agreed to the terms or 'immediate and terrible war' would recommence. The delegates signed 'the articles of agreement for a treaty' on 6 December 1921.

Under the agreement, twenty-six counties of Ireland would become the *Irish Free State, a member of the British Commonwealth of Nations, with dominion status equal to that of *Canada. A governor general would represent the British monarch, and members of the Irish legislature would be required to take an oath of allegiance. If any of the six counties of Northern Ireland (Antrim, Armagh, Down, Fermanagh, Londonderry and Tyrone) decided not to become part of the Free State, a Boundary Commission would be established to adjust the border 'in accordance with the wishes of the inhabitants'. Britain also retained ownership of the ports of Cobh and Berehaven in County *Cork, and Lough Swilly in County *Donegal for defence purposes.

In Dublin, the debate on the treaty, which began on 14 December 1921, was emotional and divisive. De Valera rejected the treaty outright. Dominion status, which some argued gave Britain too much influence in Ireland and the oath of allegiance took up most of the debate. There was less discussion on *partition.

The treaty was ratified by the Dáil on 7 January 1922, by 64 votes to 57. De Valera resigned as president (to be replaced by Griffith) and led the anti-treaty faction out of the Dáil following elections in June 1922. The *Civil War commenced on 28 June 1922. P.E.

Anglo-Irish War, the (January 1919–July 1921). Campaign of guerrilla warfare against the British army and *RIC by the *IRA, also known as the War of Independence. On 21 January 1919, 27 (of the 73) *Sinn Féin elected members (who had won seats in the December 1918 general election) who were not in jail, or on the run, formed the Irish *parliament, *Dáil Éireann, and declared the creation of an independent Irish *Republic. On the same day, the South Tipperary Brigade of the *Volunteers ambushed and killed two policemen escorting explosives to a quarry at Soloheadbeg in County *Tipperary. This incident is generally seen as the start of the War of Independence. The conflict, which lasted until 11 July 1921, had three distinct phases: the IRA campaign against the RIC; the struggle between the IRA and the *Auxiliaries/*Black and Tans; the use of IRA flying columns and the search for a peaceful solution.

The Volunteers (who in August 1919 renamed themselves the *IRA) adopted guerrilla tactics, striking quickly and fading back into the countryside. While, in theory, command lay with Cathal *Brugha, the minister for defence, the nature of guerrilla warfare made it necessary for local commanders to maintain complete control, while the Dáil was forced to endorse and take full responsibility for their actions.

Following the Soloheadbeg ambush, Cathal Brugha issued an order authorising the shooting of soldiers and policemen, and RIC barracks were targeted by the IRA as a source of weapons. In the Dáil, Éamon *de Valera proposed a motion that RIC members be 'ostracised'. Recruitment fell drastically, as policemen became social outcasts and the victims of intimidation. Many resigned and, in the countryside, barracks became deserted as RIC officers were transferred to larger urban centres. By the summer of 1919, over 50 policemen had been killed, and during Easter 1920, the IRA, in a gesture of defiance, burned many of the abandoned barracks throughout the country.

In June 1919, de Valera, who had escaped from jail in England in April, travelled to the United States to raise funds and support for the recognition of the Irish Republic. During his absence, Michael *Collins emerged as the chief intelligence coordinator of the IRA campaign. Early in the war, he successfully established a counterintelligence network and organised a 'squad' to eliminate government spies.

When the situation spiralled out of control, *Lloyd George refused to send in the army because this would have given the conflict the status of a war. Instead, 5,000 former *First World War soldiers were recruited to support the RIC. They were called the Black and Tans from the colours of their uniform. Another group, the Auxiliaries, which was made up of 1,500 ex-British army officers, was formed in August 1920. The IRA's guerrilla tactics, however, proved to be unbeatable. This led to the brutal Black and Tan campaign of terror and reprisals exemplified by the murder on 19 March 1920, of Tomás *MacCurtain, lord mayor of Cork, in front of his wife and family.

As the atrocities escalated, Lloyd George attempted to find a political solution by introducing the *Government of Ireland Act, which partitioned Ireland and for which no Irish MPs of any persuasion voted when it was passed on 23 December 1920. Under this legislation, two parliaments were to be set up, one in Dublin for 26 of the 32 counties and one in Belfast for the other six. The act failed to bring peace. *Sinn Féin ignored it and the *Ulster unionists only reluctantly accepted it.

On *Bloody Sunday, 21 November 1920,

11 British agents were assassinated in Dublin by Collins' squad. In reprisal, that same afternoon the Auxiliaries fired into the crowd during a Gaelic football game in *Croke Park, killing 12 people and wounding 60 others. That night, three prisoners, Peadar Clancy, Dick McKee and Conor Clune were also shot while (according to *Dublin Castle) 'trying to escape'. A week later, 17 Auxiliaries were killed at an ambush at Kilmichael, County *Cork, and as a result, martial law was declared in Counties Cork, *Kerry, Tipperary and *Limerick on 10 December. A day later, British forces were ambushed outside Cork and in retaliation, parts of Cork City were burned.

In December 1920, de Valera returned from the United States to find a full-scale war in progress. The IRA had perfected the tactic of the flying columns – where groups of up to 30 men operating mostly in *Munster, *Connacht and South Ulster, would launch ambushes and surprise attacks. These men remained permanently on the run and were hidden and supported by the local population. On 25 May 1921, the IRA mounted a largescale offensive, when they attacked and burned the Customs House in Dublin, the headquarters of British taxation and administrative services in Ireland.

By the summer of 1921, both sides realised that a political solution was essential. The war had cost the British government over £20 million since 1919 and the behaviour of the Black and Tans and Auxiliaries had become a great embarrassment. The IRA was short of weapons and ammunition and people were tired of the ongoing violence. On 8 July, de Valera and General Macready, the commander in chief of British forces in Ireland, agreed to a cease-fire. The truce came into effect on 11 July 1921, but preliminary negotiations between de Valera and Lloyd George in London failed to secure any agreement. In October 1921, Irish delegates arrived back in London to negotiate what would become the *Anglo-Irish Treaty. P.E.

Anglo-Norman Conquest. The Normans, from northern France, conquered England in 1066. A century later, some of their descendants in Wales and England invaded Ireland. Unlike the invasion of England, the Anglo-Normans came to Ireland by invitation.

In 1166, the deposed king of *Leinster, Dermot *MacMurrough, went to King *Henry II of England asking for help to regain his kingdom. MacMurrough had abducted the wife of Tiernan O'Rourke, a local chieftain, 14 years previously. O'Rourke was one of the enemies who drove MacMurrough out of Ireland. Some writers have drawn the parallel to the legend of Troy and exaggerated the episode's significance in leading to the invasion. Dermot's plea for help to Henry II to restore his kingdom, however, initiated the Anglo-Norman Conquest.

With Henry's permission, Dermot recruited several hundred Anglo-Norman soldiers and their leader *Strongbow. In return, Dermot offered Strongbow the succession of his kingdom and his daughter, Aoife, in marriage. Dermot returned to Ireland in August 1167, with Norman soldiers. After Strongbow's arrival with 1,000 men in August 1170, Dermot secured Leinster and the cities of Waterford and *Dublin. Dermot died in 1171. Henry II feared that Strongbow had become too powerful and might try to recover his lost earldom of Pembroke. Also, Henry wanted to avoid condemnation for the murder of Thomas à Becket at Canterbury (29 December 1170). The pope had encouraged the king to take Ireland because the church there had not reformed sufficiently. Henry arrived near Waterford on 17 October 1171, with 400 ships and 4,000 men, and asserted lordship over his Norman subjects and several Irish kings. He returned to England in April 1172, leaving Strongbow as his representative in Ireland.

The invasion was followed by a colonisation and settlement. English law and institutions were introduced – later including a *parliament, under the English crown. By the late thirteenth century, English rule was effective over two-thirds of the island. Anglo-Norman tenants settled much of Leinster and *Munster. English and Welsh landless labourers also arrived. The settlement was part of a wider population expansion and movement in north-western Europe.

At first the Normans built wooden *castles, on artificial mounds, or mottes. Later they constructed stone castles, many of which survive today, such as those at Carrickfergus and Ballymote. The Normans developed *agriculture on the estates around their manors and founded towns, including Sligo, New Ross and Drogheda. Some settlements, such as Shanid in Limerick, were mainly military or administrative; others, like Carlow and Kilkenny, developed as centres of commerce.

The colony expanded and was consolidated in the thirteenth century, but it was only a partial conquest. Gaelic culture survived alongside that of the settlers and large areas remained outside English law. The colony declined in the fourteenth century and there was a revival in the power of the Irish lords. In spite of laws against such assimilation, many settlers had adopted the culture of the native Irish. English military campaigns failed to turn the tide, and in the fifteenth century the Norman rulers concentrated on consolidating an area around Dublin known as the *Pale. In two books, *A Topography of Ireland* and *The Conquest of Ireland*, Gerald of Wales, a contemporary writer, gives a valuable account of the Anglo-Norman conquest, although he depicts the Irish as a barbarous, uncultured race. P.D.

***Annals of the Four Masters*, the.** A compilation of annals that records the history of Ireland from early times to 1616. The work, *Annála Ríoghachta Éireann*, was written between the years 1632 and 1636 by the Franciscan brother Mícheál Ó Cléirigh with the aid of Cúchoigríche Ó Cléirigh, Cúchoigríche Ó Duibhgeannáin and Fearfeasa Ó Maoilchonaire, who were collectively known as 'the four masters'. Ó Cléirigh had many enemies in the Catholic University of Louvain and the finished product was heavily criticised there for going beyond just collecting material on the lives of Irish *saints. The work is dedicated to its patron, Fearghal Ó Gadhra (a member of parliament for *Sligo). B.D.

Antrim, County. Maritime county in the extreme north-east, in the province of *Ulster, one of the six counties of *Northern Ireland. The county has an area of 1,092 square miles and a population of est. 562,216 (1996). Only 20 miles across the Irish Sea from *Scotland at its closest point, Antrim has served as a conduit linking the two *Celtic peoples for nearly two millennia. In fact, Scotland draws its very name from an Antrim-based Irish tribe, the *Scots, who expanded into the west of Caledonia from their kingdom of Dál Riata during the fourth and fifth centuries.

County Antrim is known for the beauty of its rugged coastline. Located in the north of the county, the *Giant's Causeway is a spectacular collection of thousands of black basalt columns which were formed, geologists believe, approximately 60 million years ago. In the north-east, the world-famous green Glens of Antrim stretch inland from the sea. *Belfast, Antrim's and Northern Ireland's capital and largest city, is located in the southern part of the county.

In the late medieval and early modern periods, Antrim and the west of Scotland were linked by the Lordship of the Isles headed by the Scottish MacDonald dynasty. During the late sixteenth and throughout the seventeenth centuries, a heavy influx of Scottish settlers radically altered the religious composition of the county. By the early eighteenth century, the county had the largest *Protestant population on a percentile basis of any county in Ireland. In the 1790s, Antrim was at the forefront of the *United Irish Movement and, along with neighbouring *Down, was one of only two Ulster counties to rise during the *Rebellion of 1798. Today, Antrim's population is mostly Protestant and *unionist. The economy of the county is mostly agricultural, with some *textile production. Belfast has many different industries, including shipbuilding. Bushmills *distillery, in the village of Bushmills, produces a famous *whiskey. J.P.

Aosdána. State-funded association of artists engaged in *literature, *music and visual arts. Established in 1981 and administered by the *Arts Council, Aosdána aims to honour artists who have made a significant contribution to the arts and to assist members to devote their energies fully to art. Membership is confined to no more than 200 artists of distinguished creative and original work. Members must be born in Ireland or a resident for five years. They are eligible to receive a *Cnuas*, or annuity, for five years. A maximum of five new members may be elected annually. Particular achievements are recognised through the award of *Saoi*, of which there are only five at any time. M.S.T.

Apprentice Boys. A Masonic-style organisation that shares the *Orange Order's goal of *Protestant supremacy. The organisation was established in 1814 in memory of apprentice boys who, in defiance of city governors, shut the gates of Derry (Londonderry) City on Catholic troops loyal to *King James II on 7 December 1688. The city subsequently withstood a Jacobite siege (known as the Siege of *Derry) from 18 April to 31 July 1689. The Apprentice Boys represent a complex tradition of heroism, defence of liberty, religious intolerance and, more so than other loyal orders, plebeian steadfastness. The annual Apprentice Boys march in the centre of Derry symbolised Protestant domination of this predominantly Catholic city. The civil rights march of 5 October 1968, challenging the Protestant monopoly of local political power, is often considered the beginning of the modern *Troubles. M.M.

Aran Islands, the. A group of three islands off the coast of County *Galway and County *Clare. The biggest of the three is Inishmore (population of 836), the smallest Inishmaan (population of 216) and the other Inisheer (population of 217). The islands get their name from the Irish word *Ára*, which means 'a kidney', and by extension a ridge or a back of land. The Aran Islands are renowned because of their archaeological interest and because they have produced or inspired several important writers. *Irish is the main language of the islands and it is not surprising, therefore, that its authors should write in both Irish and English.

The most famous of these is Liam *O'Flaherty (1896–1964), who celebrates the life of the island in his short stories *Dúil* (1953), as well as in his autobiography *Shame the Devil* (1934), and in some of his novels, such as *The Black Soul* (1934). The poet Máirtín *Ó Direáin (1910–88) left Inishmore when he was 18 years old, but the island became the central image in his poetry as a refuge from the awfulness of the modern world. Another native of the Aran Islands, Breandán Ó hEithir (1930– 90), a nephew of Liam O'Flaherty, was a bilingual journalist, broadcaster and novelist who cast a sardonic eye on Irish life in his numerous writings. Perhaps the most famous writer to explore the islands is the playwright John Millington *Synge (1871–1909). After a brief stay in Inishmore, he perfected his Irish in Inishmaan and he based the strange and exotic *Hiberno-English of his plays on the rhythms, cadences and syntax that he heard in the native

O'Brien's Castle on Inisheer, Aran Islands

language. Synge's *The Aran Islands* (1907) is a travel book that is also a piece of personal reflection and examination. Other noteworthy visitors to the islands included Samuel *Ferguson, Dr William *Wilde, and the scholars John *O'Donovan and Eugene *O'Curry. The American filmmaker of Irish descent Robert O'Flaherty made his famous documentary film *Man of Aran* in 1934. In recent years the author and cartographer Tim Robinson (1935–) has lovingly mapped the islands as well as exhaustively written about every aspect of the landscape, history and archaeology in *Stones of Aran* (1986 and 1995).

*Dún Aengus, perched on the high cliffs above the Atlantic Ocean, is the most prominent of several prehistoric cashels, or *hill-forts, on the islands. It is attributed in legend to the Fir Bolg, but its real age is disputed. There was certainly some settlement there as early as 800 BC, but Dún Aengus reached its most developed form in the early *Christian period. Aran sweaters, which have become very popular, are traditionally hand-knitted from thick local wool by women on the island. According to one legend, each family used a different knitting pattern so that drowned fishermen could be identified by their sweaters. Since the opening up of the island to tourism, these sweaters have become an important business and can no longer be seen as a cottage industry. At the height of the summer season as many as 2,000 visitors may come to the islands every day. A.T.

architecture. Over the centuries, Irish architecture has reflected disparate outside influences and has assimilated the styles of the many peoples who have set foot on the island's shores.

Early Neolithic builders (c.3700–2000 BC) constructed defensive forts and burial mounds. Some of these still survive, such as *Newgrange (c.3100 BC), the famous *passage-graves, and the dry-stone wall forts *Dún Aengus (Inishmore, *Aran Islands) and An Grianán Aileach (County *Donegal). Over 30,000 *raths, enclosures surrounded by earthen embankments, still mark today's landscape.

In AD 432, the arrival of Christianity in Ireland brought a new architecture. Religious settlements on *Skellig Michael (County *Kerry) consisted of a basic church and a group of *beehive huts inside a walled enclosure. Gallarus Oratory (County Kerry), an isolated chamber used for single meditation, was built with inward sloping stone walls in the shape of an upturned boat. Larger monastic settlements, built between the ninth and twelfth centuries, survive at *Clonmacnoise (County *Offaly) and *Glendalough (County *Wicklow). Religious craftsmen built *high crosses, carved with biblical scenes, at these sites and *round towers, made possible by the development of lime mortar.

Following the *Anglo-Norman invasion in 1169, Irish religious architecture adopted a Romanesque style, with carved geometric ornament around doorways and arches. From the twelfth century on, Romanesque architecture incorporated detailed exterior carvings in small churches and cathedrals, such as those at Kilkenny, Lismore and Cashel. *Christ Church cathedral, Dublin (c.1172), and *St Patrick's owe more to an emerging Gothic style, whose innovative flying buttresses and rib vaults allowed vast interior spaces. Secular Norman architecture included 'motte and bailey' *castles, four-storeyed rectangular stone towers called 'keeps' and larger, fortified castles, such as *Dublin Castle, Carrickfergus Castle (County *Antrim) and King John's Castle, Limerick City (c.1200).

During the late Middle Ages (c.1400 to 1650), as the Anglo-Norman power was consolidated across the country, the construction of regional family castles and monastic settlements increased. The majority of Irish castles date from this period, including Clare (County *Kilkenny) and *Blarney (County *Cork).

Alongside the construction of larger stone buildings for the commercial and religious elite, a tradition of 'vernacular' rural architecture – peasant homes, barns and agricultural sheds, and minor commercial premises – developed. Irish cottage-builders used local materials, including stone, clay, sods, grass and straw. The ground-plan of cottages included a door opening onto a central room, which had the hearth as its social and working centre, and bedrooms off to each side. The exterior was often whitewashed. Commercial premises in towns had two storeys, the lower for the business and upper for the living quarters.

The period between the Battle of the *Boyne (1690) and the Act of *Union (1800) may be the high point of Irish architecture. Neo-Palladianism propounded the study of ancient Roman architecture and featured pedimented windows, tight symmetry, Doric-columned porticos and granite materials. Sir Edward Lovett *Pearce (1698–1733) was responsible for the *Parliament House in Dublin (1722–39) and *Castletown House (c.1720s) (County *Kildare). Richard Castle (d. 1751) created a large series of country palaces in the classical style, including Westport (1731) (County *Mayo), Carton (1739) (County Kildare) and Russborough (1742) (County Wicklow). Other buildings constructed at this time in Dublin, in the Georgian style, include *Leinster House (1745), the Rotunda Hospital (1752–57), William Chambers' Marino Casino and *James Gandon's Custom House (1781–91).

After the Act of Union, as the country declined economically and socially, architecture reflected the slump. Once-grand Georgian buildings fell into disrepair. However, some significant buildings did go up during the Victorian era, including the Italian-Renaissance-style Amiens Street Railway Station (1844) and the traditionally-classical Broadstone Railway Station (1850), both in Dublin. Throughout the century, the growing confidence of *Catholicism was mirrored in the construction of a number of cathedrals, including St Patrick's in Dundalk (1830s).

Following independence in 1922, there were no significant efforts to create an Irish style, and a modernist and international style flourished: flat, concrete and rational. A stripped-down, bare-classicism was used in several buildings during the early days of the *Free State, including the Gresham Hotel on O'Connell Street, Dublin (1925), and Cork City Hall (1935–36). Art Deco was used in cinemas, such as the Dublin (1928–29) and Cork (1931–32) Savoys. Full-blown modernism arrived in the 1930s with Desmond Fitzgerald's Dublin Airport (1937–40) and Michael *Scott's private house 'Geragh' in Sandycove, Dublin (1937–39). Michael Scott created Busáras, the glass-fronted corporate headquarters of the national bus company in 1945. By the 1960s, controversial buildings in the dominant bland modern style of the era were being built on the ruins of Dublin's elegant, eighteenth-century-classical architecture. Also in Dublin, Desmond O'Kelly's Liberty Hall, Ireland's first skyscraper, was finished in 1965 and the infamous tower blocks of Ballymun (in the process of being demolished) were constructed in 1966. Michael Scott, Ronald Tallon and Reginald Walker designed modernist office blocks in the capital, including the Dublin Corporation Civic Offices at Wood Quay (1994–95). Sam Stephenson planned the Central Bank of Ireland on Dame Street (1980). By the 1990s, however, the limits of modernism had been reached. A new interest among younger architects in the eclecticism of post-modernism produced enthusiasm for inner-city renewal schemes, including preserving the old Georgian buildings, modern apartment units, livable communities and the creation of car-free residential zones. At the forefront of these developments was the architectural collective Group '91, which masterminded the rebirth of one of Dublin's oldest and most dilapidated neighbourhoods, Temple Bar. Construction at the beginning of the twenty-first century appears to be waning, as many international companies are rethinking their commitment to Ireland.

Irish architecture has been the product of local histories and international influences. A.K.

Ardagh Chalice. One of the greatest surviving masterpieces of ecclesiastical metalwork of the eighth century in Europe. It was found in 1868 near Ardagh, County *Limerick, with a smaller chalice and four brooches dating from the ninth/tenth century, by a boy hunting rabbits. Standing on a conical base and with broad handles of Late Antique inspiration, this wine chalice is made of silver, richly decorated with gold, glass and other materials, including amber. It is also ornamented beneath the rim, around the neck and even under the foot with a feast of filigree patterns. The chalice is on display in the *National Museum in Dublin. P.H.

Armagh, Book of. Ninth-century Irish manuscript which is the most important source for our knowledge of the life and writings of St *Patrick. It is the only early manuscript that can be dated in the 800s with any degree of reliability. An inscription states that Ferdomnach wrote it at the behest of Torbach, who was abbot of Armagh in the years 807 and 808. This small-format book includes St Patrick's own *Confessio*, a copy of the New Testament and the Life of St Martin of Tours. Its illustrations, such as the Four Evangelist symbols, are drawn in monochrome brown ink with as firm a hand as the more colourful counterparts in the **Book of Kells*. It is now in the library of Trinity College, *Dublin. P.H.

Armagh, County. Inland county in the province of *Ulster, one of the six counties of *Northern Ireland. Armagh has an area of 483 square miles and a population of est. 141,585 (1996). The county is highly fertile and *agriculture is a staple of its economy. Known in song as 'the orchard of Ireland', Armagh has a strong fruit-growing industry. Its hilly southern portion includes some of the most beautiful scenery in Ireland, such as the spectacular mountain Slieve Gullion. In the north, where Armagh borders Lough Neagh, lies the Lurgan valley with its industrial towns. *Linen was once a major industry and it is still manufactured today. Throughout the county are remnants of some 400 *raths, or ring forts, including the magnificent Navan Fort (c.700 BC) which was once the capital of the *pre-Christian kings of Ulster. Two miles west of the city of Armagh, this fort, known as Emhain Macha in Irish *mythology, was where King Conor Mac Nessa held court with his Red Branch Knights, whose stories feature the great hero *Cúchulainn and the tragic lover Deirdre. From the seventh century, Armagh has been the ecclesiastical centre of the *Catholic church in Ireland. This is attributed to Armagh's close association with St *Patrick (c.400s). Written in the ninth century, the *Book of Armagh* (807), portions of which contain accounts of the life of Patrick, is one of Ireland's most important early medieval monastic works.

Armagh was severely affected by the *Nine Years War (1593–1603). The devastation of the conflict was compounded by the subsequent *'Plantation of Ulster', in which Gaelic Catholic landowners had their lands confiscated and granted to English and Scottish 'undertakers', who in turn replaced much of the native population with *Protestant settlers from Britain. The transfer of land ownership from Catholic to Protestant in Armagh was completed with the *Cromwellian Settlement. By 1700, almost all the land in the county was held by Protestant *landlords, with the native Catholics confined to the boggy and mountainous south. During the 1780s and 1790s as the county's population grew (Armagh was the most densely populated county in Ireland at the time), political tensions exploded into open conflict between Protestant Peep O'Day Boys and Catholic *Defenders in 1785. The *Government of Ireland Act (1920) and the *Anglo-Irish Treaty of 1921 made Armagh one of the six Ulster counties that would constitute Northern Ireland. The failure of the *Boundary Commission to attach South Armagh to the *Free State in 1925 left the almost entirely Catholic population of that region greatly dissatisfied. The sectarian demographics of the county have made Armagh one of the flashpoints of the *'Troubles'. Natives of Armagh include writer George *Russell (known as AE) and poet Paul *Muldoon. J.P.

Arms Crisis of 1970. Political scandal involving *Republic of Ireland cabinet ministers. In August 1969, at the height of the *Northern Ireland conflict, as *Derry and *Belfast were swept by riots and pogroms in which loyalist mobs burned out Catholic neighbourhoods, *Taoiseach Jack *Lynch implied that military force might be supplied to protect Northern *nationalists and reiterated Irish unity as the only long-term solution. As probably intended, this brought British troops onto the streets of *Northern Ireland, but *republican ambitions, north and south, had been raised. Republicans in the ruling *Fianna Fáil Party believed that Lynch's words (in a national television address) had to be acted upon. Some backed covert military aid to the vulnerable nationalist areas in *Northern Ireland. The development of militant anti-partitionism, in parallel with long-term diplomatic strategy, was advocated to prevent the Northern Ireland issue from regaining balance. Direct aid included money to Northern defence groups, limited arms training for selected individuals and sponsorship of traditional republican figures over the then Marxist *IRA leadership. Though relatively unimportant in the crystallisation and organisation of the Provisional IRA, this Irish government support was important in providing a certain legitimacy for militant irredentism. The matter became public on 6 May 1970, when two Fianna Fáil ministers, Neil Blaney (agriculture and fisheries) and Charles *Haughey (finance), were dismissed by Taoiseach Jack Lynch for allegedly misappropriating government money for the purchase of arms. Charges against Blaney were dropped in July, and in October 1970, Haughey and three other defendants were acquitted of all charges. Haughey's involvement with the republican cause was supported by some sections of southern opinion. Lynch remained Fianna Fáil leader and Blaney was expelled from the party. Haughey became minister for health in Lynch's new cabinet in 1977, and after Lynch resigned in 1979, Haughey was elected leader of Fianna Fáil and subsequently served as Taoiseach. M.M.

army, Irish. The Irish army has its origins in the split among *republicans over the *Anglo-Irish Treaty of 1921. While most rank-and-file members of the *IRA rejected the treaty, most of the general headquarters staff accepted it. Michael *Collins, commander in chief of the new army, used the pro-treaty IRA faction to create the nucleus of the *Irish Free State army. This force, better equipped and eventually numerically superior to its anti-treaty opponents, prevailed in Ireland's bitter *Civil War (June 1922 to May 1923). The rapid demobilisation of the approximately 58,000-man force after the Civil War, as well as dissatisfaction with the political direction taken by the Free State government regarding Irish unification, led to an unsuccessful mutiny by some officers in May 1924. Ever since, the Irish army has accepted without question the principle that it is subordinate to the elected government. During the Second World War, the poorly equipped army, which rose to a maximum strength of 41,000 in March 1941, served as a symbol of Ireland's neutrality and independence but could have done little to prevent an invasion of the country. After the Second World War, successive Irish governments neglected to build up an army that could deter an aggressor. Instead, the army has served an important role in aid to the civil power, especially during the *Troubles, and it has also been deployed on United Nations duty, particularly in the Congo (where nine Irish peacekeepers were killed in November 1960), Cyprus, Lebanon and East Timor. B.G.

Arts Council, the (An Chomhairle Ealaíon). Ireland's principal organisation of arts funding and advisor on arts matters. Established in 1951 and operating under the Arts Acts of 1951, 1973 and 2003, the council aims to promote and stimulate public interest in the arts. It commissions and publishes research and information, and undertakes a range of development projects, often jointly with other public sector or non-governmental agencies. The Arts Council has 12 members and a chairman, who serve voluntarily and are appointed for five years by the minister for Arts, Sport and Tourism. The twelfth Arts Council was appointed in 2003. (Web site: *www.artscouncil.ie*.) M.C.

Arts Council of Northern Ireland, the. *Northern Ireland organisation for the funding of the arts. Established in 1962, as successor to the Committee for the Encouragement of Music and the Arts (CEMA) of 1942, it became a statutory body in September 1995, consulting external advisors on the allocation of funds made available by the government and the National Lottery. Its function is to develop and improve the knowledge, appreciation and practice of the arts in *Northern Ireland, and to increase public access. (Web site: *www.artscouncil-ni.org*.) M.C.

Ashe, Thomas (1885–1917). Revolutionary. Born in Lispole, County *Kerry, Ashe was a school principal by profession and member of the *Gaelic League and the *Irish Republican Brotherhood. He commanded the Fingall *Volunteers and fought against the *RIC at Ashbourne, County *Meath, during the 1916 *Easter Rising. Ashe was sentenced to death in May 1916 but his sentence was later commuted to life imprisonment. Released in August 1917, he was rearrested shortly afterward for sedition. Ashe died in *Mountjoy Prison, Dublin, while on *hunger strike for prisoner of war status. His funeral at *Glasnevin Cemetery on 30 September 1917, proved a turning point in the *republican rally, with the Volunteers wearing uniform in public for the first time since the Easter week surrender. A volley of shots was fired over the grave and an oration was delivered by Michael *Collins. P.E.

Asquith, Herbert Henry (1852–1928). British Liberal prime minister responsible for the third *home rule bill. Asquith was first elected to parliament in 1886 and in 1892 became home secretary under William Ewart *Gladstone. In 1908, he succeeded Henry Campbell-Bannerman as prime minister. Asquith introduced the third home rule bill into the Commons in April 1912. This bill granted Ireland its own parliament with power over all internal affairs, with the exception of taxation and the police force. In addition, Ireland would continue to send 40 MPs to Westminster. The alliance between the Liberals and the *Irish Parliamentary Party ensured its passage through the Commons, but it was defeated in the House of Lords. The provisions of the 1911 Parliament Act (by which a veto in the House of Lords amounted merely to a two-year delay) meant that Asquith's home rule bill was due to become law in 1914. Considerable opposition by *Ulster unionists led to fears that Ireland was on the brink of a civil war by early 1914. The onset of the *First World War, however, led to the suspension of the home rule bill until the end of the conflict. In 1915, Asquith yielded to demands for a coalition government, but in December 1916 he was forced to resign and was replaced by David *Lloyd George. This caused a catastrophic split in the Liberal Party, which went into decline after 1918. Asquith remained party leader until 1926 and became a peer in 1925. P.E.

Aughrim, Battle of (12 July 1691). Last battle of the Williamite War, considered the bloodiest battle fought in Ireland. After the Williamite forces had taken Athlone and crossed the *Shannon on 30 June 1691, the *Jacobite forces under the French Marshal, the Marquis de St Ruth, made a stand at Aughrim, near Ballinasloe, County *Galway. The Williamite army was led by the Dutch general, Baron van Ginkel. The Battle of Aughrim was more important than the more famous Battle of the *Boyne, fought a year earlier, in deciding Ireland's fate. As at the Boyne, the Jacobite army consisted of French and Irish troops while the Williamites had British and Continental regiments.

The Jacobites were in a good defensive position behind a marsh, but were outmanouvred by the Williamite cavalry. Before he could organise a countermove, St Ruth was beheaded by an enemy cannon ball. He had left no clear instructions to his subordinates and had positioned the most daring and gifted Irish commander, Patrick *Sarsfield, at the rear. The Jacobites were defeated and routed. The fleeing army lost 7,000. This defeat marked the end of the Jacobite cause. The Jacobites fell back upon Galway City, which, in turn, was captured by the Williamites. By this stage, many French troops had been recalled and the remaining Jacobite army was forced to make a stand at Limerick, where they were besieged. The failure of French reinforcements to arrive in time led to their surrender and the Treaty of *Limerick. T.C.

Australia, the Irish in. The Irish comprised approximately one-third of the convict and free settler emigrants to the newly established British colony of Australia. Irishmen were well represented in the *First Fleet*, the first ship of colonists from England, which arrived in New South Wales in January 1788. On board were Captain David Collins and John White, both Irishmen who held the important positions of judge advocate and chief physician, respectively, in the inaugural colonial administration. The *First Fleet* also contained Irish-born convicts who had been sentenced in England

and their marine guards. The proportion of Irish in the colony increased rapidly from 1791 when the first transport of Irish convicts reached Australia from Cobh, County *Cork.

The mass deportation of *Defenders and *United Irishmen to the colony between 1793 and 1805 created a substantial community of experienced *republican revolutionaries whose plots and uprisings created considerable ferment in 1800. The Castle Hill Rising of March 1804 (fought at Vinegar Hill) was overwhelmingly an Irish affair, which led to the first declaration of martial law in Australia. The comparatively benign tenure of Governor Lachlan Macquarie facilitated the assimilation of the disaffected Irish after 1810. By then ex-United Irishmen William Redfern and James Meehan played vital roles in developing health care and surveying the expanding Australian colonies. As the major phase of the convict transportation to Australia drew to a close in 1853, in part spurred by Irish-Australian lobbying, the continued *emigration of Irish families maintained a strong sense of ethnic identity. Ninety thousand Irish emigrants arrived in the Australian state of New South Wales between 1836 and 1886, while numerous others went to the newer state territories of Victoria, Queensland, South Australia, Western Australia and Tasmania. The extent and pace of the influx owed much to the discovery of gold, the availability of affordable land and generally good employment prospects. Almost 400,000 Irish emigrants went to Australia and New Zealand between 1850 and 1921. The distinctive contribution of the Irish in Australia took many forms, not least the creation of a sizable Roman Catholic community and the adoption of a variant of *Gaelic football as a major sporting code.

Trade unions and the political fronts of the labour movement were also heavily indebted to Irish immigrants and their descendants who were well represented at every level of colonial society. Irish miners at Ballarat goldfield, Victoria, were the focal point of a highly significant and violent protest in 1854 at the Eureka Stockade. The stand against perceived administrative injustice and incompetence found an articulate figurehead in Peter Lalor, a native of County *Laois, who subsequently became Speaker of the Victorian assembly. In 1880, the Irish community and its supporters collected the huge sum of £95,000 for famine relief in Ireland.

The profusion of Irish cultural, religious and political organisations mirrored that of the North American experience. Between the 1880s and 1914, the Irish in Sydney and Melbourne offered strong moral support for *home rule in their native country. The onset of the *First World War in 1914 and the repercussions of the 1916 *Easter Rising lessened Irish Australian support, although such revolutionary bodies as the *Irish Republican Brotherhood continued to maintain a presence in Australia. The percentage of Irish-born in Australia dropped after 1945 owing to a relaxation of restrictions on non-English-speaking applicants and other domestic and international factors, but the numbers increased in the 1950s and again in the 1980s. Relations between the Irish and Australians further improved in the 1990s and Australia remains a major destination for Irish visitors and emigrants. R.OD.

Auxiliaries, the. Military support for the *RIC during the *War of Independence. Formed in July 1920, the Auxiliaries were recruited from former British army officers to combat the *IRA. Because the British government did not recognise the conflict as a war, the Auxiliaries were made a division of the RIC. By November 1921, they were 1,900 strong. They operated independently in armed patrols striking at will. Shocked at their behaviour, their commander, Brigadier General Frank Crozier, resigned. T.C.

B

Bacon, Francis (1909–92). Painter. Bacon was born in *Dublin and raised in County *Kildare, where his father, a retired British army captain, trained horses. His family moved to London in 1914, when the British army was mobilised for war, and returned to a rebellious Ireland in 1917. A witness to a turbulent time in Ireland, Bacon moved to London in 1925. He visited Berlin in 1928 and lived in Paris until 1930. Influenced by German expressionism, French surrealism and Picasso's work, Bacon only began to paint when back in London in 1930. He produced expressionistic, distorted figurative work influenced by photography and set in surreal spaces. The inclusion of his 1933 *Crucifixion* painting (a recurring theme) in Sir Herbert Read's influential *Art Now: An Introduction of the Theory of Modern Painting and Sculpture* (1933) brought him to the attention of leading art collectors. His 1945 triptych *Three Studies for Figures at the Base of a Crucifixion*, painted in protest of the Second World War, established his reputation. In 1998, Mr John Edwards, his sole heir, donated the painter's studio to the *Hugh Lane Municipal Gallery. M.C.

Balfe, Michael William (1808–70). Composer and singer. Born in *Dublin, Balfe was apprenticed to Charles Edward Horn in London in 1823. He was commissioned by La Scala in Milan to write music for the ballet *La Pérouse* in 1826. In Paris, in 1827, Balfe met the composer Gioacchino Rossini, who arranged tuition and an engagement to sing Figaro at the Théâtre des Italiens. In 1830, Balfe married the Hungarian singer Lina Rosa. He returned to London in 1833 and wrote many operas for Drury Lane, notably *The Siege of Rochelle* (1838) and *The Bohemian Girl* (1843). C.D.

Ballagh, Robert (1943–). Painter and draughtsman. Born in *Dublin, Ballagh is a member of *Aosdána. He has designed **Riverdance* stage sets, logos, book jackets, postage stamps and currency. His style is much influenced by his early architectural training and an interest in photography. The cruciform *Portrait of Noel Browne* (1985) with stones tumbling out onto the floor demonstrates Ballagh's technical skill and innovation. An organiser of the*Irish Exhibition of Living Art in the 1970s, Ballagh believes in the wider social responsibility of the artist. He helped form the Association of Artists in Ireland in 1981 to improve artists' working conditions. He served on the executive committee of the UNESCO-affiliated International Association of Artists from 1983 to 1986. His international work led to paintings such as *Man Drawing a Recumbent Woman* (1984) for the Dürer Haus in Nürnberg. More recently, in works such as *The Bogman* (1997) Ballagh has painted events in his life that include imaginary landscapes and incorporate Gaelic texts and natural materials. He is vice president of the Ireland Institute and a member of Le Chéile/Together, Irish Artists Against Racism. M.C.

Banville, John (1945–). Novelist, literary editor. Born in Wexford town, Banville is best known for the tetralogy consisting of *Doctor Copernicus* (1976), *Kepler* (1981), *The Newton Letter* (1982) and *Mefisto* (1986), and a trilogy made up of *The Book of Evidence* (1989), *Ghosts* (1993) and *Athena* (1995). *The Book* *of Evidence* was shortlisted for the Booker Prize and awarded the Guinness Peat Aviation Award in 1990. Stylistically masterful, Banville's work draws on European art, history and literature and has a subtle philosophical dimension. In the tetralogy, Banville explores the relationship between scientific and imaginative truth. The trilogy investigates the gap between artistic perfection and personal weakness. Other work includes the novels *Birchwood* (1973), *The Untouchable* (1997), *Shroud* (2002) and a number of plays and screen-plays. For many years, Banville was literary editor of the *Irish Times* and is now that newspaper's chief literary critic. G.OB.

bardic schools. The name generally given to schools of *poetry in Ireland and *Scotland between 1200 and 1700. Although schools of poetry existed from before historic time, in the fifth century these bardic schools involved the professional training of poets (a training that sometimes took up to seven years). The schools became hereditary among certain families, particularly the Ua Dálaigh (O'Dalys) and the Ua hUiginn (O'Higgins). These families usually received patronage from a chieftain. Instruction was mainly oral, but the reading of manuscripts was also taught. The poets composed in a very formal language, which was standardised throughout the Gaelic world. The metres used were based on a complicated and subtle relationship between vowels and consonants and involved a deep and precise knowledge of assonance, rhyme, alliteration and sound concordance. This formal language was originally based on the spoken tongue of the thirteenth century, but became remote from common speech as the living language evolved in the following centuries. Poets moved freely between Ireland and Scotland as we see in the career of Muireadhach Albanach Ó Dálaigh (c.1180–1230), for example, who worked for, or wrote poems for, patrons in *Ulster, *Connacht, *Munster and Scotland. Most of this poetry is directly related to the patronage of a chieftain and is therefore eulogistic, satirical, genealogical, or commemorative, but there is also a large body of religious poetry and some strikingly passionate personal poems. A.T.

Barry, Gerald (1952–). Composer. Born in Clarecastle, County *Clare, Barry, who trained in *Dublin, Amsterdam (Peter Schat), Cologne (Karlheinz Stockhausen, Mauricio Kagel) and Vienna (Friedrich Cerha), is renowned for a highly individual style that can blend theatrical extremes of virtuosity, humour and unexpected pathos. His first opera, *The Intelligence Park* (Almeida Festival, London, 1991), was both controversial and successful; his second, *The Triumph of Beauty and Deceit* (1995), marked a rare venture into the world of television opera. His orchestral music is renowned for its excitement and energy. Notably, his 1988 BBC Henry Wood Promenade Concerts commission, *Chevaux-de-frise* and *The Conquest of Ireland* (1995) – which set to music texts from the eponymous book by Giraldus Cambrensis – and the frenetic demands of his *Second Piano Quartet* (1996) are known literally to have left blood on the keyboard. M.D.

Barry, James (1741–1806). Historical painter. Barry was born in *Cork. Supported by Edmund *Burke, he was first acclaimed in 1763 for the innovative use of Irish subject matter in his painting *The Conversion by St Patrick of the King of Cashel.* He went to London in 1764 and in 1766 to Rome, where he studied art for five years. In 1775, he was elected to the Royal Academy where he became professor of painting in 1782. His neo-classicist and republican prints, such as *The Phoenix* and *Philoctetes*, were highly prized by political radicals in Ireland. Barry worked unpaid on a series of pictures known as *The Progress of Human Culture* for the Great Room of the Society of Arts in London for many years from 1777. He wrote extensively in defence of history painting. M.C.

Barry, Sebastian (1955–). Dramatist, poet and novelist. Born in *Dublin (the son of actress Joan O'Hara) and educated at Trinity College, Dublin, Barry is considered one of Ireland's leading young playwrights. He has written volumes of poetry, such as *The Water-Colourist* (1983) and *The Rhetorical Town* (1985) and several works of fiction for adults and for young readers, including his more recent novel *The Whereabouts of Eneas McNulty* (1998). Barry's prose is characterised by a linguistically idiosyncratic, sensuous quality. His works often reflect on Irish history through personal memory, and several of his plays purport to do so through the history of his own family, although Barry has stated that the plays are concoctions. *In Prayers of Sherkin* (1991), which is based on a true story, human kindness prevails over strict religious principles when Fanny Hawke, a member of a dwindling Quaker-like sect, decides to marry an outsider. Barry's real breakthrough as a playwright came in 1995 with the much acclaimed *The Steward of Christendom*, a moving portrayal of Thomas Dunne, the *Catholic chief superintendent of the Dublin Metropolitan Police. From his deathbed, Dunne (played brilliantly by Donal *McCann) reflects on a life torn by political allegiances in the days of James *Larkin and Michael *Collins and a career ultimately assigned to oblivion by the *Anglo-Irish Treaty. In *Our Lady of Sligo* (1998), Barry focuses on the Irish middle-class in the stifling conservatism of the post-independence era through the eyes of the main character, the alcoholic, dying Mai O'Hara (played superbly by Sinead *Cusack). *Hinterland* (2002) was controversial as some critics felt the play's plot and protagonist, Johnny Silvester, were too closely modelled on the life and person of Irish politician Charles *Haughey. In *Whistling Psyche* (2004), a nineteenth-century surgeon James Barry practises as a man but is really a woman. J.C.E.L.

Barton, Robert (1881–1975). *Republican politician. Born into a *Protestant family in Glendalough, County *Wicklow, Barton was a British army officer in *Dublin during the *Easter Rising of 1916. He converted to republicanism and was the *Sinn Féin minister for agriculture (1919–21) in the first *Dáil Éireann. Barton (a cousin of Erskine *Childers) was a member of the delegation that signed the *Anglo-Irish Treaty, but joined the anti-treaty forces in the *Civil War. After the war, he retired from political life. S.A.B.

Beckett, Samuel Barclay (1906–89). Playwright, novelist, Nobel Prize winner (1969). One of the most inventive writers of the twentieth century, Samuel Beckett revolutionised modern drama with his minimalist plays associated with the theatre of the absurd. Born on 13 April 1906, in Foxrock, County *Dublin, the younger son of an affluent *Protestant quantity surveyor and an intensely religious mother, Beckett was educated at Portora Royal School, Enniskillen, County *Fermanagh. During his college years at Trinity College, Dublin, he came to love the cinema and its silent comic masters, especially Charlie Chaplin and Buster Keaton, who would inspire his work.

In 1928, Beckett moved to Paris (as a lecturer in English at L'Ecole Normale Supérieure) where he established a lasting friendship with Thomas MacGreevy, poet and later director of the *National Gallery, Dublin. In Paris, he also became the devoted disciple of his fellow Dubliner James *Joyce. Contrary to rumour, Beckett was never Joyce's secretary, but, like many of the writer's admirers, he ran errands for him, including reading out loud to the nearly blind writer.

His first publication was an essay on Joyce's *Finnegans Wake* entitled 'Dante ... Bruno. Vico.. Joyce' (1929). Beckett's first short story, 'Assumption', which deliberately lacked a plot, appeared in the magazine *transition* in 1929, and in 1930 he published a long, witty, erudite and arcane poem, *Whoroscope*. After a brief period as a lecturer in French at Trinity College, Dublin (1930–31), Beckett, penniless and plagued by ill health, lived in Germany, France and England. His short study, *Proust* (1931), explores the breakdown of the relationship between the subject and the object, also the theme of an influential essay on contemporary poetry in Ireland, 'Recent Irish Poetry', in *The Bookman* (1934). His first novel, the Joycean extravaganza *Dream of Fair to Middling Women*, written in 1932, remained unpublished until 1993. *More Pricks than Kicks* (1934), a self-consciously pedantic volume of short stories, was followed in 1938 by *Murphy*, a novel that parodies the icons of the *Irish Literary Revival. *Murphy* had been initially turned down by virtually all British and American publishers but was finally published by Routledge & Son, Ltd., in 1938. In this wonderfully funny book, Beckett invented one of his first prototypical characters – the outcast – a lone indolent, young Irish man down on his luck in London just as Beckett himself was at the time.

Beckett preferred occupied France to Ireland at peace during the Second World War and became a member of the Resistance movement. Together with his friend Suzanne Dumesnil (who would later become his wife), he left Paris to avoid arrest in August 1942 and settled in Roussillon in the Vaucluse. In the three dark years they spent there, Beckett wrote *Watt*, which was published only years later, in 1953, by Merlin Press. This novel, a comic attack on rationality, contains darker tragic undertones of Beckett's war experience.

After he returned to Paris in 1945, Beckett began to write in French to divest his style of moribund literary influences. *Mercier et Camier*, written in 1946, was his first novel in French, followed by a trilogy, *Molloy* (1951), *Malone Dies* (1951) and *The Unnameable* (1953). The trilogy's fragmented narration and interior monologues reflect the theme of the split between human perception and objective reality. The vacuity of modern society is further explored in Beckett's minimalist plays, including *Waiting for Godot* (1948–49), *Endgame* (1957), *Krapp's Last Tape* (1958) and *Happy Days* (1961). *Godot*, under Roger Blin's direction, opened in Paris in 1953 to great (if not unanimous) critical acclaim, and Beckett's years of poverty and obscurity were over. In this masterpiece of the theatre of the absurd, a movement that revolutionised drama, Beckett strips language and bares the human soul. Beckett's anti-heroes are marginal, barely surviving on the edges of life, in garbage dumps, ditches, gutters, lunatic asylums, searching for a meaning that remains elusive. For all the bleakness, isolation, alienation and loneliness, there is an extraordinary element of humour, poetry and humanity. 'I can't go on, I'll go on' (*The Unnameable*) encapsulates both Beckett's and his characters' anguish and unwillingness to give up.

Beckett's later writing moves closer to silence, but its irony and endurance stops short of pessimism and despair. Plays and prose are increasingly stripped of all but the essentials of character, setting and action. *Breath* (1969), an anti-dramatic, plotless play lasting 30 seconds, consists of a heap of rubbish, a breath and a cry. Work for television includes *Eh Joe* (1966), *... but the clouds* (1976) – based on Yeats' *The Tower* – and *Ghost Trio* (1976).

He also made a film called *Film* (1963), which was premiered at the New York Film Festival in 1965 and is now considered a classic. Evident throughout Beckett's work are the scepticism and rigour of the *Anglo-Irish literary tradition and his own sceptical response to his Protestant inheritance. His distrust extends to traditional literary and dramatic forms, and to language deadened by habitual use, which ultimately became a significant thematic and formal concern. He died in 1989 and is buried in Paris. M.S.T., L.R.

beehive huts. Roughly hemispherical huts, built without mortar on the corbel principle – layers of stone placed in a circle, decreasing in circumference as they rise until closed by a single stone at the top. The best-known examples are on *Skellig Michael and on the *Dingle Peninsula in County *Kerry, but others are found on islands farther north along the coast. With few modern exceptions, these are likely to date from the early Middle Ages (AD c.500–1000). Sometimes explained as temporary dwellings for shepherds, beehive huts most likely served as shelters or hostels for *pilgrims. P.H.

Behan, Brendan (1923–64). Playwright and writer. Behan is famous for his political views, satire, wit, drunkenness and storytelling. Born on 9 February 1923, in the Holles Street Hospital in *Dublin, he grew up in a working-class part of the inner city and left school at the age of 14. Behan had an incisive mind and was mainly taught by his father, Stephen, who read him tales by Dickens, Zola and Galsworthy. His family also instilled in Behan his socialist views and his rebel ideals. From the age of nine, he served in a youth organisation connected to the *IRA and in the 1930s was an IRA messenger boy.

In 1939, Behan was arrested on a sabotage mission in England and was sentenced to three years in Borstal, a reform school for boys. This experience became the impetus for one of his most famous works, the autobiographical *Borstal Boy* (1958) and its sequel, *Confessions of an Irish Rebel* (1965).

After his release, Behan returned to Ireland, but in 1942 was sentenced to 14 years for the attempted murder of two detectives. He

Brendan Behan

was released four years later under a general amnesty. After spending another month in jail in 1948 for drunk and disorderly conduct, Behan decided to leave Dublin for Paris, where he lived for two years..

Behan's first play, *The Quare Fellow*, based on his prison experiences, was first performed in 1956 and soon gained critical success. In the play, Behan attacked capital punishment and society's hypocrisy in matters of sex, politics and religion. Other plays include *An Giall* (1958), subsequently translated and adapted by Behan and Joan Littlewood for the Theatre Workshop in London as *The Hostage* (1958). Almost completed at the time of Behan's death, *Richard's Cork Leg* was first produced by Alan Simpson as part of the 1972 Dublin Theatre Festival. Behan's plays often use song and dance and direct addresses to the audience, which show the influence of Bertolt Brecht on his writing style. By the late 1950s Behan had gained much critical attention, which ultimately led to his downfall and death. His early discipline eventually gave way to prolonged drinking bouts and self-destructive incidents. In March 1964, Behan collapsed in the Harbour Lights Pub and died on 20 March in a Dublin Hospital at the age of 41. T.F.

Belfast. Capital of *Northern Ireland. The name derives from the Irish, *Béal Feirsde*, meaning the 'mouth of the river'. In the nineteenth century, Belfast was Ireland's main industrial city and, since 1921, capital of Northern Ireland. Although a settlement had existed since the seventh century, the town was founded by Sir Arthur *Chichester in 1603 for English and *Scots settlers. It became a borough in 1613 represented by two MPs in the Irish *parliament. In the eighteenth century, the first industries, particularly *linen, began to develop along the valley of the River Lagan.

Belfast was a *Presbyterian town with a reputation for radical politics. It supported the *American Revolution and the *1798 United Irishmen's Rebellion. The rebellion resulted in a conservative backlash and, as Belfast began to prosper after the Act of *Union, the town became more loyalist in character.

By the 1830s, Belfast was the world's main producer of linen and, after the coming of the railways in the 1840s, its harbour, Belfast Lough, became a major port. By the end of the century, the town supported a *textile industry, shipbuilding, engineering, rope manufacturing, *whiskey production and tobacco. In 1888, it officially became a city.

The population rapidly expanded as people came from Scotland, England and other parts of Ireland seeking work. By 1901, there were 349,180 inhabitants, most of whom were *Protestants loyal to Britain. There was, however, a significant minority of *Catholics. From the 1840s on, Belfast became the scene of violence, riots and even sustained street warfare between these two groups. After 1886, the *Ulster Protestant opposition to *home rule led to increasing clashes with the Catholic minority. The founding of Northern Ireland in 1920 was marked by months of violence in which hundreds of Catholics were driven from their homes. The city's demographics and its segregated neighbourhoods stem mainly from this time.

Belfast's politics reflected its religious make-up. Catholics were concentrated in certain areas, such as the Falls Road and in general were poorer and employed, if at all, in non-skilled industry. They supported *nationalist candidates and had little impact on city government. Backed by the *Orange Order, *unionist politicians dominated local government and parliamentary representation. The sectarian dichotomy continues to this day.

Belfast has been a battleground during the present Northern Ireland conflict, with riots, bombings and murders. Almost half of the fatalities and some of the worst atrocities occurred there. Due to the increase in the Catholic population, Belfast is no longer a Protestant-dominated city. In 1998, Alban Magennis of the *Social Democratic and Labour Party was elected as the first Catholic mayor and unionist parties no longer have a majority on the city council.

In recent decades, its economic profile changed as the traditional industries, particularly textiles and shipbuilding, declined. Nevertheless, with a population around 350,000, Belfast remains the second largest city in Ireland and the dominant economic centre of Northern Ireland. Prospects for further economic growth have been enhanced by the promise of peace following the *Good Friday Agreement of 1998.

Belfast sits in a bowl created by hills at the mouth of the River Lagan, which divides it in two. Ben Madigan, sometimes called Napoleon's Nose, overlooks the city to the north. Belfast is essentially a Victorian city and little of its eighteenth-century *architecture remains. The most famous building is the elaborate City Hall in Donegall Square. Most of the population live in sprawling suburbs constructed in the 1970s and 1980s. T.C.

Bell, the. Famous literary magazine (1940–54). Founded and edited by Seán *Ó Faoláin (1940–46) and Peadar O'Donnell (1946–54), The *Bell* was the leading Irish periodical of its time. Showcasing the work of established Irish writers and new talent, the journal published short stories; *poetry; literary, *theatre and *cinema criticism; and articles on important political and social issues. Ó Faoláin's editorials and essays attacked *Catholic clericalism, puritanism, *censorship and anti-intellectualism; peasant and bourgeois conservatism; and chauvinistic Gaelic *nationalism that preserved a mythical past isolating Ireland from the realities of the present and prospects for the future. The *Bell* provided liberating intellectual light in a dark and dreary period of Irish history. L.J.MC.

Bergin, Mary (1949–). Traditional *music tin whistle player. Born of musical parents in County *Dublin, she learned to play at age nine, winning many awards during traditional music's revival in the 1960s. Bergin is also the mainstay of the all-female band Dordán. Her first album *Feadóga Stáin* (1979) remains seminal. F.V.

Berkeley, George (1685–1753). Anglo-Irish philosopher and Anglican bishop of Cloyne. Born in *Kilkenny, Berkeley attended Trinity College. By 1713, he had published his major philosophical works. He travelled in Europe, briefly settled in Rhode Island (then a British colony) and returned home in 1731. He became bishop of Cloyne in 1734. Berkeley was a staunch, though unorthodox, defender of Christianity and a brilliant critic of the newly emerging scientific worldview which, he believed, endangered Christianity by replacing traditional theistic conceptions of the universe with that of a godless universe of matter in motion. Berkeley's response was both ingenious and implausible: he denied the existence of matter. His universe contained only minds and ideas; material bodies were merely ideas organised in regular patterns by an omnibenevolent God. Berkeley also offered insightful criticisms of Newtonian calculus and gravity, published a revolutionary treatise on vision, wrote proposals for dealing with poverty and proclaimed the medicinal virtues of tar water. Modern metaphysical idealism (the view that material reality does not exist) and scientific instrumentalism (the view that science does not explain anything but is merely a useful organising and predictive tool) are directly traceable to Berkeley's writings. M.L.

Best, George (1946–). *Soccer player. Born in *Belfast, Best was a precocious talent who joined Manchester United at age 15. He became one of the first soccer superstars of his generation. Best was a key member of the Manchester United team that won the European Cup in 1968 and was named European Player of the Year. He left the club prematurely in 1973, feeling the pressures of stardom and the effects of alcohol abuse. Best never regained the consistency that rated him one of the greatest players in the world. He finished his career at an array of clubs in Britain, Ireland and America before retiring in the early 1980s. He played 37 times for *Northern Ireland. F.S.

Binchy, Maeve (1940–). Journalist and bestselling fiction writer. Born in *Dublin, Binchy began her career as a schoolteacher. In 1968, she was hired to write for the *Irish Times* and continues to write columns, demonstrating her wit as well as her insights into domestic life. Her work is wide-ranging, encompassing novels, short stories, journalism, plays and television screen-plays. Binchy's first novel, *Light a Penny Candle* (1982), reveals themes common in subsequent works: relationships among friends and family, daily life in rural Ireland, individual and social tragedy and the damaging legacy of secrets kept. Binchy's bestselling novel *Circle of Friends* (1990) was made into a popular film. This story of girlhood friends addresses issues of growing up female in Ireland, the claustrophobia of small-town life and the economic disparities of class and religious membership that have defined the national culture. Other novels include *Echoes* (1985), *Firefly Summer* (1987), *Silver Wedding* (1988), *Glass Lake* (1994), *Evening Class* (1997) and *Tara Road* (1998). Binchy's collections of short stories include *The Copper Beech* (1992), *The Return Journey* (1998) and *The Lilac Bus* (1984). *This Year It Will Be Different and Other Stories* (1996) is an anthology of Christmas tales. K.MI.

Birmingham Six Case (1974). Legal case of six innocent men who spent 16 years in prison. On Thursday, 21 November 1974, 21 people were killed and 182 injured by bombs in two Birmingham pubs, the Mulberry Bush and the Tavern in the Town. The bombs had been planted by an *IRA unit, which had failed to give a warning, allegedly due to out-of-order public phones. That night, six Irishmen were detained by the Special Branch at Heysham Ferry Port. All but one were on their way to *Belfast to attend the funeral of James McDade, an IRA man killed while trying to plant a bomb in Coventry. The six men were Robert Gerard Hunter, Patrick Joseph Hill, Noel Richard McIlkenny, William Power, John Francis Walker and Hugh Daniel Callaghan. All, except Walker, who was from Derry, were natives of Belfast. Nearly all the men had *republican backgrounds. Forensic tests seemed to indicate that some of the men had been in contact with explosives. Only later were these tests proved unreliable. When handed over to the Birmingham police, the six men were badly beaten and subjected to considerable psychological pressure. Under duress, some of them signed confessions. On 15 August 1975, all six were convicted of murder and sentenced to life imprisonment. One appeal was dismissed in 1976 and at a second hearing in 1980, Lord Justice Denning denied appeal on the grounds that a frame-up was unthinkable. The Birmingham Six were finally released in 1991, having been found innocent after spending 16 years in prison. This case was but one of a number of serious miscarriages of justice involving innocent IRA suspects in Britain in the past few decades, which have seriously undermined confidence and credibility in the British legal system. The cases, however, have also resulted in some very basic improvements in a judicial process whose failures are a cause of concern to other minorities in Britain, as well as the Irish. M.M.

Birr telescope. Located in Birr, County *Offaly, this was the largest telescope in the world during the nineteenth century. Also known as the 'Leviathan of Parsonstown', it was built by William Parsons, the Third Earl of Rosse, in the early 1840s. When completed in 1845, the telescope contained a 72-inch mirror, mounted in a 56-foot tube, weighing over 3 tons. It was surpassed in size only in 1917 by the Hooker telescope at Mount Wilson in California. P.E.

Black and Tans. British ex-soldiers recruited to reinforce the *RIC during the *War of Independence. The RIC was unable to respond to *IRA attacks and military reinforcements were seen as essential. Because the British government would not admit that it was fighting a war, special recruits, mainly British ex-soldiers and sailors, were drafted to reinforce the RIC. Since regulation uniforms could not be supplied quickly enough, they were fitted in a mixture of RIC black jackets and army khaki trousers. Hence, they were nicknamed the Black and Tans, which also happened to be the name of a famous pack of foxhounds. Although a distinct unit, the *Auxiliaries were usually referred to as Black and Tans.

Between January 1920 and November 1921, 9,500 men had enlisted. With little or no police training, they were sent out to reinforce RIC barracks mainly in *Dublin, *Connacht and *Munster. The Black and Tans were notorious for their campaign of reprisals directed against civilians and property in response to IRA attacks. Originally overlooked by the authorities, this pattern of reprisals soon became official government policy. The Black and Tans gained a reputation for brutality and ruthlessness, particularly following incidents such as the burning of Cork City and the 'Sack' of Balbriggan, County *Dublin. Rather than defeating the IRA, such tactics alienated people even more from the RIC and increased support for the *republicans. Such was their reputation that in popular speech the War of Independence is still often referred to as the Black and Tan War. T.C.

Blair, Tony (1953–). British Labour prime minister, 1997 to present. Two weeks after his landslide victory, Blair visited *Northern Ireland and pledged to make the *peace process a top priority for his government. He encouraged the *IRA to restore its cease-fire by not insisting on decommissioning of arms as a prerequisite to *Sinn Féin's involvement in official peace negotiations. Blair also set a firm 9 April (Holy Thursday) 1998 deadline for the resolution of the all-party peace talks.

As the deadline approached, Blair worked aggressively to save the peace negotiations from collapse. He spoke openly with all sides, especially with *Ulster Unionist Party leader David *Trimble and urged Taoiseach Bertie *Ahern and US President Bill Clinton to remain active in the process. Blair's determined leadership was crucial to the *Good Friday Agreement.

Blair has faced difficulties in preserving the fragile peace accord. Extremists on both sides want it to fail. His ministry has struggled to resolve controversies over decommissioning, policing, Orange parades – especially Drumcree – paramilitary punishment beatings and the IRA's links with rebels in Colombia. Through it all, however, Blair has remained committed to implementing the Good Friday Agreement. R.D.

Blarney. See **Cork, County**.

Blasket Islands, the. Group of islands off the *Dingle Peninsula. Uninhabited since 1953, the Blaskets were a mecca for linguists and anthropologists during the early years of the Gaelic, or *Irish Language Revival (1905–30). A large corpus of Gaelic autobiographies emerged from the islands in the 1930s, most notably Tomás *Ó Criomhthain's *An tOileánach* (1929), Muiris *Ó Súilleabháin's *Fiche Bliain ag Fás* (1933) and Peig *Sayers' *Peig* (1936). In recent years the ownership of the Great Blasket, the largest of the islands, has become the subject of a complex legal wrangle in which relatives of the last inhabitants successfully challenged legislation to classify the island as a national heritage park. One of the smaller islands, Inishvickillane, is owned by former *Taoiseach Charles *Haughey. B.D.

Bloody Friday (1972). A day of mass carnage caused by *IRA car bombs. In *Belfast, on Friday, 21 July 1972, within one hour 26 bombs exploded, two of which (one at Cavehill Road, the other at Oxford Street bus station) killed 11 people and badly injured 130. *Television chose to cover the conflict without sanitisation and the image of dismembered bodies being shovelled into bin bags induced revulsion. The IRA, which had up to then insisted that civilians must bear the collateral costs of their campaign, was itself shaken by such a visceral atrocity. They were quick to blame the authorities for not reacting with sufficient efficiency to their warnings. Much of the IRA's credibility (accumulated through relatively selective targeting, British errors such as *Bloody Sunday and carefully timed cease-fires and policy initiatives) was wasted. Determined to limit the IRA's capacity and capitalising on the crisis, the British government sent the army back into 'No-Go Areas', notably the Bogside in Derry City, on 31 July (Operation Motorman). The same day, IRA no-warning bombs killed or fatally injured nine civilians in Claudy, County *Tyrone. M.M.

Bloody Sunday (I). Sunday, 21 November 1920. A day of atrocities at the peak of the *War of Independence. On this Sunday, Michael *Collins' Special Intelligence Unit, known as 'the Squad', shot dead 12 and injured five other suspected British agents operating in *Dublin. The victims, part of a spy network known as the Cairo Gang, led by Colonel Aimes and Major Bennett, had been brought from England to fight Collins and his organisation. Collins chose this Sunday because there was a big GAA (*Gaelic Athletic Association) football game in *Croke Park and Dublin would be unusually crowded. The night before, the *Auxiliaries had raided Vaughan's Hotel and just missed Collins and his top men who were finalising their plans. In another raid, two *IRA leaders, Peadar Clancy and Richard Kee, were captured and, along with another prisoner, Conor Clune, were tortured and shot dead on 21 November, supposedly 'trying to escape'.

At eight o'clock in the morning, members of the Squad, together with Dublin IRA members, converged on eight different addresses. Nineteen men, some of whom may not have been agents, were roused from their sleep and shot, some in front of wives or girlfriends. Most of the assassins got away, but one group was intercepted by an Auxiliary patrol and had to shoot their way out. One IRA man, Frank Teeling, was captured. By the time word was sent to Croke Park to cancel the game between *Tipperary and Dublin, it was too late. The crowds had already gathered. During the game, a contingent of Auxiliaries surrounded the stadium to search for suspects. They opened fire on the crowd with rifles and machine guns, killing 13. They claimed later to have come under attack, but it is generally believed that this was an act of revenge for the IRA's attack that morning. T.C.

Bloody Sunday (II). Sunday, 30 January 1972. Day of atrocity in Derry City, when British soldiers opened fire on civilians. Following the introduction of *internment without trial in August 1971, the *Northern Ireland Civil Rights Association (NICRA) reactivated its campaign of mass protest demonstrations. All such marches were banned as being illegal. A demonstration was held on 30 January 1972, in Derry. Estimates of the number of marchers vary. Some observers put the number as high as 20,000, whereas the Widgery Report (the report of the British government inquiry into the tragedy) estimated the number at between 3–5,000. A section of the crowd rioted at the William Street British army barricade. The army ordered the First Battalion, Parachute Regiment to begin an arrest operation. At approximately 4:10 p.m., soldiers began to open fire on the marchers in the Rossville Street area. By about 4:40 p.m. the shooting ended with 13 people dead and a further 13 injured from gunshots, one of whom later died. The Widgery Report, released in April 1972, was rejected by the *nationalist community and many others who were present on that day, as a cover-up.

Established in 1998, the Saville Tribunal, authorised by British Prime Minister Tony *Blair and headed by an international panel, has reopened the Bloody Sunday case to examine (among other issues) whether the soldiers came under fire first. The British soldiers claimed to have come under sustained attack by gunfire and nail bombs. None of the eyewitness accounts say they saw any guns or bombs being used. No soldiers were injured in the operation; no guns or bombs were recovered at the scene of the shooting. It seems that the elite soldiers, hyped up and expecting to make contact with the *IRA, reacted to some innocuous signal by methodically targeting men of military age.

Bloody Sunday was the end of the civil rights movement in *Northern Ireland. There was a massive upsurge of IRA violence following the incident as large *Catholic areas in Derry and *Belfast virtually withdrew from the state, becoming 'No-Go Areas' dominated by the IRA. Though Bloody Sunday had been the responsibility of the British army, the devolved *Stormont government fell victim and was suspended on 24 March 1972. Direct rule by the United Kingdom government in London was imposed. The Saville Tribunal is expected to issue its report in 2005. M.M.

Blueshirts, the. Political organisation. The Blueshirts organisation was formed on 9 February 1932, as the Army Comrades' Association for ex-soldiers of the *Irish Free State army. After the *Fianna Fáil victory in a general election on 16 February 1932, *Cumann na nGaedheal supporters rushed to join the Army Comrades' Association. On 22 February 1933, Éamon *de Valera fired General Eoin *O'Duffy, who was the *gárda commissioner. O'Duffy became the association's leader and renamed it the National Guard. Mimicking their European counterparts, the guard adopted blue shirts as the party uniform and became known as the Blueshirts. Under O'Duffy, the Blueshirts embraced fascist ideology and paramilitary structure. After a planned march on *Dublin in August 1933 was banned by de Valera, the movement lost its momentum. In an attempt to revive its fortunes, the Blueshirts merged with Cumann na nGaedheal and the Centre Party to form a new political party, *Fine Gael (United Ireland Party), with O'Duffy as president.

However, O'Duffy was unstable and soon broke away to organise the Blueshirts as a separate organisation. They formed a volunteer brigade to fight on the Fascist side in the *Spanish Civil War but had an inglorious career there. The movement enjoyed popular support for a brief period but faded into obscurity after Spain. T.C.

Blythe, Ernest (1889–1975). Politician and *Irish Free State minister. Born in Magheragall, Lisburn, County *Antrim, Blythe became a member of the *Gaelic League and the *IRB while working as a clerk in the civil service in *Dublin. Imprisoned during the 1916 *Easter Rising, he later supported the *Anglo-Irish Treaty and held a number of ministries (local government, 1922–23, finance, 1923–32 and vice president of the executive council, 1927–32) under *Cumann na nGaedheal. While minister for finance, he took considerable criticism for his decision to cut the old-age pension by a shilling, but he is also remembered for his support of the *Irish language and creating a state subsidy for the *Abbey National Theatre. He retired from politics in 1936 and became managing director of the Abbey Theatre from 1941 to 1967. His tenure there was considered highly controversial. P.E.

Bodley, Seóirse (1933–). Composer, conductor, lecturer, pianist. Bodley's youth in *Dublin coincided with the period when the newly formed *Radio Éireann Symphony Orchestra was introducing Irish audiences to a wide spectrum of orchestral music. His earliest work, including *Music for Strings* (1952), shows the influence of established European masters such as Bartók. Studies in Stuttgart (Johann Nepomuk David, composition, Hans Müller-Kray, conducting) broadened his outlook as shown in the *First Symphony* of 1959. He was appointed lecturer in music at University College, Dublin, in the same year. Influenced by the music and ideas he encountered at the Darmstadt Summer School, Bodley was the first Irish composer to seriously engage with the European avant-garde, as shown in the orchestral 'Configurations' (1967). In the 1970s, Bodley surprised audiences with his juxtaposition of avant-garde techniques and evocations of traditional Irish *music ('A Small White Cloud Drifts Over Ireland', 1976). He has continued to produce works of both tonal and serial orientation. M.D.

Boer War, the Irish in (1899–1902). The Irish fought on both sides of this British military campaign in southern Africa. The British attempted to seize control of two independent republics, Transvaal and the Orange Free State, where large deposits of gold and diamonds had been discovered. 22,000 Boers, 25,000 British troops and 12,000 African auxiliaries died within three years, and tens of thousands were displaced and many Boer civilians perished in British concentration camps. Irish regiments in the British army suffered heavy casualties at Colenso and Spion Kop, and the sieges of Ladysmith and Mafeking. Losses sustained by the Royal Dublin Fusiliers were commemorated by a memorial in St Stephen's Green, *Dublin, on a site originally intended for a statue of Wolfe *Tone. The activities of Irish pro-Boer commandoes led by Major John *MacBride and Arthur Lynch were acclaimed by leading Irish *nationalists, especially Arthur *Griffith whose newspaper, the *United Irishman*, helped define the *republican ideology of *Sinn Féin. The Treaty of Vereeniging ended the conflict on 31 May 1902, on favourable terms to the Boers, who went on to create the new country of South Africa. R.OD.

bogs. Seventeen percent of the land surface of Ireland is covered in bog. The word bog stems from the Irish word for 'soft' – *bogach*. Boglands began to form in Ireland about 8,000 years ago. The peat, or turf, is composed of 95% water and 5% rotted plants, animal remains, pollen and dust. Because of the large amount of rain that falls in parts of Ireland, much of the land is waterlogged and the micro-organisms that cause decay are unable to survive. Dead plants and animals gradually accumulate to form turf. 'Blanket bog' is found in many of the counties on the western seaboard, while 'raised bogs' (which are slightly higher than the rest of the countryside) are to be found in the midlands. Turf is still commonly used as a source of fuel. It has been harvested by the state company Bord na Móna since the 1930s and served as an invaluable source of alternative energy during the Second World War. B.D.

Bogside, the Battle of (1969). Siege of *nationalist/*Catholic neighbourhood in Derry City that brought the British army into the *Northern Ireland conflict. Beginning in October 1968, when a civil rights demonstration was attacked (5 October) by the *RUC in Derry City centre, tensions escalated. Twice, in January and April 1969, RUC incursions into the Catholic Bogside area led to intensive rioting and police brutality.

Sectarian passions were stoked by the *Orange Order's marching season, which in Derry peaked with the *Apprentice Boys' parade past the Bogside. Rioting was anticipated and the Derry City Defence Committee prepared to defend against the police incursions. On 12 August the Apprentice Boys' march was indeed assaulted at the Bogside's perimeter. The RUC, followed by a loyalist mob, entered the Bogside, only to be forced back. Two days of siege followed, as residents fought tear gas and armoured cars with stones and petrol bombs. In the course of battle, Jack *Lynch, then *Taoiseach, in a television address announced that 'the Irish government can no longer stand by and see innocent people injured and perhaps worse'. With the RUC exhausted, the *Stormont government was faced with the option of throwing the *B-Specials into the fray, or asking for direct aid from Britain. They opted for the latter and, late in the afternoon of 14 August 1969, British troops entered the centre of Derry. M.M.

Boland, Eavan (1944–). Poet and literary critic. Daughter of a diplomat and a painter, Boland was born in *Dublin and educated in London, New York and Trinity College, Dublin. One of Ireland's leading contemporary

Eavan Boland

poets, Boland has been at the centre of debates about feminism and the role of the woman poet in the Irish canon.

Her poetry gives expression to the unremembered lives of women who are 'outside history'. She deals frankly with issues such as childbirth, menstruation and masturbation and celebrates the domestic. The collections *The War Horse* (1975) and *In Her Own Image* (1980) explore the relation between domestic and political violence. Her nine volumes of poetry include *The Journey and Other Poems* (1986), *An Origin like Water: Collected Poems* (1996), *In a Time of Violence* (1994) and *Against Love Poetry* (2001). She is author of an autobiographical study, *Object Lessons* (1995), and a pamphlet, 'A Kind of Scar' (1989), about women writers' relationship with the Irish nation. Since 1996, Boland has taught at Stanford University in Palo Alto, California. M.S.T.

Boland, Gerald (1885–1973). Politician. Born in Manchester, England, to Irish parents and educated at the O'Brien Institute, *Dublin, Boland (brother of Harry) joined the Irish *Volunteers, and during the 1916 *Easter Rising, fought at Jacob's biscuit factory. He was imprisoned for his part in the rising. Boland was a member of the *Dáil (TD for Roscommon) from 1923 to 1961 and was a founder member of *Fianna Fáil in 1926. He was appointed minister for posts and telegraphs in 1933 and minister for lands in 1936. As minister for justice from 1939, Boland introduced strong measures to suppress the *IRA, including *internment without trial, military courts and special criminal courts. He lost his seat in 1961 but continued to work in politics as a senator until 1969. C.D.

Boland, Harry (1887–1922). *Republican. Born in *Dublin on 27 April 1887, Boland was educated at Synge Street *Christian Brothers School and at the De La Salle College, Castletown, County *Laois. He was a member of the GAA (*Gaelic Athletic Association) and a renowned *hurler, who played for Dublin in the 1908 All-Ireland Senior Championship. Boland became a member of the *IRB in 1904 and was responsible for having Michael *Collins, his close friend, initiated into the organisation in London. He was imprisoned for his role in the 1916 *Easter Rising and, after his release from prison, he helped reorganise the Irish *Volunteers and was elected secretary of *Sinn Féin in 1917. A member of the First *Dáil and part of the Irish envoy to America during the *War of Independence, Boland fell under the influence of the charismatic Éamon *de Valera. He opposed the *Anglo-Irish Treaty (1921) and worked tirelessly to prevent the *Civil War. Following its outbreak, he sided with de Valera and the republicans against the new *Free State government. Boland was shot in Skerries, County *Dublin, by a party of Free State soldiers, who had been sent by Michael Collins to arrest him. Boland died a few days later on 1 August 1922. P.E.

Boland, Kevin (1917–2001). Politician. Born in *Dublin (son of Gerald and nephew of Harry), *Boland was *Fianna Fáil TD (1957–70), minister for defence (1957–61), minister for social welfare (1961–66) and minister for local government (1966–70). He resigned from government in 1970 in sympathy with ministers Neil Blaney and Charles *Haughey, who had been dismissed by *Taoiseach Jack *Lynch in the *Arms Crisis. Boland founded the party Aontacht Éireann, which never won popular support. A committed *republican, he remained active in extra-parliamentary politics as a regular critic of Irish government policy on *Northern Ireland. Boland unsuccessfully challenged the constitutionality of the 1973 *Sunningdale Agreement in the Irish Supreme Court, arguing that the Irish government had no authority to recognise British sovereignty over *Northern Ireland. J.D.

Bolger, Dermot (1959–). Poet, publisher, novelist, playwright. Born in *Dublin, Bolger highlights the city's unglamorous north side in his work. As founder of Raven Arts Press, he edited a number of influential anthologies and published much distinctive new writing. His prolific output includes the prize-winning play *The Lament for Arthur Cleary* (1989) and the novel *The Journey Home* (1990). G.OB.

Boole, George (1815–64). Mathematician and logician. A shoemaker's son from Lincoln, England, Boole was self-taught and became a schoolmaster at 16. He was the first professor of mathematics at Queen's College, *Cork, where he taught from 1849 until his death. (Boole Hall at University College Cork was named after him.) Boole is widely regarded as the father of modern symbolic logic. Abstract descendants of Boole's algebra of logic (Boolean algebras) continue to be studied today and have useful applications in fields such as computer science and quantum theory. M.L.

Boru, Brian (Bóruma) (c.941–1014). High king of Ireland from 1002 to 1014. Born in *Munster, Brian Boru was the youngest of 12 sons of Bebinn and Cennedi, who were members of the Dál Cais tribe.

In 965, Brian's brother Mathgamain seized the throne of Munster from the Éoganacht rulers. On the death of his brother, Brian established himself as the king of Munster. He invaded Ossory in 983 and by 997 had control of South Ireland. In 1002, Brian made himself *Ard-Rí* (high king) of Ireland, becoming the first monarch outside the *O'Neill dynasty to claim such authority. He was described in the **Book of Armagh* as the emperor of the Irish.

In his expeditions to the north in 1002 and 1005, Brian took hostages and collected tributes from local kings. Much of these monies were used to rebuild monasteries and to restore the libraries, which had been burned by the *Vikings. As his power increased, relations with some of the native lords and Norse rulers on the Irish coast deteriorated. In 1013, the Vikings of Dublin and the *Leinster Irish united against him and a decisive battle was fought at *Clontarf, near Dublin, on 23 April 1014. Brian's army annihilated the forces of the Leinster-Viking alliance, but he was hacked to death in his tent by Norsemen fleeing the battlefield. M.T.D., P.E.

Boston, the Irish in. The earliest Irish arrived in Boston in the seventeenth century and came from the northern counties of Ireland. Because they spoke English, were *Presbyterian and possessed marketable skills, they were accepted by the Puritans. Their support of the rebellion against the oppressive British tax policies further guaranteed their place in the life of the colony. Irish *Catholics from the southern counties of Ireland, by contrast, generally avoided Massachusetts during the colonial period because of its punitive laws against Catholic priests. During the *American Revolutionary War (1775–83), however, as a result of friendly relations with France, attitudes toward the small Catholic population became more tolerant.

During the 1820s and 1830s, attitudes

changed as restrictive British land policies in Ireland caused large numbers of Catholics to leave Ireland for America. Their increasing numbers produced sporadic outbreaks of violence by native Bostonians who feared the impact of unskilled workers on the city's economy and the influence of Catholicism on their Protestant institutions. The influx of Irish Catholic *immigrants in the wake of the disastrous potato *Famine during the mid-1840s caused even greater consternation. In an effort to stop further immigration, nativists organised the American Party, also called the Know-Nothings, that swept the northern states. Because of the increasing volatility of the slavery issue, however, in 1856 the Know-Nothing candidate failed to win the presidency.

During the *American Civil War (1861–65), the Boston Irish formed two separate Irish regiments and fought gallantly to preserve the Union. After the war, they gained a measure of social acceptance and used money from army service or war work to move out of the waterfront into nearby neighbourhoods. Taking menial jobs in municipal services and public utilities, they paved the way for future generations to eventually become managers and executives in many of these same enterprises.

At the same time, the Boston Irish moved into political positions long denied them. At the ward level, they provided their immigrant constituents with the necessities of life; at the city level they revived the Democratic Party and groomed their own candidates. In 1884, Hugh O'Brien became the first Irish-born Catholic to be elected mayor of Boston; in 1901 Patrick Collins became the second. In 1905, John F. Fitzgerald was the first Boston-born Irish Catholic to serve as mayor and in 1914 he was succeeded by James Michael Curley, who unified the city's ethnic neighbourhoods and dominated Boston politics for more than 30 years.

By the late 1940s, the decades of political and ethnic division had contributed greatly to Boston's financial breakdown and physical deterioration. With the defeat of Curley in 1949, a succession of accommodationist mayors of Irish American background, like John B. Hynes, John F. Collins and Kevin H. White, did much to lessen traditional social and religious rivalries. They also convinced Irish political leaders to work closely with Yankee business leaders to revitalise the city's economy and launch an ambitious programme of urban renewal. During the decades from 1950 to 1970, a 'New Boston' emerged that set the city on a new and more progressive direction. In 1960, John F. *Kennedy, a native Bostonian, was the first and only Irish American Catholic to be elected president of the United States (1961–63). His father, Joseph Kennedy, had made a fortune on Wall Street and was ambassador to England in the 1930s. The Kennedy success story has inspired many Irish Americans. Bostonians of Irish background now assume new and more responsible positions not only in politics, religion, sports and education, but also in law, finance, science and the fine arts. T.H.OC.

Bothy Band, the. Hugely influential traditional *music group, which ran from 1974–79. It drew its tunes from old repertoire, but in presentation was guided by the modern-music impetus of bouzoukist Dónal *Lunny. Its key players remain influential – Matt Molloy (*Chieftains), Tríona Ní Dhomhnaill and Mícheál Ó Domhnaill (Nightnoise), Kevin Burke (Patrick Street) and Paddy Keenan. F.V.

Boucicault, Dion (1820–90). Playwright. Born Dionysius Lardner Boursiquot in *Dublin, he became the most popular and influential playwright of his generation and was known before his death as the 'Irish Shakespeare' for his prodigious production of some

150 plays. Boucicault was married three times (once bigamously) but, in spite of these affronts to Victorian sensibilities, his talent was widely admired and his plays dominated the English-speaking world.

Boucicault began his career as an actor under the stage name of Lee Moreton and worked throughout England. At age 20, he submitted *A Lover by Proxy* to Covent Garden. Although rejected by the manager, Boucicault's next effort, *London Assurance* – a brilliant comedy about the upper-classes that influenced both Oscar *Wilde and George Bernard *Shaw – was eventually accepted and opened to immediate success in 1841. Boucicault was seen as a prodigy by the London theatre community. His work appeared throughout Soho and his wealth grew exponentially. Boucicault, however, generous with his money, quickly squandered his new fortune and turned to hackwork and translating French plays to maintain his lavish lifestyle. Several unwise business agreements nearly bankrupted him, but he survived by pandering to the public's love of melodrama. Many thought that, had he not sold out, he would have been a great playwright.

During his life, Boucicault's work was performed in London, Dublin, New York, Paris and Australia. His plays contain sharp dialogue and are theatrically inventive spectacles, but for the most part lack genuine social analysis. Boucicault was an early champion of the royalty system and several of his plays, including *London Assurance* (1841), *The Octoroon* (1859), *The Colleen Bawn* (1860) and *The Shaughraun* (1874), are still enjoyed by audiences today. P.J.H.

Boundary Commission. Established under Article Twelve of the *Anglo-Irish Treaty of 1921, this body was to adjust the boundary between the *Irish Free State and *Northern Ireland 'in accordance with the wishes of the inhabitants'. The Free State government assumed that the commission would recommend the transfer of large parts of counties *Tyrone and *Fermanagh and smaller sections of *Armagh, *Down and *Derry to its jurisdiction. In this scenario, Northern Ireland, reduced to four counties, would not be politically or economically viable and this would eventually lead to reunification. Due to a number of factors (including the *Civil War), the commission did not meet until November 1924. It was chaired by Richard Feetham, a South African judge, with J. R. Fisher and Eoin *MacNeill representing Northern Ireland and the Irish Free State, respectively. Feetham ruled against the use of a plebiscite and argued that the terms of the Anglo-Irish Treaty combined with economic and geographical considerations prevented him from radically altering the border. In November 1925, a summary of the commission's final report was leaked to the *Morning Post*, a British conservative paper. It stated that the Free State was to receive parts of County Fermanagh and southern Armagh but would lose a section of East Donegal. This caused considerable embarrassment for the Free State government, which had expected to acquire at least two northern counties without the loss of any territory. W. T. *Cosgrave, leader of the Free State, concerned about political stability, favoured suppressing the report (which was only released in the 1960s as a historical document). A tripartite agreement was signed in London on 3 December 1925, which revoked the powers of the Boundary Commission. The border was to remain unchanged while the provisions for the Council of Ireland were in effect abolished. Under the agreement, the Free State was also released from some of the financial commitments contained in the treaty. P.E.

Bowen, Elizabeth (1899–1973). Novelist, short story writer. Chronicler of 'the Big House', Bowen is one of the last great *Anglo-Irish writers. Born in *Dublin, she inherited her estate in Doneraile, County *Cork, from an unbroken line of *Cromwellian forefathers. She published a finely written description of the mansion in *Bowen's Court* (1942) and the house appears, *inter alia*, in an early novel *The Last September* (1929). Her novels are full of subtle sensibility; an influence is Henry James but James updated and leavened with Irish realism as well as poetry. *The Death of the Heart* (1938) is mainly regarded as her greatest work, but *The Heat of the Day* (1949) has grittier writing, impelled by her memories of the trials and ambiguities of the Blitz during the Second World War. It contains an Irish section, which depicts 'The Big House' in wartime gloom. A beautiful late novel *The World of Love* (1955) establishes an elegiac romantic tone. Bowen was a superb short story writer. She was also an important writer of place and travel; she published a street-by-street meditation on Rome and two intimate portraits of Dublin, *The Shelbourne Hotel* (1951) and *Seven Winters: Memoirs of a Dublin Childhood* (1942). Elizabeth Bowen has been accused of being a British spy in Ireland during the war, but this was in reality ancillary to her social life on her visits to her native country. She was an indefatigable hostess and lover, richly endowed with vision and pleasure. J.L.

boxing. A hugely popular *sport at amateur level, boxing has been declining in recent years. Local boxing clubs are found in rural towns and in working-class neighbourhoods of most cities throughout Ireland. National titles are contested annually on an All-Ireland basis and champions from north and south represent Ireland at international competitions like the Olympics. The financial base is too small to support a professional circuit. Irish boxers sometimes go to the United States or Britain to turn professional and several, including Dubliners Steve Collins and Michael Carruth and Belfast's Wayne McCullough, have gone on to become world champions. The most famous Irish champion of recent times was featherweight Barry McGuigan, who became known as 'The Clones Cyclone'. His career lasted until 1989 and for some time he was based in *Belfast under the management of local promoter Barney Eastwood. F.S.

Boycott, Captain Hugh Cunningham (1832–97). English ex-army officer. Captain Boycott was appointed agent for the vast estate of Lord Erne in County *Mayo in 1879. During the *Land League's campaign for tenants' rights, as a form of social protest, Charles Stewart *Parnell urged the ostracism of anyone opposed to the reforms. In Mayo, the locals refused to work for Captain Boycott because he rejected the peasants' meagre demands for fair rents and wages. The situation became so desperate that British loyalists were imported to harvest the lands under the protection of an entire army regiment. Captain Boycott's name entered the English language as a synonym for social ostracism. J.OM.

Boydell, Brian (1917–2000). Composer. Born in *Dublin, Boydell is one of the leading Irish composers of the twentieth century. He was an accomplished musician and musicologist, who wrote a number of influential works on Irish musical history. His best-known compositions include *In Memoriam Mahatma Gandhi* (1948), *Symphonic Inscapes* (1968) and *Masai Mara* (1988). A.S.

Boyle, Robert (1627–91). Irish-born physicist, founder of modern chemistry and pioneer in the use of the scientific method. Born in Lismore, County *Waterford, Boyle was the first chemist to isolate and collect a gas. In 1662, he formulated Boyle's law (under conditions of constant temperature, the pressure and volume of a gas are inversely proportional). In the area of chemistry, he noted the difference between a compound and a mixture and argued that matter was composed of corpuscles of various sorts and sizes. P.E.

Boyne, Battle of the (12 July 1690). Battle fought between King *James II and *William III. Actually it took place on 1 July 1690 (it became the twelfth after Britain adopted the Gregorian calendar). It is the most famous battle of this conflict because both kings were present. William of Orange wanted the British throne to give him the resources to carry on the Netherlands' war against France. After the Glorious Revolution (1688), Louis XIV of France believed that James would enter the war on his side. James II arrived in Ireland, where he was still recognised as king, with an army consisting partly of French troops. William followed him. Against advice, James made a stand at the River Boyne, near Drogheda, County *Louth. The battle was little more than a skirmish. James panicked when part of his army was outflanked by the Williamite cavalry and ordered a retreat. He himself fled to *Dublin and was soon on a boat to France, leaving his army behind. William's victory assumed a symbolic importance for *Protestant *unionists and is to this day commemorated annually by the *Orange Order. T.C.

Branagh, Kenneth (1960–). Actor, director. Born in *Belfast to a working-class family, Branagh moved with his parents to Reading, England, at the age of nine. He studied acting at the Royal Academy of Dramatic Arts (RADA) in London and, at 23, joined the Royal Shakespeare Company, where he had leading roles in *Henry V* and *Romeo and Juliet*. Branagh played the title role in Graham Reid's *Billy* trilogy of TV plays (1982–84), a rare screen representation of Northern Irish *Protestantism. He soon formed his own company, the Renaissance Theatre Company and, at 29, directed and starred in the film *Henry V* (1989), which won him Best Actor and Best Director Oscar nominations. In 1993, he brought Shakespeare to mainstream audiences with his film adaptation of *Much Ado About Nothing* (1993). At 30, he published his autobiography and at 34 directed and starred as Victor Frankenstein in the big-budget adaptation of Mary Shelley's *Frankenstein* (1994) with Robert De Niro as the monster. In 1996, Branagh wrote, directed and starred in a lavish adaptation of *Hamlet*. Recently, he appeared in the films *Celebrity* (1998), *Wild Wild West* (1999) and *Rabbit-Proof Fence* (2002). He has stated in interviews that he feels 'more Irish than English'. Branagh maintains links with cultural institutions in *Northern Ireland and in 1998 made a public appeal in favour of the referendum on the *Good Friday Agreement. H.L.

Breathnach, Breandán (1912–85). *Uilleann piper, writer, traditional *music collector. His sharp intelligence and commitment made him ideological champion of the traditional music revival. Breathnach's publications (especially the journal *Ceol*, tune-book series *Ceol Rince na hÉireann* and text *Folk Music and Dances of Ireland*) remain landmarks. The revival of uilleann piping by Na Píobairí Uilleann, the collecting of songs by University College Dublin's Department of Irish Folklore and the founding of the Irish Traditional Music Archive are indebted to his vision. F.V.

brehon law. Legal system of ancient Ireland. The Irish word for a judge is *breitheamh* and it is from the genitive plural of this word, *breithiún*, that the term brehon laws is derived for the ancient laws of Ireland. The earliest surviving versions of these laws date from the seventh and eighth centuries AD and exhibit a strong Christian overlayer on older native tradition. The laws continued in practice for a long time, in large areas of Ireland, even surviving Norman and English lordship down to the seventeenth century. There is a great deal of variation in rationale and prescription within the law texts, but in general they reflect the society of their time – rural, tribal and hierarchical. The usual method of settlement of disputes was for the offending party to pay honour-price to the victim or to the victim's relatives. Such honour-price varied according to one's social status, with the main distinction being between those of lordly rank and those freemen of the farming-class. Beneath these were the unfree, tenants without surety, individuals from outside the tribe and slaves. Social mobility was, though difficult, possible between all these classes. There were some other beneficial aspects to the laws, such as the right of *women to own property and protective clauses for children. D.OH.

Brendan, Saint (AD c.500–577). Sailor, navigator and holy man. Baptised Mobhí, he was born near Ardfert, County *Kerry, possibly before AD 500. His name was closely associated with a once-active pilgrimage to the summit of Mount Brandon on the *Dingle Peninsula. His renown spread across Europe in the Middle Ages through the *Navigatio Brendani*, an anonymous account written in Latin c.800, which tells of his fabulous island-hopping voyage undertaken by *currach with 12 disciples in search of the Promised Land of the Saints. Characteristics of the various islands described could suggest a route starting in Kerry, passing the *Aran Islands and continuing to the Faroes, Iceland, Greenland and an 'Island of Grapes' – perhaps the east coast of the North American continent – before finally returning to Ireland to recount his adventures for posterity. He died in 577 at Annaghdown, County *Galway, where his sister had a convent, and was buried at *Clonfert in the same county, where a cathedral with a great Romanesque doorway now stands. P.H.

Brennan, Maeve (1917–93). Short story writer and journalist. Born in *Dublin the daughter of Ireland's first ambassador to America, Brennan lived in the United States from the age of 17. She worked for the *New Yorker*, but suffered from mental illness and died destitute. Her incisive stories of Dublin middle-class life are collected in *The Springs of Affection* (1997). *The Long-Winded Old Lady* (1997) is a collection of her entertaining journalism. G.OB.

brewing. See **distilling and brewing**.

Brigid, Saint (450–523). Irish *saint. Born in Faughert, she is often referred to as 'the Mary of the Gaels'. The most famous legend associated with Brigid tells how a local chieftain would only give her the amount of land that her cloak would cover to build a convent. Her cloak began to spread miraculously until the chieftain begged her to stop it. The area that was covered by the cloak became the site of Brigid's famous convent in *Kildare. The *Cros Bhríde* (St Brigid's Cross) is still woven from rushes and placed under the rafters of houses on her feast day (1 February). It is reputed to bring health and good fortune to the household for the coming year. St Brigid is regarded as a special patron of farm animals, and many holy wells are dedicated to her name, some of which are said to have the power to cure sterility and blindness. B.D.

Brooke, Sir Basil (1888–1973). Politician, prime minister of *Northern Ireland (1943–63). A Tory landowner, Brooke became prime minister during the Second World War because he was considered the best candidate to mobilise Northern Ireland's war effort. He was so successful in this that he enjoyed British goodwill well into the 1950s. His traditional conservatism, however, frustrated the postwar generation of British politicians. The *unionist establishment, conscious that automatic British goodwill could no longer be taken for granted, eased him from office in 1963 as an embarrassing anachronism. M.M.

Brosnan, Pierce (1953–). Actor. Born in Navan, County *Meath, Brosnan moved to London in 1964, where he made his acting debut in 1976. His first film role was in *The Long Good Friday* (1981). Television work included the detective series *Remington Steele*. He played numerous film and television roles before being cast as James Bond in *Golden Eye* (1995), which was followed by *Tomorrow Never Dies* (1997), *The World Is Not Enough* (1999) and *Die Another Day* (2002). Other films in which Brosnan has starred include *Dante's Peak* (1997), *The Thomas Crown Affair* (1999) and *Evelyn* (2002), which he also produced. J.C.E.L.

Brown, Christy (1932–81). Novelist and poet. Born to a working-class family in Crumlin, *Dublin, Brown was almost completely paralysed from birth by cerebral palsy. His mother taught him to read and Dr Robert Collis taught him movement coordination and speech. After he learned how to type using his foot, he wrote a memoir of his childhood, *My Left Foot* (1954), an insightful account of the mind of a handicapped child and working-class life in Dublin. *Down All the Days* (1970), a fictional re-creation of the same autobiographical theme, combines gritty realism with lyrical language. It is generally considered his finest work. Later novels, *A Shadow on Summer* (1973), *Wild Grow the Lilies* (1976) and *A Promising Career* (1982) are less compelling. His first volume of poetry, *Come Softly to My Wake* (1971), was a bestseller. He married Mary Carr in 1972. They bought homes in Ballyheigue, County *Kerry and in Somerset, England. *My Left Foot* was filmed by Jim *Sheridan (1990) to much acclaim. C.D.

Browne, Noel (1915–97). Politician and medical doctor. Dr Browne came to prominence in the 1940s as a campaigner for a national programme to eradicate tuberculosis, which was rampant in Ireland at that time. He joined the political party *Clann na Poblachta in 1946 (when it was established by Seán *MacBride) and was elected to the *Dáil in 1948. Minister for health in the coalition government from 1948 to 1951, Browne is popularly credited with solving the tuberculosis crisis. He sought to introduce free pre- and postnatal medical services through the bill known as the 'Mother and Child Scheme'. This was opposed by the medical lobby supported by the *Catholic church, which believed in limiting state involvement in social welfare and family matters. Dr Browne's own inflexibility and the unwillingness of his colleagues to have what they saw as an unnecessary public dispute with the Catholic church led his party leader, Seán MacBride, to demand Browne's resignation. He was re-elected to the Dáil as an independent in 1951, as a *Fianna Fáil TD in 1954, and again as an independent in 1957. He founded the National Progressive Democrats in 1958 and was elected as their TD in 1961. In 1963, Browne joined the *Labour Party and was a Labour TD from 1969 to 1973. He split from Labour in 1977 and was an independent (and briefly *Socialist Labour Party) TD from 1977 to 1982. In 1990, he ran against Mary *Robinson for the Labour Party nomination in the Irish presidential election, but was heavily defeated. While his difficulties in working with others left him on the margins of political life, Browne remained a hugely popular political figure until his death. J.D.

Bruce, Edward (died 1318). Younger brother of the king of *Scotland (1306– 29), Robert Bruce. Between 1306 and 1314, Robert Bruce, Scotland's greatest national hero, and Edward waged a relentless guerrilla war against the English occupying forces. This campaign culminated in the decisive Battle of Bannockburn in 1314, which was England's greatest defeat in the Middle Ages and ensured the survival of Scotland as an independent nation.

During his reign, Robert Bruce attempted to create a pan-Celtic state incorporating Ireland and Scotland, a plan that came tantalisingly close to fruition. In 1316, Edward invaded Ireland and proclaimed himself king. He allied himself with several native Irish rulers and together they won a series of victories against the *Anglo-Norman lords. Robert himself joined Edward in Ireland for a time. The defeat and death of Edward Bruce at Faughart, near Dundalk, in October 1318, ended one of the greatest what-ifs of Irish history. J.P.

Brugha, Cathal (1874–1922). *Republican revolutionary. Born in *Dublin and educated at Belvedere College, Brugha joined the *Gaelic League in 1899 and became a member of the Irish *Volunteers in 1913. During the *Easter Rising of 1916, he was second in command (under Éamonn *Ceannt) at the South Dublin Union. Between 1917 and 1919 he was chief of staff of the Irish Volunteers. Brugha was elected temporary Príomh-Aire (chief minister) at the first meeting of *Dáil Éireann and was minister for defence until January 1922. An opponent of the *Anglo-Irish Treaty (1921), he joined the republican side during the *Civil War and was shot by government forces in Dublin on 5 July 1922. He died two days later. P.E.

Bruton, John (1947–). Politician, *Taoiseach. Member of *Dáil Éireann for *Meath since 1969, Bruton served in several ministries (especially finance and industry) in the coalition governments of 1973–77, 1981–1982 and 1982–1987. *Fine Gael Party leader from 1990 to 2001, he became Taoiseach in December 1994 in a three-party 'rainbow coalition'. During his administration, partly because of a reduced corporate tax policy, economic growth doubled, inflation and unemployment were reduced, and a budget deficit was turned into a surplus. In February 1995, he and British Prime Minister John *Major issued a Framework Document (arising from the *Downing Street Declaration of 1993) guiding *Anglo-Irish/ Northern Irish relations that became a foundation stone of the *Good Friday Agreement of 1998. In 1995, his government supported a narrowly successful referendum campaign for a constitutional amendment allowing *divorce in Ireland. His term as Taoiseach ended in 1997 when an opposition coalition came to power. In 2001, Michael Noonan replaced Bruton as leader of Fine Gael. J.P.MC.

Bryce, James; First Viscount Bryce of Dechmont (1838–1922). Liberal politician and academic. While chief secretary for Ireland (1905–07), Bryce promoted schemes for devolution and the improvement of Irish university *education. As a *Belfast-born *Presbyterian, Bryce's support for *home rule was tempered by his concern for the interests of *Ulster Protestants. A regius professor of civil law at Oxford University (1870–93), Bryce published numerous studies of constitutional politics, most notably *The American Commonwealth* (1888). He was British ambassador to Washington (1907–13). S.A.B.

B-Specials. Special police unit in *Northern Ireland. The *Ulster Special Constabulary, or 'Specials', was formed in 1920 by the British administration to prevent anti-*republican vigilantism. There were three sections: A, B and C. The A and C Specials, consisting of full- or part-time auxiliaries, were disbanded in 1925, but the reserve 'B-Specials' were retained and deployed during the various *IRA campaigns in Northern Ireland. *Catholics shunned the force and were not welcome in it. Some believe that because the B-Specials were a crass demonstration of ethnic hegemony, they alienated Catholics out of all proportion to their actions. The Specials, fired by zeal and knowledgeable of local circumstances, were effective in suppressing subversion, at least in rural areas. In *nationalist areas, the Specials were seen as a state-sponsored vigilante force, and one of the original goals of the *Northern Ireland Civil Rights Association (NICRA) was their disbandment. Their deployment in urban areas, against civilians and in front of cameras was controversial, and the use of British troops was preferred to their full mobilisation in 1969. In 1970, they were replaced by a regular army/militia hybrid, the *UDR. M.M.

Burke, Edmund (1729–97). Politician, orator, political thinker. Born in *Dublin, Burke studied at Trinity College and the Middle Temple in London. Abandoning legal study for literary interests, he began editing the *Annual Register* in 1758 and in 1764 joined Samuel Johnson and Oliver *Goldsmith in London's 'Literary Club'. Burke married Jane Mary Nugent, the daughter of an Irish *Catholic doctor, in 1757. From 1759 to 1764 he was private secretary to William *Hamilton, chief secretary for Ireland, and in 1765 to the Marquess of Rockingham. The same year, he was elected MP for Wendover. Burke's *Thoughts on the Cause of the Present Discontents* (1770) was critical of the monarchy's control of parliament.

A superb orator, he delivered his ''Speech on American Taxation' (1774) and 'Speech on Conciliation with America' (1775) in sympathy with the grievances of the American colonies. He served as MP for Bristol from 1774, and for Malton from 1780. The same year, Burke introduced a bill for economic reform to prevent royal or executive domination of parliament through patronage. Burke was Paymaster of the Forces in Rockingham's ministry in 1782, but upon Rockingham's death, he resigned. He returned to the same post in the short-lived Fox-North coalition in 1783. From 1786 to 1788 he championed the impeachment of Warren Hastings, governor general of Bengal, for abuses by the East India Company.

In 1790 Burke published his *Reflections on the Revolution in France*, a brilliant condemnation of *republican ideas, which remains a classic statement of conservative thought. The next year, he broke with many Whig allies on the issue of *France and published his *Appeal from the New to the Old Whigs and Thoughts on the Revolution in France*. His opposition to the *French Revolution, however, did not prevent him from championing relief for Irish Catholics in his 1792 *Letters to Sir Hercules Langrishe*. After retiring from parliament in 1794, Burke continued to criticise the French Revolution in works like *A Letter to a Noble Lord* (1796) and *Letters on a Regicide Peace* (1796). He died in 1797. J.P.MC.

Burke, Joe (1939–). Traditional *music accordionist. Born in Loughrea, County *Galway, Burke was influenced by earlier generations of Irish American musicians such as Michael *Coleman. He reflects the local style of key composer Paddy Fahy, but seminal accordionists Paddy O'Brien and Joe Cooley were also mentors. Burke has become iconic to generations of players. F.V.

Butler, Hubert (Marshall) (1900–91). Essayist and critic. Born in *Kilkenny and educated at St John's College, Oxford, Butler was strongly committed to the cooperative movement, local affairs and minorities' rights. A scholar and polyglot particularly interested in Eastern European affairs, he was censured for his stance on the Roman Catholic church's role in Croatia. He campaigned for nuclear disarmament and the right to choose in the divisive abortion referendum in the 1980s. His essays are collected in *Escape from the Anthill* (1986), *Grandmother and Wolfe Tone* (1990) and *In the Land of Nod* (1996). M.S.T.

Butt, Isaac (1813–79). MP, barrister and founder of the *home rule movement. Born in Glenfin, County *Donegal, Butt was the only son of a Church of Ireland rector. Educated at Trinity College, Dublin, he was professor of political economy at the college between 1836 and 1841, and became a barrister in 1838. Butt was originally a *unionist who argued against Daniel *O'Connell's *Repeal movement. However, the appalling level of poverty within Ireland and the failure of the British government to deal with the *Famine led to his growing disillusionment with direct British rule of Ireland. As a barrister, Butt had defended *Fenian leaders and was convinced that there was a political solution to what had caused the Fenian Rebellion. In 1869, he became president of the Amnesty Association, which sought amnesty for the Fenian prisoners.

Butt founded the home rule movement by establishing the Home Government Association in 1870, and then the Home Rule League in 1873. In the general elections of 1874, Home Rule candidates won 59 seats in the House of Commons (out of a total of 103 for Ireland) and subsequently organised themselves into the *Irish Parliamentary Party (later known as the Nationalist Party), with Butt as leader. Butt's conservative nationalism envisaged a home government for Ireland within a federal system centred in Westminster. Interpreted by some as a conversion to nationalism, Butt's vision of home rule can be seen as an extension of his conservative politics. Ireland's problem could be solved only within the context of the empire and not as an independent state.

In parliament, Butt proved to be an ineffective leader, unable to control the many elements within the party and unwilling to use radical tactics to obtain Irish reform from British Prime Minister Benjamin Disraeli. He did not support the policy of obstruction (where the rules of the House of Commons were used to obstruct day-to-day business) introduced by fellow Home Ruler Joseph Biggar and later backed by Charles Stewart *Parnell. In 1877, Parnell replaced Butt as chairman of the Home Rule Confederation of Great Britain. In February 1879, Butt narrowly won a vote of confidence as party leader. At this stage, his health was failing and he died on 5 May 1879. He is buried at Stranorlar, County Donegal. J.OM.

Byrne, Gabriel (1950–). Actor, producer, director and author. Born in *Dublin and educated at University College, Dublin, Byrne began acting with the Focus Theatre. He appeared in the *RTÉ series *The Riordans* and *Bracken* and has acted in a number of critically acclaimed West End and Broadway productions. His film work includes *Excalibur* (1981), *Miller's Crossing* (1990), *Into the West* (1992), *Little Women* (1994), *The Usual Suspects* (1995) and *The Man in the Iron Mask* (1998). He co-produced *In the Name of the Father* (1993) and made his directing debut with *The Lark in the Clear Air* in 1996. P.E.

Byrne, Gay (1934–). Broadcaster, entertainer, media personality. Born in *Dublin, Byrne started his broadcasting career on Irish *radio in 1958. In 1962, he began producing and hosting *The Late Late Show* for Irish *television. Originally proposed as a summer filler, this highly entertaining show has become the world's longest-running live talk show. Under Byrne, it became a forum for public discussion on social and political issues and had a modernising influence on contemporary Ireland. From the 1970s, he hosted a *radio show, which was also highly influential. Recipient of many awards for broadcasting, he retired from *The Late Late Show* in 1999. P.E.

camogie. Outdoor field game similar to *hurling and played by women of all ages. The *Gaelic Athletic Association has actively promoted camogie by setting up Cumann Camógaíochta na nGael (The Camogie Association) in 1904. Not surprisingly, camogie is most popular in the hurling heartlands of *Munster and the counties *Kilkenny and *Galway. F.S.

Canada, the Irish in. The Irish established a notable presence in Canada during the eighteenth century, when large sections of North America were contested by the British and French governments. While individuals and small groups of Irish migrants certainly visited the future state of Canada in the early 1600s, the Anglo-French wars of the mid- to late 1700s brought much greater numbers in the uniforms of both sides. The tendency of Irish-born *emigrants to sympathise with the French perspective and the periodic enforcement of anti-*Catholic legislation ensured that large-scale Irish immigration to the Canadian colonies was discouraged prior to 1800. *Newfoundland, however, was then already heavily populated by people of Irish extraction because of long-established ties with *Waterford, *Wexford and *Cork.

Ontario and Quebec received huge volumes of Irish immigration between the 1820s and 1860s, with a sustained and heavy flow of people arriving after the *Famine. As many as 100,000 Irish may have landed in Quebec in 1847, although the settlers moved in both directions over the US/Canadian border. An estimated 329,000 Irish immigrants entered Canada between 1841 and 1850, particularly Ontario and New Brunswick. Estate clearances in Ireland, moreover, resulted in concentrated bursts of settlement in Quebec and elsewhere in the 1850s, when approximately 19% of Ontarians and 6% of Quebec residents had been born in Ireland. Census data reveal that the four provinces comprising the Dominion of Canada in 1871 contained 24.3% persons of Irish ethnicity (compared with 20% English, 15% Scots and 31% French), making Canada among the most Irish places in the world. This prominence was reflected in every facet of the country's political and cultural evolution. R.OD.

Canary Wharf Bombing (1996). *IRA bombing of London's financial district. The bomb attack in London on Friday, 9 February 1996, which killed two people, caused millions of pounds worth of damage and ended the IRA cease-fire, which had been in force since 31 August 1994. Though IRA violence did return to *Northern Ireland, the IRA's intention was to concentrate on spectacular targets in Great Britain. Many of their plans were frustrated by efficient British intelligence operations. In 1997, the IRA cease-fire was resumed. M.M.

Carleton, William (1774–1869). Novelist and short story writer. Born in County *Tyrone to an Irish-speaking peasant family, Carleton was self-educated. His stories were published in two collections, both entitled *Traits and Stories of the Irish Peasantry* (1830, 1833). His best-known novels include *The Black Prophet* (1847) and *The Tithe Proctor* (1849), indictments of the peasants' living conditions during the Great *Famine, and *Willie Reilly and his Dear Colleen Bawn*, a popular romantic melodrama. In Carleton's distinctive narrative, spirited, often grotesque characters speak a colourful *Hiberno-English. His early rejection of *Catholicism and the politics of resistance evolved into a more sympathetic but complex relation with the peasantry. M.S.T.

Carlow, County. Ireland's second smallest county, located inland in the south-east, in the province of *Leinster. The county covers an area of 346 square miles and has a population of 45,845 (2002 census). Surrounded by mountains and hills, Carlow is mainly undulating farmland. The Blackstairs Mountains form the border with *Wexford; the highest peak is Mount Leinster (2,610 ft.). The rivers Barrow and Slaney run through the county. The county capital is Carlow, on the Barrow, in the north-west of the county. Tullow, in the north on the Slaney, is a well-known angling town.

Carlow town developed around a *Norman motte-and-bailey fort, built in 1180. The fort was succeeded by Carlow Castle, but little remains of this. The ruins of many other medieval *castles can be seen in the county. In the fourteenth century, the county was of strategic and military importance, being located on the border of the *Pale, and was the scene of much fighting between Irish chieftains and English armies. In the *Rebellion of 1798, hundreds of rebels were killed in Carlow, and a rebel leader from neighbouring County Wexford, Father John Murphy, was captured and hanged in Tullow.

One of the first colleges for the training of *Catholic priests, St Patrick's College, was opened in Carlow town in 1793. The town also has a Catholic cathedral, built in 1833. Carlow, along with Mallow, in County *Cork, is one of the two centres of Ireland's sugar industry. The country's first sugar beet factory opened in Carlow in 1926 and it still employs hundreds of workers. Today Carlow is a busy market and industrial town. Besides sugar, dairy farming and crop production are the county's main economy. Carlow's most interesting archaeological monument is the 5,000-year-old Browne's Hill *Dolmen, a granite structure with a 100-ton capstone, two miles east of Carlow town. The remains of a seventh-century monastic settlement and a medieval abbey can be seen at St Mullins, on the east bank of the Barrow. P.D.

Carolan, Turloch (1670–1738). Harpist and composer. Born in County *Meath, Carolan moved with his family to County *Roscommon, where he was blinded by smallpox at age eighteen. He was educated in *harp playing courtesy of a local patron and began a career as an itinerant musician playing in the 'big' houses of Gaelic and 'new' *Anglo-Irish landowners. Carolan is one of Ireland's most renowned composers of words and music. His melodies have a distinctly Irish flavour, but also show the influence of the popular Italian music of the era, notably that of Corelli. Most of Carolan's music survives and is still widely played today. Carolan's life and work is minutely documented in *Carolan – The Life, Times and Music of an Irish Harper* by Dónal O'Sullivan in 1958 (republished in 2001). F.V.

Carr, Marina. (1964–). Playwright. Born in *Dublin, Carr grew up near Tullamore, County *Offaly, in the Irish midlands. As a student at University College, Dublin, she was involved in the Drama Society and wrote her first play, *Ullaloo*. This was followed by a Beckettian play in the absurdist mode, *Low in the Dark* (1989). Carr found her own voice with *The Mai* (1994) and *Portia Coughlan* (1996), both of which were performed at the *Peacock Theatre, and *By the Bog of Cats* (1998), which premiered at the *Abbey Theatre. The heroines in these powerful tragedies, whose themes include marital strife, murder and incest, suffer from an excess of passion that ends in suicide. The midlands setting of these plays, which includes the use of its flat but exotic accent, functions both as a realistic rural landscape and a mythical backdrop – what Carr has called 'a crossroads between the worlds'. The Druid Theatre's production of *On Raftery's Hill*, a violent play also on the theme of incest, was staged in 2000. The play *Ariel* opened at the 2002 Dublin Theatre Festival. J.C.E.L.

Carrantuohill. Ireland's highest mountain (3,414 ft./1,039m.). Situated in the MacGillycuddy's Reeks, a mountain range in County *Kerry, Carrantuohill is made up mostly of coarse-grained sandstone. The name derives from the Gaelic *Carrán Tuathaill*, meaning the reversed sickle, because its crescent of jagged rocks is facing inward rather than outward. A popular climb, it is usually approached from a rocky gully called 'The Devil's Ladder'. B.D.

Carrowmore. Extensive megalithic cemetery, possibly started in the fifth millennium BC. Much depleted by stone-quarrying, it was formerly the largest known collection of megalithic tombs in Ireland or Britain. Two miles west of Sligo town, the tombs include *passage-graves and *dolmens with stone circles, some excavated by a Swedish multi-disciplinary team. P.H.

Carson, Ciaran (1948–). Poet. Carson was born in *Belfast and educated at Queen's University, Belfast. The local idiom of Belfast pervades his writing. The voice of the storyteller, improvising and weaving tall tales and digressions, dominates his poems. Long lines and a combination of the colloquial and the poetic distinguish his style. A surreal, occupied cityscape is tenderly conjured in *Belfast Confetti* (1989) and *The Irish for No* (1987). The collection *Opera et Cetera* (1996) has been compared to *Muldoon's poetry because both poets reflect on the power of language to mislead. Carson has also published a novel, *Last Night's Fun* (1996), and a collection of prose reflections on the Belfast of his childhood, *The Star Factory* (1998). An ambitious 77 sonnet sequence, *The Twelfth of Never* (1999), was followed by *Selected Poems* in 2001. M.S.T.

Carson, Edward (1854–1935). Politician, barrister, *unionist leader. Born in *Dublin to a liberal family, Carson became a famous barrister who successfully defended the Marquess of Queensberry in Oscar *Wilde's libel suit (1895). He was appointed solicitor general for Ireland in 1892. The same year, Carson was elected as a unionist MP for Dublin University (Trinity College, Dublin). The Liberal government, elected in 1906, introduced a *home rule bill for Ireland in 1912. The *Ulster Unionist Council (UUC), set up in 1905 to represent all shades of unionism in the north, invited Carson to Ulster to organise resistance to home rule. Carson's rhetoric was belligerent, because behind the scenes he was urged on by his militant Ulster-born colleagues.

As leader of the UUC, Carson was acutely aware that, while seditious language and the impressively drilled and armed *UVF, established in 1912, gave weight to *loyalist resistance, they also threatened civil disorder, which was potentially disastrous for Irish unionism's support in Britain. Carson's strategy was to make home rule for Ireland unworkable by forcing the exclusion of Ulster from its operation. Unionists formed a majority in only four of the nine Ulster counties, however, and with neither side prepared to back down, civil war in Ireland seemed imminent in 1914. The *First World War intervened and Carson committed his people to the war effort and served in the British wartime government.

Following the *Easter Rising of 1916 and the rise of *Sinn Féin, Carson rejected attempts by Irish unionists to find an all-Ireland compromise. Though an all-Ireland unionist himself, he felt honour-bound to save the loyalists in Ulster from any form of Dublin rule. Carson was pressed to accept the premiership of the new devolved government of *Northern Ireland, established in *Belfast in 1920 (ruling six of the nine counties of Ulster), but, an Irish unionist at heart, he declined in favour of James *Craig. M.M.

Cary, (Arthur) Joyce Lunel (1888–1957). Writer. Born in *Derry, Cary studied art in Edinburgh and Paris (1907–09), and law at Oxford (1909–12). He served in the Red Cross in the Balkan Wars 1912–13, joined the Nigerian Colonial Service in 1913 and fought in the Cameroons during the *First World War. Cary settled in Oxford with his family in 1920 and devoted himself to writing. He is best known for *The Horse's Mouth* (1944), which is considered a classic. A savage portrayal of the anti-social nature of artistic genius, this novel (the third of a trilogy) examines the conflict between individual freedom and responsibility, a theme that runs throughout Cary's work. He also wrote four novels about Africa: *Aissa Saved* (1932), *An American Visitor* (1933), *The African Witch* (1936) and *Mister Johnson* (1939). Other notable publications include *Castle Corner* (1938), *Power in Men* (1939) and *The Case for African Freedom* (1941). His autobiographical novel, *A House of Children* (1941), which recalls childhood summers in Inishowen, County *Donegal, was awarded the James Tait Black Memorial Prize. In 1958, *The Horse's Mouth* was made into a film directed by Ronald Neame and starring Alec Guinness. C.D.

Casement, Sir Roger (1864–1916). British diplomat, Irish revolutionary. Following a remarkable career in the British colonial service, Roger Casement was knighted in 1911. He championed humanitarianism and opposed exploitation of native workers in such outposts of the empire as central Africa and South America. In 1913, he retired from government service and became actively involved in the burgeoning Irish *nationalist movement. Convinced that an Irish revolution needed Germany's military support, Casement went to Berlin to lobby for an arms shipment for the *Easter Rising. His return to Ireland was disastrous. In April 1916, Casement and two accomplices landed on the coast of *Kerry, put ashore by a German submarine. Casement was arrested almost immediately and charged with 'high treason' for collaborating with Germany, England's enemy during the *First World War. Casement's famous trial was swift, only four days. To compromise him, the government leaked his diaries, which contained graphic homosexual references. Although they were never introduced as testimony, these diaries influenced the entire trial. Casement's supporters claimed the diaries were forgeries. Today, the general consensus is that the diaries are genuine. Having deliberated for one hour, the jury found him guilty of 'high treason'. In spite of many appeals and the sympathy garnered by his numerous supporters, Casement was hanged in August 1916. J.OM.

Cashel, Rock of. Rock rising above County *Tipperary's Golden Vale and bearing one of the most imposing collections of ecclesiastical monuments in Ireland. Originally a fortress and allegedly where St *Patrick baptised a king of *Munster, it was handed over to the church in 1101 and became the seat of the province's archdiocese. Its oldest surviving building is perhaps the *round tower of circa 1100, followed by Cormac's Chapel (1124–34), Ireland's most complete stone-roofed church in the Romanesque style. The chapel, built in sandstone by Cormac Mac Carthaigh, king of South Munster, contains the country's oldest frescoes. The roofless cathedral dates from the thirteenth century. Its western end was never completed; a fortified bishop's palace was built later in its place. The twelfth-century Cross of St Patrick is now housed in the museum, in the fifteenth-century Hall of the Vicars' Choral at the entrance to the Rock. The cathedral was burned in 1495 and again in 1647, repaired in 1686 and again in 1729, but finally abandoned in 1749. P.H.

Castlereagh, Viscount (Robert Stewart) (1769–1822). Politician, chief secretary of Ireland (1797–1801). Born in County *Down, Castlereagh was the son of the Marquess of Londonderry, a descendant of Scottish *Presbyterian settlers, who had converted to the established *Protestant church for political reasons. Castlereagh played a key role as chief secretary of Ireland during the period of crisis that centred on the *Rebellion of 1798. Along with his superior Lord Cornwallis (Viceroy, 1798–1801), he bore responsibility for suppressing the rising. Both men tried to bring peace to Ireland after the rebellion, but were hampered by ultraconservative members of the Protestant ascendancy on the local and national levels. Between 1799 and 1800, Castlereagh worked to bring about the Act of *Union and resigned along with Cornwallis and William Pitt when King *George III blocked *Catholic Emancipation in 1801. From 1812 until his death by suicide in 1822, Castlereagh served as the foreign secretary of Great Britain. In this capacity, he was one of the central figures at the Congress of Vienna, which dictated the terms of peace to a defeated Napoleonic *France. J.P.

castles. The Irish had started building castles before the coming of the *Normans in 1169, yet none survive that we know of. The first Norman fortifications were made of earth-ring-works and motte-and-baileys. Shortly after their arrival in Ireland, the Normans were building large stone castles such as Trim in County *Meath, which consists of a tall central tower surrounded by a somewhat later curtain wall. Trim Castle and Carrickfergus Castle in County *Antrim – the most extensive in Ireland – show the Norman barons living in the towers and the soldiers in the barracks within the wall. One type of castle that remained popular until the sixteenth century was the rectangular tower with a round bastion at each corner. The Edward *Bruce invasion of 1315–18 brought castle building to a temporary halt, and when it started again in the fifteenth century (or possibly before), the builders were not only the Normans who had 'become more Irish than the Irish themselves', but in most cases the native Irish as well. However, instead of being military barracks as the Norman castles had been, these later medieval fortifications were really family residences with only a few retainers. They are, therefore, more correctly called *tower houses, though generally they bear the name castle. Usually with three storeys above a vaulted basement, they were status symbols, though often sparsely furnished inside. Blarney (County *Cork) and Bunratty (County *Clare) are among the largest of their kind; the latter, now furnished in the style of circa 1600, offers medieval banquets. Though probably over 2,000 tower houses were built during the fifteenth and sixteenth centuries, only a few survive in any way intact. A handful have been restored with success, but historical records usually give little information about the families that originally built tower houses. By the early seventeenth century, a manorial style had developed with large windows allowing more gracious living among their inhabitants, who were becoming increasingly English-orientated. The *Cromwellian period saw an end to castle building in Ireland, except for those built largely in the Victorian period, which were erected to impress the neighbours (like the earlier tower houses, but without any fortifications). P.H.

Castletown House. The first and largest Palladian-style country house in Ireland, located in Celbridge, County *Kildare. The original design by Alessandro Galilei (1691–1737) influenced the architecture of *Leinster House and the White House in Washington, DC. The building was commissioned in 1722 by William Conolly (1662–1729), speaker of the Irish House of Commons, and its construction was overseen by Sir Edward Lovett *Pearce. Castletown House has been recently restored and furnished in period style. S.A.B.

***Cathach*, the.** Ireland's oldest *manuscript, written around 600 (possibly by the hand of St *Colm Cille). *The Cathach* (or 'Battler') *Psalter* is now preserved in the *Royal Irish Academy in *Dublin. The enlarged initial letters of the Psalms were ornamented in monochrome with crosses, spirals and fish. P.H.

Cathleen Ni Houlihan. Allegorical representation of Ireland as woman and mother derived from the Gaelic **aisling* (dream or vision) tradition. With the exile of the Gaelic chieftains and establishment of the *Anglo-Irish Ascendancy, eighteenth-century Irish *bardic poetry incorporated more explicitly political motifs. The beautiful yet unattainable fairy woman featured in traditional love poetry became an impoverished, sorrowful woman – described alternately as *seán bhean bhocht* ('poor old woman'), *Róisín Dubh* ('little dark rose'), or *Caitlin Ni Houlihan* – whose only hope is the removal of English oppression and the return of her exiled husband and/or sons. Such political yearnings were given especially vivid expression in W. B. *Yeats' and Lady *Gregory's *Cathleen Ni Houlihan* (1902). In the play, Cathleen, 'the poor old woman' (originally performed by Maud *Gonne), personifies Ireland and prompts a young bridegroom to abandon his wedding plans and join the French forces of 1798 fighting for the restoration of her four green fields. E.S.M.

Catholic Emancipation Act (1829). Legislation that gave *Catholics the right to sit in *parliament. Since the *Reformation and the passing of the *Penal Laws (1695–1709), Catholics were excluded from political life, had limited access to *education and were prohibited from owning property. They could not practise their religion freely without fear of harsh penalties. By the end of the eighteenth century, an ongoing campaign for full civil and political rights for Catholics had led to a series of *Relief Acts (1774, 1778, 1782), which enabled British and Irish Roman Catholics to acquire property. In addition, the Relief Act of 1793 gave Catholics the right to vote in elections, but not to sit in parliament. Catholics continued to be barred from holding high office in the government or judiciary. Various bills that were introduced (including those by *Henry Grattan and William Conyngham Plunkett) fell short of full emancipation mostly because of the resistance of the House of Lords and King George IV.

On 12 May 1823, Daniel *O'Connell, the 'Liberator', along with Richard Lalor Sheil, established the Catholic Association, which aimed to achieve full Catholic emancipation 'by legal and constitutional means'. Ordinary people were encouraged to join by paying a small subscription (known as 'Catholic rent') of one shilling a year. Approximately 400,000 Catholics became members. The association held mass meetings throughout the country and mounted an organised publicity campaign to highlight Catholic grievances. In 1825, the government, alarmed at the power of the organisation, suppressed it, but O'Connell formed a new organisation, the New Catholic Association and the campaign continued.

In 1828, O'Connell was elected MP for County *Clare in a landmark victory, but refused to take his seat in parliament until the anti-Roman Catholic oath was lifted. Faced with the threat of nationwide disturbances, in 1829, Prime Minister *Wellington and Home Secretary Robert Peel advised the king to grant emancipation. Under the Roman

Catholic Relief Act, which was enacted on 13 April 1829, the oaths of allegiance, supremacy and abjuration were replaced with an oath that pledged loyalty to the crown without recognising the monarch as the head of the church. Catholics could now enter parliament and sit as MPs at Westminster. They could also hold all public offices with the exception of lord chancellor, monarch, regent, lord lieutenant of Ireland and any judicial appointment in any ecclesiastical court.

However, on 13 February 1829, a bill suppressing the Catholic Association was passed along with a disenfranchise bill which raised the franchise from the 40-shilling-freehold qualification to £10 per householder. The change drastically reduced the number of poorer voters from approximately 100,000 to 16,000. O'Connell disagreed with this change but did not consider it grounds for rejecting the Emancipation Act. While middle-class Catholics benefited from emancipation, those members of the Catholic peasantry who lost their vote saw no betterment of their political position within society. For many, emancipation may have represented only a symbolic victory. M.T.D., P.E.

Catholic Relief Acts (1774–93). A series of acts during the late eighteenth century repealing many of the restrictions of the *Penal Laws (1695–1709). Under this discriminatory legislation, *Catholics were excluded from political life, had limited access to education and were prohibited from owning property.

In 1760, the Catholic Committee was established by Charles O'Connor and Dr John Curry to exert pressure on the British government for relief. Some progress was made in 1774 when parliament passed an act allowing Catholics to take an *oath of allegiance, which did not deny the articles of their faith. The war between France and Britain, which began in 1778, convinced many British politicians that in the interests of imperial security, Catholics should receive significant relief.

In 1778, Gardiner's First Relief Act was passed, allowing Catholics to own land on a 999-year lease and enabling them to inherit land, providing they took an oath of allegiance. In 1782, Gardiner's Second Relief Act was introduced for those Catholics who had taken the 1778 oath. This act permitted them to purchase and own freehold land, and some restrictions were lifted on the bearing of arms and on *education. After much petitioning by the Catholic Committee, Hobart's Catholic Relief Act was passed in 1793, giving the right to vote to 40-shilling-freeholders, as well as the right to bear arms and to hold some positions in civil office. However, the act failed to give Catholics what they most wanted, the right to sit in parliament. This would change in 1829 with the *Catholic Emancipation Act. M.T.D., P.E.

Catholicism. Principal religion in the *Republic of Ireland. For over 1,500 years, the Roman Catholic church in Ireland has occupied an exceptionally important place in the lives of the Irish people. Approximately 90% of the Republic of Ireland's population and about 75% of those living on the island are Roman Catholic. Although Catholicism's origins in Ireland preceded the arrival of St *Patrick in the fifth century, his ministry as a bishop marked the beginnings of a serious campaign to convert the Irish people. Patrick's substantial success, and that of his successors, resulted in large part because they incorporated the pagan *Celtic practices of the day into *Christianity. For example, *Samhain, the pagan festival of the dead celebrated on 1 November became the feast days of All Saints (All Hallows) and All Souls. By the sixth century, Irish monks had established a tradition of extreme asceticism in monasteries throughout the country. Monasticism quickly became the dominant church organisation in Ireland, proving more amenable to

Irish society than the more centralised episcopal model. During the Dark Ages on the European continent in the seventh and eighth centuries, monasteries such as *Glendalough and *Clonmacnoise enjoyed a golden age as repositories of western civilisation's literature and art. Monasteries sent missionaries such as St *Colm Cille and St *Columbanus to evangelise Europe.

The *Viking raids of 795 led to the destruction of many monasteries and to the end of the golden age. The monasteries that survived became increasingly integrated with the political and secular life of the day. By the middle of the twelfth century, the Synod of Kells established a traditional diocesan structure for Ireland consisting of 26 dioceses in four episcopal provinces: Armagh, Dublin, Cashel and Tuam. The *Norman invasion later that century seriously disrupted these reforms and led to Irish-Norman warfare and disputes over ecclesiastical titles and offices. The Irish church suffered from continued factionalism and corruption for over three centuries as the native Gaelic Irish and the Norman invaders and their descendants struggled for political control of the country.

Beginning in the mid-sixteenth century through the 1760s, the British government, with the exception of a few short years, proscribed the Catholic church in Ireland, subjecting its clergy and laity to persecution and confiscating its property. In the 1530s, the English and Irish *parliaments declared *Henry VIII to be the head of, respectively, the English and Irish churches, thus substituting royal for papal authority. Henry VIII's *Reformation establishing a new state *Protestant church was consolidated by his daughter *Elizabeth I, who began in 1560 to impose legal penalties on those who refused to conform. When Irish Catholics supported King Charles I during the English Civil War in the 1640s, Oliver *Cromwell, the leader of the anti-royalist, parliamentary forces, reconquered Ireland and repressed the church, massacring thousands and stripping Irish Catholics of the vast majority of their land. The persecution of Catholics ceased briefly under the Catholic King of England *James II in the 1680s. Following his defeat at the Battle of the *Boyne in 1690 by the forces of William of *Orange and the Treaty of *Limerick the following year, a series of *Penal Laws were passed designed to exclude Catholics in matters of property, trade, politics and religion. Bishops were deported and banned from returning to Ireland. After 1770, however, the church began to emerge as a national institution when the British government, in the wake of Enlightenment ideas and the war with America, relaxed its enforcement of the Penal Laws to grant Irish Catholics *de facto* religious toleration.

During the last quarter of the eighteenth century, Catholics won partial relief from the Penal Laws, including in 1793 the right to vote. Irish bishops supported the Act of *Union (1800) between Great Britain and Ireland on the understanding that Britain would concede *Catholic Emancipation, the right of a Catholic to sit in parliament. Emancipation languished until 1829. During this period, Daniel *O'Connell and the Irish bishops resisted parliament's plan to control the appointment of Irish bishops in return for Catholic emancipation. Irish Catholics, clerical and lay alike, united under O'Connell and the bishops to win emancipation in 1829. This alliance fostered the development of an identity that was self-consciously Irish and Catholic.

The Catholic church was severely hampered by a lack of clerical manpower exacerbated by Ireland's rising population between 1750 and 1845. The Great *Famine of the mid-1840s decimated the population, reducing it from eight to six million people through death and emigration. The reduced population, ironically, afforded the Irish church a priest-to-people ratio that allowed the Irish pastoral mission to flourish in the second half of the nineteenth century. Under Cardinal Paul *Cullen, archbishop of Dublin from 1852 to 1878, the Irish episcopacy spearheaded a devotional revolution marked by the building of schools and churches, the expansion of parish missions and sodalities, and the reform of the Irish clergy's personal conduct and administration of the sacraments. By 1900, Irish Catholics had become the most pious Catholics in the world with close to 90% attending weekly Sunday Mass.

The church also gradually gained control of the nation's *educational system and remained a vital part of the Irish political system. During the 1880s, the church sided with Charles Stewart *Parnell on the question of land reform, but turned against him after he was named a defendant in a divorce case. Its support of the *Free State forces during the *Irish Civil War solidified the church's political influence. The Irish *Constitution of 1937 recognised the Catholic church as having 'a special position' in Irish society. (This clause was removed from the constitution in 1973.) Catholicism had so infused Irish life that the terms *Irish* and *Catholic* had become almost interchangeable. The partition of Ireland into north and south resulted in no similar ecclesiastical division for the Catholic church in Ireland. Discrimination against the minority Catholic population in Northern Ireland originally gave rise to the civil rights movement in the late 1960s and later to the *Troubles between Protestants, who are predominantly unionists, and Catholics, who are predominately nationalists.

Through continued immigration well into the twentieth century, the Irish version of Catholicism dominated the church throughout the English-speaking world. Irish *missionaries further extended Irish Catholic influence. Orders such as the Holy Ghost and Columban Fathers and the Sisters of Mercy were founded in the nineteenth and twentieth centuries to spread the faith to Africa, Latin America, Asia and India. In recent years, Catholicism's hold on the Irish people has weakened in the wake of changes in the country, the reforms of the *Second Vatican Council in the 1960s and widespread allegations of clerical sexual abuse. The Irish church has consistently supported the *peace process for the resolution of the conflict in *Northern Ireland. M.P.C.

Cavan, County. Inland county, one of the three *Ulster counties in the *Republic of Ireland. The county, which stretches over 745 square miles, has a population of 56,416 (2002 census). Cavan town is the county capital and the cathedral centre of the diocese of Kilmore. Before the English conquest, the O'Reilly clan dominated the area, which was then known as Breifni, which also includes *Leitrim.

Cavan is essentially agrarian. Throughout the county there are 365 lakes. The southern part, with its fertile, rolling hills and tidy towns, borders and resembles *Leinster. The north, rugged, mountainous and thinly populated, blends elements of *Connacht and Ulster. The north-west parish of Killanagh in the barony of Tullyhaw, dominated by the mountain Cuilcagh (2,199 ft.), is a scenic area, still largely undiscovered by tourists. Close to the mountain's base, the *Shannon Pot, a pool fed by a spring, is the source of Ireland's longest river. Cavan is also the source of the Erne, the river that produces the lovely lake country of *Fermanagh. A few hundred yards from the Shannon Pot, in the townland of Moneygashel, are interesting early *Celtic archaeological sites – a ring fort and sweat house with instruments and ornaments of the times. Ring forts are also common in other parts of the county.

The remains of Cloghoughter Castle, on an island in Lough Oughter, offers the best example of the native Irish style of circular tower *castles of the thirteenth to fifteenth centuries. Owen Roe *O'Neill, the leading general of the Catholic Confederation, died there in 1649. At Drumlane near Belturbet are the remains of a twelfth-century *round tower. In 1726, Jonathan *Swift wrote *Gulliver's Travels* in the home of his friend Thomas Sheridan near the town of Virginia.

Celebrated personalities with Cavan connections include: Philip Sheridan, American Civil War general; Archbishop John Charles McQuaid; Francis *Sheehy Skeffington; actor T. P. McKenna; and writers Shane Connaughton, Dermot Healy and Tom McIntyre. Two films, *The Playboys* (1992) and *The Run of the Country* (1995), based on Connaughton's novels, were filmed in and near the town of Redhills. William Percy *French's 'Come Back Paddy Reilly to Ballyjamesduff' has become the county anthem, sung wherever Cavan people gather. A.ML., L.J.MC.

Ceannt, Éamonn (1881–1916). Revolutionary and signatory of the 1916 *Proclamation of the Irish Republic. Born in County *Galway, Ceannt worked as a clerk in the Treasury Department of Dublin Corporation. In 1900, he became a member of the *Gaelic League and in 1908 joined *Sinn Féin. Membership of the *IRB followed in 1913, and by 1915 he had been initiated into the Supreme Council. He was court-martialled for his role in the 1916 *Easter Rising (where he commanded the *Volunteers in the South *Dublin Union area) and was executed in *Kilmainham Gaol on 8 May 1916. P.E.

Céide Fields, the. Archaeological site. Located on spectacular sea cliffs, near Ballycastle in County *Mayo, the Céide Fields is believed to be 5,000 years old, making it the oldest enclosed landscape in Europe. Extensive excavating in the 1980s revealed an integrated farm landscape of field walls, dwellings and numerous megalithic tombs that had been trapped in time by the growth of the surrounding *bog. The fields cover an area of 24 square miles. B.D.

céilí. 1. An Irish word denoting, particularly in the north, a social visit or gathering. 2. In *Scotland, it indicates music and song performance, with some dance. 3. Over all of Ireland it was adopted to denote an organised, public, traditional Irish social *dance. The first of these was held by the *Gaelic League among Irish migrants in London in 1897, based on similar Scottish assemblies. The dances were popular quadrilles and waltzes, but in the 1920s peculiarly Irish social dance-forms were created and revived for such *céilithe*, visually similar to English and Scottish 'country' dances, but performed to Irish *music. Bands dedicated to these were initially described as 'players' or 'orchestras'; the earliest to use the term *céilí* band may have been Frank Lee in London, in 1918. Dublin piper Leo *Rowsome formed the first *céilí* band in Ireland – the *Siamsa – in 1922, and starting in 1926, Irish *radio promoted the Ballinakill, Aughrim Slopes, Moate and Athlone *céilí* bands. With the shift in dancing out of private houses to schools and purpose built halls, *céilí* bands flourished, some becoming hugely popular. Many, like the McCuskers, played to exiles in the United States and Britain. The Gallowglass Céilí Band was professional and most – like The Tulla which has run from 1947 until the present day – made LP recordings. Hundreds proliferated at parish and national levels up until the 1960s and several still enjoy popularity today. F.V.

Céitinn, Seathrún (c.1580–1644). Historian and poet in Irish. Of Anglo-Norman heritage, Céitinn (sometimes Anglicised as Geoffrey Keating) became the greatest historian of Gaelic Ireland. Originally, he received native *bardic education, which would later inspire a series of traditional poems. Céitinn also studied in Bordeaux and Reims having been ordained as a priest in Ireland. The several theological works he wrote in the manner of the counter-Reformation use a strong, literate colloquial prose style, new to the *Irish language. His major work is *Foras Feasa ar Éirinn*, a history of Ireland, which he composed from native sources probably between 1629 and 1634. This history was copied by scribes and poets and remained the basic text through which the Irish understood themselves for the next 200 years. His best poetry, 'Óm Sceol ar Ardmhagh Fáil' ('At the News from Fal's High Plain') and 'A Bhean Lán de Stuaim' ('O Woman Full of Guile'), is passionate and intricate, combining personal anguish with a political vision. A.T.

Celtic mythology. The ancient *Celts had many local deities, but the most important were a basic divine couple responsible for the material prosperity of the tribe. The father-deity was usually associated with the sky and the mother-deity with the earth. Irish *manuscript compilations featuring these deities date from the medieval period – such as *Lebor na hUidre*, or **Leabhar na hUidre (The Book of the Dun Cow)* and *Lebor na Nuachongbhála* (known as the *Book of *Leinster*) – but many of the actual texts are copies from periods stretching back to as early as the seventh century AD. There are indications that the earliest Celtic sources in Ireland used variants of widespread Indo-European names for this couple. Devos was the designation of the male sky-deity, but this name became calcified in Celto-Irish tradition as *dago-devos* ('good sky'), which survived in the form *Daghdha*. The female personification of rivers and the fertile soil also followed the Indo-European pattern, being known as Danu, but she was usually referred to as the *Mór-Ríoghan* ('great queen'). Various aspects of the material and cultural landscape were connected to these deities and both play a leading role in the great primordial battle of Irish mythology, Cath Mhuighe Tuireadh, that was reputedly fought between two sets of deities at Moytirra in County *Sligo. In that battle, the Tuatha Dé Danann ('people of the goddess Danu') defeated the Fomhoire ('under-spirits').

Basic to much of the early mythological lore was the relationship between the dead and the living, which was reflected in the system of computing time. The dark half of the year, representing the dead, preceded the bright half, representing the living; and similarly the night preceded the day. This mutual dependency between dead and living seems to have been the teaching of the *druids, and from it flowed the notion that inspiration could come from the world of the dead and also that the setting sun in the west was entering the otherworld. Also prevalent was the notion that a bright deity, called by variants of the name Fionn (Irish for fair or bright), alternated in influence with a dark deity called Donn (Irish for dark).

The most dramatic deity was Lugh, who led the Tuatha Dé Danann to victory at the Battle of Moytirra. He is the Irish form of the pan-Celtic Lugus and was the master of all skills and trades and the patron of the harvest. He is described as a prophesied youth and he slew his tyrant-grandfather Balar, who had a scorching eye that destroyed all on which it looked. Other outstanding figures who reflect Celtic deities were the marvellously handsome Aenghus, the seer-warrior Fionn Mac Cumhaill (or Finn McCool) and the superhero *Cúchulainn. Gods of specific crafts appear in the form of the master-smith Goibhniu, the ubiquitous leech Dian Cécht and the wondrous mariner Manannán.

Several rivers bear the nicknames of the goddess of fertility of the land, Danu or Anu. For example, the names for the rivers *Shannon and Boyne come from *Sionainn* ('the old one') and *Bóinn* ('bright cow'). Other names represented social aspects of the divine mother – most notably the warrior-queen Meadhbh ('the intoxicating one') who was originally the goddess of sovereignty. Brighid ('the highest one') was the patron of poetry and of milk, and her cult survived strongly in the devotion to her Christian namesake, St Brighid, or St *Brigid. The goddess could be envisaged as either young and beautiful or old and ugly. In the latter guise, she is widely represented in literature and folklore as the Cailleach Bhéarra ('hag of Beare'), who, legend claims, lived longer than anybody else ever in Ireland and put several rocks and islands in their present position in the landscape. There are also many legends concerning fairy queens who reign from palaces in great rocks and hills; these derive from the goddess-image in a more localised context. The old manuscripts, mostly the work of Christian monks, and these traditions survived easily side by side with *Christianity in Ireland. D.OH.

Celtic Revival. See **Irish Revival**.

Celts. Speakers of a language that was predominant throughout much of central and western Europe – including Ireland – in the Iron Age. A Celtic dialect of Indo-European was developing in central Europe from around 2,000 BC, and from the eighth century BC a thriving culture is evidenced from that region. More clearly identifiable as Celtic are the 'Hallstatt' culture from east of the Alps in the seventh and sixth centuries BC and the *La Tène culture from the area between the sources of the Rhine and the Danube two centuries later. These Celtic people had been spreading westward for some time, establishing strong lordships in France (then known as Gaul) and the Iberian Peninsula. Later expansions brought groups of Celts southward into northern Italy and eastward as far as the Black Sea and even into an area of Asia Minor.

Since the sixth century BC, Celtic groups had crossed to Britain and set up kingdoms, assimilating the indigenous people. Some claim that the Celticisation of Ireland was a gradual process due to commercial contacts with Britain and Gaul, but it is difficult to explain in this way the complete substitution of Celtic for other languages in the country. It appears that, from the fourth century BC for the next 200 years or so, small but compact groups of Celtic-speaking warriors from Britain landed in Ireland and established power centres, which, through a combination of military and commercial success, became dominant. The early occurrence of Celtic art styles in Ireland – such as the designs on the Turoe Stone in County *Galway, dating from the first century BC – supports this theory.

The basic social structure of Celtic society was established in early Ireland. A particular territory was under the control of a tribe, which held it by arms and, when necessary, by arrangements with stronger neighbours. The belief in a divine ancestor was general, but individual tribes could vary and elaborate this so as to underline their own particular identity. The general social division was into three classes: the nobility, the common people and the bondmen, or slaves. The latter seem to have consisted generally of captives taken in war. All three classes, and the gradations of them, were linked together by an elaborate system of clientage.

From the third century AD, the continental Celts were under increasing pressure from the Roman legions. After their communities in northern Italy, in eastern Europe and in the Iberian Peninsula were decimated by the Romans, Gaul itself fell to Julius Caesar in a series of campaigns from 58 to 50 BC. The destruction of continental Celtdom was completed in the succeeding generations, as Roman, Germanic and Slavic peoples took over the Celtic areas, but dialects of the Celtic language survived in scattered areas until the fourth century AD, or perhaps even later. Britain too was conquered by the Romans, but the Celtic speech survived strongly there until pushed from the east by the Anglo-Saxon invaders from the fifth century AD onward. Migrations from the south-west of Britain, meanwhile, brought a Celtic language back to the continental landmass, where it survived as Breton. Ireland alone was untouched by the Roman legions and in this western isle a Celtic culture continued to flourish. The Celtic language developed into *Irish (sometimes called Gaelic) and in this form assimilated the culture of later *Viking, *Norman and English settlers. By the sixteenth century, Ireland was under strict English control and the native civilisation began to break down, but the Irish language, even under continuing pressure, still survives today. D.OH.

censorship. The Film Censorship Act of 1923 set the stage for more than four decades of Irish cultural policy. Although the *Free State *Constitution of 1922 endorsed the separation of church and state, in practice, the new government invariably followed the church's lead on issues of morality. *Divorce and birth control were proscribed and in 1926, the government established a Committee of Enquiry on Evil Literature, which led to the Censorship of Publications Act of 1929. This law authorised the banning of books or periodicals that were perceived as generally 'indecent or obscene' or that contained discussions of – or even allusions to – issues offensive to *Catholic morality. The specific criteria of 'obscenity' were determined behind closed doors by a Censorship Board, rather than in the courts. Formed in 1930, the first board consisted of five members appointed by the minister of justice and approved by the Catholic church and academic community. The board relied on vigilant members of the public to submit books, with the offending passage(s) marked, for review. This system meant that books could be banned on the basis of one phrase taken out of context, that years could pass between a book's publication and its banning and that some books, like James *Joyce's *Ulysses* (1922), which was immediately deemed pornographic and banned in the United States (until 1933) and England (until 1936), were never banned in Ireland. However, *Ulysses* was rarely available in Irish bookstores until 1967.

Beginning in the 1930s, censorship policies seriously affected Irish literary culture. Many of the works of a budding generation of writers were banned on moral, rather than political or ideological, grounds. While Seán *O'Faoláin's collection of short stories *Midsummer Night Madness* (1932), for instance, contained biting critiques of the physical force nationalism that had fuelled the Irish revolution, it was banned for its allusions to frustrated sexual desire and adultery. The banning of Kate *O'Brien's *The Land of Spices* (1941) for a single sentence alluding to a homosexual affair became a *cause célèbre*, foreshadowing a wave of bannings in the 1940s and 1950s for depictions of sexuality. Three of Benedict *Kiely's novels, including *There Was an Ancient House* (1955), which contained a description of female nudity, were banned. Highly critical of provincial Ireland, John Broderick's *The Pilgrimage* (1961) was banned for its treatment of homosexuality. John *McGahern's second novel, *The Dark*, was banned in 1965 for its descriptions of masturbation and the author was dismissed from his job as a primary school teacher. Most of Edna *O'Brien's fiction published during the 1960s was banned for its alleged assault on Irish womanhood through portraits of grim, unhappy marriages and extramarital affairs. Rather than appeal or protest the decisions of the Censorship Board, O'Brien and many other writers simply left Ireland. The list of Irish literary exiles between the 1930s and 1960s – the most intensive period of literary censorship – includes Samuel *Beckett and Brian *Moore, whose first four novels, including *Judith Hearne* (1955) – which was later renamed *The Lonely Passion of Judith*

Hearne – were banned. O'Faoláin, however, remained behind to combat censorship and Irish cultural isolationism in the journal, the **Bell*, which he edited between 1940 and 1946. Frank *O'Connor, one of O'Faoláin's most vocal allies, eventually left Ireland for the United States in 1952.

While there was no official *theatre censorship in Ireland (unlike in Britain), the theatre was affected by the censorship climate. In 1957 the director of the Pike Theatre, Alan Simpson, was arrested on charges of obscenity because of a reference to a contraceptive in his production of Tennessee Williams' *The Rose Tattoo*. The following year, the Dublin Theatre Festival was cancelled when Seán *O'Casey and Beckett withdrew their plays in protest at the archbishop's refusal to sanction the staging of Alan McClelland's stage adaptation of James Joyce's *Ulysses*.

In 1967, the government revised the Censorship of Publications Act. A new stipulation withheld from the public any book or periodical deemed 'obscene' for a period lasting no more than 12 years. Following this amendment, almost 5,000 titles were made available in Ireland. Censorship, however, remained a dominant cultural force in Ireland in the 1970s and 1980s. The outbreak of the *Troubles in *Northern Ireland, beginning in 1968, culminated in close surveillance of journalistic reportage of *IRA activity and opinion in the press, *radio and *television. The laws upholding media censorship began to be dismantled in 1993 when the *Downing Street Declaration announced the London and Dublin governments' decision to include the IRA and its political wing, *Sinn Féin, in a series of peace talks.

While the Health, or Family Planning, Act of 1979 ensured that the subject of contraception would no longer be prohibited, the Censorship Board turned its attention to abortion and pledged to limit Irish *women's access to information about the availability of abortions in Great Britain. Although the right to abortion in the *Republic of Ireland is still denied, two constitutional referenda were passed in 1992 securing both the right to information and the right to travel to obtain an abortion. While a Censorship Board continues to exist in the Irish Republic, its activities are significantly more limited and primarily directed toward pornography. Lee Dunne's *The Cabfather* (1975), which was the last Irish novel to be banned, was finally released in Ireland in 1988. E.S.M.

Charlton, Jack (1935–). Former Irish *soccer manager. Born in Ashington, Northumberland, in the north of England, Charlton played as centre-half in England's victorious World Cup team of 1966. He was made an honorary Irish citizen in recognition of his success as manager of the Irish soccer team from 1986 to 1996. During these ten years, the *Republic of Ireland qualified for the European Championships in 1988 – the first major tournament that Ireland contested in soccer. The Republic of Ireland later reached the quarter finals of the World Cup in Italy in 1990, and won a famous victory against Italy in Giants Stadium, New York, on the way to qualifying for the last 16 of the 1994 World Cup. Charlton retired as Irish manager in 1996. B.D.

Chester Beatty Library. Library collection of manuscripts and art. The library was donated to the Irish state by Chester Beatty (1875–1968) in 1950, because he did not like the recently elected Labour government in Britain. Born in New York, Beatty made his fortune in mining and became a British subject in 1933. An avid collector, he spent his wealth on Middle Eastern and Oriental manuscripts and books, most of which are richly and elaborately decorated. The Indian miniatures are among the best in the world. As well as treasures from the world of Islam, China and Japan, the library holds Burmese, Thai and Tibetan manuscripts.

Beatty was made an honorary Irish citizen and was given a state funeral on his death. The library recently moved to *Dublin Castle. T.C.

Chicago, the Irish in. Chicago and its Irish grew up together. In 1837, Chicago was a frontier town when Irish workers arrived to dig the Illinois and Michigan Canal, the engineering feat that connected the Great Lakes with the Mississippi River. By 1843, Irish *immigrants were 10% of the city's 7,580 residents. As Irish emigration intensified during and after the Great *Famine, their ranks swelled to 18% of Chicago's 1860 population. However, massive numbers of European newcomers between 1870 and 1924 diversified the city's ethnic and racial mix, reducing the Irish share to only 7% by 1890. The arrival of many African Americans and Hispanics in the twentieth century further diminished Irish demographics.

Despite their small numbers, the early arrival of the Irish in the city, combined with their political and English language skills, enabled them to make a distinctive imprint on Chicago's character and history. They shaped its politics, influenced Irish nationalism, dominated the *Catholic hierarchy and church institutions and defined many urban neighbourhoods.

Because Anglo-*Protestants from the east first settled the city, the mostly *Catholic Chicago Irish confronted the same prejudices experienced by their countrymen in *Boston, *New York and Philadelphia. Hostility and discrimination resulted in an Irish Catholic subculture that used politics as an avenue for advancement. By the end of the nineteenth century, Irish Catholic men were prominent in City Hall and had positions of political influence in the police and fire departments, and on construction projects with city contracts.

Like the Irish in other American cities, those in Chicago helped create a political machine that dominated the city's politics from the late nineteenth throughout the twentieth and into the twenty-first centuries. Since 1893, eight of the city's mayors have been Irish Catholics: John Patrick Hopkins (1893–95), Edward F. Dunne (1905–07), William E. Dever (1923–27), Edward J. Kelly (1933–47), Martin J. Kennelly (1947–55), Richard J. Daley (1955–76), Jane Byrne (1979–83) and Richard M. Daley (1989 to present). Richard J. Daley was the most powerful politician in Chicago history. He influenced the nomination of John F. *Kennedy for president in 1960 and made sure he carried the important state of Illinois. During the Democratic National Convention in 1968, Mayor Daley helped Hubert Humphrey become the Democratic presidential nominee, much to the anger of radical protesters in the streets. Although the Irish generally entered politics to enrich themselves and their supporters with city contracts and jobs, by the twentieth century their politicians had become more professional in approaching the complex problems of urban government. They also excelled in integrating other ethnic and racial groups into their political machine.

Until recently, unlike Irish politicians in other cities, those in Chicago were reluctant to use their local power to launch state or national political careers. Downstate Illinois seemed too rural, small-town, Protestant and Republican to offer solid support for a Chicago Irish Catholic candidate.

The Irish also gave shape to a vigorous Catholic church in Chicago. While several Irishmen served as bishops and archbishops of the Chicago Diocese, it was the neighbourhood parishes that centred the daily lives of Irish Americans, at once sheltering them from nativist hostility and transforming them into modern American Catholics. Despite the conservatism that characterised Irish American Catholicism, the Chicago experience also developed a liberal dimension. Opportunities of a frontier town enlarged the vision of its people. Chicago Catholic bishops proved more tolerant of Irish *nationalists than those on the East Coast. They also championed organised labour and the New Deal, New Frontier and Great Society social agendas. Irish leaders of Chicago Catholicism did much to harmonise the conflicts that often divided various ethnic groups, unifying both church and city. Although many Chicago Irish Catholics were hostile to the African American Great Migration to the north, some of their clergy and laity founded the Catholic Interracial Council in 1945 and made the city the headquarters for a national organisation.

Chicago's Irish women became a major force in the city's teaching and nursing professions. In 1920, Archbishop Mundelein estimated that 70% of Chicago public school teachers were Irish.

Chicago Irish writers like Finley Peter Dunne, James T. Farrell, Kate McPhelim Cleary and Clara E. Laughlin are known for their description of urban realism, tracing the Irish experience from Famine immigrants, through working-class hardships and discrimination, to the prosperous middle-class. E.McM.

Chichester Clarke, James (1923–2000). Prime minister of *Northern Ireland, 1969–71. Chichester Clarke narrowly succeeded the liberal Terence *O'Neill in April 1969. He continued reform programmes, but was forced to call on the British army in support of the *RUC in August 1969 after loyalist mobs burned out *Catholic areas in *Belfast and other cities. The resurgent *IRA militarism, which had been dormant for years, increased pressure for a tough security policy. In February 1971, Chichester Clark resigned, complaining that Britain was not providing enough troops and that *unionists expected draconian solutions. M.M.

Chichester, Arthur; Baron Chichester of Belfast (1563–1625). English soldier and administrator. For his military service during the *Nine Years War (1593–1603), Chichester was granted Belfast Castle to which he added estates in *Antrim, *Down and Inishowen, County *Donegal. As lord deputy (1605–15), he was forced by King James I to suppress *Catholicism and disrupt the clan system by establishing Scottish colonies in Ireland. Chichester was lord treasurer of Ireland (1616–25) and his son, Arthur, was created First Earl Donegal in 1647. S.A.B.

Chieftains, The The leading Irish traditional *music group. The Chieftains was formed in 1963 by *uilleann piper Paddy Moloney with some of his colleagues in Seán *Ó Riada's experimental group Ceoltóirí Chualann – fiddler Martin Fay, whistle player Seán Potts, flute and concertina player Michael Tubridy and bodhrán player Davey Fallon. They turned professional in 1975 and today only Moloney remains of the original lineup. The present band was joined by fiddler Seán Keane in 1968, by *harpist and pianist Derek Bell (d.2002) in 1974, by flute player Matt Molloy in 1979 and by singer/bodhrán player Kevin Conneff in 1980. The Chieftains broke a trail for traditional Irish music all over the world, inspiring many other Irish groups that enjoy popularity and critical acclaim today. Their albums typically incorporate folk music from other countries, but their playing of strict Irish traditional music with the highest calibre of instrumental soloists is considered exemplary. The first of their 50-plus albums (*Chieftains*, 1963) remains iconic and highly respected within the genre. Other albums of note include: *Bonaparte's Retreat* (1977), *The Chieftains in China* (1987), *Irish Heartbeat – With Van Morrison* (1988) and *Santiago* (1996). F.V.

Childers, Erskine Hamilton (1905–74). Son of Robert Erskine *Childers and fourth president of Ireland. Born in London, educated at Cambridge, Childers became advertisement manager of Éamon *de Valera's paper the *Irish Press* in 1931. First elected to the *Dáil in 1938, Childers held a number of positions under successive *Fianna Fáil governments, including Tánaiste between 1969 and 1973. He was inaugurated as Irish president on 25 June 1973 and died from a heart attack while in office on 17 November 1974. P.E.

Childers, Robert Erskine (1870–1922). Author and *nationalist. Born in London, Childers was a veteran of the *Boer War and an accomplished sailor, who wrote the mystery novel *The Riddle of the Sands* in 1903. He became an advocate of *home rule and used his boat, the *Asgard*, to smuggle weapons to the Irish *Volunteers in July 1914. During the *First World War, he volunteered for the Royal Navy. In 1921 he was elected to the *Dáil. Childers was secretary of the Irish delegation to the *Anglo-Irish Treaty conference, but was opposed to the agreement as signed. He was a *republican propagandist during the *Civil War and was court-martialled for the unauthorised possession of a gun (given to him by Michael *Collins for personal protection a few months earlier). Childers was executed on 24 November 1922. P.E.

Christ Church Cathedral. The *Dublin diocesan cathedral of the *Church of Ireland. This church was founded in 1038 by King Sitric Silkenbeard in the centre of *Viking Dublin. A part of the choir dates from the late twelfth century and the nave was completed in the thirteenth. Damaged by a roof collapse in 1562, the cathedral was restored by the distiller Henry Roe in the 1870s and recently again refurbished. Its extensive crypt reopened in 2000. P.H.

Christian Brothers, Irish. *Catholic religious teaching order. Founded in 1802 by Edmund Ignatius *Rice, the Institute of Irish Christian Brothers was dedicated to educating Ireland's impoverished youth in the catechism of the Catholic faith. Over the next 75 years, the Christian Brothers established 294 schools in Ireland which, by 1878, were staffed by more than 400 brothers teaching over 33,000 students ranging in age from four to seventeen. By 1838, the Brothers had separated from the government's National System of *Education, in keeping with the Irish bishops' plans to establish strictly denominational schools. In order to meet the needs of Catholic Ireland's rising middle-class during the mid-nineteenth century, the Brothers expanded their curriculum to include the full array of secular subjects and established a style of strict discipline in their classrooms, which became legendary. They also formalised their teaching of the Catholic religion by emphasising the sacraments, rituals and devotions. This contributed to making Irish Catholics the most practising Catholics in the world until the *Second Vatican Council. Alone among nineteenth-century Irish educators, the Brothers taught Irish history, *poetry, culture and, after 1878, the *Irish language. This emphasis on Irish culture fostered *nationalism. The Brothers' graduates included veterans of the 1916 *Easter Rising such as Patrick *Pearse, Arthur *Griffith and Éamon *de Valera. By the early twentieth century, the primary focus of the Brothers' ministry had shifted to the teaching of Irish *immigrants and their children in *Canada, *Australia, *New Zealand and the United States. Recent scandals involving the physical and sexual abuse of students have diminished the prestige of the order. M.P.C.

Christianity in Ireland, early (fifth century AD). There are indications that small numbers of Christians were in Ireland before St *Patrick's arrival, but most likely these were slaves and merchants from Roman Britain. There may also have been some missionaries, one of whom, called *Palladius, is actually mentioned. The mission of Patrick in the fifth century

AD covered large areas of the north and the midlands and he made a considerable number of converts among the lower-classes and some among the nobles. By the time of his death, his missionary work, together with Christianity's consistent body of doctrine and growing prestige throughout the continent, had given widespread appeal to the new religion in Ireland.

Within a generation or two, the episcopal nature of Patrick's organisation was giving way to a new system, consisting of monasteries with or without a bishop in charge. This was already becoming the trend in Britain in Patrick's time and was particularly suitable to the Irish context. The numerous small kingdoms needed separate missionary stations and local rulers tended to confer special parcels of land on the clerics. The monasteries grew and by the mid-sixth century had become the prime agency for change in the country. The ascetic life of hermits added to the impetus; many of these hermits became founders of new monasteries in faraway places. The career of the celebrated Columba (called Colm *Cille in Irish) illustrates the several aspects of this development. By birth a member of the leading clan in the country, he influenced all by his personal piety. He founded monasteries in different areas and then began a mission to the Picts of *Scotland.

So vibrant had the monastic Christianity of Ireland become by the year AD 664, that the Roman church authorities had difficulty in persuading the general body of Irish monks to accept the new standard method of computing the date of Easter. The Irish church was notable in other ways, also. Having its origins in a peaceful transition, it thrived in a context that had much continuity with native customs and beliefs. There had been some opposition, led by the *druids, but in time the saintly monks came to resemble the druids themselves in public perception. A good example of such continuity and integration of *Celtic customs and beliefs is well-worship. The druids had a cult of sacred springs and the Christian missionaries often resorted to the same places to perform mass baptisms. Thus in Irish folk practice, the holy well remains a centre of local religious practice and miraculous cures are attributed to it. D.OH.

Church of Ireland, the. Principal *Protestant church in Ireland and state church from 1560 to 1869. While the *Reformation began in Ireland under *Henry VIII, it was not until the Act of Uniformity (1560) during *Elizabeth I's reign that the monarch was officially head of the church. All Irish people were required by law to attend Protestant services or be fined. Worship was ordained according to the *Book of Common Prayer*. Apart from the confiscation of ecclesiastical buildings and lands, little progress was made in imposing Protestantism on the Irish people. Because of the relative poverty of the life of a clergyman, few clerics of a high calibre were attracted to careers in the Church of Ireland, and those English clergy who did come were handicapped by a lack of knowledge of the *Irish language. While there were some efforts to found new primary and grammar schools that could have propelled evangelisation, only a very few were opened. Not until Trinity College was founded in 1592 was there a national academy for the training of ministers. Even then, the mission of the Church of Ireland was mainly focused on the English-speaking, mostly newcomer population.

The character of the Church of Ireland in the early seventeenth century was shaped by the puritanism of its leadership, most notably James *Ussher, archbishop of *Armagh. Ussher emphasised the continuity of the heritage of the Church of Ireland from the earliest phase of Irish Christianity. Bishop William Bedell of Kilmore, sometime provost of Trinity, was exceptional in his dedication to preaching through the Irish language. The middle decades of the century were extremely disruptive for the organisation of the Church of Ireland as the *Rebellion of 1641 badly affected many Protestant communities and the counter-Reformation flourished under the auspices of the Catholic *Confederation of Kilkenny. Only with great difficulty were diocesan and parochial structures later re-established. After the brief restoration of *Catholicism under *James II, the church leadership closed ranks with the Protestant political and social ascendancy to impose rigid laws known as the *Penal Laws for the exclusion of Catholics and *Presbyterians or dissenters from the mainstream of national life. Though there were some notable exceptions in the eighteenth century, such as Jonathan *Swift and William King, the quality of leadership in the Church of Ireland was not inspiring on the whole and organisation languished.

In 1800, the churches of Ireland and England were united at the time of the Act of *Union. Challenges to Irish Protestantism came from the breakaway Methodist church and the rise of an evangelical movement within the Church of Ireland. The Evangelicals engaged in a vigorous campaign of proselytising among Catholics and promoted *education. The controversy over the payment of *tithes by non-members of the church to its clergy flared in the 1830s and was solved by a government compromise. Prime Minister William *Gladstone's government in the 1860s considered the Church of Ireland's place in Irish life to be disproportionate to its relatively small membership, and in 1869 parliament enacted the disestablishment of the Church of Ireland and ended its endowment. Provision was, however, made for the church's continuing mission and the payment of its clergy. A process of thorough internal reorganisation ensured that, after the *partition of Ireland in 1921, the church survived as an all-Ireland institution. C.L.

churches, early. In early Irish *Christianity, churches were built of wood or occasionally of earth – presumably small boxlike structures with corner beams (*antae*). But the double church for monks and nuns at *Kildare, as described by St *Brigid's seventh-century biographer Cogitosus, suggests a larger, taller building with chapels and drapes, as well as painted images. *Hisperica Famina*, another text of the same period, describes a church of massive timbers with a central altar, a western porch and four steeples. Stone churches became more popular after AD 800, but wooden churches continued to be built in the twelfth century. P.H.

Churchill, Winston S. (1874–1965). British politician and prime minister, 1940–45 and 1951–55. A towering figure on the world stage, Churchill played a pivotal role in Irish history on a number of occasions during his long political career.

Though a Conservative for most of his life, Churchill defected to the Liberal Party for a time, beginning in 1904. While a Liberal, Churchill backed his party's policy of *home rule for Ireland and supported the home rule bill of 1912. Later, when it appeared that *unionists were prepared to resort to violence to prevent home rule from going into effect, Churchill came to support the *partition of Ireland as a means of avoiding civil war. Partition was eventually legislated in Britain's *Government of Ireland Act of 1920.

Following the truce in Ireland's *War of Independence (1919–21), Churchill, as colonial secretary, was a member of the British team that negotiated the *Anglo-Irish Treaty of 1921, which created the twenty-six-county *Irish Free State as a dominion within the *Commonwealth.

Churchill had a significant impact on *Anglo-Irish relations as Britain's prime minister during the Second World War. As a committed imperialist, Churchill considered Ireland's proclamation of neutrality in the war an illegal act by a Commonwealth nation and was particularly incensed by Éamon *de Valera's refusal to grant the British access to the three ports reserved for the Royal Navy's use in the Anglo-Irish Treaty (ports that Churchill's predecessor Neville Chamberlain had formally turned over to the Irish government in 1938). Early in the war, Churchill was prepared to seize the ports, but he was dissuaded by military advisors, who argued that the cost of such a takeover would be greater than any gain. Even after the German threat to British security diminished later in the conflict, Churchill still considered neutrality a stain on Ireland's honour.

Despite his respect for many Irish *nationalists, Churchill's commitment to preserving the British empire prevented him from fully accepting the twenty-six counties' growing independence after 1921. T.D.

cinema. 'Irish film' describes both films produced in Ireland and world cinema with Irish themes. Up to the end of the twentieth century, only about 200 of the world's roughly 2,000 films with Irish themes were Irish productions. Film-making, which began in Ireland in the early twentieth century, was originally dominated by North American and British companies. From the 1920s through the 1950s, both foreign and indigenous filmmakers helped to build a national cinema based on historical themes and set on Irish soil. Varieties of *nationalism marked films such as *The Lad from Old Ireland* (1910), *Rory O'More* (1910), *Ireland a Nation* (1914), *Willie Reilly and His Colleen Bawn* (1920), *Irish Destiny* (1926), *Man of Aran* (1934), *The Dawn* (1936), *Odd Man Out* (1947) and *Shake Hands with the Devil* (1959). Perhaps the most famous Irish film is John Ford's *The Quiet Man* (1952), a romantic comedy set in an idealised landscape. *Ryan's Daughter* (1971), directed by David Lean, was also immensely popular and because of its spectacular cinematography of the *Kerry landscape, it was a huge boost to tourism in Ireland in the 1970s. In 1958, Seán *Lemass, then minister for industry and commerce, created Ardmore Studios, a permanent commercial facility for film production located in *Wicklow. The studios were frequently hired by both American and British producers.

Since the 1950s, an Irish documentary film genre has developed, with George Morrison, Liam O'Leary, Robert Monks, Colm Ó Laoghaire and Louis Marcus as key early figures. The organisation *Gael Linn produced *Irish-language cinema newsreels, as well as the 90-minute historical films *Mise Éire (I Am Ireland)* (1959) and *Saoirse* (*Freedom*) (1961). More recently, *Northern Irish independent filmmaker John T. Davis directed *Shell Shock Rock* (1978), which treats punk rock in *Northern Ireland and *Power in the Blood* (1990), which depicts evangelism in Ireland. Britain's Channel Four commissioned videos and films for television, providing support for Irish filmmakers during the recession-ridden 1980s. Nationalist workshop collectives such as Derry Film and Video produced documentaries such as Anne Crilly's *Mother Ireland* (1988), an exploration of nationalist iconography. Desmond Bell's *The Last Storyteller?* (2002) presents the life of folklorist Seán Ó hEochaidh, while his *The Hard Road to Klondike* (1999) deals with migration.

During the 1970s and 1980s, feature filmmakers such as Thaddeus O'Sullivan (*On a Paving Stone Mounted*, 1978), Bob Quinn (*Poitín*, 1978), Cathal Black (*Pigs*, 1984) and Joe Comerford (*Reefer and the Model*, 1988), working mostly in 16 millimetre, addressed social issues such as *economic stagnation, unemployment, *emigration and political turmoil. Based on a newspaper story, Peter Ormrod and John Kelleher's *Eat the Peach* (1986), which explores unemployment and smuggling in a border town, achieved considerable box office success in Ireland. The first Irish Film Board (Bord Scannan na hÉireann, 1981–87), established to promote national cultural expression, funded Neil *Jordan's *Angel* (1982), the story of a jazz musician who witnesses a paramilitary shakedown and murder. Pat Murphy's films *Maeve* (1981) and *Anne Devlin* (1984) took a feminist approach to Irish nationalism. Pat O'Connor's *Cal* (1984), based on Bernard MacLaverty's novel, romanticised the *Troubles, echoing the style of earlier British and American films such as John Ford's *The Informer* (1935) and Carol Reed's *Odd Man Out* (1947). Margo Harkin's study of teen pregnancy, *Hush-a-bye Baby* (1989), and Crilly's *Mother Ireland* (1988), along with Pat Murphy's work, formed a body of film directed by *women and concerned with women's issues. By 1992, a second film board was established under the leadership of Michael D. Higgins, then minister for arts, culture and the *Gaeltacht. The Irish Film Centre and the National Film Archive opened in *Dublin during the same year, and the magazine *Film Ireland* quickly established itself as the journal of Irish filmmaking. Flourishing around the Irish Film Centre, film festivals proliferated in cities throughout the island: Belfast, Cork, Derry, Dublin, Galway and Limerick. A second generation of women directors includes Mary McGuckian (*Words Upon the Window Pane*, 1994; *This Is the Sea*, 1998; *Best*, 2000) and Trish McAdam (*Snakes and Ladders*, 1995).

Although commercial success has often been elusive for Irish filmmakers, in 1989, Jim *Sheridan's *My Left Foot*, based on Christy *Brown's autobiography, became the first Irish film to win Academy Awards (for best director, best actor and best supporting actress). Sheridan's later films treat rural decline (*The Field*, 1990), the Troubles (*Some Mother's Son*, 1996 – produced by Sheridan, directed by Terry George; *The Boxer*, 1997) and Irish life in the US (*In America*, 2002). In 1991, Roddy *Doyle's novel about a rock group, *The Commitments*, filmed by British director Alan Parker, achieved international success. Neil Jordan won an Oscar in 1992 for *The Crying Game*, which remade the Troubles genre by emphasising issues of race and sexuality. Among Jordan's 15 films are *The Butcher Boy* (1998), adapted from Patrick *McCabe's novel, in which Jordan turns to domestic violence and insanity in a small Irish town, and *Michael Collins* (1996), a bio-epic.

Since the 1990s, when Ireland underwent extensive modernisation and integration into the global economy, Irish and Irish-related filmmakers have wrestled with the economic need for Hollywood levels of distribution in order to remain competitive on the world market. However, many Irish films receive only limited distribution and short theatrical runs. British director Ken Loach's *Hidden Agenda* (1990) fictionalises the *Stalker Affair in thriller fashion, while Paul Greengrass' *Bloody Sunday* (2002) re-creates in docudrama style the events of 30 January 1972, in *Derry. Mike Newell's *Into the West* (1992) joined John Sayles' *The Secret of Roan Inish* (1994) in exploring Irish *folklore to appeal to a young audience. Alan Parker's *Angela's Ashes* (1999) capitalised on the success of Frank *McCourt's story of counter-migration. *The Last September* (1999) adapts Elizabeth *Bowen's classic novel. Less popular films include Thaddeus O'Sullivan's *Nothing Personal* (1995), which joins Sheridan's *The Boxer* (1997) and Marc Evans' *Resurrection Man* (1998) in presenting a peace-process view of sectarian violence. Gerry Stembridge's *Guiltrip* (1996) is a study of domestic violence. John Boorman's *The General* (1997), Paddy Breathnach's *I Went Down* (1997) (screenplay by Conor *McPherson) and Thaddeus O'Sullivan's *Ordinary Decent Criminal* (2000) explore the criminal underground in Ireland. Scottish director Peter Mullan's controversial film *The Magdalene Sisters* (2002), set in a 1960s Magdalene Laundry (or Irish homes for unwed mothers), won the top award, the Golden Lion, at the Venice Film Festival. The chief problems facing Irish filmmaking in the early twenty-first century remain competition with Hollywood and distribution. C.H.

Civil War. See **Irish Civil War**.

Clan na Gael. Irish American revolutionary organisation. Founded in *New York in 1867 by Jerome J. Collins, Clan na Gael (also called the United Brotherhood) came to dominate the Irish *republican movement in America. During the 1880s, the Clan was led by 'The Triangle' of Alexander Sullivan, Michael Boland and Denis Feeley who were committed to carrying out dynamite explosions in British cities. Clan na Gael gave *Parnell valuable assistance and support during the *Land League agitation and the campaign for Irish *home rule. Reformed in 1900 with John *Devoy as its main leader, the organisation took part in preparations for the *Easter Rising of 1916 and sought to assist the German war effort against Great Britain. During the *War of Independence, Éamon *de Valera and John Devoy disagreed about the best means of securing American recognition for an Irish republic. With the long-standing connection between the Clan and the *IRB now severed, the organisation split. One faction, under Devoy, recognised the *Anglo-Irish Treaty, while another, led by Joseph McGarrity, rejected compromise and continued to support *IRA activity into the 1930s. Clan na Gael finally ceased activity after McGarrity's death in 1940. S.A.B.

Clancy Brothers, the. Irish folk group. The group was formed in *New York in 1959, by Tom, Pat and Liam Clancy of County *Tipperary and Tommy Makem of County *Armagh. Their first recording was of topical and popular 'rebel' ballads delivered in an upbeat, good-time style to the 'folk' instruments banjo and guitar. Their style and rejection of normal stage formality created instant popularity. A performance on the Ed Sullivan Show led to coast-to-coast recognition in the United States. In Ireland they became a 'pop' hit, and their style created a fashion that for many was an introduction to traditional *music. F.V.

Clancy, Willie (1918–73). *Uilleann piper. Born in Miltown Malbay, County *Clare, Clancy initially *step-danced and played whistle and flute. He took up the uilleann pipes having heard travelling player Johnny Doran in 1936. Tutored by Doran and by Leo *Rowsome and influenced by Séamus Ennis and John Potts, he won the major *Oireachtas award in 1947. Clancy established an international reputation, which drew many aficionados to his hometown each summer to hear him play. Upon his death, his one-time jocular reference to this activity as 'a summer school' was taken up by teacher Muiris Ó Róchain, Séamus MacMathúna of CCÉ (*Comhaltas Ceoltóirí Éireann) and local musicians who created Scoil Samhraidh Willie Clancy (the Willie Clancy Summer School), held annually in July ever since. The festival opens in Miltown Malbay with a lecture tribute to Breandán *Breathnach and its 1,500 students are joined by several thousand musicians and aficionados to create a unique carnival of traditional *music. F.V.

Clann na Poblachta. *Political party. Clann na Poblachta was founded in 1946 by a group of *republicans and economic and social radicals. Led by former *IRA leader Seán *MacBride, the party won two out of three by-elections before its first national contest in 1948 when it won 13.2% of the national vote. The party helped form the first coalition government, but was fatally damaged by the split between MacBride and Noel *Browne over the controversial *health bill known as the 'Mother and Child' Scheme. Clann na Poblachta never regained its initial strength and it was disbanded in 1965. J.D.

Clannad. Music group. Started in 1970 by *Donegal natives Máire, Pól and Ciarán Brennan and cousins Pádraig and Noel Duggan, Clannad performed *Irish language songs set to arrangements of traditional tunes. Local festival success was followed by a tour of Germany and major sound track commissions, one of which, 'Robin of Sherwood', won a British Academy Award in 1984. They became influential stylists and hugely popular in Europe. 'Enya' Brennan joined the group in 1979 but left in 1982 to pursue a hugely successful solo career in popular music. F.V.

Clare, County. Maritime county in the south-west of Ireland in the province of *Munster. Clare (1,332 square miles) has a population of 103,333 (2002 census). The county is surrounded by water: the Atlantic Ocean to its west; Lough Derg, the largest of the River *Shannon's lakes, on its east; Galway Bay to the north; and the Shannon estuary on its south. Clare is renowned for its spectacular and rugged beauty. A dramatic coastline runs northward from Loop Head to Ballyvaughan on the shores of Galway Bay. The Cliffs of Moher rise 700 feet above the Atlantic Ocean. The Burren, a geological and botanical marvel, resembling a lunar landscape, occupies a large portion of the north-western part of the county. *Prehistoric *dolmens, such as Poulnabrone, a Neolithic burial chamber dating from 3800 BC, rise starkly above the limestone plateau.

Mullaghmore, a spectacular site of limestone hills, lies in the centre of the Burren, close to the village of Corofin. In the eastern section of the county on the shore of Lough Derg, are the picturesque villages of Killaloe, Mountshannon and Scarrif.

Clare has a long and rich musical tradition and is considered one of the major centres of traditional Irish *music. Tulla, Kilfenora, Kilrush and Miltown Malbay in particular, which hosts the annual Willie *Clancy Summer School – a weeklong festival of traditional music, song and *dance – are known for the unique Clare style of traditional Irish music. Famous musicians associated with the county include Sharon *Shannon, Junior Crehan, Tommy *Peoples, Jackie Daly and Noel Hill.

The rich and colourful *folklore of the county includes the Biddy Early legend: a wise woman in the vicinity of the village of Feakle who reputedly could cure all manner of ailments and often ran afoul of the clergy. The writers Edna *O'Brien and Brian *Merriman are natives of the county.

Clare's economy is based on tourism, *agriculture and some multinational industry, mostly based in Shannon International Airport.

County Clare holds a unique place in Ireland's political history. It was here that two of the country's greatest *nationalist leaders were first elected to *parliament, Daniel *O'Connell in 1828 and Éamon *de Valera in 1917. Between the tenth and twelfth centuries, the Dál Cais dynasty, which was centred in the eastern part of Clare, reached the peak of its power under Brian Bóruma (*Boru). John Holland, the inventor of the submarine, was born in Liscannor. Ennis, the county's capital, is the first totally online community in the country. J.OM.

Clarke, Austin (1896–1974). Poet, dramatist, novelist, critic and broadcaster. Born in *Dublin, Clarke was educated at University College, Dublin (UCD). He was associated with literary revivalists Douglas *Hyde, George *Russell (AE) and W. B. *Yeats, and was influenced by Standish *O'Grady and Matthew Arnold. Clarke replaced his mentor Thomas *MacDonagh as lecturer in English at UCD when MacDonagh was executed for his part in the *Easter Rising of 1916. Clarke's first publication, *The Vengeance of Fionn* (1917), an epic poem, earned him recognition and comparison with Yeats, with whom he had an uneasy relationship. The breakdown in 1919 that caused him to be hospitalised for over a year is described in the long poem *Mnemosyne Lies in Dust* (1966).

From the early 1920s until 1937, Clarke worked in London as a literary journalist. Yeats nominated him in 1932 as a founding member of the *Irish Academy of Letters, which aimed to combat *censorship. Clarke's distinctive, influential experiments with Gaelic prosody are a feature of his collection *Pilgrimage and Other Poems* (1929), set in the late medieval period.

After he returned to Ireland, Clarke combined regular literary reviews in the *Irish Times* with poetry broadcasts on *Radio Éireann. In 1938 he published *Night and Morning*, whose intense, troubled poems are concerned with the loss of religious faith. The following year, he and Robert Farren founded the Dublin Verse-Speaking Society and in 1944, the Lyric Theatre Company, which staged verse drama at the *Abbey Theatre or the *Peacock. Beginning with *The Son of Learning* (1927), Clarke wrote 21 verse plays. From 1955, his poetry enjoyed new audiences as he satirised church and state with Swiftian indignation and passionately defended the poor. The acclaimed *Ancient Lights* (1955) earned him the sobriquet 'local complainer'. In the long poems of his old age, such as *Tiresias* (1971), he turned to erotic subject matter to indicate his resistance to the pieties of his age. Two polished volumes of autobiography (*Twice Round the Black Church*, 1962, and *A Penny in the Clouds*, 1968), two critical studies and the posthumously published *Collected Poems* (1974) show Clarke's remarkable range. He is generally regarded as one of the most accomplished Irish poets of his generation. M.S.T.

Clarke, Harry (1889–1931). Illustrator and stained glass artist. Influenced by the Art Nouveau style, Clarke, a Dubliner, is best known for his jewel-like stained glass windows found throughout Ireland, England, Scotland and Wales. As a contributor to the Irish Arts and Craft Movement, he designed eleven highly acclaimed windows for the Honan Chapel, in the grounds of University College, *Cork. He also illustrated H. C. Andersen's *Fairy Tales* (1916) and E. A. Poe's *Tales of Mystery and Imagination* (1919). A founder of the Dublin Painters' Group in 1921, Clarke took over his father's church-decorating business in *Dublin. His Geneva Window with scenes from twentieth-century *Irish literature, commissioned by the Irish government in 1925 as a gift to the League of Nations, was rejected as unsuitable in 1931 and is now in the Wolfsonian Museum in Miami Beach, Florida. His final work, *The Last Judgment*, is in St Mary's church Newport, County *Mayo. M.C.

Clarke, Thomas. (1857–1916) Irish *republican. Having emigrated from Ireland to America in 1880, Clarke joined *Clan na Gael. In 1883 he embarked upon a dynamiting mission to England, where he was arrested and sentenced to life imprisonment. On his release in 1898, Clarke went back to America but returned to *Dublin in 1907. A founder of the *IRB military council, he supervised preparations for the *Easter Rising of 1916. First signatory to the *Proclamation of Independence, Clarke was court-martialled and executed on 3 May 1916. S.A.B.

Clonfert cathedral. Clonfert *Church of Ireland cathedral in East *Galway is the burial place of the great Kerry sailor, St *Brendan, who died in 577. Parts of the west gable, with projecting antae at the corners, are among the oldest surviving parts of the structure (which probably replaced an earlier wooden church around the eleventh century). Around 1200, the doorway was added. It is Ireland's most intricately ornamented Romanesque doorway, decorated with interlaced bosses, human and animal heads, as well as geometrical and floral ornaments, culminating above in a pointed gable. Carved from friable sandstone, its details are weathering badly. The cathedral became *Protestant at the *Reformation in the sixteenth century. The cathedral is on the World Monument List. P.H.

Clonmacnoise. Sixth-century monastery. One of the most important monastic ruins in Ireland, Clonmacnoise in County *Offaly was the crossroads of Ireland where the east-west thoroughfare, the Eiscir Riada, crossed the north-south-flowing *Shannon River. Around 545, St Ciarán founded a monastery here that thrived for over 1,000 years until looted by the English in 1552. Royal patronage in return for burial rights made it a rich centre for arts, crafts and the study of Irish history and *folklore.

Ireland's oldest all-Irish *manuscript, **Leabhar na hUidre (Book of the Dun Cow)*, was completed here by 1106. The surviving ruins include the country's largest pre-Norman cathedral, St Ciarán's tomb-shrine and two *round towers. Three *high crosses and examples of the great collection of cross-decorated memorial slabs are now housed at the site's Interpretative Centre. A *Norman *castle nearby, of c.1200, guarded the river crossing, where remains of a wooden bridge of c.800 have recently been discovered. P.H.

Clontarf, Battle of (1014). Battle fought by Brian *Boru and the forces of *Munster against the *Vikings of *Dublin, the *Leinster Irish and their Scandinavian allies. Traditionally seen as a struggle between the Irish and the Vikings for the sovereignty of Ireland, the battle was really the culmination of an internal struggle between Irish provincial rulers for the control of Ireland. The battle began at dawn on 23 April and, by that evening, Brian's forces had gained the upper hand and defeated the Leinster-Viking alliance. There were many losses on both sides. Brian himself was slain in his tent and his son Murchadh was killed on the battlefield. While the battle removed the threat of Norse domination in Ireland, it did not totally extinguish their presence or influence. Many returned to their strongholds in Dublin, *Waterford and *Wexford, which they continued to control until the *Anglo-Norman invasion in 1169. M.T.D., P.E.

Coghlan, Éamonn (1952–). Athlete, middle-distance runner. Born in *Dublin, Coghlan finished fourth in two successive Olympic games (1976 and 1980) but will be best remembered for his victory in the 5,000 metre final at the World Championship of 1983. He set six world records at 1,500 metres, 2,000 metres and the mile indoors, for which he became affectionately known as 'the Chairman of the Boards'. B.D.

Coleman, James (1941–). Conceptual artist. Born in County *Roscommon, Coleman studied in *Dublin, Paris, London and Milan. He represented Ireland at the Venice Biennale in 1978 and exhibited at the L' Imaginaire Irlandais show in Paris in 1996. His interactive installations use light, sound, slide, video and live performance, making the spectator reconsider the meaning of art and its objectives. M.C.

Coleman, Michael (1891–1946). Musician. Born at Killavil, County *Sligo, an area abundant in music, Coleman is the most influential fiddle player in Irish traditional *music. In 1914, he emigrated to the United States, where he began recording in 1921. The Depression interrupted his career, but he resumed recording and radio work in 1936. Coleman's albums reflect the traditional music style of Sligo and have become part of the canon of Irish traditional music. His collected recordings have been re-released on CD. F.V.

Collins, Michael (1890–1922). *Nationalist, revolutionary, *Civil War commander, govern-

Michael Collins

ment minister – Michael Collins remains one of the enduring legends of modern Irish history. During the height of the *War of Independence (1919–21), Collins was reputedly one of the most wanted men in the British empire. However, only a few months later, he would play an important role in the negotiations leading to the *Anglo-Irish Treaty and eventually the formation of the *Irish Free State.

Michael Collins was born near Clonakilty, in County *Cork, on 16 October 1890. The youngest of eight children, he witnessed at an early age the suffering of the Irish peasantry caused by absentee *landlords and absentee government. Ireland had not had a home government since the Act of *Union of 1800. The *Famine of the 1840s, the revolutionary *Fenians and *Parnell's failed *home rule movement would all shape his political awareness.

After a primary education, Collins went to London in 1906 to join an older sister and to take a clerical position in the Post Office Savings Bank. An avid reader, Collins studied nationalist literature and history, and as he moved to other jobs, he learned accounting and finance, skills that he would later use in his political career.

In 1909 in London, Collins was sworn into the the *IRB. After the outbreak of the *First World War, he went to *Dublin and took part in the *Easter Rising of 1916. After one week, the rising was quelled, 15 leaders were executed by firing squad and many rank-and-file militants, including Collins, were jailed in Frongoch, Wales.

While in the military prison, Collins displayed the leadership qualities and dominant personality that would later distinguish him as a brilliant military and political leader. The executions raised such anti-British sentiments that the authorities stopped further executions and, in December 1916, released Collins and many of the other rebels.

Back in Ireland, Collins was appointed financial officer of *Sinn Féin, a political party committed to an independent and free Ireland. In the December 1918 general elections for the House of Commons, Collins assisted in getting a majority (73 of 105) of Sinn Féin candidates elected throughout Ireland. These candidates refused to take their seats in the House of Commons and on 21 January 1919, set up their own parliament in Dublin, called *Dáil Éireann, with Éamon *de Valera as president.

For Britain, Ireland's declaration of independence at the first Dáil meeting was a serious crisis. Michael Collins, who was the minister of finance, organised a Dáil loan to finance the new government. As director of intelligence of the *IRA and the leader of the IRB, Collins was also one of the military campaign strategists in the *Anglo-Irish War of Independence. He set up an effective system of counterintelligence and coordinated a secret campaign of assassinations of pro-British *police and agents throughout Ireland. The British commissioned a special anti-terrorist unit – the notoriously ruthless *Black and Tans – to defeat Collins' campaign. Collins responded with increased guerrilla warfare. By July 1921, the British Prime Minister David *Lloyd George agreed to a truce, followed by talks with Sinn Féin's President Éamon de Valera in London.

When further talks were arranged in October 1921, in a brilliant feat of what some historians have called Machiavellian manipulation, de Valera prevailed on the 'outlawed terrorist' Michael Collins to be part of the Irish delegation, while de Valera would remain in Ireland as head of the provisional government. Collins protested fiercely (he claimed not to be a politician and did not want to become a scapegoat for what could be only a treaty compromise), but eventually agreed to come out of 'hiding' and travel to London, to join the rest of the Irish delegation. Led by Vice President Arthur *Griffith, minister for foreign affairs, the delegation had full plenipotentiary power from the Dáil, but, rather ambiguously, were also ordered to refer any treaty draft back to Dublin before final agreement.

Collins was to play a major role in the negotiations with the British delegation, which included the Prime Minister Lloyd George, Winston *Churchill and Arthur Neville Chamberlain. The talks lasted from 11 October to 6 December 1921, when a compromise was reached and Articles of Agreement for a Treaty were signed. The *Anglo-Irish Treaty recognised an Irish Free State consisting of twenty-six of Ireland's thirty-two counties. The treaty (which also included a controversial *oath of allegiance to the crown) was fiercely debated in the Dáil and was accepted by a slim majority (64/57) on 7 January 1922. Collins viewed the treaty as a stepping stone to complete independence, but many accused him of selling out.

In June 1922, a few months after the anti-treaty republicans occupied the Four Courts building in Dublin, *Civil War broke out. Michael Collins, chairman of the Provisional Government and head of the Free State forces, desperately wanted an end to the violence. In late August 1922, he travelled to his home area in County Cork for an apparently routine recognisance trip. Some claim a meeting with the anti-treaty leaders was being negotiated. As Collins' convoy passed through Beal na mBláth, a sniper's bullet killed him instantly. He was only 31 years old. The Civil War ended in May of the following year. J.OM., L.R.

Collins, Patrick (1911–94). Painter. Born in Dromore West, County *Sligo, Collins is a semi-abstract, lyrical landscape painter whose work, in contrast to hard-edge modernism, can be described as *Celtic romanticism with an emphasis on nature and the Irish past. A member of *Aosdána, he lived in *Dublin and France and had a major retrospective in Dublin, *Cork and *Belfast in 1982. M.C.

Colm Cille, Saint (521–597). One of Ireland's three patron *saints (together with St *Patrick and *Brigid). Born of royal stock at Gartan, County *Donegal, St Colm Cille (*Columba* in Latin) was a missionary and founder of monasteries in *Derry, Durrow and *Iona. Tradition says that he illicitly copied a manuscript from his old teacher St Finnian of Moville. The controversial copy Colm Cille made may be the **Cathach*, the oldest surviving manuscript in Ireland. Colm Cille raised an army against the king, who had sided with Finnian and, after the Battle of Culdreimne (561), Colm Cille was banished. During his exile, he founded his most influential monastery on the island of Iona (Inner Hebrides), from where he Christianised the Picts in *Scotland. He is buried on Iona. P.H.

Colum, Padraic (1881–1972). Poet and dramatist. Born in *Longford and educated at University College, Dublin, Colum was inspired by the *Irish Revival movement while still an undergraduate. His first play, *Broken Soil*, was produced by the Irish National Theatre Society in 1903. This was followed by *The Land* (1905) and *Thomas Muskerry* (1910). Colum's plays portray the lives of small farmers and peasants, introducing a new realism to Irish Revival drama. In 1914, he and his wife emigrated to the United States, where they both taught comparative literature at Columbia University, in New York City. His first collection of poetry, *Wild Earth* (1916), displayed the dramatic lyricism for which he is famous. *Collected Poems* was published in 1953. Colum based his collections of children's stories, *At the Gateways of the Day* (1924) and *The Bright Islands* (1925), on a survey of Hawaii's native myths, legends and folklore. His many other popular children's books include *A Boy in Eirinn* (1913), *The King of Ireland's Son* (1916) and *The Adventures of Odysseus* (1918). In 1958, he published *Our Friend James Joyce* in collaboration with his wife Mary Maguire. Colum was the last living link with *Yeats, *Synge, Lady *Gregory and the heyday of the Irish Revival. C.D.

Columbanus, Saint (543–615). Irish monk and *saint. St Columbanus was a trail-blazer among the Irish monks who became pilgrim-exiles to spread the word of God on the European continent. Born in 543, he studied in Bangor, County *Down, and left for *France in 591. There he founded monasteries, first at Annegray and then at Luxeuil, which added a new impetus to French monasticism. Expelled in 610, Columbanus moved to Switzerland, where he left his pupil St Gall at a place where a famous monastery (St Gall) later developed, before crossing the Alps to make his own final foundation at Bobbio in Northern Italy. He died there in 615. Columbanus wrote a very strict monastic rule for his monks, passionately defended his Irish viewpoint on the date of Easter against no less a person than the pope, and was a poet and brilliant letter writer in Latin. Fiery yet humble, fallible but contrite and forgiving, he was an important figure in forging a link between the classical civilisation of the Mediterranean and the monastic culture of his native land. P.H.

Comhaltas Ceoltóirí Éireann (CCÉ). The major revival organisation of Irish traditional *music. Founded in 1951 by musicians, including piper Leo *Rowsome, CCÉ is committed to the preservation and spread of traditional Irish music, song and *dance. It organises classes for Irish music education throughout the year and competitions focused on a series of festival events called *fleadh cheoil*. The most prestigious of these is the All-Ireland *Fleadh Cheoil*, held annually in different towns all over Ireland. CCÉ grew rapidly and adopted a democratic, political-style pyramid structure with local, county and provincial branches that elect a national congress and leadership. It also has branches in Britain, Scotland and the United States. F.V.

Commonwealth (of Nations). An association of states comprising the United Kingdom and some former British dependencies. Formally established in 1931 as an outgrowth of the British empire, the Commonwealth (including such countries as Canada, Australia and New Zealand) acknowledges the British crown as its symbolic head. During the nineteenth and early twentieth centuries, a number of British dependencies gained dominion status, which combined a degree of practical independence with a profession of loyalty to the crown. The 1921 *Anglo-Irish Treaty gave the new *Irish Free State dominion status within the Commonwealth. The 1931 Statute of Westminster was passed by the British parliament largely because of extensive lobbying by Irish delegates at the imperial conferences of 1926 and 1930. The statute recognised the dominions as free and equal members of the Commonwealth, and acknowledged the sovereign right of each dominion to control its own domestic and foreign affairs and to establish its own diplomatic corps. Ireland's passage of the 1948 *Republic of Ireland Act marked the state's withdrawal from the Commonwealth. T.D.

Communist Party. The first Communist Party of Ireland was formed in 1921, when members of the Socialist Party of Ireland merged with the Communist International. James *Connolly's son, Roddy Connolly, led the tiny party and the writer Liam *O'Flaherty was also a founding member. In 1924, James *Larkin's Irish Worker League replaced the party as the group affiliated to the Comintern. Larkin's son, also named James Larkin, was a leading party member. In 1928 a group of Irish communists went to Russia for political training.

In 1932, *Belfast communists successfully organised a strike of workers on relief schemes for the unemployed, uniting *Catholic and *Protestant workers. The Communist Party of Ireland, reformed in 1933, recruited volunteers to fight on the Republican side in the *Spanish Civil War and several party members died in Spain.

Between the 1930s and 1950s, the church and the press were fiercely anti-communist and at times public activity was impossible. In 1970, the communist groups in *Northern Ireland and the *Republic of Ireland reunited as a new Communist Party of Ireland. It remained closely aligned with the Soviet Union. The party's occasional election candidates have received insignificant support, but its members have been influential in *trade unions, notably in Belfast and in various protest movements in Northern Ireland and the Republic of Ireland. The party survives, but as a force on the far left it lost out in the 1970s and 1980s to the *Workers' Party and more recently to Trotskyist groupings such as the Socialist Party. P.D.

Confederate War (1641–53). See **Rebellion of 1641** and **Confederation of Kilkenny.**

Confederation of Kilkenny, the (1642). Assembly of Confederate *Catholics (Gaelic Irish and Old English allies) organised in 1642 to govern territory held as a result of the *Rebellion of 1641. In May 1642, the Irish Catholic clergy, along with members of the Catholic nobility and prominent merchants and lawyers, met at *Kilkenny to discuss means of controlling the rebellion. An alternative government for Ireland was proposed and an oath was drafted to bind together all the Catholic Confederate Allies. In October 1642, the first General Assembly of Confederate Catholics was held at Kilkenny. The assembly met annually until 1648, but it never succeeded in gaining total control of Ireland's administrative structure. The confederation itself was marked by considerable confusion and squabbling and was formally dissolved in January 1649. P.E.

Congreve, William (1670–1729). Playwright and librettist. Born in Yorkshire, England, Congreve moved to Ireland where his father was commander of the garrison in Youghal. He attended Kilkenny College and Trinity College, Dublin, and studied law in London. His literary friends included Sir Richard Steele, Alexander Pope and Jonathan *Swift. Congreve's first play, *The Old Bachelor* (1693), was a huge success at the Theatre Royal in London. His restoration comedies, of which the best known are *Love for Love* (1695) and *The Way of the World* (1700), a comedy of manners, are masterly, witty and subtle. Although he retired from playwriting in 1700, he collaborated in translating Molière's *Monsieur de Pourceaugnac*. M.S.T.

Conn of the Hundred Battles. Legendary figure from the Red Branch Cycle of *Celtic history. Conn was a king of Ireland, AD circa 177–157, son of Rechtmar, husband of Becuma. Conn discovered, by accident, the *Lia Fáil* (stone of destiny), which supposedly screamed under the feet of a rightful king the same number of times as he would have reigning heirs. A version of the story still survives in the 'Sword in the Stone' episode of Arthurian legend. Conn's kingdom, the northern half of Ireland, was later divided into the two provinces of *Ulster and *Connacht (which derives from his name). J.MD.

Connacht. One of the four provinces of Ireland. This north-west province, which covers an area of 6,838 square miles, has a population of 464,050 (2002 census). Connacht is the least arable but one of the most beautiful provinces of Ireland. Its name derives from the Connachta, followers of *Conn of the Hundred Battles, a branch of the Venii tribe in *pre-Christian Ireland. The province consists of the counties *Roscommon, *Galway, *Mayo, *Leitrim and *Sligo. Connacht is known for such tourist attractions as: Galway Bay, Claddagh, now part of Galway City and famous for the Claddagh ring, the Irish-speaking *Aran Islands and *Connemara, with its famous marble, ponies and bogs. During the *Cromwellian Settlement, the dispossessed *Catholic Irish landowners were sent to Connacht. Oliver *Cromwell is reputed to have said: 'To Hell or to Connaught'. J.MD.

Connemara. Area of County *Galway that is situated west of the Corrib and stretches between the townlands of Barna and Carna. One of the most scenic areas of Ireland, Connemara has a vibrant Irish-speaking community with a rich tradition of **seán-nós* singing, *dancing and sailing. In recent years, the area has become something of a media enclave, and the *Irish-language *television and *radio stations (TG4 and Raidió na Gaeltachta) as well as the *newspaper *Foinse* are all based there. South Connemara is the largest *Gaeltacht in the country. B.D.

Connolly, James (1868–1916). Labour leader, revolutionary. Connolly was born in Edinburgh into extreme poverty. His parents were Irish immigrants. An avid reader familiar with the works of Karl Marx, he learned Irish *nationalism from an uncle who was in the *IRB. Connolly's early experiences of work and poverty turned him to *socialism. He first came to Ireland as a young soldier in the 1880s and later, back in Edinburgh, he became involved in labour politics. In 1896, Connolly set up the Irish Socialist Republican Party in *Dublin and established and edited the *Workers' Republic*, the party's journal. His best works as a socialist journalist and pamphleteer are collected in *Labour in Irish History* (1910) and *The Reconquest of Ireland* (1915).

His socialism made little headway in Ireland, and in 1903 he took his family to the United States, where he encountered other socialist thinkers, who added an international dimension to his own ideology. In 1910, Connolly returned to Dublin to run the Socialist Party of Ireland. He was also appointed the *Belfast organiser of the Irish Transport and General Workers' Union (ITGWU). He organised Belfast's dock workers and secured a pay raise for striking seamen and firemen. During the women *linen workers' unsuccessful strike of 1911, he set up the Irish Textile Workers' Union. In 1912, with James *Larkin, Connolly founded the Irish *Labour Party in association with the Irish Trade Union Congress.

During the *home rule crisis, Connolly clashed with William Walker, the leading labour *unionist in Belfast and alienated the nationalists under Joseph Devlin because he disagreed with Devlin's reluctant acceptance of the exclusion of parts of *Ulster from home rule. His opposition to the *First World War made him even more unpopular in Belfast and he was glad to be recalled to Dublin to take over the ITGWU.

As commandant of the *Irish Citizen Army, Connolly planned a workers' rebellion, but in January 1916, he agreed to join the IRB's planned insurrection. During the *Easter Rising, he was with Patrick *Pearse and other leaders in the General Post Office in Dublin and was one of the signatories of the *Proclamation of the Irish Republic. Connolly was severely wounded in the fighting and after his court-martial – following the rebels' defeat – had to be tied to a chair to be executed.

He is universally recognised as a national hero even though Ireland never embraced socialism. His legacy is disputed, with both constitutional socialists and republican militants claiming him. T.C.

Connor, Jerome (1876–1943). Sculptor. Born in Annascaul, County *Kerry, Connor lived in America until his return to Ireland in 1925. His best-known works include the Robert *Emmet statue, at the National Gallery in Washington, DC, and the *Lusitania* Memorial, in Cobh, County *Cork. M.C.

Conor, William (1881–1968). Painter and lithographer. Born in *Belfast, Conor studied in Belfast, Paris and London. Best known for his compassionate depictions of Belfast working people, Conor also painted landscapes and portraits. His 1932 mural on the growth and history of *Ulster is in the Ulster Museum. His work as a war artist in the *First and Second World War is in the Imperial War Museum, in London. He exhibited at the Paris Salon and in London, *Dublin, Belfast and New York. There is a collection of his work in the Ulster Museum and in the Ulster Folk Museum. M.C.

Constitution of Ireland, the. (*Bunreacht na hÉireann* in the Irish language.) The supreme law of the state. It was adopted by plebiscite in 1937 and is the successor of the Constitution of *Dáil Éireann (1919) and the Constitution of the *Irish Free State (1922). The 1919 Constitution was a brief document, adopted by the First Dáil in 1919 as part of *Sinn Féin's campaign for international recognition of Ireland's right to independence. The Free State Constitution (1922) was the first constitution of an independent Ireland but lacked popular legitimacy as the British government insisted that the provisions of the *Anglo-Irish Treaty (1921) be incorporated into the document. It was also amendable by a simple majority of the Dáil throughout its life, and 41 of its 83 articles had been amended by 1937, adding to the pressure for a new constitution.

The 1937 Constitution states that all legislative, executive and judicial powers of government 'derive under God from the people'. It sets out the form of government and defines the powers of the president and the two Houses (Dáil and *Seanad) of the *Oireachtas (legislature). It also defines the structure and powers of the courts, sets out the fundamental rights of citizens and contains a number of directive principles of social policy for the general guidance of the Oireachtas. The Constitution originally described the national territory 'as the whole island of Ireland, its islands and the territorial seas'. In 1998, as part of the *Good Friday Agreement, the Constitution was amended to define the Irish nation as the people of the island of Ireland (and its citizens abroad). It gave up the jurisdictional claim over the area constituting *Northern Ireland and asserted the will of the Irish nation to create a united Ireland, by consent and through peaceful means.

The Constitution, which may be amended only by referendum, outlines what are considered the fundamental rights of the citizen. The definition of rights in the Constitution covers five broad headings: personal rights, the family, *education, private property and *religion.

In addition to the personal rights specifically provided for in the words of the Constitution, the courts have held that there are other personal or 'Unenumerated Rights' which 'result from the Christian and democratic nature of the State', and are implicitly guaranteed by the Constitution. Citizens, and in certain cases non-citizens, have the right to apply to the courts for constitutional protection and for a ruling on whether specific legislation is constitutional.

There have been 27 amendments to the Constitution since 1937. The Constitution originally provided for a three-year transition period during which amendments could be made by the Oireachtas without a referendum. This was used twice: in 1939, on the eve of the Second World War, to alter the provisions on a state of emergency; and in 1941, to protect emergency legislation from being declared unconstitutional by the courts. The other amendments, all carried by referenda, are:

- 3rd (1973): to permit EEC (European Economic Community) membership
- 4th (1973): to lower the voting age from 21 to 18
- 5th (1973): to remove the 'special position' of the Catholic church from the Constitution
- 6th (1979): to protect adoption from court challenges
- 7th (1979): to allow more universities representation in Seanad Éireann (This has not so far been implemented.)
- 8th (1983): to prohibit abortion, specifically to guarantee 'the equal right to life of the unborn' (This was interpreted in 1992 by the Supreme Court as allowing for abortion in certain limited circumstances.)
- 9th (1984): to allow non-citizens certain voting rights
- 10th (1987): to permit the ratification of amendments to the EC (European Community) Treaties (the Single European Act)
- 11th (1992): to permit the ratification of amendments to the EC Treaties (the Maastricht Treaty on European Union or EU)
- 12th (1992): to overturn a Supreme Court judgment allowing abortion where a pregnant woman was threatening suicide (It was defeated on the same day as the 13th and 14th were passed. The numbering was not, however, altered.)
- 13th (1992): to prohibit the courts from using the anti-abortion clause (the 8th amendment) in the Constitution to restrict the right of pregnant women to travel abroad (This arose following an injunction by the high court – though later overturned on appeal – that prevented a pregnant 14-year-old victim of sexual assault from travelling to the UK for an abortion.)
- 14th (1992): to prohibit the courts from using the anti-abortion clause in the Constitution to restrict the publication of material informing people about abortion services in other jurisdictions
- 15th (1995): to permit divorce legislation (The original constitution had prohibited divorce.)
- 16th (1996): to authorise the courts to refuse bail
- 17th (1997): to guarantee cabinet confidentiality
- 18th (1998): to permit the ratification of amendments to the EU Treaties (the Amsterdam Treaty)
- 19th (1998): to introduce changes in the Constitution consistent with the *Belfast Agreement
- 20th (1999): to constitutionally guarantee a system of local government
- 21st (2001): to outlaw the death penalty in any circumstances
- 23rd (2001): to allow for the ratification of the proposed International Criminal Court
- 26th (2002): to permit the ratification of the EU Treaty of Nice.
- 27th (2004): to remove the automatic right to Irish citizenship of persons born in Ireland if neither of the parents is an Irish citizen or qualifies for Irish citizenship.

(There are no 22nd, 24th and 25th amendments because the referenda on those issues were rejected or withdrawn.) (Web site: *www.irlgov.ie*.) J.D.

Coole Park. Estate near Gort, County *Galway, associated with the *Irish Literary Revival. Coole Park was the home of Lady (Augusta) *Gregory, the dramatist, folklorist and translator. She married Sir William Gregory of Coole Park and lived there after his death in 1892. W. B. *Yeats spent frequent holidays there from 1897, and he and Lady Gregory collected folklore in the surrounding countryside. In 1919 Yeats wrote the poem 'The Wild Swans at Coole', and later, 'Coole Park, 1929'. J. M. *Synge, Edward *Martyn and others also frequently visited the estate.

The three-storey house was built around 1770, and there are woods, a river and a lake on the estate. In 1927, the estate was sold to the Forestry Commission and Lady Gregory was allowed to live there until her death. The house was demolished in 1941. Today Coole Park is open to the public as a wildlife park, with an indoor exhibition. The famous 'Autograph Tree' can still be seen, bearing the carved initials of Yeats, Synge, Seán *O'Casey, George Bernard *Shaw, Douglas *Hyde, George *Russell (AE) and George *Moore. P.D.

Cork, County. Ireland's largest and most southerly county, in the province of *Munster. Stretching over 2,895 square miles, the county has a population of 448,181 (2002 census), of which 123,338 live in the county capital, Cork City. The name derives from *Corcaigh*, the marshy land where St Finbarr founded his sixth-century monastery. The rivers Lee, Bandon and Blackwater flow eastward to divide the county into three geographical areas dominated by various mountain ranges (Caha, Miskish, Boggeragh and Nagles), some of which reach heights of over 2,000 feet. The county's coastline is heavily indented with bays (such as Bantry, Dunmanus) and fine harbours (Cork and Kinsale). Cork City is a major port for international car ferries, freight and occasional passenger liners, while Cobh (called Queenstown until 1922) was where most nineteenth-century Irish *emigrants boarded transatlantic ships to America. Ringaskiddy in Cork harbour is an important industrial centre, and Midleton farther east produces famous Irish whiskies. West Cork, with its spectacular seashore and gently rolling landscape, attracts many visitors.

In early times, Cork was part of Desmuma, the south Munster territory of the Eóganacht, dominated by the MacCarthys, who resisted the *Normans in the later Middle Ages. Cork's many medieval *castles include Blarney Castle, approximately five miles from Cork City. The word blarney has become synonymous with good-natured banter, repartee, flattery, or cajoling talk. According to one story, it was Queen *Elizabeth I (1533–1603) who first coined the term blarney, meaning 'flattery', in a reference to the *Anglo-Irish aristocrat the Earl of Blarney whose home was Blarney Castle. In modern times, the Irish tourist industry has mythologised Blarney Castle: the legend goes that those who kiss 'the Blarney stone', a particular spot of one of Blarney's parapet walls, will be endowed with the gift of eloquence, 'the gift of the gab'.

Cork was planted by Elizabethan English, including the poet Edmund *Spenser (c.1552–99), who wrote most of his poetic works, notably the allegorical epic *The Faerie Queene* (1590–96), in his Kilcolman Castle. Efforts to defeat the English with Spanish aid came to naught in 1601 at the Battle of *Kinsale – a town now known as the gourmet capital of Ireland.

Cork City, the third largest city in Ireland, built 'on the banks of my own lovely Lee', in the words of the county's most famous song, has various industries such as *distilling, *brewing, oil refining and pharmaceuticals. University College, Cork (UCC), founded in 1845 as Queen's University, is now (since 1909) a major constituent college of the National University of Ireland. Cork City is also a centre of the visual arts. It is home to the Crawford Gallery, the Honan Chapel, with a fine collection of church furnishings (including stained glass windows) and Fota House, with its impressive array of paintings and an arboretum. The county has produced many distinguished artists, including the painters James *Barry, Daniel *Maclise and Patrick *Scott. Many writers were born or lived in Cork, such as: Edith Oenone *Somerville, Lennox *Robinson, Elizabeth *Bowen, Seán *Ó Faoláin, Frank *O'Connor, William *Trevor and the poet Seán *Ó Riordáin. Other distinguished Corkonians include the composer Seán *Ó Riada, the founders of two religious orders of *nuns, Nano *Nagle and Mary Aikenhead, the *nationalist Thomas *Davis, the *Fenian John O'Mahoney, the revolutionaries Tom Barry and Michael *Collins, and Taoiseach Jack *Lynch. P.H.

Corkery, Daniel (1878–1964). *Nationalist writer and teacher. Born in Cork City, Corkery was educated there at the Presentation Brothers' secondary school and at St Patrick's College, *Dublin. After returning to Cork to teach, he became involved in the *Irish Language Revival and joined both the *Gaelic League and *Sinn Féin. With his close friends Terence *MacSwiney and Con O'Leary, Corkery founded the Cork Dramatic Society, for which he wrote plays in both the English and Irish languages. A prolific and lifelong writer, Corkery contributed to the *Leader* newspaper and wrote many excellent short stories, plays and one of Ireland's best novels, *The Threshold of Quiet* (1917). His work consistently stressed the importance of respecting Irish traditions that he believed had been slighted and neglected by elitist elements within the *Irish Literary Revival movement. Corkery had a tremendous influence on the intellectual and literary development of some of Cork's brightest young minds, such as Seán *Ó Faoláin and Frank *O'Connor. Following the *Anglo-Irish War and the *Civil War, Corkery's ultra-*republican cultural nationalism became bitter and exclusive. He rejected most of the work of the Literary Revival (J. M. *Synge being somewhat of an exception), as merely provincial English writing and insisted that true *Irish literature must reflect public involvement in land, religion and nationalism and, hopefully, find expression in the *Irish language. These opinions pervaded his best-known books *The Hidden Ireland* (1924) and *Synge and Anglo-Irish Literature* (1931). Corkery's narrow view of Irishness attracted considerable support but alienated Ó Faoláin and O'Connor, who argued for a more inclusive definition of nationality. L.J.MC.

Corrigan-Maguire, Máiréad (1944–). Cofounder of the Peace Movement in *Northern Ireland in 1976. Born in *Belfast, Corrigan-Maguire founded the Peace Movement with Betty Williams in response to the deaths of three of her sister's children, who were killed on 10 August 1976. The children were struck by a runaway car driven by an *IRA volunteer who had been shot dead by the British army. The movement was later renamed the Community of Peace People. Corrigan and Williams, as representatives of the Peace Movement, received the 1976 Nobel Prize for Peace (awarded in October 1977). C.D.

Corrs, the. Music group. The Corrs are a family pop band from Dundalk, County *Louth, consisting of Andrea, Caroline, Jim and Sharon Corr. They combine pop, folk and *dance with traditional Irish *music and good looks. The US ambassador to Ireland, Jean Kennedy Smith, spotted them in a small *Dublin club and invited them to play at the

World Cup celebrations in Boston in 1994. This attracted the attention of Atlantic Records and their debut album *Forgiven not Forgotten* was released in 1995. It sold over two million copies and a second album, *Talk on Corners*, was released in 1997. Their album, *In Blue*, came out in 2000 and *Borrowed Heaven* in 2004. B.D.

Cosgrave, Liam (1920–). *Fine Gael leader and *Taoiseach. Son of W. T. *Cosgrave, the first leader of the *Irish Free State, Cosgrave was elected to the *Dáil in 1943. In 1955 as minister for external affairs, he supervised Ireland's entry into the *United Nations. He succeeded James *Dillon as Fine Gael leader in 1965. Cosgrave became Taoiseach and leader of a National Coalition government in 1973 and played an important role at the *Sunningdale Conference. Following the government defeat in the 1977 general election, he resigned as Fine Gael leader. He retired from politics in 1981. P.E.

Cosgrave, William Thomas (1880–1965). First president of the executive council of the *Irish Free State. Born in *Dublin, Cosgrave joined *Sinn Féin in 1905 and was elected to municipal government in Dublin in 1909. He was sentenced to death for his part in the 1916 *Easter Rising, but the sentence was commuted. A member of the First *Dáil, he supported the *Anglo-Irish Treaty of 1921 and became chairman of the Provisional Government after the deaths of Michael *Collins and Arthur *Griffith in 1922.

From December 1922 until March 1932, he was the president of the executive council of the Irish Free State. In 1923, at the end of the *Civil War, he founded *Cumann na nGaedheal. A cautious and conservative politician, he successfully led the Free State during the Civil War and is credited with establishing stable parliamentary democracy in Ireland.

Following defeats in the 1932 and 1933 general elections, Cumann na nGaedheal merged with the Centre Party and the *Blueshirts in 1933 to form *Fine Gael under the control of Eoin *O'Duffy. Within a year, O'Duffy resigned and Cosgrave took over as party leader until his retirement in 1944. P.E.

Costello, John A. (1891–1976). Lawyer, politician and *Taoiseach. Costello was born in *Dublin and took part in the *Easter Rising of 1916. From 1926 to 1932, he was attorney general of the *Irish Free State and its delegate to the League of Nations. He served as Taoiseach from 1948 to 1951, and again from 1954 to 1957 in coalition with other minority parties in what are known as the first and second interparty governments. During his first term, the *Republic of Ireland Act (1948) was passed. P.E.

Coulter, Phil (1942–). Songwriter. Born in *Derry, Coulter studied music at Queen's University, *Belfast. In London, he teamed up with Bill Martin and wrote 'Puppet on a String', which won the 1967 Eurovision International Song Contest, as well as 'Congratulations', which was the Eurovision runner-up in 1968. In the 1970s, he produced albums with *Planxty and wrote the song 'The Town I Loved So Well'. Since the 1980s, he has concentrated on popular music and in 1997 became a visiting professor at Boston College. Major appearances include four sell-out concerts at Carnegie Hall and an outdoor performance on Capitol Hill, Washington, with the National Symphony Orchestra before an audience of 600,000 people. P.E.

Council of Europe. European international organisation, established on 5 May 1949. Ireland was one of the ten founding member states of the Council of Europe. There are now 41 members. Established in the aftermath of the Second World War, the council sought to secure peace and prosperity, through reconciliation and cooperation between states. The organisation was the first to introduce enforceable human rights standards into international law, through the European Convention on Human Rights. The council created the European Court of Human Rights to enforce these standards. Today, the Council of Europe is primarily concerned with the protection of human rights, the spread of pluralist democracy and the rule of law. It opposes discrimination against minorities, xenophobia, racism and drug abuse, and seeks to promote Europe's cultural heritage in all its diversity. J.D.

Craig, James First Viscount Craigavon (1871–1940). Politician, prime minister of *Northern Ireland, 1921–40. Born in *Belfast to a wealthy distiller and farm owner, Craig became *unionist MP for East Down in 1906. During the third *home rule crisis (1911–14), he was Edward *Carson's right-hand man, enjoying a familiarity with *Ulster that Carson lacked. Craig succeeded Carson as leader of the *Ulster Unionist Party (UUP) in February 1921 and became prime minister of the new devolved government in Belfast in June 1921. To consolidate the state's security, Craig organised the almost wholly *Protestant Ulster Special Constabulary. Concerned with preserving unionist hegemony, he redrew electoral districts and abolished *proportional representation in elections to the devolved parliament in 1929. Though he claimed that he was anxious not to egregiously oppress the *Catholic *nationalist community, he did admit in 1934 that 'We are a Protestant parliament and a Protestant people'. Increasingly inattentive to duties, he died in 1940 while still in office. M.M.

crannógs. Man-made, usually circular, lake islands. They consist of piles of stones as a foundation, covered by brushwood and earth, and with palisades enclosing one or more houses. Modern examples at Craggaunowen (County *Clare) and the National Heritage Park at Ferrycarrig (County *Wexford) show what crannógs would originally have looked like. Probably Bronze Age in origin, crannógs were still used in Ireland as late as the 1600s. P.H.

Croagh Patrick. Mountain in *Mayo (near Westport), where St *Patrick is said to have fasted for 40 days to obtain the right to judge the Irish people on Judgment Day. A popular annual *pilgrimage is made to the summit on the last Sunday in July, probably a Christian version of an earlier, pagan, Lughnasa Festival. Prehistoric monuments and an oratory (c.490–880) have been found here. P.H.

Croke Park. The national headquarters of the *Gaelic Athletic Association (GAA), located in *Dublin's north inner city. It is named after Archbishop John Croke, first patron of the GAA, and was acquired by the association in 1911. The major games of *hurling and *Gaelic football are played there, notably the annual All-Ireland finals in September. In November 1920, on what became known as *Bloody Sunday, British forces killed 12 people during a football game between Dublin and Tipperary. The park was reconstructed in 2002 as a bowl stadium with an all seated capacity of 79,500. (Web site: *www.gaa.ie*.) K.W.

Cromwell, Oliver (1599–1658). *De facto* head of the English parliamentary regime in the late 1640s and, from 1653, lord protector. Cromwell landed in Ireland on 15 August 1649, and from then until his return to England on 29 May 1650, he seized the south and east of Ireland from an Irish Catholic/ Royalist alliance in a lightning campaign. He was, claims Denis Murphy's *Cromwell in Ireland* (1883), 'a great, bad man'. 'Great' in, for example, the tempo and decisiveness of his siege operations which, apart from his botched storm of Clonmel, County *Tipperary, enhanced his already formidable reputation as a military leader. 'Bad' in that he was cast as the principal personification of English violence in Ireland for atrocities associated with the storming of Drogheda, County *Louth and *Wexford. The better-documented events at Drogheda show that there was no whole-scale massacre of troops and townspeople. However, royalist troops at the Millmount surrendered, apparently, on promise of quarter and were subsequently killed.

Eyewitness testimony of Thomas Wood, a *Cromwellian soldier, suggests that an unquantifiable number of women and children were killed in and around St Peter's church. This severity was exceptional in the context of the English Civil Wars, though not by the grimmer standards of the Thirty Years War in central Europe. The same might be said for the killing of 2,000 soldiers and civilians at Wexford and, specifically, the massacre of civilians congregated at the Bull Ring.

Cromwell might better be judged by the fact that, in contrast to his conflict with the Scots, in Ireland he was motivated by religious and ethnic hatred. He had made his unremitting hostility to *Catholicism abundantly clear: 'I meddle not with any man's conscience. But if by liberty of conscience you mean liberty to exercise the mass ... that will not be allowed of'. In particular, he was driven by the conviction that Irish Catholics shared a collective blood-guilt for atrocities against *Protestant settlers in the *Rebellion of 1641, and therefore insisted on a punitive postwar settlement. This insistence prolonged (1649– 53) and intensified the human suffering and destruction of the reconquest. Henry Cromwell, the son of Oliver Cromwell, governed Ireland from 1655–59. He tried to broaden the base of his support beyond the religious zealots and the army to encompass the 'Old Protestant', or pre-1640 settler, interest. This involved veering toward an Episcopalian church settlement and abandoning proposals of whole-scale transplantation of the Catholic Irish to *Connacht. Henry Cromwell was one of those who personified the 'kingship' party that advocated a more durable and generally acceptable constitutional settlement in England and Ireland. To counter this threat, the Long Parliament, abolished by Oliver Cromwell and reinstated after his death, dismissed Henry Cromwell from the lord deputyship in June 1659. P.L.

Cromwellian Settlement, the. Confiscation of land of Irish *Catholics in retribution for the *Rebellion of 1641, laying the foundations of long-term *Protestant ascendancy. The preamble of the 1652 Act for the Settlement of Ireland disavowed any intent to extirpate 'the entire nation', and the act concentrated on punishing Irish Catholic landowners according to their 'respective demerits'. 'Delinquency' encompassed not only those landowners who held high military or civil office in the confederate Catholic and, later, royalist regimes, but also those who had simply stayed at home and paid taxes.

The scheme of forfeiture envisaged the landowner surrendering his entire estate and transplanting to the reserved part of *Connacht, chosen for its remoteness. There he would, in theory, acquire lands equivalent to a proportion (the proportion varied according to his delinquency) of his original estate. In the ensuing scramble, most landowners did not actually acquire any lands in Connacht. The beneficiaries of the confiscation were 'Adventurers' who had lent money to finance the reconquest a decade before and soldiers who received their back pay in land grants. As land was the basis of social and economic power, the Cromwellian Settlement represented a profound and irreversible disempowerment. Before the war of 1641–52, Catholics owned about 60% of Irish land; by the 1660s (even after limited adjustments by Charles II) they owned only about 20%.

Even more radical schemes of 'ethnic cleansing' and mass transplantation to Connacht were seriously advocated and justified by the charge that Catholics shared a collective blood-guilt for the massacre of Protestants in the 1641 *Rebellion. The expression 'To Hell or to Connacht', which has been attributed to Cromwell, summarises his attitude to the fate of the dispossessed Irish. In the words of one of its advocates, Richard Lawrence, Ireland was, or soon would be, 'an empty prepared hive to receive its swarms' of English settlers making them 'equal or more considerable than the Irish'. Ultimately, in the absence of sufficient immigration, the government tacitly accepted that the mass of the rural population (as opposed to those living in larger urban centres) would not be uprooted.

The Cromwellian regime smashed the institutional fabric of the Catholic church but was notably unsuccessful in converting the Irish to Protestantism. In part this was due to sectarian divisions within Protestantism but also, apparently, through despair that Irish Catholics were unregenerate. P.L.

Cronin, Anthony (1926–). Poet, critic and novelist. Born in Enniscorthy, County *Wexford and educated at University College, Dublin, Cronin was appointed cultural advisor to the *Taoiseach Charles J. *Haughey in 1980. He created *Aosdána, an affiliation of Irish artists, in 1983. *Dead As Doornails* (1976), a memoir of the literary scene in 1950s *Dublin, has perhaps been Cronin's most successful work. His style is analytical, often ironic, always scholarly. As a columnist with the *Irish Times* (1976–80 and 1983– 87), he earned a reputation as a debunker of myths and hard-hitting critic of Irish political and social affairs. A selection of his writings for the *Irish Times* newspaper was published as *An Irish Eye* (1985). Other works include *The Life of Riley* (1964), a comic novel; *The End of the Modern World* (1989) and *Relationships* (1992), both volumes of poetry; *A Question of Modernity* (1966), a critique of the work of James *Joyce; *No Laughing Matter* (1989), a biography of Flann *O'Brien; and *Samuel Beckett: The Last Modernist* (1996). C.D.

Cross of Cong. Elegant processional cross, dating from circa 1125. The cross was commissioned by the High King Turlough O'Connor to house a relic of the True Cross, which was covered by a rock crystal at the centre of one side. The shaft and undulating arms are decorated with ornamental glass studs and panels bearing animal interlace typical of the Irish variant of the Scandinavian Urnes style. Arguably the finest piece of Irish twelfth-century metalwork, the cross was probably made in a *Roscommon workshop. It is now on display in the *National Museum of Ireland. P.H.

Cross, Dorothy (1956–). Installation artist and printmaker. Born in *Cork, Cross studied in Cork, Leicester, Amsterdam and San Francisco. Using found objects and photography, she explores psychoanalytic issues of identity, gender and authority. She represented Ireland at the Venice Biennale in 1993. M.C.

crosses, high. Tall stone crosses with decorative carving. High crosses are Ireland's greatest contribution to European sculpture of the first millennium. These crosses were erected at monasteries to edify and teach both monks and laity through biblical representations carved on many of them. High kings helped commission them from the ninth to the twelfth century. Fine examples are found at Moone (County *Kildare), Monasterboice (County *Louth), *Kells (County *Meath), *Clonmacnoise (County *Offaly) and *Cashel (County *Tipperary). P.H.

Cruise O'Brien, Conor (1917–). Diplomat, politician and man of letters. Born in *Dublin and educated at Trinity College, Cruise O'Brien worked at the Department of External Affairs from 1944. Among his varied writings are literary criticism (often under the pseudonym Donat O'Donnell), a study of the *Parnell era, *Parnell and His Party* (1957), and an appreciative analysis of Israel and Zionism, *The Siege* (1986). From 1956 to 1961, he was a member of the Irish delegation to the *United Nations. In 1961, he was part of the UN mission in the newly independent Congo, but resigned in protest against deference to western interests. From 1962 to 1965, he was vice chancellor of the University of Ghana, and from 1965 to 1969 held a chair at New York University (where he actively agitated against American Vietnam policy). In 1969, as a member of the *Labour Party, Cruise O'Brien was elected to *Dáil Éireann for Dublin Northeast. He was minister for posts and telegraphs in the 1973–77 coalition government. His book *States of Ireland* (1972) appreciated the position of the *unionists and condemned *nationalist irredentism. He sat in the *Seanad for Trinity College from 1977 to 1981. His 1992 book *The Great Melody* is a sympathetic study of Edmund *Burke. His newspaper columns interpreted the recent *Northern Ireland *peace process as appeasement of *Sinn Féin and the *IRA. In the 1990s he joined the independent UK Unionist Party. He is married to Máire *Mhac an tSaoi, the *Irish-language poet. J.P.MC.

Cúchulainn. One of the best-known Irish *mythological figures. In the legend, a smith named Culann was hosting a party for the high king of *Ulster, Conchubhar Mac Neasa. The king had forgotten to tell Culann that a boy, Setanta, would be joining them later and Culann unleashed his famous hound to guard the house. On his arrival, Setanta was attacked by the hound and to defend himself he threw a *sliotar*, or *hurling ball, into the dog's throat, killing it instantly. Culann was angry at the death of his favourite hound, but Conchubhar decreed that Setanta would take its place, thus earning the name Cúchulainn – or Culann's hound. Cúchulainn is also famous for his single-handed defence of Ulster against the army of Maeve, queen of Connacht, which culminated in the slaying of his best friend Ferdia. He was eventually killed by his enemies when he spurned the attentions of Mór-Ríoghain, the goddess of war.

Following the publication of Standish *O'Grady's *History of Ireland: Cuculain and his Contemporaries* (1880), Cúchulainn became a symbol of heroism for many Irish nationalists and writers, including Patrick *Pearse, W. B. *Yeats and James *Stephens. A bronze statue of Cúchulainn by Oliver *Sheppard was installed in the GPO (General Post Office) in *Dublin to commemorate the *Easter Rising. B.D.

Cullen, Cardinal Paul (1803–78). *Catholic ecclesiastic. Born in County *Kildare, Cullen served as rector in the Irish college in Rome, before being appointed archbishop of *Armagh in 1849. He was subsequently appointed archbishop of *Dublin, where he remained until his death. Cullen was a moderate *nationalist, whose main concern was to strengthen and advance the position of the Roman Catholic church in Ireland. A staunch advocate of denominational *education, he was responsible for the Synod of Thurles' (1850) condemnation of the Queen's Colleges, which had been established as secular *universities by Sir Robert Peel in 1848. Cullen launched a devotional revolution that dramatically changed the nature of Catholicism in Ireland and throughout the diaspora. His conservative Catholicism and his commitment to centralised authority and discipline within the church proved lastingly influential. A.S.

Cullen, Shane (1957–). Painter. Born in County *Longford, Cullen has had exhibitions in Ireland, Europe and the United States. His *Fragments sur les Institutions Republicaines IV* reproduces the messages smuggled out of *Belfast prison by *hunger strikers in the 1980s. M.C.

Cumann na mBan. *Nationalist league of *women. Cumann na mBan (League of Women) was set up in 1914 as a female auxiliary to the Irish *Volunteers. It absorbed Inghinidhe na hÉireann (Daughters of Ireland), the women's nationalist organisation founded in 1900. When the Volunteers split on whether or not to fight for Britain in the *First World War later that year, the majority of Cumann na mBan members voted to side with the smaller group of volunteers who opposed fighting and whose motto was 'we serve neither king nor kaiser, but Ireland'. Women in Cumann na mBan were trained in first aid, signaling, dispatch riding and other auxiliary roles, but were not allowed in combat. They served in all but one of the 1916 *Easter Rising revolutionary locales, and it was a Cumann na mBan member, Elizabeth O'Farrell, a hospital midwife, who delivered the surrender. O'Farrell, a white-collar, professional worker, was a typical Cumann member, though some factory workers were involved in Cumann na mBan as well.

After the rising, the Cumann became involved mainly in keeping the memories of the rising alive, raising money for prisoners, holding meetings and other commemorative events, and electioneering in the 1918 general election, at which *Sinn Féin won its famous victory. In the *War of Independence, 1919–21, Cumann members helped to run *Dáil courts and local authorities and produced the *nationalist newspaper the *Irish Bulletin*. Most members opposed the *Anglo-Irish Treaty (1921) and at least 400 Cumann na mBan members were imprisoned during the *Civil War. It was Cumann na mBan that conceived the Easter Lily as a commemorative symbol in 1926. In the 1930s, Cumann na mBan was active on the left wing of the *republican movement, but would never again achieve the prominence or the level of activism that it had attained in the years 1914–23. C.C.

Cumann na nGaedheal. *Political party. Launched in April 1923, Cumann na nGaedheal (Party of the Irish) formed the governments of the *Irish Free State until 1932. *Sinn Féin members who supported the *Anglo-Irish Treaty founded the party and William T. *Cosgrave, the first president of the executive council of the Free State government, became the party's first and only leader.

Cumann na nGaedheal's national organisation never attracted the levels of popular participation that characterised Sinn Féin and later, *Fianna Fáil. Its local leaders tended to be prominent businessmen, members of the professions and large farmers. Its popular support at elections derived largely from its achievements in setting up the new state and fear of renewed civil war. The party consistently defended the treaty settlement and, after the *Civil War, introduced harsh legislation to deal with continued *IRA activity, including a severe Public Safety Act which followed the assassination of the party's minister for justice, Kevin *O'Higgins, in 1927.

As the party of law and order, Cumann na nGaedheal attracted the support of merchants and shopkeepers and it was closely identified with larger farmers and the cattle trade. The export trade to Britain formed the basis of its economic policy. Although it founded several semi-state companies, the party was little concerned with industrialisation and was ideologically opposed to state intervention to improve conditions for the working-class or urban poor.

In the first post-Civil War general election in August 1923, Cumann na nGaedheal received 39% of the vote. It never surpassed this level of support. It remained in government when Fianna Fáil entered the *Dáil in August 1927. Fianna Fáil defeated the party in the general election of February 1932 and in the January 1933 election Cumann na nGaedheal support fell again. The party then merged with other conservative groups, the National Centre Party and the National Guard (the *Blueshirts), to form the *Fine Gael party in September 1933. P.D.

currach. Boat with light wooden frame of laths, covered formerly with leather but now with canvas and tar. Currachs are found in varying designs along the coasts of Ireland. Though the oars are narrow and featherless at the end, currachs are very fast and manouv-rable and ride high on the waves, as seen in Robert O'Flaherty's film *Man of Aran* (1934). It was probably in such a currach that St *Brendan set off on his famous voyage. In 1976/77, Tim Severin used a large modern example with sail – the *Brendan*, now displayed at Craggaunowen, County *Clare – to show that the saint could have reached America in such a craft. (In Kerry and the south-west, the Irish word for currach is *naomhóg* (meaning 'a saint's boat'). P.H.

Curragh Mutiny, the (1914). Military protest during the *home rule crisis of 1914. When the *UVF threatened armed resistance to home rule, the government considered deploying troops in the province. The British commander in chief in Ireland, General Sir Arthur Paget, agreed that officers from *Ulster could 'disappear' during the operation, but no other officers, even those with Irish connections, were given such choice. In March 1914, at the Curragh military camp, County *Kildare, 60 cavalry officers, led by Brigadier General Hubert Gough, offered their resignations rather than 'move against Ulster'. The War Office refused to accept the resignations. The men were assured by the secretary of state for war and the chief of the imperial general staff that there was no intention of using troops in Ulster. Both these officials were forced to resign when the Prime Minister Herbert *Asquith rejected the assurance. However, because of fear of an army crisis, the plan was abandoned. T.C.

Cusack, Cyril James (1910–93). Actor. Born in Kentani, Kenya, Cusack arrived in Ireland as a young boy, where he played children's parts in melodramas performed by his stepfather's travelling theatre company. Educated at University College, Dublin, Cusack performed in most major theatres in Ireland and Britain, including the *Abbey Theatre and the *Gate in Dublin, the Royal Shakespeare Company and the English National Theatre. With his own theatre company, which specialised in classical and Irish theatre (including *Shaw, *Beckett and *Synge) and which engaged actors like Siobhán *McKenna and Jack *MacGowran, he toured in Ireland and elsewhere. His film career began with a childhood role in *Knocknagow* in 1917 and ended in 1990 in *My Left Foot*. Other films include *Odd Man Out* (1947), *Shake Hands with the Devil* (1959), *Sacco and Vanzetti* (1974) and *True Confessions* (1981). C.D.

Cusack, Sinead (1948–). Actress. Born in Dalkey, County *Dublin, Sinead, like her younger sisters Niamh and Sorcha, followed her father Cyril *Cusack into the acting profession. She began her career at the *Abbey Theatre, Dublin, and subsequently appeared in numerous television productions and feature films, including *Hoffman* (1970) and *Stealing Beauty* (1996). However, Sinead Cusack is best known for her work as a classical actor with the Royal Shakespeare Company (RSC). Nominated for a Tony Award in 1984, she received the *Evening Standard* Award for Best Actress in 1998 for her portrayal of Mai in Sebastian *Barry's *Our Lady of Sligo* at the National Theatre in London. In 2002, she played the role of Cleopatra in the RSC production of Shakespeare's *Anthony and Cleopatra*. In 1978, she married fellow actor Jeremy Irons, with whom she has two sons. S.A.B.

D

Dáil Éireann. Irish parliament. Derived from the Old Irish word meaning an assembly, Dáil has, in modern times, been used to describe the Irish House of Representatives, that is, the lower house. The Dáil, together with the senate, or *Seanad Éireann, and the president, make up the *Oireachtas. The first Dáil Éireann (assembly of Ireland) was a controversial and revolutionary body, which first met in the Mansion House, Dublin, on 21 January 1919. It was convened by the *Sinn Féin party following their overwhelming victory in the historic general election of December 1918, at the end of the *First World War. Sinn Féin won 73 of the 105 seats allocated at that time to Ireland in the British parliament. In keeping with party policy since its foundation in 1905, Sinn Féin refused to take its seats at Westminster. Instead, they called an assembly of all elected Irish representatives to an All-Ireland parliament, Dáil Éireann, and declared Ireland an independent republic.

Dáil Éireann continued to operate underground during the *War of Independence (1919–21), establishing Sinn Féin courts as alternatives to the British system and winning the support of the people and local authorities, who gave their loyalty and revenue to the Sinn Féin minister for local government, W. T. *Cosgrave. Michael *Collins as minister for finance raised a national loan, while the *Volunteers, now known as the *IRA pledged to defend the republic. IRA Chief of Staff Richard *Mulcahy reported to the defence minister, Cathal *Brugha. After the *Anglo-Irish Treaty (1921), the new twenty-six-county parliament was also called Dáil Éireann. It came together in *Leinster House on 9 September 1922, during the *Civil War, but it was boycotted by Éamon *de Valera and his Sinn Féin anti-treaty republicans, because TDs had to take an *oath of allegiance to the British monarch in order to participate. In 1926, de Valera and some of his anti-treaty supporters founded *Fianna Fáil, a new *republican party, and entered the Dáil in August 1927, maintaining the oath was merely 'an empty political formula'.

The roles and functions of the modern Dáil Éireann, as the elected House of Representatives of the Oireachtas are set out in the *Constitution of 1937. All citizens aged 18 or over (the age limit was 21 until 1974) in the twenty-six counties are entitled to vote and to contest elections. Elections take place in multi-seat constituencies (there are 42 at present) consisting of three, four and five seats. Each *Teachta Dála* or TD represents 20–30,000 of the population and constituencies are redrawn at intervals of not longer than 12 years. There are currently 166 members in Dáil Éireann – up from 138 in the 1940s, and up to 50 of these are from the greater *Dublin area, in line with population trends.

TDs are elected by a system of *proportional representation that gives each citizen a single transferable vote. This system favours the smaller parties and makes single-party government difficult, but it is also very fair to minorities. The Constitution (Article 16.5.0) limits the Dáil to a maximum period of seven years, but current legislation imposes a five-year limit. The chair/speaker of the Dáil is called the *Ceann Comhairle* and is automatically included as a TD in any new Dáil. Under the 1937 Constitution, the Irish government is responsible to Dáil Éireann alone and the *Taoiseach, as head of the government, must be able to command a majority of the House. The Taoiseach can dissolve the Dáil at any time by submitting his resignation and that of the government, to the president. The president can exercise one of the few real political powers open to him/her (Article 13.2.2) and may, in his/her absolute discretion, refuse to dissolve the Dáil. If, however, the resignations are accepted, a general election will follow. The right to amend or initiate bills, in the Upper House, or Seanad Éireann, does not extend to money bills, which are exclusively the domain of the Dáil.

Dáil Éireann (and Seanad Éireann) have been televised since 1990 and the televising of committees began in 1993. The Irish parliament remains predominantly English-speaking, although simultaneous translation services were provided over two decades ago. *Leinster House, acquired by the new *Irish Free State in 1924, has been the seat of both Dáil Éireann and Seanad Éireann ever since. N.ÓG.

dance. Dance in Ireland has been divided between participatory traditional dance and theatre dance, with a few cross-overs between the two. As theatre dance developed in Ireland, it sought to draw on the rich heritage of traditional dance. **Riverdance* is the most popular example of merging *step-dancing tradition with theatricality. *Set- and step-dancing reached their height in the nineteenth and early twentieth centuries, but received a setback with the Public Dance Halls Act of 1935, which required that all dances be licensed and operate under strict supervision, prohibiting informal dancing in private houses or in public. Today, traditional dance is largely competition-based and is overseen by the Irish Dancing Commission (An Coimisiún le Rincí Gaelacha) and the Organisation for Irish Dance (An Cómhgháil le Rincí Gaelacha). However, a revival of set-dancing in the 1980s has led to increased participation at the social level.

Performance dance developed within the theatre as part of drama productions. John Ogilby (1600–76), who established the Theatre Royal, Smock Alley, in Dublin, was a dancing master who first came to Ireland to instruct the children of the lord lieutenant, the Earl of Stafford. Ogilby's dances for Smock Alley were character dances as part of plays. *Pompey* (1663) featured 'an Antick dance of Gypsies', 'a Military Dance' and 'a Grand Masque'.

Theatrical productions continued to provide the only outlet for dance performance, and it was not until William Butler *Yeats appointed Ninette de Valois (1898– 1998) to establish the Abbey School of Dance that dance was affirmed outside of drama. As well as providing the dance sequences for the plays at the *Abbey Theatre, de Valois also created dance works such as 'Faun' and 'The Drinking Horn'.

In 1947, Joan Denise Moriarty (1920– 92) formed the Cork City Ballet, an amateur company that performed annually with the Cork Symphony Orchestra. Its repertoire ranged from short dances to single acts of classical repertoire to original works. Moriarty worked with Irish composers such as Aloys Fleischmann (1910–92) and visiting guest artists, such as Anton Dolin (1906–83) and Marina Svetlova (1922–). Cork City Ballet's success led to the creation of the professional Irish Theatre Ballet in 1959, which disbanded in 1964 after an unsuccessful merger with the Dublin-based National Ballet. In 1973, Moriarty formed another Cork-based company, the Irish Ballet Company, which 10 years later became the Irish National Ballet. Throughout her career, Moriarty explored merging dance styles and collaborated with composer Seán* Ó Riada (1931–71), who was pioneering the use of traditional music within classical musical forms, to create *West Cork Ballet* (1961) and *Billy the Music* (1974). Her most successful work was *The Playboy of the Western World* (1977), set to music by the *Chieftains.

Dance entered cultural consciousness as the century progressed, and when a national *television network (Telefís Éireann) was launched on 1 January 1960, the opening ceremony featured a dance, set in Dublin Airport in front of a new Boeing plane. Irish Theatre Ballet appeared on national television on three occasions, and in 1966, Cork City Ballet recorded 13 dance programmes called *An Damhsa*.

The national folk theatre *Siamsa Tíre was founded by Father Pat Ahern in 1974 and for many years led the way in mixing folk dance styles with theatre. Dublin Contemporary Dance Theatre emerged in 1979, performing a repertory of contemporary dance. However, in 1989, the Arts Council withdrew funding to the company and to Moriarty's Irish National Ballet. Most companies now work in the contemporary idiom and the most prominent are the Irish Modern Dance Theatre, the Dance Theatre of Ireland, Daghdha and Coiscéim. M.S.

Darcy, Patrick (1598–1668). Politician. Born in *Galway into an Old English family, Darcy was elected MP for Navan in 1634. A gifted lawyer and skilled negotiator, he played a prominent part in the *Confederation of Kilkenny. The central contention of his treatise *An Argument Delivered* (1643) was that no legislation should have effect in Ireland without first being ratified by an Irish *parliament. This argument exercised a major influence over subsequent Irish constitutional thinkers, notably William *Molyneux, George *Berkeley and Jonathan *Swift. A.S.

Davis, Thomas Osborne (1814–45). Writer and cultural *nationalist. Born in Mallow, County *Cork, where his father was a doctor in the British army, Davis was educated at Trinity College, Dublin, and was called to the bar in 1837. He first attracted attention in 1839 in a famous speech in Trinity to the Dublin Historical Society, in which he made a forceful case for the study of Irish history as a means of preserving Irish national identity. With Gavan *Duffy and John Blake *Dillon, Davis founded the **Nation* newspaper in 1842, which published scores of essays concerning the *Irish language, *literature, history and *music, by a group of Romantic writers known collectively as *Young Ireland. Sincere and charismatic, Davis became the group's principal figure, emphasising Irish cultural self-reliance and political unity. His plea that Irish writers and artists create works that would be 'racy of the soil' inspired intellectuals of his generation and helped launch the *Irish Revival (also known as Celtic Revival).

In politics, Davis was a *Repealer and an admirer of Daniel *O'Connell, but the Liberator's retreat from Repeal after 1843 disappointed Davis and Young Ireland's political activists, who were impatient with, and critical of, O'Connell's constitutional methods. Religious tensions also affected his relationship with O'Connell, whose rabid *Catholic supporters attacked Davis' ecumenical spirit and support for nondenominational *university *education.

Davis died suddenly from an attack of scarlet fever in September 1845. His influence on cultural nationalists persisted long after his death. His inspirational works were continually reprinted in nationalist journals and other publications. His ballads 'A Nation Once Again' and 'The West's Awake' remain popular to this day. L.MB.

Davitt, Michael (1846–1906). *Nationalist, *socialist, founder of the *Land League. Davitt was born in Straide, County *Mayo, to small-tenant farmers. In 1850, his family was evicted for nonpayment of rent. They moved to England, where in 1857, at age 11, Davitt lost his right arm in an accident while working in a cotton mill. Unable to work, he attended the local Wesleyan school and the Mechanics' Institute, where he became influenced by the ideas of the Chartist movement.

Davitt joined the *Fenians in 1865, and in May 1870, he was arrested in London on suspicion of gunrunning. He received a 15-year sentence and served over seven years in very difficult conditions in Dartmoor Prison before being released in December 1877.

After a brief visit to Ireland where he was appalled by the conditions of tenant farmers in County Mayo, he travelled to America to visit his family (who had moved there in 1870). In the United States, he met John *Devoy, the Fenian leader of *Clan na Gael. Along with Charles *Parnell and Devoy, Davitt was one of the architects of the 'New Departure', whereby constitutional nationalists, Fenians and land agitators agreed to work together toward achieving agrarian reform. In 1879, Davitt established the Land League, with Parnell as president, to end evictions and reform the system of land ownership in Ireland. Influenced by the ideas of Henry George, the American single-tax socialist, Davitt, however, distanced himself from the struggle for general agrarian reform and peasant proprietorship preferring, instead, land nationalisation. This idea never gained popular support and eventually led to his falling out with Parnell.

Davitt was elected on four separate occasions to the Westminster parliament where he sided with the anti-Parnellities. In parliament, he campaigned tirelessly for social reform and for an end to the *Boer War.

Davitt was also a prolific journalist and writer, whose first book, *Leaves from a Prison Diary*, was published in 1885. Other works include *Within the Pale* (1903), dealing with anti-Semitism in Russia, and *The Fall of Feudalism in Ireland* (1904). In 1890, Davitt set up and edited his own socialist newspaper *Labour World*. He died in Dublin on 30 May 1906 and is buried in Straide, County Mayo. P.N., P.E.

Davitt, Michael (1950–). Poet in the *Irish language and literary activist. Davitt was the main force behind the new Irish poetry that started with the journal *Innti* in 1970. This movement superseded the Irish obsession with tradition as a closed system and tapped into the international rock and pop culture of the 1960s and 1970s. With wit and panache, Davitt organised poetry readings as if they were pop concerts. A formidable performer himself, Davitt wrote poetry that ranges from the deeply felt lyric to the funny, clever and dramatic. His mixture of the serious and the less solemn is characteristically Irish. His collections include *Gleann ar Ghleann* (Valley on Valley; 1982) and *An Tost a Scagadh* (Silence to Sift; 1983). Translations of his work are found in *The Bright Wave (An Tonn Gheal*; 1986), *The Field Day Anthology* (1992) and *Freacnairc Mhearcair: The Oomph of Quicksilver* (2000). A.T.

Day-Lewis, Cecil (1904–72). Poet. Born in County *Laois and raised in England, Day-Lewis was educated at Oxford where he was later appointed professor of poetry. He became poet laureate of England in 1968. With Louis *MacNeice, Sir Stephen Spender and W. H. Auden, he was a member of the MacSpaunday group that promoted social change. Among his writings are several poetry collections, including *From Feathers to Iron* (1931), *Poems in Wartime* (1940) and *An Italian Visit* (1953); an autobiography, *The Buried Day* (1960); translations of Virgil and Valéry and, as Nicholas Blake, a series of detective novels. *The Whispering Roots* (1970) explores his complex relationship with his Irish ancestry. *The Complete Poems of C. Day-Lewis* was published in 1992. M.S.T.

Day-Lewis, Daniel (1957–). Actor. Born in London, Daniel was the second child of poet Cecil *Day-Lewis and actress Jill Balcon. Always more interested in acting than in academics, he dropped out of boarding school in his early teens and was given a small part in the film *Sunday, Bloody Sunday* (1971). He studied acting at the Bristol Old Vic and also performed with the Royal Shakespeare Company before returning to screen acting in 1982. His first major supporting role was in *The Bounty* (1984), but it was with more prominent parts in *My Beautiful Launderette* and *A Room with a View* (both 1986) that he gained international acclaim. Known for the intensity with which he prepares his roles, Day-Lewis has played a great variety of characters, including a Czech surgeon in *The Unbearable Lightness of Being* (1988) and a cerebral palsy sufferer in *My Left Foot* (1989), based on the book by Christy *Brown, for which role he won the Academy Award for best actor. The latter film reconnected him with his Irish roots and he became an Irish citizen and resident. Other films in which he has starred include *The Last of the Mohicans* (1992), *In the Name of the Father* (1993), *The Age of Innocence* (1993), *The Crucible* (1996), *The Boxer* (1997) and *Gangs of New York* (2002). J.C.E.L.

Deane & Woodward. Architectural firm. Deane & Woodward, one of nineteenth-century Ireland's most influential architectural practices, bore the names of its founders Sir Thomas Deane (1792–1871) and Benjamin Woodward (1816–61). Based at first in *Cork and then in *Dublin, they designed as one of their first projects Queen's College (now University College) in Cork in 1845– 49. Their work on the Museum Building in Trinity College, Dublin (1852–57), and the former Kildare Street Club (1856–61) showed the influence of Pugin and Ruskin on their designs and led to further commissions in England: the Oxford Museum and the Crown Life Office in Blackfriars (1856–58). After Woodward's death, the Deane dynasty continued the practice for decades. P.H.

Deane, Seamus (1940–). Writer, critic. Widely regarded as one of the most influential Irish literary critics of his generation, Deane is also a distinguished poet and novelist. Born in *Derry and educated at St Columb's College, Queen's University, Belfast, and Cambridge University, he is now professor of Irish Studies at Notre Dame University. Deane distinguished himself as a poet with the publication of *Gradual Wars* (1972) and *History Lessons* (1983). His work investigates the ways in which Irish literary and political culture can be understood as a response to the experience of colonisation. Deane was a founding member of the *Field Day Theatre Company, which re-energised Irish *theatre and cultural criticism in the 1980s. Although often controversial, Field Day sought to engage with the problems of contemporary Irish society and culture, particularly those precipitated by the *Northern Ireland conflict. His academic publications include: *Celtic Revivals: Essays in Modern Irish Literature* (1984), *A Short History of Irish Literature* (1986), the groundbreaking *Field Day Anthology of Irish Writing* (1991) and *Strange Country: Modernity and Nationhood in Irish Writing Since 1790* (1997). Deane has also published a novel, *Reading in the Dark* (1996), which was short-listed for the Booker Prize. P.J.M.

de Brún, Bairbre (1954–). Politician, *Northern Ireland minister for health (1999–), leading member of *Sinn Féin. De Brún was born in *Dublin and joined Sinn Féin in 1984. She is a fluent Irish speaker and was, until her election to the Northern Ireland assembly in 1998, a teacher of French and Irish in Northern Ireland's first Irish medium secondary school. She was a leading member of the Sinn Féin negotiation team in the talks leading to the 1998 *Belfast Agreement. E.C.

De Danann. Traditional *music group. This innovative traditional band was formed in Spiddal, County *Galway, in 1974. Led by the virtuosity of fiddler Frankie Gavin and bouzouki player Alec Finn, the band has acted as a launch pad for some of Ireland's greatest singers, including Dolores Keane, Mary Black, Maura O'Connell, Eleanor Shanley and Tommy Fleming. They have experimented with Irish American vaudeville songs ('Star Spangled Molly', 1978), black gospel music ('Half Set in Harlem', 1991), as well as covering well-known Beatles and Queen numbers. B.D.

Defenders, the. A secret society which sprang up in County *Armagh in the mid-1780s to 'defend' *Catholics from sectarian attacks from the *Protestant Peep O'Day Boys. It spread through Catholic *Ulster in the 1790s, feuding with the *Orange Order, and formed an alliance with the *United Irishmen. The Defenders faded after the *Rebellion of 1798 and slowly mutated into the Ribbonmen during the first half of the nineteenth century. K.W.

Delaney, Ronnie (1935–). Irish Olympic athlete. Born in Arklow, County *Wicklow, Delaney graduated from Villanova University, Pennsylvania. In 1954, he became the seventh athlete in history to run a mile in under four minutes. In 1956, he won the gold medal in the 1,500-metre race at the Melbourne Olympic Games, setting a new Olympic record of 3:41.2. P.E.

Democratic Unionist Party (DUP). One of the two main *unionist political parties in *Northern Ireland. (The other is the *Ulster Unionist Party [UUP].) The DUP was formed in September 1971 by Ian *Paisley, currently its leader, and Desmond Boal, who was then member of the *Stormont parliament for Shankill. Boal declared that the party would be 'right-wing in the sense of being strong on the constitution, but to the left on social policies'. The party succeeded the *Protestant Unionist Party. The DUP has participated in Northern Ireland local government elections, various local assemblies, Westminster general elections and elections to the European parliament. Capitalising on discontent with the pro-*Good Friday Agreement Ulster Unionist Party, the DUP increased its vote by more than 50% in a Westminster general election in the autumn of 2001. With 22.5% of the total, it was the second largest party in Northern Ireland. The DUP in 2004 had five Westminster members of parliament (Ian Paisley, Peter Robinson, Iris Robinson, Nigel Dodds and Gregory Campbell) and one member of the European parliament (Jim Allister). In 2003, the DUP became the largest single party in the Northern Ireland Assembly. M.M.

Derry, County. One of the six counties in the province of *Ulster, which make up *Northern Ireland. Derry (816 square miles) has a population of est. 213,035 (1996). The county is bounded on the north by the Atlantic Ocean, and on the east and west by the Lower Bann and the river Foyle, respectively. Derry City, the county capital, was the site of a monastery founded in the sixth century by St *Colm Cille (Columba) who, according to legend, saved the poets from being banished from Ireland. The ancient territory of Tír Eoghain (named after the son of the early Irish King Niall of the Nine Hostages) occupied most of the county, which remained Gaelic in power and culture until the *Flight of the Earls in 1607 ended Gaelic hegemony in Ulster. King James I of England granted the confiscated lands of these native chieftains to English settlers after 1609. These settlers, mostly Londoners, named the county Londonderry and some of the smaller towns, such as Draperstown, after their trades and occupations. The English settlers were joined in the middle of the seventeenth century by dissenting *Presbyterians from *Scotland, many of whom, disappointed at not finding the religious liberty they yearned for, later left for North America.

(These *Scots-Irish made up a sixth of the total population by the time of the United States' Declaration of Independence.) During the Siege of *Derry in 1689, the city, protected by its stout walls built three-quarters of a century earlier, withstood a long onslaught by *Jacobite forces. (Derry's are perhaps the last circuit of town walls to be built anywhere in Europe.) Derry had a significant naval base on the Foyle during the Second World War where American troops were stationed. The city was the scene of civil rights unrest in the late 1960s, which led to the *Northern Ireland conflict, or the *Troubles. The county's economy includes *textiles, farming and light industry. The Nobel Prize-winning poet Seamus *Heaney was born in Toome, County Derry, and the well-known poet and literary critic Seamus *Deane was born in Derry City. P.H.

Derry, Siege of (1689). During the Williamite War, on 18 April 1689, Derry (Londonderry) locked out *James II with cries of 'No surrender!' thus beginning the siege. Major Baker (replaced after his death by John Mitchelbourne) and Reverend Walker took over the command of the 30,000 civilians, mostly refugees, and 7,000 troops in the city. The Jacobites lacked cannons, equipment and troops for an attack but blockaded the city. On 28 July two ships broke through the blockade in Lough Foyle, and the siege ended on 31 July. In commemoration of the siege, the *Apprentice Boys of Derry parade annually in August. T.C.

de Valera, Éamon (1882–1975). The figure of Éamon de Valera towered over Irish politics for more than half a century, from the *Easter Rising of 1916 into the 1970s. *Nationalist, revolutionary, shrewd Machiavellian politician, fervent Irish *Catholic, *Taoiseach and president of Ireland, de Valera more than any other political leader shaped modern Ireland.

He was born in New York City in 1882 to *immigrant parents, Catherine Coll, an Irish domestic worker and Juan Vivion de Valera, a Spanish sculptor. In 1885 his mother, who was widowed the previous year, sent the child to Ireland to be raised by his grandmother in the family's small cottage in Bruree, County *Limerick.

Éamon de Valera

De Valera excelled in school, won a scholarship to the prestigious Blackrock College and qualified in 1905 as a teacher of mathematics from the Royal University, Dublin.

The Ireland of his childhood was a cauldron of political turmoil – *Parnell, the *Land Wars and *Fenianism. Increasingly attracted to the burgeoning nationalist movement, de Valera became a member of the *Gaelic League in 1908 and in 1913 joined the Irish *Volunteers, a nationalist militia.

Three years later, in the Easter Rising of 1916, de Valera commanded the defence of Boland's Mills, a strategically located factory in Dublin. He was arrested and sentenced to death along with the other leaders, but his sentence was commuted partly because of his American citizenship and partly because the executions were arousing mass sympathy for the rebels. Back in Ireland after his release from prison in 1917, de Valera enjoyed hero status as the senior surviving commander of the rising. He threw himself wholeheartedly into the campaign of the new political party *Sinn Féin and won a parliamentary seat for East *Clare in the election of June 1917.

Charismatic and politically savvy, de Valera became both president of Sinn Féin and of the Irish Volunteers, its military wing. In 1918, he was again arrested and imprisoned in Lincoln Prison in England, for his part in an alleged 'German plot'. The following year, he escaped with the help of Michael *Collins and Harry *Boland.

An Irish parliament representing the thirty-two counties, the *Dáil, was convened on 21 January 1919 and declared Ireland a free and democratic republic in blatant defiance of the British government. De Valera was elected its first president. Shortly after, he went to the United States to raise money and support for Irish independence. He spent 18 months exhaustively travelling the United States and raised $5 million, but he alienated some *Irish American leaders and failed to gain US government recognition for the new Irish Republic.

On his return to Dublin in December 1920, de Valera was critical of some of the methods of guerrilla warfare Michael Collins had developed during the *War of Independence. In July 1921, a truce was called and de Valera went to London for discussions with *Lloyd George, the British prime minister. No progress was made but further negotiations began in October.

The *Anglo-Irish Treaty was finally negotiated in December 1921 by an Irish delegation from which de Valera was conspicuously absent. He had prevailed on Michael Collins to take part in the final treaty negotiations in London while he, de Valera, remained in Dublin to preserve unity and ensure acceptance of the final agreement. Some historians have argued that de Valera knew that the nationalist ideal of an Irish republic was not a likely outcome and in a Machiavellian move conveniently separated himself from the treaty compromise.

After a pro-treaty vote of 64 to 57, de Valera, who was opposed to the compromise, immediately rejected the treaty and resigned from the Dáil. In the spring of 1922, anti-treaty republicans occupied the *Four Courts building in Dublin, precipitating the *Civil War. De Valera crisscrossed Ireland during this period, arguing the case for the republic with passionate rhetoric. He was, however, criticised by some republican supporters for his 'external association' theory of an independent republic within the Commonwealth. De Valera was to regain influence with the republicans only after their military leader Liam Lynch's death in 1923.

After Michael Collins' death in August 1922, the Civil War dragged on until May 1923 when the republican forces called a cease-fire.

In August 1923, de Valera was arrested while contesting the general election in Ennis, County Clare, and after his release from jail, a year later, he decided to take his place in constitutional politics. In November 1925, he failed to get Sinn Féin to recognise the new twenty-six-county *Free State Dáil and he resigned as president. Many of his republican colleagues in Sinn Féin were outraged, but such was de Valera's power of persuasion that in 1926 he brought most of the Sinn Féin supporters into his newly founded political party, *Fianna Fáil. The new party remained abstentionist, objecting to the *oath of allegiance required by all Dáil members. However, they entered the Dáil in August 1927, reluctantly taking the oath of allegiance (de Valera's and the republicans' main objection to the *Anglo-Irish Treaty).

In the general election of September 1927, Fianna Fáil won 44 seats and narrowly failed to form a coalition government. De Valera had reinvented himself politically, a process that would be complete in 1932 when Fianna Fáil came to power. De Valera would govern for the next 16 years, solidifying Fianna Fáil's power and quelling any threats from the die-hard *IRA purists – his older colleagues from Sinn Féin – and also from the *Blueshirts. He founded the *Irish Press*, a pro-Fianna Fáil newspaper with a broad national agenda, in 1931.

In 1932, de Valera abolished the oath of allegiance, the most controversial issue of the 1921 treaty. He also refused to pay land annuity payments to Britain, causing the *Economic War. Internationally, de Valera played an important role in the League of Nations, as president of the council in 1932 and later as president of the assembly.

In 1937, de Valera drafted a new *Constitution, reflecting his conservative doctrinairism. In an ingenious political move, he extended the jurisdiction of the new constitution to cover the entire island of Ireland. Although Ireland remained neutral during the Second World War, the country suffered economically well into the 1950s when emigration peaked.

De Valera's greatest achievement was to create a constitutionally stable government in post-colonial Ireland, but his vision of a nationalist, self-sufficient Ireland isolated the country economically, politically and culturally. He resigned in 1959 as Taoiseach and served two terms as president from 1959 to 1973. He died in 1975. J.OM.

de Vere, Sir Aubrey (1814–1902). Poet and author. Born in County *Limerick, de Vere was influenced by his friend William Wordsworth. An intimate of Tennyson and Robert Browning, de Vere travelled extensively in Italy (1839–44) before publishing his collection of romantic poems, *The Waldenses* (1842). In *English Misrule and Irish Misdeeds* (1848), de Vere declared his Irish sympathies and he became a Roman *Catholic in 1851. In 1854, he was appointed professor of political and social science in the Dublin Catholic University, where he developed an interest in Irish legend and history. His works include *The Legends of St Patrick* (1872) and *Recollections* (1897). S.A.B.

Devlin, Denis (1908–59). Poet, translator and diplomat. Devlin was born in Greenock, Scotland, and educated at Belvedere College and University College, Dublin. His and Brian Coffey's early poems were published jointly in *Poems* (1930), and Samuel *Beckett favourably reviewed his *Intercessions* (1937). Posted to the United States, he met poets Robert Penn Warren and Alan Tate who edited his *Selected Poems* (1963). A modernist poet, he wrote about the anxiety of human existence and the conflict between human beings, an impersonal god whom Devlin calls 'the heavenly foreigner', and external reality. M.S.T.

Devoy, John (1842–1928). *Irish American political activist. Born in County *Kildare, John Devoy was one of the original *Fenians and in 1866, he was imprisoned for his part in the outlawed Fenian movement. In 1871, his prison sentence was commuted in exchange for self-imposed exile to the United States. From his arrival in *New York, Devoy would immerse himself in Irish American political activism. He was one of the main architects of Irish American support for Charles Stewart *Parnell and the *Land Wars of the 1870s, the *Easter Rising of 1916 and later for Éamon *de Valera's money-raising tours in the United States. He later broke with de Valera and supported the *Anglo-Irish Treaty and the new *Free State government.

Patrick *Ford, editor of the *Irish World*, persuaded Devoy that *nationalism needed a popular cause, like the war on landlordism, to mobilise the Irish masses. In June 1879, Devoy, Parnell, future leader of the *Irish Parliamentary Party, and Michael *Davitt, a founder of the *Land League, negotiated the 'New Departure', under which Irish American nationalists would support both *home rule and land reform. In 1900, Devoy became one of the leaders of *Clan na Gael, an Irish American revolutionary organisation dedicated to Irish independence, and maintained close ties to the *IRB.

Among Devoy's more adventurous exploits is the masterminding of the escape by seven Irish political prisoners from Western *Australia and their successful trip to the United States on the ship *Catalpa* in 1876. He was an early supporter of John Holland, an Irish immigrant, who designed the first underwater vessel – later called the submarine. Devoy's autobiography *Recollections of an Irish Rebel* (1929) is a firsthand account of Irish political activism in the United States. J.OM.

Dillon, Gerard (1916–71). Painter. Born in *Belfast, Dillon was a landscape and figure painter, who studied briefly at Belfast College of Art before living in London and *Dublin. Inspired by *Connemara, he produced Chagall-like surreal work with strong autobiographical content. He exhibited regularly at *Irish Exhibition of Living Art from 1943 until 1969, when he withdrew from the Belfast show in support of northern *nationalists. M.C.

Dillon, James (1902–86). Politician, *Fine Gael leader (1959–65) and noted orator. Born into a distinguished political dynasty (son of John *Dillon), he was first elected to the *Dáil in 1932 and became vice president of Fine Gael in 1933, when it merged with the Centre Party. Dillon resigned from the party during the Second World War because he disagreed with Fine Gael's support for *neutrality. During the coalition (interparty) governments, he was minister for *agriculture, a sector he managed to rebuild following the damage of the *Economic War. In 1952, he rejoined Fine Gael and his era of leadership is seen as a period of consolidation for the party. P.E.

Dillon, John (1851–1927). Politician. Militantly anti-*landlord during the *Land War, Dillon (son of John Blake *Dillon) served four prison terms in the 1880s. He was *Irish Parliamentary Party MP for *Tipperary (1880–83) and for East *Mayo (1885–1918). After the party split in 1891 following the *O'Shea divorce case, he aligned with the anti-Parnellites. When the party reunited, in 1900, with the Parnellite John *Redmond as chairman, Dillon supported the new leader and thereafter the two men provided effective leadership in anticipation of *home rule. On Redmond's death in 1918, Dillon became chairman. In the following general election in December 1918, *Sinn Féin crushed his party and Dillon lost his East Mayo seat to Éamon *de Valera. L.MB.

Dillon, John Blake (1816–66). Irish *nationalist politician. The son of a shopkeeper from Ballaghadereen, County *Mayo, Dillon graduated from Trinity College, Dublin, and became a lawyer in 1841. He was one of the founders of the **Nation* newspaper in 1842 and became a member of the *Repeal Association. Dillon joined the *Young Ireland movement in 1846 and led the 1848 insurgency at Killenaule, County *Tipperary. After the uprising, he escaped to the United States where he practised law. In 1855, Dillon returned to Dublin under amnesty and became secretary to the Irish National Association in 1864. Elected as MP for County Tipperary in 1865, he opposed *Fenianism and joined British radicals in campaigning for land reform. S.A.B.

Dingle Peninsula. Peninsula in County *Kerry, jutting into the Atlantic Ocean on the southwest coast of Ireland. The town of Dingle stands near the end of the peninsula. Some of the most beautiful *Munster *Irish is spoken in the *Gaeltacht areas on the peninsula. The *Blasket Islands at its western tip produced such literary classics as *An tOileánach (The Islandman)* by Tomás *Ó Criomhthain and storytellers like Peig *Sayers. In 1579 a Spanish military expedition was annihilated at Dún an Óir on Smerwick Harbour and nine years later a *Spanish Armada vessel foundered off Slea Head. Many archaeological sites and *beehive huts may be associated with an ancient *pilgrimage to *Mount Brandon (3,127 feet) in honour of St *Brendan. P.H.

distilling and brewing. Alcohol has long had a prominent and controversial place in Irish culture. Brewing and distilling have been, and continue to be, important industries in Ireland's *economy. Although neither industry was ever a large-scale direct employer, the vast network of distillers, brewers, distributors, publicans and 'spirit grocers' (there were over 14,000 licensed sellers of alcohol in Ireland in 1836) has formed a vital segment of the Irish middle-class from the eighteenth century to the present day.

We don't know when distilling started or if, prior to the 1160s, what the Irish were distilling was something we would call *whiskey today. Production of whiskey, or *uisce beatha* (the Irish for 'water of life'), probably began sometime after the eighth century when Irish missionaries brought Mediterranean distillation techniques to the British Isles. Distilling spirits from barley became more common from the twelfth century and was a ubiquitous craft industry in Ireland from the fifteenth century onward. Duties, taxes and the licensing of retail sale of spirits, wine and beer became an important source of revenue for the English government from the later sixteenth century, even though endemic corruption, evasion and subversion of the same became a characteristic feature of Irish public culture for the next three centuries. Custom duties on imported spirits established from 1661, nevertheless, encouraged Irish whiskey production, and by 1765 there were 946 registered stills in Ireland, which together produced over 715,000 proof-gallons of spirit. At the same time, great quantities of illicit distillation of whiskey were produced all over the country. The industry, under steady pressure from imports, illicit distillation and government regulation that favoured larger producers, consolidated over time. Production increased steadily for most of the nineteenth century, with the exception of the 1840s, the years of Father Mathew's temperance crusade and the Great *Famine. Whiskey production became more geographically concentrated, primarily in *Dublin and *Cork. Steady consolidation in the industry continued into the twentieth century, as Irish distillers lost export ground to Scottish producers and domestic consumption levelled out. Three active distilleries remained in Ireland at the end of the twentieth century – Midleton Distillery in County Cork (where whiskeys such as Paddy, Power, Jameson and the premium Midleton Reserve are currently distilled); Cooley Distillery in County *Louth (a twentieth-century distillery where Connemara, Locke and other specialty whiskeys are made); and Bushmills Distillery in County *Antrim which makes varieties of the famous whiskey of the same name.

Beer, brewed in Ireland from ancient times, remained a popular drink, especially in urban areas, despite the rise in spirit consumption from the early modern period. At the end of the eighteenth century, there were hundreds of breweries in Ireland, with larger producers concentrated in Dublin and Cork and with many retail brewers throughout the country. Into the early decades of the nineteenth century, Irish brewers faced declining consumption as well as increasing competition from larger high-quality English producers, as well as from domestic spirit production and West Indian rum. However, from 1850 to 1914, Irish beer production tripled, with the *Guinness Brewery in Dublin becoming the world's largest brewer. By 1914, 40% of Irish beer production was exported and beer exports made up over 3% of all Irish exports. Over the course of the twentieth century, the Irish brewing industry consolidated dramatically, while beer production continued to rise. *Guinness (now owned by international drinks giant Diageo) operates breweries in Dublin, Belfast, Kilkenny and Dundalk. Cork City has two large breweries: Beamish and Crawford, producers of Beamish stout and Lady's Well Brewery, where Murphy's stout and other beers are produced. In recent years, micro-breweries and brew pubs, such as the Irish Brewing Company in County *Kildare and the Carlow Brewing Company (whose old recipe micro-brews have won international recognition), have begun to re-emerge across Ireland. P.A.T.

divorce. Divorce was relatively freely available under the old *Celtic law system, but in the centuries following the *Anglo-Norman invasion, Ireland adopted the English system of law, which restricted divorce. In the nineteenth and early twentieth century, for example, each individual divorce required a separate act of the British parliament and was, therefore, only available to the wealthy. Divorce was totally prohibited by the first *Free State government in 1926 (as part of a *Catholic conservative policy programme including censorship and a ban on contraception). Although *Northern Ireland remained part of the United Kingdom, the *unionist government used its devolved legislative powers to limit the liberalisation of divorce legislation – even as reforms were introduced in Britain. The new Irish state's *Constitution, which was adopted by referendum in 1937, included a prohibition on divorce. During the 1970s and 1980s, in response to the growing problem of marital breakdown, the state reformed family law in such areas as custody of children, maintenance of a dependent spouse and the division of property. However, this did not amount to a comprehensive law dealing with separation and divorce remained banned.

The first attempt to amend the constitutional ban came in 1986, when the *Fine Gael–*Labour coalition government proposed a referendum on divorce. *Fianna Fáil officially allowed its members to campaign on either side, but a majority of the party opposed the measure. The measure was defeated with a 63.5% 'no' vote. Subsequent analysis suggests that only one-third of the public was morally or socially opposed to the measure. However, the middle ground almost unanimously voted against it, because the government's legislative plans for the introduction of divorce were unclear, raising fears about *women's welfare entitlements and property rights in particular. In the aftermath of this defeat, comprehensive legal separation was introduced as a solution to marital breakdown. The only outstanding issue was the right to remarry. A second referendum in 1995 to remove the constitutional ban on divorce was supported by all the main political parties, but passed only by a tiny 50.3% majority. Following this referendum, the *Dáil passed appropriate legislation making divorce available in the *Republic. E.C.

Dixon, James (1887–1970). Painter. A fisherman and small farmer from Tory Island, County *Donegal, Dixon was encouraged to paint by artist Derek *Hill. The naiveté of his landscape paintings, exhibited in *Belfast in 1966 and recently at the *Irish Museum of Modern Art (IMMA), is an important quality for modern painters. M.C.

Doherty, Willie (1959–). Photographer and video artist. Born in *Derry, Doherty studied in *Belfast. He worked initially in black and white, with superimposed captions on photographs of *Northern Ireland that commented upon its media representation. He moved on to colour without text, and he uses video extensively – in increasingly complicated technical formats – which undermine stereotypical interpretations of the *Northern Ireland conflict. M.C.

Poulnabrone Dolmen, the Burren, County Clare

dolmens. Stone Age megalithic tombs. Dolmens consist of between three and seven uprights carrying a capstone weighing up to 100 tons, as at Browneshill, County *Carlow. These massive structures were probably erected by means of a removable ramp. Poulnabrone Dolmen, County *Clare, has been radiocarbon-dated to 3800–3200 BC. It housed 22 burials. P.H.

Donegal, County. The most northerly county in Ireland and one of the three in the province of *Ulster that are part of the *Republic of Ireland. The county capital is Lifford. One of Ireland's most scenic counties, Donegal (area of 1,876 square miles) has a population of 137,383 (2002 census). The county has a spectacular 200-mile coastline and its rugged interior regions are dominated by the majestic Mount Errigal. Slieve Liag in the south of the county boasts the highest sea cliffs in Europe (1, 972 feet).

The county is often referred to as Tír Chonaill or 'the land of Conall'. The High King Niall of the Nine Hostages who ruled between 379 to 405 carved up much of west Ulster between his two sons, Conall and Eoghan. Conall received most of Donegal, while his brother Eoghan was given Tyrone (*Tír Eoghain* – the land of Eoghan) and Inishowen (Eoghan's island). The term *Tír Chonaill*, therefore, refers only to those parts of County Donegal outside of the Inishowen peninsula.

St *Colm Cille has a strong association with the county. He is reputed to have been born in Gartan in 521 and is believed to have spent some time in Glencolumbcille and Tory Island.

The O'Donnell clan ruled most of Donegal until the *Flight of the Earls in 1607 shattered the dynasty's control of the county, which now became known as Donegal, or *Dún na nGall* – 'the fort of the foreigner'.

A large cottage industry has been built in the county around tweed, especially in the towns of Ardara and Downings. Killybegs is a major fishing port and Bundoran, a popular seaside resort. Among Donegal's many tourist attractions are Glenveagh Castle and National Park and the magnificent art collection of Glebe House. The county's most important archaeological site is the Grianán of Aileach, a circular stone fort that dates back to the Iron Age and was reputed to have been the residence of various northern chieftains.

The **Annals of the Four Masters*, the famous compilation of annals that records the history of Ireland from early times to 1616, was written between the years 1632 and 1636 at the Donegal Abbey, by the Franciscan brothers collectively known as 'the four masters'. Each year thousands of pilgrims visit Station Island in Lough Derg, known as St *Patrick's Purgatory. A typical retreat lasts for three days and participants go without sleep or food (except for black tea and toast) and walk barefoot around the rocky island saying prayers. Much of the county is Irish speaking. B.D.

Donleavy, J. P. (1926–) Writer. Born in Brooklyn, New York, and educated at Trinity College, Dublin, Donleavy became an Irish citizen in 1967. His work is marked by wit, pessimism and bawdiness. *The Ginger Man*, a partly autobiographical novel that evokes Donleavy's riotous student days in *Dublin, is widely acknowledged as a classic. Considered scandalous, the book was rejected by numerous publishing houses, but established a cult following after its initial 1955 publication in Paris. Donleavy and his hedonistic anti-hero Sebastian Dangerfield became known to a wider audience in the 1960s, when publishers in other countries overcame their fears about its contents. *The Ginger Man* overshadows Donleavy's subsequent work, such as *Meet My Maker the Mad Molecule* (1964), *The Saddest Summer of Samuel S* (1966), *The Beastly Beatitudes of Balthazar B* (1968) and *The Destiny of Darcy Dancer: Gentleman* (1977). M.E.

Down, County. Ireland's most easterly county, in the province of *Ulster, one of the six counties of *Northern Ireland. Down (957 square miles) has a population of est. 454,411 (1996). The name comes from the Dún, or fortification, which also forms part of the placename Downpatrick, which is the county capital. The town is also named after St *Patrick, who worked in the area in the fifth century and died at Saul in County Down (though where he is buried is unknown). In ancient times, the county formed part of the kingdom of Ulidia, or the Ulaidh people, divided between the Dal Fiatach in eastern Down and the Uí Echach in the west of the county. *Viking settlements have left little trace, but the *Norman invasion left its mark on the county. The Norman John de Courcy, who overran the county late in the twelfth century, built *castles at Dundrum and Greencastle. Four centuries later, Down was further colonised by Scots planters who added to the racial and religious mix. Bordered by Belfast Lough on the north and the Mourne Mountains to the south (rising to a height of 2,796 feet at Slieve Donard), the county has both highlands and undulating terrain of plain and low hills. The long and lovely inlet, Strangford Lough, separates the Ards Peninsula from the main body of the county. In the inlet is Mahee Island, with its excavated early Christian monastery at Nendrum. Bordering on Strangford Lough's shores is Mount Stewart House, the eighteenth-century mansion of the Marquess of Londonderry, set in one of the finest gardens in Ireland. *Dolmens (e.g., Legananny), castles like Dundrum, abbeys such as Inch, as well as churches old and new, dot the Down landscape. The Ulster Folk and Transport Museum at Cultra splendidly conjures up the past of this historic county. The first canal in Britain or Ireland was built in County Down between 1731 and 1742, linking the town of Newry with Lough Neagh. The county also has majestic scenery and attractive coastal towns and villages, including Rostrevor, Ardglass and Strangford. Newcastle has a fine championship golf course 'where the mountains of Mourne sweep down to the sea', in the words of the famous song by Percy *French. Holywood claims to be one of the first golf courses founded in Ireland. Holywood and Bangor (the site of another early monastery) are now practically suburbs of the city of *Belfast and make up a considerable proportion of the population of the northern part of the county. Distinguished natives of Down include: Sir Hans Sloane (1660–1753), founder of the British Museum; Captain Francis Crozier (1796–1848), second in command to Sir John Franklin in the ill-fated search for the north-west passage; John Butler *Yeats, artist and father of the poet W. B. *Yeats and the artist Jack B. *Yeats; and the composer Sir Hamilton *Harty. P.H.

Downing Street Declaration (15 December 1993). Important statement by British Prime Minister John *Major and Irish *Taoiseach Albert *Reynolds committing both governments to the *peace process in *Northern Ireland. Talks had been going on between the British and Irish governments and four constitutional Northern Ireland political parties since 1991. The Downing Street Declaration re-asserted the *Anglo-Irish Agreement's principle that Northern Ireland's status could not be changed without the consent of its people. The declaration committed the Irish government to introduce and support changes in the Irish *Constitution (specifically, the claim of sovereignty over the entire island of Ireland) and it formally asserted that the United Kingdom had no selfish, strategic, or economic interest in Northern Ireland. Finally and perhaps most importantly, the declaration opened the way for Northern Ireland parties with paramilitary links to join negotiations if the parties committed themselves to exclusively peaceful methods and agreed to abide by the democratic process. The Downing Street Declaration is considered one of the main factors leading to the *IRA's historic cease-fire of 31 August 1994, which was followed by the *loyalist cease-fire of 13 October. Those cease-fires eventually made it possible for *Sinn Féin and two small loyalist parties – the *Ulster Democratic Party and the *Progressive Unionist Party – to participate in the multiparty talks that concluded with the signing of the 1998 *Good Friday Agreement. T.D.

Doyle, Roddy (1958–). Novelist. Born in *Dublin, Doyle taught school in the north Dublin suburb of Kilbarrack, on which he based his 'Barrytown trilogy' – *The Commitments* (1987), *The Snapper* (1990) and *The Van* (1991). These novels' depiction of life in a Dublin housing estate, the characters' resilience and irreverence, and Doyle's informal style struck a fresh note in Irish writing. The Booker Prize-winning *Paddy Clarke Ha Ha Ha* (1993) depicts with deceptive lightness the frailty of family life and introduces the violence and frustration developed more fully in *The Woman Who Walked into Doors* (1996). Doyle's other works include the novel *A Star Called Henry* (1999) and a number of plays and screen-plays. G.OB.

Drennan, William (1754–1820). *Republican, founding member of the *United Irishmen. Born into a *Belfast *Presbyterian family, Drennan studied philosophy in Glasgow and medicine in Edinburgh. He set up a medical practice in *Belfast in 1778 and was soon drawn to the patriot politics of the *Volunteer movement, which sought parliamentary reform. By late 1791, two years after his move to Dublin, Drennan was one of the founders of the United Irishmen, closely associated with Theobald Wolfe *Tone, Thomas Addis Emmet, Dr William McNeven and other radicals who campaigned for the democratisation of the Irish government and emancipation of *Catholics. Drennan convinced his fellow United Irishmen to adopt elements of masonic *modus operandi* and nomenclature. He was tried in May 1794 for publishing a seditious libel, after which he drew back from high-profile political activities. Although aloof from paramilitary republicanism, Drennan contributed prose and verse to United Irish organs and wrote the popular 'Wake of William Orr' in late 1797. He avoided serious persecution during the *Rebellion (of 1798) period but was jeopardised not only by the outbreak of open conflict in May 1798 but by his subsequent closeness to the *Emmet family. Drennan retired from medicine in 1807 and returned to Belfast, where he published the *Belfast Monthly Magazine*. He died in February 1820. R.OD.

Drew, Ronnie. See **Dubliners**.

druids. The directors of religion and philosophy among the ancient *Celts. The word druid (Old Irish *druí*, Modern Irish *draoi*) derives from ancient Celtic *dru-wid-os*, meaning 'one of great knowledge'. Classical authors, such as Livy, Pliny and Julius Caesar, made frequent reference to the druids of Celtic Gaul and Britain, stating that they were wise men who had supernatural knowledge, whose judgments were respected and who oversaw various religious and social rituals. Early Irish literature shows that the institution of druidism was also well established in Ireland, the druid being considered an expert in antiquarian knowledge, in clairvoyance and in prophesying. Druids were reputed to negotiate peace settlements between warring factions, to divine the identity of future kings by sleeping on bull hides and to gain inspiration from the dead by sojourning near burial mounds. More fanciful accounts have them casting spells for the discovery of thieves, covering themselves with magical 'cloaks of concealment', and causing storms and thunderbolts to impede the progress of hostile armies. It is obvious that the rhetoric uttered by druids was considered sacred and they themselves were at pains to project the importance of their profession. On public occasions, they wore colourful ceremonial garments decorated by the feathers of various birds. They convened for training and ritual in quiet groves, and various traditions portray the oak, the hazel and the rowan as trees sacred to them. There are various references to the many years spent in learning to be a druid, the teacher being an established druid with many students under his direction. D.OH.

Dublin. Capital of the Irish *Republic and its political, economic and cultural centre. Situated on the east coast, Dublin straddles the River Liffey. The city has been immortalised in poems, novels and plays by some of the greatest writers of the English language, including James *Joyce and Seán *O'Casey. Evidence of habitation around Dublin dates back to 5000 BC. The *Celts developed at least two settlements near the Liffey, and the city's Irish name, *Baile Átha Cliath* (the Town of the Hurdle Ford) refers to an ancient river crossing. During the golden age of early *Christianity, Dublin was home to several churches, monasteries and hermit huts. In AD 841, the *Vikings established a settlement where the River Poddle joined the Liffey, in an area known as Dyfflin or in Irish *Dubh Linn* (black pool), from which the city's name is derived. By the early tenth century, Dublin was a prosperous trading town, and after the *Anglo-Norman invasion, the city became the centre of Anglo-Norman, and later English, power in Ireland.

Dublin remained a small, walled town with approximately 9,000 residents until an influx of *Protestant refugees from Europe dramatically increased its population at the end of the seventeenth century. In the eighteenth century, economic prosperity led to the development of Georgian Dublin, which became known as 'the second city' in the British empire. Dublin spread beyond its old walls, developing along a gridiron pattern of squares and streets. Modern Dublin's centre, with the beautiful St Stephen's Green and the Georgian architecture of Merrion Square, Ely Place and Fitzwilliam Square, dates from this period. After the Act of *Union (1800) and the abolishment of the Irish *parliament, members of the ascendancy returned to England and the city fell into decline. By the end of the nineteenth century, Dublin had some of the worst slums in Europe.

In the twentieth century, Dublin was the centre of labour and political unrest, from James *Larkin's protests, the Lockout of 1913, to the 1916 *Easter Rising and the *War of Independence. The shelling of the *Four Courts in the city's centre in June 1922 started the *Civil War. Between 1922 and 1932, the *Irish Free State government, preoccupied with re-establishing law and order, was unable to deal adequately with the city's many social problems. The programme of slum clearance that *Fianna Fáil started when the party came to power in 1932 was later postponed during the Second World War because of a shortage of building material. Thirty-four people were killed when the city was bombed by the German air force in May 1941. The 1960s and 1970s saw a renewed period of expansion. Ireland's membership of the European Economic Community (now known as the *European Union) brought an infusion of wealth and prosperity, revitalising Dublin as a political, economic and cultural centre. Tourism became a major industry. The *Northern Ireland conflict was felt directly in Dublin on 17 May 1974, when three car bombs exploded without warning during rush hour, killing 26 people. The *Dublin Bombing, the biggest murder case in the Republic of Ireland, remains unsolved.

While development in the city slowed during the recession of the 1980s, the 'Celtic Tiger' economy of the 1990s ushered in an era of unprecedented growth and led to the emergence of a modern cosmopolitan capital. Today, Dublin covers an area of 44.4 square miles, with a population of approximately half a million. Dublin, with one of the fastest-growing urban economies in Europe, is an international centre of information technology and financial services. About 80% of the workforce is employed in the service sector. Twenty per cent work in manufacturing – engineering, pharmaceuticals and *brewing and distilling, most notably the *Guinness Brewery at St James' Gate, which was founded in 1759. Prosperity has led to soaring property prices, traffic congestion and suburban sprawl. Problems such as inner-city decay, deprivation in some suburban areas and crime remain serious challenges.

Dublin's thriving cultural and social life boasts the world-renowned *Abbey and *Gate Theatres and, perhaps, the greatest conversationalists in the world. There are numerous galleries, restaurants and over 800 pubs, including the Brazen Head, which claims to have been in business since 1198, and Davy Byrne's, the setting for one of the episodes of Joyce's *Ulysses*. Other attractions include *Dublin Castle, Trinity College, which was founded by *Elizabeth I in 1592 and is home to the *Book of *Kells*, the *Phoenix Park, one of Europe's largest parks, *Christ Church cathedral, *St Patrick's cathedral and the Dublin Writers' Museum. The city has an extraordinarily vibrant Anglo-Irish literary tradition starting with such eighteenth-century writers as Jonathan *Swift and Oliver *Goldsmith. Bram *Stoker, Oscar *Wilde and George Bernard *Shaw were natives of the city, as was William Butler *Yeats, one of the greatest modern poets in the English language. Yeats, along with playwrights Lady *Gregory and Edward *Martyn and novelist George *Moore, helped found the Abbey Theatre, which became famous through the plays of John Millington *Synge and Seán *O' Casey, who were also Dubliners. Every 16 June, known as Bloomsday, the city celebrates the life of one of its greatest writers, James Joyce. Other twentieth-century writers associated with the city include Samuel *Beckett, Brendan *Behan and Christy *Brown. The Dublin literary tradition continues today with writers such as Roddy *Doyle and Maeve *Binchy. P.E.

Dublin bombings (1974). *Loyalist bombings in the *Republic of Ireland. On 17 May 1974, 26 civilians were killed in three car bomb explosions in Dublin City centre and seven in an explosion in Monaghan town. The attacks were carried out by loyalist activists from *Northern Ireland. These related incidents represent the greatest loss of life in a single day as a result of the *Northern Ireland conflict. The Dublin government did not pursue leads as vigorously as might have been expected, afraid perhaps of the violence spilling over the border. Persistent allegations have been made of 'dirty war' involvement in the atrocity by elements of the state security forces in Northern Ireland. M.M.

Dublin Castle. The centre of British authority in Ireland until 1922. Dublin Castle was built by King *John of England in 1204. The original castle corresponded in extent with the present Upper Castle Yard, flanked on each corner by a great circular tower, beneath one of which – the Powder Tower – an earlier *Viking fortification was excavated. Other than these towers, much of the existing structure is the result of extensive rebuilding between 1730 and 1800, and this includes the first-floor, state apartments where Irish *presidents are inaugurated and where John F. *Kennedy was received in 1963. The castle has been recently adapted as a forum for *European Union and other meetings and also for state tribunals. P.H.

Dublin, County. Maritime county in the province of *Leinster. Though Dublin, with 356 square miles, is ranked only thirtieth in size among the Irish counties, it is by far the most heavily populated, with 1,122,600 inhabitants (2002 census), almost a third of Ireland's total population of 3,917,336 (2002 census). The city of *Dublin, Ireland's capital and the county capital, with almost half a million inhabitants, is the administrative, financial and cultural centre of the country. It is also the centre of the Irish railway network and it contains the country's largest port. Dún Laoghaire, in south County Dublin, is also an important centre for car ferry traffic between Ireland and the United Kingdom. Other prominent urban centres include the towns of Swords, Malahide, Balbriggan and Skerries. One of the world's greatest golf links courses is in Portmarnock, in north County Dublin.

The county is bounded to the north by County *Meath, to the east by the Irish Sea, to the west by counties *Kildare and Meath and to the south by County *Wicklow. The landscape is generally flat and low lying, except in the south where the county borders the Wicklow Mountains. The main rivers include the Dodder, the Tolka and the Liffey, which rises south-west of Dublin City in Wicklow and travels approximately 50 miles before entering the sea at Dublin Bay. The coastline stretches for over 70 miles and includes the islands of *Lambay, Ireland's Eye and St Patrick's Island near Skerries.

Manufacturing and service industries are generally confined to the capital, while a significant fishing industry is centred in the towns of Howth and Skerries. *Agriculture remains an important, although declining, sector of the county's economy. Farms tend to be small, with cattle, barley and potatoes the chief products. A market gardening industry is concentrated in the northern part of the county, especially around the villages of Rush and Lusk and the area around Kinsealy. The explosion of development in the capital in the last decade has transformed the rural landscape outside the city, creating a vast low-density suburbia. The Flood Tribunal, established in 1997, has investigated charges of improper planning decisions and political corruption in land development in north County Dublin.

Human habitation in the county can be traced back to Mesolithic hunter-gatherers who dwelt in the hills to the north and south of Dublin City over 6,000 years ago. The county's historical sites include: Neolithic dolmens at Woodtown; *Viking remains at Wood Quay; monastic and church buildings such as *Christ Church cathedral, St Mary's abbey, St Doulagh's church and St Catherine's well at Balgriffin; and *castles at Dalkey, Swords and Malahide. From the twelfth to the sixteenth century, the county formed a significant part of the *Pale. During the twentieth century, Dublin City was the site of many important political and cultural movements and events, including the 1916 *Easter Rising, the birth of the *Irish Revival and the start of the *Civil War. The county also has its own literary history: Flann *O'Brien's *The Dalkey Archive* is set in the south County Dublin picturesque seaside town of Dalkey, while the opening chapter of James *Joyce's *Ulysses* is set in a Martello tower in Sandycove, where Joyce lived with Oliver St John *Gogarty, the inspiration for his character Buck Mulligan. P.E.

Dubliners, the. Music group. This popular ballad-group was formed in O'Donoghue's music bar in *Dublin in 1962. The original group included Barney McKenna, Luke Kelly, John Sheahan, Ciarán Bourke and Ronnie Drew. Kelly (d. 1984) was a passionate singer and Drew's gravelly bass became renowned. Dublin street-song was their core material, sung in local accents and set to superb arrangements with strong traditional instrumentals. F.V.

Duffy, Sir Charles Gavan (1816–1903). Politician, author, journalist. Born in County *Monaghan, Duffy was largely self-educated. In 1842, he founded the **Nation* weekly newspaper, the voice of the *Young Ireland revolutionary movement, with Thomas *Davis and John Blake *Dillon. He was in prison twice: once for sedition in 1844 and again, just before the *Rising of 1848, which he supported. Duffy started the Tenant League with James Fintan *Lalor and others in 1850, and was elected MP for New Ross in 1852. Duffy was a co-founder of the short-lived Independent Irish Party. After its collapse, he *emigrated to *Australia in 1855 and became prime minister of Victoria in 1871. From a Young Ireland revolutionary, Duffy had become a mainstream politician in the new world and was knighted in 1873. His political memoirs include *Young Ireland* (1880), *Four Years of Irish History 1845–49* (1883), *My Life in Two Hemispheres* (1898) and *A Bird's Eye View of Irish History* (1882). C.D.

Dún Aengus. *Prehistoric stone fort. Dramatically sited above a 200-foot cliff on Inishmore (*Aran Islands), Dún Aengus has multiple walls, the innermost one defended by stone stakes known as *chevaux-de-frise*. The date of construction is uncertain, but recent excavation showed human activity in the interior from about 800 BC onward. P.H.

Dunlop, John Boyd (1840–1921). Inventor and industrialist. Born in Dreghorn, Ayrshire, in *Scotland, Dunlop established a veterinary practice near *Belfast in 1867. He independently reinvented and pioneered the manufacture of commercially practical pneumatic rubber tires. (The first pneumatic rubber tire was patented by Robert William Thompson in 1845.) Dunlop's first design, consisting of a rubber inner tube, covered by linen tape and an outer tread of rubber, was made in 1887. The Dunlop Company began the mass production of tires in 1890 but in 1896 Dunlop sold both his patent and business for £3 million. This business, which ultimately developed into Dunlop Rubber Company, Ltd., greatly facilitated the development of motor transport. S.A.B.

Durrow, Book of. A copy of the Gospels and one of Europe's most important *manuscripts surviving from around AD 700. Of uncertain provenance (Ireland or Britain), the *Book of Durrow* was long kept at the site of the Columban Monastery at Durrow, County *Offaly, before being given to Trinity College, Dublin, in the seventeenth century. The manuscript is richly adorned with spiral and interlace ornament. P.H.

E

Easter Rising (24–29 April 1916). Rebellion which set in motion the events that brought about the creation of an independent Irish republic. The outbreak of the *First World War in August 1914 changed the course of Irish history by indefinitely postponing the *home rule bill and providing the impetus for the rising. The leader of the *Irish Parliamentary Party, John *Redmond's support of the war and the looming threat of conscription outraged an increasing number of nationalists, who came to see the war as an opportunity to separate from Britain.

The rising was originally planned by the *IRB in May 1915 to happen in one of three circumstances: a German invasion of Ireland, the introduction of conscription into the British army in Ireland, or if the war seemed likely to end without either of these two occurring. A group consisting of Seán *MacDiarmada, Thomas *Clarke, Patrick *Pearse, Joseph Mary *Plunkett and Thomas *MacDonagh worked on the details of the rising. In January 1916, James *Connolly, commandant of the *Irish Citizen Army, who was planning a rising separately, was persuaded to join the nationalist cause. The plans were kept secret within the IRB and even the commander in chief of the Irish *Volunteers, Eoin *MacNeill, was not told. When the rising happened, almost everybody, including British intelligence, was taken by surprise.

The original plan envisaged a countrywide rebellion launched under the guise of Irish Volunteer manoeuvres on Easter Sunday, 23 April 1916. However, a German ship, the *Aud*, carrying arms for the rising, was intercepted by the royal navy off County *Kerry and was scuttled on 22 April 1916. Eoin MacNeill, commander in chief of the Volunteers, cancelled all manoeuvres for Easter Sunday when he discovered their true purpose. On Good Friday he was talked into collaborating because he was persuaded that the government was about to arrest Volunteer leaders. On Saturday, however, aware that the government had no intention of striking and hearing of the capture of the *Aud*, he changed his mind and issued an order calling off the rebellion. The order was published on Easter Sunday in the form of an advertisement cancelling all Volunteer manoeuvres throughout the country for that day. This prevented most of the country from joining in the rebellion.

Nevertheless, the leaders decided to go ahead in *Dublin with whatever forces they could muster. At this stage, it was clear that the military feasibility of the rising was questionable but they believed that some gallant, symbolic gesture on behalf of Ireland's right to be a sovereign nation had to be made. They hoped that their actions and, if necessary, their sacrifice would rekindle the spirit of Irish *republicanism. On Easter Monday, 24 April, about 1,000 Volunteers and 200 members of Connolly's Irish Citizen Army seized the General Post Office (GPO) and other strategic sites in Dublin. From the GPO, Pearse read out the *Proclamation of the Irish Republic, declaring Ireland a sovereign republic and announcing a provisional government. It is the first declaration of independence in history that specifically mentions *women.

Over the next two days, the British army under Sir John Maxwell and reinforcements brought in from the *Curragh Camp, County *Kildare, *Belfast and Athlone, surrounded rebel positions. Street fighting continued for a week during which many buildings were destroyed. British artillery and a gunboat, the *Helga*, bombarded key rebel positions, including the GPO and Liberty Hall, headquarters of Connolly's Irish Transport and General Workers Union. Although there were some sporadic incidents in *Wexford, *Galway, Ashbourne, County *Dublin and County *Meath, there was no widespread uprising. The British sealed off Dublin and the population outside of the capital was not fully aware of what was happening. On 29 April to prevent further bloodshed, Pearse, who had been appointed first president of the Republic and head of the provisional government, surrendered. The last rebel outpost to hand over its arms was Boland's Mills under the command of Éamon *de Valera.

Sixty-four rebels had been killed, along with 132 crown forces and 230 civilians. Although initially the rising had little popular support, the British reaction to the rising provoked widespread sympathy for the rebels and their cause. The murder of Francis *Sheehy Skeffington, a well-known pacifist, the killing of civilians in North King Street by British soldiers and the implementation of martial law antagonised most people. The execution of the leaders (Patrick Pearse, Thomas Clarke, Thomas MacDonagh, Joseph Plunkett, Edward Daly, Michael O'Hanrahan, Willie Pearse, John *MacBride, Éamonn *Ceannt, Michael Mallin, Seán Heuston, Cornelius Colbert, Seán MacDiarmada, James Connolly and the hanging of Sir Roger *Casement) turned public opinion totally against the British and made martyrs of the executed rebels. Éamon de Valera was spared, supposedly, because he was a US citizen. The executions unleashed massive support for the republican cause and the ideal of an independent Ireland. *Sinn Féin's sweeping victory in the 1918 general election and the formation of the first *Dáil in January 1919 paved the way for the *War of Independence. T.C.

Economic War, the (1932–38). Economic and political dispute between the *Irish Free State and Britain. The Economic War began in 1932, when Éamon *de Valera's *Fianna Fáil government introduced legislation to abolish the *oath of allegiance to the British crown and refused to pay Britain the land annuities (repayments of British loans for land purchase). The British government retaliated by imposing duties and quotas on Irish imports, mainly on cattle and dairy produce. The Irish government responded with duties on British coal, iron, steel and machinery.

Since almost all Irish exports were to Britain, the measures considerably damaged trade, particularly the cattle trade, but all sections of the Irish *economy were affected. The Free State government and the Fianna Fáil party, however, turned the conflict to its political advantage using rhetoric about national self-sufficiency and sacrifice in the face of a foreign oppressor. In the opposing political camp, the damage to the cattle trade was one cause of the emergence of the short-lived *Blueshirt movement.

In 1934, relations between the two countries improved with the first of three 'coal-cattle' pacts. The British cabinet moved toward negotiations, which began in January 1938. In April that year, a series of agreements on trade, finance and defence repealed most of the special duties and restrictions on imports to each country. The land annuities issue was settled for a one-time single payment of £10 million and the Irish ports which had been retained by the British under the terms of the *Anglo-Irish Treaty were returned. P.D.

economy. For centuries before independence, Ireland had been an agrarian economy that was largely bypassed by the nineteenth century Industrial Revolution that transformed Britain and several European countries. The earlier *plantations (*Munster in the sixteenth century, *Ulster in the seventeenth) displaced the native *agricultural population in favour of a landed gentry. The land was partially returned to later generations of farm-labouring classes by a series of *land acts in the late nineteenth century. The Great *Famine in the 1840s was an economic catastrophe brought about by the potato blight and the government's failure to provide relief. Britain traditionally regarded Ireland as a source of cheap food and labour to support her rapidly expanding economy, a practice enshrined in Britain's economic policies both pre- and post-Irish independence.

Ireland gained political independence from Britain in 1922, but the fledgling Irish economy did not assume any real semblance of economic independence until the latter part of the century. Average incomes in Ireland were approximately 60% of those in Britain in 1913, when British living standards were among the highest in Europe. This relative situation had changed little by 1990, though, by then, British living standards had fallen well below the richer economies of mainland Europe. Through its dependence on Britain's relatively poorly performing economy, in terms of trade and labour market links, Ireland's own economic progress was arrested. The new state depended heavily on agriculture in the 1920s as a key supplier to the British market in an era of free trade, but the industrial sector was almost nonexistent. The *Fianna Fáil government, which assumed power in 1932, instituted a policy of strong protectionism buttressed by high external tariff barriers, later endorsed by no less an economist than John Maynard Keynes. The objective was to develop the indigenous manufacturing base by guaranteeing exclusive access to the domestic market to home-based suppliers. The policy was inspired by the *nationalist government of the day and compounded by an *Economic War with Britain that limited access to the British market. Legislation was passed also to restrict the level of foreign ownership of Irish manufacturing firms. The manufacturing sector expanded significantly during the 1930s, with a concentration on basic industries such as food, clothing and *textiles, and wood and *furniture. However, the policy proved completely inadequate to prepare the young economy for the rigours of operating in a free trade environment in the post-war era of the 1940s and 1950s. The manufacturing sector had stagnated, inefficiencies were rampant and output quality was poor, all of which were inevitable consequences of heavy protectionism. As Europe recovered and boomed in the 1950s, the Irish economy remained depressed. *Emigration was massive and the population was declining, while on the economic front, balance of payments crises constrained economic growth. A radically new approach was required and arrived in the shape of a strategy document, 'Economic Development', prepared by T. K. *Whitaker, the then secretary of the department of finance, in 1958.

This paved the way for a radical reorientation of industrial policy toward an outward-looking economy that focused on making Ireland an attractive location for foreign direct investment (FDI) and on building up the economy for participation, eventually, in the European model of economic integration. Generous fiscal and financial incentives were used to attract overseas firms to locate in Ireland. Over a period of 40 years, the industrial sector was radically transformed from being heavily dependent on the home market in highly protected, Irish-owned, inefficient firms to a modern export-oriented, largely, though not exclusively, foreign-owned and strongly competitive manufacturing sector. This transformation was not without pain as the transition to free trade that commenced in the 1960s was accelerated in the 1970s when Ireland joined the European Economic Community (1973) and many indigenous firms contracted or closed. The government also invested in building up the economy's infrastructure and its human capital through the introduction of free second-level *education in the 1960s. This led in time to a significant increase in an educated and up-skilled workforce, which proved critical to the attractiveness of Ireland as an industrial and international services centre in the 1990s. The infrastructure was seriously inadequate for the needs of a modern economy (note that Ireland was classified officially as a 'developing economy' in 1971) and European structural funds were vitally important in the 1990s to raise investment levels in the economy to about 30% of Gross Domestic Product (GDP) over a sustained period of time.

The gains to agriculture were a critical influence in encouraging Irish voters to join the European Community in 1973, though this sector has declined significantly since then and now accounts for less than 10% of GDP. The decision to join the *European Union (EU) (then known as the EEC) was of key long-term strategic importance to the economy and has sustained the flow of FDI from overseas firms wishing to locate their European manufacturing base in Ireland (as, for example, Dell, Apple and Intel). Ireland enjoyed sustained economic growth from 1959 to 1973, but was severely affected by the two oil crises of the 1970s. The economy suffered from macroeconomic mismanagement during the late 1970s, when excessive spending by government severely curtailed the scope for fiscal flexibility during the depressed years of the 1980s. Government debt to GDP ratio was constantly rising and peaked at over 110% in 1986; average and marginal tax rates were excessive and emigration began to rise once more. The economy appeared to be unmanageable during these difficult years and at one stage the threat of International Monetary Fund (IMF) intervention was looming.

However, a period of 'expansionary fiscal contraction' was initiated in 1987: government spending was severely cut and the social partners (government, major *trade unions and business organisations) embarked on a series of pay and tax agreements which ensured that moderate wage increases were guaranteed in exchange for generous tax concessions. Employment expanded from 1.1 million to 1.7 million from 1993 to 2000, reflecting the boom conditions of the 1990s; returned emigrants and a substantially increased female participation in the workforce contributed to this boom. The debt to GDP ratio had stabilised at 32% in 2003/4 and the size of government in the economy is now one of the smallest in Europe.

Today, Ireland is among the richest economies in the world and was recently ranked fifth in a league table of economies based on incomes *per capita*, higher than that of the UK and above the average of the European Union. This surge of economic growth since 1993 (almost 10% annually from 1995 to 2000) was unprecedented and the Irish economy became known as the 'Celtic Tiger'. Even though the standard of living improved dramatically for many Irish people, poverty levels still persist in certain sectors and locations in the country. In 2001–2, Ireland's economy slowed down, in tandem with the international economy, though it still recorded above average GDP growth rates over 6%. In 2003, GDP growth slumped to 1.4 % but rebounded in 2004, with steady employment gains. Even with the slowdown, the transformation of the economy, including the structural adjustments created during the years of the 'Celtic Tiger', has remained intact. D.A.D.

Edgeworth, Maria (1767–1849). Novelist and educationalist. Born in Black Bourton, Oxfordshire, Edgeworth came to Ireland in 1782 and lived on the family estate at Edgeworthstown, County *Longford, from then until her death. Initially, she was an influential writer of children's books and of works of educational theory, but her best-known work is her first novel, *Castle Rackrent* (1800). The book, with its original use of *Hiberno-English and critique of *Anglo-Irish society, earned her an international reputation. She wrote three other novels on the challenges to Anglo-Ireland after the Act of *Union, notably *The Absentee* (1812) and several novels depicting London society in a satirical light, including *Belinda* (1801). Unlike *Castle Rackrent,* these works were substantially influenced by her father's liberal *unionism. After the publication of *Ormond* in 1817, the same year her father died, she published just two other novels, both with English settings. G.OB.

education. Ireland's long tradition of education is reflected in the country's cultural heritage. The *bardic schools of *pre-Christian Ireland helped to preserve and transmit the history of its earliest inhabitants. This system of learning, secular and oral in nature, involved the memorisation of tales and myths and was central in the education of poets (**fili*) and judges (*brehons). The great monastic schools such as Clonard and *Clonmacnoise, which provided the first organised learning based on literacy in Ireland from the fifth century onward, served as a sanctuary of learning during Europe's Dark Ages. Ireland was known as *Insula Sanctorum et Doctorum*, the 'Island of Saints and Scholars'.

The *Protestant *Reformation ended the monastic system (the monasteries were closed), denying most *Catholics access to education. Wealthier Catholics began travelling abroad to Irish colleges, which had been established on the continent. In 1592, Trinity College was founded in Dublin to further the growth of *Protestantism and English culture in Ireland. Under the *Penal Laws, the Catholic church was forbidden from having any role in education. In reaction, a system of hedge schools (in open fields or in primitive buildings) developed. Teachers financed by the local population taught a mixture of spelling, reading, arithmetic and religion. During this time, Protestant evangelical groups such as the Baptist Society began establishing schools in an attempt to convert the Catholic population.

The *Catholic Relief Acts at the end of the eighteenth century allowed the widespread establishment of schools in towns and cities by religious orders such as the Irish *Christian Brothers. The Kildare Place Society, set up in 1811, provided nondenominational education and within 20 years had over 137,000 pupils attending its associated schools. In 1831, the government established the National Board of Education to organise a system of state-sponsored national primary schools, one of the first of its kind in Europe. The board had the power to cover the cost of building schools, provide schoolbooks and contribute to teachers' salaries. Catholic and Protestant students were to be educated together for every subject with the exception of religious instruction. Despite these efforts, integration failed and, by the late 1860s, most national schools were denominational in nature. The Intermediate Education Act of 1878 introduced a common curriculum and examination system and established a Board of Commissioners to oversee the secondary schools system.

Three 'Queen's Colleges' were established in 1845 in *Belfast, *Cork and *Galway in an attempt to undermine the demand for the *repeal of the Act of *Union. These colleges were to be non-religious with no theology faculties. They, however, failed to attract any support from the Catholic population and were labelled 'godless' by the Catholic hierarchy, who in 1854 established the Catholic University in Dublin. In 1879, the British, in a fresh attempt to solve the university question, dissolved the 'Queen's Colleges' and established in their place the Royal University. The Irish Universities Act, 1908, created two separate *universities: the National University of Ireland (NUI) and Queen's University. (The colleges in Galway, Cork and Dublin became part of the National University and the College in Belfast became Queen's University.) Trinity College remained independent of these changes.

At present, there are four universities in the *Republic of Ireland: The NUI (with its constituent universities and colleges – NUI Dublin, NUI Cork, NUI Galway, NUI Maynooth, the Royal College of Surgeons and the National College of Art and Design); the University of Dublin (Trinity College); the University of Limerick; and Dublin City University. Northern Ireland has two universities: Queen's University at Belfast and the University of Ulster with campuses in Belfast, Derry, Jordanstown and Coleraine. For 2002/2003 the total number of students in all three sectors of education was 920,274. The budget figure for 2004 was just over 6 billion. The Department of Education and Science is responsible for the administration of primary, post primary and special education and directs state and European support for universities and third-level colleges. State spending in education in 2000 totalled more than £2.5 billion. Nearly 50% of secondary school graduates advance to college and university level.

Education in *Northern Ireland is administered centrally by the Department of Education for Northern Ireland and locally by five education boards. In 2001/2002, 346,663 students were attending primary and secondary education. While the law guarantees that every school is open to all pupils regardless of religious denomination, most Catholics attend schools owned by the Catholic church and financed by public funds, while Protestant and other non-Catholic children generally attend state schools. Integrated state schools also exist but they account for only a small percentage of enrolled students. At least 44.3% of students go on to higher education, the highest rate in the United Kingdom. P.M.D., P.E.

Edwards, Hilton Robert Hugh (1903–82). Actor and producer. Born in London, Edwards joined the Old Vic Theatre just before his eighteenth birthday. In 1927 he toured Ireland with Anew *McMaster's Shakespearean Company and met Micheál *MacLiammóir, with whom he formed a personal and professional partnership that would last a lifetime. Together, they became the directors of Ireland's first Irish-language theatre, An Taibhdhearc, which opened in Galway in 1928. In the same year, MacLiammóir and Edwards founded the *Gate Theatre Company, which specialised in a modern, international repertoire. At the Gate, Edwards introduced innovations in production, design and lighting and directed over 400 productions, acting in many of them. In the 1960s, he produced and directed several plays by Brian *Friel in *Dublin, London and on Broadway. He directed a short film, *Road to Glenascaul* (1951), which was nominated for an Academy Award. From 1961 to 1963 he was head of drama at *RTÉ. He died in Dublin in 1982, four years after his partner. J.C.E.L.

Éire. Official (Irish) name for Ireland under the 1937 *Constitution. *Éire* is the Irish word for Ireland. In 1937, the Éamon *de Valera government replaced the 1922 Constitution with *Bunreacht na hÉireann* (the Constitution of Ireland), which was endorsed by the people of the *Irish Free State. Ireland was declared to be a sovereign, independent and democratic state and its name was changed from the Irish Free State to Éire, which was used until the *Republic of Ireland Act (passed in December 1948 but came into effect in April 1949) officially declared Ireland a republic. P.E.

Elizabeth I (1533–1603). Queen of *England (1558–1603). Elizabeth I consolidated the *Reformation in England with a new Act of Supremacy (1559) and continued the process of administrative centralisation in Ireland that had begun under *Henry VIII. During her reign, the international religious and political conflicts of the Reformation and counter-Reformation caused political instability and social upheaval in Ireland. The continued *Catholicism of most of the Irish people posed a particular security dilemma for the queen and her ministers. When the pope excommunicated Elizabeth in 1570, the Old English settlers in Ireland, upon whom the crown had partly depended to maintain control, were torn between their continued faith in the Roman church and loyalty to their queen. Increasingly, the Gaelic lords, who had also remained Catholic, looked to Spain, the most aggressive counter-Reformation power, for assistance against English dominance. Under the leadership of Hugh *O'Neill, the second Earl of Tyrone, resistance of the Gaelic lords to English impositions resulted in the *Nine Years War (1593–1603). The Irish *army and a small Spanish invasion force were defeated decisively by the English led by Lord Mountjoy at the *Battle of Kinsale, County *Cork, in 1601. In 1607, four years after Elizabeth's death, O'Neill and several other prominent Gaelic lords left Ireland for exile on the continent (an event popularly known as the *Flight of the Earls) and the old Gaelic social order came to an irrevocable end. F.B.

emigration and immigration. Over the centuries, the Irish have emigrated throughout the world. Although the Irish have departed for various reasons, the bulk of Irish emigration resulted from the effects of British political and economic domination. The English *plantations of Ireland during the sixteenth and seventeenth centuries displaced Irish *Catholics from their lands, sent thousands fleeing into political exile in Europe and forced others into indentured servitude in the West Indies or North America. During the eighteenth century, nearly 300,000 *Scots-Irish Dissenters, most of them descendants of the *Ulster settlers, emigrated to America's frontier to escape their second-class status in Ireland.

Irish emigration from 1815 to 1914 dwarfed all earlier periods. Catholic peasants, deprived of land ownership rights and relying almost exclusively on the potato crop, suffered greatly during periods of economic depression and famine caused by crop failure. In general, the poorest and sickest emigrants, those looking for seasonal work, or seeking to retain closer ties with Ireland, crossed the Irish Sea to Great Britain. Beginning in the early nineteenth century, *Australia was a destination for Irish convicts. Throughout that century, Australia and *New Zealand attracted a core of ambitious and adventurous Irish settlers and the occasional Irish rebel. However, the vast majority of nineteenth-century emigrants, particularly from the Great *Famine years, settled in *America, where they flooded cities from *New York to San Francisco and soon dominated municipal politics and the Catholic church. Many Irish during this period also went to *Canada and *Newfoundland.

After the *First World War, American immigration restrictions and the Great Depression slowed the flow of Irish emigrants to the United States. After Ireland's independence, most twentieth-century Irish emigrants moved to Great Britain to seek jobs. During the 1980s and 1990s, America became a popular choice for educated and skilled young Irish emigrants seeking greater opportunities. The *Whitaker Plan and Ireland's entry into the European Economic Community (EEC, now known as the *EU) sparked an economic recovery that led to many Irish people returning from abroad during the 1970s. The Irish *economy declined again during the 1980s, only to rebound dramatically during the 1990s. Dubbed the 'Celtic Tiger', this vigorous economy caused immigration to overtake emigration and Ireland for the first time ever experienced an influx of immigrants. Some are of Irish descent but a sizable number are Eastern Europeans or Africans seeking asylum, or entering illegally. At the beginning of the twenty-first century, as the Irish economy slowed, racism and intolerance became serious problems. R.D.

Emmet, Robert (1778–1803). Revolutionary and *nationalist icon. Born in *Dublin into a highly educated *Protestant family of *Tipperary and *Kerry origins, Emmet was educated at Trinity College, Dublin, where he displayed great talent for oratory, chemistry and mathematics. Under the influence of his brother, Thomas Addis Emmet, a founding member of the Society of *United Irishmen, the younger Emmet joined the society in December 1796. He was obliged to withdraw from Trinity College in April 1798 when suspected of sedition but remained a committed United Irishmen. Emmet was part of the Dublin leadership throughout the *Rebellion of 1798 and by January 1799 was a figure of national standing. He travelled to Scotland in the summer of 1800 to confer with associates imprisoned at Fort George before illegally going to Hamburg and Paris to petition the French government to invade Ireland. Highly active in Irish radical circles on the continent, Emmet sought support for a French-backed revolution in Ireland in the Irish communities of the Iberian Peninsula, Switzerland, Holland and many parts of *France. He returned to Ireland in October 1802 after he conferred with Napoleon and Talleyrand on the anticipated French renewal of war with Britain. Along with Thomas Russell, William Dowdall and Philip Long, Emmet organised the remnants of the United Irishmen to assist the French in a planned rebellion or invasion. An explosion in an arms depot exposed the plot and forced Emmet to act without the French in Dublin on 23 July 1803. Violence also broke out in *Kildare, *Down, *Antrim and County Dublin. Emmet went into hiding but was eventually apprehended by Town Major Henry Sirr in the Harold's Cross section of Dublin on 20 August. Brought to trial for treason on 19 September, Emmet made the most famous speech from the dock in Irish history and accepted his inevitable capital sentence with a fortitude that won him the praise of his enemies. Emmet was executed in Thomas Street, Dublin, the following day in front of a massive crowd. The circumstances of his death, youth and tragic relationship with Sarah Curran made him a romantic figure to nineteenth-century nationalists who were largely unaware of his life as a revolutionary. R.OD.

England. England held sovereignty over Ireland from the *Anglo-Norman Conquest of 1169–71 until the creation of the *Irish Free State in 1922, with *Northern Ireland still remaining part of the United Kingdom. The long relationship between the two countries has always been a troubled one. Efforts by the English to maintain and expand their political, economic and cultural dominance were met by continual resistance from the Irish. From 1171 until 1541, the English crown ruled over Ireland as a lordship through feudal relationships with the native Gaelic aristocracy. Despite some colonisation by English settlers, who often became more Irish than the Irish themselves, effective control remained limited to the *Pale, an area around *Dublin. During the sixteenth century, the Tudor monarchs attempted to expand administrative control over Ireland and replace the traditional *brehon laws with English common law. As part of this effort, *Henry VIII was formally proclaimed 'King of Ireland' in 1541. The Protestant *Reformation launched by Henry VIII had profound and traumatic consequences, because the majority of the Irish people, including most of the Old English settlers, remained faithful to the Roman *Catholic church. After the defeat of a rebellion (the *Nine Years War, 1593–1603) led by Hugh *O'Neill and the subsequent exile of several of the most prominent Gaelic nobles (the *Flight of the Earls, 1607), the English government stepped up their policy of plantation, whereby Protestant English and Scottish settlers would consolidate England's control over its colony.

When conflict between Charles I and parliament plunged England into civil war during the 1640s, the Irish people rose in widespread rebellion (*Rebellion of 1641) against the new settlers and formed the *Confederation of Kilkenny. After the triumph of parliamentary forces, the campaigns of Oliver *Cromwell in Ireland during 1649–50 brutally repressed both royalist and Catholic Irish. As part of the *Cromwellian Settlement, England confiscated the lands of the remaining Catholic landowners in *Leinster, *Munster and *Ulster, with many of them being forcibly removed to *Connacht. During the 'Glorious Revolution' of 1689–91, *James II, who had been deposed largely because of his uncompromising Catholicism, sought to use Ireland, with its large Catholic population, as a base to recapture the English throne. After the defeat of James' forces at the Battle of the *Boyne (1690) and the final *Jacobite stand at Limerick (1691), the British government allowed the *Protestant ascendancy of *Anglo-Irish landowners to establish political, economic and social control over Ireland by means of extensive *Penal Laws (which discriminated against the Catholic majority) and, through the eighteenth century, to run Ireland largely as it saw fit. The Protestant ascendancy increasingly sought a degree of legislative autonomy for Ireland and, in 1782, achieved a *parliament with substantially increased, though still limited, powers. Radical *republican ideas emerged to challenge British rule during the 1790s with the formation of the *United Irishmen. The failed, though very bloody, *Rebellion of 1798, was followed by the Act of *Union (1800), whereby Ireland became a part of the United Kingdom of Great Britain and Ireland. (*Scotland had been part of the United Kingdom since 1707.) The union provided Ireland with representation in the British House of Commons, though the country continued to be administered by an appointed lord lieutenant and chief secretary. Although all 100 Irish MPs were initially Protestant, the *Catholic Emancipation movement (members of parliament under the leadership of Daniel *O'Connell) achieved in 1829 the right of Catholics to sit in parliament. During the 1840s, O'Connell launched an unsuccessful movement to *repeal the union and establish an Irish parliament (based in Dublin) that would be chosen by a democratic majority of the Irish people. For the more radical *nationalists of the conspiratorial *IRB, the inadequate response of the British government to the Great *Famine of 1845–51 underlined the need for an independent Irish republic, to be achieved by violent means if necessary. After the Famine, Irish *emigration increased to cities in England such as Liverpool, London and Manchester. Despite facing considerable prejudice, the contribution of Irish emigrants to English society and culture has been considerable. Throughout the nineteenth century, the British government administered Ireland with a mixture of coercive and conciliatory policies: it suppressed republican rebellions in 1848 and 1867, as well as sporadic agrarian agitation, while it also funded *education and economic development programmes, established local government institutions and provided incremental measures of land reform. During the 1880s, Charles Stewart *Parnell created a disciplined Irish Party in the House of Commons that sought to achieve *home rule. After the conversion of Liberal leader William Ewart *Gladstone to this viewpoint, his party introduced unsuccessful home rule bills in 1886 and 1893. *The First World War delayed implementation of a third home rule bill, which passed the House of Commons in 1914 despite *unionist opposition. The *Easter Rising of 1916 and the subsequent emergence of *Sinn Féin as the predominant political party in Ireland led to the *Anglo-Irish War of 1919–21. Negotiations resulted in the *Anglo-Irish Treaty (1921), which founded the *Irish Free State. Home rule was, in the end, implemented only in the six northern counties that had opposed it so vehemently. Although the Free State remained initially a dominion within the British *Commonwealth, the treaty effectively ended British sovereignty over the country, except for *Northern Ireland, which still remains part of the United Kingdom. F.B.

English writers in Ireland. The *Anglo-Norman Gerald of Wales (c.1146–1223), also known as Giraldus Cambrensis, is perhaps the first English writer to undertake the task of explaining Ireland and the Irish to the civilised world. Gerald wrote: '[The Irish] are so barbarous that they cannot be said to have any culture'. His two books *The History and Topography of Ireland* (1188) and *The Conquest of Ireland* (1189) remained immensely influential upon successive generations of English settlers and conquerors until the nineteenth century.

While there were a number of English-born writers in Ireland from the thirteenth through the fifteenth century who wrote in English, Norman-French and Latin, it was the reconquest of Ireland in the sixteenth and seventeenth centuries that gave rise to a flowering of both literary and polemical writing by new English settlers and visitors. The most famous, talented and perhaps most influential of these was Edmund *Spenser (1552–99). Spenser's major works, including his *Amoretti* and *Epithalamion* (1595), as well as his great allegorical epic, *The Faerie Queene* (1590 and 1596), written at Kilcolman Castle in County *Cork, are profoundly influenced by Ireland as both a real and a symbolic place. Convinced that Gaelic culture had to be destroyed to establish civility and *Protestantism, Spenser in *A View of the Present State of Ireland* (written 1596, printed 1633) advocates a harsh military campaign for the subjugation of the Irish, 'a people altogether stubborn and untamed'. His prescription for the taming of Ireland's 'licentious barbarism' was carried out very thoroughly by Oliver *Cromwell some 50 years later.

In the eighteenth century, there were many distinguished *Anglo-Irish writers but very few English writers of any great significance in Ireland. However, some of the greatest English writers of the nineteenth century spent time in Ireland. Anthony Trollope (1812–82) lived and worked in *Offaly and *Tipperary from 1841 to 1859 and wrote his first two novels *The Macdermots of Ballycloran* (1847) and *The Kellys and the O'Kellys* (1848) during that period. John Henry (Cardinal) *Newman (1801–90) resided in *Dublin from 1851 to 1858, during which time he delivered the lectures published as *Idea of a University* and became the founding rector of the Catholic University of Ireland. Although Newman found his Irish sojourn difficult, it did not prevent him from making statements such as 'If I were an Irishman I should be (in heart) a rebel'. A fellow Oxford convert and disciple of Newman, Gerard Manley *Hopkins (1844–89) was appointed professor of classics at University College Dublin in 1884, where he wrote his final 'terrible sonnets'.

One of the most important nineteenth-century English writers on Ireland, John Stuart Mill (1806–73), never set foot there. Mill's many writings on Ireland, such as *The Condition of Ireland* (1846–47), *Principles of Political Economy* (1848–71) and *England and Ireland* (1868), were so sympathetic to the plight of Irish tenants that in the early 1850s, as he reports in his autobiography, leaders of 'the popular party in Ireland' (probably the Tenant League) 'offered to bring me into parliament for an Irish County'.

Another eminent Victorian, William Makepeace Thackeray (1811–63) published in 1843 *The Irish Sketch Book*, one of the liveliest of the many travel books written by English visitors to Ireland. This genre goes back to the seventeenth century and includes *An Itinerary* (1617) by Fynes Moryson, who was impressed by the mildness of the winter, the greenness and fertility of the fields and the medicinal properties of the *whiskey. The most influential traveller's account of eighteenth-century Ireland was Arthur Young's *A Tour in Ireland* (1780), which was praised by Maria *Edgeworth and later by *nationalists, and remains an important source of information about both landlords and the peasantry of the time. In the twentieth century the tradition has continued in such works as H. V. Morton's *In Search of Ireland* (1931), V. S. Pritchett's *Dublin, A Portrait* (1967) and Tim Robinson's *Stones of Aran* (1986 and 1995). In contrast to many earlier visitors, modern writers strive to resist stereotypes, whether hostile or sentimental. In the 1940s the English poet John Betjeman wrote: 'The Irish are not mad and spooky and vague and dreamy, as some of them would have us think, but extremely logical. It is we who are the other things'. J.MCD.

Ennis, Séamus (1919–82). *Uilleann piper, singer, raconteur, broadcaster and collector. Born in Finglas, *Dublin, Ennis learned from his father and local musicians to play the pipes. He collected songs for the Folklore Commission in the late 1940s and worked on music programming with *Radio Éireann. In the 1950s, his pioneering BBC radio show *As I Roved Out* played a key part in the traditional *music revival. In later decades, he was best known for exceptional music performances. A 'school' dedicated to his memory is held in North County Dublin each autumn, and a cultural centre named after him was opened in the village of Naul in 2001. F.V.

Enniskillen Bombing (1987). *IRA bombing in *Northern Ireland. On Sunday, 8 November 1987, 11 people – 10 *Protestant civilians participating in a Remembrance Day Ceremony at the town's cenotaph and one member of the *RUC – were killed in a bomb attack in Enniskillen, County *Fermanagh. The attack was carried out by the IRA, who claimed that the bomb had been detonated prematurely 'by mistake'. Revulsion at the atrocity was widespread and it represented a landmark in public reaction against Provisional IRA militarism. For the first time, Gerry *Adams, speaking for Provisional *Sinn Féin, chided the IRA for lack of care in its operations. M.M.

Eriugena, John Scottus (c.810–c.877). Philosopher. Born and monastically educated in Ireland, Eriugena was a Greek scholar and the most productive systematic philosopher between the fifth and eleventh centuries. Between 850 and 877, he taught at the court of Charles the Bald, King of the Franks, where he was advisor to the king. During this time, he also translated Greek patristic and neo-platonist works into Latin, became embroiled in a dispute on predestination and produced (c. 866) his systematic treatise, *De Divisione Naturae*. The book attempted the first complete rational explanation of Christianity. Its unorthodox combination of pagan pantheism with Christian theism led to its papal condemnation in 1225. M.L.

Ervine, David (1954–). *Unionist politician. Chief spokesman for the *Progressive Unionist Party (PUP), an organisation with close links to the *Ulster Volunteer Force, Ervine is a member of Belfast City Council and of the *Northern Ireland assembly. In the 1970s, Ervine served a five-year jail sentence for possession of explosives. After his release in 1980, he entered community politics. When the main *Protestant paramilitary organisations called a cease-fire in 1994, he became a highly visible media figure. Though a firm unionist, Ervine supported the *Good Friday Agreement for securing the connection with Britain. He is critical of *nationalist, particularly *republican, attempts to push the agenda of a united Ireland. However, Ervine shares something of the paramilitary worldview and supported republican inclusion in the political process despite the *IRA's ongoing activity and its stockpile of arms. (Loyalist paramilitaries, of course, behaved likewise.) His rhetoric is generally optimistic, if given to portentous epigrams, though he is quick to explain the history of loyalist violence as reflexive. M.M.

Eucharistic Congress. Largescale Catholic assembly. Ireland's first Eucharistic Congress, convened in *Dublin in 1932, was a huge public celebration of the sacrament of the Eucharist in honour of the fifteen-hundredth anniversary of St *Patrick's conversion of Ireland. More than one million people attended mass in *Phoenix Park, attesting to Roman *Catholicism's pervasive influence on the lives of the Irish people. The congress personified the confidence and prominence of the twentieth-century Irish Catholic church prior to the *Second Vatican Council. M.P.C.

European Union (EU), Ireland's membership. In a 1972 referendum, the Irish electorate voted by a substantial majority to join the European Union (then the European Economic Community made up of six founding members). This was a landmark decision in a process initiated in 1959 by *Taoiseach Seán *Lemass and by Secretary to the Department of Finance T. K. *Whitaker to pursue a policy of *economic expansion, end Ireland's isolationist policies and lessen its economic domination by Great Britain.

Membership of the European Union has helped Ireland achieve significant levels of economic development in the last 30 years. Ireland in 1972 was the poorest of all EU member states. It has benefited substantially from the EU budget, particularly in the form of structural funding in the 1980s and 1990s (e.g., upgrading of roads and other communication networks). Benefiting also from free trade and from the Single European Market, Ireland has been able to diversify its trade with different EU countries. In excess of 60% of Irish exports now go to EU countries. Its inclusion in a unified European market has been an important factor in attracting foreign (mainly US) investment in Ireland. Multinational firms such as Dell and Intel established major European centres in Ireland. As a result, Ireland's Gross Domestic Production (GDP) *per capita* has grown from 60% of the EU average in 1960 to more than 120% in 2000. The introduction of the euro (the single EU currency) in January 2002, in Ireland and in 11 other EU economies, was the culminating point in the process of full economic integration.

Although membership of the European Union has mostly been felt at the economic level, EU-generated law has also been responsible for significant changes in areas such as employment equality (covering equality of treatment for men and *women), safety, *health and welfare at work. Politically, it has made Ireland less Anglocentric, more confident and open to outside influences. Ireland has both helped shape European Union policy and in turn been influenced by it. Because of a landmark Irish Supreme Court decision in the 1980s, it is necessary to have referenda in Ireland in relation to treaties associated with further European integration. While Ireland has endorsed by referenda major European legislation (in 1987 the Single European Act, which finalised the Single European Market; and in 1992, the Maastricht Treaty, which enabled the creation of the single currency, the euro), it narrowly rejected the Nice Treaty in 2001, which provided for EU enlargement to include parts of Eastern Europe. Ireland's veto of further EU expansion reflected a fear of competition and budgetary threats posed by the prospect of new members and, most importantly, of threats to Irish *neutrality and fear of diminished power in a restructured union. The Irish government received a Declaration by the European Union that Ireland's traditional policy of neutrality was not affected by the treaties, before holding a second referendum on the Nice Treaty in October 2002. This was passed by a nearly two to one majority.

While EU leaders aim at making the EU (now consisting of 25 member states) the most competitive economy in the world by 2020, future challenges and issues include the development of a European Security and Defence Policy (ESDP), environmental change, human rights and a wider cooperation with developing countries. Ireland's overall objectives in the EU are primarily to help protect the rights and interests of EU citizens; maintain freedom, security and justice; promote economic prosperity; and act more effectively internationally to promote peace, security and development. B.A.

ev+a. Annual open submission exhibition of art. Held in *Limerick since 1977, the exhibition is adjudicated by a single outside curator. A biennial participation of invited international artists alternates with colloquies on contemporary art and culture. The adjudicators are from around the world: in 2002 the curator was from Thailand and in 2001 from Sudan and the United States (Web site: *www.iol.ie/eva.*) M.C.

External Relations Act (1936). Act limiting the role of the British crown in Ireland's affairs. In December 1936, Éamon *de Valera used the abdication of Edward VIII as an opportunity to pass two pieces of related legislation. The *Constitution (Twenty-seventh Amendment) Act removed all references to the crown from the Irish Constitution, while the Executive Authority (External Relations) Act authorised the king to act on behalf of the *Irish Free State in external matters 'as and when advised by the Executive Council to do so'. P.E.

F

fairs. Originally, the fair was a public assembly in early Ireland. These fairs had a political and ceremonial function, particularly those in *Tara and Uisneach in *pre-Christian Ireland. The more modern fair after cultural Anglicisation bears only a slim resemblance to these medieval assemblies, but their echoes survive. The later fairs are related to markets, but are seasonal rather than regular. From the seventeenth century onward, rich landlords or merchants received royal grants, which allowed them to hold fairs, and charged tolls from the people who wished to sell their wares. Although regulated by English law, fairs retained much of their Irish character. Under the guise of buying and selling, much revelry took place.

Donnybrook Fair in *Dublin was suppressed in 1867 because of its riotous nature. Ballinasloe Fair in County *Galway specialised in the buying and selling of horses. Spancel Hill Fair in County *Clare was held at the end of June and was notorious for its gatherings of *travellers. Ballindine Fair in County *Mayo was typical in that the street trade gave way to a more organised mart in the 1950s. The Two-Mile-Borris Fair in County *Tipperary only dealt in suckling pigs, but was put out of business by the Pigs and Bacon Commission in the 1940s. The highlight of the fair was a pig-guzzling competition, where bachelors had to prove their manhood by eating as many young pigs as they could within three hours. The Oul' Lammas Fair in Ballycastle in County *Antrim takes place at the end of August each year. It is now most famous because of the song (named after the fair), which includes the lines: 'Did you treat your Mary Ann to the Dulse and Yellow man/at the old Lammas Fair in Ballycastle O!' Perhaps the most genuine of all the extant fairs is Puck Fair in Killorglin, County *Kerry, held every year from the 10 to 12 of August. A large beribboned white male goat is hoisted onto a platform and gapes bemused for three days at the revellers below. Pubs remain open all day and all night for three days. Supposedly, this ceremony of the white male goat may have a pagan origin, but it is more likely that the burghers of Kerry saw a good chance of turning some money when the chance came. A much more serious kind of fair was the Hiring Fair in East Donegal, where the children of the poor were hired out as wage slaves to the rich farmers of the lush lowlands of *Ulster and *Scotland, a practice that survived until the 1940s. A.T.

Famine, the Great Irish (1845–49). The Great Famine of the late 1840s was the worst demographic and social catastrophe in modern Irish history. The immediate cause of the calamity was the blighting of the potato crop in Ireland, in three seasons out of four, by a fungal disease – *phytophthora infestans* – to which there was no known antidote at the time. Striking first in late summer 1845, the blight destroyed one-third of that year's potato crop and three-quarters of the 1846 crop; it was less virulent in 1847, but as seed potatoes were scarce, the crop was not plentiful in 'black '47'. The 1848 potato crop was down almost 40% below average yield. By 1849 the blight was abating, but by this time Irish society had experienced a massive trauma of death, disease and *emigration. Diseases, such as typhus, dysentery and 'relapsing fever', were even more lethal than actual starvation. An added menace was an outbreak of cholera in 1849.

Precise statistics on the 'famine' calamity are difficult to establish; but the most reliable figures suggest excess mortality (i.e., famine-related deaths) of about one million, with between a million and one and a half million people estimated as having emigrated in the years 1845 to 1851. While no region or social group entirely escaped the ravages of famine and disease, the heaviest losses were experienced in the west and south-west and among children under five and adults over 65 years of age.

While the immediate cause of the calamity was the potato blight, the circumstances that left such a large portion of the population at risk to the failure of a single root crop were complex and relate to very particular economic, social and political factors operating in early-nineteenth-century Ireland. The population of Ireland had grown rapidly from the final quarter of the eighteenth century. This population growth was heavily rural-based and was encouraged by an expansion of tillage farming (driven by market demand in Britain). A growing population of rural poor in Ireland, living on small-holdings and subsistence potato plots, provided the cheap labour force for an expanding agricultural – especially tillage – sector in Ireland. While the years following the end of the Napoleonic wars in 1815 saw a slowing down in the rate of population growth in Ireland, largely due to an accelerating rise in emigration, by the early 1840s the population of Ireland was probably not far short of eight and a half million people. Some three million of this population were dependent on the potato as the staple component of their diet. This was the broad base of the Irish rural poor. For millions more of the population, the potato was an important, but not a vital, element of their diet and animal feed.

*Agriculture was the mainstay of the Irish *economy. The emergence of an industrial enclave in the north-east of the island was balanced by losses in manufacturing activity and employment in the rest of the country in the pre-Famine decades. Since the Act of *Union of 1800, Ireland was an integral part of the United Kingdom. By 1845, Ireland was fully integrated into a single free-trade economy with Britain, which by this time was the most advanced economy in the world. This very fact – that through the failure of a single root crop, massive death and suffering had been experienced in a 'region' of the most developed economy in the world – fuelled the anger of Irish *nationalists, both at the time and in later generations, prompting their denunciation of British rule in Ireland and their sustained demand for Irish self-government.

The response of the government in the pre-Famine decades to the problem of Irish poverty was to establish in the early 1840s a network of *workhouses – grim institutions for the custodial care of the utterly destitute. By 1845 the total capacity of the workhouse system was 100,000 inmates. At the height of the potato famine two years later, more than three million people would be in receipt of some form of food relief – through soup kitchens or through other channels. The workhouse system, designed to deal with 'normal' Irish poverty, was overwhelmed by the scale of the Famine calamity. During the crisis years of the Irish Famine, government policy changed direction several times: from emergency grain shipments, to public works schemes, to direct food aid and back again to the workhouses and some 'outdoor relief' paid for by taxes on Irish property. The policy was excessively bureaucratic, too rigidly bound by dominant contemporary ideas of *laissez-faire* – inhibiting state intervention in either the labour market (wages) or the commodity market (food prices) – and, in the case of some influential members of the political and administrative elite, pervaded by a notion that this horrific check on reckless Irish population growth was ultimately 'providential'. Private charity – channelled largely through religious bodies of all denominations – was considerable, though not inexhaustible, and only in a small minority of instances was famine relief tainted by an excess of religious zeal in the form of proselytising.

The Famine altered the class structure of rural Ireland, decimating the landless and cottier class. It left many landlords bankrupt and forced the sale of up to 14% of the land of Ireland. It altered the scale of Irish emigration, so that what had been a swelling stream of emigrants became a torrent and a 'culture of emigration' was established which was to be a feature of Irish socio-economic life for more than a century afterward.

The population of Ireland had fallen to 6.6 million by 1851; continuing emigration would cause it to fall to 4.4 million by 1911. The nationalist political movements of Daniel *O'Connell for *Repeal and the *Young Irelanders were overwhelmed by the horror of the Famine. But the sense of grievance at the way in which the government had responded to the crisis was to leave later generations of Irish nationalists – both at home and throughout the Irish diaspora – with a strong determination to do whatever they could, whatever was needed, to achieve an independent Irish state. G.OT.

Farquhar, George (1677/78–1707). Dramatist. Born in *Derry and educated at Trinity College, Dublin, Farquhar abandoned an early acting career after he accidentally stabbed a colleague on stage in Dublin. He moved to London, where his first two plays *Love and a Bottle* (1698) and *The Constant Couple* (1699) were well received at London's Drury Lane Theatre. As an army lieutenant, Farquhar travelled throughout England and Ireland to recruit soldiers. His play *The Recruiting Officer* (1706) draws upon these experiences. His final play, *A Beaux' Stratagem*, was a great success, but he was by then on his deathbed, possibly suffering from tuberculosis. Farquhar's genius lies in creating penetrating satire through playful and witty comedies with elaborate plots and delightfully eccentric characters. He died in poverty. C.D.

Farrell, Micheal (1940–2000). Painter. Born in Kells, County *Meath, Farrell developed from hard-edged *Celtic abstraction to engaged figurative work. He studied art in London, taught in New York and London and represented Ireland at the Paris Biennale in 1967. Along with Gerald *Dillon and other artists, he withdrew his work in protest against treatment of *nationalists from the *Irish Exhibition of Living Art in *Northern Ireland in 1969. Excluded from *ROSC, he moved to Paris and produced work in response to events in Ireland, notably monochromes of the 1974 *Monaghan and Dublin bombings and the 1977 *Madonna Irlanda* or, *The Very First Real Irish Political Picture* (*Hugh Lane Municipal Gallery). His most recent projects dealt with the Great *Famine and *Bloody Sunday. M.C.

Faulkner, Brian (1921–77). Prime minister of *Northern Ireland (1971–72). A *Protestant businessman, Faulkner was educated in *Dublin and elected to the Northern Ireland parliament as a *Unionist in 1949. As minister of home affairs (1959–63), he became known as a hard-liner in his efforts to end the *IRA violent border campaign. He served as commerce minister (1963–69) and minister of development (1969–71). A most capable unionist politician, Faulkner became deputy prime minister in 1966, but many believe that he undermined the leadership of Prime Minister Terence *O'Neill. Faulkner succeeded James *Chichester Clarke as prime minister in March 1971. By then, a war had developed between the IRA and the British army. In August 1971, Faulkner introduced *internment, under which hundreds of suspected IRA members were imprisoned without trial. The events of

*Bloody Sunday (January 1972) and internment intensified *nationalist/*Catholic opposition to the *Stormont government. Faulkner's overtures to Catholic moderates failed and in March 1972, Britain suspended the Northern Ireland government. Faulkner and his ministers resigned. In 1973, he helped negotiate a power-sharing executive for Northern Ireland, and following the agreement of a Council of Ireland at *Sunningdale, he became its head in January 1974. When a *loyalist general strike crippled Northern Ireland in May 1974, Faulkner resigned and the government collapsed, resulting in the re-imposition of direct British rule. He was made Baron Faulkner of Downpatrick in 1976. He died following a horse-riding accident in 1977. M.M.

Fay, Frank (1871–1931). Actor. Fay was born in *Dublin and, like his brother William *Fay, was educated at Belvedere College. He founded the Dublin Dramatic School and Ormonde Dramatic Society in 1898. As drama critic for Arthur *Griffith's *United Irishman* (from 1899 to 1902), he encouraged innovation on the stage. In 1902, he directed W. B. *Yeats' *Cathleen Ni Houlihan* and AE's (George *Russell) *Deirdre*. The Irish National Dramatic Society, which he had founded with his brother in 1902, became the Irish National Theatre Society (the precursor to the *Abbey Theatre) in 1903 when they joined forces with Yeats and Lady *Gregory. Frank Fay was instrumental in building up the company and trained the actors in speech. He played Naisi in AE's *Deirdre* (1902), Cuchulain in Yeats' *On Baile's Strand* (1904) and Seán Keogh in *J. M. Synge's *The Playboy of the Western World* (1907). He left the Abbey in 1908 after a dispute with Yeats, bitterly complaining of the latter's complete ignorance of acting. With his brother Willie, he departed for the United States, but attempted several times unsuccessfully to negotiate a return to the Abbey. After his return to Dublin, the Abbey School of Acting engaged him as an elocution teacher. J.C.E.L.

Fay, William George (1872–1947). Actor and producer. Fay was born in *Dublin and, like his brother Frank *Fay, educated at Belvedere College, which he left at age 16 to join a touring theatre group. He formed his own company in 1897. He produced Alice Milligan's *Red Hugh* in 1901, which W. B. *Yeats saw. Fay coached the players for a production of Douglas *Hyde's *Casadh an t-Súgáin (The Twisting of the Rope)* in 1901 and Yeats' *Cathleen Ni Houlihan* in 1902. In the same year, William, together with his brother Frank, founded the Irish National Dramatic Society, which became the Irish National Theatre Society (precursor to the *Abbey Theatre) in 1903, after they had been joined by Yeats and Lady *Gregory. William Fay acted as stage manager for the company. As an actor, he appeared in Yeats' *The Hour-Glass* (1903). From 1904, he produced plays for the Abbey Theatre, which under his direction developed its distinctive peasant drama. With his brother and the *Allgood sisters, he created the economic acting style of the Abbey players. He married Abbey actress Brigit O'Dempsey. He was successful as Christy Mahon in J. M. *Synge's *The Playboy of the Western World*, Bartley in *Riders to the Sea* and Martin in *The Well of the Saints*. In 1908 he resigned from the Abbey after complaints from its sponsor, Annie Horniman, and disagreements with Yeats. Joined by his brother, he went to the United States, where he produced Irish plays. After 1914, he worked in London and Birmingham. Fay played the part of Father Tom in the 1967 film *Odd Man Out*. With Catherine Carswell, he wrote *The Fays of the Abbey Theatre* (1935). J.C.E.L.

Feiritéar, Piaras (c.1600–53). Poet in the *Irish language. Feiritéar belonged to an aristocratic family in County *Kerry. His love poems were heavily influenced by the *amour* *courtois* traditions of continental Europe and were collected and edited by Patrick Dineen in 1903. Although he was of *Anglo-Norman descent, he sided with the native Irish in the *Rebellion of 1641 and captured Tralee Castle, which he held for 10 years. He was hanged in Killarney, County Kerry, for his part in the rebellion in 1653. B.D.

Fenians. Revolutionary movement of the second half of 1800s. The Fenian Brotherhood was started in the United States in 1858 by John O'Mahony, who, like many *Irish Americans, was disillusioned with parliamentary politics in Ireland and the waning *Young Ireland movement. On St *Patrick's Day 1858, with American backing, James *Stephens founded a secret society in *Dublin. Loosely linked with the American Fenians, the society sought the creation of an independent Irish *republic. It was so secret that, initially, it had no formal title and was known only as the Society or Organisation.

The organisation eventually took the name Fenians from the branch of the movement in the United States. (The word Fenian refers to *Fianna, the legendary army of ancient Ireland led by Finn McCool, which performed feats of superhuman heroism while protecting *pre-Christian *Celtic Ireland from invaders and intruders both human and otherwise.) Later, the organisation became known as the Brotherhood and, eventually, the *Irish Republican Brotherhood (IRB).

Stephens organised the movement in a clearly defined hierarchy with each member's knowledge of the organisation confined to his own particular section. In practice, however, security was not watertight.

The movement spread throughout Ireland drawing opposition from the authorities and the *Catholic church, which supported constitutional *nationalists. Stephens was successful in Ireland but fell out of favour with the powerful American faction. His newspaper venture, the *Irish People*, was seen as a breach of security and a means by which the movement could be infiltrated.

In 1865, the authorities, anticipating a rebellion with American backing, arrested Stephens, Jeremiah *O'Donovan Rossa and other leaders. By 1866, the Fenians were under increased pressure to organise a rebellion. There were many splits among them. Stephens escaped from jail and fled to the United States where he briefly became head of the American organisation. He was hampered, however, by a lack of resources and was replaced by *American Civil War veterans intent on rebellion as soon as possible. The American Fenians launched an unsuccessful attempt to invade *Canada in 1866.

In Ireland, the Fenians mounted a rising on 4–5 March 1867. A combination of bad weather, informers and a highly efficient British army quickly quelled the rebellion. Many of the rebels were arrested and imprisoned. The campaign for an amnesty for Fenian prisoners and outrage at the execution of three Fenians in Manchester, England, known as the *Manchester Martyrs, aroused massive public support and gave new impetus to constitutional politics, which resulted in the *home rule movement. T.C.

Ferguson, Harry George (1884–1960). Engineer. Born in Growell, County *Down, Ferguson joined his brother's cycle-repair business in 1902. He established an engineering business in 1911, importing tractors and later he designed his own tractor. His draught control system (patented in 1925) revolutionised farming methods by improving traction and making light inexpensive machines more effective. Ferguson joined forces with Henry Ford in the 1930s to manufacture his designs in the United States, but the partnership dissolved after a legal battle in 1947. In 1946, with British government backing, production of the Ferguson tractor was launched in Coventry. Ferguson set up his own US plant in 1948, but sold it to Massey-Harris in 1953. S.A.B.

Ferguson, Sir Samuel (1810–86). Poet and antiquarian. Born in *Belfast, Ferguson is best known for his translations from the *Irish, published in such collections as *Lays of the Western Gael* (1865) and *Congal* (1872). These works anticipated the interests of the *Irish Revival and influenced the young W. B. *Yeats. Ferguson was knighted in 1878 for reorganising the Irish public records office, work from which his *Ogham Inscriptions in Ireland, Wales and Scotland* (1887) partly derives. G.OB.

Fermanagh, County. Inland county in the province of *Ulster, one of the six counties of *Northern Ireland. Fermanagh (648 square miles) is one of the least densely populated counties in Ireland, with a population of est. 54,033 (1996). Bordered on the east by *Monaghan and *Tyrone, on the north by *Donegal, on the west by *Leitrim and on the south by *Cavan, Fermanagh derives its name from the Irish *Fir Manach*, meaning the tribe of Manach. The highest mountain in the county is Mount Cuilcagh (2,175 feet) on the border with Cavan. The largest lake in the county is Lough Erne and principal rivers are the Erne, the Finn, the Pettigo and the Omna.

Until their defeat at the Battle of *Kinsale in 1601, the county was dominated by the Maguire family. Following this battle and the *Flight of the Earls, the lands formerly held by the Gaelic chieftains were confiscated and given to settlers from England and Scotland. After the *Government of Ireland Act (1920), Fermanagh came under the control of the *Northern Ireland parliament.

Fermanagh is known for the Belleek pottery company, established in 1857, which produces a world-famous hand-painted porcelain. Tourist attractions include the Marble Arch, a natural limestone bridge near Enniskillen, and the monastic site on Devenish Island, founded by St Molaise in the sixth century. The main industries in the county are *agriculture, fishing, forestry and tourism. The county's capital is Enniskillen, famed as a centre of *Protestant resistance to King *James II in the 1680s. One of the Irish regiments in the British army before and during the *First World War was named the Enniskillen Dragoons, after this town. A.S.

Fianna. Legendary army of ancient Ireland led by Finn McCool. The Fianna (literally 'soldiers') were a band of fighting men whose qualifications were quite rigid: No man could be taken into the Fianna until he knew 12 books of *poetry. He had to be put into a deep hole in the ground up to his middle while nine men would go the length of 10 furrows from him and would cast their spears at him. Or he must run through the forest, pursued by other Fianna, without being harmed, upsetting his hair, or cracking a twig underfoot. The many stories of Finn and the Fianna are known as the Fianna Cycle, though the origin and dates of the various stories are spread from at least the eighth to the eighteenth centuries, in both Ireland and Scotland. J.M.D.

Fianna Fáil. *Political party. Fianna Fáil was formed in 1926 by pragmatists within the anti-*Anglo-Irish Treaty *Sinn Féin party, most notably Éamon *de Valera, who wished to engage in the political life of the new *Irish Free State. Ultimately, Fianna Fáil won the support of the vast majority of the anti-treaty public. The party was led and dominated by the personality of Éamon de Valera from its foundation until he stepped down as leader in 1959. De Valera continued to be a significant figure while serving as president, though he was almost entirely uninvolved in the day-to-day leadership of the party. Party leaders since de Valera include: Seán *Lemass (1959–66), Jack *Lynch (1966–79), Charles *Haughey (1979–92), Albert *Reynolds (1992–94) and Bertie

*Ahern (1997–). Fianna Fáil has been consistently the largest party in the *Dáil since 1932, and has been in government 1932–48, 1951–54, 1957–73, 1977–81, February–November 1982, 1987–94 and 1997–present.

Fianna Fáil was initially organised around a radical *nationalist programme, which sought to overturn those aspects of the Anglo-Irish Treaty that limited Irish sovereignty, and on a wider programme of anti-partitionism and economic development. In particular, Fianna Fáil sought to abolish the *oath of allegiance to the British monarch; secure the return of those ports still occupied by the British navy; abolish the right of judicial appeal to the British Privy Council; end the payment of land annuities to Britain; and end the right of veto on legislation held by the governor general (the British monarch's representative in Ireland). All of these objectives were achieved between 1932 and 1938, but Fianna Fáil's ultimate declaration of sovereignty came with the introduction of a new (the current) *Constitution, which was adopted by referendum in 1937.

Ireland's *neutrality during the Second World War was supported by the other parties, but the policy was associated most strongly with Fianna Fáil, and remains popular with the public, even though its real impact on the conduct of Irish *foreign policy is less clear since the ending of the Cold War.

The popularity of the party's nationalist, neutralist and economic development policies led to 16 uninterrupted years of Fianna Fáil government starting in 1932. This long period was interrupted only briefly from 1948 to 1951 and from 1954 to 1957, after which Fianna Fáil served another 16 years in government until 1973.

In the 1960s, following a long period of economic development based on protectionism and *agriculture, Seán Lemass, de Valera's successor, advocated a shift toward free trade, foreign investment and state planning. In 1972, Ireland joined the European Economic Community (now the *European Union).

Fianna Fáil returned to government in 1977 with its second-highest share of the vote ever. By 1981, the party lost power again, because of the economic crisis caused by the second oil crisis and the heightened tension in *Northern Ireland during the 1981 *hunger strikes. On their return to government in 1987, Fianna Fáil was credited with laying the ground for the rapid improvement in Ireland's economic position by negotiating the first 'social partnership' agreement between government, employers and labour unions. Since then, agreements have been renewed every three years. The party also entered its first ever coalition government (with the *Progressive Democrats) in 1989, followed by an historic Fianna Fáil/*Labour Party government between 1992 and 1994.

Fianna Fáil played a central role in the negotiation of the 1994 *IRA cease-fire and the 1998 *Good Friday Agreement. The public perception that Fianna Fáil could best manage the *peace process gave the party an electoral boost in the 1997 general election. In 2002, Fianna Fáil became the first government party in over 30 years to secure re-election – doing so with an increased popular vote and winning extra seats. In 2004, the party suffered a setback in local and European elections. J.D.

Field, John (1782–1837). Composer and pianist. Born in *Dublin, Field was apprentice to Muzio Clementi, owner of a piano manufacturing firm. He travelled with Clementi throughout Europe demonstrating these instruments. Field settled in St Petersburg in 1803, where he composed most of his mature music. His work reached an artistic peak with the Nocturnes, a romantic genre he created and named and which later inspired the work of Chopin. Field died in Moscow. S.A.B.

Field Day Theatre Company. Drama company. Founded in *Derry in 1980 by playwright

Brian *Friel and actor Stephen *Rea, the Field Day Theatre Company aimed to establish Derry as a theatrical centre and to initiate an intellectual movement that would redefine Irish political and cultural identity. Seamus *Deane, Seamus *Heaney, Tom Paulin and David Hammond joined Friel and Rea on the Board of Directors. The first production, Brian Friel's *Translations* (1980), like much of the theatre's subsequent work, explored questions of community, language and identity. Other plays included Friel's *Three Sisters* (1981) and *The Communication Cord* (1982), Tom Paulin's *The Riot Act* (1984), Derek *Mahon's *High Time* (1984), Tom *Kilroy's *Double Cross* (1986), Stewart Parker's *Pentecost* (1987), Friel's *Making History* (1988), Terry Eagleton's *St Oscar* (1989) and Seamus Heaney's *The Cure at Troy* (1990). Field Day launched a pamphlet series in 1983 with Tom Paulin's *A New Look at the Language Question*, Seamus Deane's *Civilians and Barbarians* and Seamus Heaney's *Open Letter*. In 1988, three radical international critics – Terry Eagleton, Edward Said and Fredric Jameson – contributed to the series. The company's largest undertaking was *The Field Day Anthology of Irish Literature* (3 vols., 1991), edited by Seamus Deane, which presented Irish, English and Latin texts from the earliest times to the present and included introductory essays. Two additional volumes to the anthology were published in 2002. C.D.

fili. Most easily translated as the modern word poet. In early and medieval society the *fili* was part of a learned class whose boundaries are not always clear. A *fili* could write praise poetry or satires for his chief and employer, but he might also be a genealogist, historian, grammarian, diplomat, advisor, storyteller, or professor of knowledge. This sense of the *fili* came to an end with the destruction of the Gaelic aristocratic polity in the early seventeenth century. A.T.

Fine Gael. Political party. Fine Gael was founded in 1933 when *Cumann na nGaedheal (an offshoot of the pro-treaty faction of *Sinn Féin) merged with the National Centre Party and the quasi-fascist *Blueshirt movement. Fine Gael was initially led by the Blueshirt's leader General Eoin *O'Duffy, but W. T. *Cosgrave became the party's leader in 1935. Thereafter the leaders were: W. T. Cosgrave (1935–44), Richard *Mulcahy (1944–59), James *Dillon (1959– 65), Liam *Cosgrave (1965–77), Garret *FitzGerald (1977–87), Alan *Dukes (1987–90), John *Bruton (1990–2001), Michael *Noonan (2001–02) and Enda *Kenny (2002–present). Fine Gael has served in government on six occasions: 1948–51, 1954–57, 1973–77, 1981–Feb. 82, Nov. 1982–87, 1994–97.

The party's initial pro-treaty and conservative image was further tarnished by its relationship with the Blueshirts, and it was not until 1948 that Fine Gael first entered government. Both in 1948 and 1954, Fine Gael's coalition partners rejected party leader Richard Mulcahy as *Taoiseach because of his hardline security role during the *Civil War. John A. *Costello was elected Taoiseach while Mulcahy remained as Fine Gael leader. In the 1960s, Fine Gael made overtures to the *Labour Party through a new, more centrist, policy document, 'The Just Society', in a bid to construct an alternative government to *Fianna Fáil.

Their coalition government, with the Labour Party (1973–77), was highly unpopular as they struggled to respond to the first oil crisis of the 1970s. This government implemented very repressive internal security policies in response to the heightening conflict in *Northern Ireland and was heavily defeated in the general election of 1977.

Under a new leader, Garret FitzGerald, Fine Gael positioned itself as a liberal party on social issues and won record shares of the vote in the elections of 1981 and 1982, reaching almost 40%.

A series of poor election results in the 1980s and 1990s and especially in 2002 led to a growing sense of crisis. After the 2004 elections in which Fianna Fáil lost votes, Fine Gael struggled to remain the principal opposition party. J.D.

Fitzgerald, Barry (1888–1961). Actor, stage name of William Joseph Shields. Born in *Dublin and educated at Merchant Taylor's School, Fitzgerald played with the amateur Kincora Players group and then at the *Abbey Theatre (1916–29). He took up acting full time in 1929. Fitzgerald toured the United States in 1934 and was voted the best character actor of the year by theatre critics for his performance as Fluther in Seán *O'Casey's *The Plough and the Stars*. He played the role of Fluther again in 1936 in John Ford's film version of the play. Fitzgerald moved to Hollywood in 1937 and appeared in many films, winning an Oscar for his performance as Father Fitzgibbon in *Going My Way* (1944). He also played in *The Quiet Man* (1952), directed in Ireland by John Ford, starring John Wayne and Maureen O'Hara. Fitzgerald returned to Ireland in 1959. C.D.

FitzGerald, Garret (1926–). Politician, leader of *Fine Gael and *Taoiseach. Born in *Dublin, FitzGerald worked for the Irish national airline *Aer Lingus and as a lecturer in Political Economy at University College, Dublin, before being elected to the *Dáil in 1969. Member of *Seanad Éireann for Fine Gael from 1965 to 1969, he was a member of the Dáil from 1969 to 1992. He was minister for foreign affairs (1973–77), leader of Fine Gael (1977–87) and Taoiseach (June 1981–March 1982 and November 1982–March 1987). Committed to solving the *Northern Ireland conflict throughout his political career, FitzGerald was involved in the negotiations leading up to the *Sunningdale Agreement. Later, as Taoiseach, he signed the *Anglo-Irish Agreement of 1985, which gave the Irish government a formal role in the administration of Northern Ireland for the first time. FitzGerald attempted to reform social legislation in the 1980s, but his reputation was somewhat damaged by his decision to call an anti-abortion referendum in 1983 and by the rejection of legislation on *divorce in the 1986 referendum. J.D.

Fitzgerald, Lord Edward (1753–98). Chief military strategist of the *United Irishmen. Born in London into Ireland's premier titled family, the Earls of Kildare, Fitzgerald spent much of his childhood in France prior to joining the Sussex militia in 1779 under the command of his uncle, the Duke of Richmond. Following a stint in the Twenty-sixth Regiment, Fitzgerald transferred to the Nineteenth with which he fought and was wounded during the *American Revolution. On returning to Ireland, he became MP for the borough of Athy, *Kildare, due to family patronage. Tiring of political life, Fitzgerald studied at the Military College in Woolwich, England, in 1786–88, until appointed major of the Fifty-fourth Regiment in Canada. He travelled widely on the Canadian frontier, where his adventures included induction into a Native American tribe.

A lifelong Francophile, Fitzgerald went to Paris where he liaised with Thomas *Paine, a connection that led to his dismissal from the army in 1792. Fitzgerald was disaffected with constitutional politics by 1793 because of the perpetuation of anti-Catholic laws and the climate of repression during the war against France. He was a leading member of the Society of *United Irishmen from 1796, and in June of that year he travelled secretly to Paris to encourage the French government to liberate Ireland. His mission, backed by that of Wolfe *Tone, helped bring about the attempted landing of a French army in Bantry, County *Cork, in December 1796. To protest the government's counterinsurgency policy,

Fitzgerald declined to stand for election in July 1797 and became instead the military leader of the revolutionary United Irishmen.

A wanted man from 12 March 1798, with a bounty of £1,000 on his head, Fitzgerald remained the most important dissident until his eventual arrest after a violent struggle in Dublin on 19 May 1798. The loss of Fitzgerald contributed to the failure of the *Rebellion (of 1798), which commenced four days later. He died in Newgate Prison on 4 June from wounds sustained in his capture. R.OD.

fitzGilbert de Clare, Richard. See **Strongbow**.

Flanagan, T. P. (1929–). Painter. Born in County *Fermanagh, Flanagan studied and taught in *Belfast. He is best known for his evocation of place, notably *Donegal *bog land, which inspired Seamus *Heaney's poem *Bogland*. A skilled draughtsman, he produces elegant and highly reflective work. M.C.

Flatley, Michael (1958–). Flute player and *step-dancer. Flatley was born in Chicago to parents from *Sligo and *Carlow. His father was the chair of the Irish Musicians Association in Chicago. Flatley studied dance at the Dennehy School and developed an award-winning Sligo flute style, which he perfected while spending vacations in his father's home in Gurteen, Michael *Coleman's native area. Flatley formed his own dance school and often appeared with the *Chieftains. He emerged as a star soloist in **Riverdance* and later directed his own big-stage dance show, *Lord of the Dance*. F.V.

Fleadh Ceoil. A weekend festival, literally the Irish for 'feast of music'. The name was adopted by *CCÉ (Comhaltas Ceoltóirí Éireann) for its traditional *music gatherings after 1952. It is based on competition where successful players progress from county to provincial level and then to the supreme 'All-Ireland'. The *fleadh* typically occupies all of the amenities of the host town and attracts numerous musicians, singers and dancers who perform casually in pubs and outdoor sessions. F.V.

Flight of the Earls (4 September 1607). A pivotal point in Irish history, when the last remaining of the Old Irish nobility fled the country. Hugh *O'Neill, Earl of Tyrone and his followers – Rory O'Donnell, Earl of Tyrconnell, and Cúconnacht Maguire of Fermanagh – were defeated in the *Nine Years War against Queen *Elizabeth I. To ensure that the old Gaelic system was finally broken in *Ulster, the rebels had to renounce their Gaelic titles and ancestral rights and live by English law. In return, they avoided the confiscation of their land and were pardoned.

However, English officials in Ireland tried to bring these Gaelic lords totally under English rule, if not dispossess them altogether. O'Neill and O'Donnell became involved in a secret plan with the Spanish that would have led to another rebellion. When they were summoned to *Dublin, they believed that the plot had been betrayed. Rather than face a trial and probable execution, they and their followers sailed from Rathmullen, County *Donegal, for Spain, on 4 September 1607. Their ship landed in France from where the exiles travelled to Rome. Although they probably intended to return to Ireland with Spanish troops, the earls remained in Rome until their deaths, surviving on a papal pension. Their flight is usually seen as the end of the Gaelic order in Ireland and paved the way for the *Ulster plantation. T.C.

folklore. The archive of the Irish Folklore Commission, housed at University College, Dublin, is one of the finest of its kind in the world. Because of its great variety and its surviving vibrancy, the traditional lore of Ireland has attracted much scholarly attention. Over two centuries of collecting has produced a harvest of stories, songs, *music, beliefs, customs and other lore.

Among the most colourful genres is the native hero-lore, derived from ancient *mythology and passed down from generation to generation, often in written as well as oral form. Some of these hero-tales were in medieval vellum manuscripts, whereas others circulated in paper manuscripts of recent centuries. The adventures of Fionn Mac Cumhaill (Finn McCool) and his warrior band the *Fianna were especially popular, telling of love, intrigue and great combats with sinister and magical foes. Less diffuse tales are told of other mythical heroes, such as Lugh, *Cúchulainn and the legendary ideal King Cormac Mac Airt. Religious tradition has also been very influential, patron saints of the various localities being held in high regard. These *saints, historical personages from the early centuries of Irish *Christianity – such as Caoimhghin, Ciarán and Mochua – are portrayed in legend as miracle workers who used their sacred power to banish monsters, cure illnesses and provide food for the people in time of need.

Ireland is famous for its fairy-lore. The fairies are known in Irish as the people of the *sí*, a word which originally designated a mound or tumulus, and the Irish fairies can be connected with early beliefs of how the dead live on as a dazzling community in their burial chambers. Thousands of **raths* – ancient earthenwork structures which dot the Irish landscape – are claimed to be inhabited still by the *sí*-people. This lore has been enriched by many migratory legends from the rest of Europe, with themes such as commerce between mortals and fairies, abductions and mystical journeys to fairyland.

Versions of numerous far-flung international folktales have been current in Ireland for many centuries. The simplest of these are fanciful little tales concerning animals, ornate and highly stylised wonder-tales, exemplum-type religious tales, real-life romantic tales and a wide range of short humorous anecdotes. The most popular of all these international tale-plots with Irish storytellers told of how a princess was rescued by a widow's son from the jaws of a fearsome water monster. More native in origin are the legends of historical characters and folk accounts of historical events. There are also stories concerning a variety of ghosts, revenants and spirits. A solitary female spirit, the *bean sí* (banshee), is often heard to announce by her wailing the impending death of a member of an Irish family.

Folklore has been expressed in song, in Irish and English. In Irish, 'Amhrán na mBréag' (The Song of Lies), tells of unbelievable things which the singer claims to have seen, just like a storyteller does in a tall tale. 'The Cow that Ate the Piper' is a song in *Hiberno-English based on a humorous international folktale, according to which a man thinks that a cow has eaten a piper who slept in a byre, when he finds only the boots of the piper there. Songs like 'Seven Drunken Nights' (popularised by Ronnie Drew and the *Dubliners) about a man returning home to find his wife in bed with another man play on another folktale theme.

A wide range of beliefs and practices are concerned with the life cycle, especially birth, marriage and death. In the calendar cycle, four great indigenous festivals mark the beginning of the seasons. Lá Fhéile Bríde (St *Brigid's Feast, 1 February), was originally called *oímelg*, meaning 'lactation'. The May festival Bealtaine meant 'bright fire' and marked the beginning of summer. Lughnasa, called after the god Lugh, was the harvest festival and the November feast *Samhain, when the otherworld was believed to intervene in this world with special vigour, marked the beginning of winter. Originally, the year was divided into two halves, the dark half beginning at Samhain and the bright half at Bealtaine. Much custom centres also on Christmas, Easter, St John's Night and the Feast of St Martin. D.OH.

Ford, Patrick (1837–1913). Journalist. Ford emigrated as a child from *Galway to *Boston, where anti-Irish nativism turned him into a fervent *nationalist. His New York-based *Irish World* became the largest circulating Irish newspaper in the United States. It combined grievances of Irish tenant farmers and Irish American labourers into attacks on agrarian and industrial capitalism. John *Devoy and Michael *Davitt embraced Ford's insistence that a campaign against *landlordism should be a key ingredient of Irish nationalism, thus producing the New Departure strategy. L.J.MC.

foreign policy. Since independence, Ireland's foreign policy has been historically dominated by two issues, *partition and *neutrality. In the 1960s, European integration became a priority for Ireland and in 1973, Ireland joined the *European Union (EU), then known as the European Economic Community (EEC). Successive *Taoisigh and ministers for foreign affairs have sought a solution to the *Northern Ireland conflict, most recently through the 1990s *peace process. In recent years, the *Republic of Ireland's foreign policy has also focused on third-world development and human rights issues. J.D.

Four Courts, the. Landmark of *Dublin's city centre, located at Inns Quay on the River Liffey. Built between 1786 and 1802, the structure is a masterpiece of Georgian *architecture. Part of the building was designed by Thomas Cooley, who died before its completion. The project was then taken over by James *Gandon. The building gets its name from the four courts that traditionally made up the judicial system in Ireland: Chancery, King's Bench, Exchequer and Common Pleas. Today the building continues to be the centre of the Irish court system, housing both the High Court and the Supreme Court.

The Four Courts is best known in Irish history as the site where the first shots of the *Irish Civil War (1922–23) were fired. On the night of 13 April 1922, an *IRA garrison under the command of Rory O'Connor occupied the Four Courts and other prominent buildings in Dublin in defiance of the pro-treaty provisional government headed by Michael *Collins. Following the IRA kidnapping of the provisional government's deputy chief of staff, General J. J. O'Connell, on 26 June 1922, Collins ordered the Four Courts evacuated. O'Connor and his garrison ignored the order and, in the predawn hours of 28 June, using artillery they had borrowed from the British, Collins' troops began shelling the Four Courts. O'Connor and his men surrendered two days later, on 30 June.

In the 11 months of internecine warfare that followed, it is estimated that many more Irish *nationalists killed one another than had been killed by the British during the whole of the struggle for independence between 1916 and 1921. Thus, the Four Courts – rebuilt in the aftermath of the Civil War – can be seen, on the one hand, as a symbol of the rule of law in Ireland and, on the other, as a reminder of the chaos and fratricidal bloodshed out of which modern Ireland was born. T.D.

France. Long-term cultural, economic, religious and political bonds have tied Ireland to France for much of the modern period. After the Treaty of *Limerick (1691), which effectively ended resistance to *William III, thousands of *Catholic soldiers (the *Wild Geese) fled to France, where they formed the first of the famous Irish Brigades. These units served with distinction in the French army through the Napoleonic era. Further Franco-Irish connections emerged in the late seventeenth century with the introduction of the *Penal Laws, which outlawed the *education of Catholics in Ireland. As a result of these acts, wealthy Irish Catholic families were forced to educate their sons on the continent. Throughout the eighteenth century, the vast majority of Irish Catholic clergy (also banned under the penal statutes) received their training in France. Finally, trade, both legal and illicit, had been carried on with France for centuries and Irish Catholic families were prominent in Bordeaux and Nantes. At the end of the eighteenth century, the *United Irishmen's ambassador to France, Wolfe *Tone, successfully forged an alliance with the revolutionary government. This pact nearly bore fruit when a large French fleet led by General Lazare Hoche arrived at Bantry Bay in 1796. An ill wind prevented a successful landing. A small French force under General Humbert landed in Mayo in August 1798 and scored some surprising victories before being overwhelmed at Ballinamuck in Longford. Irish *republicans continued to hope for French assistance until the English victory at Trafalgar effectively ended such dreams. J.P.

Free State. See **Irish Free State.**

French, William Percy (1854–1920). Songwriter and theatre impresario. Born in Cloonyquin, County *Roscommon, French was educated at Trinity College, Dublin, where he graduated in 1881 with a degree in civil engineering. After working as an engineer for the Board of Works for a few years, he tried journalism, painting and eventually songwriting. In 1891, French and Houston Collisson started a touring theatrical company, which was immediately successful. Together, they toured throughout Ireland, England, the United States and Canada, giving concerts of songs for which Percy French wrote the lyrics and Collisson composed the music. They also wrote and produced light operas such as *The Irish Girl*. Percy French, supposedly, wrote a song about every county in Ireland. Some of these songs are so identified with the counties they represent that they have become county anthems. This is especially true of such timeless gems as the 'Mountains of Mourne' (County *Down), 'Come Back Paddy Reilly to Ballyjamesduff' (County *Cavan) and 'Are You Right There Michael' (County *Clare.) J.OM.

French Revolution. The 1789 French Revolution inspired reformers and revolutionaries in Ireland, as in other European countries. In Ireland, the most important reform association formed in the wake of the French Revolution was the Society of *United Irishmen founded in 1791. In the early 1790s, reform clubs in *Belfast and *Dublin celebrated the anniversary of the fall of the Bastille and literature about the revolution circulated widely. Pamphlets argued for and against the revolution. Thomas *Paine's *Rights of Man* was published in seven Irish editions between 1791 and 1792. The *Northern Star* newspaper, published in Belfast, closely followed events in *France and supported the execution of the king. The revolution radicalised political reformers, who began to oppose monarchy and adopt ideas such as universal male suffrage.

In the mid-1790s, the United Irishmen formed reading societies and clubs in towns and villages. The French influence became entwined with the older *Presbyterian republican tradition and with widespread *Catholic discontent. In small towns and villages, the Catholic secret society, the *Defenders, viewed the French cause in traditional terms, as Catholic and anti-English. French symbolism was adopted in places: the 'tree of liberty' was planted and pipers played the Marseillaise.

The United Irishmen corresponded with the Jacobin Society in Paris and reported its proceedings in their publications. From 1793, the French leadership considered Ireland as a base for destabilising England. Agents from France were arrested and tried in Ireland in

1794–95. In May 1794, the United Irishmen were suppressed and, in 1795, they decided to seek French assistance in a rebellion. Wolfe *Tone arrived in France in February 1796. In December, Tone accompanied General Lazare Hoche's 43-ship fleet to Bantry Bay, County *Cork, but storms prevented a landing. During the *Rebellion of 1798 a much smaller French expedition arrived at Killala, County *Mayo, in August, but was soon defeated.

After 1798, Ireland became less and less significant to French military plans. Remnants of the republican movement still sought French help during Napoleon's reign and individual United Irishmen remained in France until 1815. The revolution left a lasting legacy in Ireland: popular politics would contain a strong element of democratic republicanism, reinforced by the French Revolution of 1848. P.D.

Friel, Brian (1929–). Playwright. Born in County *Tyrone, Friel was educated at *Maynooth College, Kildare, and St Joseph's College, Belfast. His early writings include short stories published in the *New Yorker* and radio plays broadcast by the BBC, among them *A Sort of Freedom* (1958) and *A Doubtful Paradise* (1962). An acute awareness of place characterises both the stories in *The Saucer of Larks* (1962) and his plays. The *Abbey Theatre staged *The Enemy Within* in 1962. The play focuses on the inner struggle of St Columba (*Colm Cille), torn between his patriotic love for his native Ireland and his religious calling on the island of Iona. Friel spent part of 1963 in Minneapolis learning aspects of stagecraft from Tyrone *Guthrie. His next play, *Philadelphia, Here I Come!* (1964), brought him international acclaim and enjoyed a successful run on Broadway. Its protagonist, Gar O'Donnell, is torn between his unexpressed love for his emotionally taciturn father, who runs a shop in the small *Donegal town of Ballybeg (Friel's 'anytown'), and the unknown attractions of Philadelphia. Friel represents Gar's

Brian Friel

divided psyche by portraying him as two characters, 'public' and 'private'. These early plays introduce the conflicting forces of home and exile that are pervasive in all of Friel's work. Recurring themes in his plays are the pain of loss and the inevitable necessity of change, the sacrifice, anxiety and rare triumph associated with artistic creation, the inadequacy of language and the roots of theatre in sacred ritual.

The themes of love and disillusionment link the plays *The Loves of Cass Maguire* (1966), *Lovers* (1967) and *Crystal and Fox* (1968), while *The Mundy Scheme* (1969) bitterly lampoons political life in the Irish *Republic. *The Freedom of the City* (1973), an unusually direct reaction to political violence in *Northern Ireland, suggests that there is no single perspective on truth. *Faith Healer* (1979) consists of four contradictory monologues that leave the audience to reflect on the nature of truth and mystery.

In 1980, along with actor Stephen *Rea and others, Friel founded the *Field Day Theatre Company, established in *Derry to create a 'fifth province of the imagination' that would transcend traditional sectarian and political divisions. Field Day staged plays by Tom *Kilroy, Derek *Mahon, Tom Paulin and Friel himself. Its first production was his *Translations* (1980), set in Donegal in 1833, at a pivotal moment in Irish history as the British mapped and translated Ireland's placenames into English. *Making History* (1988), whose main protagonist is Hugh *O'Neill, scrutinises the process of inclusion, exclusion and manipulation by which history is written. *Dancing at Lughnasa* (1990), released as a film in 1998, explores the atavistic forces underlying Irish society. More recent plays include *Wonderful Tennessee* (1993), *Molly Sweeney* (1995), *Give Me Your Answer, Do!* (1997), a translation of Chekhov's *Uncle Vanya* (1998) and *Performances* (2003), which continue to examine the same thematic issues from different angles. Friel's plays explore in poetic language the ways individuals and communities shape and are shaped by history, language and myth. M.S.T., J.C.E.L.

furniture. Irish furniture – like Irish art, decorative arts and architecture – was shaped by the island's ancient, *Celtic tradition, as well as its close proximity to Britain and the continent. Carvers and cabinetmakers, drawing from these resources, created some of the finest furniture in Europe that graced Ireland's grandest town houses, *castles, country houses, manors and farmhouses. The vernacular furniture of the countryside, where a majority of Ireland's population lived, was simple and functional, but incorporated elements of 'high style' design and displayed some of the finest Celtic carvings. Unfortunately, little if any Irish 'country' furniture has survived from the period before the *Famine of the 1840s because people burned it for warmth.

Prior to the seventh century AD, there is some material evidence of simple wooden beds, benches and stools. High *crosses and *manuscript illuminations between the eighth and tenth centuries, such as the *Book of *Kells*, depict a variety of forms of varying luxury. These illustrations show that wood furniture reached high levels of artistry. It was often carved with geometric forms, spiral ornament, bands of interlacing scrolls and animal decoration – features later defined as distinct characteristics of Irish furniture. Often the wood is painted or gilded, sometimes upholstered with leather or fabric, and seats are generally concave. Late-twentieth-century excavations in *Dublin show quality woodworking from the eleventh century onward. There is a paucity of furniture dating from the sixteenth and seventeenth centuries, a devastating period of war and strife. However, records indicate a variety of substantial, often elaborate high-style pieces: tables and cabinets; richly upholstered and embroidered chairs and stools of various types and sizes, some gilded, lacquered, or cushioned; and canopied bedsteads with fine curtains or hangings. Increasingly during this period, both furniture and styles were being imported from the continent and, especially, from England, adding to the complex task of identifying pieces as 'Irish'.

The eighteenth century brought, first, peace and then prosperity to Ireland and an unrivalled flowering of the decorative arts. More pieces of high-style furniture have survived from this period onward. While the patrons of the arts were generally the rich *Protestant minority who looked to Britain for furniture examples, the artists and craftsmen were almost always native Irish.

In the early 1700s, furniture of oak and walnut, as well as lacquered pieces, reflected the classical, baroque taste of Britain and the continent. By mid-century, the Irish furniture industry was thriving. As trade with the West Indies grew, mahogany became the wood of choice. At this time, the sturdy and robust characteristics that are generally associated with Irish furniture became manifest. The architectural strength of the baroque and the sensual extravagance of the rococo were seen in the central figures of aprons on tables, chairs, stools and chests: a lion head, flowers, a shell, or a grotesque mask, festooned with carvings of foliage and birds. Table and chair legs rested on paws or claw-and-ball feet. A bulge directly above the foot, generally covered with carved hair or foliage, was a particularly Irish characteristic.

By the end of the eighteenth century, the more delicate features of the neoclassical style had reached Ireland, curtailing the general robustness of Irish design. Although nineteenth-century Irish furniture continued to reflect revival styles and tastes coming from England, such as gothic and rococo, a growing interest in an Irish national identity, especially in antiquities and cultural achievements, began to emerge. In furniture, a neo-Celtic style reflected motifs from Irish history.

Starting in the 1840s, chairs, tables, settles and cabinets – typical Irish country furniture forms – were carved, painted, or engraved with interlaced, Celtic patterns reflecting earlier Irish craftsmanship, similar to the more elaborate, high-style examples. Although country furniture made by local craftsmen or journeymen carpenters tended to be humble and utilitarian, in many instances it was painted, sometimes elaborately, to add visual interest and hide inferior wood or joinery. It tended to be made of locally grown pine – a general term used for various softwoods such as Scots fir, larch, Norway spruce, or yellow pine. Often furniture was made with multiple uses, like the settle bed – a particularly Irish form that combines the uses of a bed and a bench.

Bog wood – ancient oak, yew and fir trees that had lain buried and preserved in the *bogs – became widely used due to its strength and beauty. Elaborately carved suites of furniture portrayed ambitious themes from Irish history (legends, monarchs and animals) and emblems (harps, wolfhounds and shamrocks). Around the 1850s, a distinctive style of inlaid furniture, using motifs of historic buildings, ruins and national symbols such as harps, roses, thistles and shamrocks, emerged in the region of Killarney.

As mass production and, in reaction to it, the Arts and Crafts movement began to take root, first in Britain, then in Ireland, this interest in the Irish decorative history blossomed. Design from the early *Christian period was heralded as the embodiment of Irish style and character.

Today, Irish furniture – both the vernacular furniture and its high-style counterparts – is recognised as some of the finest produced in Europe. D.S.

G

Gael Linn. A major *Irish language promotion organisation. Founded by Dónal Ó Móráin (1923–2001) in 1953, Gael Linn financed filmmaking (*Mise Éire* and *Saoirse*, with soundtracks by Seán *Ó Riada), Irish-language newsreels and children's *Gaeltacht scholarships. In 1957, it began recording traditional artists and organised cabaret Irish music in tourist venues. Its numerous recordings promoted traditional *music in Ireland. F.V.

Gaelic Athletic Association (GAA). The main sporting organisation in Ireland dedicated to the cultivation and development of the native Irish games of *hurling and *Gaelic football. Although these games existed in some form or another for hundreds of years, it was the GAA which formalised and codified the sports from its foundation in 1884. Michael Cusack (1847–1906) was the most important figure in the creation of the organisation. Drawing upon the newfound enthusiasm for spectator sports, the *Irish Revival movement, local patriotism and the exclusivist nature of other sporting organisations, the GAA flourished in its early years because of its association with the *nationalist politics of the *IRB. Within a few years the organisation was rooted in every part of the country, so that an All-Ireland Championship in hurling and football was held as early as 1887.

Hurling, a game played with sticks and a small hard light ball known as a *sliotar*, is often said to be the fastest field game in the world. Gaelic football grew out of the rough-and-tumble inter-parish brawls of the nineteenth century and is close in appearance and style to Australian Rules football. The club is the smallest unit of the association, very often based on the parish, and the best players in these clubs are chosen to represent their counties, which vie for the title of All-Ireland champions. The All-Ireland finals are seen as the most important sporting occasions in the country, dwarfing all other events, even international *rugby and *soccer games, in terms of attendance and interest. These finals will draw close to 80,000 people to *Croke Park (Dublin), which is the main stadium and the headquarters of the association. Part of the GAA's strength derives from the fact that it is an all-Ireland thirty-two-county organisation and does not recognise the border. Although for cultural and political reasons the games are played almost entirely by nationalists in the six counties of *Northern Ireland, the players are people of all social classes throughout most of the country. Gaelic football is more widespread, whereas hurling is more geographically confined. The games have developed strong local identities and regional esteem is often judged on the success of the county team. By 2004, *Cork was the most successful team in the hurling championships and *Kerry in football.

The GAA has often been involved in political controversy because of its strong stand on national issues. For many years players were not allowed to play 'foreign games', a code for rugby and soccer, and until recently members of the *RUC and the British army were not permitted into the organisation. This had as much to do with tradition as it had with harassment of players in Northern Ireland and the occupation by the British army of some local playing fields. The games have also been very popular with Irish emigrants in the United States and in Britain, and both New York and London have entered teams in the All-Ireland Championship. Ireland plays Australia from time to time in a game of compromise football rules and a compromise hurling game is often played with teams of Scottish shinty (a form of hurling particular to Scotland). A.T.

Gaelic football. A traditional form of football unique to Ireland, based upon catching and kicking and played by two teams of 15 players each. The rules of the modern form of the game (a version of which had been played for a few hundred years) were formulated by the *Gaelic Athletic Association (GAA) in 1884. Under the auspices of the GAA, Gaelic football is now played in almost every parish in the country with competitions being organised at school, college, club, county and provincial level. The pinnacle of the annual calendar is the Sam Maguire Cup presented to the winners of the All-Ireland final – an inter-county (thirty-two-county) football championship. The All-Ireland final is played in Dublin's *Croke Park, the GAA's national stadium, on the fourth Sunday of September each year. A capacity crowd of 79,500 attends the final and millions all over the world watch live television coverage.

In recent years, the sport has formed an alliance with a sister code, Australian Rules, resulting in an annual compromise rules series, which alternates between venues in Ireland and Australia. Although Gaelic football is still an amateur sport, this may change in future years as it strives to compete with other international field games. A game of Gaelic football lasts 60 minutes at club level and 70 minutes at senior inter-county level.

In 2004 County *Kerry held the record for the All-Ireland title, having won it 31 times. The record for consecutive victories is also held by Kerry, who have won it four times in a row between 1929 and 1932 and again between 1978 and 1981, together with *Wexford, who were successful from 1915 to 1918. Perhaps one of the most famous players was the legendary Mick O'Connell who won four All-Ireland medals with Kerry over three decades (1959, 1962, 1969 and 1970) and led them to victory in 1959. Other famous players include: Peter Canavan (Tyrone), John Joe O'Reilly (Cavan), Paidí Ó Sé (Kerry) and Mattie McDonagh (Galway). B.D.

Gaelic League (Conradh na Gaedhilge). Organisation dedicated to preserving the *Irish language, founded in *Dublin in 1893. The decline of the language had reached calamitous proportions by the end of the nineteenth century. The number of Irish speakers had fallen from 320,000 in 1851 to 38,000 in 1891. Language enthusiasts insisted that radical remedial steps were required to halt the decline. Eoin *MacNeill called a meeting in Dublin on 31 July 1893, at which the new organisation Conradh na Gaedhilge was set up. Douglas *Hyde was inaugurated as its first president.

The league set up language classes and had established 550 branches at home and abroad by 1908. A network of peripatetic teachers (or *timirí*) brought the language to every corner of the island and an annual Gaelic festival (An tOireachtas) was established in 1897. A weekly newspaper, **An Claidheamh Soluis*, was first published in 1899 and Patrick *Pearse was among its early editors. Though the league still exists today, its membership and influence has waned considerably. B.D.

Gaelic Revival. See **Irish Language Revival.**

Gaeltacht. A term used to describe those districts that are largely *Irish speaking. These areas are mainly in *Donegal, *Galway and *Kerry, but there are smaller pockets in counties *Cork, *Waterford, *Mayo and *Meath. Originally all of Ireland was a Gaeltacht, but the language began to recede from the late seventeenth century, initially from the towns and later from the rest of the country. The word *Gaeltacht* is a borrowing from Scottish Gaelic, originally meaning the Highlands and the people who lived there. When it was borrowed into Irish in the eighteenth century, it referred more to the people – the 'Irishry' – than to the district. It has been used to denote an area only since the late nineteenth century.

The Gaeltacht regions do not have any separate administrative arrangements, but there is a state board Údarás na Gaeltachta (the Gaeltacht Authority) that has some economic planning and development functions. There is a radio station Raidió na Gaeltachta, which serves as a unifying force between the scattered areas and also as a national Irish-language service. In the past, the Gaeltacht, poor and marginalised, suffered from heavy *emigration. Today, prosperity and easy mobility pose different problems. Parts of the Galway Gaeltacht have been swallowed up by the urbanisation of Galway City and have become extended suburbs. The romantic attraction of the west of Ireland has brought 'white settlers' who care little for the native language. On the other hand, the Gaeltacht is more aware of its identity as a separate kind of place than ever before, and the lure of cultural tourism with its attendant monies has managed to slow down the inevitable conquest of English. Some of the very best *literature in Irish in the twentieth century has come from the Gaeltacht. A.T.

Gaiety Theatre. From its opening in 1871, the Gaiety has been dedicated to presenting both musical and dramatic entertainment, including *opera and ballet. The theatre was conceived by John and Michael Gunn, whose family owned a music business in *Dublin's Grafton Street. The building, on King Street South, was designed by noted architect C. J. Phipps. Its interior was altered several times, in 1883, 1955 and 1984. Under the management of the Louis Elliman group (1936–65), the Gaiety became known for its home-produced Christmas pantomimes, starring Jimmy *O'Dea and Maureen Potter, and established annual seasons of the Dublin Grand Opera Society. Hilton *Edwards and Micheál *MacLiammóir began presenting plays at the theatre during the Second World War and had great success with MacLiammóir's own *Ill Met by Moonlight* (1946) and *The Importance of Being Oscar* (1960).

Other important dramatic productions at the Gaiety include Douglas *Hyde's *Casadh an t-Súgáin (The Twisting of the Rope)* (1901) and Seán *O'Casey's *The Bishop's Bonfire* (1955). From 1965 to 1984 the theatre was managed by Eamon Andrews studios. In the 1950s and 1960s, the Gaiety was the venue for Sunday night concerts with the *Radio Éireann Symphony Orchestra. In 1971 the theatre hosted the Eurovision Song Contest. Once referred to by MacLiammóir as 'a place of breadth and dignity', the Gaiety has staged a wide variety of entertainments, ranging from *King Lear* to *The Vagina Monologues* and from Phil Coulter to *Carmen*. J.C.E.L.

Galway, County. Ireland's second largest county, in the province of *Connacht. Extending from the Atlantic to the River *Shannon (area of 2,374 square miles), the county has a population of 208,826 (2002 census). Galway City, the county capital, straddles the divide between the barren Irish-speaking *Connemara to the west and the fertile farmland of the east. It is a vibrant, cosmopolitan city, the site of University College, Galway, a constituent college of the National University of Ireland. It is also one of Ireland's most artistic cities, with a thriving traditional *music scene and two successful *theatre companies, Macnas and the Druid Theatre. The three-week Galway Arts Festival draws large crowds in July as do the Galway Races, which take place during the first week of August. Many information technology multinationals have set up bases in the city. Traditional industries like fishing and tourism are also flourishing.

Galway City developed originally as a crossing point on the River Corrib and was ruled by 14 *Anglo-Norman families. It is still known today as 'The City of the Tribes'. During the Middle Ages, the city developed a booming trade with continental Europe and with Spain in particular. The popular city landmarks the Spanish Arch and Lynch's Castle date from this period.

A small fishing village, the Claddagh, existed long before the city proper and had its own laws, customs and chieftains. It is from this village that the famous Claddagh ring originates.

Beyond the Claddagh lies the popular seaside resort of Salthill, with fine Edwardian buildings blending uneasily with nightclubs and amusement arcades. Walking Salthill's famous promenade has been a popular form of recreation for city dwellers for many years. Galway City is also the gateway to scenic areas like *Connemara, the *Aran Islands and the Maamturk and Twelve Bens mountain ranges which lie to the west of the city. Connemara National Park covers almost eight square miles of *bogland, heath and mountains, including much of the Twelve Bens. The granite-faced Diamond Hill is perhaps the main attraction in the park. Much of Connemara has been designated as special areas of conservation (SACs) and some traditional farming practices like harvesting turf are perceived to be under threat.

The county's most famous building is the neogothic Kylemore Abbey, which was built in the 1860s and is now the monastic home of the Irish Benedictine *nuns. Galway is also the home of Ireland's only native breed of horse, the Connemara pony. Small, hardy animals, their pedigree is believed to be a cross between *Celtic horses of old and stallions that came ashore from the sunken *Spanish Armada. Originally found wild in the mountains of Connemara, they are now bred all over the world and are used particularly as riding ponies for children. Connemara marble is a unique green-coloured marble used mostly for jewellery and ornate surfaces such as altars and fireplaces. It is now practically extinct. In 1919, in the first transatlantic nonstop flight starting from Newfoundland, aviators John William Alcock and Arthur Whitten Brown landed near Clifden, in the western part of the county.

Lough Corrib, world famous for angling, is situated in mid-county. The east shore of the lake is less dramatic with vast swathes of bogland and thriving market towns like Ballinasloe and Tuam. B.D.

Galway, James (1939–). Musician. An internationally renowned flautist, Galway was born in *Belfast and educated at the Royal College of Music and the Guildhall School of Music in London and the Conservatoire National Supérieur de Musique in Paris. Galway was principal flute with the London Symphony Orchestra in 1966 and with the Royal Philharmonic Orchestra, 1967–69. He was principal solo flute with the Berlin Philharmonic Orchestra, 1969–75, where he played under Herbert von Karajan. He has pursued a solo career since and has made numerous recordings. Galway was Principal Guest Conductor of the London Mozart Players, 1999–2000. He has played at the White House and at Buckingham Palace. *James Galway: An Autobiography* was published in 1978 and the television series *James Galway's Music in Time* was aired in 1983. C.D.

Gambon, Michael (1940–). Actor. Born in *Dublin, the son of an army officer and a jeweller's daughter, Gambon moved with his family to London when he was six. His first professional acting roles were with the *Gate Theatre, Dublin, in 1962, before he joined Laurence Olivier's National Theatre the following year. He went on to appear in a number of leading roles in plays written by Alan Ayckbourn, in particular. Gambon has regularly appeared at the Royal National Theatre and the Royal Shakespeare Company in roles including King Lear, Othello, Mark Anthony and Volpone. He was critically acclaimed for his central performance in Dennis Potter's groundbreaking TV drama, *The Singing Detective* (1986). Notable film roles include Albert Spica in *The Cook, The Thief, His Wife and Her Lover* (1989). In the 1990s, he played roles in several Irish films, including the Dublin-set comedy *A Man of No Importance* (1994); *Nothing Personal* (1995), the study of Belfast *loyalist paramilitaries; and film versions of Brian *Friel's *Dancing at Lughnasa* (1998) and Elizabeth *Bowen's *The Last September* (1999). He was knighted in 1997. H.L.

Gandon, James (1743–1823). English architect who designed much of eighteenth-century *Dublin. Born in London, Gandon was a student of the renowned architect Sir William Chambers. He established his own practice in London in 1765. Gandon won the first Gold Medal for architecture at the Royal Academy in 1769 and exhibited drawings there in 1774–80. After moving to Dublin in 1781, Gandon became the leading exponent of the neoclassical style in Ireland. He designed many of Dublin's most important public works, including the Custom House (1781–91), the east and west porticos of the *Parliament House (1785–97), the *Four Courts (1786–1802), Carlisle (now O'Connell) Bridge (1794–98) and the King's Inns (1795–1808). Gandon was an original member of the *Royal Irish Academy and retired in 1808. S.A.B.

Gárda Síochána (Guardians of the Peace). Police force of the Irish *Republic. On 22 February 1922, the Civic Guard replaced the *RIC as the national *police service of the *Irish Free State. At the same time, the Dublin Metropolitan Police (DMP), which had been established in 1836 as an unarmed, apolitical force for the capital, continued to function independently. The Civic Guard was renamed Gárda Síochána na hÉireann in August 1923 and in 1925, it merged with the DMP. Michael Staines, the first gárda commissioner, rejected suggestions that the force would be armed, arguing that the gárda síochána would 'succeed not by force of arms or numbers, but on their moral authority as servants of the people'.

The murder of a gárda was regarded as a capital offence until 1990, when a Criminal Justice Act abolished capital punishment from the statute books. A referendum in 2001 made capital punishment unconstitutional. Murder of a member of the force now carries a 40-year prison sentence.

Today, the garda síochána is responsible for state security and for the enforcement of all criminal and traffic legislation. Besides these domestic duties, the force, along with the Irish *army, also performs peacekeeping duties overseas as part of Ireland's commitment to the *United Nations. The country is divided into six policing regions and as of May 2004 there are 11,900 gardaí and 1,800 civilian support staff. General management and control is the responsibility of the gárda commissioner, who is appointed by the government and is responsible to the minister for justice. P.E.

Gate Theatre. The Gate Theatre Company was founded in *Dublin in 1928 by Micheál *MacLiammóir and Hilton *Edwards. In 1930, after two seasons at the *Peacock Theatre, the company moved to its own premises, the converted assembly rooms of the Rotunda Buildings on Parnell Square East. From its beginnings, the Gate was dedicated to a modern, international repertoire, thus complementing the *Abbey Theatre's focus on Irish plays.

The Gate quickly became known for the high standard of its productions, which included works by Ibsen, Chekhov and O'Neill, as well as Irish playwrights like Oscar *Wilde, Bernard *Shaw, Denis Johnston and Mary Manning. Orson Welles and James Mason began their acting careers at the Gate Theatre. For many years after 1936, Lord Longford's theatre company, Longford Productions, shared the theatre with the original Edwards and MacLiammóir company, which increasingly toured abroad. In the final years of the founders' directorship, the theatre went into something of a decline, but it revived with the appointment of their successor, Michael Colgan, in 1983. A new translation of Ibsen's *Peer Gynt* (which was the first play produced by the Gate Company in 1928) was commissioned from Frank *McGuinness for the theatre's sixtieth anniversary in 1988. The 1991 Samuel *Beckett Festival, which presented all 19 stage plays, met with great acclaim and toured to New York's Lincoln Center and London's Barbican. Gate premieres of Irish plays include Brian *Friel's *Molly Sweeney* (1994) and Conor *McPherson's *Dublin Carol* (2000) and *Port Authority* (2001). J.C.E.L.

Gavin, Frankie (1956–). Fiddle and flute player. Born in County *Galway, Gavin is considered one of the greatest instrumentalists in traditional *music. His band *De Danann (formed 1974) has been consistently successful and innovative. Gavin's performances with such stars as Stephan Grappelli have gained him an international reputation. F.V.

Geldof, Bob (1954–). Singer. Born in Dún Laoghaire, County *Dublin, Geldof was the founding member of the new-wave band the Boomtown Rats in 1975. Moved by the plight of starving Ethiopians in 1984, Geldof assembled a gallery of stars to record 'Do They Know It's Christmas?' This evolved into Live Aid, two massive concerts that were staged simultaneously in London and Philadelphia. The concerts netted more than £50 million for famine relief, and Geldof received an honorary knighthood for his humanitarian work from Queen Elizabeth II. B.D.

George I (1660–1727). King of Great Britain and Ireland (1714–27), elector of Hanover (1698–1727). By securing the *Protestant succession and establishing a 'Whig ascendancy' in Great Britain and Ireland, the accession of George I was a setback for the *Catholic gentry in Ireland. His ministry's appointment of Englishmen to key positions in Ireland also alienated the Protestant ascendancy, thus provoking constitutional disputes between the Irish and British parliaments in 1719–20 and 1723–25. An experienced soldier, George I oversaw the defeat of the *Jacobites in northern Britain in 1715, but he remained unpopular in England due to his brusque manner and his indulgence of foreign favourites. S.A.B.

George II (1683–1760). King of Great Britain and Ireland (1727–60). George II was the last British monarch to lead troops into battle (at Dettingen in 1743) and his army suppressed a second *Jacobite rebellion in 1745–46. His government in Ireland extended the *Penal Laws in 1728, when Irish *Catholics were deprived of the right to vote in parliamentary elections. However, during the final years of George II's reign, the Catholic gentry re-emerged as a force in Irish political life. S.A.B.

George III (1738–1820). King of Great Britain and Ireland. His long and tumultuous reign (1760–1820) witnessed the loss of the 13 North American colonies, the *French Revolution, Napoleon and extended periods of personal mental collapse. In Ireland, pivotal events included Henry *Grattan's successful campaigns for economic and legislative independence in 1779 and 1782 respectively, as well as the repeal of many of the anti-Catholic *Penal Laws. Yet, the failure to grant complete *Catholic Emancipation, to which the king was obstinately opposed, coupled with the recall of the reforming Lord Lieutenant Fitzwilliam, helped trigger the *Rebellion of 1798. In turn, this latter episode resulted in the Act of *Union (1800), which abolished the Irish *parliament and established the United Kingdom of Great Britain and Ireland. J.P.

Giant's Causeway. A series of spectacular polygonal columns composed of basalt found on the north coast of County *Antrim. Geologists believe that they were formed when an ancient lava flow cooled and solidified approximately 60 million years ago during the early Tertiary period. Its name stems from a local legend that the columns were built by giants as part of a roadway to *Scotland. P.E.

Gladstone, William Ewart (1809–98). British Liberal politician and four times prime minister (1868–74, 1880–85, 1886 and 1892–94). Generally considered the most important British statesman of the second half of the nineteenth century, Gladstone had a decisive impact on Irish history. His first term as prime minister was largely focused on Irish affairs, as he declared that his primary mission was to 'pacify Ireland'. Two important pieces of Irish legislation were passed during the term: the 1869 Disestablishment of the *Church of Ireland Act and the 1870 *Land Act. In his second term, the 1881 *Land Act became law at the height of the *Land War (1879–82). Due to his progressive Irish policies, by the mid-1880s, Gladstone's Liberal Party generally received the support of *Parnell's *Irish Parliamentary Party. In 1885, Parnell showed the Liberals that they could not take that support for granted by using his party's decisive vote in parliament to force Gladstone's government from office, allowing the Conservatives under Lord Salisbury to take over. Parnell's strategy paid off in December 1885, when Gladstone publicly announced that he was prepared to support *home rule for Ireland. Parnell's party once again threw its support to the Liberals and Gladstone became prime minister for the third time in 1886. Gladstone's first home rule bill (1886) proposed a parliament in Dublin to legislate domestic matters only. The bill was defeated in the Commons and Gladstone resigned as prime minister. Gladstone's condemnation of Parnell following the *O'Shea divorce scandal in 1889 proved disastrous to the Home Rule Party, splitting it into two opposing factions. In 1893, Gladstone, again prime minister, introduced his second home rule bill, which allowed for a continued Irish presence at Westminster with its power limited to voting on Irish issues. The bill was passed in the Commons but defeated in the House of Lords. Gladstone retired a year later. P.E., T.D.

Glasnevin Cemetery. Dublin's main cemetery situated in the northside suburb of Glasnevin. The cemetery was established by Daniel *O'Connell in 1832 as a nondenominational resting-place operated by a committee. Over one million people are buried here, including Michael *Collins, Éamon *de Valera, Brendan *Behan, Peadar Kearney (who wrote the words of the Irish national anthem), Charles Stewart *Parnell, the poet Gerard Manley *Hopkins and Daniel O'Connell himself. The *Republic's first crematorium opened here in 1988. The chapel is by J. J. MacCarthy and the Finglas Road gate by William Pearse, father of Patrick *Pearse. P.H.

Glendalough. Picturesque valley in the Wicklow Hills. Glendalough is – according to its name – the valley of the two lakes, but it is also the valley of two *saints. These are Kevin, a hermit who died in 618 and around whose grave a famous monastery was later built, and Laurence O'Toole, an abbot who died in 1182 and was canonised in 1226. The latter may have erected some of the Romanesque-style buildings still surviving in the valley. The *round tower, just under 100 feet high, was restored in 1876 and is one of the best preserved in the country. The cathedral is the second largest pre-*Norman church in Ireland. Glendalough was one of Ireland's greatest places of *pilgrimages until Cardinal *Cullen banned them in 1862 because of too much 'drink and debauchery'. P.H.

Gogarty, Oliver St John (1878–1957). Physician and writer. Gogarty graduated with a degree in medicine from Trinity College in his native *Dublin in 1907 and established a successful surgical practice. By the time he published his first poetry collection, *An Offering of Swans* (1923), three of his plays – on the subject of urban poverty – had already been staged by the *Abbey Theatre. Gogarty wrote both classically inspired lyrical poetry and bawdy verse. His *Collected Poems* appeared in 1951. He also wrote several novels and a series of unreliable autobiographical accounts and reminiscences, including *As I Was Going Down Sackville Street* (1937), *Tumbling in the Hay* (1939) and *It Isn't This Time of Year at All!* (1954). He moved to the United States in 1939 and died in New York in 1957. Oliver Gogarty was the model for Malachi ('Buck') Mulligan in James *Joyce's *Ulysses* (1922). J.C.E.L.

Goldsmith, Oliver (c.1730–74). Playwright, poet, novelist. Born to a *Church of Ireland clergyman in Pallas, County *Longford and educated at Trinity College, Dublin, Edinburgh and on the continent, Goldsmith arrived in London destitute in 1756. There, he worked as a physician, an apothecary, an editor, a musician and a school custodian, before embarking on a literary career. His output was voluminous (more than 40 volumes) and varied. Struggling to make a living, Goldsmith contributed essays, reviews and letters to the new periodicals and wrote histories of England (1764), Rome (1769) and Greece (1774), and biographies of Voltaire (1761) and Turloch *Carolan (1760).

Goldsmith's famous novel *The Vicar of Wakefield* (1764), (which his friend Dr Johnson sold to rescue him from being arrested for debt) set forth some of his most enduring themes: social satire on the manners and morals of the urbane Englishman of the eighteenth century; a preference for country virtue over the corruption of the city; and a complaint against the Enclosure Laws, which turned farmland into pleasure grounds for the rich, while displacing the small farmer. Similar ideas are illustrated in his best-known poem, 'The Deserted Village' (1770), based on his childhood in the village of Lissoy, in County *Westmeath. His poem, 'The Traveller' (1764), which first brought him literary attention and his *Letters of a Chinese Citizen* (1761–62) embody his ideas of the enlightened Englishman as a citizen of the world.

His plays *She Stoops to Conquer* (1773), which has become a classic, and *The Good-Natur'd Man* (1767) were produced with great success in London. This revival of the comedy of manners style was Goldsmith's response to the sentimental, or 'weeping' comedies that dominated the theatre at the time. A bit of a court jester, sometimes ridiculous and vain, Goldsmith was valued for his simple style and loved for his generous nature. Johnson said of him, 'No man was more foolish when he had not a pen in his hand, or more wise when he had'. Edmund *Burke reportedly burst into tears on hearing the news of his death. Goldsmith's and Burke's statues on either side of the main entrance of Trinity College are *Dublin landmarks. J.MD.

golf. One of Ireland's most popular sports. When *Ulster was planted in 1606, a certain Viscount Montgomery, with an ancestral home in Ayrshire, Scotland, acquired a large portion of the Ards Peninsula in County *Down. He built a school at Newtown where the scholars had 'a green for recreation at golf, football and archery'. This is the first mention of golf in Ireland.

It was almost three centuries later, however, before the game gained a firm foothold. In 1882, Royal Belfast, founded by Thomas Sinclair, became Ireland's first, formally constituted club. Scottish regiments of the British army played a major role in the development of golf in Ireland, establishing the Curragh Golf Club (1883), Royal Dublin (1885) and Lahinch (1892).

From these modest beginnings, the island of Ireland now boasts 405 golf clubs. The geographical term is used advisedly, because there is no political border in Irish golf. Both the men's and women's games for the country north and south are governed from Dublin, by the Golfing Union of Ireland (GUI) and the Irish Ladies Golf Union (ILGU).

Though something of a latecomer to the game, by comparison with its Scottish and English neighbours, Ireland claimed a major, pioneering role in golf administration. The GUI was launched in 1891 as the world's first national union and the ILGU, which was instituted in 1893, claimed the same distinction for the women's game.

It is estimated that the world contains only 150 pure links courses – golf courses located on dune-land linking arable land with the seashore. Ireland can boast 40 of them, including such celebrated stretches as Ballybunion and Waterville in County *Kerry; Royal County Down; Portmarnock in County *Dublin; Royal Portrush in County *Antrim; Rosses Point in County *Sligo; Lahinch and the latest arrival, Doonbeg, in County *Clare. Among the major international events that the country played host to were the 1951 British Open (Royal Portrush), the only time the British Open was played in Ireland; the 1960 Canada Cup and 1991 Walker Cup (both at Portmarnock); and the 1996 Curtis Cup (at Killarney). The 2006 Ryder Cup is to be staged at the Kildare Club, 20 miles west of Dublin.

Among Ireland's leading professionals, Fred Daly won the 1947 British Open while Christy O'Connor Senior has over 30 international victories, including the World Seniors of 1977. Joe Carr, the country's leading amateur, won 40 championships, including the British Amateur three times. D.G.

Gonne, Maud (1866–1953). *Nationalist and suffragette. Gonne was born in England to a wealthy British army officer. The family moved to Ireland in 1867 and when Gonne was four her mother died. Sent to France at 19 to recuperate from tuberculosis, Gonne fell in love with Lucien Millevoye, a right-wing politician and journalist, with whom she had two children.

In 1888, Gonne returned to Ireland and threw herself into nationalist politics. In the 1890s, she led *republican protests in *Dublin and agitated among tenant farmers in the west. She campaigned for the release of *Fenian bombers, who were imprisoned in England, and like most republicans, she supported the *Boers in their war with England. Gonne visited France, England, Scotland and America to lecture and collect funds. In Paris she launched the newspaper *L'Irlande Libre*, in May 1897. Arthur *Griffith and James *Connolly were important political influences. In 1900, she founded a republican and suffragist women's society, Inghinidhe na hÉireann (Daughters of Ireland).

Gonne was the great unrequited love of the poet W. B. *Yeats, whom she met in 1889. He unsuccessfully proposed marriage to her twice (in 1891 and 1916). She was the subject of many of his poems and in 1902 she had the leading role in his play *Cathleen Ni Houlihan*. Gonne was a leading figure in the Irish National Literary Society and like Yeats, was at-

Maud Gonne

tracted to the occult.

Her relationship with Millevoye ended in 1899 and in 1903, in Paris, she married the republican and Boer War veteran, John *MacBride. They had a son, the future politician, Seán *MacBride, but separated shortly after and MacBride returned to Ireland. She remained in Paris until 1917. MacBride was executed for his part in the 1916 *Easter Rising. On her return to Ireland, Gonne adopted his surname for the first time. She was arrested in Dublin in May 1918 for *Sinn Féin activity (the alleged 'German Plot') and she spent six months in Holloway Jail, London. She opposed the *Anglo-Irish Treaty of 1921 and was imprisoned during the *Irish Civil War. During and after the Civil War, Gonne organised the Women's Prisoners' Defence League to help republican prisoners and their families. She continued to support the republican movement and her son Seán's attempts to form a constitutional republican party. In 1938, she published a memoir of her early life, *A Servant of the Queen*. Gonne is buried in *Glasnevin Cemetery, Dublin. P.D.

Good Friday Agreement, the (1998). Agreement resulting from the *peace process in *Northern Ireland. Properly known as the 1998 Belfast Agreement, this was the culmination of multiparty talks that began January 1998 to end the *Northern Ireland conflict. A number of parties participated in the talks and largely endorsed the agreement, including *Sinn Féin, under the leadership of Gerry *Adams, but not Ian *Paisley's *Democratic Unionist Party (DUP). The substance of the agreement was worked out by David *Trimble, the leader of the *Ulster Unionist Party (UUP), and John *Hume, the leader of the *Social Democratic and Labour Party (SDLP), in conjunction with the British Prime Minister Tony *Blair and the Irish *Taoiseach Bertie *Ahern. George Mitchell (who had compiled 'The *Mitchell Report' on the situation in Northern Ireland) and US President Bill Clinton played important roles in securing the final accord. The historic agreement was reached at around 5:00 p.m. on Good Friday, 10 April 1998. Trimble and Hume were awarded the Nobel Prize for Peace in 1999.

The complex plan was designed to balance the various interests:

East-West Relations

The British secretary of state would remain responsible for non-devolved matters – notably, security – and represent Northern Ireland in the government of the United Kingdom. Articles in the Irish *Constitution would be amended to withdraw its territorial claim (or any possible interpretations of a claim) over Northern Ireland, substituting an aspiration to Irish unity. The 1985 *Anglo-Irish Agreement was replaced by a new British-Irish Agreement, effectively restating the necessity for cooperation between the sovereign governments. A British-Irish Council would bring together delegates from the new devolved assemblies for Northern Ireland, Scotland and Wales, the governments of the Isle of Man and the Channel Islands and the British and Irish parliaments. The Council would meet periodically to discuss general issues.

Internal Relations
A devolved Northern Ireland assembly and government, subordinate to London, would be established. The assembly would be based on power-sharing between representatives of the *Catholic/*nationalist and *Protestant/*unionist communities. Legislation would require either parallel consent or a weighted majority of 60% of the assembly's members to become law. Subcommittees, whose membership would broadly reflect party strengths, would oversee the implementation of legislation. Each government department would be headed by a minister with full executive authority. An unelected civic forum would foster a wider consensus on social and economic matters. All parties committed themselves to making their best effort to secure paramilitary disarmament. In response, British state security would be scaled down.

North-South Relations
The all-Ireland dimension would be addressed by a North-South Ministerial Council, responsible to and limited by the Northern Ireland assembly and the Irish government. The council would seek to coordinate and harmonise transport, agriculture, education, health, environment, research, tourism and cultural heritage.

Prisoners associated with paramilitary groups on cease-fire were to be released within two years and the *RUC was to be reformed to encourage its acceptance by the entire community, especially the long-alienated nationalists. There were commitments to enhance the status of the *Irish language and a local, predominantly Protestant dialect, Ulster-Scots. Further measures to ensure fair employment were promised.

The agreement was approved in a Northern Ireland referendum by 71.1% of voters (nearly half of unionist voters opposed the accord) and by 95% in the Republic. After elections to the assembly, David Trimble of the UUP duly became first minister of the new devolved executive, with Séamus *Mallon of the SDLP as deputy first minister. Legislation to give effect to the Belfast Agreement became law in June 1998. Such issues as disarmament, or as it has become known decommissioning, have proved controversial and the assembly has more than once been suspended by the British government because of lack of progress on this issue. M.M.

Government of Ireland Act (1920). Legislation that set up *home rule with two separate parliaments for the north and the south of Ireland. During the *War of Independence, *Lloyd George's government decided to implement home rule with two separate parliaments, similar to the bill passed in 1914. This act was aimed at undermining *Dáil Éireann, the parliament established by *Sinn Féin after the 1918 election, while satisfying *unionists' demands not to be ruled from Dublin. The northern parliament was limited to six of Ulster's nine counties. (Unionists had a majority in four of the six counties.) In subsequent elections, Sinn Féin won in the south, but refused to convene a parliament under the act and remained in Dáil Éireann. Unionists had 40 of the 52 seats in the north and established their own parliament in *Belfast under the act, thus creating the state of *Northern Ireland and the *partition of Ireland. T.C.

Graham, Patrick (1943–). Painter. Born in Mullingar, County *Westmeath, Graham studied at the National College of Art and Design, Dublin, and is a member of *Aosdána. His neo-Expressionist technique and figurative content has been influential in the continuing reaction to formalism. M.C.

Grattan, Henry (1746–1820). Irish parliamentarian. Born in *Dublin where he was educated at Trinity College, Grattan attended the Middle Temple in London and was called to the Irish Bar in 1772. He was influenced by the nationalist politics of Henry Flood, MP, who advocated the independence of the Irish House of Commons from Westminster. In December 1775, Grattan accepted the patronage of Whig magnate Lord Charlemont, who brought him into the Commons as a borough MP. Grattan rose quickly to prominence owing to his considerable skills as an orator and the crisis engendered by the *American Revolution. In 1778 he was closely associated with the 'patriot' *Volunteer organisation, which gave the pro-reform party adhering to Grattan and Flood the support of an extra-parliamentary armed mass movement. This obliged Westminster to yield a large measure of legislative independence to Ireland in 1782. Grattan purchased a small estate at Tinnehinch, County *Wicklow, with a Commons grant of £50,000, and from 1790 was MP for Dublin City. Although an avid supporter of *Catholic rights and a sympathiser of the radical *United Irishmen, Grattan was falsely suspected of sedition in April 1798. His reputation was further tarnished in establishment circles during the *Rebellion of 1798, notwithstanding his temporary residence in England. An opponent of the Act of *Union, Grattan was briefly an MP in 1800 and, again, after 1804 in the Westminster parliament. He campaigned for *Catholic Emancipation until his death in London in June 1820. R.OD.

Graves, Alfred Perceval (1846–1931). Poet and educationalist. Born in *Dublin, educated at Windermere College and Trinity College, Dublin, Graves worked initially as a schools inspector in England. His father was the *Church of Ireland bishop of Limerick. Graves published the collections *Songs of Old Ireland* in 1882 and *Songs of Erin* in 1892, both in collaboration with Sir Charles Stanford. He wrote lyrics for old Irish folk tunes derived from the collection of George *Petrie. He also wrote under the pen name Father Prout and one of his most enduring songs is the comic ballad 'Father O'Flynn'. Graves was a contributor to *Punch* magazine and active in the Irish Literary Society in London. His autobiography, *To Return to All That* (1930), was written as an alternative version of the family history to that portrayed by his son, the novelist, poet and mythologist Robert Graves (1895–1985), in *Goodbye to All That* (1929). C.D.

Graves, Robert James (1796–1853). Physician after whom Graves' Disease is named. Born in *Dublin, Graves was educated at Trinity College, Dublin, and medical schools in London, Edinburgh and the continent. He took up a position as physician at the Meath Hospital in Dublin in 1821. He was president of the Royal College of Physicians of Ireland, 1843–44. Graves helped to found and edit the *Dublin Journal of Medical Science*. His enduring reputation rests on his *Clinical Lectures* (1843) and on his diagnosis of Graves' disease, or hyperthyroidism. His pioneering treatment of fever patients through 'supportive therapy' was adopted worldwide. C.D.

Greevy, Bernadette (1940–). Mezzo-soprano. Born in *Dublin, Greevy has gained international acclaim for her performances, particularly those of works by Elgar, Mahler and Brahms. In her early career she attracted the attention of Sir John Barbirolli, the noted conductor, who proved influential in promoting her career. She has won numerous national and international awards for her singing. A.S.

Gregory, Lady (Augusta) (1852–1932). Playwright, director, patron of the arts. Born into a landholding *Protestant family, Augusta Persse grew up in Roxborough House, County *Galway. In 1880, she married Sir William Gregory

Lady Augusta Gregory

and entered the social, literary and political circles of Europe's aristocracy. Lady Gregory is best known for her prominent role in the *Irish Literary Revival, as a playwright, director, editor and translator. In 1896, Lady Gregory invited William Butler *Yeats to her estate *Coole Park, a gathering place for literary and political figures. Their subsequent friendship and work became the heart of the Irish Literary Revival. Lady Gregory's role as mentor and friend to Yeats and their collaborations were critical to Yeats' development as a writer.

With Yeats and J. M. *Synge, Gregory founded the Irish Literary Theatre in 1899, which in 1904 became the *Abbey Theatre. Aiming to establish an Irish national theatre and to honour Irish culture, they staged works by Irish playwrights either based on folk literature or with Irish subjects. Later, Gregory was managing director of the Abbey Theatre and wrote or translated over 40 plays. A strong advocate of the *Irish language and folk literature, Gregory translated such Irish sagas as *Cuchulain of Muirthemne* (1902). Her other works include *Our Irish Theatre* (1914), *The Image and Other Plays* (1922) and *Irish Folk History Plays* (1912). Lady Gregory's political activism and literary work focused on restoring and promoting an Irish national literature, language and cultural identity. K.MI.

Griffin, Gerald (1803–40). Novelist. Born in Limerick City, Griffin began his literary career in London in the 1820s, where he published a book of short stories. Ill health and bad luck, however, forced his return home. His best-known work is *The Collegians* (1829), based on a local murder. Significant for its depiction of the pre-*Famine Catholic middle-class, it was also a popular success, inspiring Boucicault's *The Colleen Bawn* (1860) and, some believe, Theodore Dreiser's *An American Tragedy* (1925). Beset by doubts about his work, in 1838 Griffin burned his papers and entered the *Christian Brothers. G.OB.

Griffith, Arthur (1871–1922). *Nationalist leader, founder of *Sinn Féin. Born on 31 March 1871, in *Dublin, Griffith first worked as an apprentice in the printing trade and later became a journalist. In 1899, he launched the *United Irishman*, the first of a succession of newspapers he edited that called for an 'Irish Ireland'. Griffith's newspapers championed this ideology of cultural nationalism and political separatism, which emerged at the turn of the twentieth century and maintained that independence would be pointless if Ireland lost its cultural identity. He was also active in the *Gaelic League, a cultural nationalist organisation that promoted the *Irish language and Gaelic cultural traditions, and advocated protectionist measures to encourage greater economic self-sufficiency.

In a series of articles published in 1904, *The Resurrection of Hungary: A Parallel for Ireland*, Griffith outlined a plan of constitutional change for Ireland based on the experience of the Hungarians in the Hapsburg empire. According to his model of a 'dual monarchy', Ireland would retain its link to the British crown and share a common foreign policy, but would otherwise govern itself. In effect, Griffith argued for a status similar to what existed before the Act of *Union (1800): domestic affairs controlled by an independent Irish parliament sitting in Dublin, but one elected by a democratic majority and not dominated by *Protestant landowners, as it had been in the eighteenth century. This new constitutional order could be achieved, Griffith argued, by a policy of 'passive resistance', whereby Irish members would withdraw from the Westminster parliament and form a new national assembly in Dublin. Griffith's 'Hungarian policy' soon became known more simply as 'Sinn Féin', meaning 'we ourselves'. On 28 November 1905, Griffith founded Sinn Féin, a political organisation dedicated to promoting national political autonomy, cultural vitality and economic self-sufficiency. The new political party unsuccessfully contested the North Leitrim parliamentary constituency in 1908.

Meanwhile, in 1906, the *United Irishman* ceased publication due to legal problems and was replaced by *Sinn Féin*, which continued to promulgate Griffith's views until its suppression by the government early in the *First World War. The Sinn Féin party led by Griffith had little success until after the *Easter Rising of 1916, for which it was incorrectly held responsible because of its publicly visible radicalism. Griffith himself did not participate in the rising because he still opposed armed force. At the party convention in 1917, Griffith relinquished leadership to Éamon *de Valera, the only surviving commander of the rising.

In the elections of 1918, Sinn Féin emerged as the strongest party in Ireland, winning 73 of 105 parliamentary seats, and proceeded to implement, in essence, Griffith's policy of withdrawing from Westminster and establishing itself in Dublin as an independent national assembly, *Dáil Éireann. This move sparked the *Anglo-Irish War, which lasted from January 1919 to July 1921. In late 1921, Griffith led a delegation (which included Michael *Collins) to London to negotiate a settlement of the conflict. The *Anglo-Irish Treaty, signed on 6 December 1921, created a twenty-six-county *Irish Free State, which was still formally under the crown and within the British *Commonwealth. Although this was consistent with Griffith's 'Hungarian policy', the failure to achieve a republic for all of Ireland, and especially the mandatory *oath of allegiance to the British crown, caused an acrimonious split in the Dáil. When the treaty was narrowly ratified in January 1922, de Valera resigned as president and was replaced by Griffith. Shortly after the *Civil War erupted in June 1922, Griffith suffered a cerebral haemorrhage and died on 12 August 1922. F.B.

Guerin, Veronica (1958–96). Journalist. During her short career, Guerin won many awards for her exposés on the Irish criminal underworld. She received numerous threats and was shot in the leg in an attack on her house, before she was eventually murdered in her car in a suburb of *Dublin in 1996. Two men, connected to a Dublin criminal gang, have received life sentences for their part in her murder, but one of these convictions was overturned on appeal. The gang leader, John Gilligan, was acquitted of the charge that he had Guerin murdered but was sentenced to 28 years for drug-related offences. B.D.

Guildford Four. Notorious miscarriage of justice in England. Four innocent people spent 14 years in prison for two Provisional *IRA bombings of pubs in Guildford and Woolwich, England, in 1974. The four – Carole Richardson of London and Gerard Conlon, Patrick Armstrong and Paul Hill, all from *Belfast – were convicted of the bombings and sentenced to life in prison in 1975 on police evidence that was later found to have been tainted: coerced and fabricated confessions; altered interrogation notes; and police perjury. Prosecutors in the case were also later found to have suppressed evidence that conflicted with the confessions.

The Guildford Four became a cause célèbre in both Britain and Ireland when a number of prominent British figures – including the Catholic archbishop of Westminster, the Anglican archbishop of Canterbury, two former home secretaries and several retired judges – spearheaded a campaign to win their release. That campaign led British Home Secretary Douglas Hurd to order an inquiry into the case in 1989. This uncovered evidence of the conspiracy by police and prosecution, and a three-member appeals court overturned the convictions on 19 October 1989. Three of the four were immediately released. Paul Hill, who had also been sentenced to life for a murder in *Northern Ireland, was taken to Crumlin Road Prison in Belfast and released two days later after a hearing that lasted less than 10 minutes. That murder conviction was also overturned later.

A 1994 British government report on the wrongful convictions found that the miscarriages of justice were the result of individual failings rather than a fault in the criminal justice system.

Gerard Conlon wrote a book on his ordeal entitled *Proved Innocent* (1990), which was later the basis of the film *In the Name of the Father* (1993). T.D.

Guinness. Family of *brewers. In 1756 Arthur Guinness (1725–1803) established a brewery in Leixlip, County *Kildare, which he moved to *Dublin in 1759. The business grew under his son Arthur (1767–1855) and grandson Benjamin (1798–1868), who developed export markets in the United States and Europe. Sir Benjamin's sons, Arthur Edward (1840–1915), First Baron Ardilaun, and Edward Cecil (1847–1927), First Baron Iveagh, were generous benefactors to the city of Dublin. They oversaw the development of their brewery in St James Gate, which still produces dark, creamy stout, into one of the world's largest breweries. By 1980, the family interest in the business had fallen to just 5%, but the company continued to expand its holdings. However, the financial takeover of Guinness by Distillers in 1986 led to a fraud trial in 1990, after which the company's former chairman was found guilty of illegal manipulation of Guinness share prices. Guinness, now part of the multinational conglomerate Diageo, continues to sponsor the publication of the *Guinness Book of World Records*. S.A.B.

Guthrie, Sir Tyrone (1900–71). Dramaturge. Born in Tunbridge Wells, England, he spent his early years at Annaghmakerrig, County *Monaghan, his mother's home. Initially noted for his direction of the classical repertory at London's celebrated Old Vic Theatre, Guthrie has been internationally renowned since the 1950s. His Dublin productions included Seán *O'Casey's controversial *The Bishop's Bonfire* (1954). In 1962, he was appointed inaugural director of what became the Guthrie Theatre, in Minneapolis, where Brian *Friel studied his methods. Between 1963 and 1970, Guthrie served as chancellor of Queen's University, Belfast. Annaghmakerrig House is now an artists' retreat, in accordance with his will. G.OB.

Hamilton, Hugh Douglas (1739–1808). Portrait painter. Born in *Dublin and trained at Dublin Society Schools, Hamilton produced small oval pastel portraits, which earned him success in London. He painted large oil portraits in Italy, where he lived for 13 years. On his return to Ireland in 1792, Hamilton continued his career with full-length portraits in oils, most of which were of people opposed to the Act of *Union. M.C.

Hamilton, William Rowan (1805–65). Mathematician. Born in *Dublin, Hamilton was brilliant and precocious. A polyglot by age nine, he was appointed professor of astronomy at Trinity College and astronomer royal at Dunsink Observatory, even before graduating in classics and mathematics. He dabbled in poetry (discouraged by his friend Wordsworth) and philosophy (inspired by his friend Coleridge). He excelled in mathematics, where he favoured highly original, abstract, general approaches. He invented quaternions (the forerunners of later non-commutative algebras) and Hamiltonian dynamics (first exploited in the 1920s by Schroedinger in his wave formulation of quantum mechanics). Unhappy in love, Hamilton struggled with alcoholism until his death. M.L.

harp, Irish. The symbolic instrument of Ireland. Its present form was established over 1,000 years ago, with variations in shape being introduced up to the seventeenth century. The oldest surviving instrument, the Brian Boru harp, held in Trinity College, Dublin, dates to the fourteenth century. The older instruments were smaller and heavier and had wire strings. From the early 1800s, they increased in size, were lighter and first used gut, then nylon strings. The old harp was associated with indigenous classical *music. Its players were meticulously trained and enjoyed considerable respect in chieftains' houses in Ireland and abroad, particularly in *Scotland. Music composed by these early harpers still survives – most notably that of Turloch *Carolan (1670–1738), 200 of whose tunes survive and are still available in print. Other harpists include Ruadhrí Dall Ó Catháin (his sixteenth-century tune 'Give Me Your Hand' is still popular) and the Connellan brothers (from the seventeenth century).

Harping was largely extinguished along with the Gaelic order in the seventeenth and eighteenth centuries, and its players and repertoire were submerged in 'folk' (now called 'traditional') music. The 1792 Belfast Harp Festival, a final effort to revive harping, produced hugely valuable transcriptions by Edward Bunting, still in print today. The organisations Cáirde na Cruite and the Harp Foundation maintain the popularity of the instrument today through teaching and performance. F.V.

Harris, Richard (1930–2002). Actor. Born in Limerick City, Harris was educated at Crescent College, Limerick, and at the London Academy of Music and Dramatic Art. He wanted to be a *soccer player, but during a three-year bout with tuberculosis in his late teens he turned his mind to acting. Harris made his stage debut in 1956 in Joan Littlewood's production of Brendan *Behan's *The Quare Fellow*. His first screen role was in Cyril Frankel's *Alive and Kicking* (1958). He won the Best Actor Award at Cannes and was nominated for an Oscar for his part as a *rugby player in *This Sporting Life* (1963). Other notable films include *A Man Called Horse* (1969), *Unforgiven* (1993) and *The Field* (1990), for which he was again nominated for an Oscar for best actor. His last screen role was as Albus Dumbledore in the first two Harry Potter films in 2001/2002. Harris also had an accomplished singing career, notably in the role of King Arthur in the 1967 film version of Lerner & Loewe's musical *Camelot* and in his recordings of the songs of Jimmy Webb. His recording of *MacArthur Park* became an international hit single in 1968. C.D.

Hartnett, Michael. See **Ó hAirtnéide, Mícheál.**

Harty, Sir Hamilton (1879–1941). Composer, conductor, pianist. Born in County *Down, Harty was a church organist from the age of 12 (Magheracoll, Belfast, Bray). He quickly established his reputation as a composer and gifted accompanist after he moved to London in his early twenties. His talent as a conductor led to his appointment in 1920 to Manchester's Hallé Orchestra, often lauded under his stewardship as the finest in Britain. After leaving Manchester in 1933, he worked mainly in London. He introduced much new music (including Mahler and Shostakovich) to British audiences, premiered Walton's First Symphony in 1934 and was a renowned interpreter of Berlioz. His arrangements of Handel's Water Music and Royal Fireworks Music were staples of the symphonic repertoire. He left many fine recordings and his own Irish-inflected music – including an Irish Symphony (1904), concertos for violin (1908) and piano (1922), and the symphonic poem 'The Children of Lir' (1938) – attracted new listeners through a series of recordings by the Ulster Orchestra in the 1980s. M.D.

Haughey, Charles J. (1925–). Politician, leader of *Fianna Fáil, *Taoiseach. Born in Mayo, Haughey served as a TD from 1957 to 1992. His first ministerial post was in the Department for Justice (1961–64), where he earned a reputation as a reformer. Most notably, he introduced the Guardianship of Infants Act (1964) and the Succession Act (1965), giving wives equal legal rights with regard to the upbringing of their children and the inheritance of family property. He also effectively abolished the use of the death penalty. He served as agriculture minister (1964–66) and as a highly successful finance minister (1966–70), during which term he presided over the First Commission on the Status of *Women. He was dismissed from the government by Taoiseach Jack *Lynch and prosecuted for attempting to illegally import arms for the defence of nationalist areas in *Northern Ireland during the *Arms Crisis in 1970. Although he was found not guilty, the issue remained controversial because the extent of government involvement, including that of the Taoiseach himself, had yet to be conclusively determined. As a result of his popularity with the party grassroots, Haughey returned to government as health minister under Lynch in 1977.

In 1979, he successfully found a broadly acceptable formula for the legalisation of contraception, a daunting task given the depth of public division on the issue at that time. He was elected leader of Fianna Fáil and served as Taoiseach from 1979 to 1981, February to November 1982 and from 1987 to 1992. Haughey was personally involved in 1987 in formulating the 'Programme for National Recovery' between the government, *trade unions and employers. The programme heralded the modern 'social partnership' model of policymaking in Ireland and is generally seen as one of the reasons for the rapid economic growth in the 1990s.

A poor election result in 1989 forced Fianna Fáil to enter its first ever coalition government – with the *Progressive Democrats. Haughey was replaced as party leader in

1992. Controversy about his financial affairs has plagued him throughout his life, and since 1996 he has been subjected to a Tribunal of Inquiry regarding donations he is reported to have received during his political career. E.C.

health. Through the centuries, war and hunger brought disease. The bubonic plague epidemic of 1649–52 began in *Galway and ravaged the country, along with typhus. The famine of 1740–41 brought 'famine fever' – most likely typhus – and the Napoleonic era, of apparent prosperity and intensifying poverty, was characterised by 'the country disease' – dysentery – and typhus again. The first western European cholera epidemic, in the early 1830s, did not spare Ireland, and the Great *Famine of the following decade brought famine fever and 'relapsing fever' along with mass starvation.

During the eighteenth century, a few voluntary hospitals were set up in the cities. In the early nineteenth century it was noted that, epidemics and periodic famine aside, the Irish were among the healthiest peasantry of Europe, because of their potato diet. The Famine years, 1846–49, prompted the establishment of temporary fever hospitals and laws for the medical relief of the poor. In 1851 a medical officer (dispensary doctor) was appointed for every *workhouse in the country and people could consult him for a small fee, or for free. The several voluntary hospitals already in the cities catered mainly to the poor, and by 1861 the hospitals attached to the workhouses could take patients who were not workhouse inmates. However, before antisepsis, hospitals probably killed more people than they cured and were important mainly for the chance they gave doctors to develop skills in the treatment of disease. *Dublin obstetricians, for example, were to become world leaders in the field. (The large Irish families that persisted up to the 1960s facilitated this development.)

Health care that was brought to the people included the Jubilee and the Lady Dudley nurses, trained nurse-midwives who worked in rural areas. Set up in the years 1897–1902, these nurses were crucial in the reduction of maternal and infant mortality. Also important were the anti-tuberculosis campaign of the Women's National Health Association (1907) and the health education undertaken by the various agricultural and social organisations of this period.

People's continued good health, then as now, was more dependent upon living conditions and diet than upon medical services, however. Rural housing improved in the late nineteenth century and remittances from *America, agricultural education and a rising standard of living overall ensured a more varied diet for rural people. Poorer city people were at a terrible disadvantage, living in unhealthy tenements and lanes with inadequate sanitary facilities, an uncertain water supply and no access to clean milk even when they could afford it. The housing programmes of the 1930s and 1950s eventually replaced the worst of these slums with proper dwellings.

After the *Irish Free State was created in 1922, the workhouse system was abolished in the south, but it continued till 1945 in *Northern Ireland. In the Free State/*Republic, the public hospitals were poorly equipped and staffed, and it was not until the Public Health Act (1945), which established Public Health nurses and the creation of a Department of Health two years later, that the serious public health problems of tuberculosis and typhus were seriously tackled. In 1950, the young Minister of Health Dr Noel *Browne was forced to resign his position because of opposition from the medical profession and the *Catholic bishops to his scheme to provide free medical care for mothers and children up to the age of 16. In 1953, after a prolonged political battle involving the major political parties, the Catholic church and the medical profession, a free-for-all maternal and infant health service was finally introduced. Maternal mortality, already falling since the introduction of children's allowances in 1944, fell dramatically, as it did in Northern Ireland after the introduction of the National Health Service in 1948. Infant mortality, north and south, fell definitively in the late 1950s, due to improved living conditions and medical facilities. C.C.

Healy, Timothy (1855–1931). *Nationalist politician. Born in Bandon, County *Cork, Healy worked as a barrister and journalist. As MP for *Wexford (1880–83), he became a proficient debater and an expert at parliamentary obstruction. A leading supporter of Charles Stewart *Parnell, he served as MP for *Monaghan (1883–85), South Londonderry (1885–86) and North Longford (1887–92). Healy recommended Parnell's temporary retirement after the *O'Shea divorce case and subsequently became his most bitter antagonist. Healy was anti-Parnellite MP for North Louth (1892–1910) but became estranged from the *Parliamentary Party and joined the conciliatory nationalist group 'All for Ireland' League in 1910. Although a conservative, Healy developed sympathy for *Sinn Féin while MP for North-east Cork (1910–18) and served as first governor general of the *Irish Free State (1922–28). S.A.B.

Heaney, Seamus Justin (1939–). Poet, essayist, playwright, Nobel laureate. Born into a *Catholic family, the eldest of nine children, Heaney was brought up on a small farm, 'Mossbawn', between Catholic Toomebridge and *Protestant Castledawson in County *Derry. Educated at St Columb's College in Derry and Queen's University, Belfast, he started teaching in the English Department at Queen's University in 1966. Heaney took part in the civil rights marches in the late 1960s. From 1970 to 1971, he was a visiting lecturer at the University of California, Berkeley.

His first collection of poems, *Death of a Naturalist* (1966), is rooted in his rural, childhood experience, which Heaney makes extraordinarily vivid through his highly sensuous language. The influences of Robert Frost, William Wordsworth, Gerard Manley *Hopkins, R. S. Thomas and Patrick *Kavanagh are evident. The title of his second collection, *Door into the Dark* (1969), suggests both the mystical orientation and the sense of displacement and exposure that characterise much of Heaney's poetry. The preoccupation with digging, ploughing, fishing, peering down wells, probing secret recesses and dark interiors becomes an effort of cultural retrieval and restoration.

Wintering Out (1972) appeared at the height of the *Troubles and, as the title suggests, is concerned with endurance in bleak conditions. The poetry reflects a nostalgic longing for an idealised, lost or disappearing home, transcending the ravages of history. For Heaney, P. V. Glob's book, *The Bog People* (1969), about the discovery in Danish bogs of Iron Age sacrificial victims to Nerthus, the Mother Goddess, suggested ways of understanding the contemporary conflict in *Ulster as part of a timeless continuum of ritual tribal slaughter.

In 1972, Heaney moved from Belfast to Glanmore in County *Wicklow and was head of the English Department at Carysfort College, Dublin, between 1975 and 1981. *North* (1975) continues the attempt to define the present by exploring its relationship with the past. There are more *bog poems and poems that use *Viking mythology to comment on the present. But, increasingly, Heaney comes to question his own aestheticising procedures, insisting upon the stark reality of atrocity, which overwhelms and silences.

A new voice is heard in *Field-Work* (1979), where he struggles to affirm the 'clear light' of imaginative freedom and transcendence. In 1980, *Pre-occupations: Selected Prose 1968–1978* appeared. The following year, Heaney

Seamus Heaney

became visiting professor at Harvard and, in 1984, Boylston professor of rhetoric and poetry. His translation of the middle-Irish poem *Buile Suibhne* (*Sweeney Astray*, 1983) was published by *Field Day, the Derry theatre company which he and Brian *Friel founded in 1980. For Heaney, the outcast birdman Sweeney is a figure of the displaced artist. His next collection, *Station Island* (1984), includes the Dantesque title-poem in which he encounters a series of ghosts, among them literary figures such as William *Carleton and James *Joyce, and victims of sectarian murders, who challenge him about his allegiances and his art.

In his next collection, *The Haw Lantern* (1987), the self-scrutiny is unrelenting. A series of political 'parable poems' shows the influence of east European poets such as Zbigniew Herbert and Czeslaw Milosz. The central 'Clearances' sonnet sequence is written out of the loss of bereavement, in memory of Heaney's mother, who died in 1984. In these poems, absence and loss are transformed through the work of memory and imagination. A second volume of essays, *The Government of the Tongue* (1988), affirms the liberating and redemptive power of art in the face of political oppression. His play *The Cure at Troy*, after *Philoctetes* by Sophocles, dramatises questions of personal conscience, duty and communal loyalty.

In 1989, Heaney became chair of poetry at Oxford University. A collection of his Oxford lectures entitled *The Redress of Poetry* and his translation of *Beowulf* were published in 1995, the year in which he was awarded the Nobel Prize for literature. His recent collections of poetry, *Seeing Things* (1991), *The Spirit Level* (1996) and *Electric Light* (2001), display a buoyant confidence, a relaxed visionary quality, a new lightness of touch. E.K-A.

Henry II (1133–89). King of England (1154–89). Within a year of succeeding to the English throne, Henry secured a papal letter (*Laudabiliter*) authorising the conquest of Ireland. In 1168, he gave his consent for Dermot *MacMurrough to recruit the military assistance of Richard fitzGilbert de Clare (*'Strongbow') in his campaign to recover the kingship of *Leinster. In October 1171, Henry led a military expedition of 4,000 men to Ireland, partly to avoid the full consequences of the murder of Thomas à Becket (29 December 1170). Having secured the submission both of Strongbow and the Gaelic lords, he divided the land of Ireland into fiefs and installed a vice-regent in *Dublin, thus establishing the power of the English crown in Ireland for the first time. S.A.B.

Henry VIII (1491–1547). King of England (1509–47), responsible for the *Reformation. Henry VIII was the first monarch to rule Ireland as a king rather than 'lord'. Since the twelfth-century *Anglo-Norman Conquest, the English monarchs had ruled Ireland and its Gaelic nobility as a 'lordship' under the feudal system. Effective English control had remained largely limited to the *Pale, the area around *Dublin. After the Kildare rebellion of 1534–35, Henry sought to expand his authority. By the policy of 'surrender and regrant', the Gaelic lords were obliged to surrender their ancestral lands and pledge loyalty to the king.

In return for their submission, Henry VIII returned their lands (which were now held under the English law of primogeniture) and granted them English titles. In a further effort to enforce obedience, in 1541 the Irish *parliament passed an act whereby Henry VIII became formally king of Ireland. Although he had previously supported Rome in its struggle against the *Protestantism of Martin Luther, Henry broke with Rome and decided to 'reform' the church in his kingdom when the pope refused to dissolve his marriage to Catherine of Aragon (who had failed to provide him with a male heir).

Henry VIII's *Reformation of the church in England during the 1530s had profound consequences for the future of Ireland. The Irish aristocracy, including both the Gaelic chieftains and the 'Old English' families who had settled in the country since the twelfth century, remained largely faithful to Rome, as did the masses of the Irish peasantry. After the Reformation, the English crown increasingly sought to maintain its control over Ireland by the 'plantation' of loyal 'new English' settlers, many of whom were actually from *Scotland. F.B.

Henry, Paul (1876–1958). Painter. Born in *Belfast, Henry painted Irish landscapes using post-impressionist techniques. He trained in Belfast and Paris and worked as an illustrator in London for 10 years before going to paint on Achill Island in County *Mayo. Henry combined avant-garde techniques and traditional subject matter. His work is accessible and symbolic of political change. Henry founded the Society of Dublin Painters in 1920 to exhibit modern art. M.C.

Henry, Sam (1878–1952). Song collector. A Customs & Excise officer and a *Unionist councillor for Coleraine, County *Derry, Henry collected some 1,000 songs in the North Derry/Antrim area from 1906 until his death. Half of these were published from 1923 to 1939 as 'Songs of the People', a weekly column largely edited by him in the *Northern Constitution* newspaper. The 'Songs of the People' both preserved old local songs and presented them for new interpretation. A 632-page book collection of songs from his columns, Sam Henry's *Songs of the People* (University of Georgia Press, 1990), makes a significant contribution to the archive of Irish traditional song. F.V.

Herzog, Chaim (1918–97). President of Israel, 1983–93. Born in *Belfast, Herzog was educated at Wesley College in *Dublin and at Cambridge and London. He was a fluent Irish speaker. Herzog enrolled in the British army in 1939, graduated from the Royal Military Academy, Sandhurst, and served with distinction in Europe in the Second World War. In 1947, he emigrated to Israel and joined the Jewish underground militia, Haganah. He was appointed head of the Intelligence Department of General Staff of the Israeli Defence Force (IDF) in 1948. Herzog served as defence attaché to Washington for the IDF, 1948–50 and 1959–62, and was Israel's ambassador to Washington, 1975–78. He entered the Knesset for the Labour Party in 1981 and was elected president in 1983. C.D.

Hewitt, John (1907–87). Poet. Born in *Belfast, Hewitt remains one of the most important and influential voices in *Ulster poetry. A committed *socialist and art curator, he worked for the Belfast Museum and Art Gallery and travelled frequently to Eastern Europe. Throughout his life, he was a prolific and imaginative poet who played with language and form. Hewitt celebrated northern regionalism while simultaneously studying what it meant to come from a community fractured by sectarianism. He edited the Northern Ireland literary magazine *Lagan*, was the art critic for the *Belfast Telegraph* and was poetry editor for *Threshold*. After a stint as director of the Herbert Art Gallery and Museum in Coventry, he returned to Northern Ireland in 1972 where, as writer-in-residence at Queen's University, Belfast, he received an honorary doctorate for his profound literary contributions. Hewitt is regarded as the father figure of contemporary Ulster poetry for his attempts to scrutinise the two Northern Irish communities. His work includes *Conacre* (1943), *No Rebel Word* (1948), *The Day of the Corncrake* (1969), *The Planter and the Gael* (1970, with John *Montague) and *Kites in Spring: A Belfast Boyhood* (1980). P.J.H.

Hiberno-English. Term generally describing English as it was spoken in Ireland. Sometimes known as Anglo-Irish, or Irish English, Hiberno-English originally referred to the English of the Irish country people whose speech was directly influenced by the *Irish language. When the Irish people first came into contact with English throughout the seventeenth century, they heard it through the sound system of their own language. Having haltingly embraced it at first, by the late eighteenth century and early nineteenth century, they eventually reproduced a hybrid, which was either beautiful and exotic, or barbaric and ugly, depending on your point of view.

Hiberno-English differed from standard English in pronunciation, vocabulary and syntax, each of which was heavily influenced by Irish. In pronunciation, Hiberno-English failed to reproduce a sound such as the English *th*, as it did not exist in Irish. A classic Hiberno-English speaker would say 'turty tree tousand tistles and torns' or 'dis, dat, dese and dose', and roll the r in words such as *word* or *first*. Seventeenth-century English pronunciations have survived in Hiberno-English, such as 'tay' and 'say' for 'tea' and 'sea'. Many Irish words became part of its vocabulary, such as *galore*, *smithereens* and *kabosh*.

Many Irish authors drew inspiration from the language of the common people. In Tom *Murphy's play *A Crucial Week in the Life of a Grocer's Assistant*, one of the characters says about another: 'Heeding that hussy of a clotty of a plótha of a streeleen of an ownshock of a leibidje of a girleen that's working above in the bank'. The syntax is English but the words are Irish: *plótha* being a fool, *streeleen* a slut, *ownshock* a twit and *leibidje* an idiot. As with pronunciation, there are also older strata of demotic Elizabethan English in Hiberno-English. For example, in Ireland sick is used, which is the Elizabethan term for 'ill'. The structure of the sentence in Hiberno-English was initially much dependent on Irish. Thus, curiosities such as 'I am after doing it', or 'I do be getting my dues' or 'I bees there every day' are almost literal translations of the Irish verbs.

John Millington *Synge once seriously proposed that this mongrel speech should become the official language of the new Ireland. However, today, it is debatable whether Hiberno-English exists any longer. Most young people have an underlying desire not to speak as the country people do. While English in Ireland is spoken generally with an Irish accent, there are very few syntactical or lexicographical differences today between the English of Ireland and that of Britain. English as it is spoken in Ireland today is more influenced by American television programmes and the Hollywood culture. A.T.

Hill, Derek (1916–2000). Portrait and landscape painter. Born in Southampton, England, Hill was made an honorary citizen of Ireland in 1999 for his contribution to Ireland's artistic wealth. He is best known for his atmospheric scenes of *Donegal and Tory Island. Widely travelled, he painted for a year in *Mayo and Donegal after the Second World War. In 1954, he bought a house in Donegal, which he filled with paintings and left to the nation in 1981. He inspired and supported the school of Tory Island painting. M.C.

hill-forts. One, two, or three concentric walls usually surrounding the summit of a hill. Too extensive for permanent fortification, the area enclosed may have served as temporary refuge or for annual folk gatherings. Most were erected in the last dozen *pre-Christian centuries. P.H.

Hoban, James (c.1762–1831). Architect of the White House, Washington, DC. Born near Callan, County *Kilkenny, Hoban studied architectural drawing in *Dublin under Thomas Ivory. He emigrated to America in 1785. He won a commission to design the state capitol in Columbia, South Carolina, which was completed in 1791. In 1792, Hoban designed the President's House in Washington. Following the burning of the President's House by British forces in August 1814, Hoban oversaw the reconstruction (1817–29) of what henceforth would be known as the White House. Other buildings by Hoban in Washington included the Great Hotel (1793–95), the Little Hotel (1795) and the State and War Offices. C.D.

Hogan, John (1800–58). Sculptor. Born in County *Waterford and raised and educated in *Cork, Hogan worked in the neoclassical style in Rome for over 20 years and later in Ireland. He created many funerary monuments, commemorative works and busts of Irishmen. M.C.

Holy Cross Abbey. Cistercian abbey, founded by Dónal Mór Ó Briain in 1169. Located in County *Tipperary, the abbey gets its name from a relic of the True Cross still housed there. Rebuilt in the fifteenth century with patronage from the Butler Earls of Ormond, the monastery was suppressed during the *Reformation, but beautifully restored as a *Catholic parish church in the 1970s. P.H.

holy wells. Natural springs, found throughout Ireland and other *Celtic countries. Before Christianity, these springs were dedicated to female deities, representatives of the local earth mother deities. Holy wells are an example of how Christianity became superimposed on local pagan customs and beliefs of the *pre-Christian Celtic world. Many holy wells, according to local belief, are said to possess strange powers. Some of them are classed as healing wells, others as cursing wells and some even combine the powers of cursing and healing. There are also wells that can make the poor rich, the unhappy happy and the unlucky lucky. The wells are typically named for female *saints. J.MD.

home rule. Constitutional political movement in the second half of the nineteenth century, aimed at establishing an Irish *parliament. The concept was that the home rule parliament would legislate on domestic issues, while imperial matters such as finance, taxation and *foreign policy would remain under the control of Westminster.

The home rule movement was founded by Isaac *Butt, a former *unionist and member of parliament. Butt started questioning direct rule from Westminster as he became increasingly aware of the lack of indigenous industry and the appalling level of poverty within Ireland. A barrister who defended *Fenian rebels and president of Amnesty Association, Butt was interested in a constitutional solution to the problems which led to the Fenian rebellion.

In May 1870, Isaac Butt founded the Home Government Association to promote home rule on a federal basis. This pressure group was initially dominated by *Protestants who now saw home rule as an expression of loyalty to England and as a means of protecting both the Act of *Union and the privileged position of the ascendancy in Ireland. However, by 1873 the movement became increasingly *nationalistic and lost Protestant support. In November 1873, this organisation was replaced with the Home Rule League and 59 home rulers won seats in the 1874 election, thereby establishing a sizable Home Rule party (known also as the *Irish Parliamentary Party) in parliament. Despite this success, Butt proved to be an ineffective leader. In 1877, Charles Stewart *Parnell replaced him as chairman of the Home Rule Confederation of Great Britain. Following Butt's death in May 1879, the leadership of the Parliamentary Party went to William Shaw.

Parnell, however, was increasingly becoming Irish nationalism's most charismatic leader and by 1880 he had successfully replaced Shaw. In October 1882, the Irish National League was established as the new constituency organisation of the Home Rule Parliamentary Party. By 1886, there were over 1,000 branches throughout Ireland, responsible for funding election campaigns and contributing to MPs' salaries. Parnell at the same time organised the Parliamentary Party into a strong, closely controlled group, whose members pledged 'to sit, act and vote as one' and planned to support the political party in Westminster that offered the most concessions.

In 1885, the Conservative government attempted to win Irish support by relaxing coercion and passing the Ashbourne *Land Act of 1885. William *Gladstone, the Liberal Party leader, made no such efforts and Parnell instructed Irish voters in Britain to vote Conservative in the November 1885 election. The results were disappointing for Parnell because, even though his party won 86 seats, it failed to hold a perfect balance of power. (The Conservatives won 249 seats and the Liberals 335.) However, after Gladstone's conversion to home rule in December 1885, Parnell decided to back the Liberals.

In April 1886, Gladstone introduced his first home rule bill. It proposed the establishment of a legislature in Dublin with control over domestic matters for the whole island. Imperial matters would still be decided by Westminster (Irish peers and MPs were excluded) and Ireland would be responsible for 15% of the cost of running the British empire. The bill was defeated in the Commons by 30 votes and Gladstone resigned as prime minister. The Conservatives now took office determined to undermine home rule with a policy of conciliation, known as Constructive *Unionism. This policy held that by solving Ireland's problems of poverty and land ownership, the Irish would embrace the union with Britain and abandon the quest for home rule. Parnell realised that home rule now totally depended on an alliance with the Liberals and he spent the next four years developing this relationship.

In December 1890, the *O'Shea divorce case proved disastrous for Parnell and the Home Rule party. Gladstone stated that 'on moral grounds' he could no longer support Parnell. The party split into two opposing factions and was only reunited under John *Redmond in 1900.

In 1893, Gladstone introduced his second home rule bill, which allowed for a continued Irish presence at Westminster with its power limited to voting on Irish bills. The bill was passed in the Commons but was defeated in the House of Lords. The third home rule bill, introduced in 1912 by Prime Minister Herbert *Asquith, would give an Irish parliament power over all internal matters, except for taxation and, for a time, the police, which the British government would continue to control for six years. Ireland would also continue to send 42 MPs to Westminster under the bill. After the 1911 Parliament Act, the House of Lords no longer had veto power and could delay legislation for only two years. The home rule bill, therefore, was due to become law in 1914, but considerable opposition by *Ulster unionists placed Ireland on the brink of civil war. The onset of the *First World War caused the suspension of the home rule bill until the end of the conflict. The 1916 *Easter Rising, however, completely changed the political landscape. The nationalist *Sinn Féin party increasingly gained widespread support at the expense of the Home Rule party, which was practically wiped out in the 1918 general election. During the *War of Independence, Prime Minister *Lloyd George attempted to bring peace to the country with the *Government of Ireland Act (1920), which established two home rule parliaments – one in *Belfast and one in *Dublin. The act was completely ignored in southern Ireland where it was later superseded by the *Anglo-Irish Treaty. P.E.

Hone, Evie (1894–1955). Cubist painter and stained glass designer. Born in *Dublin, Hone studied (with fellow student Mainie *Jellet) in London and in Paris with André Lhote and Albert Gleizes. Much influenced by Irish medieval art, she worked for the stained glass workshop An Túr Gloine from 1933 to 1944 and on private commissions. Her stained glass windows can be seen in many churches in Ireland, in a few in England (including Eton College) and in Washington, DC. M.C.

Hone, Nathaniel (1718–84). Portrait painter and miniaturist. Born in *Dublin, Hone was a founding member of the Royal Academy in London in 1769. His opposition to classical Italianate painting in favour of Dutch naturalism is evident in his 1775 painting *The Pictorial Conjuror, Displaying the Whole Art of Pictorial Deception* (*National Gallery of Ireland), in which Hone satirised the British painter Joshua Reynolds. The work was rejected by the Royal Academy in 1775 and exhibited the same year by Hone in London in one of the earliest one-man exhibitions. M.C.

Hone, Nathaniel the Younger (1831–1917). Landscape painter. Born in *Dublin, Hone the Younger graduated in engineering and science from Trinity College, Dublin, in 1850. He studied painting with Thomas Couture in Paris in 1854. After 17 years painting in Barbizon and Bourron-Marlotte, France, and 18 months in Italy, he returned to Ireland to the family estate in Malahide. From 1876, he exhibited his paintings of the Malahide landscape regularly at the *Royal Hibernian Academy. M.C.

Hopkins, Gerard Manley (1844–89). English poet who spent the last years of his life in Ireland. Born in Stratford, Essex, Hopkins was educated at Balliol College, Oxford, where he was influenced by the Oxford movement and its leader, John Henry *Newman. Following Newman's example, he converted to Catholicism in 1866 and joined the Jesuit Order in 1868. Hopkins was ordained a priest in 1877 and ministered in parishes across England and Scotland. In 1884, he was appointed professor of Greek and Latin at University College, Dublin, where he taught until his death in 1889. On joining the Jesuit Order, Hopkins renounced poetry and burned most of his early poems. In 1875, however, the tragic death of a number of nuns on the ship the *Deutschland* inspired his first major poem, 'The Wreck of the Deutschland'. Hopkins continued to write poetry, mainly on religious themes but also dealing with his intense love of the beauties of nature, for the rest of his life ('The Windhover' and 'Spring and Fall'). Hopkins was an intensely original poet, innovative in his use of language and metrical forms. His unhappiness in Ireland inspired the composition of his bleak late poems (mostly in 1885), known as the 'Dark Sonnets', including 'Carrion Comfort' and 'No worst, there is none'. A.S.

horse racing. One of Ireland's major sports. Records of horse racing in Ireland date from 751 when 46 races were run with only 93 horses. In 2001, a total of 6,351 horses ran in 1,935 races for a total prize fund of almost $40 million. Currently over one million people attend race meetings every year. For a country of its size, Ireland's impact on international horse racing – from Australia to the United States and Hong Kong – has been remarkable.

The rules of racing are enforced by the Turf Club, a self-electing body, which was formed in the eighteenth century. The main organisation of the sport, Horse Racing Ireland, formed in 2001, is made up of trainers, breeders, owners and bookmakers. Racing in Ireland is financed by the government, which collects tax from the privately owned off-course betting shops. On-course betting includes both bookmakers and a state-run system called the Tote.

The two types of horse racing, steeplechasing (or jump racing) and flat racing, have become major attractions throughout Ireland. Steeplechasing originated in the south of Ireland, supposedly when two landowners raced their horses from one church steeple to another. Ever since, jump racing has been the more popular form, with major races such as the Irish Grand National at Fairyhouse, County *Kildare. Traditionally, Ireland has had a very strong presence and much success at the Cheltenham festival in Britain, commonly referred to as the 'Olympics' of jump racing. The Irish horse *Arkle*, who ran in the 1960s, is reputed to be the greatest steeplechaser of all time. The legendary Irish trainer Vincent O'Brien dominated the Cheltenham races in the 1950s, winning both the Gold Cup and the Champion Hurdle three years in a row. He won England's Aintree Grand National, one of the most prestigious horse races in the world, with three different horses.

O'Brien also achieved unprecedented international success in flat racing – the more lucrative form of the sport – and helped to revolutionise the breeding industry in Ireland. In flat racing, he won the Epsom Derby six times, the Prix de l'Arc de Triomphe three times and in 1968 the Washington International with the great *Sir Ivor*. Other great horses he trained include *Nijinsky* and *Alleged*. O'Brien's son-in-law, John Magnier, has built up the Coolmore Stud in County *Tipperary to be one of the most powerful breeding operations in the world and has employed Aidan O'Brien to train at Vincent O'Brien's old 'Ballydoyle' stables. Magnier and Aidan O'Brien are one of the most powerful racing teams in Europe today.

Ireland's most successful trainer in terms of the number of winners is Dermot Weld, who broke the record in 2000 when saddling his 2,578th winner. Weld has also made a huge impact on international racing. He saddled *Go And Go*, the only European-trained winner of an American classic, at the 1990 Belmont Stakes. Three years later, *Vintage Crop* travelled to Australia to win the Melbourne Cup.

Irish jockeys – such as Pat Eddery and Kieran Fallon on the flat and Tony McCoy over the jumps – dominate British racing. The best-known jockey based in Ireland is Michael Kinane, who has won ten home classics.

Some race meetings in Ireland have become legendary. The Galway Races in late July have been immortalised in songs and stories and continue to be a huge international tourist attraction to this day. B.OC.

Horslips. The first 'Celtic rock' band. Formed in 1970, Horslips capitalised on the traditional *music revival by fusing traditional melodies with rock and roll. One of its members was guitarist Declan Sinnott, who later became a noted rock musician. The band, which used mythic *Celtic heroes as motifs, heightened interest in the traditional until its demise in 1979. F.V.

Hugh Lane Municipal Gallery. Collection of almost 2,000 modern and contemporary works built upon the original collection of Sir Hugh *Lane. Funded by Dublin Corporation, the

Hugh Lane Gallery opened in 1933 as one of the foremost collections of modern art in Ireland. The collection is housed in Charlemont House, once the town house of James Caulfield, later First Earl of Charlemont (1728–99), and designed on classical lines by William Chambers (1723–96). The Hugh Lane Gallery offers a dynamic exhibition programme that explores multimedia expression alongside historical and retrospective exhibitions of Irish work. The gallery contains the reconstructed studio of Francis *Bacon and has a lively education and outreach programme. (Address: Parnell Square, Dublin 1. Web site: *www.hugh lane.ie*.) M.C.

Huguenots. French *Protestants who settled in Ireland in the late seventeenth century. Huguenots had been subjected to increasing persecution in France in the seventeenth century, and when the Edict of Nantes – which had granted religious toleration – was revoked in 1685, they were expelled. By 1665, small Huguenot communities had already settled in *Dublin and *Cork. About 10,000 immigrated in the 1690s; many were veterans of the Williamite armies in the recent Irish war.

Twenty-one Huguenot communities were formed. The most notable settlement was at Portarlington, in Queen's County (now County *Laois). The Huguenots made a disproportionate contribution to Irish commercial and industrial life. Near Lisburn, County *Armagh, Huguenots, such as Samuel Crommelin (who published *Essay on Linen Manufacture in Ireland*, 1705) were part of the emerging linen trade. In Dublin, the La Touche family was prominent in banking and politics. The writer of supernatural stories, Sheridan *Le Fanu, was also of Huguenot descent. Some Huguenot congregations joined the *Church of Ireland and the communities lost their distinct identity in the eighteenth and nineteenth centuries. Huguenot cemeteries can still be seen in Dublin and elsewhere. P.D.

Humbert, General (Jean Joseph Amable) (1767–1823). Leader of French military expedition to Ireland. On 23 August 1798, three frigates landed General Humbert and 1,070 French soldiers on the shore of Killala Bay, County *Mayo. About 1,500 Irish peasants joined him to liberate their country. Humbert's French professional and Irish ragtag army won victories before 8 September when it surrendered to superior forces at Ballinamuck, County *Longford. British victors treated the French captives with dignity and sent them home. They executed the Irish rebels. L.J.MC.

Hume, John (1937–). Politician. Born in Derry, Hume was a secondary school teacher and community activist. The outbreak of intercommunal violence in *Northern Ireland propelled him into the forefront of the *nationalist community leadership and, eventually, into a growing national and international role as one of the principal architects of the Northern Ireland *peace process. After the outbreak of violence in 1968, reacting against old-style politics, Hume became active in the Derry Citizens' Action Committee. In 1969, he became prominent in the *Northern Ireland Civil Rights Association (NICRA), founded specifically to advocate nonviolent change in Northern Ireland, without challenging its constitutional status as part of the United Kingdom. The following year, Hume became a founder of the *Social Democratic and Labour Party (SDLP), which was to take over from the old Nationalist Party as the vehicle for a more modern, articulate nationalism.

Hume has never held executive power, with the exception of a brief period as minister for commerce in the ill-fated power-sharing Executive in Northern Ireland in 1974. However, since assuming the leadership of the SDLP in 1979 (he resigned in 2001), he has wielded immense influence in Irish politics. Hume used this influence in three key areas: to

John Hume

promote awareness among citizens of the *Republic of Ireland about the realities of life in Northern Ireland; to lessen the fears of Northern *unionists about their political prospects in a united Ireland; and to persuade *republican militants away from armed struggle and toward the normal democratic process. The creation by the Irish government in 1984 of the New Ireland Forum to fill the vacuum created in Northern Ireland politics by the suspension of the Northern Ireland assembly was largely at his urging, and was at the core of his attempt to link north and south in a process aimed at removing violence from the political agenda.

In 1992, Hume took an even more dramatic initiative by engaging in secret discussions with Gerry *Adams, the *Sinn Féin leader, which eventually helped to bring about an *IRA cease-fire in 1997. Ironically, Hume was so successful in bringing Sinn Féin into constitutional politics, that it now rivals the SDLP as the electoral voice of northern nationalists. Unionists have maintained a certain coolness toward Hume, even as he has tried to reassure them that the *partition of Ireland will be increasingly irrelevant in a *European Union where the emphasis is on European integration and not traditional boundaries. Under his leadership, the SDLP remained committed to a united Ireland, while at the same time accepting what is effectively a unionist veto (the 'principle of consent').

Although he retired from membership of Northern Ireland's legislative assembly in 2001, he retained his membership both of the UK House of Commons (to which he was first elected in 1983) and of the European parliament (to which he was first elected in 1979). Hume, who has maintained that jobs and economic growth are the best antidote to sectarianism, has played a significant role as a facilitator of substantial investment by US companies in the long-dormant but now reviving Northern Ireland economy. US President Bill Clinton – not least because of Hume's urging – played a highly significant role in the *peace process. Hume shared the Nobel Peace Prize with David *Trimble in 1998 for his essential work for peace in Northern Ireland. J.H.

hunger strikes. A form of extreme protest throughout Irish history. Hunger strikes go back to earliest times in Ireland when they were used as a means of shaming a powerful person by fasting. In the nineteenth century, *Fenian prisoners used it to protest against their conditions.

In the twentieth century, on 25 November 1917, Thomas *Ashe, who was a rebel in the *Easter Rising, 1916, died having been force-fed while on hunger strike in *Mountjoy Jail. In 1920, Terence *MacSwiney, Lord Mayor of *Cork, and ten other *republican prisoners went on hunger strike. MacSwiney, who was transferred to Brixton prison, London, died on 25 October along with two other hunger strikers. Their deaths, particularly MacSwiney's, gained massive international publicity and huge sympathy for the Irish cause. After the *Civil War in 1923, republican prisoners in Mountjoy and *Kilmainham jails went on hunger strike demanding their release. The strike ended following two deaths.

Hunger strikes continued to be used by

republicans. Prisoners in the Maze (Long Kesh) began a campaign for the reinstatement of the special category or political prisoner status. Beginning in 1976, a refusal to wear prison clothes ('the blanket protest') escalated into the 'dirty protest' and, in 1980, into a hunger strike, which ended in confusion after the men thought mistakenly that their demands had been met. In March 1981, other republican prisoners, most notably Bobby Sands, began a hunger strike to restore special category status. At the time, the *IRA republican leadership did not approve of the strike, but later sanctioned it. In April, while still on hunger strike in prison, Sands was elected as MP for Fermanagh-South *Tyrone. He died on 5 May 1981, the 66 day of his fast. The campaign to get the government to concede to the strikers' demands mobilised thousands. The death of a further nine hunger strikers alienated many in the nationalist community and catapulted *Sinn Féin into electoral politics. T.C.

Hunt Museum, Limerick. Museum of art and *Celtic artifacts. Art historian and connoisseur John Hunt advised many collectors, including William Randolph Hearst. Hunt and his wife, Gertrude, also assembled their own eclectic collection of objets d'art, which they left in trust to the Irish people. The collection found its permanent home in the Hunt Museum, the eighteenth-century Custom House in Limerick City, which was officially opened in 1997. The collection of 2,000 items, ranging from the Stone Age to Picasso, includes a bronze horse by Leonardo da Vinci, Irish prehistoric and medieval antiquities, eighteenth-century Irish Delftware and paintings by Renoir and Yeats. P.H.

hurling. One of the national *sports of Ireland. Less widely played than *Gaelic football, hurling also attracts huge crowds, especially during the summer championship season. The game consists of two teams of 15 players each, using a stick, which is called a hurley or *camán*, and a small leather ball, a *sliotar*. Hurling is one of the fastest field sports in the world and one of the most skilful. Codified and promoted by the *Gaelic Athletic Association (GAA), the game has existed in one form or another for over three millennia with the earliest literary reference dating the game back to 1272 BC. The *Book of *Leinster*, compiled in the twelfth century, gives an account of how in 1272 BC the native Firbolg and the invading Tuatha De Danann, while preparing for battle, decided to stage a hurling match between the best players. Hurling features regularly in Irish *mythology, most famously associated with the legendary warrior *Cúchulainn, who was an acclaimed hurler.

Evolving through old Gaelic society (whose *brehon laws regulated the sport) and the *Anglo-Norman ascendancy, hurling was promoted and organised by *landlords in the seventeenth and eighteenth centuries. Contests between landowners' teams were commonplace until the agrarian agitation of the nineteenth century brought about the end of hurling in this form. Michael Cusack, one of the founders of the GAA, was a strong advocate of hurling's revival and the game, together with Gaelic football, was at the forefront of the GAA's campaign to promote indigenous sport. Today, although hurling is played throughout Ireland, the most successful teams are in the south.

There is little top-class hurling played north of a line drawn from *Galway in the west to *Dublin in the east. As in Gaelic football, the elite competition in hurling has traditionally been organised on a provincial basis, with the climax of the season being the All-Ireland final, now played on the second Sunday in September. The history of the game has been dominated by three counties, *Cork, *Kilkenny and *Tipperary, who between them account for two-thirds of All-Ireland title victories since the All-Ireland Championship system was established by the

Hurling

GAA in 1884.

In *Ulster, three counties, *Antrim, *Derry and *Down, compete for the provincial championship, but none has won the All-Ireland. Antrim reached the final on two occasions, in 1943 and 1989. *Connacht, in the west, has only one county, Galway, which contests the hurling championship. Galway has won the All-Ireland four times. *Leinster in the east and *Munster in the south are the two leading provinces in hurling. In Dublin, the most populous county in Ireland, Gaelic football is much more popular than hurling.

Kilkenny is the second-most successful county in the history of the game – a remarkable achievement for a small county. *Wexford and *Offaly also have a tradition of hurling and both have won All-Ireland finals. Munster is regarded as the home of hurling with all six of its counties having won the All-Ireland. (*Kerry's victory was a surprise as the county concentrates on and excels in Gaelic football.) Cork and Tipperary are the leading counties in Munster hurling, and their Munster finals in Thurles – regarded as the best hurling field in the country – are the stuff of legend. Cork leads with 29 All-Ireland titles in hurling. Christy Ring, from Cork, is regarded by many as the greatest hurler of all time. He played on the only team to win four successive All-Ireland finals between 1941 and 1944. Other legendary players include Mick Mackey of Limerick, Eddie Kehir of Kilkenny, John Doyle of Tipperary, Nicky Rackard of Wexford and John Keane of *Waterford.

The All-Ireland final of 1931 is credited with turning hurling into a mass spectator sport. It went to two replays before Cork overcame Kilkenny, with nearly 100,000 attending the three matches. Eight years later, the same counties played in the final, with Kilkenny winning by one point in the dramatic final of 1939. It is remembered as 'The Thunder and Lightning Final' because of the violent storm that broke ominously in the afternoon, the same day (3 September 1939) that the Second World War began. Record crowds watched the resurgent Wexford team of the 1950s, who won All-Irelands in 1955, 1956 and 1960 and reached the finals of 1951 and 1954. The famous 1926 Cork-Tipperary Munster final in Thurles ended in turmoil due to overcrowding and encroachment on the playing field. For the rescheduled game, which drew a then-record crowd of 27,000 and its replay, Tom Semple of the GAA – after whom the Thurles venue is now named – personally planned and oversaw the stewarding arrangements that made the occasion a great success. S.M.

Hutchinson, Billy (1959–). Politician and former *loyalist paramilitary. Born and raised in *Belfast's Shankill neighbourhood, Hutchinson grew up in the middle of the *Troubles. In response to *IRA violence, particularly *Bloody Friday, he joined the *UVF in 1972. In 1974, Hutchinson was sentenced to life imprisonment for the UVF-sponsored murder of two Belfast *Catholics, Michael Loughran and Edward Morgan. During his 15-year prison term, Hutchinson became an avid distance runner, received a social sciences degree and developed an interest in politics. Having left the Maze (Long Kesh) prison, Hutchinson joined the *Progressive Unionist Party (PUP) and became an active participant in the *Northern Ireland *peace process. In 1998, he earned one of the PUP's two seats in the Northern Ireland assembly. Hutchinson is a committed *socialist and a staunch supporter of the *Good Friday Agreement. R.D.

Hyde, Douglas (1860–1949). Cultural nationalist, writer, first president of Ireland (1939–45). Born in *Sligo, son of a *Protestant minister, Hyde moved to *Roscommon and while still very young developed an interest in the *Irish language. Educated at home and then at Trinity College, Dublin, he studied arts, theology and law. Hyde wrote numerous books on *folklore and *Irish literature, such as *Leabhar Sgéuluigheachta* (1889), *Love Songs of Connacht* (1893), *Beside the Fire* (1890) and *A Literary History of Ireland* (1899), and some poetry. His thought-provoking essay 'The Necessity for De-Anglicising Ireland', which he delivered in 1890 to the National Literary Society, questioned the fashion of imitating all things English while at the same time hating the English.

A friend of W. B. *Yeats, George *Moore, Lady *Gregory and other important writers of the *Irish Revival, Hyde wrote numerous plays, including *Casadh an t-Súgáin (The Twisting of the Rope)* (1901), a joint venture with Yeats and Lady Gregory, which was one of the first Irish-language plays to be acted in a theatre.

In 1893, Hyde was elected the first president of the *Gaelic League, the major force in the revival of the Irish language. His insistence that the Gaelic League should stay out of politics led to his resignation as president in 1915. He continued with his work as professor of Irish in University College, Dublin, until 1932 and was unanimously appointed Ireland's first president in 1938. G.U.L.

Hynes, Garry (1953–). Theatre director. Born in *Roscommon, Hynes founded the Druid Theatre Company in Galway in 1975 and was artistic director there until 1991. Her three-year tenure as artistic director of the *Abbey Theatre was marred by controversy and in 1995 she returned to her former position at the Druid. She directed the highly successful *Leenane Trilogy* by Martin *McDonagh, which won four Tony Awards in 1998, including one for best director. B.D.

I

Immigration. See **Emigration and Immigration.**

internment. Incarceration without trial or legal process. Internment has been used in Ireland, north and south, in every decade since *partition in 1920. The most notorious instance is part of the *Northern Ireland conflict. On 9 August 1971, to contain rising *IRA violence and specifically to foil a concerted bombing offensive, internment, or detention without trial, was introduced across Northern Ireland. In a series of dawn raids, 342 people, almost all *Catholics, were arrested and taken to makeshift camps. There was an immediate upsurge of violence and 17 people were killed during the next 48 hours. Of these, 10 were Catholic civilians who were shot dead by the British army. Internment continued until 5 December 1975. During that time, 1,981 people were detained: 1,874 were Catholic/*republican, while 107 were *Protestant/*loyalist. Seán MacStiofáin, IRA leader at the time, recalled that 'the result of the internment roundup and the interrogation excesses was that the British succeeded in bringing into combat not a diminished, but a vastly reinforced republican guerrilla army'.

Internment added to the sense of the IRA as an army. In Long Kesh (Maze) prison, in County *Antrim (an American air force base during the Second World War), all prisoners lived in 'cages', compounds of four Nissen huts surrounded by barbed wire. Each of three huts (120 feet by 24 feet) would house 40 men. The fourth was reserved for use as a canteen. Guards recognised IRA 'officers' and all communication went through the prisoners' 'Officer Commanding'. Under what became known as 'Special Category Status', prisoners were allowed to wear their own clothes and could freely associate at all times. The men imprisoned here organised themselves militarily. Lectures on tactics and arms were given and there was even drilling with dummy wooden guns. In 1973, William Whitelaw, the secretary of state for Northern Ireland, also conceded this status to convicted paramilitary prisoners. Internment and Special Category Status were phased out in 1975 as part of Britain's attempt to deal with the Northern Ireland crisis as a law and order problem. M.M.

Invincibles, the. A *nationalist secret society committed to violence. Established in *Dublin in 1881, the society grew out of the revolutionary *Fenian movement. The Invincibles sought to make Ireland ungovernable by assassinating British officials. Their most notorious act was the *Phoenix Park Murders (1882), which resulted in 26 arrests and five executions. The society ceased to function shortly after the murders. T.C.

Iona. Scottish island in the Inner Hebrides and centre of learning and piety. St *Colm Cille, or Columba, founded a monastery here in 563. He died on the island in 597. The saint's biography was written here around 700 by his successor, Abbot Adamnan. With a strong poetic tradition, Iona kept Irish annals up to 740 and many believe that the *Book of *Kells* was written there. Eighth/ninth-century high *crosses survive from the early monastery and the restored cathedral dates from the thirteenth century. P.H.

Ireland Act, the (1949). British legislative response to the *Republic of Ireland Act (1948). In the Ireland Act enacted on 2 June 1949, Westminster recognised the secession of the *Republic of Ireland from dominion status and confirmed that *Northern Ireland was part of the United Kingdom until its own parliament chose otherwise. It also allowed unrestricted travel between Ireland and Britain and granted British citizens' rights to Irish citizens living in the UK. P.E.

Ireton, Henry (1611–51). English politician and general. A commander of parliamentary forces during the English Civil War, Ireton married Oliver *Cromwell's daughter in 1646. In 1649, he went with Cromwell to Ireland and remained as lord deputy, capturing *Carlow, *Waterford, Duncannon (1650) and *Limerick (1651) where he died of fever. S.A.B.

Irish Academy of Letters. Modelled on the Swedish Academy that awards the Nobel Prize, the academy was founded by W. B. *Yeats in 1932 to reward achievement in letters and to organise writers to oppose literary censorship. George Bernard *Shaw was nominated its first president, Yeats its vice president. Twenty-five of Ireland's best-known writers were invited to become full founding members and a further ten associate members. All but seven (one of whom was James *Joyce) accepted. In 1933, the academy opposed the banning of Shaw's *The Black Girl in Search of God* without success. Among its awards were the Harmsworth Award for fiction, the Casement Prize for drama and verse, the O'Growney Prize for *Irish language publications and its highest award, the Gregory Medal. Prizes were awarded irregularly and rarely between 1940 and 1969 when commercial sponsorship led to a brief revival. The academy is currently inactive but has not been dissolved. M.S.T.

Irish America. Irish Americans represent the largest portion of the Irish Diaspora. In the 1990 US census, 44 million Americans claimed some Irish heritage. From the late seventeenth into the early nineteenth century, between a quarter- and a half-million Irish, mostly *Protestants, usually *Presbyterians, entered North America. Some *Ulster Presbyterians settled in New England and the Mid-Atlantic regions, but most chose the farmlands on the southern and northern frontiers, between Native Americans and tidewater whites. They fought on both sides in the *American Revolution. The Carnegies and Mellons date from this time. Beginning with Andrew Jackson, a number of American presidents have claimed Irish Protestant heritage, including Grover Cleveland, William McKinley, Woodrow Wilson and, more lately, Richard Nixon, Jimmy Carter, Ronald Reagan and Bill Clinton.

Since 1820, the vast majority of around six million Irish entering the United States have been *Catholic. Because of the Great *Famine, over a million left Ireland between 1845 and 1851, some on so-called 'coffin ships'. The largest portion went to the United States. Since many Americans of Ulster Presbyterian stock joined and sometimes led such anti-Catholic agitations as the Know-Nothing movement, claimed a British more than an Irish lineage and defined themselves as *Scots Irish, Irish America has had a mainly Catholic image and flavour. Not until relatively recently did many American Protestants acknowledge Hibernian backgrounds.

Transitions from economically and socially limited rural Ireland, where often Irish was the vernacular, to urban America bred poverty, alienation, neuroses, crime and broken families, exacerbating American anti-Catholic nativism.

Early Irish immigrants, mostly tenant farmers or agricultural labourers, lacked expertise to farm vast acres of rural America.

Settling in cities, initially in the north-east, they laboured on docks, in mines, on river-boats, in horse barns; dug canals; and laid railroad tracks. Dangerous occupations limited male life spans. Irish Catholics tended to emigrate as singles and, by the close of the nineteenth century, more women than men left home, taking jobs in American mills, factories or, more likely, in domestic service.

Victims of nativist bigotry themselves, many Irish Catholics, unfortunately, had little sympathy for other victims of discrimination. During the *American Civil War, Irish soldiers fought bravely on both sides. Most of those in blue did so to save the Union, not to emancipate slaves. An 1863 Draft Act provoked Irish urban riots. *New York's rampage cost over two million dollars in property damage and, more importantly, the deaths of eleven lynched African Americans, a Native American mistaken for a black, three policemen and 15 rioters. (Many of the police and soldiers who restored order also were Irish.) Much Irish racism stemmed from fears of losing jobs, ignorance and an inferiority complex. Later in the century, San Francisco's Denis Kearney campaigned to keep the Chinese out of the United States. In the 1960s, many Irish Americans opposed integrated housing and schooling out of the same fears. Anti-Semitism also has tarnished the Irish image, especially in the 1930s and 1940s, when a considerable number, especially in the east, became disciples of the infamous Father Charles Coughlin.

Following the Civil War, Irish America progressed economically and socially. In post-Famine Ireland, rising standards of living and an improved national school system meant that Irish immigrants now had more skills and education. New immigrants from southern and eastern Europe replaced the Irish on the lowest levels of the labour market. By the 1900s, many Irish Americans were skilled labourers and some middle-class professionals and businessmen. A number of women became teachers and nurses.

Many Irish Americans emotionally and financially fuelled militant *nationalist movements – the *Fenian movement and its counterpart in Ireland, the *IRB, *Clan na Gael and the *IRA – as well as constitutional nationalism – *home rule and the *Irish Parliamentary Party.

In the twentieth century, Irish Americans politically controlled most cities north of the Mason-Dixon line and had significant influence in New Orleans. Tammany Hall, the headquarters of New York City's Democratic Party, was the early model of the Irish urban political machine, one that *Chicago's Richard J. Daley perfected in the 1950s, 1960s and 1970s.

Often, Irish politicians were guilty of corruption, benefiting from graft and kickbacks. But on balance, Irish politics was more positive than negative. While urban reformers were more interested in morality than poverty, Irish politicians distributed food, coal and clothing and found jobs and paid medical and funeral expenses for impoverished constituents. Influenced by Catholic values rather than secular ideologies, Irish political machines steered the Democratic Party away from individualistic toward communal liberalism. During the 1920s, New York's multi-term governor, Al Smith, a Tammany Hall graduate, previewed much of Franklin Delano Roosevelt's New Deal agenda.

The Irish were hugely influential in the American Catholic church, operating a vast institutional structure of primary and secondary schools, colleges, hospitals and orphanages. Many of America's labour leaders have been Irish American: from Terence V. Powderly, the first grand master of the Knights of Labour in 1879, to Philip Murray and George Meany in the twentieth century.

After the Second World War, Irish America completed its difficult passage from urban ghettos to middle-class suburban neighbourhoods, from insecurity to self-confidence. Because so many women were nurses and teachers, and men worked for railroads, urban transport systems, local, state and federal governments and on police and fire departments, the Irish weathered the Depression better than most other groups. Educational benefits from the 1944 GI Bill of Rights rapidly increased Irish American economic, social and residential mobility.

Hollywood films in the 1930s and 1940s, with stars such as Spencer Tracy, Pat O'Brien and Bing Crosby playing benevolent, charming Irish American priests, did much to diminish anti-Catholicism so evident after Al Smith's loss to Herbert Hoover in the 1928 presidential election.

By the 1930s, Irish politicians had gained prominence on the national stage. James J. Farley was chairman of the Democratic Party. Frank Murphy was attorney general under FDR and later served on the Supreme Court. In 1960, John F. *Kennedy's election as the first and only Catholic president of the United States symbolised the Irish Catholic success story. Other Irish American politicians have been influential and have lobbied for direct American involvement in Northern Ireland. These include Speaker of the House Thomas P. 'Tip' O'Neill, Senate Majority Leader George Mitchell and Congressman Peter King. President Bill Clinton and Senator Mitchell were instrumental in bringing about the *peace process and the 1998 *Good Friday Agreement.

Irish Americans have also been prominent in athletics, particularly in baseball, which they once dominated (Mike 'King' Kelly, Ed Delahanty, Charles Comiskey, John McGraw, Connie Mack) and boxing (John L. Sullivan, 'Gentleman' Jim Corbett, Jack Dempsey, Gene Tunney, Billy Conn). They have been on the forefront of American entertainment with singers (Bing Crosby, Rosemary Clooney), dancers (Gene Kelly, Ray Bolger, Donald O'Connor), comedians (Jackie Gleason, Art Carney, Fred Allen) and actors (James Cagney, Spencer Tracy, Brian Dennehy, Barbara Stanwyck, Grace Kelly, Irene Dunne). John Ford may have been America's greatest film director and Eugene O'Neill its best playwright. Along with O'Neill, F. Scott Fitzgerald, Flannery O'Connor, William Kennedy, Alice McDermott, Pete Hamill and Tom Flanagan are among a long list of writers that indicate that there is an Irish dimension to the American literary tradition. (Flanagan's novels represent the very best in Irish historical fiction.)

With increasing assimilation throughout the twentieth century, many Irish Americans, middle-class and suburban, have abandoned Democratic communalism for Republican individualism. Today, for a large number of Irish Americans, ethnicity is defined in cultural rather than religious terms. It remains to be seen whether Irish identity will survive in a pluralistic American society. L.J.MC.

Irish Architectural Archive. A collection that preserves the records of Ireland's *architectural heritage. A nonprofit organisation established in 1976, the archive includes over 80,000 Irish architectural drawings from the late seventeenth to late twentieth century and over 300,000 photographs. It also holds an extensive reference library with material on Irish architects, buildings and styles. The archive has an active publications and outreach programme. (Address: 45 Merrion Square, Dublin 2. Web site: *www.iarc.ie*.) M.C.

Irish Brigades. See **Wild Geese.**

Irish Citizen Army (ICA). A workers' militia of about 350 members. The ICA was established after excessive violence was used against workers and protesters by the Dublin Metropolitan Police during the long-running industrial dispute known as the 1913 Lockout. The Irish Citizen Army was under the auspices of the Irish Transport and General Workers Union. James *Connolly, the union's acting general secretary, became its commandant. Training was provided by former British army officer, Captain Jack Whyte. Dedicated to *socialism and Irish independence, the Citizen Army was involved in the *Easter Rising of 1916. Connolly was one of the leaders executed after the rising's defeat. T.C.

Irish Civil War (1922–23). Bloody and bitter conflict, lasting from the summer of 1922 until the spring of 1923, between factions within Irish *republicanism over the terms of the *Anglo-Irish Treaty. The treaty, which ended the *Anglo-Irish War (1919–21), established an *Irish Free State with virtual independence for twenty-six (out of thirty-two) counties of Ireland, but with dominion status within the British *Commonwealth. Many republicans especially objected to the *oath of allegiance to the crown required by the treaty of all government officials. Only a few in the *Dáil objected to the *partition of Ireland and the failure of the treaty to provide for a united sovereign Ireland, because most believed that the *Boundary Commission would make territorial adjustments favourable to *nationalists and that eventually the Free State would take over (in some fashion) the six northern counties. They were much more concerned with the dominion status of the Free State, which was not the full-fledged *republic for which they had fought.

Treaty proponents, including Michael *Collins, one of the negotiators, argued that the Free State was a stepping-stone on the path to a full republic. On 7 January 1922, the second Dáil approved the treaty by a narrow 64 to 57 vote, with opponents beginning an immediate boycott of the new government. Pending the establishment of permanent institutions, sovereignty over the new Free State was shared temporarily by the Provisional Government, headed by Collins and Arthur *Griffith, who presided over the Dáil.

The political divisions over the treaty were echoed within the *IRA, with a majority opposed to any settlement that failed to achieve the republic for which they had fought. A final break between the Provisional Government and the strong anti-treaty faction within the IRA occurred in late March 1922. Defying a government ban, the IRA organised an army convention and established a new army executive to continue the struggle for a republic. On 14 April 1922, a group of anti-treaty forces led by Rory *O'Connor seized the *Four Courts and other buildings in *Dublin. They repudiated the civilian Provisional Government and formed a rival centre of authority. Meanwhile, during the protracted efforts to overcome differences over the treaty, Collins had gained valuable time to build, with British assistance, a new Free State army.

In May 1922, Collins and Éamon *de Valera made a final effort to hold the republican movement together with an electoral pact that would create a unity government in the new parliament to be elected in June. Arthur Griffith and other treaty supporters vigorously protested against this electoral alliance. The June elections demonstrated overwhelming backing for pro-treaty candidates, with only 36 anti-treaty representatives chosen out of a total of 128 seats. The anti-treaty group in the IRA then split into two further factions, with those in the Four Courts commanded by O'Connor advocating a resumption of the military campaign against Britain. Alarmed by the continued occupation of the Four Courts and the increasingly questionable ability of the Free State government to maintain order, the British government demanded action against the rebels and even threatened military intervention. When assassins killed the Northern Ireland *unionist MP Sir Henry Wilson in London on 22 June, the British escalated their pressure, holding the IRA faction in the Four Courts responsible. (Some historians have suggested that Collins himself probably ordered the assassination in retaliation for attacks on

*Catholics in *Northern Ireland.)

On 28 June, the Free State army attacked the Four Courts and, in little more than a week, the anti-treaty forces throughout Dublin had been routed. The attack on the Four Courts, however, reunified treaty opponents, including both the military forces (referred to as 'Irregulars' by the Provisional government) and politicians such as de Valera. Liam Lynch emerged as the commander of the anti-treaty militants who were strongest in the south and west of Ireland. Initially, they held *Cork and *Limerick, but the Free State army captured these strategically important cities by August. In the same month, the Free State lost two of its most important leaders. On 10 August Arthur Griffith died from a cerebral haemorrhage and, on 22 August Michael Collins was killed by an assassin's bullet in his native west Cork.

The military campaign of the anti-treaty forces suffered greatly from a lack of coordination. Guerrilla warfare fought by 'flying columns' became their predominant tactic. They resorted to theft to gain supplies, alienating many from their cause. During the Civil War, the anti-treaty forces burned many of the country houses of the landed *Anglo-Irish gentry. In October 1922, the Roman Catholic bishops issued a joint pastoral, which condemned the insurgents. Under the impetus of Richard *Mulcahy, who had succeeded Collins as commander of the Free State forces, the Dáil approved a Public Safety Bill, which took effect in October 1922 and set up military courts with draconian powers. Under this emergency legislation, which included the death penalty for illegal possession of weapons, the Free State government executed 77 political insurgents between November 1922 and March 1923. One of those executed was Erskine *Childers, a leading republican. In retaliation for the harsh new measures, Lynch ordered the targeting of pro-treaty members of the Dáil. After Deputy Seán Hales was assassinated on 7 December 1922, the Free State government ordered the immediate execution of Rory O'Connor, Liam Mellows and two other prominent leaders of the 'Irregulars'. During the course of the conflict, the government also interned over 10,000 rebels without trial. The uncompromising Lynch continued to overrule peace efforts as a new year of fighting began, but, in March 1923, he died in action. His successor, Frank *Aiken, suspended military operations on 30 April 1923 and de Valera began negotiations with the Free State government. Although no agreement could be reached on specific terms to end the conflict, on 24 May, Aiken ordered his forces to disarm and de Valera declared that, though the legitimacy of the Free State could not be recognised by true republicans, any continuation of the military struggle would for the moment be 'vain' and 'unwise'. The Free State government accepted this cessation of hostilities without either a negotiated peace or the complete disarmament of the rebels.

Civil War casualties, once thought to range as high as 4,000, are now estimated to be closer to 1,000. The war left the new state with significant economic burdens and caused deep psychological scars, which would cast a long shadow over Irish politics for decades to come. Beyond the disagreement about specific provisions of the treaty, the underlying issue in the Civil War involved whether the new state would have a democratic foundation. In the end, the will of the majority of the Irish people as expressed in open elections, which favoured acceptance of the treaty, prevailed.

Militant republicans, who regarded any settlement short of a full republic as a betrayal of the republican ideal, would continue their struggle beyond the Civil War through the following decades into the era of the *Northern Ireland Conflict. F.B.

Irish Exhibition of Living Art (IELA). An open exhibition of modernist work. Founded in 1943 by Louis *Le Brocquy in reaction to *Royal Hibernian Academy restrictions, the exhibition was supported by Mainie *Jellett and others as a democratic alternative that presented mostly abstract work. The organising committee was reconfigured in 1972 and a year later IELA ended. M.C.

Irish Free State (Saorstát Éireann). Official name of the twenty-six-county state that came into existence on 6 December 1922, one year after the signing of the *Anglo-Irish Treaty. Under the treaty, the state was to be a member of the *Commonwealth, with dominion status equal to that of Canada. The British monarch was to be represented by a governor-general, and all members of the Irish legislature were required to take an *oath of allegiance to the British crown. The Free State legislature, or *Oireachtas, consisted of two houses, the *Dáil and *Seanad Éireann.

A substantial anti-treaty faction led by Éamon *de Valera had bitterly opposed the Free State and its oath of allegiance to Britain, arguing for a free and independent *republic. After the treaty was ratified by a narrow margin, the dispute escalated into a bitter *Civil War in June 1922.

W. T. *Cosgrave was elected first president of the Executive Council in December 1922 at the height of the Civil War. It would be his task to establish a stable parliamentary democracy within the new state. Throughout the Civil War, the Free State government took strong measures to end the conflict, including the use of *internment without trial and execution (77 in all). Ultimately, these coercive measures and the government's superior resources helped the fledgling state to survive and in May 1923 the Civil War ended.

In August 1923, the fourth Dáil was elected with *Cumann na nGaedheal, the party founded by Cosgrave in April 1923, retaining power. De Valera's party, *Sinn Féin, refused to take the oath and participate in the new parliament. The absence of any effective opposition greatly strengthened the power of the new government as it attempted to re-establish law and order, rebuild the Irish *economy and assert Irish independence in foreign affairs.

In 1922, the *Gárda Síochána, an unarmed civil police force, was established. The legal system was reformed under the Courts of Justice Act (1924), which abolished both the British and Sinn Féin courts and established district and circuit courts to deal with most criminal cases and the high and supreme courts to adjudicate appeals and constitutional matters.

The Army Mutiny Crisis of 1924 represented a serious threat to the stability of the state. As the Free State government began to demobilise and restructure the army for a peacetime role, on 6 March 1924, officers issued a list of demands, which included an end to demobilisation and a guarantee that the government intended to establish a republic. Eoin *O'Duffy, appointed supreme commander of the army to deal with the mutiny, reached a compromise agreement. By successfully quelling the mutiny, the Free State established that the army was the non-political servant of the state.

In the area of economic development, the Free State government adopted a conservative policy, which was supported by banks, large farmers and the wealthy *Anglo-Irish landlord community. *Agriculture was the most important sector of the economy, involving more than half the population, but farms remained small and inefficient. The Ardnacrusha Hydro Electric Power plant and a number of semi-state companies, including the Electricity Supply Board (ESB) and the Irish Sugar Company, were established at this time. Britain was developed as Ireland's main market, and to encourage free trade, tariffs were not widely imposed. Approximately 13,000 new jobs were created in industry during this period, 1922–32.

To assert its international identity, the Free State joined the *League of Nations on 10 September 1923 and created an extensive foreign diplomatic service. In 1925, a major controversy was averted when the Free State government convinced the British to suppress the *Boundary Commission's recommendations that a part of County *Donegal be ceded to *Northern Ireland (in return for parts of County *Fermanagh and County *Armagh). The Ultimate Financial Agreement between Britain and Ireland, signed on 19 March 1926, waived certain financial claims against the Free State in return for continued payments of land annuities and pensions. The agreement was never passed by the Dáil and was later repudiated by de Valera after *Fianna Fáil came to power in 1932.

The Statute of Westminster, passed in 1931 by leaders of Commonwealth countries (with the Irish representatives particularly involved), gave dominions the right to accept, annul, or amend British legislation. The statute essentially ended British involvement in the Free State's affairs.

Cosgrave's party narrowly survived a strong challenge from de Valera's new party Fianna Fáil in the general election of 1927. Kevin *O'Higgins' assassination on 10 July renewed fears of a return to violence and the government passed a Public Safety Act, banning all revolutionary societies.

The economic depression of the early 1930s and rising unemployment led to the government's defeat in the general election of 1932. Fianna Fáil with *Labour Party support formed a government. In 1937, the *Constitution of 1922 was replaced with *Bunreacht na hÉireann*, in which Ireland was declared a sovereign, independent, democratic state and its name was changed to *Éire* (or in the English language, Ireland). P.E.

Irish Georgian Society. Ireland's *architectural heritage society. Founded in 1958 by Desmond Guinness, the society promotes the conservation of distinguished buildings and allied arts of all periods in Ireland through education and grants, planning participation, membership and fundraising. The society's main achievements include the saving of such buildings as Castletown, County *Kildare; Damer House, County *Tipperary; Doneraile Court, County *Cork; Roundwood, County *Laois; Tailors Hall, *Dublin, and 13 Henrietta Street, Dublin. (Address: 74 Merrion Square, Dublin 2. Web site: www.*irish-architecture.com*.) M.C.

Irish language. *Celtic language. Irish, Welsh, Breton, Scottish Gaelic and the extinct languages of Manx (from the Isle of Man) and Cornish (from Cornwall) form the group of Celtic languages, which share similar grammatical, phonological, syntactical and lexicographical features. The language is historically and generally known as Irish, although some people prefer to call it 'Gaelic', which is the Anglicised word for *Gaeilge*, or the Irish word for the Irish language. The most common theory put forward by linguists is that a primitive form of the Irish language arrived from the continent with Celtic invaders, colonists, or travellers some centuries before the Christian era.

Recent archaeological theory argues that the Irish language developed in Ireland over thousands of years before *Christianity, and if there was a Celtic invasion it goes much further back in time than heretofore supposed. Regardless, Irish was the only language of the country when literacy started in Ireland in the fifth and sixth centuries with the arrival of Christianity. Monks wrote it down using Latin as a model and they transcribed Irish *mythology and sagas, often of a pagan or mythological provenance. As a result, Irish *literature is the oldest continuing vernacular literature in Western Europe. The same people who wrote the *Book of *Kells* (illuminated *manuscript of the Gospels) in Latin, probably also recast or composed Irish stories in the Irish language. There is a vast corpus of early Irish literature, particularly relating to religious and legal matters. These are written in Old Irish, which gave way to Middle Irish in about the ninth century.

Although the *Viking invaders disrupted commercial and religious life, they had little impact on the language itself, lending a few paltry words of commerce and of seafaring. Irish learning became more secularised from the twelfth century onward, with the responsibility for training of scholars and poets passing to families of powerful patronage. The *Anglo-Norman invasion of 1169 did little to change this pattern, except for the introduction of the English language. Although the new language had little immediate effect, it slowly took over the entire Gaelic world from the early seventeenth century onward. The Anglo-Norman aristocracy, although always described by the native Irish as *Sasanaigh*, or English, became, in the celebrated phrase, 'more Irish than the Irish themselves'. They wrote stories and poetry in the Irish language, became patrons of art and literature, and eventually opposed English rule.

The Statute of *Kilkenny (1366) outlawed the use of the Irish language, habits and customs by the English who lived inside and outside the *Pale. *Henry VIII's 'Act for the English order, habite and language' of 1537 was a serious attempt to begin the Anglicisation of the native Irish, but was still largely directed to those who considered themselves 'the king's true subjects'. The Irish language began to come under pressure only when the Irish political system was destroyed in the seventeenth century. The defeat of the Irish by the English in the *Nine Years War, in the *Cromwellian conquest and in the ultimate war of the English succession (1689–91) reduced the Irish language to one of common speech, banished from the higher domains of government, law, commerce, education and discursive prose.

Many Irish began to turn to the English language during the eighteenth century in order to gain some power under the English system, and in the nineteenth century in order to survive. Despite this, there were probably more speakers of Irish in 1845, just before the *Famine, than ever before. But they were all poor and the vast majority of them lived in the west and in the south of the country. Most of those who died in the Famine were Irish speakers, as were most of those who emigrated in the following decade. From the middle of the nineteenth century, Irish, by now associated with poverty, defeat and hunger, became a minority language in its own country. At the turn of the twentieth century, the national *Irish Language Revival heralded a new life for the language and for the first time in hundreds of years Irish speakers were given a dignity which they had been denied.

The *Gaelic League was the most important of the language organisations that spread enthusiasm for all things Irish. The *Irish Free State came into being on the basis of a cultural as well as a political revival and, thus, it was not surprising that the new state gave proper emphasis to the language. Irish returned into domains of government, education and thought from which it had been banished since the seventeenth century. Irish was designated an official language in the first Constitution of 1922. However, the Irish-speaking areas (the *Gaeltacht) continued to shrink, albeit at a slower pace. Irish is now one of the two official languages of Ireland and has recognition for the first time in the six counties of *Northern Ireland. It has developed a strong and vibrant literature, which is a continuation of the past. There are Irish-language newspapers, radio stations and a television channel. Irish is taught to every schoolchild and plays a central role in much cultural activity. Although under constant and unremitting pressure from English, the day-to-day language in most of Ireland, Irish continues to flourish as the first language or the language of choice of many Irish people. A.T.

Irish Language Revival. Ongoing movement, beginning in the nineteenth century, to revive interest in, and use of, the *Irish language. The Irish Language Revival, also known as the Gaelic Revival, has its genesis in several learned societies that were founded to study antiquities in the nineteenth century. The most prominent of these were the Gaelic Society of Dublin (1807), the Archaeological Society (1840), the Celtic Society (1845) and the Ossianic Society (1853). Phillip Barron founded an Irish school in 1835 in *Waterford, and in 1862, Risteard Daltún from *Tipperary published *An Fíor-Éireannach (Real Ireland)*, one of the earliest attempts at an Irish language newspaper. Micheál Ó Lócháin from *Galway published the bilingual paper *An Gaodhal (the Irishman)* in *New York in 1881. New works in Irish were published by the Archbishop of Tuam, John McHale, who also translated works by authors as diverse as Thomas *Moore and Homer. There was not a united movement, however, until the Society for the Preservation of the Irish Language (SPIL) was established in 1876. SPIL succeeded in having Irish included as a voluntary subject in national schools in 1878. The Gaelic Union, an offshoot of SPIL, was founded in 1879 and published the *Gaelic Journal* from 1882 onward. Dubhghlas de hÍde's (Douglas *Hyde) essay 'The Necessity for De-Anglicising Ireland' decried the abandonment of the national tongue in favour of English. Essays by scholars such as Eoghan Ó Gramhnaigh and Eoin *MacNeill called on the nation to halt the decline of the language.

The founding of the *Gaelic League in 1893 was the most important single event in the revival of the language. By 1907, there were 600 Gaelic League branches throughout Ireland. Travelling teachers were a common sight as they moved, mainly on bicycle, from one part of a county to the next, teaching both Irish and Irish history to their classes. The cultural festival the Oireachtas was founded in 1897 for native speakers and learners alike. A sense of pride was instilled in the language after years of disrespect and neglect. The Gaelic League, with its *Feiseanna* (concerts), the Oireachtas and new periodicals such as *Fáinne an Lae* ('The Dawn of Day', 1898–1900) and **An Claidheamh Soluis* ('The Sword of Light', 1899), gave a platform to writers such as An tAthair Peadar Ó Laoghaire, Pádraig MacPiarais (Patrick *Pearse) and Pádraic *Ó Conaire, who created a new literature in Irish. Initially, many of these writers dismissed the *Irish Literary Revival of W. B. *Yeats and J. M. *Synge (which strived to create a national Irish literature in English) as a heresy and a form of British imperialism. This hard line had softened by 1905, when Pearse came to regard the Irish National Theatre as an ally rather than an enemy of the language movement.

In 1922, when part of Ireland gained independence from Britain, the Irish language was made an official language of the state. G.U.L.

Irish Literary Revival. See **Irish Revival.**

Irish Museum of Modern Art (IMMA). The main museum of modern art in Ireland. Opened in 1991 in the Royal Hospital Kilmainham under the directorship of Declan MacGonigal, the museum is directly funded by the government. The Royal Hospital was originally founded by James Butler of Kilkenny Castle (Duke of Ormonde) in 1680 as a home and hospital for aging soldiers and designed by William Robinson in 1684. Today, fully refurbished with climate-controlled galleries, the museum displays the best of Irish and international postwar art in rotating temporary exhibitions and curated shows. IMMA runs educational and community programmes and helps local art organisations throughout Ireland to set up and present exhibitions and projects. The museum hosts the annual Glen Dimplex Artists Award. (Address: Kilmainham, Dublin 8. Web site: *www.modernart.ie.*) M.C.

Irish parliament, the. See **Parliament, Irish.**

Irish Parliamentary Party. Irish *nationalist MPs in the late nineteenth and early twentieth century dedicated to *home rule. Following the general election of 1874, the Irish Parliamentary Party, a coalition of former *Repealers, Liberals and a few former *Fenians and Conservatives, with Isaac *Butt as first chair, began its existence. Butt's hesitant leadership, inattention to duties and pro-British imperialism antagonised Charles Stewart *Parnell and others demanding a more vigorous campaign for home rule. In 1879, William Shaw succeeded the deceased Butt. Following the 1880 general election, Parnell became chair and created a tightly disciplined party, unified in purpose and opinion, energised by the *Land War and heavily financed by *Irish America. Playing balance of power politics in the British House of Commons, the Irish Parliamentary Party forged an alliance with *Gladstone's Liberals, resulting in significant benefits to Ireland and two home rule bills (the first lost in the House of Commons, the second in the House of Lords).

Parnell's involvement in the *O'Shea divorce scandal in 1890 split the party and Irish nationalism. In 1900, the two branches reunited under the leadership of John *Redmond, leader of the Parnellite minority. By 1914, the Irish Parliamentary Party had won the struggle for home rule but *Ulster *unionist intransigence frustrated the victory. This disappointment, Irish casualties in the *First World War, resistance to a military draft and the popularity of the 1916 *Easter Rising martyrs led to the triumph of *Sinn Féin in the 1918 general election and, for all practical purposes, the demise of the Irish Parliamentary Party. In the Northern Ireland parliament, the remnants of the party became the *Nationalist Party. L.J.MC.

IRA (Irish Republican Army). Paramilitary organisation representing militant separatist *republicanism. Since its emergence during the *Anglo-Irish War (1919–21), the Irish Republican Army has sought to end British government in Ireland and establish an independent and unified Irish *republic by means of armed struggle. The IRA has upheld the tradition of militant republicanism that originated with the *United Irishmen in the 1790s and continued through the *IRB of the late nineteenth and early twentieth centuries. More specifically, the organisation developed from the small faction of Irish *Volunteers that launched the *Easter Rising in 1916. Despite government suppression following the rising, the Volunteers re-established themselves in 1917.

When *Sinn Féin became the dominant political party in the 1918 elections and established the first *Dáil Éireann in January 1919, the Irish Volunteers, increasingly known as the Irish Republican Army, became the official military force of the emergent state. The Dáil, however, exercised limited control over the IRA and tactical decisions were largely made by local commanders.

During the *Anglo-Irish War, Michael *Collins came to the fore as the IRA's director of organisation and intelligence. Despite few weapons, the organisation's guerrilla strategy forced the British government to negotiate a settlement. The *Anglo-Irish Treaty (6 December 1921) provided only dominion status for a *partitioned country (twenty-six out of thirty-two counties), rather than a full and unified republic, and also required an *oath of allegiance to the crown. These terms split the IRA into pro-treaty supporters of the new *Free

State and an anti-treaty republican faction. The ensuing bitter *Civil War (1922–23) was fought between the Free State army and the IRA, referred to as the Irregulars by the new government.

In 1926, Éamon *de Valera led many of the defeated republicans into constitutional politics by forming the *Fianna Fáil party; those who did not follow de Valera and were committed to a united Ireland by armed force, remained known as the IRA. In 1932, Fianna Fáil became the governing party and, in 1936, de Valera's government proscribed the IRA. For the next few decades, the IRA remained a fringe movement with very limited popular support. In 1939, the organisation undertook a brief bombing campaign in Britain and, from 1956 to 1962, its 'border campaign' targeted British military and administrative centres in *Northern Ireland. During the 1960s, its nationalist ideology became increasingly combined with socialist principles. The outbreak of 'the *Troubles' in Northern Ireland in the late 1960s led to the IRA's re-emergence to new prominence.

At the 1969 Army Convention, the organisation split on ideological grounds into the Official and Provisional IRA. The increasingly Marxist Official IRA declared a total cease-fire in the summer of 1972, and from then on the term IRA has been used for the Provisionals. The IRA (now the Provisionals) launched a military campaign to end conclusively British rule in Northern Ireland. Heavy-handed incursions by the British security forces into *Catholic neighbourhoods in *Belfast and the shooting of 13 unarmed protesters on *Bloody Sunday (30 January 1972) in *Derry re-energised the Provisional IRA. Attacks on civilian as well as military targets by IRA bombers and gunmen were countered by increasingly brutal methods by the British security forces in a seemingly endless cycle of violence.

Some of the more outrageous exploits of the IRA included the assassination of Lord Mountbatten in County *Sligo in 1979, and an explosion in Brighton, England, during the 1984 Conservative Party Conference, which nearly succeeded in killing British Prime Minister Margaret *Thatcher and other government ministers. During the *hunger strikes of 1981, a combined strategy of 'the armalite and ballot box' emerged, as Sinn Féin (the IRA's political wing) contested elections in both Northern Ireland and the Irish Republic. By the early 1990s, the stalemated military campaign led some within the republican movement, including Gerry *Adams, to question the continuation of the 'long war'. On 31 August 1994, the IRA announced a cease-fire. Although a perceived lack of progress during negotiations with the British government led the IRA to renew its military campaign with a bombing at *Canary Wharf in London on 9 February 1996, a new *Labour government headed by Tony *Blair revived the *peace process and a new cease-fire was declared by the IRA on 20 July 1997. After difficult negotiations, Sinn Féin representatives signed the *Good Friday Agreement on 10 April 1998. Since the agreement, the 'decommissioning' of weapons held by both the IRA and loyalist paramilitaries, as well as the pace of the withdrawal of British troops from Northern Ireland, have proved especially contentious. Although small groups of dissident republicans, including the 'Real IRA', continue to pursue the armed conflict, most members of the IRA have now accepted constitutional methods to achieve their aim of a unified Irish Republic. F.B.

IRB (Irish Republican Brotherhood). Revolutionary *nationalist organisation of the late nineteenth and early twentieth centuries, which was active in Ireland, Britain and the United States. Inspired by revolutionary groups on the continent, James *Stephens founded the organisation in *Dublin in March 1858 with the goal of achieving an Irish *republic by armed force. Its members became known as *Fenians after the legendary warriors of Irish *mythology. Although it was secret and oath-bound, British agents easily infiltrated the organisation. Urban workers and artisans, in particular, supported the IRB. Despite opposition from the *Catholic church because of its revolutionary ideology, many members remained devout Catholics. More militant members forced Stephens from the leadership in 1866 when he failed to deliver a promised armed rebellion. Partly because of informers, the subsequent rising that took place in Ireland in 1867 was easily put down by the authorities.

Meanwhile, in 1866, 1867 and 1871, Irish American Fenians, many of them veterans of the *American Civil War, launched unsuccessful attacks on British Canada. The execution of the three *Manchester Martyrs in England in November 1867, for their role in a policeman's death during an attempt to free Fenian prisoners, galvanised public sympathy in Ireland. The *home rule movement of the 1870s grew out of the Amnesty Association, founded in 1869 to free imprisoned Fenians. After his release in 1871, one former prisoner, John *Devoy, emigrated to the United States and proved to be indefatigable in promoting Irish American support for the IRB. In June 1879, Devoy negotiated a pragmatic agreement, the 'New Departure', with Charles Stewart *Parnell, the leader of the *Irish Parliamentary Party (from 1880) and Michael *Davitt, a founder of the *Land League, by which the Fenians would support a unified nationalist front on both home rule and land reform. Many members of the IRB opposed this temporary alliance with constitutional nationalism.

During the 1880s, Parnell's success in building a disciplined Irish party at Westminster eclipsed the revolutionary appeal of the Fenians. The revival of the IRB from a period of dormancy began with the return to Ireland in 1907 of Thomas *Clarke, who had spent 15 years in English prisons. The deferral of home rule by the British government in 1914 due to the beginning of the *First World War provided Clarke and younger colleagues, including Seán MacDermott and Patrick *Pearse, the impetus and opportunity for radical action. Accordingly, the IRB leadership organised the *Easter Rising of 1916, in which James *Connolly's Citizen Army also participated. The formation of the *Irish IRA under the leadership of Michael *Collins, an IRB member, to wage an open war against British rule from 1919 to 1921 made the conspiratorial IRB less relevant and the organisation eventually dissolved in 1924. F.B.

Irish Revival. Resurgent Irish cultural movement of the nineteenth century (also known as Celtic Revival and Irish Literary Revival). By the beginning of the nineteenth century, with the *Irish language in drastic decline, societies were formed to study the riches of the native culture – such as the Gaelic Society of Dublin (1807), the Iberno-Celtic Society (1818) and the Ulster Gaelic Society (1830). Throughout the nineteenth century, a massive corpus of the old literature was edited and translated by scholars including Eugene *O'Curry, John *O'Donovan, John O'Daly, Standish Hayes O'Grady and Whitley Stokes. European scholars were also becoming aware of the linguistic and cultural value of the Irish sources. At the same time, active forms of cultural expression emerged, such as: the *nationalist fervour of Thomas *Davis and *Young Ireland; the fresh creative voices of the poets Samuel *Ferguson and James Clarence *Mangan; and the popular folklore anthologies published by Patrick Kennedy and others. All pursued the quest for a new identity based on Gaelic sources but largely expressed through the English language.

This spirit of Irish cultural resurgence was greatly magnified by the foundation in 1884 of the *Gaelic Athletic Association to promote native games and, in 1893, of the *Gaelic League to arrest the decline of the Irish language. By the 1890s, three major literary figures had come to the forefront of this movement: the poet and dramatist W. B. *Yeats, the Gaelic scholar and writer Douglas *Hyde and Lady Augusta *Gregory, playwright, collector of folklore and translator of myth. Their work would crystallise the quest for an Irish identity and spearhead the Celtic Revival. In 1897, Lady Gregory, Yeats and others began to formulate plans for a national theatre; this led to the creation of the Irish Literary Theatre (which became known as the *Abbey Theatre in 1904). The first production (in 1899) by the Irish National Theatre was Yeats' *The Countess Cathleen*, which incorporates much of the spirit of the Celtic Revival. Cathleen represented the protective female symbol of Ireland, beautiful in form and spirit, protecting her people in time of distress. Another powerful symbolic figure of the revival was the mythological hero *Cúchulainn, who single-handedly protected his people from enemy attacks. *Irish Language Revivalists who advocated a purely Irish-language literature were suspicious of the idea of writing in English and tended to dismiss *Anglo-Irish writers as irrelevant to the Irish Revival. By 1910 a specifically Irish mode of writing in English had been established, which drew its images from myth and folklore and its language from the inflections of Irish dialect speech. D.OH.

Irish traditional music. See **music, traditional.**

Irish Traditional Music Archive (ITMA). A multimedia reference archive and resource centre in *Dublin for Irish *music, song and *dance. Founded in 1987, this nonprofit music centre (financed by the *Arts Council) has all of *Radio Éireann's (*RTÉ) and BBC's material from the 1920s until the present, as well as manuscripts, ballad sheets, graphic images, photographs, songbooks and tune notations. ITMA is constantly acquiring new material. All the major collections and performers are represented in its 15,000 printed items and 10,000 hours of sound recordings. F.V.

J

Jacobites. Followers of the *Catholic King *James II (1633–1701), from the Latin word for James, *Jacobus*. After the Treaty of *Limerick (1691), many Irish Jacobites emigrated to *France, where King James lived in exile. From there, they planned the restoration of the throne of England to the Stuarts, but successive attempts all failed, culminating in the Battle of Culloden (1746).

A literary Jacobite tradition (poetry celebrating the Stuarts' return to power) survived well into the eighteenth century. The Catholic church allowed the exiled Stuarts to nominate Irish bishops until 1766. Jacobitism in Ireland was never as strong as in *Scotland, where loyalty to the Stuarts remained firm, although some Irish participated in Jacobite conspiracies in Britain and Irish soldiers in the French army fought in the 1745 Rebellion. Some contemporaries viewed Irish recruitment into France's Irish Brigade as a Jacobite threat. By the mid-eighteenth century, however, Jacobitism was in rapid decline. T.C.

James II (1633–1701). King of England and Ireland (1685–88). James II succeeded his brother Charles II in 1685, but his reign was cut short by the 'Glorious Revolution'. His active promotion of Roman *Catholicism offended the deep-rooted anti-Catholicism of his English and Scottish subjects. His son-in-law *William of Orange, leader of the Netherlands, invaded England and deposed him (November–December 1688) primarily to forestall an Anglo-French alliance in the looming Nine Years War (1689–97).

Richard Talbot, Earl of Tyrconnell, James' appointee as commander of the army and later (1687) lord lieutenant, ensured that Irish Catholics controlled the administration and army in Ireland. Shortly after James' landing in Ireland (March 1689), all of the country except for *Derry and Enniskillen, County *Fermanagh, was brought under his control. While James sympathised with his fellow Catholics, he wanted to maintain Ireland's political subordination. He very reluctantly acquiesced in the reversal of the *Cromwellian Land Settlement and the *Irish parliament's assertion of independence from the English parliament.

James' performance as a military commander was mixed. D'Avaux, the French envoy, identified the central weakness in James' leadership: '[H]e is much taken up with little things ... passing over lightly those which are essential'. James saw Ireland as a stepping-stone to regain Scotland and England but his Irish followers did not, by and large, share his three-kingdom preoccupation. The French, James correctly observed in his *Memoirs*, were 'averse from venturing more succours than what was absolutely necessary to keep the war alive' in Ireland. James rightly rejected French advice and confronted the expeditionary force led by Marshal Schomberg in the autumn of 1689. This forced William III to lead another, larger, expedition to Ireland in 1690.

On balance, James' apparent decision to fight a delaying action at the *Boyne (July 1690) was justifiable even though the Franco-Irish army was heavily outnumbered. However, he perpetrated a gross error in switching troops from the critical river crossing at Oldbridge and suffered a psychological collapse immediately after the battle. James II was, by his later admission, 'too precipitate' in embarking for France. The Battle of the Boyne was indecisive and the Irish would fight for over another year.

James spent the remainder of his life in France, lapsing into apathy and fatalism. The Irish, as evidenced by *folklore and contemporary historiography, were ambivalent about James the man, if not James the king. Even an ardently *Jacobite historian like the Abbé Mac Geoghegan could include the barbed comment, 'Sire, if you possessed a hundred kingdoms, you would lose them'. P.L.

Jellett, Mainie (1897–1944). Cubist painter and theorist. Born in *Dublin, Jellett studied in Dublin, London and Paris. She learned an academic style from Walter Sickert but later developed an idealist version of cubism under the influence of Albert Gleizes. After harsh criticism of her abstract work, Jellett returned to a more figurative style that incorporated religious subject matter. She was a member of the Society of Dublin Painters and a founding member of the *Irish Exhibition of Living Art in 1943. M.C.

Jenkinson, Biddy (1929–). Pseudonym of an *Irish-language feminist poet and critic. Jenkinson has maintained her privacy and she refuses to be translated, believing that *Irish literature cannot be translated into English without loss. She has been published widely in Irish literary journals such as *Innti* and *Comhar*. Her poetry collections include *Báisteadh Gintlí* (1987), *Uiscí Beatha* (1988) and *Dán na hUidhre* (1991). She published her poetic manifesto in the *Irish University Review* (spring/summer 1991). Jenkinson writes with emotional intensity about femininity, motherhood and the woman's role in sustaining humankind's links with nature. C.D.

Jesuits. Catholic religious order, also known as the Society of Jesus. Ignatius Loyola founded the Society of Jesus in Spain in 1534. The Jesuits came to Ireland in 1542 during the reign of *Henry VIII. After the Council of Trent in 1563, the Jesuits promoted the Counter-Reformation, preserving Irish loyalty to *Catholicism during the *Protestant Reformation. Famed for their rigorous system of *education, the Jesuits opened 13 schools, colleges and residences in Ireland and a novitiate at Kilkenny between 1642 and 1654. After *James II's defeat at the Battle of the *Boyne in 1690, only six Jesuits remained in Ireland. The relaxation of the *Penal Laws in the mid-1700s brought a resurgence in the number of Jesuits until Pope Clement XIV, under pressure from Catholics who saw the Jesuits as overly domineering, reluctantly suppressed the order in 1773. During the order's gradual restoration between 1801 and 1814, Father Peter Kenney, the first superior of the restored order, founded the renowned College of Clongowes. Other schools opened soon after and the Jesuit reputation for education led the Irish bishops to entrust the administration of University College, Dublin, to the Society in 1883. Jesuits also played a major role in the genesis of the new National University in 1908. During the 1960s, the *Second Vatican Council inspired Jesuits to focus on issues of social justice. M.P.C.

Jews. Although officially refused residency in 1079, a number of Jews immigrated to Ireland after the *Anglo-Norman invasion. It was an English Jew in Bristol who lent *Strongbow funds that helped finance the invasion. The Irish Jews were expelled along with the English Jews in 1290 and with the exception of a few Spanish *conversos*, there were no Jews in Ireland until the *Cromwellian Settlement.

A synagogue may have existed in *Dublin as early as 1660, a cemetery in 1717 and a new synagogue in 1762. In *Cork, a cemetery existed in 1727 and a ritual slaughterer in 1753. Jewish merchants were in *Belfast in the 1750s and a Jewish butcher in 1771. Thirty Jewish families were in Galway in 1781 and a few Jews elsewhere throughout the island.

Jews, along with *Catholics, were excluded from the guilds in the eighteenth century. Legislation offering Jews citizenship was defeated in 1743. In the nineteenth century, increased persecution in Eastern Europe led to the immigration of Jews, mostly from Latvia and Lithuania, to Ireland. They settled mainly in Dublin and Cork and engaged in *furniture making, antiques and peddling. According to census figures, there were approximately 5,000 Jews in Ireland by 1911.

In the 1890s, there were anti-Jewish demonstrations in Dublin and Cork, and a major anti-Jewish boycott and attack in *Limerick in 1904. This mirrored an increase in anti-Semitism on the continent, as seen in the Dreyfus Case and the publication of *The Protocols of the Learned Elders of Zion*. Throughout the 1920s and 1930s, two Irish priests, Denis Fahey and Thomas Cahill, spread a virulent anti-Semitism premised on the *Protocols*, and Fahey greatly influenced the infamous American anti-Semite, Father Coughlin. During the Holocaust, thousands of entry requests were denied on economic and anti-Semitic grounds. After the war, a few Jews were admitted. In the 1960s, a Dublin synagogue was set on fire. To describe modern alienation and exile, James *Joyce made the protagonist of his masterpiece *Ulysses* (1922) a Jew.

Ireland refused to recognise the existence of the state of Israel until 1963, and it was only in 1996 that the first Irish ambassador took up residence. Isaac Herzog, who was Chief Rabbi of the *Irish Free State (1921–36), became Israel's first Chief Ashkenazic Rabbi and his son, *Chaim, who was born in Belfast, was Israel's president from 1983 to 1993. Dublin had two Jewish mayors, Robert Briscoe (1956 and 1961) and his son, Ben Briscoe (1988), and Cork had a Jewish mayor in 1977, Gerald Goldberg. Jewish life in Ireland continues today for the approximately 1,500 Jews located mainly in Dublin. G.M.W.

John, King of England (1167–1216). Third son of *Henry II, appointed Lord of Ireland, 1177. His visit in 1185 to Ireland was disastrous. He failed to gain the support of the *Norman *landlords or local Irish kings. John became King of England in 1199, and on a second visit to Ireland in 1210, he finally stamped royal authority on the country and introduced the common law of England. However, King John's control in Ireland suffered a setback after the barons' revolt of 1212. T.C.

Johnston, Denis (1901–84). Playwright. Born in *Dublin and educated at Cambridge and Harvard, Johnston worked as a barrister in Dublin. His disillusionment with Irish *nationalism is reflected in his satirical play *The Old Lady Says 'No!'* (1929). A play in the expressionist tradition, it depicts emotional experience rather than objective reality and draws on a wide range of quotations to create a pastiche effect. Like his other works, including the play *The Moon in the Yellow River* (1931), it is intellectually demanding. M.S.T.

Johnston, Jennifer (1930–). Novelist. Born in *Dublin, Johnston is best known for her spare, economical style. Her works focus on the struggle between loyalties – personal and political, public and private – which are often played out against the background of the decaying 'Big House'. Johnston's first novel, *The Captains and the Kings* (1972), won the *Evening Standard* First Novel Award. *The Old Jest* (1979) won the Whitbread Award and *Shadows on Our Skin* (1977) was short-listed for the Booker Prize. A collection of three novels, *The Captains and the Kings* (1972), *The Railway Station Man* (1984) and *Fool's Sanctuary* (1987) was published as *The Essential Jennifer Johnston* (2000). N.H.

Jordan, Neil (1950–). Novelist and filmmaker. Born in *Sligo, Jordan was one of the founders of the innovative Irish Writers' Co-

Neil Jordan

operative, which published his first book, *Night in Tunisia* (1976), a collection of stories. A novel, *The Past* (1980) followed, but since the release of his first feature film, *Angel* (1982), he has been known mainly as a film-maker. His writing and directing have earned him an international reputation and a number of prestigious awards. Jordan's two best-known films are *The Crying Game* (1992) and the bio-epic *Michael Collins* (1996). In both, his long-term fascination with the fabrication of personality and identity is set in the context of Irish historical violence. His screenplay for *The Crying Game* won an Academy Award. Such films as *The Company of Wolves* (1984), *Mona Lisa* (1986), *The Miracle* (1991) and an adaptation of Patrick McCabe's novel *The Butcher Boy* (1997) have the intensity and psychological complexity for which Jordan has become renowned. He has also made the Hollywood films *High Spirits* (1988), *We're No Angels* (1990), *Interview with the Vampire* (1994) and *In Dreams* (1999). Jordan has published a number of screen-plays, a novella, *The Dream of a Beast* (1983) and the novel *Sunrise with Sea Monster* (1995), entitled *Nightlines* in the United States. G.OB.

Joyce, James Augustine (1882–1941). Writer. No other writer has influenced twentieth-century literature as much as James Joyce. He is the ultimate modernist who revolutionised the novel with his inventive use of the stream of consciousness and verbal acrobatics.

Born on 2 February 1882, in *Dublin, James was the eldest of ten children in a relatively prosperous, middle-class, *Catholic family. Even as the family sank into poverty, largely because of his father's drinking, the young James received the best education from the *Jesuit schools Clongowes Wood and Belvedere College.

By the time Joyce enrolled at Dublin's Royal University (now University College, Dublin) in 1898, the family was living in the utmost squalor, hounded by debt collectors, evicted by landlords, constantly moving from one shabby house to another. Yet throughout this trauma, Joyce maintained an intellectual detachment, a trait he would later bring to a fine art form. An ambitious and independent-minded student, Joyce had his essay 'Ibsen's New Drama' published in the *Fortnightly Review* in 1900. Ibsen sent Joyce a note in which he expressed appreciation for his insights.

After he graduated in 1902, Joyce, who was becoming known in literary circles, registered at the Royal University Medical School. However, later that year, to escape Dublin's religious and social suffocation he went to Paris, where he soon gave up medicine to write verse. There, he discovered Edouard Dujardin's French novel *Les lauriers sont coupés* (1888), which he later credited for inspiring him to use interior monologue. A year later, in 1903, Joyce returned to Dublin because his mother was dying. He would later fictionalise his own emotions of that time in *Ulysses*, where Stephen Dedalus – young Joyce's fictional alter ego – is haunted by his mother's death and plagued by feelings of guilt. During this period, Joyce taught briefly at a private school and lived for a while in a Martello Tower with Oliver St John *Gogarty, who appears as Buck Mulligan in *Ulysses*. On 6 June 1904, he had his first date with Nora Barnacle, with whom he would spend the rest of his life. It is this fateful day that Joyce would immortalise in his daring novel *Ulysses*. Shortly after they met, Joyce and Nora set sail for Europe. They married 27 years later.

Joyce would live the rest of his life in self-imposed exile – first in Trieste, then in Rome, Paris and Zurich – writing some of the greatest prose in the English language about the country he left behind. Throughout, he would subject his family (Nora and their two children, Giorgio and Lucia) to the itinerant, impoverished lifestyle he had experienced as a child.

Joyce's first published work was *Chamber Music* (1907), a small volume of verse. *Dubliners*, his brilliant collection of short stories containing his first masterpiece 'The Dead', was published in 1914, after years of legal wranglings because various publishers were afraid to print material that contained objectionable language, disrespect for religion and the crown and references to real people and places in Dublin. Joyce would mine his life and the city of Dublin for all his books, creating scandal in his wake.

From 1904 to 1915, Joyce and his family lived in Trieste, during which time he would publish *Chamber Music*, finish *Dubliners*, revise *Stephen Hero* into *A Portrait of the Artist as a Young Man* and begin *Ulysses*. Earning little from teaching English, Joyce was constantly on the edge of poverty but always managed to find supporters (his brother Stanislaus, Harriet Shaw Weaver and later Sylvia Beach) to rescue him. In Trieste, he befriended Ettore Schmitz (whose pen name was Italo Svevo) and encouraged him to write his novel *Confessions of Zeno*.

Joyce's first novel *A Portrait of the Artist as a Young Man*, which had been serialised by Ezra Pound in the magazine the *Egoist*, was published only in 1916. In despair, he had once thrown the unfinished manuscript in the fireplace, but his sister who was staying with him rescued the pages from the flames. In this autobiographical novel, Joyce traces the development of the artistic sensibility and shows how the artist must escape the crippling forces of religion, family and *nationalism. Joyce's only play, *Exiles*, was rejected by W. B. *Yeats for Dublin's *Abbey Theatre in 1915 and was staged with little success (in Munich in 1919 and in New York in 1925) until Harold Pinter's 1970 production in London. In 1915, Joyce moved with his family to Zurich and after the war to Paris, where they stayed from 1920 to 1940. Suffering from chronic eye disease and bouts of blindness, he underwent many operations throughout this period. *Ulysses* was published in Paris in 1922, on Joyce's fortieth birthday, by Sylvia Beach's bookstore Shakespeare and Company. Episodes of the book had been serialised in the *Little Review* and the *Egoist* and the work was immediately recognised as a masterpiece by Pound, T. S. Eliot, Hemingway and *Beckett. In this novel, Joyce experiments with formal techniques including the stream of consciousness, allowing the reader to enter the minds of his main characters, Leopold Bloom (a middle-class Dublin Jew, who stands for modern man), Stephen Dedalus and, in the book's final episode, Bloom's wife, Molly. Structured loosely after Homer's *Odyssey*, *Ulysses* is packed with philosophical, historical, literary and mythological allusions. *Ulysses* was banned as obscene in the United States until 1933 and in Britain until 1936. Although it was never officially banned in Ireland, it was rarely available in bookstores until 1967. Today, the novel is considered one of the great books of western

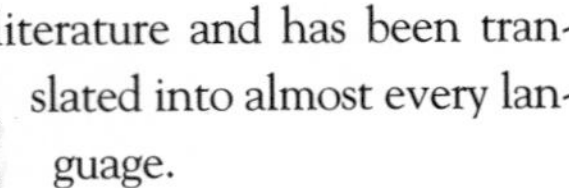

literature and has been translated into almost every language.

Joyce worked on his last book, *Finnegans Wake*, from 1923 to 1938, pushing language to its limits and creating an extravaganza of multilingual wordplay. Sections of the as yet untitled 'Work in Progress' were published in avant-garde magazines, and in 1929 Joyce orchestrated the publication of a collection of essays by 12 well-known writers, including Samuel Beckett and William Carlos Williams, to respond to the objections of the work's chief critics (who included Seán *O Faoláin). By the 1930s, the years of toil, poverty and hardship had taken their toll. Joyce's health was fragile, his daughter Lucia was mentally ill and his son Giorgio unhappily married. As the Second World War loomed, *Finnegans Wake* was published in 1939, on Joyce's fifty-seventh birthday. Received with less enthusiasm than *Ulysses*, it was described as unreadable, ridiculous and manipulative. Shortly after the outbreak of war, Joyce and Nora moved to Zurich. Joyce died there in 1941, fittingly in exile and on the move. L.R., J.OM.

Joyce, William (1906–46). Nazi propagandist and radio broadcaster. Born in New York of Irish parents, Joyce was raised in *Galway. He emigrated to England in 1922 and joined the British Union of Fascists in 1934. In 1939, he went to Germany and broadcast Nazi propaganda throughout the Second World War. He acquired the nickname 'Lord Haw-Haw' during this period. Although a US citizen, Joyce was tried and executed for treason in England on the grounds that having once used a British passport, he was considered a British subject and his Nazi propaganda was treason. The trial is unique in legal history. His remains were re-interred in Galway in 1976. S.A.B.

K

Kavanagh, Patrick (1904–67). Poet. Born in Inniskeen, County *Monaghan, Kavanagh was the eldest boy in a large, poor family. His formal education ended abruptly when he left school at age 13 to help his father on the farm and in the cobbler's shop. The end of his schooling marked the beginning of a dogged, self-taught apprenticeship in poetry. Though he wrote poems and ballads from age 12, Kavanagh's journey from local balladeer to major Irish poet was slow and painful. Discouraged from the pursuit of poetry by his practical parents, Kavanagh was eventually championed by AE (George *Russell), who published and introduced him to other writers. His first book, *Ploughman and Other Poems* (1936), was published when he was 32. Three years later, Kavanagh gave up farming and went to live in *Dublin as a professional poet and literary journalist, writing for the *Bell, Envoy, Dublin Magazine* and the *Irish Press*. Kavanagh is admired among subsequent generations of Irish poets for his brave and original stance against the rear guard of the *Irish Literary Revival. Instead of playing the set part of country poet, Kavanagh redefined the role on his own terms and with it, the Irish pastoral, most notably in his landmark volume *The Great Hunger* (1942), which depicted country life as harsh and spiritually unaccommodating, undermining more romantic views established by Revivalist writers. In 1960, after a fallow period lasting more than a decade, Kavanagh experienced a major poetic renewal with his buoyant canal poems in *Come Dance with Kitty Stobling*. Other works include an autobiographical novel, *The Green Fool* (1938), *A Soul for Sale* (1947), a novel, *Tarry Flynn* (1948), *Collected Poems* (1964), *Collected Prose* (1967) and a posthumously published novel, *By Night Unstarred* (1977). J.AR.

Keane, John B. (1928–2002). Writer and humourist. Born in Listowel, County *Kerry, Keane was the owner of a public house, which was the source of many of his stories. A prolific essayist and fiction writer, John B. Keane wrote many best-sellers in Ireland, including *The Gentle Art of Matchmaking and Other Important Things* (1973) and *Durango* (1992). Best known, however, for his 19 published plays, Keane was the most popular Irish playwright working in the second half of the twentieth century and the most undervalued by the critical establishment. What became his dramatic trilogy – *Sive* (1959), *The Field* (1965) and *Big Maggie* (1969) – depicts domineering parents and harsh conditions in mid-twentieth-century rural Ireland. Keane's plays are a mix of realism, grotesquerie and satiric wit. From 1958 onward, Keane submitted his plays to the Abbey Theatre, but only *Hut 42* premiered there in 1962. It was not until the revival of Keane's plays in the 1980s, that the national theatre took his work seriously. One of Keane's best novels is *The Bodhran Makers* (1986), an elegy for a rural community dismantled by mid-century economic trouble and migration. In 1998, Keane received the coveted Gradam Medal from the National Theatre Society for exceptional contributions to Irish theatre. C.H.

Keating, Geoffrey. See **Céitinn, Seathrún.**

Keating, Seán (1889–1977). Painter and teacher. Born in *Limerick, Keating was a leading pupil of William *Orpen at the Dublin

Metropolitan School of Art and went on to work with him in London. Elected to the *Royal Hibernian Academy in 1919, he was a professor at the National College of Art in *Dublin from 1934 to 1954 and president of the Royal Hibernian Academy from 1948 to 1962. Although using modern techniques, Keating's work defies modernist style categories because of his use of popular *nationalist subject matter. His work often engages in a visual dialogue with the work of Orpen. M.C.

keening. A practice which was common at wakes and funerals well into the twentieth century in parts of Ireland. The word is the Anglicisation of the Irish word *caoineadh*, meaning 'lament'. Keening consisted of a death-poem sung by *mná caointe* (or keening women) at a funeral. The poem praises the dead person and laments his or her loss. It was usually accompanied by wailing. It occasionally reached literary status as in the celebrated 'Caoineadh Airt Uí Laoghaire, or 'Lament for Art O'Leary', by Eibhlín Dhubh *Ní Chonaill. A.T.

Kells, Book of. North-western Europe's most famous *manuscript, containing illuminated copies of the gospels, from circa 800. The *Book of Kells* was preserved in the Columban monastery at Kells, in County *Meath, until 1653. Set up in the ninth century by monks from Iona, the monastery at Kells became the head of all the Columban monasteries. The *Book of Kells* was stolen from the monastery at Kells in 1007, but rediscovered – minus its cover – some time afterward. Iona is currently viewed as the most likely place of origin, but the book remained in Kells until the seventeenth century, when it was given to Trinity College, Dublin, where it is still preserved. The manuscript was written and illuminated by three or more hands. Its most intricate and minuscule-scale ornament of spiral, interlace, animal and key pattern decoration, as well as its portraits of Christ, Evangelists and the Mother and Child, make this book a marvel of inventiveness and exuberant colour. One element, lapis lazuli, had been imported from as far away as Afghanistan. P.H.

Kelly, Michael (1762–1826). Tenor, composer, manager, publisher. Born in *Dublin, Kelly was the earliest Irish tenor of international note. He created the roles of Don Curzio and Don Basilio in the first performance of Mozart's *Nozze di Figaro* at the Burgtheater in Vienna on 1 May 1786. His operatic career began in his native Dublin and took him to major centres in Europe, where he worked with Gluck and Mozart. He settled in London in 1787, where he performed in opera, composed for the stage, was a stage manager and music publisher, and even set himself up as a wine merchant, a venture that led him to bankruptcy in 1811. His lively *Reminiscences*, ghost-written by Theodore Hook and published in 1826, are an important firsthand source, detailing the musical scene of his time. He was praised for his musicianship, acting skills and vocal technique, but the actual quality of his voice was said to be 'wanting in sweetness'. M.D.

Kennedy, John Fitzgerald (1917–63). Thirty-fifth president of the United States (1961–63). The descendant of *Famine-era emigrants from County *Wexford, Kennedy was the first (and to date only) Roman Catholic to be elected president of the United States. Millions of *Irish Americans saw Kennedy's election in 1960 as the culmination of their community's triumph over poverty and discrimination in American society. Despite Kennedy's personal interest in Irish affairs, official American policy toward Ireland, particularly on the issue of *partition, remained unchanged during his tenure in office. This was due mainly to the United States' 'special relationship' with Britain as part of American

Muckross House, Killarney National Park, County Kerry

Cold War strategy. Nevertheless, on an emotional and symbolic level, his presidency was significant in Irish history, as many Irish people considered his rise to power emblematic of the diaspora's success. Kennedy's visit to Ireland in the summer of 1963 was met with tremendous popular enthusiasm. Likewise, his assassination in Dallas, Texas, the following November, was a source of national sorrow. T.D.

Kennelly, Brendan (1936–). Poet, dramatist, critic and professor of modern literature at Trinity College, Dublin. Born in County *Kerry, Kennelly has published over 20 books of poetry and has won the AE Memorial Prize. In his best-known poetic works – *Cromwell, The Book of Judas* and *Poetry My Arse* – he gives a voice to the marginalised and the outcast. He has also published two novels, *The Crooked Cross* and *The Florentines* and dramatic adaptations of Sophocles' *Antigone* and Euripides' *Medea*. Kennelly has edited many anthologies, including *The Penguin Book of Irish Verse*. P.E.

Kerry, County. Coastal county in the southwest of Ireland, in the province of *Munster. Kerry, covering an area of 1,855 square miles, has a population of 132,424 (2002 census). Kerry is bordered by *Cork and *Limerick to the east and by the Atlantic Ocean to the west. Known as 'the Kingdom', the county is one of the most scenic counties in Ireland and has distinctly diverse regions. The north is mostly lowland, much of it good dairy-farming country, with scattered *bogs. The south and west are mountainous and sheep-farming is the main land use. There is some fishing in the west, Dingle being the main fishing port. The coastline is rocky, with several sandy beaches and many islands. Ireland's highest mountain, *Carrantuohill (3,414 feet), is in the Macgillycuddy's Reeks range in the southern part of the county.

Kerry's mountains, coastline and the famous lakes of *Killarney make it one of Ireland's main tourist destinations. The Ring of Kerry is a famous circular drive around the spectacular Iveragh Peninsula, stretching from Killorglin to Kenmare. Other attractions include Ross Castle and Muckross House, both near Killarney; Derrynane House – once the home of Daniel *O'Connell; the annual Puck *Fair, held every August in the town of Killorglin; and the jagged *Skellig Islands, where monks established a settlement in the seventh century. The county has a great many archaeological sites and monuments. Many are concentrated on the *Dingle Peninsula and the county's only complete *round tower is in the north at Rattoo, near Ballyduff.

Kerry has never had much industry besides farming. The county capital, Tralee, is a busy market town, with a few factories and a nearby port at Fenit. Killarney, a smaller town, which has long depended on the tourist industry, is the seat of the Catholic bishop of Kerry and has a mid-nineteenth-century cathedral. Listowel, in north Kerry, is a market town. Since the *Famine, Kerry has had one of Ireland's highest *emigration rates to the United States.

The southern part of the county was little affected by the Norman and English settlements, though this only partly explains Kerry's distinct political history. The county was one of the main centres of the *Land War of the 1880s and many violent incidents occurred there during the *War of Independence. During the *Civil War, the county was the last place where the *Free State army established its authority. Free State executions and massacres in the war's last days left a lasting political bitterness in the county and strong support for *republicanism endures today.

Kerry is known for its *Gaelic football teams, which have been the country's most successful, and also for its literary tradition. The great Gaelic poets, Aodhagán *Ó Rathaille (1670–1729) and Eoghan Rua *Ó Súilleabháin (1748–84) were born in east Kerry in the Sliabh Luachra district. The *Blasket Islands produced several works of *literature in Irish, based on oral storytelling. These have been translated, including the classic autobiography *An tOileánach (The Islandman)* (1929) by Tomás *Ó Criomhthain (O'Crohan). Twentieth-century writers from north Kerry include Maurice Walsh, the *Abbey playwright George Fitzmaurice and, more recently, the writers Bryan *MacMahon and John B. *Keane and the poet Brendan *Kennelly. P.D.

Kickham, Charles J[oseph] (1828–82). Novelist and political activist. Born in Mullinahone, County *Tipperary, Kickham was coeditor of the Fenian newspaper the *Irish People*. In 1865, he was arrested and sentenced to 14 years in prison for treason. He served four years before being released due to ill health. Kickham is best remembered for *Knocknagow* (1879), a loving depiction of rural life, which is one of the most popular of all Irish novels. G.OB.

Kiely, Benedict (1919–). Writer, journalist. Born in Dromore, County *Tyrone and educated in Omagh and University College, Dublin, Kiely is a novelist, short story writer, literary critic, journalist, broadcaster and essayist. In his first book, *Counties of Contention: A Study of the Origins and Implications of the Partition of Ireland* (1945), Kiely expresses a political consciousness that recurs in the first of his ten novels, *Land Without Stars* (1947) and his last two – *Proxopera* (1977) and *Nothing Happens in Carmincross* (1985). In his four volumes of short stories, his mature novels, memoirs and travel writing, Kiely, like a traditional oral storyteller (*seanchaí*), combines whimsical fantasy and a wide-ranging, playful, often nostalgic reference to Irish lore and song lyrics, with shrewd realistic observation. He is well known also for his literary criticism, principally Poor *Scholar: A Study of the Works and Days of William Carleton* (1947) and *Modern Irish Fiction – A Critique* (1950). J.MCD.

Kildare, County. Inland county in the province of *Leinster, in the eastern part of Ireland. Kildare, covering 654 square miles, has a population of 163,995 (2002 census). Kildare derives its name from the Irish language Cill Dara, 'the church of the oak tree', a reference to a monastery near Kildare town which, it was claimed, was founded by St *Brigid. The county's principal geographic features are: the Bog of Allen, a vast expanse of low-lying moor-like land that stretches over most of Ireland's midland counties; and the flat plain of the Curragh, which covers over 1,000 acres and is six miles long and two miles wide. Kildare is the main centre for *horse racing and also for horse breeding in Ireland. Besides the race-track at the Curragh, race meetings are also regularly held at Naas, the county capital, and Punchestown. Since 1855, the Curragh has also been a principal army base in Ireland. The main rivers in the county are the Liffey, the Barrow and the Boyne. The Grand and Royal canals also run through the county.

From the late fourteenth century to the early sixteenth century, the Fitzgeralds, an *Anglo-Norman family, dominated the county. Occupying a strategic position between the *Pale and the territories controlled by the Gaelic lords, the Fitzgerald family had a strong bargaining position with the English crown. In return for their protection of the Pale, they were granted substantial local autonomy. This dominance was ended by the execution of 'Silken' Thomas Fitzgerald following his failed revolt in 1535.

County Kildare is noted for its rich pasture-land, which is particularly suited to the fattening of cattle for the Dublin market and for export outside Ireland. Tillage farming is also carried on in parts of the county.

Kildare is also home to two of the most celebrated Catholic educational institutions in Ireland: Clongowes Wood College near Clane, where James *Joyce attended boarding school and which he immortalised in *A Portrait of the Artist as a Young Man*; and St Patrick's College, *Maynooth, originally founded in 1795 as a seminary for Catholic priests. One of the major tourist attractions in the county is *Castletown House, the first and largest Palladian-style country house in Ireland, located near Celbridge. The town of Prosperous lent its name to Christy *Moore's first album, which is generally acknowledged as a classic. A.S.

Kilkenny, County. Inland county in the province of *Leinster. Stretching over 800 square miles, Kilkenny is a medium-sized county, with a population of 80,421 (2002 census). Geographically, the county is varied: the elevated Castlecomer plateau to the north, the Slieveardagh hills in the west and the hills in the south and east contrast with two low-lying valleys in the centre and east of the county. Through the two valleys flow the rivers Nore and Barrow which, like the sides of the letter V, join up at the bottom before flowing into the Celtic Sea below New Ross. The Barrow, which flows through Muine Bheag (Bagenalstown) and Graignamanagh (with its splendidly restored Cistercian abbey), forms the western boundary with *Carlow, while the Suir above *Waterford partially defines the county's southern boundary.

Kilkenny has an illustrious history: the Statute of *Kilkenny (1366) prohibited *Anglo-Normans from assimilating into Gaelic culture and the *Confederation of Kilkenny, an Assembly of Confederate Catholics (Gaelic Irish and Old English allies) held annual meetings here from 1642 to 1649. The county and city of Kilkenny preserve the atmosphere of its medieval past. The county has a number of interesting and picturesque towns and villages but the crowning jewel is the city of Kilkenny itself, known affectionately as 'the Marble City', from the fossil-rich limestone that surrounds it and which was used in many of its buildings. The cathedral and Kilkenny Castle are perhaps the most famous of these. The thirteenth-century cathedral is dedicated to St Canice, or Cainnech, after whom (*Cill Chain-*

nigh, the church of Canice) the city and county are named. The castle, founded by William the Marshal in 1192, was bought in 1391 by the Butlers, who were great benefactors to the county for centuries and who handed the castle over to the state in 1967. Since then, Kilkenny Castle, along with its fine nineteenth-century art gallery, has been open to the public.

Kilkenny City is synonymous with high-quality design and craftsmanship. The *Kilkenny Design Workshops, set up in 1963 by the Irish Export Board, made the city into a centre for innovative crafts, where many young artisans developed their skills in jewellery, pottery, weaving and *textile design. Famous natives of county Kilkenny include the philosopher George *Berkeley; the sculptor Christopher Hewetson; Edmund Ignatius *Rice, founder of the *Irish Christian Brothers; the architect James *Hoban who designed and built the White House in Washington; the scholar and editor John *O'Donovan; the painter Tony *O'Malley; and the writer Thomas *Kilroy. The Kilkenny Arts Festival, which takes place annually in August, attracts international writers and artists. P.H.

Kilkenny, Statute of (1366). A series of reactionary laws enacted by the Irish *parliament to quell the increasing assimilation of the *Anglo-Norman population into the Gaelic culture. Because the Normans were becoming 'more Irish than the Irish themselves', the statute required that only English be spoken, English law followed and English dress and manners observed. Intermarriage between the native Irish and Anglo-Norman population was also prohibited. T.C.

Kilkenny Design Workshops. The workshops were established at Kilkenny Castle by the Irish government in 1963 to develop design innovation for established Irish craft-based industries such as silversmithing, ceramics, *furniture, weaving and *textile design. The craft workers, many of whom were British, German and Scandinavian, quickly developed an outstanding reputation for graphic, industrial and craft design. The Design Workshops were closed down in 1988, but many of the craft workers established their own workshops in Kilkenny. S.A.B.

Kilmainham Gaol. Famous prison in Dublin. Opened in 1796, Kilmainham Gaol was an ordinary prison, which also housed political prisoners such as the *United Irishmen, *Young Irelanders and Charles Stewart *Parnell. Leaders of the *Easter Rising were executed here. During the *Irish Civil War, *republicans were also imprisoned and executed in Kilmainham until its closure in 1924. It was turned into a museum in 1966. T.C.

Kilroy, Thomas (1934–). Playwright and academic. Born in Callan, County *Kilkenny and educated at University College, Dublin, Kilroy taught at various universities in the United States and in Ireland. His plays include *The Death and Resurrection of Mr Roche* (1968), which addresses questions of sexual orientation, *Tea and Sex and Shakespeare* (1976), *Talbot's Box* (1977), about the personal struggle and suffering of Dublin working-class ascetic Matt Talbot, and *Double Cross* (1986), which explores the wartime careers of two Irishmen, Brendan Bracken, *Churchill's minister of information, and William *Joyce, who broadcast Nazi propaganda as 'Lord Haw-Haw'. *The Madame MacAdam Travelling Theatre* (1991), a theatrically imaginative, but poorly received, critique of 1940s ideology, was produced by *Field Day. In 1997 the *Abbey Theatre staged Kilroy's *The Secret Fall of Constance Wilde*, in which Oscar *Wilde's wife confronts her husband's double life and her own mixed emotions. Kilroy is concerned with the nature of solitude and the relationship of the outcast to the stagnant Irish society from which he has withdrawn. He became a director of Field Day Theatre Company in 1988. His historical novel, *The Big Chapel* (1971), won the *Guardian* prize for fiction. C.D., J.C.E.L.

Kinsale, Battle of (25 December 1601). Last battle of the *Nine Years War. A Spanish force, which landed at Kinsale, County *Cork, to help the Irish, was besieged by an English army under Lord Mountjoy. Hugh *O'Neill and his ally Red Hugh *O'Donnell took their forces in an epic march south from their *Ulster stronghold to assist the Spanish. The English became trapped between the Irish forces and the town. However, an attempt to relieve Kinsale ended in disaster when the Spanish failed to advance from the town and the ill-trained and ill-equipped Irish were routed by the English. The Spanish withdrew a week later. T.C.

Kinsella, Thomas (1928–). Poet. Born in *Dublin and educated at University College, Dublin, Thomas Kinsella worked for several decades in the civil service. Frequently described as the Irish T. S. Eliot, Kinsella became the most influential harbinger of modernism in Irish *poetry. Struggling out from the oppressive 'double shadow of Yeats and English verse', he constructed his identity as a poet caught between the tensions and paradoxes of the dual Irish tradition – Gaelic and English. As his work evolved, he abandoned his early lyricism in favour of the fragmented interconnectedness of his late series of longer poems and sequences.

Most influential among Kinsella's poetry collections were *Another September* (1958), *Downstream* (1962), *Nightwalker* (1968) and *Butcher's Dozen* (1972). A prolific translator from the Irish (*The Táin*, 1969 and *An Duanaire – Poems of the Dispossessed*, 1981), Kinsella also edited *The New Oxford Book of Irish Verse* (1986). In 1995, he published an historical overview of Irish poetry, *The Dual Tradition: An Essay on Poetry and Politics*. J.AR.

Kitchener, Horatio Herbert; First Earl Kitchener of Khartoum and of Broome (1850–1916). British military commander. Born in Ballylongford, County *Kerry, Kitchener enjoyed a distinguished military career in Africa and India. As commander of the Egyptian army, he conquered Sudan (1896–99) and was subsequently commander in chief of British forces in South Africa (1900–02). As secretary for war (1914–16), Kitchener rapidly expanded Britain's small professional army into a mass volunteer force of three million men. He died when *HMS Hampshire* was sunk en route to Russia in June 1916. S.A.B.

Knowth. *Passage-grave in County *Meath. Along with *Newgrange and Dowth, Knowth forms a great Neolithic cemetery on a ridge of hills north of the Boyne river, some miles upstream from Drogheda, County *Louth. It dates from around 3000 BC, making it older than the Pyramids. Knowth has two separate tombs back-to-back within a large earthen mound – one corbelled, like that in Newgrange, the other flat-roofed. Because of fallen stones, public access to the burial chambers is not feasible, but visitors can see the beautifully decorated stones on the outside of the mound and also reconstructed 'satellite' tombs around its periphery. Access is through the Brú na Bóinne Interpretative Centre on the south bank of the Boyne. P.H.

L

Labour Party, the. *Political party. The Labour Party was formed in 1912, but had only a minimal organisational existence before the foundation of the *Irish Free State. Since 1922, Labour has seen itself as the political party of the *trade union movement. In practice, however, the Labour Party had a difficult relationship with the trade unions. Though part of the European social democratic tradition, Labour has had a low level of support. Its inability to form a government on its own has reduced Labour's position in Ireland to that of a minority party, and Labour has had to make many compromises as part of coalition governments with much larger conservative parties. Its leaders have been: Thomas Johnson (1918–27), T. J. O'Connell (1927–32), William Norton (1932–60), Brendan Corish (1960–77), Frank Cluskey (1977–81), Michael O'Leary (1981–82), Dick Spring (1982–97), Ruairi Quinn (1997–2002) and Pat Rabbitte (2002 to present).

In the first election with (near) universal suffrage, in 1918, Labour stood aside to give *Sinn Féin a free run to highlight popular support for independence. This decision certainly weakened Labour in a crucial period of its development. Serving as the opposition while anti-treaty Sinn Féin boycotted the new parliament from 1922 to 1926, Labour aligned itself with *Fianna Fáil in the 1932 general election, identifying with that party's more *republican stance and its policy to end payment of land annuities to Britain. Splits and personality clashes in the *trade union movement often spilled over into the Labour Party and the party itself actually split in 1943. Labour remained a largely conservative force during this period; its position to the 'left' of Irish politics was modified by its large rural vote and the conservative policies of the trade union leadership.

In the post-Second World War period, Labour's only way of holding political office was to form coalition governments with *Fine Gael (and other small parties) in 1948–51 and 1954–57. Labour moved to the left in the late 1960s, reflecting the political mood of the time. Their 1969 election result was, however, very disappointing, and though they formed a coalition government with Fine Gael in 1973, it was from a position of relative weakness. The unpopularity of that government and its conservative economic policy in response to the oil crisis led to deep splits in the party. Labour served in government with Fine Gael again from 1981 to February 1982 and November 1982 to 1987. The splits in the party, between radicals and conservatives, were now very bitter, and Labour was under severe electoral pressure from the left-wing Workers Party, especially in *Dublin and other urban centres. Labour's relationship with trade unions also reached a low point at this time. The unions criticised Labour's compromises in government and sought to influence public policy directly, rather than rely on the Labour Party.

A period in opposition allowed Labour to re-establish some credibility. In the general elections of 1992, Labour achieved its highest-ever vote, 19.3% – mostly new middle-class supporters who deserted Fine Gael and Fianna Fáil and voters unhappy with the government's performance. The decision to enter government with Fianna Fáil was bitterly opposed by some of the party leaders' closest advisors. Labour withdrew from this government in December 1994, in a clash with Fianna Fáil leader Albert *Reynolds, and negotiated a new coalition deal with Fine Gael – based on a programme similar to that which they had had with Fianna Fáil. However, the change of government halfway through a Dáil (the first change of government without an election) was not popular and Labour was perceived to be arrogant and aloof in power. In the 1997 election, Labour's vote fell to just over 10%. The party's performance in 2002 was also a major disappointment as it failed to benefit by a shift to the left by a significant number of voters. Labour's vote fell by 2% while both the popular vote and number of seats won by Sinn Féin, the Green Party, small left parties and protest candidates increased. J.D.

lace. See **textiles**.

Lalor, James Fintan (1807–49). Land reform agitator, revolutionary. Born at Tinakill, County *Laois, and educated at Carlow Lay College, Lalor became involved in agrarian reform in the 1840s. In a series of letters to the **Nation* in 1847, he proposed rent strikes and joint resistance to eviction. He took charge of the newspaper the *Irish Felon*, successor to the suppressed *United Irishman*, following the arrest of John *Mitchel and John Martin. Lalor was arrested after the failed *Young Ireland rising in July 1848 and released fatally ill in November 1849. His influence in his own lifetime was limited, but his declaration in the *Nation* in 1847 that 'the entire ownership of Ireland, moral and material . . . is vested of right in the people of Ireland' had enduring appeal to later radical leaders such as Michael *Davitt, James *Connolly, Patrick *Pearse and Arthur *Griffith. C.D.

Lambeg drum. A handmade cylindrical drum, about three feet in diameter. Made from goatskin over an oak frame, the drum is played with canes. The first recorded use was in the eighteenth century. Associated with *Orange Order bands, Lambeg drums were used by different organisations, including the *Ancient Order of Hibernians. The decline of other band traditions means that the Lambeg drum is almost an exclusively Orange instrument today and features in a number of Orange Order events, including drumming competitions. T.C.

Lambay Island. Large island off the North *Dublin coast where St *Colm Cille is said to have founded a church, of which no trace remains. Recent excavations have shown that the island was inhabited as far back as the Stone Age, when flint and stone for axes were quarried. Roman remains were uncovered not far from the harbour in 1927, suggesting the presence of traders or settlers from Britain in the first centuries after Christ. The island is privately owned and not accessible to the public. P.H.

Land Act of 1870, the (the Landlord and Tenant [Ireland] Act). The first of a series of land acts passed between 1870 and 1909 that would radically change the relationship between *landlord and tenant and would alter the nature of land tenure in Ireland. Having become prime minister in 1868, William *Gladstone, as part of his policy 'to pacify Ireland', advocated a fairer relationship between landlord and tenant. His 1870 Act gave legal recognition to the *Ulster Custom (customary rights in Ulster that protected tenants from eviction – as long as they paid their rent – and allowed them to sell their farms) in the parts of Ireland where it had existed. Elsewhere, tenants were to be compensated for improvements made to farms and eviction for causes other than the nonpayment of rent. The Bright Clause within the act allowed tenants who wished to purchase their holdings to borrow two-thirds of the purchase price. While in no way radical, the act had huge symbolic significance in the sense that seemingly absolute landlord rights were now being questioned for the first time. P.E.

Land Act of 1881, the (the Land Law [Ireland] Act). William *Gladstone's second land act passed at the height of the *Land War. The act established the principle of dual ownership between *landlord and tenant. It granted all tenants (except those in arrears or leaseholders) the three Fs – fair rent, free sale and fixity of tenure – for which the *Land League under the leadership of Michael *Davitt and Charles Stewart *Parnell had campaigned so vigorously since 1879. Rents were to be set by a *Land Commission and fixed for 15 years, and tenants who wished to purchase their land could borrow 75% of the purchase price from the government. P.E.

Land Act of 1885, the (the Purchase of Land [Ireland] Act). Important Conservative act dealing with tenant proprietorship – also known as the Ashbourne Act. As part of Lord Salisbury's Conservative government's policy of Constructive *Unionism ('killing *home rule with kindness'), the act provided £5 million to allow tenants to borrow the entire purchase price of their holdings. Repayments were to be made over 49 years at 4% interest. Within three years, 25,000 tenants purchased land, and amending acts between 1887 and 1889 provided further funds for the scheme. In 1891, the Balfour Land Act set aside £33 million in government bonds to aid in tenant purchase and established the Congested Districts Board to provide relief for distressed areas of the country. P.E.

Land Act of 1903, the (the Irish Land Act). One of the last in a series of land acts reforming land ownership in Ireland. This act (commonly known as the Wyndham Land Act) expanded on previous land legislation by providing £100 million in loans for land purchase. Repayments were to be made over 69 years at 3.5% interest. The act, however, did not compel landlords to sell, although those who sold their entire estates were rewarded with a 12% bonus. This act, along with the 1909 Birrell Land Act (passed by the Liberal government under Herbert *Asquith), effectively ended the transfer of land tenure begun in 1870. P.E.

Land Commission. Quasi-judicial body established to enforce the terms of William *Gladstone's *Land Act of 1881. The act, passed at the height of the *Land War, authorised the Land Commission to set fair rents that would be fixed for 15 years. The commission could also purchase estates and make loans to tenants who wished to own their land. The commission was seen as an arbitrator whose work had a stabilising influence following the recent turmoil of the Land War. Later acts (1903 and 1923) expanded its functions to include redistribution of land. P.E.

Land League, the. Agrarian protest organisation that agitated for land reform during the Land War of 1879–82. The economic crisis of 1878–79 threatened Ireland's rural population with a disaster comparable to the Great *Famine. Following successful mass meetings at Irishtown and Westport, County *Mayo, in April and June, 1879, the Irish National Land League was formed in *Dublin, on 21 October, by Michael *Davitt. Charles Stewart *Parnell, then a rising star in the *Home Rule party, agreed to act as president. The Land League vowed to ameliorate the drastic plight of the Irish peasantry by fighting against unjust rents and evictions and for tenant ownership.

Now for the first time *landlords faced an organised tenant class in what became one of the greatest mass movements in Irish history. The league advocated nonviolence, preferring, instead, the more effective methods of mass meetings and social ostracism, or boycotting. However, assaults on landlords and their agents, intimidation and damage to property became widespread, and the Gladstone government quickly passed the Protection of Persons and Property Act in 1881.

The Land League vigorously campaigned for the three Fs – fair rent, free sale and fixity of tenure – and Gladstone's 1881 *Land Act, a milestone in land legislation, granted these demands to most tenants. (The 130,000 tenants in arrears and 150,000 leaseholders were, however, excluded from the act.)

Parnell could neither accept nor reject the act without losing some degree of support. If he rejected the act, his moderate supporters would desert him, but on the other hand, acceptance of the act would alienate his more militant followers, including the *Fenians who demanded more radical reforms. His solution was to abstain from voting for the legislation in parliament and to condemn the act when it was passed.

In October 1881, Parnell was arrested for making a provocative speech in *Wexford and imprisoned in *Kilmainham Gaol. From prison, Parnell issued a 'No Rent Manifesto' and the authorities responded by suppressing the league on 20 October 1881.

Parnell was released in May 1882 under the terms of the Kilmainham Treaty: he promised to restore law and order in the country, and the government, in return, would relax coercion and extend the 1881 Land Act to include those previously omitted. Following his release, Parnell refused to revive the Land League and dismantled the Ladies Land League. He now considered the land question to be solved and began concentrating solely on the issue of national self-government. Davitt, the league's chief architect, one of whose main objectives was land nationalisation, remained dissatisfied and disillusioned with Parnell. T.OCon., P.E.

Land War, the. See **Land League, the.**

landlords. Landlords in Ireland were a direct consequence of the *plantations and land confiscations of the sixteenth and seventeenth centuries. Most landlords were of Scottish or English descent, and their acquisition of land had come at the expense of the native Irish and Old English. The English system of renting land to tenants was copied, but while this worked well in England, it proved very divisive in Ireland. Landlords here represented not only a different economic class and separate culture, but also a conquering, imperial presence. Increasing agrarian agitation marked the nineteenth century, and a series of *land acts passed between 1870 and 1909 radically altered the relationship between landlord and tenant so that by the turn of the twentieth century tenant proprietorship had become a reality. P.E.

Lane, Sir Hugh Percy (1875–1915). Art dealer and collector. Lane is best known for establishing *Dublin's Municipal Gallery of Modern Art in 1908, albeit in temporary accommodation. Born in *Cork, Lane trained as a painting restorer and art dealer in London, but returned to Ireland regularly to visit his aunt, Lady *Gregory. He commissioned John Butler *Yeats in 1901 to paint portraits of leading Irish citizens and organised an exhibition of Old Masters at the *Royal Hibernian Academy in 1902. A collection of Irish paintings he assembled for display at the St Louis World Fair in 1903 was shown instead in London in 1904. After an unsuccessful campaign for a new permanent gallery of modern art on a bridge over the river in Dublin, he withdrew his gift of pictures from the Municipal Gallery and later bequeathed them to the National Gallery in London. He was director of the *National Gallery of Ireland from 1914, while continuing to live and work in London as an art dealer. After his death on the **Lusitania*, a codicil to his will bequeathing his French impressionist paintings to the City of Dublin was refused recognition by British courts. The Lane Bequest is at present still divided, with 31 paintings in the *Hugh Lane Municipal Gallery, Dublin, and the eight remaining paintings rotating every six years between London and Dublin. M.C.

Laois, County. Midland county in the province of *Leinster. Laois (covering 664 square miles) has a population of 58,732 (2002 census). Dominated by an expanse of agricultural land, the county is bound to the east by the Castlecomer plateau and the River Barrow, to the north-west by the Slieve Bloom Mountains, and to the west by the River Nore. Portlaoise, the county capital, is situated near the Rock of Dunamase, a natural outcrop topped by a fortress belonging to the twelfth-century king of Leinster, Dermot *MacMurrough. The town has one of Ireland's top security prisons. Other main market towns include Portarlington, Mountmellick, Abbeyleix and Mountrath. Abbeyleix is designated a Heritage Town and is one of the finest examples of a planned-estate town in Ireland.

There are over 1,000 historical sites and monuments in the county, some dating back over 6,000 years. These include: *pre-Christian settlement at the Heath near Portlaoise; the fifth-century monastery founded by St Comdhan at Killeshin; Norman and medieval *castles such as Ballaghmore Castle near Borris-in-Ossory and Lea Castle east of Portarlington; and Emo Court, a large neoclassical estate house, which was begun about 1790 by James *Gandon.

After the arrival of the Normans, the territory of the county was divided among seven clans. Following the fall of the Fitzgeralds of Kildare in 1534, the O'Moores (and O'Connors of *Offaly) became sworn enemies of the English government and began raiding the *Pale. During the reign of King Edward VI, both families were driven from their land and under the reign of Queen Mary, Laois became known as Queens County and the town of Portlaoise was established as the Fort of Maryborough. British *plantation failed in the sixteenth century due to bad planning and fierce Gaelic resistance. The eighteenth century, however, was a period of colonial consolidation, with Maryborough growing as an administrative centre. The population was halved from 159,930 (1841) to 73,124 (1881) because of the *Famine. In 1920, Maryborough became Portlaoise and the county was renamed Laois at the end of the *War of Independence. During the twentieth century, the county underwent considerable *economic development, based on industrialisation and the modernisation of *agriculture. Today, nearly half of the county's workforce is engaged in services, 15% in industry and 22% in agriculture. P.E.

Larkin, James (1876–1947). *Trade union leader, politician. Born in Liverpool to Irish parents, Larkin was a dock worker who embraced *socialism. In 1907, he was sent to *Belfast to organise the National Union of Dock Labourers. A charismatic leader, Larkin re-invigorated the dockers' union and tried to reduce sectarian divisions. After an employers' lockout, he organised a dockers' and carters' strike which lasted from May to November 1907. The strike was supported in other towns and even the *RIC mutinied in sympathy. Troops were brought in and, after two deaths during a riot, the union's leadership called off the strike.

Convinced that Ireland needed its own labour movement, Larkin helped to found the Irish Transport and General Workers Union (ITGWU) in 1909. Along with James *Connolly, he established the Irish *Labour Party with the support of the Irish Congress of Trade Unions in 1912. He led the workers during the Dublin Lockout of 1913, which brought him into conflict with employers and some *Catholic church leaders.

Disillusioned, he went to the United States in 1914. In 1919, he was charged with criminal anarchy for his involvement with the fledgling American *Communist Party and after a three-week trial, he was sentenced to five to ten years imprisonment. Through the intervention of liberal Democrat *New York Governor Alfred E. Smith, Larkin was released from prison in 1923. He returned to Ireland, where the trade union movement was now 100,000 strong and under new leadership. Unable to play a dominant role, Larkin broke away and followed his own militant path. He joined the Labour Party and was elected as a TD in 1943, which led to a split with the ITGWU. Larkin's legacy is the development of organised trade unionism in Ireland. T.C.

Larne Gun Running (1914). *Unionist arms smuggling event. Alarmed at the introduction of a *home rule bill, *Ulster unionists formed the *UVF. In order to arm the UVF, on 24–25 April 1914, 25,000 rifles and 3,000,000 rounds of ammunition were smuggled by boat from Germany by F. H. Crawford into Larne, County *Antrim. The boats were met by units of the UVF and the arms were distributed throughout Ulster. The *police did not interfere. The arms' military value was questionable, but the political significance was immense. It put pressure on the British government and led *nationalists to arm themselves. T.C.

La Tène. The art style of the *Celts, named after a site in Switzerland. Consisting of curvilinear and trumpet patterns, spirals, palmettes and other motifs derived from Greek designs, La Tène art developed in central Europe and reached Ireland sometime after 300 BC. Fine examples are found on the Turoe Stone (County *Galway) and the Broighter torc in the National Museum. La Tène is one of the basic styles in early *Christian Irish art. P.H.

Lavery, John (1856–1941). Portrait painter. Born in *Belfast, Lavery was trained in Scotland and France and influenced by Bastien-Lepage, Whistler and Velázquez. His painting of Queen Victoria's state visit to Glasgow in 1888 brought many portrait commissions. He lived in London and was knighted in 1918 for his work as a war artist. He is mainly represented at the *Hugh Lane Municipal Gallery, where his painting of Michael *Collins lying in state, *Love of Ireland*, 1922, can be viewed. The *National Gallery of Ireland and *Ulster Museum hold many of his works, including portraits of his wife, Lady Hazel Lavery. She was the model for the figure on the original Irish £1 note, which Lavery designed. M.C.

Lavin, Mary (1912–96). Writer. Born in Massachusetts, US, Lavin returned to Ireland at the age of 10. Her first collection of short stories, *Tales from Bective Bridge*, was published in 1942. Although she also wrote novels, including *The House in Clewe Street* (1945) and *Mary O'Grady* (1950), it was as a short story writer that she was most acclaimed. These stories, including the collections *The Long Age and Other Stories* (1944) and *In the Middle of the Fields* (1967), are largely concerned with the intimate lives of middle-class Irish families, often her own family and friends. Many of her stories appeared in the *New Yorker*, as did those of her friend Frank *O'Connor. Her fiction shows her acute powers of observation and keen insights into human nature. A.S.

law and the legal system. The law in Ireland is a common law system derived from English law. Since independence in 1922, Ireland's legal system has developed its own framework and most recently has been influenced by the laws of the *European Union (EU).

In ancient times, when Ireland was made up of a system of tribal families and provincial chiefs, a sophisticated indigenous system of *brehon law developed. This system was based on custom and the law was administered by judges who were called brehons. The oldest remaining brehon texts are from the seventh and eighth centuries, which show a pronounced Christian influence on the older brehon code. The origin of modern Ireland's legal system dates to the *Anglo-Norman invasion in 1169. Common law had been established in England by the Normans after their conquest of England in 1066. In 1171, King *Henry II landed in *Waterford and formed the King's Council to administer English law in Ireland in his absence. Originally, the council consisted of two departments, the Exchequer, headed by the treasurer, and the Chancery, headed by the chancellor, the king's chief advisor. In 1216, the *Magna Carta* was issued in Ireland. English common law began to prevail in Ireland from 1331, when King Edward III issued a writ giving the people of Ireland the same status at law as the English. As in England and Wales, judges travelled to different parts of Ireland to administer the king's law. In the beginning, these judges applied local customary laws, as the brehons had, but over time a uniform system emerged.

As the common law system developed, rules became rigid and this 'Black Letter' law system, emphasising procedure over substance, often led to unfairness. Many petitioned the king to use his prerogative power to remedy unfair legal results, giving rise to the law of equity. The courts of equity worked on a basis of fairness and rivalled the common law courts. In 1615, the king decreed that in a case of conflict between the two systems, equity should prevail. A system of precedent also developed, whereby previous decisions became binding on future decisions of the courts. Eventually, the two systems fused and the current Irish court system was established by the Judicature (Ireland) Act of 1877. Equity still prevails over the common law.

After the Act of *Union (1800) dissolved the native Irish *parliament, all Irish laws were enacted from Westminster in London. The *Anglo-Irish Treaty (1921) established the *Irish Free State, which had legislative independence from Britain. The new Irish court system now had dominion status, with an ultimate appeal to the privy council in London (or the House of Lords, the highest court of appeal in England for the *Commonwealth countries). The Irish Free State adopted a Constitution in 1922, but the existing law remained in full force and effect, unless changed by the Constitution. The 1922 Constitution prescribed a tripartite separation of powers to the executive, the legislature and the judiciary. The executive council, a cabinet elected by the legislature, consisted of the king of England and the two houses of the *Oireachtas, the *Dáil and the *Seanad.

The Irish *Constitution of 1937 defined a new legal order. Ireland became a *republic in all but name and this document now forms the basis of Ireland's legal system. Like the 1922 document, the Constitution of 1937 outlined the principal institutions of state and certain fundamental individual rights. The 1937 Constitution revised the courts system: it designated the supreme court and high court as the highest constitutional courts in Ireland and also recognised courts of 'Local and Limited Jurisdiction'.

Today, law in Ireland is divided into civil and criminal areas. Civil law deals with private relationships and the settling of disputes between civilians and between individuals and the state. The responsibility is on the injured party to initiate proceedings. Criminal law deals with public wrong. The office of the director of public prosecutions generally prosecutes these cases on behalf of the state and victims are not directly involved in the process except as witnesses. As in other common law countries, an accused person is presumed innocent until proven guilty beyond reasonable doubt.

The Irish courts are divided into four

major divisions. In civil cases smaller claims are dealt with by the district court, larger claims by the circuit court and the high court has unlimited jurisdiction. The supreme court is the ultimate court of appeal.

In criminal law, the district court deals with summary offences (misdemeanours) with the power of sentence up to two years imprisonment. The circuit court deals with indictable offences (felonies), except murder and rape, which are heard by the central criminal court. The circuit court and the central criminal court are conducted before judge and jury. Appeals are dealt with by the court of criminal appeal, or, when a point of law is involved, by the supreme court. There is also a special criminal court for terrorist offences, which has no jury.

The supreme court consists of a chief justice and eight judges. Cases are decided by a panel of three or five judges. The supreme court has a consultative as well as an appellate jurisdiction. The president may refer proposed legislation to the supreme court to test that legislation's constitutionality, and the high court and circuit court may consult the supreme court on a point of law that may arise throughout a trial.

The legal profession in Ireland consists of solicitors and barristers, a division inherited from the English system. In most cases, a person must first consult a solicitor for legal advice. Generally, barristers are not permitted to deal directly with the public. Usually, solicitors deal with non-contentious work such as the transfer of property, the making of wills, the administration of estates, the formation of companies and the preparation of cases for court. Solicitors advocate in the district court and to a growing extent in the circuit and high court. Barristers specialise in litigation and usually concentrate in a specific area. They generally practise in the circuit court, high court and supreme court. Barristers continue to wear wigs and gowns in court, although this mandatory requirement was abolished in 1995. In 2000, Ireland had 5,500 solicitors and 1,300 barristers, a dramatic increase over the past 20 years. To become a solicitor or barrister in Ireland one studies law at university for three to four years as an undergraduate. University law graduates interested in becoming barristers or solicitors engage in a training programme of approximately three years involving both practical experience and academic work (either at the Honourable Society of Kings Inns or the Law Society of Ireland, respectively). A non-law graduate can independently prepare for entrance exams to the Law Society of Ireland to become a solicitor, or attend a diploma course organised by the Honourable Society of Kings Inns to become a barrister. T.O.C.

Leabhar na hUidhre. The oldest surviving *manuscript written entirely in Irish. It gets its name 'The Book of the Dun Cow' because, in the late Middle Ages, its vellum was thought to have come from a greyish-brown cow owned by St Ciarán, the sixth-century founder of the monastery at *Clonmacnoise, County *Offaly. Most of the manuscript was written there by two monks, one of whom was killed in 1106. It contains the oldest copy of the famous epic *Tain Bó Cuailnge (The Cattle Raid of Cooley)* and other stories from the Ulster Cycle of Tales (e.g., *The Destruction of Da Derga's Hostel)*, as well as historical and religious tracts. Used as a ransom payment for a prince in 1359, it is now in the library of the *Royal Irish Academy. P.H.

Le Brocquy, Louis (1916–). Painter. Le Brocquy, probably Ireland's most distinguished living painter, was born in *Dublin. He studied chemistry before studying art in European museums, where he was especially impressed by the precision of tonal values of Spanish painting. In 1943, a year after the *Royal Hibernian Academy rejected his painting *The Spanish Shawl*, Le Brocquy helped organise the *Irish Exhibition of Living Art (IELA). His cubist-influenced *Travelling People*, 1946, and *Tinkers Resting*, 1946 (Tate Gallery), preceded a series of grey isolated figures as in *The Family*, 1951 (*National Gallery of Ireland), which won a major award at the Venice Biennale in 1956. He moved to London in 1946 and to France in 1958, where he began to produce white torso paintings. Le Brocquy's interest in Polynesian and *Celtic head cults, combined with his early employment as a scientific illustrator, helped produce an obsessive series of human heads. From 1964, he painted images of anonymous ancestral heads, such as *Reconstructed Head of an Irish Martyr*, 1967 (Smithsonian Institution), which developed in 1975 to monochromatic images of heads of writers and painters such as W. B. *Yeats, Samuel *Beckett, James *Joyce and Francis *Bacon, among others. Le Brocquy has also painted watercolour landscapes, illustrated books and designed tapestries, and he is widely represented in public and private collections. Since 1996, he has returned to painting more corporal images. In 2000, he returned to live and work in Ireland. M.C.

Lecky, William Edward (1838–1903). Historian. A graduate of Trinity College, Dublin, Lecky carried out extensive research in Irish archives for his monumental *History of England in the Eighteenth Century*. The last five volumes were devoted to Ireland and refuted James Anthony Froude's negative analysis of Irish culture and society. As Liberal *Unionist MP for Dublin University (1895–1902), Lecky supported the establishment of a *Catholic *university in Ireland but was firmly opposed to *home rule. He was awarded the Order of Merit in 1902. S.A.B.

Ledwidge, Francis (1887–1917). Poet. Born in Slane, County *Meath, and educated at the local national school, Ledwidge worked as a miner and road maker. His early poems appeared in the *Drogheda Independent* and gained the attention of Lord Dunsany, who organised the publication of his first collection, *Songs of the Fields* (1915). Ledwidge joined the British army at the outbreak of the *First World War. He survived the Gallipoli landing but was killed in Flanders in 1917. *Complete Poems* was published in 1919. Ledwidge's tragic life experiences – a failed romance, the trauma of the *First World War and the execution of friends and fellow poets after the *Easter Rising of 1916 – added to the melancholy of his poetry, which remained centred on the immediate beauty of the local and the pastoral. C.D.

Le Fanu, (Joseph) Sheridan (1814–73). Novelist and short story writer. Born in *Dublin and descended both from *Huguenot stock and the family of Richard Brinsley *Sheridan, Le Fanu is best known for his ghost stories and Gothic novels. His most famous novel is *Uncle Silas* (1865), but his international reputation is based on such stories as 'Green Tea' (1869) and 'Carmilla' (1872). James *Joyce draws on Le Fanu's *The House by the Churchyard* (1863) in *Finnegans Wake*. G.OB.

Leinster. One of the four provinces of Ireland. The province, which covers an area of 7,645 square miles, has a population of 2,105, 449 (2002 census). Leinster consists of the counties *Carlow, *Dublin, *Kildare, *Kilkenny, *Laois, *Longford, *Louth, *Meath, *Offaly, *Westmeath, *Wexford and *Wicklow. The name derives from Laighan, which in ancient Ireland was the territory of the Laigini, a powerful tribe in *pre-Christian Ireland. In the twelfth century, the Leinster King Dermot *MacMurrough sought help from the English King *Henry II to regain his kingship, initiating the *Anglo-Norman Conquest. Ireland's capital, the city of *Dublin, is on the Irish Sea, in the eastern part of the province. J.OM.

Leinster, Book of. One of the three great collections (including **Leabhar na hUihre [The Book of the Dun Cow]* and MS. Rawlinson B.502, the latter in the Bodleian Library in Oxford) of Old Irish poems, tales, histories and genealogies of kings and *saints. Housed in the Library of Trinity College, Dublin, the *Book of Leinster (or Lebor na Nuachongbhála)* was compiled or transcribed by a bishop of Kildare at the behest of Dermot *MacMurrough's tutor in the mid-twelfth century. P.H.

Leinster House. Palladian mansion. Designed by Richard Cassels (1690–1751) in 1745 for James FitzGerald, Earl of Kildare (1722–73), this mansion stimulated the development of Merrion Square as the centre of fashionable society in *Dublin. Its design is thought to have influenced Irish architect James *Hoban, who designed the White House in Washington DC. The mansion was bought by the *Royal Dublin Society in 1815 and then purchased by the Irish government in 1925 to accommodate both houses of the Irish *parliament. Leinster House remains the centre of Irish government and provides a focal point for several of Ireland's cultural institutions. S.A.B.

Leitrim, County. Maritime county in the province of *Connacht. Leitrim, with an area of 613 square miles, has the smallest population, 25,815 (as per 2002 census, which shows the first increase in the county's population since record keeping began). Historically, the reason for so few inhabitants was that the county's poorly drained land forced many to leave in search of a better living elsewhere. Because of this, the county's landscape, which is divided into two separate sections north and south of Lough Allen, remains unspoiled and majestic. The name comes from *Liath Druim*, the grey ridge, suggesting the hilly terrain that takes up much of the county. Interspersed, however, are a number of coarse angling lakes (Melvin, Macnean, Allen and Gill), which it shares with *Roscommon, *Fermanagh and *Sligo.

Traditionally, Leitrim was the territory of the O'Rourkes of Breifne, but the areas around the eastern end of Lough Gill were taken over by the English Jacobean planters in the early seventeenth century. An English settler built Parke's Castle around 1620 on Lough Gill. Excavations in the 1980s showed this to be the site of the home of Brian, one of the last O'Rourke chieftains.

Leitrim has the shortest coastline of any Irish maritime county, a mere three miles near Tullaghan, where it is wedged in between Sligo and *Donegal. Its main boating activity is based in the fine inland marina at Carrick-on-Shannon, the county capital. Leitrim's second major town is Manorhamilton. Dromahair has a seventeenth-century *castle and the fine Franciscan friary of Creevelea, one of the last houses of the order to be founded before the *Reformation. The accomplished stained glass artist Wilhelmina Geddes (1887–1955) was a native of Drumreilly and the writer most associated with the county is John *McGahern who, though born in *Dublin, has made his home on a farm near Fenagh. P.H.

Lemass, Seán (1899–1971). Irish revolutionary, politician and *Taoiseach, 1959–66. Born in *Dublin, Lemass joined the Irish *Volunteers at the age of 15 and served under Éamon *de Valera during the *Easter Rising of 1916. He would become one of de Valera's lifelong supporters. In the *War of Independence (1919–21), Lemass was an officer in the *IRA but spent much of the conflict in prison. During the *Irish Civil War, he followed de Valera into the *republican anti-treaty camp. In 1924, he was elected *Sinn Féin TD for South Dublin but refused to take his seat in the *Free State Dáil (in keeping with his party's policy of abstentionism).

When de Valera broke with Sinn Féin in

1926, Lemass helped him found the *Fianna Fáil party. The following year, Lemass entered the Dáil and in 1932, when Fianna Fáil took power, Lemass became de Valera's minister for industry and commerce. He held that position until 1940, when he became minister for supplies, an important and powerful post, considering the wartime shortages facing neutral Ireland during the Second World War.

Though the youngest minister in the first Fianna Fáil government, Lemass became one of the most influential and was chosen as de Valera's Tánaiste in 1945–48, 1951–54 and again in 1957–59. When de Valera resigned as Taoiseach and leader of Fianna Fáil to run for president of Ireland in 1959, Lemass succeeded him in both positions.

As Taoiseach, one of Lemass' chief goals was to modernise Ireland's economy. Under his leadership, Fianna Fáil abandoned its traditional protectionism and adopted free trade policies. This more outward-looking approach to Irish policy-making is illustrated by two of Lemass' best-known initiatives: Ireland's bid for membership in the European Economic Community (EEC) – now the *European Union – in 1961; and his 1965 meetings with *Northern Ireland's Prime Minister Terence *O'Neill (the first such meetings any Irish head of government had held with his Northern counterpart since 1925). Although Ireland's initial EEC application was unsuccessful, the country's eventual entry into the community in 1973 is often credited to Lemass' overhaul of the Irish *economy during the 1960s. Due largely to his promotion of economic planning and trade liberalisation, Irish economic growth during the decade was phenomenal: the standard of living rose by 50%, which helped lead to a population increase of 100,000 between 1961 and 1971, the highest growth level recorded since the state was founded. Lemass' pragmatic leadership and the success of the economy during his years in power also helped modernise Irish politics, as the nation's *political parties began to focus increasingly on economic and social issues and to place less emphasis on Civil War antagonisms.

Due to deteriorating health, Lemass resigned as Taoiseach and Fianna Fáil leader in 1966. He was succeeded by Jack *Lynch. T.D.

Leonard, Hugh (1926–). Playwright, pseudonym of John Keyes Byrne. Born in Dalkey, County *Dublin, and educated at Presentation College, Dún Laoghaire, Leonard worked for the *Land Commission, 1945–59. Later, he worked as script editor for Granada Television and the *Abbey Theatre. The play *Da* (1973), a portrayal of an uneasy son and father relationship, is arguably his masterpiece and has enjoyed many revivals. It received a Tony Award in 1978 and was filmed in 1988 by Matt Clark, starring Martin Sheen. *A Life* (1980), a play that developed the autobiographical theme of *Da*, was also produced on Broadway. Other plays, such as *The Patrick Pearse Motel* (1971) and *Suburb of Babylon* (1983), satirised contemporary Irish life. Television scripts include *Strumpet City* (1979), *The Irish RM* (1985), *Troubles* (1987) and *Parnell and the Englishwoman* (1988). Leonard has also written two volumes of autobiography, a memoir, *Rover and Other Cats* (1990) and three novels, *The Off-shore Island* (1993), *Parnell and the Englishwoman* (1993) and *A Wild People* (2002). C.D.

limerick. A short, humorous and often nonsensical verse of five lines that have a particular pattern of rhyme (aabba) and rhythm. Lines 1, 2 and 5 are of three feet and rhyme, and lines 3 and 4 are of two feet and rhyme. The rhythm is anapestic. Generally, a person or situation is being lampooned, often in a bawdy or irreverent way. How this poetic form originated and how it came to be named after *Limerick, the city and county in Ireland, remains a mystery. Local lore has it that the eighteenth-century Irish poet and Limerick native Andreas McGrath composed in this five-line metre, which was based on an ancient Irish verse form. Another theory is that the limerick was first invented in the eighteenth century by a Limerick student at Trinity College who composed these witty ditties in classical Greek and Latin to poke fun at his fellow students and teachers. The practice became a fad on campus and eventually limericks were being composed in English also. The limerick is also said to have originated from a folk song in which the refrain is 'Will you come up to Limerick?' as each listener contributed an impromptu verse. Supposedly, in the eighteenth century, members of the Irish Brigade returning from France brought back this song. Edward Lear popularised this form of light verse with the publication of his *Book of Nonsense* in 1846. L.R., J.OM.

Limerick, County. Inland county in the province of *Munster. The county, 1,064 square miles, has a population of 175,529 (2002 census). Very fertile areas of the county, especially in the east and centre, are part of the 'Golden Vale', where dairy farming thrives. The *Shannon forms the northern border of County Limerick for a total of 48 miles, almost until the river reaches the Atlantic Ocean. The Shannon was a commercial waterway used by travellers and traders, who probably brought the many gold objects dating from the Late Bronze Age, around 700 BC., that have been discovered throughout the county.

Cnoc Fírinne and the Knockainey hills are ancient sites once associated with the *Celtic otherworld. The Benedictine Abbey of Glenstal on the slopes of the Slieve Felim hills is one of the most vibrant spiritual centres in Ireland today. Limerick City is the largest urban area in the mid-western region, with a population of 54,058. The *Vikings founded Limerick City in a sheltered position at the top of the Shannon estuary in 922 and were con-

King John's Castle, Limerick City

quered in 967 by the O'Brien King of Munster, Brian *Boru and his brother. In the thirteenth century, Limerick City fell to the *Anglo-Normans. The Normans also expelled the O'Donovan chieftains southward to *Cork and *Kerry, allowing the Norman FitzGeralds to take over the lands west of the city, where they built *castles at Adare, Carrigogunnel, Askeaton, Shanid, Glin and Newcastle West. Limerick has more surviving examples of ceremonial halls (in some of these castles) than any other county. In 1691, Limerick City was under siege and witnessed the culmination of the campaign of King *William of Orange to end the Stuart monarchy. King *James II had fled to *France after the Battle of the *Boyne a year before, and the Treaty of *Limerick in 1691 marked the end of *Catholic Ireland's alliance with the *Jacobean cause.

In the eighteenth century, the Croom area of the river Maigue became a centre for poets writing in Gaelic including, among others, the Clare-born Brian *Merriman, who wrote the *Midnight Court*. English-language authors associated with Limerick include Gerald *Griffin, Kate *O'Brien, Frank *McCourt, poet Aubrey *de Vere and his bilingual successor Michael *Hartnett. Artists include Dermod O'Brien and Seán *Keating. The *Hunt Museum in Limerick City has one of the finest art collections anywhere in the country and Limerick boasts one of the best art colleges in Ireland.

The University of Limerick, with a heavy

emphasis on *technology, has had significant impact on the city's economic and cultural life. The famous Ardagh Chalice, now in the *National Museum in Dublin, was found in County Limerick, not far south of Foynes. The latter, which served as a transatlantic seaplane base in the 1930s and 1940s, is still a small but busy port. Adare is a particularly picturesque village with thatched cottages and a Tudor-style manor house (now a hotel). The *Young Irelander William Smith *O'Brien and various members of the O'Malley clan, are among the best-known political names associated with Limerick history. Éamon *de Valera, though born in *New York, spent his childhood in Bruree, a village in the southern part of the county. Limerick City was famous for its hams and those five-line verses (*limericks), sometimes nonsensical but always funny, whose origin and connection with Limerick, city or county, has yet to be satisfactorily explained. P.H.

Limerick, Treaty of (3 October 1691). Treaty ending the Williamite War. Signed by the *Jacobite and Williamite commanders at the end of the Siege of Limerick, the treaty ended the war between *James II and *William III. In exchange for surrendering, the Jacobites were granted free passage for themselves and their families to France. Those who remained were granted limited rights (similar to those enjoyed by *Catholics under Charles II). The *Protestants who dominated *parliament in *Dublin, however, reneged on these concessions and soon began to enact the *Penal Laws. The *Wild Geese felt betrayed and took as their battle cry, 'Remember Limerick and the treachery of the English'. T.C.

Linehan, Rosaleen (1937–). Actress. Born in *Dublin, Linehan studied at University College, Dublin, and first became known as a comedienne in revues and on *radio and *television. Her diverse career includes performances in plays by George Bernard *Shaw, Oscar *Wilde, Seán *O'Casey, Oliver *Goldsmith and Shakespeare. In 1989, she was nominated for a Tony Award for her performance on Broadway in Brian *Friel's *Dancing at Lughnasa*. Her one-woman show *Mother of All the Behans* played in England, Scotland, France and New York. In 1997, she gave a memorable performance as Winnie in Samuel *Beckett's *Happy Days* at the Lincoln Center Festival. Other roles include Lady Bracknell in Wilde's *The Importance of Being Earnest* at the *Abbey Theatre, Mommo in Tom *Murphy's *Bailegangaire* at the Royal Court Theatre, Madam Arcati in Noel Coward's *Blithe Spirit* at the Guthrie Theatre in Minneapolis and Mary Tyrone in Eugene O'Neill's *Long Day's Journey into Night* at the *Gate Theatre. She has also appeared in many films, including the film of *Happy Days*. L.R.

linen. See **textiles**.

literature in English. The beginning of Irish literature in English is often dated to the sixteenth century when the Tudor re-conquest of Ireland brought about a flowering of writing in English. However, a number of English works survive from the Middle Ages. Friar Michael of *Kildare (born c.1280) is the first known English-language poet in Ireland. He is included in an important collection of Irish material known as *Harley 913* (c.1330). The collection also contains the celebrated anonymous *Hiberno-English burlesque fantasy *The Land of Cokaygne*. One of the most interesting and self-conscious users of an 'Old English' form of the language in the Elizabethan age was Richard Stanihurst (1547–1618), who contributed a section on Ireland to Holinshed's *Chronicles* (1577) and translated the first four books of Virgil's *Aeneid* (1582).

The term *Anglo-Irish to describe literature in Ireland, while controversial, carries a special significance in the eighteenth and nineteenth centuries, not only because until the early twentieth century most Irish writers of English were of ascendancy background, but also because many of them dealt with the colonial experience of divided identity. Many of the most distinguished 'English' writers of the eighteenth century were in fact either of Irish birth or lived a significant part of their lives in Ireland. Of these, Jonathan *Swift (1667–1745) and Oliver *Goldsmith (1728–74) are the best known. Swift's 'savage indignation' at the grossness of 'that animal called man' in his great satires *A Tale of a Tub* and *Gulliver's Travels* reflects his experience of being caught between two identities as well as his rage at the gross injustice of English treatment of both the native and Anglo-Irish. However, to adapt the Duke of Wellington's notorious retort to the suggestion that his Irish birth made him an Irishman ('being born in a stable does not make one a horse'), being born in Ireland does not necessarily make one an Irish writer. Many of those who were born there – such as Sir Richard Steele (1672–1729), George *Farquhar (1677–1707) and Laurence *Sterne (1713–68) – show little detectable influence of Ireland in their art. Conversely, neither Richard Edgeworth (1744–1817) nor his daughter Maria *Edgeworth (1767–1849) were born in Ireland, but Maria is universally regarded as a major Irish writer. While her *Castle Rackrent* (1800) is by no means the first Irish novel, as is often claimed, it is the first to rank among the finest European novels of its time. *The History of Jack Connor* (1752) by William Chaigneau (1709–81) was the first novel to address the question of Irish identity and it was followed by numerous novels by Thomas Amory (c.1691–1788), Henry Brooke (1703–83), Charles Johnstone (1719–1800), Frances Sheridan (1724–66) and many others. The first half of the nineteenth century produced a large body of Irish fiction, including works by Lady *Morgan (1775–1859), William *Carleton (1794–1869), Gerald *Griffin (1803–40) and Sheridan *Le Fanu (1814–73).

Everything that changed the western world between 1776 and the 1830s also changed Ireland and Irish culture: revolutionary *republicanism, *nationalism, romanticism, the beginning of industrialism. Specifically, the *Rebellion of 1798 and the new forms of political consciousness brought by it, together with the effects of the Act of *Union, created new and sharper divisions and competing senses of identity. Sentimental and romantic images of Ireland's past, especially in the poetry and songs of Irish writer Thomas *Moore (1779–1852), appealed to a large European audience. Later writers and critics distanced themselves from 'the sweetest lyrist of [Ireland's] saddest wrong' as Shelley called him, but Moore's *The Irish Melodies* and *National Airs* remained immensely influential on Irish culture, writing and political consciousness for over a 100 years.

The chief literary enterprise of the nineteenth century, 'inventing Ireland', is primarily attributed to the *Literary Revival, which began in the 1890s, with W. B. *Yeats (1865–1939) playing a prominent part. A cultural revival had, however, started much earlier. Beginning in the late eighteenth century, there was a concerted effort to preserve the *Irish language and *music, and to rediscover Irish literature, history and *folklore. Yeats acknowledged his indebtedness to many of these precursors, especially to Carleton, James Clarence *Mangan (1803–49), Sir Samuel *Ferguson (1810–86) and Douglas *Hyde (1860–49). By the time Lady Augusta *Gregory (1852–1932), John Millington *Synge (1871–1909) and others helped Yeats launch the Irish Literary Theatre (which became the *Abbey Theatre in 1904), there were many competing and overlapping forms of Irish nationalism in place, some focused on political self-determination, some on cultural renewal and some on the restoration of the Irish

From the Literary Map of Ireland (Tourism Ireland)

language. Although Patrick *Kavanagh's dismissal of the Literary Revival as 'a thoroughgoing English-bred lie' is unfair, the revival was overwhelmingly Anglo-Irish in personnel and taste and had a tense relationship with more *Catholic and politically singleminded movements such as *Sinn Féin. During the late nineteenth and early twentieth century, novels such as *Knocknagow* by Charles *Kickham (1828–82) and those of Canon Patrick Sheehan (1852–1913), which addressed political and social themes from nationalist and Catholic perspectives, enjoyed a large popular readership both within Ireland and among Irish emigrants.

As in the eighteenth century, many Anglo-Irish writers *emigrated to London, and some of the chief figures in late-nineteenth-century English literature were Irish-born, notably Oscar *Wilde (1856–1900) and George Bernard *Shaw (1856–1950), who not only continued the tradition of Irish dominance in drama that had started in the early eighteenth century, but were consciously Irish in maintaining a critical perspective on English culture. Another Irish figure in the London literary scene was novelist Bram *Stoker (1847–1912). Stoker, who was Henry Irving's theatrical agent, is best known for his famous novel *Dracula* (1897), which is deeply indebted to the tradition of Irish Gothic fiction, especially to Le Fanu's vampire tale 'Carmilla' (1872). One of the most popular, prolific and influential figures in nineteenth-century *theatre was Dion *Boucicault (1820–90), whose Irish plays (especially *The Colleen Bawn*, 1860), were immensely successful not only in Ireland, but in London and America.

The Literary Revival, especially as embodied in the work of Yeats and Synge, has continued to enjoy esteem and influence until the present, but, since Irish independence in 1922, literature in English can hardly be called 'Anglo-Irish'. There is, however, a distinguished subcurrent of Anglo-Irish writing, which includes the novelists Elizabeth *Bowen (1900–73), Molly Keane (1905–96) and William *Trevor (b. 1928), the great playwright Samuel *Beckett, the poet Richard Murphy (b. 1927) and the essayist Hubert *Butler (1900–90). The main tradition of twentieth-century Irish literature derives from the extraordinary work of James *Joyce (1882–1941) and from the 1920s until the 1960s constituted a kind of loyal opposition to the dominant *Catholic puritanism and philistinism of the Irish *Free State (later the *Republic of Ireland). The leading writers in this period were Liam *O'Flaherty (1896–1984), Seán *Ó Faoláin, (1900–90), Frank *O'Connor (1903–66), Patrick Kavanagh (1904–67), Flann *O'Brien (1911–66), Brendan *Behan (1923–64) and outstanding women such as Kate *O'Brien (1897–1974), Mary *Lavin (1912–96) and Edna *O'Brien (b. 1930).

The past 30 years have seen the flowering of a very diverse body of literature both in the Republic and in *Northern Ireland. While there are many exceptions to the generalisation, those from the south increasingly tend (somewhat in the spirit of Joyce), to see themselves as citizens of the international republic of letters, while those in *Northern Ireland are understandably concerned with the *Troubles and with conflicting forms of Irish identity. Ireland has four Nobel Prize winners for literature (George Bernard Shaw, W. B. Yeats, Samuel Beckett and Seamus *Heaney). The remarkable number of internationally acclaimed living poets (Thomas *Kinsella, John *Montague, Eavan *Boland, Paul *Muldoon and Seamus Heaney), dramatists (Brian *Friel, Tom *Murphy and Sebastian *Barry) and writers of fiction (John *Banville, John *McGahern, Roddy *Doyle) enables contemporary Ireland to exert an influence on the world far in excess of its size or political power. J.McD.

literature in Irish. Composition of literary material, particularly myth, saga and poetry goes back to the *prehistoric period in Irish, making Irish literature the oldest continuing tradition in western Europe. Many of the sagas and some of the poetry reflect a society that can be dated to the first or second centuries BC. *Christianity brought literacy in Latin and Roman script in the middle of the fifth century. Literature in Irish has its written beginnings in the monasteries that fostered the golden age of Irish art. Apart from a few poems and jottings which may be dated to the sixth century, the earliest extant material we have are lyric poems written by Irish monks on the margin of manuscripts in the eight century. These are simple, intense and passionate. Certainly older, but written down somewhat later, are the great heroic stories of kings and gods. The most famous of these is the **Táin Bó Cuailnge* (The Cattle Raid of Cooley) – the story of a jealous queen and two bulls and *Cúchulainn – which is often seen as the Irish epic. It is remarkable that the most significant of this early literature is in prose, even though the **fili* is often seen as a continuation of the *druid and possessing magical powers. The *Viking invasions destroyed a lot of the monasteries and by the twelfth century Irish literature had come under the patronage of secular families. These families supported the *bardic poets and their schools and helped compile and preserve the great manuscript books in which most of the medieval literature has survived. The most famous of these books are **Leabhar na hUidhre* (The Book of the Dun Cow) and *The Book of *Leinster.*

A greater European influence can be detected after the Norman colonisation. The common stock of romantic tales took root and helped to shape the traditional Irish stories of the *Fianna. The tradition of *amour courtois* was developed among the aristocracy and eventually made its way into the folk tradition. Works of European literature were translated into Irish. The great rupture in this literature takes place as a result of the English conquest in the early seventeenth century, although, paradoxically, some of the greatest poetry and most powerful prose grew out of the struggle. Dáibhí *Ó Bruadair's (1625–98) life and poetry reflect the story of his times and kind: a life begun with patronage and ended in poverty. Seathrún *Céitinn's *Foras Feasa ar Éirinn (A Basis of Knowledge About Ireland)* is a compendium of Irish history, written in the 1630s, which inspired Irish people for 200 years. But the destruction of the aristocracy also exposed a literature of the common people. The eighteenth century, in particular, was a century of song-poetry, composed by the impoverished and cherished by the destitute. Although often painful and lamenting as in the poetry of Aodhagán *Ó Rathaille (c.1670–1729), or rhetorically political as in the songs of Seán Clárach Mac Domhnaill (1691–1754), this song-poetry includes such lively compositions as Brian *Merriman's *Cúirt an Mheán Oíche (The Midnight Court*, 1780).

Prose had been reduced to a trickle by the nineteenth century and the language went into serious decline after the *Famine. The *Irish Revival of the 1880s and the *Gaelic League, however, had as one of their aims the revitalisation and modernisation of literature in Irish. As a result, the twentieth century has been one of the richest of all. The novel was born, the short story escaped from *folklore, poetry reinvented itself, drama appeared from nowhere and seriously intellectual discursive prose appeared for the first time since the seventeenth century. In fact, for all its longevity as a tradition, there has been more writing in Irish in the twentieth century than in all other centuries put together. Perhaps the most significant author was Máirtín *Ó Cadhain (1906–70), whose novels and short stories married traditional language of a most developed kind with a modern and wild sensibility. In poetry, Seán *Ó Ríordáin (1916–77) used his own personal investigations as the basis of his finely wrought and often scary lyricism. At the beginning of the twenty-first century, contemporary writing in Irish is vibrant. A.T.

Lloyd George, David (1863–1945). British politician, British prime minister (1916–22). One of the most important figures in British politics in the early twentieth century, Lloyd George had a profound impact on Irish history. Born in Wales, Lloyd George emerged from humble circumstances to become a dynamic figure in British politics. As MP for Caernarfon Boroughs (1890– 1945), he championed Welsh causes and as chancellor of the Exchequer greatly improved social welfare services. Prime minister from 1916 to 1922, Lloyd George led Britain through the *First World War and the Paris peace negotiations. In 1917, he established the Irish Convention to seek a settlement of the political crisis in Ireland. He was, however, condemned by Liberal opinion in Britain for his apparent approval of 'official reprisals' against suspected *republicans by the British army and *'Black and Tan' police, which intensified the violence and brutality of the *Anglo-Irish conflict during 1920 and 1921. Nevertheless, Lloyd George successfully negotiated the *Anglo-Irish Treaty which ended the *War of Independence and led to the creation of the *Irish Free State. He was forced to resign as prime minister in October 1922 in part because of Conservative dissatisfaction with the terms of the Anglo-Irish Treaty. In 1945, he was made an earl (First Earl Lloyd George of Dwyfor). Lloyd George is the author of several books, including *War Memoirs* (6 vols., 1933– 36). S.A.B.

Longford, County. Inland county in the province of *Leinster. After Leitrim, the landlocked county of Longford (421 square miles) is the second-least populated county in Ireland, with 31,127 inhabitants (2002 census). Primarily *agricultural, the county has some light industry and *textile production. The reputation of being a flat midland county is not really justified. The western part, bordering the River *Shannon, is certainly low-lying, but to the east of Longford town, the land is higher, reaching 912 feet at Carn Clonhugh. A much lower hill, Slieve Calry, is identified with the Brí-Leith of ancient Irish *mythology, residence of Midir of the Tuatha Dé Danann tribe. At the foot of Slieve Calry is the village of Ardagh, where there is an old church dedicated to St Mel, Longford's patron *saint, and where Oliver *Goldsmith is said to have mistaken a convent for an inn, an event recalled in his play *She Stoops to Conquer*. Goldsmith (1728–74) was supposedly born at Pallas, not far from Ballymahon. A younger contemporary was Richard Lovell Edgeworth (1744–1817), author and inventor after whom the village of Edgeworthstown (also known as Mostrim) was called. He was also father of Maria *Edgeworth (1767–1849) who, though born in England, spent most of her life in County Longford, where she wrote *Castle Rackrent* (1800) and corresponded with her friend Sir Walter Scott. Other writers from Longford include Leo Casey, author of songs and ballads, and the poet Padraic *Colum.

In early times, Longford's leading family was the O'Farrells, lords of Annaly, who defended the county against Norman invaders. A fine example of motte and bailey, erected by Hugh de Lacy in the twelfth century, overlooks the town of Granard. Other ancient monuments include the fine, but little-known, *dolmen at Aghnacliff and the Cistercian abbey of Abbeylara. During the *Rebellion of 1798, a combined French and Irish force was defeated by the British under Lord Cornwallis at Ballinamuck. Longford's best-known modern politician is Albert *Reynolds (born in Roscommon), the *Republic's *Taoiseach from 1992 to 1994. P.H.

Longley, Michael (1939–). Poet. Born in *Belfast to English parents, Longley was educated at Trinity College, Dublin. Along with Seamus *Heaney, he is associated with the Northern Group founded in Belfast by Philip Hobsbaum, and is one of the few poets of his generation who stayed in Belfast throughout the *Troubles. Known for his exquisitely crafted nature poems, Longley has also written some of the best political poems of his generation. Longley's themes and subjects reflect his background in classics. *No Continuing City* (1969), his first book, depicts home both as a place of brutal violence and reunited family. Political violence intrudes on its fragile civility. However, rural *Mayo provides an alternative setting for meditation. The collections *Gorse Fires* (1991) and *The Weather in Japan* (2000) integrate the personal, communal and universal, but approach the *Northern Irish troubles obliquely, in order to show how they disrupt domestic, private life. *Tuppenny Stung*, a short autobiography, appeared in 1994. M.S.T.

Lough Derg Pilgrimage. Catholic *pilgrimage. Long regarded as the most difficult pilgrimage in Christendom, this journey to St *Patrick's Purgatory, or Station Island, in County *Donegal, continues to take place between 1 June and 15 August each year. Today, the pilgrims spend three days on the island and perform a series of penances, including vigils and fasting. A widely popular religious practice before the Great *Famine (1845–51), the pilgrimage was transformed during the Irish devotional revolution (1850–75), which condemned indigenous religious practices in an effort to normalise Irish *Catholicism. In their tourist handbook of 1853, *Connemara and the West of Ireland*, Mr and Mrs Samuel Carter Hall reassured readers that the pilgrimage to Lough Derg and 'similar evil customs' were dying out. E.S.M.

Louth, County. Maritime county in the province of *Leinster. Ireland's smallest county, only 318 square miles, Louth is, however, more heavily populated (101,802; 2002 census) than other larger counties because it has the major towns of Drogheda and Dundalk near both its northern and southern extremities. These two towns together account for just over half the county's population. The most strikingly beautiful part of the county is the Cooley Peninsula, which looks across the border with *Northern Ireland to the majestic Mourne Mountains in County *Down. On the peninsula are the active port of Greenore, a small *whiskey *distillery and the historic town of Carlingford (renowned for its oysters). The Cooley Peninsula is most famous for the legendary epic **Táin Bó Cuailnge* (The Cattle Raid of Cooley), which chronicles Queen Maeve of *Connacht's attempts to carry off a prized bull from Cooley so that her herd could equal that of her husband's. To the west of Dundalk is a standing stone that tradition associates with the death of *Cúchulainn, the hero of the *Táin Bó Cuailnge*.

The county's southern border is the river Boyne, scene of the fateful Battle of the *Boyne (1690), in which King *William of Orange defeated the forces of King *James II and changed the course of Irish history. More than three centuries earlier, the Scottish King Edward *Bruce's invasion of the county cost him his life at Faughart, where he is buried. Faughart is also the acknowledged birthplace of St *Brigid, Ireland's foremost female *saint. The high *crosses at Monasterboice are among the most impressive and best preserved in Ireland. In Mellifont, the Cistercians founded their first Irish monastery in the twelfth century. The church of St Peter in Drogheda houses the head of Ireland's only canonised martyr, St Oliver *Plunkett.

Louth, at one time on the cusp of Gaelic Ireland and the English-dominated *Pale, has some fine *castles and *tower houses, including Carlingford Castle, Castle Roche and Roodstown. St Laurence's Gate in Drogheda is a symbol of the strength of this once-fortified town on the river Boyne. Nearby, a viaduct over the river constructed for the Dublin-Belfast railway line was regarded as the great engineering feat of mid-nineteenth-century Ireland. On the northern side of the estuary is Beaulieu, dating from the 1700s, one of the first country houses in Ireland to be built without fortifications. An Grianán, the vibrant home of the Irish Countrywomen's Association, is north of Drogheda. Notable figures from Louth include: the painter Nano Reid, architect Michael *Scott and the economist T. K. *Whitaker. P.H.

Lover, Samuel (1797–1868). Novelist, songwriter and painter. Born in *Dublin, Lover established himself as a miniaturist and marine painter. He published *Legends and Stories of Ireland* (1831) with his own illustrations. In 1835, Lover moved to London, where he published the stage-Irish novels *Rory O'Moore* (1837) and *Handy Andy: A Tale of Irish Life* (1842). He devised a successful stage show entitled *Irish Evenings*, which featured his own songs and sketches, and toured England and the United States. He wrote over 300 Irish songs in all. Samuel Lover was the grandfather of Victor Herbert (1859–1924), the celebrated Dublin-born cellist and writer of Broadway musicals. C.D.

Loyalists. People who support the continued existence of Northern Ireland as part of Britain. *See* **Unionism**.

Lunny, Dónal (1947–). Musician and producer. Lunny is a bouzouki, guitar and bodhrán player, composer, arranger and producer. He popularised the modern 'Irish bouzouki'. Lunny experimented with different instruments as accompaniment in Irish *music and championed the style of 'pitching' of notes on the bodhrán. He has been an influential figure in all modern presentations of traditional music ranging from his pop band Emmet Spiceland (1960s), to *Planxty (1972–75), *Bothy Band (1974–79), Moving Hearts (1981–84), solo work with rock and traditional musicians and the 'trad-rock' band Coolfin (1998–99). F.V.

Lusitania (7 May 1915). *First World War maritime tragedy. The Cunard Liner *Lusitania* was sunk in 1915 by a German submarine, off Kinsale, County *Cork, with the loss of 1,198 people. Fearing that further incidents would incite the United States into entering the war, Germany temporarily ceased its campaign of unrestricted warfare in the Atlantic. P.E.

Lynch, Jack (1917–99). Politician, *Taoiseach, leader of *Fianna Fáil. Born in Cork City, Lynch worked as a civil servant and as a barrister. He was also an extremely skilled *hurler who won eight All-Ireland medals with Cork. Member of the *Dáil from 1948 to 1981, a government minister from 1957 to 1966, Lynch was Taoiseach from 1966 to 1973 and again from 1977 to 1979. He was leader of Fianna Fáil from 1966–79, having been selected as a compromise at a time when the party was bitterly divided between supporters of Charles *Haughey and George Colley. Initially, Lynch was perceived as a weaker political force, overshadowed by these two great rivals. In the early years of the *Northern Ireland conflict, 1968–70, he was severely tested, but his position within the party was strengthened when he dismissed Charles Haughey and Neil Blaney from the cabinet, for alleged gunrunning to northern *nationalists, during the *Arms Crisis in 1970. He was a hugely popular political leader and, in the 1977 general election, led Fianna Fáil to its largest victory since 1938. Haughey replaced Lynch as leader of Fianna Fáil two years later after a series of by-election defeats. J.D.

M

MacBride, Major John (1865–1916). Politician, revolutionary. Born in County *Mayo, MacBride was active in *republican circles in the west of Ireland before emigrating to South Africa in 1896. While there, he organised the *Irish Brigade, which fought on the Boer side in the *Boer War. After the war, MacBride settled in France, where he married Maud *Gonne. The couple had one son, Seán *MacBride, who founded Amnesty International. On his return to Ireland, MacBride resumed his republican activities and served on the Supreme Council of the *IRB. He took part in the *Easter Rising of 1916 and was executed along with the other leaders in May 1916. A.S.

MacBride, Seán (1904–88). *IRA leader, politician, Nobel Peace Prize winner. Born in Paris, Seán was the son of John *MacBride (who was executed for his part in the *Easter Rising of 1916) and *republican activist Maud *Gonne MacBride. He was a member of the IRA in the *War of Independence, took the anti-treaty side in the *Civil War and remained active in the IRA until the enactment of the 1937 *Constitution (serving from 1936 to 1937 as its chief of staff). MacBride formed *Clann na Poblachta in 1946. He was elected to the *Dáil from 1948 to 1957 and was minister for external affairs between 1948 and 1951. A founding member of Amnesty International, MacBride was a barrister, who specialised in human rights cases. He was UN Commissioner for Namibia in Africa from 1973 to 1976. In 1974, MacBride was awarded the Nobel Peace Prize, as chairman of Amnesty International. In later years, he was a constant critic of the British government's human rights record in *Northern Ireland. J.D.

MacDiarmada, Seán (1884–1916). Revolutionary. Born at Kiltyclogher, County *Leitrim, MacDiarmada moved to *Belfast in 1902, where he joined the *IRB in 1906. He was crippled in 1912 by an attack of poliomyelitis. In 1915, MacDiarmada became a member of the military council of the IRB. He fought at the GPO (General Post Office) in *Dublin during the *Easter Rising in 1916 and was one of the seven signatories of the *Proclamation of the Irish Republic. He was executed on 12 May 1916. C.D.

MacDonagh, Thomas (1878–1916). Poet and revolutionary. Born in Cloughjordan, County *Tipperary, and educated at Rockwell College, Cashel, MacDonagh lectured in English literature at University College, Dublin. In 1908, he helped Patrick *Pearse open St Enda's School in *Dublin. He joined the Irish *Volunteers in 1913 and the *IRB in 1915. MacDonagh was a signatory of the *Proclamation of the Irish Republic, issued at the beginning of the *Easter Rising in 1916, and was in command of Jacob's factory in Dublin during the weeklong fight. He was executed on 3 May 1916. His volumes of poetry, inspired by his deep Catholicism and the *Irish Literary Revival movement, include *Through the Ivory Gate* (1903), *Lyrical Poems* (1913) and *Poetical Works* (1916). A play, *When the Dawn Is Come*, was produced by the *Abbey Theatre in 1908. MacDonagh's most significant work is *Literature in Ireland*, a book of essays (published posthumously in July 1916) in which he proposed the existence of an 'Irish Mode' of literature that applied the distinctive rhythms and patterns of Gaelic to *Hiberno-English speech and writing. C.D.

MacGonigal, Maurice (1900–79). Landscape and portrait painter. Born in *Dublin, MacGonigal was a pupil of William *Orpen. He went on to teach at the Dublin Metropolitan School of Art and National College of Art, Dublin, where, along with Seán *Keating, he continued Orpen's formal academic tradition. He exhibited his paintings often at the *Royal Hibernian Academy, where he was president from 1962 to 1977. M.C.

MacGowan, Shane (1957–). Singer. Born in London of Irish parents, MacGowan was the founding member of the Irish punk band the Pogues. Hits include the duet with Kirsty MacColl 'Fairytale of New York' (1987). Their most famous album was *Rum, Sodomy and the Lash* (1985), which includes such perennial favourites as 'A Pair of Brown Eyes' and 'Dirty Old Town'. He has been heavily influenced by the writings and the hedonistic lifestyle of Brendan *Behan. MacGowan is regarded as one of the most accomplished lyricists in modern rock music. He broke with the Pogues in the mid-1990s to set up a new band called the Popes. B.D.

MacGowran, Jack (1918–73). Actor. MacGowran was born in *Dublin and educated by the *Christian Brothers. He worked as a clerk in an insurance office but turned to acting in the early 1940s. He played at the *Gate and *Abbey Theatres, and in 1950 joined the Radio Éireann Repertory Company. John Ford brought him to Hollywood to act in *The Quiet Man* (1952). After his return to Ireland, MacGowran formed his own theatre company, the Dublin Globe Theatre. In 1954, he moved to London, where he worked for television and acted successfully in the West End. Around this time, he became interested in the works of Samuel *Beckett and would eventually be one of Beckett's most respected interpreters. Beckett wrote the radio play *Embers* (1959), which won the Prix Italia, and *Eh, Joe* (1966), a short piece for television, for him. MacGowran also had notable performances in the plays of Seán *O'Casey. MacGowran's film work includes *Darby O'Gill and the Little People* (1959), *The Fearless Vampire Killers* (1967) and *The Exorcist* (1973). In 1971 he received the New York Critics' 'Actor of the Year' Award for his brilliant performance in *Beginning to End*, a one-man show based on material from Beckett plays. He died in New York in 1973. J.C.E.L.

Macken, Walter (1915–67). Novelist, actor, playwright. Born in *Galway, where he is fondly remembered, Macken wrote his first story at the age of 12 and left school at 17 to join the Galway theatre An Taibhdhearc. There he acted, directed, built sets and wrote plays in Irish. During the 1940s and 1950s, Macken acted at the *Abbey Theatre and appeared in a number of films. In 1948, he played the lead role on Broadway in M. J. Molloy's *The King of Friday's Men*. Macken's own play *Home is the Hero* (1953) was made into a film in 1959, with Macken himself in one of the lead roles. The film was nominated for a Golden Bear Award at the Berlin Film Festival. Macken also wrote the film script for Brendan *Behan's *The Quare Fellow*.

A prolific and best-selling author, Macken wrote with passion and drama about ordinary people struggling in extraordinary circumstances. His works are often set in or around Galway and reflect *Catholic and *nationalist values. His numerous historical novels include the trilogy: *Seek the Fair Land* (1959), a treatment of the *Cromwellian migrations; *The Silent People* (1962), about the Irish *Famine; and *The Scorching Wind* (1964), which follows two brothers through the bitter struggles of the *War of Independence and the *Civil War. *Rain on the Wind* (1950), a romance set in Galway, is probably his most popular novel, while Macken himself favoured *I Am Alone* (1949), which was banned upon publication. He died suddenly in 1967, a year after his appointment as artistic director of the Abbey Theatre. J.C.E.L.

MacLiammóir, Micheál (1899–1978). Dramatist, actor, writer. MacLiammóir, man of the theatre, wit and conversationalist, was the talking piece of the city of *Dublin for 60 years. For many of these, Madame Jammet offered him lunch in her famous restaurant. Born in England as Alfred Willmore, he lived in Dublin since he was a young man and became the most prominent Irish actor of his day. In the late 1920s, he met his life partner Hilton *Edwards, with whom he founded the Irish-language theatre An Taibhdhearc in Galway and the renowned *Gate Theatre (1928) in Dublin. He gave the young Orson Welles his first acting job at the Gate Theatre, launching him on a brilliant and famous career.

MacLiammóir was more Irish than Oscar *Wilde, on whom he modelled his style and wit. His most lucrative performance as an actor was his one-man show *The Importance of Being Oscar*, which he published as a book in 1963. He was an elegant and serious writer in both Irish and English; among his most delightful publications were *Put Money in Thy Purse: The Filming of Orson Welles' Othello* (1952) and *Each Actor on His Ass* (1961). MacLiammóir had an almost esoteric sense of camp. For him living was theatre and theatre an opportunity for provocation and lyricism. He was a king of many parts in his adopted country. J.L.

Maclise, Daniel (1806–70). Painter. Born in *Cork, Maclise became a member of the Royal Academy in 1840. He was known for painting entertaining Irish themes and for illustrating caricatures of Irish life. His use of antiquarian detail and large scale is most evident in the 1854 romantic history painting *The Marriage of *Strongbow and Aoife* in the *National Gallery, Dublin. M.C.

MacMahon, Bryan (1909–98). Short story writer, novelist and playwright. MacMahon was born in Listowel, County *Kerry, where he worked for over 40 years as a schoolteacher and headmaster. In the 1940s, he contributed poems and stories to the **Bell*. A collection of short stories entitled *The Lion Tamer* (1948) was followed in 1952 by a novel, *Children of the Rainbow*. MacMahon closely observes rural village life, with a passionate awareness that this way of life is fast disappearing. Due to his enthusiasm, the voices in his stories are at times over-insistent. His best-known play, *The Honey-Spike*, was produced at the *Abbey Theatre in 1961; rewritten as a novel in 1967, it depicts the travails of a young *traveller couple expecting a child and displays MacMahon's knowledge of Shelta, the travellers' language. In 1966 his pageant commemorating the *Easter Rising of 1916 was staged by the *Gaelic Athletic Association at *Croke Park. MacMahon had a strong interest in the *Irish language and *folklore and translated the autobiography of Peig *Sayers (1974). He was one of the driving forces behind the Listowel Writers Week. MacMahon's autobiography, *The Master*, was published in 1992. J.C.E.L.

MacMahon, Tony (1939–). Musician and television producer. MacMahon is an accordionist, television producer and ideologue within traditional *music. Born in Ennis, County *Clare, he was inspired as a child by the playing of accordionist Joe Cooley and piper Felix Doran. With Séamus *Ennis, MacMahon developed a formidable interpretation of slow airs. During his 26 years of television work with *RTÉ , he increased music popularity with the programmes *Aisling Geal*, *Ag Déanamh Ceol*, *The Long Note*, *The Pure Drop* and *Come West Along the Road*. F.V.

MacManus, Terence Bellew (1823–60). Irish *nationalist. A native of County *Fermanagh, MacManus established a successful shipping agency in Liverpool. He joined the *Repeal Association and *Young Ireland and was transported to Tasmania for his part in the uprising of 1848. He escaped to the United States in 1852 and died in poverty in San Francisco. His funeral in *Dublin in 1861 gained national attention for the *IRB. S.A.B.

MacMathuna, Ciarán (1925–). Collector and radio presenter of traditional *music programmes. His name is synonymous with the traditional music revival. In contrast to earlier broadcasts' emphasis on **céilí* bands, MacMathuna promoted the solo voices, the music of little-known people and small places, bringing such styles as *Clare, East *Galway and *Sligo to national attention. His major shows, *Ceolta Tíre* and *Job of Journeywork*, ran for some 15 years. F.V.

MacMurrough, Dermot (Diarmait MacMurchada) (d. 1171). King of *Leinster. In the struggle for the high kingship of Ireland, Dermot was defeated by Rory *O'Connor, high king of Ireland. After Dermot abducted the wife of O'Rourke, a local chieftain, O'Rourke deposed him and took his lands. Dermot fled to England in 1166 and sought the help of *Henry II, who gave Dermot a letter of permission to recruit mercenaries. In 1167, Dermot returned to Ireland with Norman, Flemish and Welsh mercenaries. His most important recruit among the Normans in Wales was Richard fitzGilbert de Clare, nicknamed *Strongbow. In return for his aid, Strongbow was promised the kingship of Leinster after Dermot's death and Dermot's daughter, Aoife, in marriage. Strongbow invaded Ireland in 1170 and soon most of Leinster was under Norman control. By the time of Dermot's death, the *Norman Conquest was well under way. To the Irish, Dermot was known as *Diarmait na nGall* (Dermot of the Foreigners) and he is generally seen as having initiated the Anglo-Norman Conquest of Ireland. T.C.

MacNeice, Louis (1907–63). Poet. Born in *Belfast and raised in Carrickfergus, County *Antrim, where his father was an Anglican clergyman, MacNeice was sent to English schools from the age of 10. He attended Marlborough College and later Merton College, Oxford, where his contemporaries included W. H. Auden, Stephen Spender and Cecil *Day-Lewis. In 1940, after a decade of university lecturing, he joined the BBC where he worked as a writer and producer for 20 years.

MacNeice's tendency toward irony, pessimism and classical learning, as well as his considerable lyric gift, were already apparent in his 1929 debut, *Blind Fireworks*. On his return from the *Spanish Civil War in 1936, he became linked with Auden and to the English school of left-leaning 1930s poets. His most ambitious work from this period is *Autumn Journal* (1939), a verse-journal in 24 cantos that brought together a broad panorama of autobiography, history and the politics of Ireland, Britain and Europe. MacNeice cut loose from the 1930s poets with *Springboard* (1945) and *Holes in the Sky* (1948), and later *Ten Burnt Offerings* (1952) and *Solstices* (1961). He also wrote radio plays and translations, including *The Agamemnon of Aeschylus* (1936). His unfinished autobiography, *The Strings are False*, was published in 1965. J.AR.

MacNeill, Eoin (1867–1945). Historian and politician. Born in Glenarm, County *Antrim, MacNeill was vice president of the *Gaelic League, professor of early Irish history at University College, Dublin, and chief of staff of the Irish *Volunteers. In 1914, he opposed John *Redmond's plea to the Irish Volunteers to support the British in the war, prompting Redmond to found the rival National Volunteers. On the eve of the *Easter Rising of

1916, MacNeill issued a countermand order calling off the Irish Volunteer participation in the rebellion. Member of *Dáil Éireann and minster for education (1922–25), he was also the *Free State member of the *Boundary Commission (1924–25). He withheld his signature from its final report and resigned, insisting that the commission had misinterpreted its mandate. J.P.MC.

MacSwiney, Terence (1879–1920). Politician. Born in Cork City, MacSwiney was a founding member of the Cork Dramatic Society, for which he wrote a number of plays, including *The Revolutionist*. In 1913, he played a prominent role in the foundation of the Cork *Volunteers. He complied with Eoin *MacNeill's order calling off the *Easter Rising of 1916 and was responsible for persuading Kerry Volunteers not to join the rising. In 1919, MacSwiney refused to take his seat in the British parliament and instead joined the first *Dáil as *Sinn Féin representative for West Cork. In March 1920, he became lord mayor of Cork City, but in August of that year, at the height of the *War of Independence, he was arrested on charges of sedition. MacSwiney went on *hunger strike, drawing worldwide attention to the cause of Irish *nationalism. On 24 October 1920, he died in Brixton prison, after 74 days on hunger strike. His funeral was one of the largest ever held in Cork City. A.S.

Maguire, Brian (1951–). Painter. Born in *Dublin, Maguire uses an expressionist style to comment on sociological and political alienation of contemporary life. He is one of the most successful of the new Irish expressionists. M.C.

Maher, Alice (1956–). Painter and sculptor. Born in *Tipperary, Maher studied in *Limerick, *Cork, *Belfast and San Francisco. Using painting and sculpture, she parodies and reverses traditional themes and associations to discomfort the viewer in surrealist fashion. M.C.

Mahon, Derek (1941–). Poet, verse dramatist, critic and scriptwriter. Mahon was born in *Belfast and educated at Trinity College, Dublin. He is one of a renowned generation of northern Irish poets who emerged in the 1960s, including Michael *Longley and Seamus *Heaney. A brilliant master of forms from an early age, Mahon is a mandarin poet, whose literary influences include fellow sceptical *Protestant writers Louis *MacNeice and Samuel *Beckett. Admired for their technical elegance and perfect-pitch lyricism, the poems of *Night Crossing* (1968), *Lives* (1972), *The Snow Party* (1975) and *Courtyards in Delft* (1981) are austere and fastidious: few, but precise details, a limited palette of colour, controlled tone and unyielding landscape. Early on, Mahon experimented with epistolary verse, which became his primary form after 1986. *The Hudson Letter* (1995) and *The Yellow Book* (1997) adopt a contemporary conversational idiom and experiment with a longer, more flexible line. Other publications include *Collected Poems* (1999), *Journalism* (1996), verse plays such as *Racine's Phaedra* (1996) and his verse translation, *Words in the Air: A Selection of Poems by Philippe Jaccottet* (1998). M.S.T.

Major, John (1941–). British prime minister, 1990–97. Major succeeded Margaret *Thatcher as Conservative Party leader and prime minister, and initiated the 1990–92 Brooke-Mayhew talks with the main *nationalist and *unionist parties in *Northern Ireland. Between 1990 and 1994, he approved secret negotiations between the British government and *Sinn Féin and signed the *Downing Street Declaration (1993), which opened the door for paramilitary organisations' political wings to enter all-party negotiations if they committed themselves to exclusively peaceful methods and agreed to abide by the democratic process. Despite ongoing negotiations with Sinn Féin, Major expressed outrage when the US government granted Sinn Féin leader Gerry *Adams a visa to the United States in January 1994. Adams' US visit was followed by an *IRA cease-fire that began in August 1994.

By demanding IRA arms decommissioning before he would include Sinn Féin in official peace negotiations, Major missed the opportunity for a permanent peace in Northern Ireland during his tenure. The IRA, furious that Major had trumpeted decommissioning to satisfy unionists, ended their cease-fire in February 1996 by bombing *Canary Wharf in east London. Thus, although Major played an instrumental role in moving the *peace process forward, the *Good Friday Agreement came only after the election of Tony *Blair's Labour government in 1997. R.D.

Mallon, Séamus (1936–). Politician. Born in Markethill, County *Armagh, the son of a headmaster and a nurse, Mallon was a teacher. After becoming involved in the civil rights movement, he helped form the *Social Democratic and Labour Party (SDLP). Mallon was committed to peaceful *republican *nationalism and his election to the deputy leadership of the SDLP in the late 1970s signalled the eclipse of that party's *socialist wing. In 1981, he was nominated to the Irish *senate by the then *Taoiseach Charles J. *Haughey, and in 1982 to the eventually abortive Northern Ireland assembly. While his leader, John *Hume, concentrated on influencing international public opinion and the British and Irish governments, Mallon often took the lead in intraparty negotiations within *Northern Ireland. Following the *Good Friday Agreement, he was appointed deputy first minister to David *Trimble in the Northern Ireland assembly. When John Hume resigned the leadership of the SDLP in 2001, however, Mallon vacated his public positions (as deputy first minister and deputy leader of the SDLP) to make way for a younger generation. M.M.

Manahan, Anna (1924–). Actress. Born in *Waterford, Manahan studied under Ria Mooney at the Gaiety School of Acting and played with the *Edwards/*MacLiammóir Company at the *Gate. Highlights in a remarkable career include roles in the notorious 1957 Pike Theatre production of *The Rose Tattoo*, which led to the arrest of its director, Alan Simpson, on charges of obscenity; *Big Maggie*, written for Manahan by John B. *Keane; and Brian *Friel's *Lovers*, for which she received her first Tony nomination in 1968. Manahan has also appeared in such films as *Hear My Song* (1991) and *A Man of No Importance* (1994). Her role as the widow Mag in the box-office hit *The Beauty Queen of Leenane* by Martin *McDonagh won her a Tony Award in 1998. B.D.

Manchester Martyrs (23 November 1867). Execution of William O'Meara Allen, Michael Larkin and William O'Brien. In September 1867, two leading *Fenians, Thomas Kelly and Timothy Deasy, were arrested in Manchester on suspicion of terrorism. An attempt to free them led to the death of a police officer, Sergeant Brett. Twenty-nine arrests were made and Allen, Larkin and O'Brien were convicted and executed for the killing. Their execution produced a great wave of sympathy for the 'Manchester Martyrs'. The alleged last words of the executed men, 'God Save Ireland', were later made into a song by T. D. Sullivan. P.E.

Mangan, James Clarence (1803–49). Poet and translator. Born in *Dublin, Mangan grew up in poverty but received an education through a charitable priest and learned several European languages. He worked at the Ordnance Survey Office from 1833 to 1839, where he associated with the scholars George *Petrie, John *O'Donovan and Eugene *O'Curry. These scholars provided Mangan with translations of Old Irish poems that he re-created into his own peculiar style of English. His works include the two-volume *Anthologia Germanica*, comprising translations of modern German poetry and *Poets and Poetry of Munster* (1849, posthumously). Some of his finest poetry was written in 1846 in response to the spread of the *Famine and published in the **Nation* newspaper. These lyrical ballads, composed in a haunting style, include 'Dark Rosaleen', 'A Vision of Connaught in the XIII Century', and 'Sarsfield'. Addicted to opium and alcohol, always flamboyantly attired, yet destitute and depressive, Mangan had all the characteristics of the romantic genius. He died of cholera, weakened by malnutrition. He was relatively unknown in his lifetime but is now recognised as the leading Irish poet of the mid-nineteenth century. C.D.

manuscripts, illuminated. The 'Island of Saints and Scholars' was famous for its manuscripts, a number of which were painted in monastic scriptoria. The oldest decorated example is the **Cathach* of circa 600, followed by the *Book of *Durrow* around a century later, and reaching its zenith in the *Book of *Kells* of circa 800 (the latter two possibly written in Ireland). The Abbey Library of St Gall in Switzerland has an important collection of Irish illuminated manuscripts of roughly the same period. Others are scattered in libraries around Europe. Illuminated manuscripts of later periods include the twelfth-century *Book of *Leinster* (Library of Trinity College, Dublin), which also contains important historical material. P.H.

Markievicz, Constance Gore-Booth, Countess (1868–1927). *Republican, revolutionary, politician. Born Constance Gore-Booth in London, Markievicz was brought back by her family to their Irish estate at Lissadell House, County *Sligo, shortly after her birth.

Constance Markievicz

She studied painting in London and Paris and in 1900 married a Ukranian-Polish count, Casimir Markievicz, who was also a painter. The marriage failed and in 1903 she settled in *Dublin, where she was associated with the *Gaelic League and leading figures in the *Abbey Theatre.

In 1908 Markievicz joined *Sinn Féin and a year later she founded Na Fianna, a republican-led militaristic boy-scout organisation. She joined Maud *Gonne's *Inghinidhe na hÉireann* (Daughters of Ireland) and contributed to suffragette and *nationalist newspapers. During the Dublin lockout of 1913, Markievicz assisted James *Larkin and the Dublin workers' families and in 1914 she became an officer in the *Irish Citizen Army, prompting the resignation of its secretary, Seán *O'Casey.

She fought in the *Easter Rising of 1916 and was sentenced to death along with the other leaders. Her sentence was commuted to penal servitude for life and she was released in 1917. In 1918, Markievicz was elected as a Sinn Féin MP – the first woman to be elected to the British House of Commons. In keeping with Sinn Féin's policy of abstention, she refused to take her seat in the British parliament. She was minister for labour in the first *Dáil. Markievicz vehemently opposed the *Anglo-Irish Treaty and supported the republican side in the *Irish Civil War. She was arrested in December 1923 for campaigning for the release of republican prisoners and went on *hunger strike. In 1926, she joined *Fianna Fáil and in June 1927 was re-elected to the Dáil. She died a month later. P.D.

Martyn, Edward (1859–1923). Playwright. Martyn was born into a Catholic *landlord family in County *Galway and educated at Beaumont and Oxford. He was a bachelor, a devout Catholic, a fluent Irish speaker, president of *Sinn Féin (1905–08), co-founder of *Feis Ceoil* (the National Music Festival) and devotee of ecclesiastical music and art. With W. B. *Yeats and Lady *Gregory, he founded the Irish Literary Theatre (1899) that evolved into the *Abbey Theatre. His preference for the drama of ideas led him to co-found, with Thomas *MacDonagh and Joseph Mary *Plunkett, the Theatre of Ireland in 1906. His plays include *The Heather Field* (1899) and *The Tale of a Town* (1902). M.S.T.

Maturin, Charles (Robert) (1780–1824). Novelist. Maturin was born in *Dublin, educated at Trinity College, Dublin, and ordained in 1803. The landscape of the west of Ireland and Maturin's interest in Irish affairs inspired *The Milesian Chief* (1812), first published under the pseudonym Dennis Jasper Murphy. *Bertram* (1816) is a successfully staged tragedy in blank verse. *Melmoth the Wanderer* (1820), a powerful novel, is his most enduring work. Its plot and narrative form are complex and the settings are typically Gothic or exotic. Among its themes are madness, persecution, religious mania and unrequited passion. M.S.T.

Maynooth, St Patrick's College. National Seminary of Ireland and later a college of the National University. Founded in 1795 by an act of parliament, the Royal College of St Patrick's at Maynooth (known colloquially as Maynooth) has been the principal seminary for the training of secular priests in Ireland for more than 200 years. During this time, more than 10,000 men have been ordained, a remarkable average of 50 per year. In order to replace the seminaries that were lost on the continent after the French Revolution, the Irish bishops in 1795 pressured the British government to create a seminary. Maynooth established the bishops as an influential political force in Ireland. Stability came slowly to Maynooth; six presidents served there in its first 18 years. In 1845, the government increased its annual grant and, by 1853, over half of the priests serving in Ireland were Maynooth graduates. These men reformed the *Catholic church between 1850 and 1900, consolidating a devotional revolution that made Irish Catholics the most pious in the world. St Patrick's became a Pontifical University in 1896 and its College of Arts and Sciences became associated with the National University in 1910. Lay students entered Maynooth in the 1970s. In 1997, the College of Arts and Sciences and the Pontifical University, including the seminary, separated. Today the much smaller seminary is attempting to adapt to changes in contemporary Ireland. Most of Ireland's leading ecclesiastics were educated at Maynooth, including Eugene O'Growney, early editor of the *Gaelic League's *Gaelic Journal* and William Walsh, archbishop of Dublin, 1885–1921. M.P.C.

Mayo, County. Maritime county in the province of *Connacht in the west of Ireland. The third largest county in Ireland (2,156 square miles), Mayo has a population of 117,428 (2002 census). It is bordered on the east by *Sligo and *Roscommon and on the south by *Galway. While the central part of the county contains some of the most fertile land in Connacht, the eastern and western regions are largely barren. Most of the county's population lives in this central area, in towns such as Castlebar, the county capital, Ballina and Westport. The latter is a picturesque, lively town, which was planned by an English architect, James Wyatt, in the eighteenth century. Achill Island in the north-west of the county (connected by a causeway) is known for its dramatic scenery, well described in Heinrich Böll's book *Irish Journal*. The barony of Erris in the west of the county contains the largest blanket *bog in Ireland. The most famous mountain in Mayo is *Croagh Patrick, a site closely associated with St *Patrick and one of the most enduring pilgrimage sites in Ireland. In the village of Knock, in 1879, some local people claimed to have seen an apparition of the Virgin Mary and the town has been known as a holy place ever since. The *Céide Fields on the north coast of Mayo is a noted archaeological site, where the remains of a human settlement, including stone walls, field patterns, houses and megalithic tombs, some 5,000 years old, were preserved by the blanket bog.

The population of the county has never recovered from the *Famine. From a peak of 388,817 in 1841, it had declined to 117,428 in the 2002 census. In the sixteenth century, Grace *O'Malley, or Granuaile, a member of a prominent local family, won considerable notoriety for smuggling, piracy and resistance to the English. Michael *Davitt, the *Land League leader, was born in Straide and the National Land League was first established at a meeting in Daly's Hotel in Castlebar on 16 August 1879. Captain *Boycott, whose name has become a word in the English language, was a landlord's agent at the height of the *Land War in the county. Mary *Robinson, the respected former Irish president, was also born in the county. Mayo is a largely agricultural county, although fishing and tourism are of increasing importance to the local economy. A.S.

Mary McAleese

McAleese, Mary (1951–). President of Ireland, law professor, journalist and civil rights activist. Born in *Belfast into a *Catholic family, McAleese grew up in a *Protestant area, near Ardoyne. The family was forced to move in the early 1970s when their home was machine-gunned and they were advised for their own safety not to return. In another sectarian attack, her deaf brother was badly beaten. McAleese succeeded Mary *Robinson as Reid Professor of criminal law at Trinity College in 1975 and in 1979 joined *RTÉ as a journalist. She was involved in campaigns for prisoners' rights, gay rights and the ordination of women as Catholic priests, but opposed abortion. In 1987, her appointment as director of Queen's University's Institute of Professional Legal Studies met with intense *unionist opposition. In 1994, she was appointed provice-chancellor of the university, the first Catholic woman to reach such a position. Selected as the *Fianna Fáil candidate for the 1997 presidential election (in preference to former *Taoiseach Albert *Reynolds), McAleese was elected with 58.7% of the popular vote, the largest percentage vote for any presidential candidate to date, surpassing even Éamon *de Valera's first election. J.D.

McAliskey, Bernadette Devlin (1947–). *Nationalist, *socialist, politician. Born into a poor *Catholic nationalist family in Cookstown, County *Tyrone, McAliskey won a scholarship to Queen's University, Belfast. She became involved with the *People's Democracy student civil rights organisation, which was established in the aftermath of an infamous *RUC attack on a Derry demonstration in October 1968. A socialist *republican, McAliskey campaigned as the 'Unity Candidate' acceptable to both republicans and traditional nationalists, in a by-election to the Westminster seat of mid-Ulster in April 1969. On a massive anti-unionist turnout, she was elected at the age of 22 as the youngest member of the United Kingdom parliament, which she electrified with a dramatic and undiplomatic maiden speech.

During the Battle of *Bogside in August 1969, McAliskey urged resistance to RUC incursion and was later sentenced to six months imprisonment for riotous behaviour. Her increasingly radical stance alienated moderate Catholics and she lost her seat in 1974. In February 1981, McAliskey (her married name) was seriously injured in an attempt on her life when loyalist gunmen entered her home. The same year, she played a leading role in the National H-Block Committee established to support the demands of the *hunger strikers. She rejected the *Good Friday Agreement as an unacceptable betrayal of republican principles. M.M.

McCabe, Eugene (1930–). Writer. Born in Glasgow, McCabe returned to Ireland at a young age. His first major play, *The King of the Castle* (1964), provoked considerable controversy for its unflinchingly realistic portrayal of Irish rural life. The most important of his later works are the trilogy of plays for television on the *Northern Ireland crisis, *Victims* (1976), one part of which was published that year as a short novel with the same title, and the novel, *Death and Nightingales* (1992), which deals with political and domestic violence in late-nineteenth-century Ireland. A.S.

McCabe, Patrick (1955–). Writer. Born in Clones, County *Monaghan, McCabe trained as a teacher in *Dublin. He has an economical writing style, rich in local idiom and frequently tinged with the macabre. *The Butcher Boy*, which was shortlisted for the Booker Prize in 1992, is undoubtedly his masterpiece and is regarded as one of the best Irish novels of the twentieth century. The *film *The Butcher Boy*, co-written with Neil *Jordan, was received with great acclaim in 1998. The book was also made into a play called *Frank Pig Says Hello*. Other novels include *Music on Clinton Street* (1986), *Carn* (1989), *The Dead School* (1994), *Breakfast on Pluto* (1998), *Mondo Desperado* (1999) and *Emerald Germs of Ireland* (2000). He has also written many plays and adapted some of his novels for the stage. B.D.

McCann, Donal (1943–99). Actor. Born in *Dublin, McCann is widely regarded as one of the greatest modern Irish actors. He appeared in numerous films and television programmes, but his greatest performances were on the stage, especially in the widely acclaimed roles in Sebastian *Barry's *The Steward of Christendom* (1995) and Brian *Friel's *Faith Healer* (1979). McCann battled with alcoholism and depression for most of his life. At his best, McCann had a charisma and force unequaled by any other Irish actor of recent times. He won major critical praise for his brilliantly controlled performance in John Huston's film *The Dead* (1987). A.S.

McClure, Robert John Le Mesurier (1807–73). Explorer. Born in *Wexford and educated at Eton and Sandhurst, McClure joined the British navy in 1824 and served in the Arctic expeditions of 1836 and 1848. In 1850, he was second-in-command on an expedition to find the missing Arctic explorer Sir John Franklin. McClure discovered Baring's Island, penetrated the Barrow Strait and discovered the North-west Passage. He returned to England in 1854 and was knighted. McClure later served in the China Seas. He published his Arctic adventures, *Voyages*, in 1884. C.D.

McCormack, John (1884–1945). Operatic and concert tenor. Regarded as one of the greatest singers of the twentieth century, McCormack was born in Athlone, County *Westmeath, and educated at the Marist Fathers School in Athlone and at Summerhill College, *Sligo. In 1902, at *Feis Ceoil* (the National Music Festival), he won a gold medal in the tenor competition and, the following year, he travelled to Italy to study under Vincenzo Sabatini. McCormack made his operatic debut in 1907 at Covent Garden, London, in *Cavalleria Rusticana*. By 1909, he was singing opera in Chicago and Boston and with the New York Metropolitan Opera Company. Following a tour of Australia in 1911, he began a successful career on the concert stage. McCormack became an American citizen in 1919 and was made a papal count in 1928 in recognition of his services to Catholic charities. P.E.

McCormick, F. J. (1889–1947). Actor. Stage name of Peter Judge. Judge was born in Skerries, County *Dublin, the son of a *brewery manager. During a brief career in the civil service in London and Dublin, he took part in amateur dramatics and adopted a stage name. In 1918, he joined the *Abbey Theatre Company, where he was taught elocution by Frank *Fay. McCormick appeared in over 500 plays, most notably in those by Seán *O'Casey. He brilliantly created the role of Joxer Daly in O'Casey's *Juno and the Paycock* (1924), opposite an equally brilliant Barry *Fitzgerald as Captain Boyle. Eileen Crowe played the part of Mary Boyle and she and McCormick were married in 1925. He was cast as Jack Clitheroe in O'Casey's *The Plough and the Stars* (1926). When riots broke out in the Abbey Theatre during the opening week of the play, McCormick attempted to quiet the audience by saying, 'Don't blame the actors. We didn't write this play'. The actor and O'Casey had been close friends, but the remark led to a rift that never healed. McCormick toured the United States five times and received numerous offers, but never wanted to leave the Abbey. He played several film roles, including the part of Shell in Carol Reed's *Odd Man Out* (1947). J.C.E.L.

McCourt, Frank (1930–). Writer. Born in Brooklyn, New York, McCourt was taken back to Ireland as a child, at the height of the Depression. At 19 he returned to New York, where he became a high school teacher. *Angela's Ashes*, his funny and poignant memoir of an impoverished *Limerick childhood, published in 1996, won a Pulitzer Prize, sold millions of copies around the world and was made into a film by Alan Parker. A sequel *'Tis*, was published in 1999. M.E.

McDonagh, Martin (1970–). Playwright. Born in London, the son of Irish immigrants, McDonagh grew up in England. However, the family regularly visited Ireland on summer holidays, inspiring McDonagh to write about the isolation of Irish rural life. His first darkly comic trilogy of plays, the *Leenane Trilogy* (*The Beauty Queen of Leenane*, *A Skull in Connemara* and *The Lonesome West*), set in the west of Ireland, rapidly won international acclaim after their initial productions at the Druid Theatre in *Galway in 1996–97. The plays went on to be major successes in London and on Broadway. McDonagh's play *The Cripple of Inishmaan*, the first of a projected *Aran Trilogy*, was first performed at the National Theatre in London in 1997. It was followed in 2001 by *The Lieutenant of Inishmore*, a bloody farce satirising Irish terrorists. The play was turned down by several theatres and eventually staged by the RSC at The Other Place, Stratford-upon-Avon. Inspired as much by television soaps and films as by playwrights like J. M. *Synge, Tom *Murphy and David Mamet, McDonagh's work characteristically juxtaposes melodrama, comedy and violence. A.S.

McGahern, John (1934–). Novelist and short story writer. Born in *Dublin, McGahern grew up in Cootehall, County *Roscommon, where his father was a police sergeant and his mother a schoolteacher. He qualified as a teacher at St Patrick's College, Drumcondra, and later studied at University College, Dublin.

McGahern's first novel, *The Barracks*, the dark, intensely moving story of a police sergeant's wife who is dying of breast cancer, was published in 1963. His second novel, *The Dark* (1965), was banned under the Censorship of Publications Act and McGahern was dismissed from his teaching position in Clontarf, Dublin, without official explanation. Written in an unusual mix of third, second and first person narrative, the novel depicts stages in the relationship between an adolescent boy and his difficult, widowed father. Effectively barred from teaching in Ireland, McGahern lived in England, Spain and the United States before settling in County *Leitrim in 1974, where he still lives on a farm. His novels *The Leavetaking* (1974, revised version 1984) and *The Pornographer* (1979) chronicle this period in his life. Primarily a novelist, McGahern has published four books of short stories, *Nightlines* (1970), *Getting Through* (1978), *High Ground* (1985) and *Collected Stories* (1992). The story 'Korea' was made into a film by Cathal Black in 1995.

Frequently set in the northern midlands, McGahern's novels are dark, fiercely lyrical portrayals of the isolation and claustrophobia of rural Ireland. Recurring themes are the tensions within the family, fear of poverty and starvation, the repression of emotions and sexuality, and the struggle to choose between ambition and security, set within the ritual cycle of the farming seasons and the church calendar. McGahern's meticulous prose style – the result of much cutting and paring – is honed to a fine art in *Among Women* (1990), whose protagonist, Michael Moran, is loved by the women in his family regardless of his difficult temperament. The novel was shortlisted for the Booker Prize. *That They May Face the Rising Sun* (2002, *By the Lake* in the American edition) is a broader but loving portrayal of a year in the life of a rural community. While the earlier novels *The Barracks* and *The Dark* have more raw intensity, *Among Women* and *That They May Face the Rising Sun* show a profound understanding of human nature. J.C.E.L.

John McGahern

McGuckian, Medbh (1950–). Poet. McGuckian was born in *Belfast and educated at Queen's University, Belfast. Her radically innovative poetry emerged in the 1980s and was labelled post-modernist by critics. McGuckian's poems, which strive to map female identity and states of mind, are playful, enigmatic and often elusive, written in a fluid, highly associative, expansive style. Dominant images include hearth and garden, but traditional metaphors such as germination, light and water are given new resonance. Collections include *The Flower Master* (1982), *On Ballycastle Beach* (1988), *Selected Poems* (1997) and *Shelmalier* (1998). She has translated Nuala *Ní Dhomhnaill's poetry into English. M.S.T.

McGuinness, Frank (1953–). Playwright. Born in Buncrana, County *Donegal, McGuinness is one of Ireland's leading contemporary playwrights. His first play, *Factory Girls* (1982), is a sympathetic portrayal of the lives of working-class women in his native Donegal. He is best known for his award-winning play *Observe the Sons of Ulster Marching Towards the Somme* (1985), an empathetic study of *loyalist involvement in the *First World War. His other plays include: *Carthaginians* (1987), a dramatic meditation on the impact of sectarian violence on the citizens of Derry set in a graveyard; *Someone Who'll Watch Over Me* (1992), inspired by the hostage takings in Beirut, which was a major success on Broadway and in London; and *Mutabilitie* (1997), a dense play set in sixteenth-century Ireland. McGuinness' plays are bold explorations of issues relating to gender, class, religion and politics. He has also written adaptations of classic European plays and screenplays for film and television. A.S.

McGuinness, Martin (1950–). *Republican, *Sinn Féin politician. Born into a *Catholic family in *Derry, McGuinness was drawn to republican activities in the wake of the civil rights movement (*Northern Ireland Civil Rights Association; NICRA). By 1972, he was the second in command in the Provisional *IRA in Derry. McGuinness was capable, dedicated and ruthless, and in a meritocratic IRA, whose older leadership was depleted by continual arrests, he advanced quickly. He was part of an IRA delegation that met with Secretary of State William Whitelaw in July 1972. Subsequently, he rose to the national leadership of the IRA and allegedly served as chief of staff periodically. Nevertheless, he served little time in jail and his close and stable family life was not seriously disrupted. McGuinness provided a militant cover for Gerry *Adams' drift toward constitutional politics in the late 1980s. He was personally committed to the *peace process, though he pursued tactical use of armed struggle to strengthen the republican hand up to the IRA cease-fire of 1996. He has served as Sinn Féin's chief negotiator since 1990. After the *Good Friday Agreement, McGuinness was elected as Sinn Féin MP for mid-Ulster and appointed minister of education in the Northern Ireland assembly. M.M.

McKenna, Siobhán (1923–86). Actress. Born in *Belfast and raised as an Irish speaker, McKenna was educated at University College, Galway. She acted in An Taibhdhearc, the *Irish-language theatre in Galway, and joined the *Abbey Theatre in 1944, where she acted with F. J. *McCormick and Cyril *Cusack. Among her most memorable roles were Pegeen Mike in *Synge's *The Playboy of the Western World* (which she played for the first time in 1951) and *Shaw's Saint Joan. She first played the part of Joan in her own Irish translation at the Taibhdhearc, where she modelled her performance on her mother, a woman of remarkable faith. She later won international acclaim for the role in productions in London in 1954 and on Broadway in 1956. *Here Are Ladies* (1970), a one-woman show, was a huge hit in London and the United States. She appeared in eight films, notably *Dr Zhivago* (1965). C.D.

McMaster, Anew (1894–1962). Actor, manager. Born in *Monaghan, McMaster made his acting debut in 1911 with Fred Terry's company. In 1925 he founded his own touring company (he was actor, manager and director) to bring Shakespearean plays to the Irish provinces. Revered in rural Ireland, McMaster also took his company on tours of the Near East and Australia. While his own acting style was in the grand manner of an older tradition that was rapidly going out of fashion, his Shakespearean Company served as a training ground for a number of innovative actors and directors. Micheál *MacLiammóir (whose sister McMaster married) met his future partner Hilton *Edwards while touring with McMaster. Harold Pinter spent two years with the company and subsequently praised McMaster's magnificent performances as Othello. Later in his career, McMaster had successful seasons at the *Abbey Theatre in Dublin with actors such as Sir Frank Benson and Mrs Patrick Campbell. J.C.E.L.

McPherson, Conor (1972–). Playwright. Born in *Dublin, McPherson first made his mark at the Dublin Theatre Festival in the early 1990s. His work deals mostly with the underbelly of Irish society. The best-known plays include *This Lime Tree Bower* (1995), which played at the Bush Theatre, London, and *The Weir* (1997), a box-office hit on Broadway. His quirky film *I Went Down* (1997) won the Best Screenplay Award at the San Sebastian Festival. He also wrote the screenplay for the film *Saltwater*. B.D.

Meagher, Thomas Francis (1823–67). Politician. Born in County *Waterford, Meagher was active in the *Repeal association in the early 1840s. Closely associated with other *Young Ireland leaders like John *Mitchel and Charles Gavan *Duffy, he ultimately grew disillusioned with the conciliatory policies pursued by Daniel *O'Connell. One of the founders of the Irish Confederation, the organisation established in 1847 by the Young Ireland leaders opposed to O'Connell, Meagher was sentenced to transportation to Tasmania for his part in the *rebellion of 1848. He escaped to America, where he worked as a journalist. Meagher fought on the Union side in the *American Civil War and reached the rank of brigadier general. From 1865 to his death, he served as secretary of the Montana Territory. His fiery oratory won him the nickname of 'Meagher of the sword'. A.S.

Meath, County. Maritime county in the province of *Leinster in the eastern part of Ireland. The county, covering an area of 904 square miles, has a population of 133,936 (2002 census). Bordered on the east by *Dublin and the Irish Sea, on the north by *Louth, *Monaghan and *Cavan, on the west by *Westmeath, and on the south by *Offaly and *Kildare, Meath is known as 'the Royal County' because the high kings of Ireland were believed to have been crowned at the Hill of *Tara. The county derives its name from the Irish *midhe*, meaning 'middle', the name of the fifth province in early *Christian Ireland, which was dominated by the southern branch of the *O'Neill family. This included lands now in counties Meath, Westmeath, Cavan and *Longford. The boundaries of the present-day county were formed in the twelfth century, when King *Henry II granted these lands to Hugh de Lacy.

The land is generally flat, apart from the hills of Loughcrew in the west of the county. The principal rivers in the county are the Boyne and the Blackwater. The Battle of the *Boyne, one of the turning points in Irish history, was fought at Oldcastle in July 1690. Major archaeological attractions include the megalithic *passage-graves at *Newgrange and *Knowth, which are believed to have been built around 3200 BC. The main towns in the county are Navan, the county capital, Trim and Kells, which is well known for its association with the celebrated *Book of *Kells*. It is believed that most of the book was written and illustrated in *Scotland, probably at the monastic settlement at Iona, before it was brought to Kells for its protection in the ninth century. The manuscript was kept in the monastery until 1541 and since 1661 it has been held by Trinity College, Dublin. County Meath is noted for its rich grasslands, ideal for raising cattle. A.S.

Mellifont, the Treaty of (1603). Treaty ending the *Nine Years War. After the Battle of *Kinsale, Hugh *O'Neill surrendered to Lord Mountjoy not knowing that Queen *Elizabeth I had died. The terms were favourable to

O'Neill. He was pardoned for taking part in the war and remained an earl, retaining ownership of his lands. T.C.

Merriman, Brian (c.1749–1805). Poet in the *Irish language. Author of one great masterpiece, *Cúirt an Mheán Oíche*, or *The Midnight Court*, Merriman was born in County *Clare and was a teacher of mathematics. He died in Limerick City. His great poem of more than 1,000 lines in perfect rhyming couplets describes how the women of Ireland bring the men to court for their neglect and sexual cowardice. It is a rambunctious, hilarious and dramatic poem. Scholars are divided as to whether there is a personal or even a political 'message' in the poem. Merriman is poking fun at the human condition and providing great entertainment while doing so. A.T.

Mhac an tSaoi, Máire (1922–). Poet and scholar. Daughter of the politician Seán MacEntee and married to the writer Conor *Cruise O'Brien, Mhac an tSaoi was educated at University College, *Dublin, and the Sorbonne, Paris. She became a lawyer in 1944 and served in the Department of Foreign Affairs abroad from 1947 to 1962. Her poetry combines traditional forms and metres with a contemporary idiom. Her intimate knowledge of Gaelic literature enriches her frank and unsentimental poetry. Among her themes are the pain of loss, women's sexuality and the roles thrust upon them. Mhac an tSaoi was highly influential on the generation of women poets that followed her, including Eavan *Boland and Nuala *Ní Dhomhnaill. Collections of poetry include *Margadh na Saoire* (1956), *An Cion go dtí Seo* (1987) and *Trasládáil* (1997). M.S.T.

Midleton, Colin (1910–83). Painter. Born in *Belfast, Midleton worked as a damask designer and then studied art. He experimented with many modernist styles of European painting while still prioritising content. Midleton exhibited regularly at the *Irish Exhibition of Living Art and produced an important body of modernist work. M.C.

missionaries, Irish. Irish priests, brothers and *nuns commissioned to spread the *Catholic faith in foreign countries. The roots of Irish missionary activity extend back to the sixth century and the age of Irish monasticism when Irish monks travelled to Europe to spread the gospel. Modern Irish missions date from the early 1800s when the Irish *Christian Brothers opened schools in England. Later, they expanded their ministry to the United States. John Hand founded All Hallows College in *Dublin in 1842 as a seminary to train Irish men to serve as diocesan priests exclusively in foreign dioceses. Hundreds of All Hallows priests staffed parishes, especially in America. During the same period, Catholic religious teaching orders began to send members overseas and new orders were instituted specifically to establish foreign missions.

The Presentation Sisters, founded in Ireland in 1775, established a mission to Calcutta in 1841. The Sisters of Mercy, established in 1831 by Catherine Elizabeth McAuley, extended their mission during the 1840s to the United Kingdom, Australia, Canada and, under the leadership of Mary Frances Xavier Warde, to the United States. The White Fathers began a mission to Africa in 1860. The African mission eventually numbered almost half of all Irish missionaries in its ranks. In the twentieth century, new orders such as the Columban Fathers (1916) were founded and grew rapidly until the *Second Vatican Council. The Irish foreign missions grew as part of Ireland's devotional revolution and played a critical role in the development of Irish Catholicism as a worldwide phenomenon. M.P.C.

Mitchel, John (1815–75). Politician, revolutionary, writer. Raised in Newry, County *Down, and educated at Trinity College, Dublin, Mitchel was a lawyer by profession. He joined the *Young Ireland group and wrote the life of Hugh *O'Neill for their 'Library of Ireland' series. After Thomas *Davis' death, Mitchel became editor of the **Nation* and a full-time writer and national figure. The Great *Famine deeply affected him and in his book *The Last Conquest of Ireland*, he blamed Britain and the *landlord system for the devastation caused by the Famine.

Mitchel called for an active, and if necessary violent, campaign to end British rule in Ireland. His colleagues thought him too militant and he founded his own paper, the *United Irishman*, in February 1848. A few months later, he was tried for the new crime of treason felony and sentenced to 14 years *transportation to *Australia. His *Jail Journal* is a classic of prison literature. Mitchell escaped from Australia to America in 1853 and his wife and children followed him there. He earned a living as a journalist and was actively involved in *Irish American politics, particularly in the *Fenian movement. During the *American Civil War, Mitchel supported the Confederate South. He returned to Ireland to run as an abstentionist candidate for Westminster. Disqualified from parliament because he was an escaped convict, he was elected a second time as an MP for *Tipperary, but died soon after on 20 March 1875. T.C.

Mitchell Report. Central document in the *Northern Ireland *peace process. On 28 November 1995, the British and Irish governments established an International Body to examine the decommissioning of illegal arms, one of the primary obstacles to peace negotiations involving all of Northern Ireland's political parties. The International Body, chaired by former US Senator George Mitchell, issued its report on 22 January 1996. The report accepted that Northern Ireland's paramilitary groups need not decommission any arms prior to all-party negotiations, but it set out six principles to which all parties must adhere in order to move the peace process forward. These six principles, which came to be known as the 'Mitchell principles', involved a 'total and absolute commitment': 1) to democratic and exclusively peaceful means of resolving political issues; 2) to total disarmament of paramilitary organisations; 3) to verification of disarmament by an independent commission; 4) to renounce the use of force or the threat thereof to influence all-party negotiations; 5) to agree to abide by the terms of any agreement reached in all-party negotiations and to resort to democratic and exclusively peaceful methods in trying to alter any aspect of such an agreement; 6) to urge that 'punishment' killings and beatings be stopped and to take steps to prevent them.

When the peace negotiations began on 10 June 1996, all the political parties present had to make a clear commitment to the Mitchell principles in order to participate. Because the *IRA had called off its 1994 cease-fire in February 1996, *Sinn Féin did not meet the requirements for participation in the June talks. The resumption of the IRA cease-fire in July 1997, however, allowed Sinn Féin to enter the negotiations on 9 September 1997. T.D.

Moloney, Mick (1944–). Singer, banjo player, researcher and writer. Born in County *Galway, Moloney was involved in the 1960s 'folk' movement in *Dublin, particularly in the seminal group the Johnstons. In the United States since 1973, he has established a distinguished career as the leading scholar of Irish *music. His Green Fields of America ensemble of musicians and dancers represented the strength of, and gave muscle and status to, Irish American music. Moloney has written extensively on Irish music and has contributed to some 60 recordings, broadcasting and film work. In 1977, he founded the Folklife Center in Philadelphia and in

1999 he received a National Endowment for the Arts Award. F.V.

Molyneux, William (1656–98). Political writer and scientist. As surveyor general and chief engineer (1684–88 and 1691–98), Molyneux was responsible for supervising military and civil construction in Ireland. A founder of the Dublin Philosophical Society (1683–1708), he published many important works on optics and mathematics. Molyneux was elected MP for Trinity College, Dublin (1692–98). His most influential book, *The Case of Ireland's Being Bound by Acts of Parliament in England Stated* (1698), critically examined Ireland's constitutional status and questioned the English parliament's claim to authority over the Irish *parliament. Molyneux used the 'natural right' ideas of his friend John Locke to argue that because there was a contract between ruler and ruled, legitimate government was dependent upon securing the consent of those governed. By denouncing taxation without consent and legislation without representation as unnatural, Molyneux sought to demonstrate that Ireland was bound only by the laws enacted by its own parliament. S.A.B.

Monaghan, County. Inland county, one of the three counties of the province of *Ulster in the *Republic of Ireland. Monaghan (500 square miles) has a population of 52,772 (2002 census). Its name is derived from the Irish *Muineachán*, 'the place of the shrubs'. The county is bordered on the east by *Louth and *Armagh, on the north by *Tyrone, on the west by *Fermanagh and *Cavan, and on the south by *Meath. The principal rivers in the county are the Finn and the Blackwater. The Slievebeagh Mountains along the north-west border of the county separate it from Tyrone. Among the principal lakes in the county are Lough Erne, Lough Eaglish, Lough Muckno and Glaslough.

Monaghan was dominated by the MacMahon family until the execution of Aodh Rua MacMahon in October 1590. The county was subsequently divided between the remaining native chieftains and a small number of English settlers. This so-called 'native plantation' was largely successful in introducing English land-owning systems into the county. It also meant, that unlike other Ulster counties, Monaghan was not part of the 'Ulster *Plantation'. The county remained predominantly *Catholic in population; in 1901, for example, its population was 74% Roman Catholic, with the remainder being divided almost equally between Anglicans and *Presbyterians. After *partition, the county was incorporated into the *Irish Free State. The principal towns in the county are Monaghan town, the county capital, Clones and Castleblayney. The experience of poor small farmers in Monaghan in the early years of the independent Irish state is powerfully captured in works like *Tarry Flynn* and *The Great Hunger* by the Inniskeen-born poet Patrick *Kavanagh. Charles Gavan *Duffy (1816–1903), a *nationalist leader who became prime minister of Victoria, in Australia, was born in Monaghan. A.S.

Montague, John (1929–). Poet. Montague was born in New York of Irish parents, but sent back to Ireland at an early age to live with relatives. He grew up in County *Tyrone and was educated at University College, Dublin, and Yale. His poetry explores the conflicts and continuity in the lives of individuals and their communities, and the manner in which the past shapes the present. *Death of a Chieftain* appeared in 1964. The resentment and anger about family matters and *Ulster politics in the poems of *The Rough Field* (1972), *A Slow Dance* (1975) and *The Dead Kingdom* (1984) give way to a long-suffering but celebratory tone in *Mount Eagle* (1988). Montague is sceptical about the narrow cultural and *nationalist ideals that dominated the early decades of the *Irish Free State. His best love poems, such as 'All Legendary Obstacles', are intense, spare and technically adroit. His other publications include The *Figure in the Cave and Other Essays* (1989), *Collected Poems* (1995), *Love Present and Other Stories* (1997) and *Smashing the Piano* (1999). M.S.T.

Moore, Brian (1921–99). Novelist. Born in *Belfast, Moore is *Northern Ireland's best-known novelist. At the outbreak of the Second World War, he joined the Air Raid Precautions Unit, and later described some of his experiences during the bombardment of Belfast in his novel *The Emperor of Ice-Cream* (1965). From 1943, Moore worked for the British government in North Africa, Naples and Marseilles. After the war, he moved to Canada, where he worked as a newspaper reporter. He became a Canadian citizen in 1953. He moved to the United States in 1959 and settled in California. A prolific, popular writer and excellent storyteller, Moore addresses such modern Irish preoccupations as exile, identity, *nationalism and the *Catholic faith. Among his best-known novels are *The Lonely Passion of Judith Hearne* (1955), set in Belfast (which was originally banned in Ireland); *The Great Victorian Collection* (1975), which mixes realism with surreal elements; and *Black Robe* (1985), set in seventeenth-century Canada. Several of his novels have been made into films. G.OB.

Moore, Christy (1945–). Singer, songwriter, musician and social activist. One of Ireland's most popular entertainers, Christy Moore was born in Newbridge, County *Kildare, into a musical and politically conscious family. Strongly influenced by the folk music revival in the United States in the late 1950s and 1960s, Moore sought out the almost extinct pure traditional Irish *music. His early album *Prosperous* (1970) is a natural blend of American folk song influence and Irish traditional sounds such as *uilleann pipes and tin whistle. This classic album contributed to the revival of Irish traditional music. Moore's own songs

Christy Moore

are characterised by their humorous and satirical comments on Irish culture and politics. He was also the driving force behind the bands *Planxty and Moving Hearts. J.OM.

Moore, George (1852–1933). Novelist. Born at Moore Hall, Ballyglass, County *Mayo, Moore studied art in Paris before turning to fiction. Novels such as *Esther Waters* (1894), considered scandalous in their day, introduced a modern, European dimension to Irish fiction. An autobiographical trilogy, *Hail and Farewell* (1911–14), is a notorious account of his involvement in the *Irish Revival. He also published an influential collection of stories, *The Untilled Field* (1903). From 1911 until his death, Moore lived in London. G.OB.

Moore, Thomas (1779–1852). Poet and lyricist. Born in *Dublin to a *Catholic merchant family, Thomas Moore published more than 40 volumes, mostly of verse and song. Educated at Trinity College, Dublin, and at the Inner Temple in London, he never practised law but instead turned to writing. Moore contributed *nationalist pieces to his friend Robert *Emmet's journal the *United Irishman*. After publishing a translation of the Greek poet Anacreon (1800) and other volumes of poetry, in 1808 Moore published the first two volumes of his most famous work – *Irish Melodies* (it had grown to eight volumes by 1834). Though many of the songs are openly nationalistic, treating such issues as sedition, violence, Lord Edward *Fitzgerald and the martyred Robert Emmet, they were a great success with English audiences, due in part to Moore's insistence on singing them himself with great passion in London drawing room society.

Ireland, betrayed and misruled, remained the main theme of most of Moore's lengthy career. In patriotic times, Moore was considered 'Ireland's National Bard', and in revisionist days, a trivial and sentimental rhymer. His other works on Irish history include: *Memoirs of Captain Rock, the Celebrated Irish Chieftain* (1824) and a four-volume *History of Ireland* (1835–46), as well as a *Life of Lord Edward* [Fitzgerald] (1831). His oriental romance, *Lallah Rookh*, earned him an unusual £3,000 advance in 1817, along with critical success. In 1848, he collected his numerous books of poetry on nationalistic, political, philosophical and religious subjects into 10 volumes.

Moore is also famous for his friendship with Lord Byron. The two poets met in 1811 and Moore became Byron's literary executor and custodian of Byron's memoirs upon the latter's death in 1824. Moore burned the scandalous memoirs at the request of Byron's widow (and half sister) and in 1830 published his own edited collection, *Letters and Journals of Lord Byron, with Notices of his Life* in two volumes. Today he is neglected by literary critics but his songs (such as 'The Harp that Once', 'Let Erin Remember' and 'The Minstrel Boy') remain enormously popular and are considered classics of Irish cultural nationalism. J.MD.

Morgan, Lady (1783–1859). Novelist. Born Sydney Owenson in *Dublin, the daughter of an actor, she first gained attention as a singer and harpist. Her compositions *Twelve Original Hibernian Melodies* (1805) anticipated Thomas *Moore's melodies and made her a celebrity. She is best known for novels that helped to shape romantic conceptions of Ireland, particularly *The Wild Irish Girl* (1806), but also *The O'Briens and the O'Flaherties* (1827). Invited to become a member of the Marquis of Abercorn's household, she married the house surgeon in 1812. She also wrote books on France and Italy. In 1837, she left Dublin for London, where she later died. G.OB.

Morris, Locky (1960–). Conceptual artist and sculptor. Born in *Derry, Morris studied sculpture in *Belfast and Manchester. His identification with local conditions can be seen in a piece of sculpture on emigration commissioned by Derry City Council and situated outside its offices. M.C.

Morrison, Van (1945–). Songwriter, musician. Born in *Belfast, Van Morrison grew up in a musical household. His father was a lover of jazz, blues and spirituals. As a teenager, Morrison wrote many songs and started a rock and roll band, called THEM. Encouraged to go to London during the mid-1960s, the band was enormously successful in the UK and had two top ten hits, 'Here Comes the Night' and 'Gloria', both written by Morrison and both still recognised as rock classics. It was the heyday of 1960s British rock and roll in 'Swinging London', at the time the home of the Beatles, the Rolling Stones, Eric Clapton and David Bowie. The commercialism and manipulation of the record industry proved too much for the young Morrison and he left London in 1967. He did not record again until 1969, when his album *Astral Weeks* was released. Recorded in the United States, it was universally recognised as one of the greatest albums of rock and roll. A string of classics followed. He pushed his own creative limits, combining jazz and blues influences and eventually returning to his Irish roots to record a unique album with the *Chieftains, *Celtic Heartbeat* (1987). J.OM.

by + © BPFallon/bpfallon.com

Van Morrison and Michelle Rocca

Mountjoy Jail. Prison dating from 1850. This *Dublin jail has housed many thousands of inmates in its history, ranging from petty thieves to notorious murderers and famous figures in Irish history. Several of the Invincibles, a militant nationalist group, were executed in the jail for the *Phoenix Park murders in 1883. Brendan *Behan's experiences as a prisoner in Mountjoy were described in his play *The Quare Fellow* (1954). After the *Easter Rising of 1916, a *hunger strike was mounted by *republican prisoners which culminated in the death of Thomas *Ashe in September 1917. On 14 October 2001, 10 *Volunteers, who had been tried and executed in the jail by British military court-martial in 1920–21, were honoured with a state funeral and the remains of nine of them were re-interred in Glasnevin Cemetery, Dublin. Now a medium-security prison with a capacity of 670, Mountjoy is the main prison in the Irish *Republic for adult males. S.A.B.

Mulcahy, General Richard (1886–1971). *Irish Free State minister and *Fine Gael leader. Mulcahy was born in *Waterford, and educated at Mount Sion *Christian Brothers School and later at Thurles. He was a member of the *Gaelic League and the Irish *Volunteers, and was interned for his role in the *Easter Rising of 1916. Upon his release, he was appointed director of training of the Volunteers and later its chief of staff. A member of the first *Dáil and supporter of the *Anglo-Irish Treaty (1921), he succeeded Michael *Collins as commander of the military forces of the Provisional Government during the *Civil War. He served as minister for defence under the *Cumann na nGaedheal government but resigned over the *Army Mutiny. A TD for *Dublin and *Tipperary, he became leader of Fine Gael following the resignation of W. T. *Cosgrave in June 1944. Mulcahy served as minister for education during the interparty governments before retiring from politics in 1961. P.E.

Muldoon, Paul (1951–). Poet, playwright, essayist. Muldoon was born into a *Catholic family in Portadown, County *Armagh, and grew up near a village called The Moy. He was educated at St Patrick's College, Armagh, and at Queen's University, Belfast, where Seamus *Heaney was his tutor. After university, he worked for the BBC in *Northern Ireland as a radio and television producer.

Muldoon's poetry, with its suspicion of systems, myths and visions, its notions of fluid identity and its constant awareness of alternative possibilities, has been significantly influenced by Louis *MacNeice. In his early collections, *New Weather* (1973), Mules (1977), *Why Brownlee Left* (1980) and *Quoof* (1983), Muldoon writes on themes of hybridity and border crossing between diverse histories, languages and cultures. 'The More a Man Has the More a Man Wants', a sequence of 49 sonnets based on the Trickster cycle of the Winnebago Indians, parodies the traditional quest journey. These poems destabilise the sense of place and time, delight in elaborate digressions and verbal pyrotechnics, and dramatise an ironic negotiation between the poet's native attachments and his cosmopolitan literary and historical sensibility.

Since 1990, Muldoon has taught at Princeton University. The work after *Quoof* (his last book before leaving Ireland) elaborates the idea of departure and metamorphosis. The long title poem of *Madoc* (1990) explores interconnection and 'mixed marriage' – between old and new worlds, fact and fiction, nationalism and imperialism, poetry and politics and different kinds of discourse. The parenthetical titles of the individual poems are the names of philosophers, but 'Madoc – a Mystery' resists any coherent philosophical outlook or belief.

The *Annals of Chile* (1994) contains the moving lament, 'Incantata', on the death of his lover, the painter Mary Farl Powers, while 'Yarrow', an elegy for his mother, closes the volume. In *Hay* (1998) Muldoon continues to demonstrate his formal ingenuity with examples of the ghazal, pantoum, haiku, villanelle and sestina. The volume includes imitations of other Irish poets such as W. B. *Yeats and Michael *Longley, poems on the *Troubles, and the ambitious 'The Bangle (Slight Return)', a series of 30 sonnets, moving between the Australian outback, Virgil and a Parisian restaurant.

In 1998, he became the Clarendon Lecturer at Oxford University. His Clarendon lectures, an idiosyncratic review of Irish literary history, were published under the title *To Ireland, I* (2000). He has also published a play, *Six Honest Serving Men* (1995), a libretto, *The Shining Brow* (1993), two books for children and translations from the Irish. Muldoon was awarded the Pulitzer Prize in 2003. E.K-A.

mummers. Participants in mumming, a costumed, masked ritual related to Christmas. This ritual dates to medieval times and survives in the east and north of Ireland. Mumming has associated rhymed verse, part originally of folk plays with legendary and historical heroes such as St *Patrick, Brian *Boru, or Daniel *O'Connell, and may also involve music. F.V.

Munster. One of the four provinces of Ireland. The province, which covers 9,526 square miles, has a population of 1,101,266 (2002 census). Munster consists of the counties *Clare, *Cork, *Kerry, *Limerick, *Tipperary and *Waterford. The name derives from Muma, an ancient kingdom in the south of Ireland, which was later divided into Deas Mumhan (Desmond), south Munster and Tua Mumhan (Thomond), north Munster. The province has some of Ireland's most beautiful scenery, including the rugged coastlines of counties Clare, Cork and Kerry, the Lakes of Killarney and the Burren. The famous Battle of *Kinsale in 1601 ended the *Nine Years War rebellion of the *Ulster Irish chieftains and effectively abolished the old Gaelic order. J.OM.

murals, Belfast wall. Political wall paintings. Belfast has a long tradition of *loyalist murals. The first one, painted around 1908, depicted the Battle of the *Boyne in 1690, when Protestant King *William III defeated Catholic King *James II. The murals were – and for the most part still are – painted on 12 July to commemorate the Battle of the Boyne. Unlike the old murals, the new ones are more intentionally anti-nationalist and anti-Catholic. The sinister images are threatening and are meant to be.

The emergence of murals on the *nationalist side dates from the *hunger strikes. In the spring and summer of 1981, hundreds of murals were painted by *republicans. From the very beginning, republican murals portrayed the 'armed struggle' (unlike the loyalist murals). This was less so in the 1990s as the *peace process unfolded. M.M.

Murphy, Thomas (Bernard) (1935–). Playwright. Born in Tuam, County *Galway, the youngest of 10 children, Murphy left school at 15 and trained as a fitter-welder and later as a vocational teacher. In his spare time, he took part in amateur dramatics. His first play, *On* *the Outside*, jointly written with his friend Noel O'Donoghue, won the manuscript prize at the All-Ireland Amateur Drama Competition in 1957. *The Iron Men*, which won script competitions and was revised as *A Whistle in the Dark*, was scathingly rejected by the *Abbey Theatre's managing director, Ernest *Blythe. Often compared to Harold Pinter's *The Homecoming*, which it predates, the play was staged in London, where several reviewers misunderstood the play's violent characters as accurate depictions of all Irishmen. Murphy lived in England between 1962 and 1970. Irish productions of the powerful and tragic *Famine* (1968) and the psychological fairy tale *The Morning After Optimism* (1971) were well received, but *The Orphans* (1968) was a failure. *The Sanctuary Lamp* (1975) was successful but controversial because it expressed disillusionment with organised religion. Murphy was disappointed by the critical response to *The Blue Macushla* (1980), a play based on the idiom of gangster films, but three subsequent plays, *The Gigli Concert* (1983), *Conversations on a Homecoming* (1985) and *Bailegangaire (Town Without Laughter)* (1985, with Siobhán *McKenna as Mommo in her final, brilliant performance) were highly acclaimed and cemented his reputation as one of the foremost playwrights of his generation.

Characterised by what Brian *Friel has called the 'pure theatricality' of their language, Murphy's plays focus on social, institutional, familial and personal breakdown against the backdrop of a changing Ireland. The characters in these plays are on a quest to overcome tragedy and despair; their attainment of spiritual wholeness often involves a leap of faith. With *Too Late for Logic* (1989), Murphy seemed to be looking for new directions. In 1994 he published a novel, *The Seduction of Morality*. A play based on its themes and characters, *The Wake* (1998), was well received, as was *The House* (2000). In October 2001 the Abbey Theatre celebrated Tom Murphy's career with a season of six of his plays. J.C.E.L.

music, classical. The *harp as the national symbol attests to the importance of music in Irish life. The instrument is found on Irish coins and official documents, such as passports. Not a great deal is known of the early history of music in Ireland. Much material held in churches was lost through the ages, and the tradition of the *bardic harpers, professional performers in the employ of the Irish nobility, was oral. The first harp festival was held in *Belfast in 1792, when the tradition had suffered nearly two centuries of decline. The music survives only in transcriptions of the style of the time, by the *Armagh organist, Edward Bunting.

*St Patrick's cathedral in *Dublin established a choir in 1432. A pair of organs was acquired in 1471 by *Christ Church cathedral, where two English madrigal composers, John Farmer (from 1595 to 1599) and Thomas Bateson (from 1608 to 1630), served as organists. Bateson was the first music graduate of the University of Dublin (Trinity College) in 1615 and the city acquired its first theatre in Werburgh Street in 1638.

In the eighteenth century, Dublin, then the second city in the British empire, entered what has been called a 'golden age' of music. British and European musicians came to Dublin and some of them settled there, including Johann Sigismund Kusser (1660–1727), a pupil of the great Lully, composer to Louis XIV, and the Italian composer Francesco Geminiani (1687–1762), one of the great violin virtuosos of his day. The greatest musical event in eighteenth-century Ireland was the premiere of Handel's *Messiah* on 13 April 1742, in Mr Neale's Great Musick Hall, Fishamble Street, Dublin. An audience of 700 was able to fit in the hall because ladies' hoops and gentlemen's swords were prohibited. The best-known Irish composer to emerge in the eighteenth century was John *Field (1782–1837), known as the inventor of the nocturne, and an important influence on Chopin and on composers in Russia, where he spent most of his life. Field's limpid style and easy melodic filigree were much admired (Liszt prepared an edition of the Nocturnes). The music of the *Cork-born composer, pianist and organist, Philip Cogan (c.1748–1833), who was Thomas *Moore's teacher, is still performed.

Many of the more gifted Irish musicians of the nineteenth century chose to leave Ireland, where the patronage and social glitter of the eighteenth century had faded after the Act of *Union (1800). Dublin-born Michael *Balfe (1808–70) and *Waterford-born William Vincent Wallace (1812–65) were among the most successful composers of English opera in the nineteenth century, and their two most popular works, *The Bohemian Girl* and *Maritana*, were recorded in recent years. Hamilton *Harty (1879–1941) and Charles Villiers *Stanford (1852–1924), the most important Irish composers of the early twentieth century, also worked mainly abroad. However, musicians also came to Ireland from Europe. Pianist and composer Michele Esposito (1855–1929), who trained in Naples, came to the Royal Irish Academy of Music (RIAM) in 1882. The RIAM, which was founded in 1848, was the main music school in Dublin and in 1890 launched a Dublin Municipal School of Music for the working-classes, which survives today as the DIT Conservatory of Music and Drama. Würzburg-trained Heinrich Bewerunge (1862–1923) taught chant and organ at St Patrick's College, *Maynooth, from 1888. Munich-born Aloys Fleischmann (1910–92), whose father had been cathedral organist in Cork from 1888, was appointed professor of music at University College, Cork, at the age of 24. Fleischmann, Frederick May (1911–85) and Brian *Boydell (1917–2000) were the most important figures in the first generation of modern Irish composers.

The national broadcasting service, *Radio Éireann, formed a symphony orchestra in 1947, but in general the young Irish state did not greatly encourage or support classical music for many years. A national concert hall was not opened until 1981. A national conservatory and opera company have not yet been established. Composers like Gerald *Barry (1952–), Ian Wilson (1964–), Donnacha Dennehy (1970–) and Jennifer Walshe (1974–) have won international attention, as have many Irish performers. Recently, an infrastructure of institutions has been created, including most importantly, the Music Network, a national music development organisation (supported by the *Arts Council since 1986) that promotes and fosters the careers of Irish musicians at home and abroad. M.D.

music, popular. Following the establishment of Ireland's national *radio service, which started broadcasting on 1 January 1926, Irish *dance and traditional *music, which up to then had been notably regional, became nationally available. After the Second World War, Ireland, like Britain, came increasingly under the influence of American music and culture. On the radio people listened to the big band music of the swing era, such as Glenn Miller, and in ballrooms throughout Ireland people danced to this music. In Dublin's Theatre Royal, meanwhile, big band performers such as Stan Kenton and Count Basie played to enthusiastic audiences. People could also tune in to the BBC and the American Forces Network (AFN) and hear all varieties of American music, from big band, to jazz and the emerging rock and roll of the 1950s. Elvis Presley galvanised and sometimes appalled the Irish population (as much as the American and European). From the mid-1950s, pockets of rock and roll sedition emerged, and by the late 1950s and the early 1960s, pop charts became an essential phenomenon on the radio. European-based radio stations such as Radio Luxembourg broadcast far more pop-oriented music than Irish radio.

Replacing the big bands, the show bands

came into being in Ireland to compensate for the lack of live appearances by American and other international stars who could be heard only on the radio. From the late 1950s into the early 1970s, show bands performed the pop hits of the day in dance halls all over Ireland. While there was discipline, rigour and style in their execution of the pop tunes of the day, show bands performed little, if any, original material. Through the 1960s, as Ireland changed socially and economically, up to 700 bands toured the length and breadth of the country, including the Clipper Carlton, the Royal Showband, the Miami and the Dixies, which achieved almost cult status. Some of Ireland's internationally known rock stars got their start in show bands, most notably Van *Morrison (1945–) with the Monarchs and Rory Gallagher (1949–95) with the Fontana Showband. Unlike most other bands of the time, these two show bands interspersed obscure rhythm and blues songs with familiar pop chart tunes. In 1963 in Belfast, Morrison founded the rock group THEM, which was successful in the British charts until it broke up in 1966. Morrison's 1968 album *Astral Weeks* is highly regarded as one of the most important rock records of all time. Gallagher, meanwhile, formed Taste in 1965. This band split up in 1970, but by that time Gallagher was viewed as a *bona fide* electric guitar hero. Even after his untimely death in 1995, he is rightly regarded as one of the finest exponents of the electric guitar.

In the 1970s, Irish pop started to make it into the British charts with the folk group the *Dubliners, Celtic rock band *Horslips, singer/songwriter Gilbert O' Sullivan (1946–) and rock band Thin Lizzy. The latter's front man and main songwriter, Phil Lynott (1951–86), is regarded as one of hard rock music's most gentle, romantic lyric writers. Two emerging Irish rock bands in the late 1970s that were inspired by Thin Lizzy were the Boomtown Rats and *U2. The former, after several successful years, imploded in 1982 and its leader Bob *Geldof (1954–) went on to develop Live Aid in 1985. U2 is one of the most successful rock bands in the world. Through a mixture of shrewd marketing, an inordinate level of self-belief and a back catalogue of remarkably resilient pop/rock songs, U2 has remained at the top of the industry for over two decades. While they remain a guiding light for Irish rock, few Irish bands have followed in their footsteps and none has come close to their success.

From the 1980s and 1990s onward, however, many Irish pop and rock bands have succeeded in topping charts internationally: the Undertones, Chris de Burgh (1947–), the Pogues, Sinéad *O'Connor (1966–), Enya (1961–), the Cranberries, the Saw Doctors, Boyzone, the *Corrs, Boyzone's former lead singer Ronan Keating (1977–), Westlife (a pop band that has become the only act to reach number one with their first seven releases), Samantha Mumba (1982–), Divine Comedy and Ash. T.C-L.

music, traditional. The indigenous music of Ireland. Mostly 'folk' music, it was created and performed locally for the entertainment and ritual usage of the plain people. The bulk of its repertoire dates to the nineteenth and the eighteenth centuries. However, traditional music also incorporates the music and ethos of the classical court musicians, the *harpists, whose art was submerged into folk music with the destruction of the Gaelic order after the sixteenth century. This stream of higher artistic consciousness was carried on in classic *uilleann pipe music and in fiddle music and today is expressed on all instruments. The term traditional has been favoured among players since circa 1900, implying a synergy of artistic pedigree, political awareness and musical integrity.

Traditional music at its broadest incorporates instrumental music (some tunes linked to specific dances), song in Irish and English

Harry Benagh and Jackie Daly at the Crosses of Annagh, County Clare

(some melodies are played as instrumentals) and social and performance dancing. Its repertoire is largely of the island, closely tied to Gaelic music in Scotland and, particularly in song, owing much to older English ballads. This amalgam includes tunes from ancient to modern that have been passed on in a largely oral process over several hundred years. Less-favoured pieces fell into disuse, preferred items underwent change according to personal taste, misinterpretation, or memory lapse, compounding a slowly changing core of tunes and song which remain universally recognised and played. Printed sources from the mid-1800s onward retained once-forgotten items, making possible their re-assessment and re-incorporation into the oral process. Beginning in the early 1900s, recorded music preserved actual personal styles of playing and led to a national style on a particular instrument (for example, in fiddle music *Coleman's became the standard). Since the introduction of cassette technology in the late 1960s, there has been even greater fluidity in movement of styles and repertories. Today 3,000 CDs of traditional Irish music are available between Ireland, Britain and the United States.

Instruments

Traditional music is played on the *harp, the *uilleann pipes, fiddle (violin), concert flute (wooden, open-hole model), chromatic (button) accordion, melodeon, concertina, tin whistle and banjo. Snare drum was originally used as rhythmic percussion (in **céilí* bands), but since the 1960s the bodhrán (single-sided frame drum) has achieved huge popularity. Accompaniment initially involved piano on early 1900s recordings, but today is largely done on guitar and an Irish version of bouzouki. Other instruments used include keyboards, mandolin, harmonica, spoons and bones – in all, 37 different types of instruments.

The Music

The oldest forms of traditional music are the slow airs and marches, some dating to the sixteenth century. The jig, *dance music in 6/8, 12/8 and 9/8 time, is referenced first in the 1670s. The reel in 4/4 time came from Scotland in the late 1700s, the hornpipe also in 4/4 time came from England in the same period, and the polka in 2/4 time, the mazurka in 3/4 time, and the waltz from Europe in the mid-1800s. These tunes, having entered Irish music, acquired various Irish regional accents and styles, which render them utterly distinct from the originals. This trend continues up to the present, with popular tunes being borrowed from other cultures and ultimately becoming acculturated by subtle change of timing and rhythmic emphasis. *Donegal, for instance, has a repertory of 4/4-time Scottish strathspeys locally known as 'highlands'.

Regional Styles

While all styles were originally locally based, the music has five major styles with a variety of articulation, repertoire, instrument and context. The different styles involve combinations of basic playing techniques – use of bow in fiddle, of wind in flutes and concertinas and so forth, basic note decoration, tempo and rhythm. Originally (and still) geographically associated, these are now also widely disseminated by recordings and their adoption is a matter of personal taste or choice. All are defined on fiddle. The five major styles are: Donegal (fiddle based, subtle decoration, emphatic bow use,

Scottish influence), *Sligo (fast tempo, highly ornamented), East *Galway (minor keys, variable modality, melody centred, slow tempo), *Clare (slower tempo, melody centred, selective decoration) and Sliabh Luachra (North *Cork/*Kerry, using polkas and 12/8 'slide' jigs, rhythm-dominant, fiddle based). On flute, a *Leitrim style (breathy, rhythmic) and a *Roscommon (florid ornament) are prominent, while on uilleann pipes regional styles have given way to individual styles because of the lack of local players.

Song

The major song styles are *seán-nós* in the *Irish language; *Ulster ballad style; 'old' ballads in English; a more standardised, widespread *a cappella* ballad style in the English language with regional variants; and a popular ballad style with accompaniment. Major distinctive styles within Irish-language song are found in South Ulster, in West Donegal, Connemara, Kerry and Ring (County *Waterford).

Collectors

Despite the existence of an oral tradition, the work of nineteenth-century idealists in committing the repertoire and lyrics of Irish music to print has been both invaluable and influential. Edward Bunting compiled the first major collection of instrumental music in 1796. Other collectors include: George *Petrie, Patrick Weston Joyce, Henry Hudson, James Goodman, Francis O'Neill, Frank Roche and Breandán *Breathnach for instrumental music; and Charlotte Brooke, Eugene *O'Curry, Maighréad Ní Annagáin & Séamus Clandillon, Sam Henry, Joseph Ranson and Séamus Ennis for song. The Department of Irish Folklore at University College, Dublin, has also contributed to the preservation of Irish music.

Revival

Traditional music was carried in the tailspin of the *Irish Language Revival at the end of the nineteenth century. Traditional song was seen as a vehicle for language and dance as a social bonder. When, in the wake of the 1935 Public Dance Halls Act and in response to social change, Irish social dancing moved to specialised halls, ensembles capable of providing the necessary repertoire and volume (*céilí* bands) were formed. By the late 1950s, the majority of dancing in Ireland was to modern music provided by show bands and traditional music was rarely performed. In 1951 a group of dedicated players, backed by Irish Americans who knew and loved Irish music from the recordings of a couple of generations of Irish immigrants, formed an organisation to revive traditional music, called *Comhaltas Ceoltóirí Éireann (CCE). Spearheading the revival around the same time, Ciarán *MacMathuna was promoting solo instrumental performance on the *radio and the classical composer Seán *Ó Riada was experimenting with different forms of indigenous music. In 1968, Breandán Breathnach's Na Píobairí Uilleann body was formed to promote uilleann piping. Such organisations as the Irish World Music Centre (IWMC) (a postgraduate study facility with an ethno-musicological overview and a special interest in Irish traditional music at University of *Limerick), the *Irish Traditional Music Archive (1987) and the harpists group Cáirde na Cruite (1960), and various summer schools and competitions have contributed significantly to the flourishing of traditional music today. F.V.

Mythology. See **Celtic mythology.**

Nagle, Nano (1718–84). Foundress of the Presentation Sisters Order of Nuns. Nagle came from a *Catholic landowning background and ran several schools for poor children in *Cork City, from the 1750s. In 1776, she set up the Sisters of the Charitable Instruction of the Sacred Heart of Jesus in Cork. The first of the socially active female congregations in Ireland, it was formally recognised, in 1802, as the Presentation Sisters and spread rapidly to become one of the largest and most widely distributed Roman Catholic female congregations in the world. C.C.

***Nation*, the.** Weekly *nationalist newspaper. Founded in 1842 by Thomas *Davis, John *Dillon and Charles Gavan *Duffy, the *Nation* served as the chief vehicle for the dissemination of the *Young Ireland movement's views. Though the ideas expressed in the paper were varied, the *Nation* provided the most thoroughgoing expression of Irish cultural nationalism between its founding and 1897, when it ceased publication. Many of its writers, including such important political and literary figures as John *Mitchel, Thomas Francis *Meagher, William *Carleton and James Clarence *Mangan, urged the Irish people to resist British domination, extolled the qualities of early Celtic culture and celebrated the contributions of Ireland's Gaelic heritage to world civilisation. In keeping with its nationalist ethos, the newspaper promoted the revival and preservation of the *Irish language. T.D.

National Archives. The official archives of the Irish government. Established in 1988, the National Archives are an amalgamation of the Public Record Office of Ireland (founded 1867) and the State Paper Office (founded 1702). Located at Bishop Street in *Dublin, the archives hold the records of Irish government departments, the courts and other state agencies, the Church of Ireland, and documents from private sources. Most records date from the nineteenth and twentieth centuries and are open to inspection by members of the public. (Address: Bishop Street, Dublin 8. Web site: *www.national archives.ie.*) S.A.B.

National Botanic Gardens. Gardens founded by the *Royal Dublin Society in 1795 to serve the scientific and agricultural communities of Ireland. Dr Walter Wade, who laid out the grounds, introduced exotic plants from around the world. The Botanic Gardens were placed under government control in 1877 and now cover 50 acres on the river Tolka at Glasnevin, a suburb of *Dublin. They contain a wonderfully large plant collection of more than 20,000 species, herbaceous borders, a rose garden, a rockery, an arboretum and pond, as well as Burren areas. The recently restored curvilinear range of glasshouses (constructed 1843–69) are a fine example of the work of the Dublin iron-master Richard Turner, who also designed the glasshouse at Kew Gardens (England). A new education and visitor centre opened in September 2000 and the gardens continue to serve scientific functions and delight visitors of all ages. S.A.B.

National Gallery of Ireland, the. Inaugurated in 1864, the gallery houses the national collection of Irish art from the late sixteenth century to the mid-twentieth century, as well as a collection of European master paintings from the fourteenth to the twentieth centuries. Among the most important eighteenth-century painters on display are Nathaniel *Hone the Elder, George Barrett and Thomas Roberts. The nineteenth-century collection has excellent examples of the group known as the Irish Impressionists (Nathaniel *Hone the Younger, Walter *Osborne and Sarah Purser). The sculpture collection from the seventeenth to the nineteenth century includes many Irish portrait busts. The building was adapted from Lanyon's original plan by Francis Fowke. A new Millennium Wing designed by Benson and Forsyth houses Irish *painting and *sculpture galleries. The work of Sir William *Orpen, Paul *Henry, Mainie *Jellett and Louis Le *Brocquy can be viewed in the new wing.

An education programme arranged around exhibition themes provides constant lectures and tours. A centre for the study of Irish art, a Yeats Archive, a multimedia facility and a national portrait collection are also planned. (Address: Merrion Square West, Dublin 2. Web site: *www.national gallery.ie*.) M.C.

National League, the. Constituency organisation of the *Irish Parliamentary Party. Following the 1882 Kilmainham Treaty, Charles Stewart *Parnell considered the land question to be solved and turned his attention to national self-government, or *home rule. On 17 October 1882, the Irish National League was established in *Dublin to aid in the constitutional struggle for home rule. While Parnell was the driving force behind the organisation, its constitution was drawn up by Timothy Harrington and T. M. *Healy. The league, in theory, was to be governed by a committee of 48 members but, in reality, power always remained in the hands of the Parliamentary Party. By 1886, there were over 1,000 branches nationwide, each responsible for financing election campaigns and MPs' salaries. The league continued this essential function until the Home Rule party split in 1890. P.E.

National Library of Ireland. Ireland's national library dedicated to the collection and preservation of materials of Irish interest. The National Library was established in 1877, being founded upon the library of the *Royal Dublin Society. Originally located in *Leinster House, the library moved to its present building on Kildare Street in 1890. The National Library's collections consist of close to one million books and extensive files of *newspapers, prints, drawings, maps and *photographs. Important documents housed at the library include Giraldus Cambrensis' twelfth-century accounts of the topography and conquest of Ireland (*Topographia Hiberniae* and *Expugnatio Hibernica*) and the Ormond deeds, a major source for the medieval history of Ireland. The collection of manuscripts contains 1,200 Gaelic manuscripts, including the fourteenth-century *Book of Magauran* and the papers of famous Irish writers (such as W. B. *Yeats and Seán *O'Casey) and political personalities (such as John *Redmond and Roger *Casement). The Genealogical Office, which originated in 1552 as the Office of Arms, was incorporated into the library in 1943. The National Library's Photographic Archive opened in Temple Bar in 1998. A genealogical advisory service for family historians is currently available for personal callers to the library. (Address: National Library of Ireland, Kildare Street, Dublin 2. National Photographic Archive, Meeting House Square, Temple Bar, Dublin 2. Genealogical Office, 2 Kildare Street, Dublin 2. Web site: *www.nli. ie*.) S.A.B.

National Museum of Ireland. Ireland's national museum consists of collections of archaeology, history, decorative arts and natural history. Established in 1877, the National Museum acquired the scientific collections of the *Royal Dublin Society, which now form the basis of the Natural History Museum. In the 1890s, the museum also received the *Royal Irish Academy's collection of antiquities and it continues to preserve the natural and cultural material heritage of Ireland. Archaeological and historical collections are displayed at the National Museum, on Kildare Street. They include a collection of weapons, tools and artifacts from the *Viking burial grounds at Kilmainham and Islandbridge, the largest such collection outside Scandinavia. The archaeological collection also contains the National Treasury, with outstanding examples of Celtic and medieval art such as the *Tara Brooch, the *Ardagh Chalice and the *Cross of Cong. The Broighter Hoard is a treasure of gold objects (*La Tène-style torc or neckband, a miniature sailing boat with oars, a bowl and two necklaces) dating from around the last century BC, which were found at Broighter, County *Derry, in 1896. Also, displayed here is the Derrynaflan Hoard, which consists of liturgical church metalwork, comprising a chalice, a paten with support and a strainer, all covered by a large bronze basin. The hoard was discovered in 1980, on the bog-island of Derrynaflan, County *Tipperary. The high-quality die-stamped ornament and enamelled studs of the paten and stand would argue for an eighth-century date for both of them, whereas the stylised filigree of the chalice would suggest a date for it in the following century.

The museum's collection of croziers (wooden staffs, often enshrined in metal, used by Irish abbots from the eighth to the twelfth century) and reliquaries is unique in Europe and includes decorative examples from *Clonmacnoise, County *Offaly, and Lismore, County *Waterford. The Natural History Museum on Merrion Street holds an extensive collection of zoology and the National Museum in Collins Barracks exhibits decorative arts, history and folklore. (Address: National Museum of Ireland, Archaeology and History, Kildare Street, Dublin 2. National Museum of Ireland, Decorative Arts and History, Collins Barracks, Benburb Street, Dublin 7. National Museum of Ireland, Natural History, Merrion Street, Dublin 2. Web site: *www.museum.ie*.) S.A.B., P.H.

Nationalism. Irish nationalism emerged as an ideology during the late eighteenth century. Since then, two distinct, though interrelated traditions have developed: constitutional nationalism, which has sought to achieve substantial political autonomy by working through the existing parliamentary system, and 'physical force' nationalism, which has sought a complete separation from British rule by means of armed revolt. There are also cultural nationalists who have sought to preserve the indigenous Gaelic cultural traditions, particularly the *Irish language.

The constitutional and 'physical force' traditions have never been mutually exclusive. Many gains have been achieved by the constitutional movement only because of an implicit threat of mass violence, and proponents of 'physical force' have at times adopted parliamentary means to achieve their own strategic objectives. Generally, the constitutionalists have regarded the achievement of an independent Irish state as a gradual process and have been willing to accept less than complete autonomy. By contrast, the 'physical force' movement has insisted on the immediate achievement of an Irish Republic. Cultural nationalists, meanwhile, have argued that the achievement of any degree of political autonomy would be meaningless if the 'soul' of the nation – its language and cultural traditions – was lost.

Inspired by the republicanism of the *French Revolution, the *Society of United Irishmen was founded in Belfast in October 1791. It called on Irishmen of all religious denominations to overthrow British rule. The unsuccessful *Rebellion of 1798, however, exacerbated sectarian divisions and led to the Act of *Union and formal political union with Britain in 1800. Although non-sectarianism has ever since remained a guiding principle of Irish nationalism and many of its leaders have been Protestants, Irish nationalism has drawn its support largely from among Catholics. This occurred because British identity was avowedly Protestant and the British state overtly discriminated against Catholics.

In the 1820s, the first significant constitutional nationalist movement emerged, led by Daniel *O'Connell. Using grassroots organisation of the Irish peasantry, the *Catholic Emancipation movement achieved the right of Catholics to sit in the British parliament in 1829. Catholic priests actively participated in the movement, part of an increasingly close relationship between *Catholicism and nationalism. A similar constitutional movement led by O'Connell during the 1840s to *repeal the Act of Union failed. Meanwhile, a group of younger men known as *Young Ireland, which included Thomas *Davis, called for more forceful measures. Davis, in particular, placed great emphasis on cultural revival and the preservation of the *Irish language. Even before an abortive rising in 1848 during the Great *Famine, however, many of Young Ireland's leaders had been arrested.

Following the catastrophe of the Famine, which many nationalists blamed on British misgovernment, Irish *emigrants to America played an increasingly prominent role in supporting and funding Irish nationalist organisations, including the secret, oath-bound *IRB, founded in 1858. The *Fenians, as its members were popularly known, attempted a rebellion in 1867, but it proved to be an ill-organised fiasco. In the late 1870s, Fenians joined constitutionalists in a 'New Departure' to achieve fair terms of land tenure for Irish tenant farmers. In the 1880s, agrarian agitation and constitutional protest resulted in the emergence of a disciplined Irish party in the British parliament led by Charles Stewart *Parnell. Dedicated to achieving *home rule for Ireland, the so-called *Irish Parliamentary Party frequently held the balance of power at Westminster.

In 1890, Parnell fell from power due to personal scandal and, during the following decade, nationalist energies shifted to the cultural sphere, where such organisations as the *Gaelic League, founded in 1893, promoted the Irish language and the revival of the native culture. During the first decade of the twentieth century, political nationalism re-emerged through both a revived Parliamentary Party led by John *Redmond, which put home rule back on the agenda at Westminster, as well as new 'advanced' nationalist organisations, such as Arthur *Griffith's *Sinn Féin, founded in 1905, which sought a combination of political autonomy, cultural revival and economic self-sufficiency. When resistance from *unionists in *Ulster blocked autonomy for all thirty-two counties and the *First World War delayed implementation of home rule, a revived IRB staged the *Easter Rising of 1916. Although the rising was brutally repressed and 15 of its leaders were executed, a transformed Sinn Féin emerged after the war as the strongest political formation in Ireland and led the struggle for independence between 1919 and 1921. Under the *Anglo-Irish Treaty negotiated in December 1921, twenty-six counties became a self-governing dominion, though still formally under the crown. However, the *Constitution of 1937 made the twenty-six counties a republic in everything but name and, in 1948, the government officially proclaimed the *Republic of Ireland. The goal of a republic consisting of the entire island of Ireland remains elusive and Northern Ireland's six counties remain part of the United Kingdom. During the *Troubles in *Northern Ireland, which began in 1968, the traditional divisions within Irish nationalism have been recapitulated, with the *Social Democratic and Labour Party (SDLP) representing the constitutionalist approach and Sinn Féin, which is indissolubly, if indefinably, linked to the *IRA, representing the 'physical force' tradition. Under the leadership of Gerry *Adams, Sinn Féin renounced violence and turned to constitutional politics. The party was involved in the negotiations leading to the *Good Friday Agreement and its members now participate in the new institutions created by the agreement. A dissident group of republicans rejected the Good Friday Agreement and still adhere to the 'physical force' tradition of nationalism. F.B.

Nationalist Party of Northern Ireland. Name given to the nationalist MPs in the *Northern Ireland parliament. The Nationalist Party was not a proper party but a collection of local groups and organisations united mainly in their opposition to *unionism and characterised by *Catholicism. The party dominated politics in the Catholic community until the advent of the *civil rights movement in 1968. After Seán *Lemass' visit to *Stormont, Eddie McAteer, the leading Nationalist MP, was persuaded to become the leader of the opposition, in effect recognising the Northern parliament's legitimacy. The party would soon be eclipsed by the *Social Democratic and Labour Party (SDLP) as the *Troubles progressed. T.C.

Neeson, Liam (1952–). Actor. Born in Ballymena, County *Antrim, Neeson was an amateur boxer before taking up the theatre. The director John Boorman cast him in *Excalibur* (1981) having seen him at the *Abbey Theatre in *Dublin. His debut on Broadway was in *Anna Christie* in 1993, which won him comparisons with Marlon Brando and a Tony nomination. In 2002, he starred on Broadway in Arthur Miller's *The Crucible* to great acclaim. He received an Oscar nomination for the leading role in Steven Spielberg's *Schindler's List* (1993). Neeson starred in Neil *Jordan's 1996 bio-epic *Michael Collins* and in

Liam Neeson

such films as *Suspect* (1987), *Husbands and Wives* (1992), *Rob Roy* (1995) and *Star Wars: The Phantom Menace* (1999). M.E.

neutrality. Principle of Irish *foreign policy since the Second World War. The roots of Irish neutrality go back to the *War of Independence (1919–21), when Irish *republicans argued that the policy would allow an independent Ireland to respect legitimate British security interests without itself being drawn into a war involving the United Kingdom. Despite Irish aspirations, however, the *Anglo-Irish Treaty of 1921 granted Britain the use of three Irish ports (Berehaven, Cobh and Lough Swilly) and such other facilities as might be needed in time of war, effectively making Irish neutrality unfeasible.

The situation changed in 1938, when British Prime Minister Neville Chamberlain, following negotiations with Éamon *de Valera, agreed to give the Irish government unconditional control of the treaty ports, in return for Ireland's pledge that no foreign power could use Irish territory as a base of attack on Britain. When the Second World

War began in September 1939, Ireland announced that it would remain neutral. Over the following six years, de Valera's government kept Ireland out of the war, despite often bitter criticism from Britain and the United States. (Partly to defuse this criticism, de Valera secretly authorised informal military and intelligence cooperation with the allies.) Ireland continued to remain neutral after the war. In 1949, the Irish coalition government then in power declined to join NATO, citing *partition as a reason for not participating in an alliance involving Britain. In recent years, suggestions that increasing inter-European cooperation should include a military component have sparked renewed debate in Ireland over the precise nature of Irish neutrality. T.D.

Newfoundland, the Irish in. The Irish became established in Newfoundland because of the annual cod-fishing expeditions to the territory from the west coast of England and the south coast of Ireland. While intermittent contact with Newfoundland was not unknown prior to the seventeenth century, Irish ships, traders and fishermen were regularly in what became Canadian waters from the 1670s.

*Waterford was then a major staging and provisioning port for English fleets heading to Newfoundland. Together with *Wexford and *Cork, Waterford provided the bulk of the Irish population that eventually over-wintered and settled in Newfoundland. By the 1770s, around 5,000 men and 100 ships left Irish ports annually for seasonal work in Newfoundland and several permanent communities were established there. Anglo-French conflict and bouts of anti-*Catholic persecution failed to reverse the trend of Irish migration, and in 1784 the British authorities tolerated the first Catholic mission in *Canada. In 1800, *United Irishmen within Newfoundland's garrison attempted an anti-British revolt which testified to the strength of connections between the colony and their native country. Approximately half the Newfoundland population was of Irish birth or extraction by 1836, a proportion sustained into modern times. The distinctive features of this community included the retention of regional accents from Ireland's southern maritime counties and the survival of the *Irish language and traditions in Newfoundland, or what they called *Talamh an Éisc*, 'the land of the fish'. R.OD.

Newgrange. *Passage-grave in the Boyne Valley, in County *Meath. Newgrange is Ireland's most famous prehistoric monument, built about 500 years before the Pyramids and a millennium before Stonehenge. Under a large mound some 280 feet in diameter and 36 feet high, a 66-foot-long passage leads to a burial chamber 20 feet high. The grave is renowned for the rising sun shining into it for 17 minutes as it climbs over the horizon at the winter solstice a few days before Christmas. Accessible from the chamber are three burial niches, two with stone basins (possibly for cremated bone). The beautifully carved stone at the entrance, others in the tomb chamber, as well as some of the 97 large recumbent slabs forming the mound's kerb, are decorated with a variety of geometrical designs, including the triple spiral unique to Newgrange. Enclosing this Stone Age mound are 12 out of the original 38 upright boulders which once formed a

Detail in Newgrange, Neolithic Passage Grave, Co. Meath

Bronze Age circle around it. Newgrange is accessible only through the Brú na Bóinne Interpretative Centre on the south side of the Boyne. P.H.

Newman, John Henry (1801–90). English educator and cardinal. Newman was the first rector of Dublin Catholic University. Educated at Trinity College, Oxford, he became vicar of St Mary's, Oxford, in 1828. After travelling widely in southern Europe, Newman began his *Tracts for the Times* (1833) and in 1835 joined the 'Oxford movement', an attempt to revitalise the Church of England by reviving certain Roman Catholic doctrines and rituals. In 1837, Newman published a defence of Anglo-Catholicism, Romanism and Popular Protestantism. He converted to Roman Catholicism and was ordained a priest in 1846. Newman established oratories at Birmingham (1847) and London (1850). He reinvigorated Catholic *education in Ireland and served as the rector of Dublin Catholic University (1854–58). He was made a cardinal in 1879. S.A.B.

newspapers. More than 150 titles are published in Ireland each week, between daily, weekly and provincial papers. Traditionally, there has been a clear distinction in the political affiliations of the major newspapers. The *Irish Independent*, which was founded by William Martin Murphy in 1905, supported *Fine Gael, while the *Irish Press*, which was set up by Éamon *de Valera in 1931, was a vehicle of the *Fianna Fáil party. The *Irish Times*, established in 1859, catered to the *Protestant minority and the urban middle-class, but in the 1960s it became more liberal.

These lines of political demarcation have become less evident in recent years. The *Irish Press* ceased production in 1995 after decades of financial and industrial strife. The *Irish Independent* broke with traditional affinities in the general election of 1997, when it urged its readers to vote against the government of the day, of which Fine Gael was the dominant party.

The *Irish Times* is regarded as Ireland's premier newspaper. It places particular emphasis on free thinking, with columnists such as Fintan O'Toole, Mary Holland (d. 2003), Vincent Browne and John Waters carrying on the tradition of Flann *O'Brien and John Healy. Geraldine Kennedy became the first woman editor of the *Irish Times* in 2002. Its Web site, *www.Ireland.com*, is a fine example of electronic publishing.

In recent years, the *Cork Examiner* has been reinvented as a national newspaper – the *Irish Examiner* – which competes with the *Irish Independent* for the middlebrow market. Irish editions of British tabloids – the *Star*, the *Sun* and the *Irish Mirror* – have also made great inroads into the market in recent years.

In *Northern Ireland, the ethos of the main newspapers is still determined along political and sectarian grounds. The *Irish News* is bought mostly by nationalists, while the *Newsletter* and the *Belfast Telegraph* are seen to have *unionist leanings. The Sunday newspapers in the *Republic are also divided along these lines, though not as rigidly. The *Sunday Business Post* and *Ireland On Sunday* are nationalistic in their outlook, while the *Sunday Independent* professes to reach out to the unionist community. The Irish edition of the *Sunday Times* might have some claim to be the first all-Ireland newspaper, with healthy sales among both communities, north and south. The *Sunday Tribune* has built up a considerable reputation for investigative journalism and exposés on political sleaze, while the Irish-language weekly *Foinse* is a bright and breezy publication combining national news with regional issues and a particular emphasis on the *Gaeltacht areas. The *Evening Herald*, which is part of the Independent Group, is Ireland's best-selling evening paper. (Web sites: *www.irish examiner.com*; *www.independent. ie*; *www.*

sunday-times.co.uk; www.irelandonsunday .com; www.sbpost.ie; www.news-letter. co.uk; www. tribune.ie; www.belfasttele graph. co.uk; www. foinse.ie; www.irishnews.com.) B.D.

New York, the Irish in. New York City has been home to the Irish for three centuries. Beginning in the 1600s and through the 1700s, most of the Irish entering New York were *Ulster *Protestants with farming and mercantile backgrounds. In 1830, Irish *immigrants numbered about 20% of New York City's population. By the middle of the nineteenth century, however, economic, social and political pressures in Ireland forced greater numbers, especially *Catholics, to emigrate. The *Famine accelerated this exodus, driving 848,000 men, women and children to New York between 1847 and 1851. This unprecedented onslaught of destitute, ill and unskilled immigrants burdened the city with its first social service crisis, resulting in the creation of institutions such as the Emigrant Savings Bank, an Emigrant Commission and the first Immigration Station at Castle Garden. Their arrival also stretched the limits of existing institutions like the Almshouse Department, the Lunatic Asylum, Bellevue Hospital and the House of Refugees. For the next 50 years, the flow of Irish continued despite improved economic, social and political conditions in Ireland. This altered the profile of the typical Irish immigrant to single Catholics in their twenties, more than half female.

Irish immigrants became productive citizens, finding work mostly as domestics, day labourers, teachers and civil servants. In 1873, John Holland, a former *Christian Brother, arrived in New York. He designed and launched the first submarine in 1878 in Paterson, New Jersey. In 1858, the Irishman John O'Mahoney established the *Fenian Brotherhood in New York. John *Devoy, the *Fenian rebel, came to New York in 1871 and went on to become an editor and journalist. Éamon *de Valera, one of modern Ireland's greatest politicians and statesmen, was born in Manhattan in 1882 to an immigrant mother who sent him back to Ireland when he was two and a half years old to be raised by her family in County *Limerick. Many famous Irish figures made New York their home, from Thomas Addis Emmet, who became attorney general of New York (1812–13), to the great Irish tenor, John *McCormack.

The Irish left indelible marks on New York's Catholic church and politics. Under the leadership of Archbishop John Hughes, a native of County *Tyrone, and a succession of Irish and Irish American bishops, priests and *nuns, the Catholic church grew from a minor denomination with two churches in 1820 to a major institution with 60 by 1860. The church also established St Vincent's Hospital (1849), the New York Foundling Hospital (1870), St Patrick's cathedral (1879) and many other schools, hospitals and orphanages.

One of the darker, more complex episodes of the Irish experience in New York was the 1863 Draft Riots. Angered by unfair conscription laws ($300 could buy an exemption), primarily Irish mobs rioted for four days, causing more than $2 million in damage, the deaths of 3 policeman, 15 rioters and 11 lynched African Americans, before police and soldiers, many of them Irish, restored order. The violence reflected fear and frustration in the Irish community with anti-Irish discrimination, Irish fatalities in the war and the prospect of competing with freed slaves for jobs.

Beginning with 'Honest' John Kelly, who took charge of Tammany in 1871, the Irish, one-third of the population in 1880, dominated city politics for more than 70 years years.Tammany Hall was the headquarters of the Democratic Party in New York City and would become synonymous with Irish machine politics tinged with corruption and 'graft'. In 1918, Tammany-backed Al Smith, son of Irish immigrants, won the first of four elections for governor of New York and in 1928 became the first-ever Catholic to run for president. William O'Dwyer, who emigrated from County *Mayo with his brother Paul (later a famous human rights activist), was the city's only Irish-born mayor (1946–50) of the century.

The Depression and the Second World War slowed emigration from Ireland. Following the war, as their economic status improved, many of the Irish moved out of city neighbourhoods and jobs. In 1950, first- and second-generation Irish represented less than 6% of the city population. Two waves of immigrants between 1945 and 1960 and again between the early 1980s and 1990s, led to a healthy resurgence of Irish immigrants in the city, bringing such talent as the *Clancy Brothers and Tommy Makem, Milo *O'Shea and Frank *McCourt.

The St Patrick's Day parade, the symbol of the Irish in New York since 1766, remains a show of political unity, ethnic pride and a forum for issues and controversy in the community. In the twenty-first century, the Irish are still emigrating to New York, despite Ireland's unprecedented economic prosperity. L.D.A.

New Zealand, the Irish in. The Irish emigrated to the British colony of New Zealand from the late eighteenth century and ultimately formed a sizable minority within the white population of the islands. Irish-born sailors participated in James Cook's Pacific voyages in the 1770s, and the establishment of a penal colony in New South Wales (Australia) in January 1788 increased the Irish contact with New Zealand. Irish soldiers in the British military were well represented in New Zealand garrisons after 1847 and the post-*Famine exodus led to the migration of thousands of free settlers to the southern hemisphere. Emigrants from the province of *Munster were particularly drawn to New Zealand, as were men and women from the nine counties of *Ulster. By the 1860s, when the discovery of gold increased the drawing power of the country, approximately 18% of New Zealand's population was of Irish stock, and the proportion was considerably higher in Westland. The tendency of Irish women to marry outside their cultural circle accounted for significant intermarriage with Scots and English families. William Ferguson Massey of *Derry became premier of New Zealand in 1891 and fellow Ulsterman John Balance of *Antrim attained the office in 1912. Thomas Bracken, a native of County *Monaghan, composed the national anthem of New Zealand, 'God Save New Zealand'. Irish New Zealanders played a large role in labour politics and a recent premier, Jim Bolger, is the son of *Wexford immigrants. R.OD.

Ní Cathasaigh, Máire (1956–). Harpist. Born into a music family in Bandon, County *Cork, Ní Cathasaigh learned the instrument from age eleven and went on to win all major awards. She was the first *harp player to teach at *Comhaltas Ceoltóirí Éireann's annual Scoil Éigse. As a professional player, Ní Cathasaigh bridges the old harp-playing traditions and modern-day traditional Irish *music. She has interpreted the harp music of Turloch *Carolan extensively and her droning technique for the performance of *dance music has been hugely influential. F.V.

Ní Chonaill, Eibhlín Dhubh (c.1743–c.1801). Poet in the *Irish language. A widow (and Daniel *O'Connell's aunt), Ní Chonaill is famous for her one literary composition – 'Caoineadh Airt Uí Laoghaire' ('The Lament for Art O'Leary'). This lament, or *keen or death poem, is considered one of the greatest poems written in Ireland or Britain in the eighteenth century. Composed on the murder of her husband by the forces of the British crown in 1773, this lament is a passionate outburst of love, of loss and of horror against fate, narrow-mindedness and misfortune, and against *Protestantism and England's rule of law. A.T.

Ní Chuilleanáin, Eiléan (1942–). Poet and lecturer. Born in *Cork, Ní Chuilleanáin was educated at University College, Cork, and Oxford. She teaches medieval and Renaissance English at Trinity College, Dublin. Ní Chuilleanáin's central theme, developed over successive volumes, is the emergence of female subjectivity from historical images of confinement – towers, nunneries, statuary, veils. Her poetry is notable for its incisive intelligence, its sustained and striking images, its wealth of careful detail and its sensitive evocations of women's experiences in history and myth. Among her collections are *Acts and Monuments* (1972), *The Rose-Geranium* (1981), *The Magdalene Sermon* (1989) and *The Brazen Serpent* (1994). M.S.T.

Ní Dhomhnaill, Nuala (1952–). *Irish-language poet and critic. Born in Lancashire, England, to Irish-speaking parents, Ní Dhomhnaill was raised in County *Tipperary but spent long periods in the Irish-speaking district of *Kerry. She was educated at University College, Cork, and lived for some years in Turkey. Ní Dhomhnaill holds a key position as both a senior woman poet and a leading Irish-language poet. Her poetry is written exclusively in the Irish language, but is widely translated into English by well-known Irish poets. She collaborated with poet Micheál *Ó hAirtnéide to produce the bilingual *Selected Poems/Rogha Dánta* (1988) and with Paul *Muldoon in *The Astrakhan Cloak* (1991). Ciaran *Carson, Seamus *Heaney, Michael *Longley and Muldoon are among the translators of *Pharaoh's Daughter* (1991), and Medbh *McGuckian and Eiléan *Ní Chuilleanáin translated *The Water Horse: Poems in Irish* (1999). Collections in the Irish language include *An Dealg Droighin* (The Blackthorn Brooch) (1981) and *Féar Suaithinseach* (Miraculous Grass) (1984). Much of her imagery is drawn from the *Munster folk tradition she encountered in Kerry and from *Catholic symbols. A poem such as 'The Fairy Hitch Hiker' is typical in that it combines a contemporary, humorous idiom, sophisticated technique and a feminist social awareness. M.S.T.

Ní Ghráda, Máiréad (1896–1971). Dramatist. Ní Ghráda was a prolific writer of short plays, which were both experimental and popular. She is primarily known for *An Triail* (The Trial), first performed in *Dublin in 1964. The play caused a stir at the time as it dealt with the plight of a young unmarried mother and her abandonment by lover, family and society. *An Triail* is still regularly produced. A.T.

Nine Years War, the (April 1593–March 1603). *Ulster rebellion against Queen *Elizabeth I. Between 1593 and 1603, reacting against growing interference by the English administration in land issues in Ulster, Hugh *O'Neill of Tyrone and Red Hugh *O'Donnell of Tyrconnell led a rebellion against the crown, known as the Nine Years War. King Phillip II of Spain sent troops to assist the Irish. Arriving in Kinsale, County *Cork, in September 1601, the Spanish forces were quickly besieged by an English army led by Lord Mountjoy. Rebel forces from Ulster moved south to relieve the Spaniards, but in the Battle of *Kinsale, on Christmas Eve, 1601, the combined Irish and Spanish forces were defeated.

In March 1603, the Treaty of *Mellifont formally ended the rebellion. The new English king, *James I, wanted to ensure that the old Gaelic system was broken in Ulster in particular, and so under the treaty, the rebels had to give up their Gaelic titles and ancestral rights and live by English law. In return, they avoided the confiscation of their land and were given a pardon.

The *Flight of the Earls occurred four

years later, when O'Neill and over 90 other Ulster chiefs, dissatisfied with their new positions and fearing future retaliation, sailed for the continent. P.E.

Norman invasion. See **Anglo-Norman Conquest.**

North Strand Bombings (31 May 1941). Bombings of parts of *Dublin during the Second World War. The Luftwaffe bombed parts of the city, leaving 34 dead, 90 injured and 300 houses destroyed. The North Strand was worst hit but bombs also landed on South Circular Road, Terenure and Sandycove. At the time, the Irish government believed that British interference in German wireless signals, the so-called 'beam', had put the Luftwaffe planes off course. Recent research, however, indicates that the bombing was deliberate, a warning to the Irish government to remain neutral. After the war, Germany accepted responsibility and paid £327,000 in compensation to the Irish state. T.C.

Northern Ireland. Constituent part of the United Kingdom since 1920. Northern Ireland has a population of 1,685,267 (2001 census). Made up of the six *Ulster counties, *Antrim, *Armagh, *Down, *Fermanagh, *Londonderry and *Tyrone, Northern Ireland was created by the *Government of Ireland Act (1920), through which Britain tried to disengage from Ireland. Britain assumed that the two *home rule administrations created by the act would eventually become one through the proposed Council of Ireland. The *Anglo-Irish Treaty of December 1921 and the subsequent Free State Act (1922) left Northern Ireland as per the Government of Ireland Act: six counties of Ulster that guaranteed a *unionist majority, even though the new state could not deliver political consensus from its minority (39%) nationalist population. The powers of parliament and government (from the mid-1930s centred in Stormont Castle and known as *Stormont) were constitutionally modelled on Westminster, but remained limited and, particularly in financial matters, dependent on London. With *Civil War in the south and an *IRA campaign within its borders, the new state's birth was accompanied by constitutional, political and economic uncertainties and insecurities. This experience would influence the northern government's expectations of, and attitudes toward, respectively, governments in Dublin, Great Britain and the *Catholic/nationalist minority within its borders. A *Protestant state for a Protestant people in the north stood as counterbalance to the Catholic state for a Catholic people that was the *Irish Free State.

While it initially intended to accommodate the Catholic minority (e.g., one-third of posts in the police were reserved for Catholics, although they were never taken up), discrimination against nationalists became endemic. In the early 1920s, in particular, the state used the *RUC to serve both as police and in a military capacity to suppress *republican insurrection, which in turn reinforced nationalist alienation from the state. More than ever, religious identities became political identities. Catholic noncooperation and Dublin's hostile rhetoric only confirmed unionists' perceptions that nationalists wanted to destroy their state. Socially, the period between the two world wars saw the consolidation of two mutually hostile groups. This was a time fraught with economic difficulties: high unemployment, an increasing population, a decline in the staple industries of shipbuilding, *linen and *agriculture and, compared to Britain, a poor standard in all areas of public service.

Northern Ireland, however, benefited from the Second World War. The southern Irish state's (*Éire) *neutrality made Northern Ireland an essential part in the British war effort. Its agriculture was modernised, its government strengthened; its economy improved overall and with it came general prosperity. Britain promised and delivered parity of social services for the postwar period. The *Ireland Act (1949) confirmed the constitutional position of Northern Ireland, reassuring unionist governments. Britain's financial aid allowed Northern Ireland to move economically and in terms of social policy well ahead of the *Republic. While unionists had primarily hoped to consolidate their position within their own constituencies through the adoption of these policies, nationalists benefited at least as much – given their over-representation in the disadvantaged sections of society – particularly in areas of health and education. This helped to loosen their allegiance to Dublin and made them more willing to accept the northern state on a day-to-day basis. By the second half of the 1950s, some Catholic middle-class groups were beginning to reject the *Nationalist Party's abstentionist and ineffective approach and to debate a fuller integration of the minority population into the state.

The 1960s saw an increased growth in confidence among the Catholic middle-classes. This coincided with Prime Minister Terence *O'Neill's administration's policies of economic planning and modernisation, in which, it was hoped, Catholics might participate and thus accept the state. Civil rights groups emerged demanding equal status for all citizens of Northern Ireland. This began to alienate the conservative section of unionism and soon counter-demonstrations were mounted. By the late 1960s, politics had moved onto the streets and made Prime Minister O'Neill's standing within his own party increasingly difficult. As rioting and attacks by and against, the police multiplied, the Unionist governments from 1969 to 1972 tried to stem the tide by granting most of the civil rights demands. But it was too late: the revival of latent violent sectarianism had made Northern Ireland ungovernable. The most recent *Troubles would last for almost 30 years. In 1972, Stormont was dissolved and direct rule of Northern Ireland from Westminster was implemented.

During the following 15 years, British governments attempted by various means to create a political middle ground in which the liberal wings of unionism and nationalism could work together and end paramilitary violence. This proved impossible to achieve, not least because of the nature of direct rule itself, which made regional politicians powerless and focused all attention on Britain. Ultimately, paramilitary violence (by such groups as the *IRA, INLA, the *UVF and the *UDA) was accepted as a defensive necessity by each side. Both nationalism and unionism had split into more moderate and radical factions. The *Anglo-Irish Agreement of 1985 was Britain's last attempt at creating a consensus of the middle ground, now with active support from Dublin, which up to then had offered very little but hostile rhetoric. Dublin's involvement was unacceptable to unionists, thus dooming hopes that the agreement would lead to a cessation of violence.

The emergence of *Sinn Féin, the political wing of the IRA, as a political party in the wake of the *hunger strikes, probably encouraged a U-turn in British politics in Northern Ireland. With the interest and support of the Dublin government, it seemed feasible to work from the outside in: if the paramilitaries of both sides could be persuaded to substitute politics for the armed struggle, a way forward might be found. This was enthusiastically supported by John *Hume's SDLP (Social Democratic and Labour Party), but initially met with hostility from unionists. Only after David *Trimble became leader of the *Ulster Unionist Party was progress made. Trimble eventually realised that there was no way back to a unionist Stormont government and compromises in the form of power-sharing would have to be made. After long negotiations, the *Good Friday Agreement was signed in 1998 and a new form of devolved government began, based on 'parity of esteem' for both traditions. To accommodate the difficulties of governing Northern Ireland, the agreement institutionalised sectarianism: no legislation can be passed without a majority percentage from each of the sectarian sides supporting it. The Good Friday Agreement faced many obstacles: decommissioning of arms, continuing sectarian violence on the streets and radical splinter paramilitaries on both sides. During the first years of the new century, the new Northern Ireland assembly survived shakily, under pressure in particular from the substantial section of unionists who were unwilling to accept cooperation with Sinn Féin. S.W.

Northern Ireland Civil Rights Association (NICRA). Civil rights community organisation. Formed in January 1967, NICRA was inspired particularly by the campaigns of Martin Luther King in the United States. The association's organisation was modelled on the British National Council for Civil Liberties. The founding committee, which represented a spectrum embracing left-wing, radical and liberal *unionist and *nationalist opinion, included Noel Harris, Conn McCluskey, Fred Heatley, Jack Bennett, Michael Dolley, Kevin Agnew, John Quinn, Paddy Devlin, Terence O'Brien and Robin Cole. Its aim was to reform, not overthrow, *Northern Ireland. NICRA's basic demands were 'one man, one vote' in local elections, an end to gerrymandering, outlawing discrimination, and reform of the security apparatus (the disbandment of the *B-Specials and the repeal of the Special Powers Act). Like civil rights organisations in the United States, NICRA organised marches to publicise its case. The first march was on 24 August 1968, in Dungannon, County *Tyrone, to protest discrimination in housing allocation practised by the unionist-controlled local council. The march, which was attended by 4,000 people, attracted media attention. The next march, on 5 October 1968, in *Derry, was attended by a large crowd, including the *Nationalist leader Eddie McAteer and other *Stormont MPs. McAteer and Westminster MP Gerry Fitt were both injured when the *RUC attacked the marchers with batons. This violence is seen as the beginning of the *Troubles. NICRA brought public attention to bear on Northern Ireland and put pressure on the British government to introduce reforms. A series of protests and demonstrations followed. The unionist authorities viewed NICRA as a front for the *IRA and resisted NICRA's demands for reform. The RUC responded violently to its demonstrations and the *UVF planted bombs in order to destabilise the region. NICRA was eventually overshadowed by the outbreak of communal violence and paramilitary campaigns. T.C.

Northern Ireland conflict (1968–97). *Northern Ireland was created by the *Government of Ireland Act in 1920 under pressure from *Ulster unionists who threatened war if included in an all-Ireland parliament. *Nationalists never accepted its legitimacy and have continually sought reunification with the rest of the island. Northern Ireland has not enjoyed one decade without violence or paramilitary campaigns since its formation.

The most recent conflict was sparked by the unionist authorities' violent reaction to the protest marches of the *Northern Ireland Civil Rights Association. The unionist government believed that NICRA was a front for the *IRA, although an independent investigation subsequently refuted this. The *RUC attacked NICRA's peaceful protests and widespread rioting resulted. The *UVF, a *loyalist paramilitary organisation, planted a series of bombs in 1969, which it tried to blame on the IRA, hoping that the reforming Prime Minister Terence *O'Neill would be replaced with a hard-line unionist. As violence spread in 1970, British troops were brought in, initially to relieve the RUC and protect *Catholic areas from attack.

Walls, known as 'Peace Lines', were erected between Catholic and *Protestant areas in *Belfast to keep rioting factions apart.

The attacks on nationalist districts resulted in a revival of the IRA, which had been inactive since the early 1960s. The renewed IRA soon split over tactics. The Provisionals emerged as the stronger faction and conducted a military campaign against the *Stormont government and the security forces. The other faction, the Officials, carried on for a few years before giving up violence in favour of left-wing politics. On the loyalist side, the UVF was joined by the *Ulster Defence Association (UDA) in a campaign of random assassinations of Catholics.

On 9 August 1971, the government of Northern Ireland introduced *internment without trial. On 30 January 1972, which became known as *Bloody Sunday, British soldiers shot dead 13 civilians in *Derry during a mass demonstration against internment without trial. In response to this tragedy, the IRA escalated its campaign. Recruitment to loyalist groups increased after *Bloody Friday, 4 March 1972, when IRA bombs killed 11 in Belfast. The intense violence – 180 people were killed in 1971 and 496 in 1972 – convinced the British to suspend the local parliament and appoint a secretary of state to govern the region directly from London. An attempt to bring peace by the formation of a power-sharing government in 1974 was brought down by a loyalist strike. The violence continued despite sporadic attempts at finding a political settlement. The IRA continued its activities in *Northern Ireland and in Britain, while loyalist paramilitary groups, often in collusion with the security forces, maintained their attacks on Catholics.

In 1979, Margaret *Thatcher became the British prime minister. She was determined to defeat the IRA. Thatcher took a hard line when IRA prisoners in Long Kesh (Maze) went on *hunger strike, demanding the restoration of political status. Ten prisoners died on hunger strike, including Bobby Sands, who had been elected MP for *Fermanagh/South Tyrone before his death.

Sands' election to parliament and *Sinn Féin's public campaign on behalf of the hunger strikers showed Sinn Féin's growing political influence. The 1985 *Anglo-Irish Agreement, in which the British and Irish governments agreed to consult on Northern Ireland issues in an attempt to end the violence, provoked, however, a unionist backlash. The IRA continued its campaign of violence despite public revulsion at actions such as the *Enniskillen bombing in 1987, which killed 19 people.

The arrival of John *Major as prime minister in 1990 opened the way for renewed talks. The groundwork had been laid by negotiations between John *Hume and Gerry *Adams. Tortuous discussions between Dublin and London led to a framework document for negotiations involving all political parties and both governments. This led to the signing of the *Downing Street Declaration on 15 December 1993, in which the British and Irish governments agreed that it was a matter for the Irish people, north and south, to decide the future of the island. On 31 August 1994, the IRA – and shortly after, the loyalist groups – declared a cease-fire. However, the negotiations broke down and the IRA resumed military activities in February 1996.

After general elections in Ireland and Britain, in which Bertie *Ahern became *Taoiseach and Tony *Blair prime minister, talks began again. In July 1997, the IRA reinstated its cease-fire and in September of that year Sinn Féin became a full participant in the negotiations. This time around, with the active involvement of Ahern, Blair, US President Bill Clinton and Senator George Mitchell, who was the US Special Envoy to Northern Ireland, an agreement was reached on Good Friday 1998, known as the *Good Friday Agreement.

Although endorsed by the people of Ireland, the agreement is still not fully implemented. Dissident republicans opposed to it planted a bomb in *Omagh, County *Tyrone, in 1998, killing 29 people. The IRA began decommissioning its arsenal in October 2001. Loyalist paramilitaries continue to attack Catholics. The *UDA dissolved its political wing and came out against the agreement. Sectarian attacks and communal violence in flashpoints, like north *Belfast, continue. Over 3,600 people have died in the conflict. T.C.

Nuns. In the twelfth and thirteenth centuries, there were Augustinian, Cistercian and Franciscan nuns. The *Reformation and the counter-Reformation brought change, not only in the suppression of the religious life, but in the tightened regulations governing nuns. There were only nine convents in Ireland in 1731, belonging to the Poor Clares, the Carmelites and the Dominicans. The major increase in the number of nuns in Ireland occurred in the early nineteenth century, though the first of the modern, socially active congregations, the Presentation, was effectively established by Nano *Nagle in Cork in 1776. The Irish Sisters of Charity followed in 1815, the Loreto in 1821, and the Sisters of Mercy in 1828. Congregations such as the Sacred Heart, the Sisters of St Louis and the Ursulines came in from abroad. Most nuns worked with the poor in schools, asylums, hospitals, orphanages, hostels, evening classes and (for those allowed to go outside the convent) sick visitation. Some orders ran fee-paying boarding schools, which were preparing pupils for university entrance examinations by the late nineteenth century. The number of nuns multiplied by eight between 1851 and 1911 and continued to grow until well into the twentieth century. Nuns alone made up 4.6% of the female workforce in 1961.

The religious life offered *women challenging work and often considerable authority, in a democratic community. The convent also gave middle-class women independence of day-to-day male authority. Convent entrants were, mostly, middle-class women in their early to mid-twenties, who brought a dowry with them. Many sisters, cousins, or friends seem to have entered convents at the same time and nieces followed aunts into the religious life. Dowry-less girls, from artisan or small-farming backgrounds, entered the convent as lay sisters. These sisters, like lay brothers in orders of priests, did the domestic work and could not aspire to positions of authority in the house. The distinction that marked off lay sisters from other nuns was abolished by the *Second Vatican Council in the 1960s.

By the early twentieth century, nuns were very important agents of the state, as national teachers, industrial school and reformatory managers and *workhouse nurses. This reinforced their considerable social authority and status. Numbers of recruits to the religious life remained high, up to the 1970s, by which stage Irish nuns had established flourishing convents on all five continents. C.C.

O

oath of allegiance. Pledge of loyalty by members of the Irish *Dáil to the British crown, required between 1922 and 1933. The *Anglo-Irish Treaty of December 1921, which conferred dominion status on the new *Irish Free State, included a provision stipulating that future members of the state's parliament would be obliged to take an oath swearing that they would be 'faithful to H. M. King George V, his heirs and successors by law in virtue of the common citizenship of Ireland with Great Britain.'

Such an oath was unacceptable to many *republicans in Ireland and was the focus of much of the treaty debate in the *Dáil in January 1922. Led by Éamon *de Valera, opponents of the treaty argued that the acceptance of dominion status would represent a betrayal of the *republic and that the oath of allegiance to the crown would perpetuate British colonialism in Ireland. In the end, the Dáil ratified the treaty 64 to 57. Continued republican opposition to the treaty settlement culminated in the *Irish Civil War (1922–23) between the Free State and *IRA forces. The fledgling Free State survived the Civil War, which ended in May 1923. De Valera and his followers in the *Sinn Féin party refused to recognise the Free State as a legitimate political entity and, for the first years of the state's existence, refused to take Dáil seats to which they were elected, due primarily to their aversion to the oath. By 1925, however, de Valera had grown frustrated with the political impotence of this abstentionist policy. He therefore broke with Sinn Féin that year and in 1926 created the *Fianna Fáil party. The following year, de Valera took the oath and led his followers into the Dáil, insisting that the oath was an empty political formula that he and other Fianna Fáil members could take 'without being involved, or without involving their nation, in obligations of loyalty to the English crown'.

In March 1932, de Valera formed the first Fianna Fáil government in the history of the state. Within days of taking office, he began dismantling the provisions of the Anglo-Irish Treaty. In May 1932, the Dáil passed a bill removing the oath, but it was delayed in the *Seanad and not abolished until after another general election in May 1933, in which de Valera's party won an overall majority. T.D.

O'Brien, Edna (1934–). Novelist and short story writer. Born in Tuamgraney, County *Clare, O'Brien moved to England in 1959 where she has spent her entire writing career. She first came to prominence with *The Country Girls'* Trilogy (reissued in 1986 with an epilogue) – *The Country Girls* (1960), *The Lonely Girl* (1962, reissued in 1964 as *The Girl With Green Eyes*), and *Girls in Their Married Bliss* (1963). These novels have a strong autobiographical undercurrent and their candour about female sexuality and the patriarchal structure of Irish life was considered scandalous. The books were banned by the *Censorship of Publications Board until 1975. In novels such as *August Is a Wicked Month* (1964) and *Casualties of Peace* (1966), O'Brien examines the fates of isolated, abandoned women living lives of emotional impoverishment in fashionable and exotic locales. In these works, O'Brien draws on her familiarity with the international film community during the 1960s and early 1970s and her rather bleak opinion of its superficiality.

Edna O'Brien

Although O'Brien lives in England, her fiction has a predominantly Irish focus. In *A Pagan Place* (1971), she returns to the County Clare landscape of the trilogy. Just as outspoken as the earlier work, the book is more psychologically sophisticated. This Irish setting is also particularly prominent in the collections of short stories *The Love Object* (1968) and *Returning* (1982), reflecting the recurring themes of home and homemaking throughout her work. The novel *Time and Tide* (1992) explores another of her perennial subjects, motherhood, in the context of contemporary issues and events. Such later works as *House of Splendid Isolation* (1994) and *Down by the River* (1996) address such taboo topics as the Provisional *IRA and incest. O'Brien's non-fiction includes *Mother Ireland* (1976), *Arabian Knights* (1977) and *James Joyce* (1999), whose influence she has frequently acknowledged. *In the Forest* (2002) is a controversial novel based on a series of murders in County Clare that shocked Ireland. G.OB.

O'Brien, Flann (pen name of Brian O'Nolan), (1911–66). Writer. Born in County *Tyrone and raised in *Dublin, O'Brien was educated at University College, Dublin. While still a student, he wrote reviews and pamphlets (including some bawdy ones in Old Irish) under the first of many pen names, Brother Barnabas. Later, he wrote under the name Myles na Gopaleen. James *Joyce praised his first novel, *At Swim-Two-Birds* (1939), as 'a really funny book'. Also described as an anti-novel, *At Swim-Two-Birds* is a wild parody of Irish myth, popular culture and classical education, several of whose fictional characters come to life to plague their author. The book did not sell well partially because of the war, but it has since become a classic. His next book, *The Third Policeman*, was completed in 1940 but rejected by publishers and eventually published in 1967. His satirical and playful column 'Cruiskeen Lawn' in the *Irish Times* delighted readers for 26 years. The column featured wordplay; jokes in Irish and Latin; and merciless satire of vernacular speech, journalism and cliché. The novel *An Béal Bocht* (1941) gained immediate popularity among the *Irish language enthusiasts whom it satirised, but attracted critical attention only when it was published in English under the title *The Poor Mouth* (1964). Three plays by O'Brien were staged unsuccessfully in 1943, *Faustus Kelly*, *The Insect Play* and *Thirst*. Other works include the novels *The Hard Life* (1961), *The Dalkey Archive* (1964) and *Slattery's Sago Saga*, which was incomplete at the time of his death. Flann O'Brien's fiction is characterised by self-reference, demolition of literary convention and pretension, and a linguistic inventiveness that rivals *Beckett and Joyce. M.S.T.

O'Brien, Kate (1897–1974). Novelist, dramatist and essayist. O'Brien was born in *Limerick and educated at University College, Dublin. The success of her play *Distinguished Villa* (1926) led her to write full-time and her first novel, *Without My Cloak* (1931), was enthusiastically received. Subsequent novels deal with the conflict between individuals' desire to be free and moral and social constraints. O'Brien's style is intense and realist and her typical central characters are convincing feminists and

*Catholics. *Mary Lavelle* (1936) was banned, as was *The Land of Spices* (1941), because of one offending sentence. *That Lady* (1946) explores the relationship between Spain's Philip and Ana de Mendoza. *Farewell Spain* (1957) and *My Ireland* (1962) are highly distinctive travel books and *Teresa of Avila* (1951) is a study of the Spanish saint. M.S.T.

O'Brien, William Smith (1803–64). *Nationalist politician. Born in Dromoland, County *Clare, O'Brien came from a *Protestant landowning family. As Tory MP for Ennis (1828–31), he campaigned for *Catholic Emancipation and improvements to poor relief and *education in Ireland. While MP for County *Limerick (1835–49), he joined the *Repeal Association but in 1846 broke with Daniel *O'Connell and joined the Irish Confederation. Sentenced to death in 1848 for leading the *Young Ireland insurrection, O'Brien was reprieved and transported to Tasmania. Pardoned in 1854, he returned to Ireland but took no further part in politics. S.A.B.

Ó Bruadair, Dáibhí (1625–98). Poet in the *Irish language. Born in County *Cork, Ó Bruadair spent most of his life in County *Limerick. He received training in a *bardic school and was particularly fond of the *Dán Díreach* (classical syllabic verse). His poems, *Duanaire Dháibhidh Uí Bhruadair*, were collected and edited by S. C. MacErlean in 1910. They chart the declining status of the poet with the upheaval of the old Gaelic order that resulted from *Cromwell's reign of terror and the Treaty of *Limerick. B.D.

O'Byrne, Fiach MacHugh (c.1544–97). Powerful chieftain of sixteenth-century Ireland. A native of Ballinacor in the mountainous Glenmalure district of County *Wicklow, O'Byrne, with his military acumen and resources, posed a major threat to the Anglo inhabitants and administrators of County *Dublin. The inability of the Elizabethan invaders to neutralise O'Byrne resulted in his being pardoned by the crown in February 1573. On 25 August 1580, a major punitive expedition of English forces under Lord Deputy Grey de Wilton into O'Byrne's stronghold of Glenmalure was virtually annihilated. This defeat of the English forces inspired survivor Edmund *Spenser to write *The Faerie Queen* and obliged the English Queen *Elizabeth to pardon O'Byrne in 1581. Renewed efforts to capture him in March 1594 led to the temporary loss of his Ballinacor home to English occupation until late 1596. O'Byrne, who had forged strong links with the influential *Ulster *O'Neill and O'Donnell families, was eventually trapped and summarily executed on 8 May 1597. R.OD.

Ó Cadhain, Máirtín (1906–70). Writer in Irish, scholar, language activist. Ó Cadhain is considered the foremost Irish prose-writer of the mid-twentieth century. A native speaker, who received no secondary education but finished his career as professor of Irish in Trinity College, Dublin, Ó Cadhain is author of short stories ranging from the anti-romantic rural to the post-modern fantastic. He is best known for his novel *Cré na Cille (Graveyard Earth)*, a story in which all the characters are dead but who speak the most lively and vibrant vernacular while savaging and excoriating one another. A.T.

O'Casey, Seán (1880–1964). Dramatist. Born in *Dublin (as John Casey) into a poor *Protestant family, O'Casey had to support himself with manual labour well into his forties. Poverty, his father's early death and an eye ailment disrupted his education, and only through remarkable resilience would O'Casey overcome these obstacles and become one of Ireland's most important dramatists. His six-volume autobiography, beginning with *I Knock at the Door* (1939) and finishing with *Sunset and Evening Star* (1954), offers an animated record of his difficult childhood and adulthood.

O'Casey's writing career began not in *belles-lettres* but in politics, with his first book, *The Story of the Irish Citizen Army* (1919), which exposes O'Casey's *socialist beliefs, to which he remained faithful the rest of his life. His character sketches of labour and *nationalist figures such as Jim *Larkin, James *Connolly and the Countess *Markievicz foreshadow the dramatist O'Casey was to become. Between 1920 and 1923, the *Abbey Theatre rejected four of his plays, but he was encouraged to continue writing by Lady *Gregory, W. B. *Yeats and Lennox *Robinson.

Never fully a part of the *nationalist movement, O'Casey demythologises in his major plays key events of the nationalist struggle – the *Easter Rising, the *War of Independence and the *Irish Civil War. *The Shadow of a Gunman*, which had a brief premiere in April 1923 at the end of the Abbey's season, casts a critical look at Ireland's War of Independence (1919–21) by depicting its devastating impact on Dublin's slum dwellers. The play enjoyed a successful run when the Abbey reopened in the autumn and was a success in Britain and the United States a few years later. In 1924, *Juno and the Paycock*, considered O'Casey's masterpiece, proved immediately popular and continues to be produced in Ireland and elsewhere. One of O'Casey's most entertaining works, the play presents the Irish Civil War (1922–23) as a series of selfish and irresponsible tirades between feuding parties. *The Plough and the Stars*, which dramatises the 1916 Easter Rising, had a rocky start at the Abbey in 1926, when nationalists interrupted the show on the fourth night to protest O'Casey's representation of the heroes of the rising. Like *Juno and the Paycock*, the play exposes Ireland's nationalists as misguided and conceited and their rebellion as a licence for the mob to wreck and loot.

The success of these plays (known as the Dublin trilogy) gave the Abbey the financial lift it badly needed. Although the theatre supported O'Casey during the weeklong disturbances aroused by *The Plough and the Stars*, Yeats rejected in 1928 O'Casey's next play, *The Silver Tassie* (1929), an experimental play with surrealist scenes of the *First World War. O'Casey was embittered by the Abbey's decision and decided to live permanently in England where he had moved in 1926.

The Dublin trilogy's unsympathetic rendering of Irish nationalist politics underwent quiet revision in some of O'Casey's middle plays, *The Star Turns Red* (1940), *Red Roses for Me* (1943), *Purple Dust* (1945) and *Oak Leaves and Lavender* (1947). In *Purple Dust*, for instance, O'Casey appears conciliatory toward the Irish nationalist tradition when he targets English colonialism as a force victimising the native peasantry. O'Casey's later expressionist plays, *Cock-a-Doodle Dandy* (1949), *The Bishop's Bonfire* (1955), *The Drums of Father Ned* (1959) and *Behind the Green Curtains* (1962), consolidated his reputation as an innovative dramatist, but brought him little financial success.

O'Casey was involved much of his life in confrontations with his Irish contemporaries. In 1926, O'Casey engaged in a public debate with the prominent nationalist and feminist agitator Hanna *Sheehy Skeffington, who harshly criticised *The Plough and the Stars*. Another quarrel in 1958 proved equally dramatic when the Dublin Theatre Festival censored Alan McClelland's dramatisation of James *Joyce's *Ulysses*. O'Casey and Samuel *Beckett withdrew their own plays in protest and O'Casey further banned for five years all productions of his plays in Ireland. S.M.M.

Ó Conaire, Pádraig (1882–1928). Writer in the *Irish language. Born in *Galway, Pádraig Ó Conaire was in the vanguard of the Gaelic Revival (*Irish Language Revival) in the early years of the twentieth century and is often credited with launching Gaelic literature into a modern era. He was greatly influenced by French and Russian literature and his collection of short stories *Scothscéalta* (Best Stories; 1956) is often compared to the works of Maupassant. He was one of the first Gaelic writers to examine themes that dealt with life outside the rural *Gaeltacht areas. His expressionist novel *Deoraíocht* (Exile; 1910), for example, explores the misfortunes of an Irish cripple in London and stemmed from his own period of exile there. Though regarded by many as the first professional Gaelic writer, it is thought that he earned no more than £700 in total from his work. He had a severe drinking problem and died destitute in 1928. B.D.

O'Connell, Daniel (1775–1847). Lawyer and politician. Born in Carhan, County *Kerry, O'Connell was raised in Derrynane by his uncle, a *Catholic landowner. He attended school in France, where the excesses of the *French Revolution fostered his lifelong abhorrence of violence. His commitment to nonviolence was later reinforced by the savagery of the *Rising of 1798, which in his view resulted in the further repression of Irish Catholics.

O'Connell studied law at Lincoln Inns in London between 1794 and 1796 and was called to the Irish Bar in 1798. He joined the Munster Circuit and, with his knowledge of the *Irish language and insight into the character of the people, he built up a large law practice. He was brilliant in rebuttal, in cross-examining witnesses and in convincing juries of the merits of his clients' cases, particularly when defending individuals charged with violent offences during the *tithe war (1830–38). Physically imposing, O'Connell projected a public image that embodied a chieftain's pride and a hero's strength. He married his cousin, Mary O'Connell, in 1802; they had eight children during a long and happy marriage.

O'Connell's first political appearance came in 1800, when he opposed the Act of *Union. When *Catholic Emancipation did not follow the passage of the act, he joined the campaign for civil rights for Catholics. In 1824 O'Connell transformed Irish political life by forming the Catholic Association. To finance the organisation he instituted the 'Catholic Rent', a penny per month collected after Mass by the clergy. This alliance with the *Catholic church created a nationwide political movement. O'Connell then forced the emancipation issue forward in 1828 by standing for election for Clare, at a time when Catholics were excluded from parliament. A master of political theatre that both entertained and educated his audiences, O'Connell organised massive meetings across the country. He won an overwhelming victory against the government candidate and the entire country waited to see if he would be allowed to take his seat. Government ministers, fearing an uprising, conceded Catholic Emancipation in April 1829. O'Connell, known thereafter as 'the Liberator', emerged as the unrivaled leader of the Irish nation. His masterly use of the implied threat of violence to wring reform from the government became one of his principal political weapons.

O'Connell, who was not a republican, respected the institutions of British government, including parliament and the monarchy. However, he was determined, as an Irishman and a Catholic, to bring about the *repeal of the Act of Union and the re-establishment of a parliament in Ireland. He gave up his law practice to devote himself to politics. A special collection called the 'O'Connell Tribute' was made annually to compensate him for sacrificing his legal fees.

After the general election of 1832, O'Connell became the leader of 39 Irish MPs who had pledged to fight for repeal. O'Connell and his fellow MPs cooperated with the Whigs to promote reform and in 1835, when his party held the balance of power in the House of Commons, the O'Connellites and the Whigs formalised this alliance in the Litchfield House Compact. This agreement brought about the administrative reform of *Dublin Castle and the alteration of the method of paying *tithes, a much hated tax on the produce of land paid to support the *Protestant Church of Ireland by non-church members and Catholic tenant farmers.

In 1841, O'Connell was elected lord mayor of Dublin, the first Catholic to hold that office in 150 years. He upheld the *laissez-faire* economic doctrines of Adam Smith and Benthamite utilitarianism. O'Connell also earned a European-wide reputation as a political radical. He supported national liberation movements, parliamentary reform, Jewish emancipation and the abolition of slavery. When the Tories took power in 1841, O'Connell revived the repeal campaign, which he believed could be won through the constitutional means of nonviolent mass agitation. Subscriptions to his Repeal Association, through the 'Repeal Rent', approached £50,000. He organised so-called 'monster meetings' attended by many thousands of people. The authorities became concerned with the intimidating size of the crowds and the potential for violence. After a reputed three-quarters of a million people assembled on the Hill of *Tara in 1843, the government decided to prohibit the next meeting, scheduled at *Clontarf. O'Connell, unwilling to risk bloodshed, cancelled the meeting, but he was arrested, charged with conspiracy, sentenced to a year's imprisonment and fined. He spent three months in prison before a successful appeal was made to the House of Lords. He was devastated both emotionally and physically by the experience of the trial and the imprisonment. His health failing, he continued to speak out for repeal, but without effect. O'Connell's last speech in the House of Commons, in 1847, told of the suffering generated by the *Famine. He died in Genoa en route to Rome. According to his wishes, his heart was sent on to Rome and his body was returned to Ireland for burial. O'Connell's reputation for securing Catholic Emancipation through constitutional agitation was diminished in some nationalists' eyes by his failure to win repeal through the same means. His legacy among later generations of Irish nationalists, however, lay in the creation of an enduring model of constitutional politics based on strong leadership, party organisation and institutional support from the Catholic church. L.MB.

O'Connor, Frank (1903–66). Short story writer. Born Michael O'Donovan in *Cork City, O'Connor is considered one of the masters of the short story. His experiences during the *War of Independence provided the basis for his first collection, *Guests of the Nation* (1930), the title story of which is among his best-known works. His *Collected Stories* (1981) includes such masterpieces as: 'My Oedipus Complex' and 'First Confession', which draw on his impoverished childhood; 'The Long Road to Ummera' and 'The Majesty of the Law', set in traditional rural Ireland; and 'The Mad Lomasneys' and 'A Set of Variations', which depict the urban *Catholic lower middle-class of O'Connor's youth. A recurring theme is independence and these stories portray the spectrum of difficulties and compromises constituting the moral landscape of the newly created *Irish Free State. Told in a conversational style, with a wry sense of humour and compassion, these realistic stories capture the humanity of ordinary Irish people.

Some of his work reflects the influence of one of his schoolteachers, Daniel *Corkery. Early in his career, O'Connor worked as a librarian. Later, he was a director of the *Abbey Theatre, for which he wrote plays and where he worked closely with W. B. *Yeats. Like many of his contemporaries, O'Connor had some of his work banned, including his translation of the risqué eighteenth-century Irish poem *The Midnight Court* (1946). O'Connor also wrote in many other literary forms, including poetry, novels – *The Saint and Mary Kate* (1932) and *Dutch Interior* (1940) – biography and literary criticism. Among these are the autobiographical *An Only Child* (1961) and *My Father's Son* (1968); *Kings, Lords and Commoners* (1959), his translations of early Irish poetry; *The Lonely Voice* (1964), a critical study of the short story; and *The Backward Look* (1967), a history of Irish *literature. His travel books, confined to Ireland, are vehicles for his sharp criticisms of the state of the nation, particularly with regard to the maintenance of its *architectural heritage. O'Connor also wrote a good deal of outspoken journalism. During the 1950s, he was based largely in the United States, where he taught at Harvard, Northwestern and Stanford and was a regular contributor to the *New Yorker*. He returned to Ireland in 1961. G.OB.

O'Connor, James Arthur (c.1792–1841). Landscape painter. Born in *Dublin, O'Connor was based in London from 1822. His early topographical paintings were followed by romantic and picturesque representations of idealised Irish scenes. M.C.

O'Connor, John (1947–). Pianist. Born in *Dublin and educated in Dublin and Vienna, O'Connor is particularly noted for his performances of works by Beethoven and Mozart. He has also championed the works of the Irish composer John *Field. O'Connor has recorded widely and is professor of piano at the Royal Irish Academy. A.S.

O'Connor, Rory (d. 1198). King. Rory O'Connor succeeded his father Turlough as king of Connacht in 1156 and became high king of Ireland ten years later. He had more power than any Irish king before him, especially after he had successfully expelled Dermot *MacMurrough from his *Leinster kingdom. O'Connor was set to rule over a united Ireland, but MacMurrough's invitation to the Normans in 1169 to come and help restore him to his Leinster kingdom initiated the *Anglo-Norman invasion. The Treaty of Windsor in 1175 forced Rory to accept an Ireland divided between the Irish and the Normans and he returned to being king of Connacht only, subject to the overlordship of King *Henry II of England. The Normans largely ignored the treaty and Rory was deposed in 1186. He died 12 years later at Cong Abbey, County *Mayo, and was buried at *Clonmacnoise, County *Offaly. P.H.

O'Connor, Sinéad (1966–). Singer. Born in *Dublin, O'Connor achieved some success with her debut album *The Lion and the Cobra* (1987), but it was her version of Prince's 'Nothing Compares 2 U' (1990) that propelled her to celebrity status. The single topped the charts in 17 countries. O'Connor has spoken openly about her troubled childhood. She caused intense controversy when she tore up a picture of the pope on the American television show *Saturday Night Live* in 1992 and when she refused to allow the American national anthem to be played at one of her concerts in 1990. O'Connor was ordained as a priest in the dissident Irish Orthodox Catholic and Apostolic church in

Sinéad O'Connor and Shane MacGowan

1999 and changed her name to Mother Bernadette Maria. B.D.

O'Connor, Thomas Power (1848–1929). Journalist and politician. Born in Athlone, County *Westmeath, and educated at Queen's College, Galway, O'Connor (popularly known as 'Tay Pay') was *nationalist MP for Galway (1880–85) and Liverpool's Scotland division (1885–1929). 'Tay Pay' chronicled Irish parliamentary life in newspapers such as *T. P.'s Weekly* and published books, including *The Parnell Movement* (1886) and *Memoirs of an Old Parliamentarian* (1929). A well-loved figure at Westminster, O'Connor became the first president of the UK Board of Film Censors in 1917. S.A.B.

O'Conor, Roderic (1860–1940). Landscape, portrait and still-life painter. Born in *Roscommon, O'Conor studied art in *Dublin and Antwerp and lived in France from 1886. Influenced by Gauguin and van Gogh, his Brittany landscapes and peasant portraits show his move from post-impressionism to expressionism and his distinctive use of Fauvist stripes of pure colour. M.C.

Ó Criomhthain, Tomás (1856–1937). *Irish language writer of the *Blasket Islands. Born on the Blasket Islands, Ó Criomhthain taught himself to read and to write Irish as an adult, having been deprived of his native language by the Anglicised education system. A visiting schoolteacher persuaded him to write his life story on the model of works by Maxim Gorky and Pierre Loti. His book *An tOileánach (The Islandman*; 1929), ostensibly an autobiography, is also an objective description of Blasket Island life. 'It is as cold as the rock from which it was hewn, as sharp as the wind from the Atlantic and as objective as a hawk on the wing'. He also wrote poetry in unbroken lines. A.T.

O'Curry, Eugene (1796–1862). Professor, archaeologist and translator. He worked with John *O'Donovan in the Ordnance Survey of Ireland and as a cataloguer in the *Royal Irish Academy and British Museum. O'Curry became the first professor of Irish history and archaeology in the Catholic University of Ireland. His collection of lectures, *The Manners and Customs of the Ancient Irish*, remains an authoritative text to this day. P.H.

O'Dea, James (Jimmy) Augustine (1899–1965). Comedian. Born in *Dublin, O'Dea studied to be an optician in Edinburgh, but became interested in amateur theatre and in 1927 formed a partnership with producer and scriptwriter Harry O'Donovan. Gentle, sad-eyed and short-legged, O'Dea gained international renown as one of the great comedians of his era. He created a gallery of Dublin characters, the most famous of which was Biddy Mulligan, 'The Pride of the Coombe'. A master of comedic timing, O'Dea starred in annual pantomimes at Dublin's Royal and Gaiety Theatres for nearly 40 years. He also performed in *The Irish Half-Hour*, which was broadcast on BBC radio during the Second World War, and appeared in a number of films, including *Darby O'Gill and the Little People* (1959) (as king of the fairies). O'Dea influenced many younger comedians like Maureen Potter, who appeared with him in television comedies during his final years. J.C.E.L.

Ó Direáin, Máirtín (1910–88). Poet in Irish. Born on Inishmore, in the *Aran Islands, Ó Direáin is widely recognised as the begetter of modern Irish poetry. He published his first collection, *Coinnle Geala (Bright Candles*; 1942), out of his own pocket and continued to compose prolifically until his death. His early poetry is sentimental, but he later developed a hard edge and a noble voice. A.T.

O'Doherty, Brian (1934–). Conceptual artist. Born in County *Roscommon, O'Doherty has from 1969 exhibited his work under the name of Patrick Ireland, in protest against British military presence in *Northern Ireland. Educated in *Dublin, he lives and works in New York as artist and professor of art. M.C.

O'Donnell, (Red) Hugh (c.1571–1602). One of the last great Gaelic chieftains and a key rebel leader in the *Nine Years War. Also known as Red Hugh O' Donnell, he was the son of Sir Hugh O'Donnell, the lord of Tír Conaill. As a teenager, he was kidnapped by the English Lord Deputy Sir John Perrott who feared the growing threat to the British government posed by the O'Donnell family. He was held prisoner in *Dublin Castle, before escaping in 1592. In May 1592, he became chief of the O'Donnells. Between 1593 and 1603, in a reaction against growing interference by the English administration in land issues in *Ulster, O'Donnell and Hugh *O'Neill of *Tyrone led a rebellion against the crown, known as the Nine Years War. King Philip II of Spain sent troops to assist the Irish rebels. Arriving in Kinsale in September 1601, the Spanish forces were quickly besieged by an English army led by Lord Mountjoy. O'Donnell and O'Neill marched south, to relieve the Spaniards, but in the battle of *Kinsale, on Christmas Eve, 1601, the combined Irish and Spanish forces were defeated. O'Donnell was sent to Spain for further help. He was received by King Philip II, who promised additional forces for the Irish rebels. O'Donnell, however, fell ill at Simancas and died there in September 1602. P.E.

O'Donovan, John (1809–61). Antiquarian, scholar and historian. John O'Donovan documented ancient Ireland in the letters that he wrote for the Ordnance Survey. He also edited many old texts for the Irish Archaeological Society. His crowning achievement was his seven-volume edition of *The *Annals of the Four Masters* (1848–51). P.H.

O'Donovan Rossa, Jeremiah (1831–1915). *Republican. Born in Rosscarbery, County *Cork, O'Donovan founded the Phoenix National and Literary Society in 1856. After being imprisoned for *Fenian activities (1865–71), he went to America where, as a leader of the Fenian Brotherhood, he organised a 'skirmishing fund' for a war against Britain. His newspaper, the *United Irishman*, was outspoken in its support for the Fenian 'dynamite campaign' (1881–85) in England. O'Donovan Rossa died in New York and his funeral in *Dublin was the occasion for a famous graveside oration by Patrick *Pearse. S.A.B.

O'Duffy, Eoin (1892–1944). *Fine Gael and *Blueshirt leader. Born in County *Monaghan, O'Duffy was appointed deputy chief of staff of the *IRA during the *War of Independence. A supporter of the *Anglo-Irish Treaty, he became commissioner of the *Gárda Síochána in 1922 and was also chief of staff of the army. When he was dismissed in February 1933 by Éamon *de Valera, he became the leader of the *Blueshirts (Army Comrades Association), a quasi-fascist organisation. He was also the first leader of Fine Gael but resigned from the party in September 1934. In 1936, O'Duffy organised the Irish Brigade to fight for Franco in the *Spanish Civil War. P.E.

O'Faolain, Julia (1932–). Writer. Born in London, Julia O'Faolain is the daughter of Seán *Ó Faoláin. A fiction writer, translator and language teacher, O'Faolain explores a wide variety of political, historical and religious themes, with particular attention to women's experiences. In Irish and foreign settings, O'Faolain's characters grapple with the mores and expectations of church and state. *No Country for Young Men*, a Booker Prize finalist in 1980, reveals the effects of the Irish political landscape on three generations of a family involved in the republican struggle.

Other fiction includes *We Might See Sights and Other Stories* (1968), *Man in the Cellar* (1974), *Women in the Wall* (1975), *Daughters of Passion* (1982), *The Obedient Wife* (1982) and *The Irish Signorina* (1984), as well as translations under the name Julia Martines. O'Faolain also edited a collection of essays, *Not in God's Image: Women in History from the Greeks to the Victorians* (1973). K.MI.

O'Faolain, Nuala (1946–). Journalist and novelist. Born in *Dublin, O'Faolain lectured in literature at University College, Dublin, and was a television and radio producer for the BBC and *RTÉ. Beginning in the 1980s, she produced three ground-breaking series on women for RTÉ: *Women Talking*, *The Women's Programme* and *Plain Tales*. She is an award-winning opinion columnist for the *Irish Times*.

O'Faolain's memoir *Are You Somebody? The Accidental Memoir of a Dublin Woman* (1996), which was a best-seller in both Ireland and the United States, deals frankly with sex, family and alcoholism in Ireland since the 1950s. Her memoir courageously documents her struggle to define herself outside of the traditional gender role she was expected to fulfil. In 2001, she published her first novel, *My Dream of You* and in 2003 another memoir, *Almost There*. N.H.

Ó Faoláin, Seán (1900–91). Short story writer, editor, intellectual. Born John Whelan in Cork City, where Daniel *Corkery was an early mentor, he assumed the Irish form of his name in 1918. Educated at University College, Cork, where he received an MA in both Irish and English, he was a Commonwealth Fellow at Harvard from 1926 to 1929. His experiences as publicity director on the *republican side during the *War of Independence and the *Civil War form the basis of a number

Seán Ó Faoláin

of stories in his first collection, *Midsummer Night's Madness* (1932). More stories followed during the 1930s, as well as three novels – *A Nest of Simple Folk* (1934), *Bird Alone* (1936) and *Come Back to Erin* (1940). The most noteworthy novel, *Bird Alone*, was banned by the Irish censors. Its protagonist's conflicts with church and society typify the stifling atmosphere that prevailed in Ireland in the first half of the twentieth century. During the 1930s, Ó Faoláin started exploring the Irish historical legacy in his biography of Daniel *O'Connell, *King of the Beggars* (1938), and later in a controversial travel book, *An Irish Journey* (1940), in *The Great O'Neill* (1942), a biography of Hugh *O'Neill, and in *The Irish* (1947).

In 1941, Ó Faoláin founded the *Bell*, the most important literary and cultural periodical to appear since the establishment of an independent Ireland. Liberal in outlook and defiant in tone, it criticised Irish society's theocratic and autocratic tendencies. Ó Faoláin resigned the editorship in 1946 and devoted himself to the short story, producing such incisive stories as 'Lovers of the Lake', 'Up the Bare Stairs' and 'The Woman Who Married Clark Gable'. In these stories, passion conflicts with society's mores. His *Collected Stories* (1983) includes stories with an international flavour such as 'Foreign Affairs' and 'The Faithless Wife'. He also published an autobiography,

Vive Moi! (1965), and a final novel, *And Again?* (1979). His revision of *Vive Moi!* (1993) was more personally revealing. During the 1950s, Ó Faoláin taught at Princeton, North-western and Boston College. Among his other works are two travel books on Italy and several works of criticism, notably *The Vanishing Hero* (1956), a study of the modern novel. G.OB.

Offaly, County. Inland county in the province of *Leinster. The county has 772 square miles and a population of 63,702 (2002 census). 'In a quiet water'd land stands Saint Kieran's city fair' are the poetic words used by the Offaly poet T. W. Rolleston (1857–1920) to describe *Clonmacnoise, the monastic jewel in Offaly. One of the country's most important centres of craftsmanship and learning in the medieval period, Clonmacnoise produced a wealth of *manuscripts, annals and high *crosses. The 'water'd land' refers to its location beside the *Shannon, which forms the county's western boundary with *Galway and *Roscommon. The eighteenth-century Grand Canal divides the county north and south. The Boyne River bounds the eastern part of the county near Edenderry. In the south, the Slieve Bloom Mountains rise to a height of 1,733 feet. But most of the county is made up of the lowlands around the Shannon and extensive turf-*bog, where some of Ireland's oldest settlement remains dating from around 7000 BC were discovered at Lough Boora.

The county capital, Tullamore, is famous for its Tullamore Dew Irish *whiskey and Irish Mist liqueur. Birr, an elegant town, is renowned for its giant *Birr telescope of 1845, with which the Third Earl of Rosse (1800–67) discovered spiral nebulae. Birr Castle demesne now houses the famous telescope and also has gardens and a science centre. A monastery, founded by St *Colm Cille (or Columba) at Durrow near Tullamore, was the source of the famous seventh-century *Book of *Durrow*, now one of the greatest treasures in the Library of Trinity College, Dublin. During the *plantation of English settlers under Mary Tudor in 1556, the county was renamed King's County after Mary's husband, King Philip II of Spain. One famous piece of art preserved in Offaly is the beautiful twelfth-century metalwork shrine of St Manchan in Boher parish church. A pair of fine Romanesque churches at Rahan date from the same period. Aspects of nineteenth-century life in Offaly are preserved in some of the novels of Anthony Trollope (1815–82), written when he was postmaster in the town of Banagher. The county's economy consists of *agriculture and turf production by the state-owned company Bord na Móna. P.H.

O'Flaherty, Liam (1896–1984). Writer. Born on Inishmore, the largest of the *Aran Islands, O'Flaherty briefly studied for the priesthood at Rockwell College, County *Tipperary, before joining the Irish Guards Regiment. He was discharged in 1917 and thereafter suffered from nervous exhaustion. He married writer Margaret Barrington in 1926. Becoming disillusioned with the radical politics he had championed in 1921, he roamed Ireland, England, Europe and the Americas throughout the late 1920s. His first novel was *Thy Neighbour's Wife* (1923). Dostoyevski's influence is evident in the bleakness of *The Informer* (1925) – which was successfully adapted for cinema – *Mr Gilhooley* (1926) and *The Assassin* (1928). *Famine* (1937), *Land* (1946) and *Insurrection* (1950) form a trilogy on Irish nationalism. He was a founding member of the *Irish Academy of Letters, and several of his novels, including *The Black Soul* (1924), were banned. O'Flaherty brings the traditional storyteller's art to his most successful short stories in both English and Irish. The narrative voice in the collections *Spring Sowing* (1924) and *Dúil* (1954) is oral, vigorous and lyrical. *Two Years* (1930) and *Shame the Devil* (1934) are autobiographical volumes. M.S.T.

O'Flynn, Críostóir (1927–). Writer in Irish and English. Born in Limerick City, O'Flynn is a rhetorical but extremely readable autobiographer in both *There Is an Isle: A Limerick Boyhood* (1998) and *Consplawkus* (1999). The latter is a diatribe against the bureaucracy of Ernest *Blythe's directorship of the *Abbey Theatre, *Irish language politics and the inept clerical control of the state educational system. O'Flynn possesses an enrapturing dry style, redolent with comic detail. His collection *Sanctuary Island* (1971) contains remarkable short stories. O'Flynn is an exuberant poet; his intense regionalism is exemplified by 'Summer in Kilkee' (1984), which is centred around the famous hostelry of the brothers Scott. His work in Irish includes the fantasy-like *Learairí Lios an Phúca* (Sketches of the Devil's Fort; 1968) and the collection of poems *O Fhás go hAois* (From Growth to Age; 1969). Three of his plays in Irish were running at the same time in 1968: *Is é A Dúirt Polonius* (So Said Polonius), *Cóta Bán Chríost* (produced in English as *The Order of Melchizedek*) and *Aggiornamento*. Above all, O'Flynn adheres to the strict discipline of the good storyteller. J.L.

Ogham. Oldest written form of the *Irish language. Notches in groups of one to five, on, diagonally across, or on either side of a central line, form letters of a 20-letter alphabet. (The alphabet has 19 letters but there is also a symbol for ng, which makes up the twentieth 'letter'.) Ogham inscriptions from the third to the eighth centuries AD are found on memorial stones in Ireland's southern maritime counties, mostly in *Cork and *Kerry. P.H.

O'Grady, Standish James (1846–1928). Writer. Born in Castletown Berehaven, County *Cork, and educated in classics at Trinity College, Dublin, O'Grady popularised the ancient Irish saga material, which had been collected and translated by antiquarians and scholars during the first half of the nineteenth century. His two-volume *History of Ireland (The Heroic Period*, 1878 and *Cuculainn and His Contemporaries*, 1880) featured the legendary *Ulster hero, *Cúchulainn, and inspired the cultural *nationalism of the *Irish Literary Revival as well as the *Gaelic League. O'Grady himself, however, was a staunch *unionist with aristocratic interests. He portrayed Cúchulainn as a conservative hero who honoured tradition and prevented the need for revolution in ancient Ireland. Like Samuel *Ferguson before him, O'Grady hoped to convince the *Anglo-Irish *landlords that the salvation of the faltering ascendancy lay in embracing the Gaelic past, which could heal the breach between the *Protestant elite and *Catholic majority. This in turn would create a sense of cultural identity fully compatible with the union.

The sense of optimism that pervaded his *History of Ireland*, however, was short-lived. In his attacks on the *home rule bill of 1886, Toryism and Irish democracy, O'Grady condemned Irish landlords for neglecting their responsibilities as the country's natural leaders. In 1900, he founded the weekly periodical, *All-Ireland Review*, in one last effort to spur the slumbering aristocracy into opposing the threats of the blossoming Irish nationalism and democracy. Disillusioned by the increasingly nationalist public culture that emerged in the wake of the *Easter Rising of 1916, O'Grady left Ireland permanently in 1918 and died on the Isle of Wight in 1928. E.S.M.

Ó hAirtnéide, Mícheál (1941–99). Poet. Born in County *Limerick, Ó hAirtnéide (who published in English as Michael Hartnett) worked in various jobs, but mostly lived on his writings. Author of more than 30 books of poetry in English and Irish and of translations, he appeared to abandon the writing of English in favour of Irish in the mid-1970s with his collection *A Farewell to English* (1974). He continued, however, to write in both. His original poetry, the best of which is brought together in *Selected and New Poems* (1994), can range from the tender to the rhetorical. These styles are also reflected in his brilliant translations of the seventeenth-century Irish poets Dáibhi *Ó Bruadair, Pádraigín Haicéad and Aodhagán *Ó Rathaille. A.T.

O'Higgins, Kevin (1892–1927). Politician. Born in Stradbally, County *Laois, O'Higgins was a member of the first *Dáil in 1919. An articulate supporter of the *Anglo-Irish Treaty, he became minister for home affairs (later retitled justice) in the *Free State government in 1922. A vigorous opponent of the anti-treaty faction during and after the *Civil War, he initiated controversial emergency legislation (internment without trial) and empowered the judiciary rather than the military to carry out these laws. O'Higgins also developed an unarmed national police force, the *Gárda Síochána, and purged militant *republican sympathisers from the Free State army during the Army Mutiny Crisis of March 1924. He advanced unpopular Intoxicating Liquor legislation in 1924 and 1927, curbing the operating hours and numbers of drinking establishments in Ireland. In 1925, he played a decisive role in the controversial *Boundary Commission negotiations. O'Higgins advanced the autonomy of the Irish Free State within the British *Commonwealth. He was sensitive to northern *unionists, who, he believed, would be persuaded toward unification by collaboration rather than by threats or demands. On 10 June 1927, he was assassinated by three *IRA members. J.P. MC.

Oireachtas. Ireland's national parliament and legislature. The Oireachtas consists of the *president (*an tUachtarán*) and two Houses: a House of Representatives elected by popular vote (*Dáil Éireann) and a Senate (*Seanad Éireann) made up of six members elected by graduates of the older universities, 43 elected by members of local authorities and 11 nominated by the incoming *Taoiseach after a general election. The functions and powers of the Oireachtas are set out in the *Constitution. Legislation must be passed by the Dáil and Seanad and signed by the president. The Dáil, which is also known as the parliament, however, has the power to override Seanad objections and amendments by a simple majority. The president does not have a veto and is obliged to sign bills passed by the Dáil and Seanad, unless he or she decides to send the bill to the Supreme Court to test its constitutionality, or, if at the request of a majority of the Seanad and at least one-third of the Dáil, the president calls a referendum on the bill. This second provision has never been used. J.D.

O'Kelly, Alanna (1955–). Conceptual artist. O'Kelly studied in *Galway, *Dublin and London. Her work is about the position of the female in the contemporary environment. She uses many different media including performance. M.C.

O'Kelly, Aloysius C. (1850–c. 1935). Painter. Born in *Dublin, O'Kelly studied painting in Paris. He developed his realistic style in Brittany, Ireland, North Africa, England and America and exhibited widely. His images for the *Illustrated London News* were collected by Vincent van Gogh. He often concealed his identity, age and movements, possibly due to his *nationalist activities and on occasion he exhibited under the pseudonym 'Arthur Oakley'. M.C.

O'Leary, John (1830–1907). *Fenian leader. In 1848, while a student at Trinity College, Dublin, O'Leary was briefly imprisoned for taking part in a raid on police in his native county of *Tipperary. A contributor to the **Nation*, he visited America on behalf of the

*IRB in 1859. Back in Dublin, O'Leary was an editor of the Fenian newspaper the *Irish People* (1863–65). He was imprisoned for nine years (1865–74) for Fenian activities, after which he lived in exile in Paris, where he continued to participate in *republican politics. In 1885, he returned to Dublin where he became prominent in literary society and influenced W. B. *Yeats, whose poem 'September 1913' contains the lines 'Romantic Ireland's dead and gone/It's with O'Leary in the grave'. S.A.B.

Omagh Bombing (August 1998). Real IRA (a dissident group of the *IRA) bombing in *Northern Ireland. On Saturday, 15 August 1998, a car bomb tore through the town centre in Omagh, County *Tyrone. The blast killed 29 people and injured 220 others. The massacre, which occurred months after the *Good Friday Agreement, was the largest loss of life in a single incident in Northern Ireland during the current *Troubles. A warning call was placed 40 minutes before the blast, but the caller's directions apparently caused people to be moved closer to the bomb-laden vehicle. The Real IRA claimed responsibility for the bombing. This dissident *republican group wanted to undermine the *peace process and the *Good Friday Agreement. The incident caused almost unanimous revulsion and hardened in many the resolve for peace.

The *RUC Chief Constable Ronnie Flanagan created a special task force to investigate the bombing. Recently, the Northern Ireland Police Ombudsman Nuala O'Loan has harshly criticised Flanagan and the RUC for failing to prevent the bombing despite two prior warnings about plans to attack Omagh and for the task force's flawed investigation. R.D.

O'Malley, Donogh (1921–68). Politician. Born in *Limerick, O'Malley was elected to the *Dáil in 1954. A leading figure in the modernising wing of *Fianna Fáil in the 1960s, he was minister for health from 1965 to 1966 and minister for education from 1966 to 1968. His most lasting achievement was the abolition of fees for secondary *education and the introduction of financial aid for *university education. His promising political career was abruptly ended by his death in 1968. A.S.

O'Malley, Ernie (1897–1957). Revolutionary and writer. Born in Castlebar, County *Mayo, O'Malley studied medicine at University College, Dublin, and after the 1916 *Easter Rising, joined the *Gaelic League and the *IRA. He travelled throughout Ireland organising the IRA structure and was wounded several times. Captured and tortured in 1920, O'Malley escaped from *Kilmainham Gaol in 1921. He opposed the 1921 *Anglo-Irish Treaty and helped lead the anti-treaty occupation of the *Four Courts in April 1922. He escaped, went on to organise *republican forces in *Ulster and *Leinster, but was captured and imprisoned in November 1922 while critically wounded. When released in 1924, still weak from wounds and effects of a *hunger strike, O'Malley travelled through Europe by foot absorbing the culture and studying Renaissance painting in museums. He went to America in 1928 with Frank *Aiken to raise funds for the *Irish Press*. O'Malley stayed there for seven years travelling and writing, and returned to Ireland in 1935 and married American sculptor Helen Hooker. The publication of his first volume of autobiography, *On Another Man's Wound* (1936, published in the United States as *Army Without Banners*), covering the years 1916–21, brought him literary acclaim. He wrote many articles about Ireland and the arts and collected modern paintings. M.C.

O'Malley, Grace (c.1530–c.1603). Female chieftain of the O'Malley clan, also known as Granuaile. Born in County *Mayo, Grace was the daughter of Owen O'Malley, chieftain of the seafaring O'Malley clan during the turbulent era of *Henry VIII's conquest of Ireland. Grace O'Malley has become a legend for her daring exploits as a pirate queen and warrior who resisted the English. According to one legend, her nickname Granuaile derives from 'Grainne Mhaol' or 'bald Grace' because once she cut her hair in order to look like a boy so that she could accompany her father on a sea voyage. Her name more likely derives from 'Grainne Umhaill' after her father's territories (Umhall). She was married twice but her independence and reputation as a warrior are legendary. At the height of her power, Grace had 20 ships and raided many English merchant ships. In 1577 she was caught and imprisoned, but arranged her own release. One famous story recounts how when Grace went to London to petition for her son's release and her lands (as a widow she had no rights), Queen *Elizabeth I granted Grace a pardon and a pension. Another legend tells of how, when she was refused hospitality at Howth Castle, outside *Dublin, she kidnapped the son of the Earl of Howth. The ransom she requested was that an extra place be always set at the banquet table, a tradition maintained to this day. J.OM.

O'Malley, Tony (1913–2003). Expressionist landscape painter. O'Malley worked in St Ives, Cornwall, from 1959 and painted in County *Kilkenny where he was born. He was a member of *Aosdána. His flat, modernist works are inspired by nature and history. M.C.

O'Neill dynasty. Powerful Gaelic dynasty, based in *Ulster. The O'Neill dynasty was descended from Niall Glundúb, an Irish high king of the tenth century. Niall of the Nine Hostages (Niall Naoighiallach) is the legendary ancestor of the O'Neills. The 'nine hostages' refer to his raids in the fifth century, described in ninth-century texts. The O'Neills began to assert great influence in Ulster from the late twelfth century onward. The dynasty comprised many branches, the most important of which was the Tyrone line. The heads of this branch (who bore the title Uí Néill) exerted great authority in the north of Ireland throughout the late Middle Ages, commanding the allegiance of several other Irish families. However, there was intense rivalry between the Tyrone O'Neills and other branches, most notably with the O'Neills of Clandeboye. This lasted into the early 1600s, sometimes leading to military conflict. The O'Donnells of Tír Conaill (*Donegal) were also fierce rivals of the O'Neills.

The last truly Gaelic chief of this dynasty was Hugh *O'Neill, who was 'Uí Néill' from 1593. Hugh, like his predecessors, strongly resisted the spread of English power in Ulster. He was the most prominent military commander of what was the final stand by Gaelic Ireland against England, the *Nine Years War (1594–1603). After defeat at the Battle of *Kinsale (1601), in County *Cork, O'Neill fled Ireland in 1607 (known as the *Flight of the Earls).

The O'Neills, however, continued to be prominent in Irish affairs. In the mid-1600s, for instance, Sir Phelim O'Neill and Owen Roe *O'Neill played a major part in the *Rebellion of 1641 and the wars waged by the *Confederation of Kilkenny throughout the 1640s. Other members of the dynasty were to gain prominence as soldiers and statesmen on continental Europe. In particular, some members of the family entered into the Spanish nobility.

Today, the O'Neill clan association, which was established in the 1980s, has as its clan leader a Spanish nobleman, Don Carlos O'Neill, the twelfth Marquess de La Granja, fifth Marquess Del Norte and Conde de Benagiar. J.C.

O'Neill, Francis (1848–1936). Musician, collector and writer. Born in West *Cork, O'Neill went to sea at age 16 and after extraordinary exploits came to join the Chicago police in 1873, becoming chief of police in 1901. He was a flute player, fiddler and piper. President of the Chicago Irish Music Club, he collected tunes from immigrant Irish musicians and read voluminously about indigenous Irish *music. His most important books are the seminal collection of 1,850 tunes *The Music of Ireland* (1903) and the hugely popular *The Dance Music of Ireland*. Other works include the theoretical book *Irish Folk Music – A Fascinating Hobby* (1910) and the widely used *Irish Minstrels and Musicians* (1913). F.V.

O'Neill, Hugh (1550–1616). Second earl of Tyrone, last 'Uí Néill' (head of the *O'Neill dynasty). Born in Dungannon, after his father's death, O'Neill was brought up in England by Sir Henry Sidney, former English lord deputy of Ireland. He was sent back to Ireland in 1568 in an attempt to increase the English crown's influence in *Ulster. O'Neill initially proved a loyal servant of the crown and commanded a horse troop within the English forces that suppressed the Desmond Rebellion in *Munster in 1569. He first aroused English suspicions of his loyalty in 1588, when he sheltered survivors of the *Spanish Armada. In 1591 he aided the escape of Red Hugh *O'Donnell from *Dublin Castle. In 1595, one year after the other Gaelic lords of Ulster, including Red Hugh O'Donnell, had rebelled against the English crown (the so-called *Nine Years War), he was inaugurated as 'the Uí Néill' according to Gaelic Irish political tradition. He was subsequently proclaimed a traitor by the crown and, with encouragement from Spain, he joined the rebellion of the Ulster Gaelic lords. In 1598 he won a notable victory over the English at the Battle of the Yellow Ford. The following year, he outwitted the English commander, the Earl of Essex, by getting him to agree to a cease-fire that *Elizabeth I did not want, which contributed to Essex's downfall. The next English commander to face O'Neill, Lord Mountjoy, was more successful against the Ulster lords, using the effective tactic of destroying their resources.

In September 1601, Spanish aid for the Irish arrived at Kinsale, County *Cork, on the south coast of Ireland. In December 1601, on Christmas Eve, O'Neill along with his main ally, Red Hugh O'Donnell, suffered defeat in the Battle of *Kinsale at the hands of Mountjoy. This effectively marked the end of the Nine Years War, though a peace treaty between the Ulster lords and the crown was not signed until 1603, at *Mellifont, County *Louth. This treaty was considered to be too lenient by many within the crown administration, however, and O'Neill and the other rebels were constantly harassed by the Dublin government during the subsequent years. This led to their flight to continental Europe in September 1607, (the so-called *Flight of the Earls). Hugh O'Neill died in exile, in Rome, in 1616. J.C.

O'Neill, Máire. See **Allgood, Molly.**

O'Neill, Owen Roe (c.1599–1649). Leading military commander of the *Confederation of Kilkenny during the Confederate Wars and nephew of Hugh *O'Neill. Owen Roe spent his early years in continental Europe in the Spanish military service in Flanders (present-day Belgium). He returned to Ireland one year after the outbreak of the *Rebellion of 1641, becoming the commander of the Confederation of Kilkenny's *Ulster army. This brought him into conflict with Scottish forces, which had been sent to protect Scottish settlers in Ulster. In 1646, he defeated the Scots at the Battle of Benburb, County *Tyrone. However, political divisions within the Confederation of Kilkenny prevented him from taking full advantage of this victory. O'Neill was closely associated with the political faction led by Archbishop Rinuccini, the papal Nuncio, causing the rival pro-Ormondist faction to declare him a traitor in 1648. In early 1649, he reached a cease-fire agreement with the pro-

Terence O'Neill

Cromwellian forces in Ulster. He died in November 1649, before he could come into conflict with Oliver *Cromwell's army, which had landed in Ireland the previous August. J.C.

O'Neill, Terence Marne (1914–90). Politician, prime minister of *Northern Ireland from 1963 to 1969. O'Neill spent most of his first 30 years outside Northern Ireland and he never internalised its passions. His meeting with Seán *Lemass, prime minister of the *Republic, in 1965 caused a sensation, but O'Neill preferred inclusive rhetoric to substantive civil rights reform. At the outbreak of the *Troubles in 1968, O'Neill attempted to secure broad cross-community support in the February 1969 'Crossroads Election'. He failed and was forced to resign by *unionist antipathy. His legacy was a unionism shaken out of its complacency and bitterly divided. M.M.

opera. Until recently, opera in Ireland was dominated by the works of Italian composers and a handful of the more popular nineteenth-century German and French standards. The first Italian opera heard in Ireland was *La Cascina*, a burletta (or light comic opera) by Giuseppe Scolari, performed by the Amici family touring company in *Dublin in January 1761. In 1777, Dubliners heard their first full-length Italian opera, Gazzaniga's *L'isola d'Alcina*, and a month later, Piccini's *La buona figliuola*. Michael *Kelly, the Dublin-born tenor who would later create the roles of Basilio and Curzio in Mozart's *Le nozze di Figaro*, appeared as a boy singer in the Piccini opera. Mozart's *Così fan tutte* was first performed in Dublin, at Crow Street, in 1811 and *Figaro* and *Don Giovanni* in September 1819. During the late eighteenth and early nineteenth centuries, Italian operas were produced in Dublin at irregular intervals, especially in the years 1781, 1782, 1808, 1811 and 1819. There were also occasional productions of English opera, as well as Italian and French works sung in English translation.

The 4,000 seat Theatre Royal in Hawkins Street, which opened in 1821, presented operas of the Italian *ottocento* composers Rossini, Donizetti and Bellini, and later Verdi. A series of spectacular Italian opera seasons featuring the world's best singers (including Grisi, Viardot, Lind, Patti, Mario, Rubini and Lablache) continued almost every year until the theatre was destroyed by fire in February 1880.

Although the rebuilt Royal had a successful performance of Wagner's *Der Ring des Nibelungen* cycle in 1913, the centre of operatic activity in Dublin after 1880 was the considerably smaller *Gaiety Theatre. Up to the outbreak of the Second World War, touring companies performed operas at the Gaiety and in provincial centres, usually in English translations. The Carl Rosa Opera Company, which first performed at the Gaiety in 1875, presented the Irish premieres of Puccini's *La Bohème*, *Tosca* and *Madama Butterfly*, as well as operas by the Italian *verismo* composers.

The earliest and still best-known Irish-born opera composer is Michael William *Balfe (1808–70), who wrote some 30 operas in English, Italian and French. His most important operas include *The Siege of Rochelle* (1835), *The Bohemian Girl* (1843) and *The Rose of Castille* (1857). *Waterford-born William Vincent Wallace is best remembered for his opera *Maritana* (1845). Charles Villiers *Stanford (1852–1924) wrote 10 operas, including *Seamus O'Brien* (1896) and *The Travelling Companion* (post. 1925), which were generally better received in Germany than in Britain and Ireland. Most of these Irish operas had their premieres in London. Victor Herbert (1859–1924), who was born in Dublin and educated in Germany, composed all of his more than 50 stage works, mostly operettas and Broadway musicals, in the United States. His only serious opera, *Natoma* (Philadelphia, 1911), featured John *McCormack in the leading tenor role. Ireland's most important contemporary composer is Gerald *Barry (1952–). Two of his works, *The Intelligence Park* and *The Triumph of Beauty and Deceit*, have won critical success at British contemporary opera festivals.

After 1945, opera in Ireland was supported by voluntary organisations, enthusiastic groups who put on short seasons in *Belfast, *Cork, *Limerick, *Galway and smaller provincial centres with amateur choruses, *ad hoc* orchestras and hired-in professional principals. The most important one, the Dublin Grand Opera Society, by the mid-1950s, had an annual opera season of seven weeks, usually in original languages, with major principals and conductors from Ireland, Britain and mainland Europe and the Radio Éireann Symphony Orchestra.

Wexford Festival Opera, founded in 1951 with a policy of staging unfamiliar repertory, has become world-renowned. Three new productions play to packed houses every October. Opera Ireland (formerly the Dublin Grand Opera Society) mounts four new productions from the mainstream international repertoire, in two weeklong seasons. The Anna Livia International Opera Festival gives two works during late summer, while the Opera Theatre Company (OTC) tours regularly and sometimes commissions and performs works by contemporary composers. Today, all of these companies are professional organisations.

Famous Irish singers include Michael Kelly in the eighteenth century, Limerick-born soprano Catherine Hayes (1818–61), tenors John O'Sullivan (1878–1955) from Cork and John McCormack (1884–1945) from Athlone and *Mayo soprano Margaret Sheridan (1889–1958). More recently, sopranos Heather Harper from Belfast and Suzanne Murphy from Limerick, and Dublin mezzo-sopranos Ann Murray and Bernadette Greevy have established international reputations. J.A.

Orange Order, the. *Loyalist political organisation. The Orange Order grew out of a *Protestant secret society, the Peep O'Day Boys, which fought with the Catholic *Defenders, over land in *Ulster in the 1790s. Following a victory over the Defenders in September 1795, the Peep O'Day Boys formed the Orange Order. Named after *William III, Prince of Orange, victor of the Battle of the *Boyne, the organisation sought to defend the monarchy and the Protestant ascendancy.

The *French Revolution had radicalised Irish politics and the landed-gentry class believed that the Orange Order could counteract the revolutionary Society of *United Irishmen. Under *landlord patronage, the order became synonymous with reactionary politics. It spread throughout Ireland and in March 1798 the Grand Lodge of Ireland was formed to coordinate the 470 Orange lodges throughout the country. The *Yeomanry (part-time militia) was dominated by Orangemen and when the United Irishmen's *Rebellion broke out in 1798, the Yeomanry quashed the rebellion and persecuted the rebels.

Although the Orange Order initially opposed the Act of *Union (1800) because William *Pitt, the British prime minister, had promised *Catholic Emancipation, Irish Protestants flourished under the union. The Orange Order became the union's staunchest defender and membership spread throughout the British Isles, with support at the highest levels of government. The king's brother, the Duke of Cumberland, was the order's Grand Master. Its marches, however, were often accompanied by violence and its politics were extreme. A parliamentary commission condemned the order as a threat to political stability, and at the duke's urging, it was dissolved. Individual lodges continued to exist and in 1846 the order was revived, this time without gentry support. It was strongest in Ulster and its activities continued to be marked by violence. After incidents such as Dolly's Brae in which several people were killed, the Party Processions Act outlawed marches. With its mix of Protestantism and opposition to *home rule, the order remained popular, and William Johnston in the 1870s galvanised it as the respectable voice of the landed gentry against the radical *Land League. With renewed aristocratic patronage, the order united landlords and ordinary Protestants in a new dynamic *unionism.

The Orange Order was the driving force of the *Ulster Unionist Party and the *UVF, providing the geographic and organisational framework on which both operated. After *partition in 1920, the order's processions of men in orange sashes and bowler hats, parading behind banners and bands, personified *Northern Ireland. Almost all unionist politicians and every prime minister and the vast majority of the *RUC, have been Orangemen. Its hundreds of annual marches have been demonstrations of Protestant strength and warnings to the Catholic minority. Its biggest event, held annually on 12 July commemorates the Battle of the *Boyne. As these marches go through or pass by Catholic areas, the order has been accused of heightening tension during the *Northern Ireland conflict. Riots often follow. Local residents' opposition to them in recent years has increased, most notably in Drumcree, Portadown, County *Armagh, where since 1995, the march, or its banning, has often resulted in violence, involving loyalist paramilitaries and the British army. T.C.

Ó Rathaille, Aodhagán (c.1670–1729) Poet. Ó Rathaille is generally seen as one of the finest poets in the *Irish language between the seventeenth and the twentieth centuries. His main themes are the dispossession of the Irish nobility, the hope of a Jacobite return and his own fall from grace and status as a poet. His life was a struggle to maintain or to attain patronage. The MacCarthys were his native masters, but they were dispossessed by the Anglicised Brownes who cared little for his, or for any, art. Although his early poems are often conventional, he is best remembered for his passionate outpourings of anger in the work of his middle and late period. His 'Valentine Brown' is a savage attack on the upstart who has taken his master's lands, although it is tempered by a kind of haughty pity that characterises much of his best poems. Ó Rathaille is one of the first and finest writers of *aisling, or vision poetry, in which the poet dreams of a return of a saviour – usually one of the Stuarts – who will bring Ireland to her former glory. The most authoritative collection of his poetry is *Dánta Aodhagáin Uí Rathaille* (Poems of Aodhagán Ó Rathaille) published for the Irish Texts Society in 1911. He has been well served in translation by Frank *O'Connor and Michael *Hartnett. A.T.

O'Reilly, John Boyle (1844–90). *Fenian and journalist. A native of County *Meath, O'Reilly lived in England before returning to Ireland to join the *IRB. After enlisting in the British army in order to recruit soldiers for the Fenians, O'Reilly was arrested and transported to Western Australia. He escaped to the United States in 1868 and became a supporter of *Clan Na Gael. In 1870, he joined the staff of the Boston *Pilot* and later became its owner/editor. In 1876, O'Reilly helped to organise the rescue of Fenian convicts from Australia aboard the *Catalpa*. O'Reilly also wrote novels (*Moondyne*, 1880, and *In Bohemia*, 1886) and edited *The Poetry and Songs of Ireland* (1889). S.A.B.

Ó Riada, Seán (1931–71). Musician, composer, arranger. Born in County *Cork to parents full of cultural idealism, Ó Riada learned classical violin, piano and music theory from the age of seven. He studied music at University College, Cork, and joined Radio Éireann as a music director in 1953 for two years. He played in Paris before returning to do arrangements for the Radio Éireann Light Orchestra and Radio Éireann Singers. He became interested in the traditional *music revival and developed a theatre score for Bryan *MacMahon's play *The Honey Spike*. The musicians who performed the score formed his ensemble Ceoltóirí Chualann. In the 1960s, this group presented music on the weekly *radio shows *Reacaireacht an Riadaigh* (Ó Riada's Recording Session) and *Fleadh Cheoil an Raidió* (Radio Music Festival), which were hugely popular and influential.

Appointed as a lecturer in music at University College, Cork, in 1963, Ó Riada moved to Cúil Aodha, County Cork, where he continued composing and formed a choir, Coir Chúil Aodha (now run by his son Peadar). He made some 700 arrangements for his traditional group, 25 orchestral arrangements of Irish tunes and 120 choral arrangements of Irish songs. His influential radio lecture series *Our Musical Heritage* was published as a book. His music scores for George Morrison's films *Mise Éire* (1959) and *Saoirse* (1961), which used traditional melody in an orchestral format, are groundbreaking, as was his score for the film of *The Playboy of the Western World* (1962). With his ensemble Ceoltóirí Chualann, Ó Riada made a huge impact on traditional music. His jazz-style arrangements forced the recognition of traditional music as a valid artistic expression, inspiring and influencing a generation of musicians. F.V.

Ó Ríordáin, Seán (1916–77). Poet in Irish. Ó Ríordáin is generally recognised as the best of the postwar poets. His work is characterised by a constant wrestling between tradition and modernity, and by an even greater struggle of a conscience torn by the Catholic scruples of his time, particularly in his first collection, *Eireaball Spideoige* (Robin's Tail; 1952). He was wracked by ill health all his life and the tenuousness of existence is explored in his finest collection, *Brosna* (Firesticks; 1964). Despite this darkness, Ó Ríordáin's poetry also contains a quirky humour and exciting wordplay (as in the poem 'Siollabadh', which captures the rhythms of a busy hospital ward). In his weekly column in the *Irish Times* from the late-1960s to the mid-1970s, he explored social, political and literary themes in a distinctive prose style. A.T.

Orpen, William (Newenham Montague) (1878–1931). Portrait painter, teacher and war artist. Born in Stillorgan, County *Dublin, Orpen won many prizes as a student at the Dublin Metropolitan and the London Slade Schools of Art. In London, influenced by the work of French artists Chardin and Watteau and Dutch artist Rembrandt above all, he exhibited regularly from 1899 with the New English Art Club (NEAC). Works of that period such as *The Mirror*, 1900 (Tate Gallery, London), and *The Portrait of Augustus John*, 1900 (National Portrait Gallery, London), show influences of Whistler. From 1903 to 1905, he ran the Chelsea School of Art with Augustus John. While working as a portrait artist in London, Orpen taught regularly at the Dublin Metropolitan School, from 1902 to 1914, where he exerted much influence on Irish painters such as Seán *Keating, Leo *Whelan and Patrick *Tuohy.

In 1907, he continued the series of portraits of famous contemporary Irishmen which John B. *Yeats had started for *Hugh Lane's collection. Orpen's *Homage to Manet*, 1909 (Manchester City Art Galleries), depicts stalwarts of the New English Art Club who rejected the teaching of the Royal Academy in favour of the realism of impressionism. Exhibited at the NEAC, the painting is an admission of the influence of Manet. Before leaving Ireland to become Official War Artist in France from 1917 to 1918 and Official Artist of the Paris Peace Conference in 1919, Orpen did three non-commissioned paintings – *Sowing New Seed*, 1913 (Adelaide Art Gallery, Australia), *The Western Wedding*, 1914 (location unknown), and *The Holy Well*, 1916 (*National Gallery of Ireland). These paintings mediate the conflict between the traditional and the modern by the representation of the Irish landscape and established symbols of Irishness. M.C.

Osborne, Walter F. (1859–1903). Genre and portrait painter. Born in *Dublin, Osborne studied in Dublin and Antwerp. His work developed from careful paintings of continental and English rural villages and cottage gardens to charming impressionistic paintings of Dublin. M.C.

Ó Searcaigh, Cathal (1958–). Poet in *Irish. Born in the *Donegal *Gaeltacht, Ó Searcaigh has written extensively about a sense of place and the loneliness of exile. Much of his writing deals with homosexual love. He has published seven collections of poetry: *Miontragóid Chathrach* (A Small City Tragedy; 1975), *Tuirlingt* (Landing; 1978; with Gabriel Rosenstock), *Súile Shuibhne* (Sweeney's Eyes; 1987), *Homecoming/An Bealach 'na Bhaile* (1993), *Na Buachaillí Bána* (The White Boys; 1996), *Out in the Open* (1997). *Ag Tnúth leis an tSolas* (Longing for Light; 2000) contains the best of his previous collections along with a volume of new poems. His work has been translated into many languages. B.D.

O'Shea, Katharine (Kitty) (1845–1921). Mistress and later wife of Charles Stewart *Parnell. Born in Essex, England, she married Captain William Henry O'Shea in 1867. The marriage failed and, in 1880, her relationship with Parnell began. Captain O' Shea remained quiet about the affair, hoping to gain from an inheritance that Katharine expected from her wealthy aunt, Mrs Benjamin Woods. However, when the aunt died in May 1889, the inheritance was contested and Katherine was unable to give Captain O'Shea his settlement of £20,000. He filed for divorce and in November 1890, Parnell was named as a co-respondent. The scandal that followed ruined his political career and split the *Home Rule party. Katharine married Parnell in June 1891. Four months after his death, she disappeared from public life. T.OCon., P.E.

O'Shea, Milo (1926–). Actor. As a schoolboy in his native *Dublin, O'Shea played small parts for the *Edwards/*MacLiammóir Company. At age 19, after acting with a touring company and taking lessons at Ria Mooney's Gaiety School of Acting, he joined the Dublin Players' Theatre. In the early 1950s he toured the United States and Canada, and on his return to Ireland appeared in a variety of plays, musicals, pantomimes and revues. The part of Leopold Bloom in Joseph Strick's film *Ulysses* (1967), based on the book by James *Joyce, brought him international recognition and led to appearances on Broadway (where he made his debut in *Staircase* in 1968) and film roles, including in Franco Zeffirelli's *Romeo and Juliet* (1968). Other films include *Barbarella* (1968), *The Verdict* (1981), *The Matchmaker*

(1997) and *The Butcher Boy* (1998). O'Shea has also acted for television, notably with Anna *Manahan in the series *Me Mammy*, written by Hugh *Leonard. More recently he has appeared on the sitcom *Frasier*. He lives in New York. J.C.E.L.

O'Siadhail, Mícheál (1947–). Poet and linguist. Born in *Dublin, O'Siadhail was educated at Trinity College, Dublin, and the University of Oslo. A member of *Aosdána and formerly professor at the Dublin Institute for Advanced Studies, he published works on linguistic studies, such as *Córas Fuaimeanna na Gaeilge: na Canúinti agus an Caighdeán* (Sound System of Gaelic: The Dialects and the Standard; 1975) and *Téarmaí Tógála agus Tís as Inis Meáin* (Building and Housing Terms from Inishmaan) (1978) and Irish and English poetry collections, including *An Bhliain Bhisigh* (The Leap Year; 1978), *Hail! Madam Jazz* (1992) and *A Fragile City* (1995). His verse treats the precarious position of human beings on the edges of the dominant culture but its tone is often optimistic. M.S.T.

Ossian. Legendary Gaelic bard. Ossian is said to have associated with the third-century warriors at the court of *Tara and to have related their exploits to St *Patrick. In 1762–63, the Scottish writer James Macpherson (1736–96) published translations of two epic poems recounting the exploits of the legendary Irish hero Fionn Mac Cumhaill (or Finn McCool) (as Fingal), which he attributed to Ossian. The publication of these poems made Ossian's name familiar throughout Europe but provoked a literary controversy over the work's authenticity. S.A.B.

Ó Súilleabháin, Diarmuid (1932–85). Novelist in the Irish language. Ó Súilleabháin is part of the first wave of modernist novelists in Irish who abandoned plodding social realism and went straight for the imagination. Although his experimentalism was untempered by any sense of linear narrative, his novels, particularly *Dianmhuilte Dé* (The Hardmills of God; 1964) and *Caoin Tú Féin* (Weep for Yourself; 1967), were read with enthusiasm in the 1960s and 1970s. His most accomplished novel is *An Uain Bheo* (The Time Alive; 1968), which exposes the seamy side of power. A.T.

Ó Súilleabháin, Eoghan Rua (1748–84). Poet in *Irish. Ó Súilleabháin is colloquially known as 'Eoghan of the sweet mouth' because of the musicality of his poetry. His poetry became renowned throughout *Munster because it was set to popular tunes. Ó Súilleabháin entered folklore as a type of the clever and verbally witty word spinner. 'Im Leabaidh Aréir' (In Bed Last Night) may be his finest example of word music unencumbered by sense, whereas 'Ceo Draíochta' (Magical Mist) is an almost perfect *aisling composed at a time when that genre had lost much of its force. His wandering life finds expression in his wandering style. He is the greatest Irish poet who ever lived who had little to say. A.T.

Ó Súilleabháin, Muiris (1904–50). Writer, autobiographer. His autobiography *Fiche Blian ag Fás (Twenty Years a'Growing*; 1933) is one of the three classics of the Blasket autobiographies. Translated by George Thomson and by Moya Llewelyn Davies in 1933, this book describes the author's youth on the *Blasket Island, his leaving of the island and his induction into the *Gárda Síochána, or Irish *police force. Bordering on sentimentality, his autobiography brought a lightheartedness to rural writing that had been missing until then. A.T.

O'Sullivan, Seán (1906–64). Portrait painter and graphic artist. Born in *Dublin, O'Sullivan studied in Dublin, London and Paris. He exhibited many works, mostly portraits and some landscape paintings, at the *Royal Hibernian Academy for almost 40 years. He designed stamps, provided book illustrations and made posthumous drawings of the 1916 *Easter Rising leaders. The *National Gallery of Ireland has a collection of his drawings of prominent Irishmen and women and the *Abbey Theatre has a collection of his portrait paintings. M.C.

O'Sullivan Sonia (1969–). Athlete. Born in Cobh, County *Cork, Sonia O'Sullivan, a middle- and long-distance runner, is considered Ireland's greatest female athlete. She was favoured to win two gold medals at the Atlanta Olympics in 1996 but failed to finish the 5,000 metre final (due to illness) and did not qualify for the 1,500 metre final. O'Sullivan, however, went on to win an Olympic silver medal in the 5,000 metre at the Sydney Olympics in 2000. She also won a silver medal in the 1,500 metre at the World Championships in 1993 and a gold medal in the 3,000 metre at the European Championships of 1994. She was also World Student Games champion at 1,500 and 2,000 metre in 1991. Sonia created history in 1998 by winning both the long and short course events at the World Cross-Country Championships in Marrakesh. B.D.

O'Toole, Peter (1932–). Actor. Born in *Connemara and raised in Leeds, England, O'Toole was part of the wave of provincial actors and dramatists who broke the elitist stranglehold on the London stage in the 1950s. In 1962, he won international stardom and the first of seven Oscar nominations for the title role in David Lean's *Lawrence of Arabia*. Other signature performances include his roles in *Becket* (1964), *The Lion in Winter* (1968), *Goodbye Mr Chips* (1967) and *The Ruling Class* (1972). In 2003, O'Toole was awarded an honourary Oscar. M.E.

Ó Tuairisc, Eoghan (1919–82). Writer. Ó Tuairisc was born in Ballinasloe, County *Galway. His first novel, *Murder in Three Moves* (1960), was a thriller, but he is best known for his work in Irish. His historical novel *L'Attaque* (1962), which deals with the French invasion of Ireland in 1798, is a classic of the genre. *Dé Luain* (Monday; 1966) is a blow-by-blow account of elements of the 1916 *Easter Rising while 'Aifreann na Marbh' (Mass for the Dead), his poetic tribute to the victims of Hiroshima, was published in his collection *Lux Aeterna* (1964). B.D.

Ó Tuama, Seán (1926–). Scholar in the *Irish language, dramatist and poet. Ó Tuama is one of the few professors of Irish in modern times who championed the importance of literature and opposed the desiccated tradition of Germanic philology prevalent for most of the century. He inspired a generation of Irish poets and literary scholars. A stylist in prose and poetry, Ó Tuama established a tradition of literary drama almost single-handedly. His selected poems are published in a bilingual edition *Rogha Dánta/Death in the Land of Youth* (1997) and his literary essays in *Repossessions: Selected Essays on the Irish Literary Heritage* (1995). A.T.

P

Paine, Thomas (1737–1809). English radical political thinker. Paine was a radical pamphleteer who influenced republican thinking in North America, France and Ireland in the 1780s and 1790s. Born in Thetford, England, into a Quaker family, Paine became interested in the French Enlightenment as a young man. Paine's hugely popular *Common Sense* appeared in January 1776, the same year that the 13 colonies in America declared independence. The book highlighted the lack of civil liberties in the British empire. Paine met George Washington in America before moving to Paris in 1789, where he associated with progressive liberals from Ireland, Britain and all parts of continental Europe. Paine's *The Rights of Man*, part one, was printed in early 1791 and was widely pirated in Ireland where the debate over Edmund *Burke's denunciation of the *French Revolution created a huge controversy. Paine mixed in the same Parisian circles as Irish radicals Lord Edward *Fitzgerald and Henry and John Sheares and was made an honourary *United Irishman. His *Age of Reason* was viewed by some in 1796 as a step back from earlier political extremism but he remained one of the most admired and notorious men of his times. He died in New York in 1809. R.OD.

painting. The earliest known painting in Ireland is found on megalithic pottery. The abstraction and decoration of megalithic carvings and medieval *manuscripts continue to influence Irish painting today.

Easel paintings, mostly portraits, survive in Ireland only from the late seventeenth century. Limited patronage and shortage of schools sent Irish artists to London, leaving major landowners to employ visiting portrait painters. Garret Morphey's (c.1650–1716) *Caryll, third Viscount Molyneux of Maryborough*, c.1700, is an early example of Irish portraiture. James Latham (1696–1747) from County *Tipperary and Philip Hussey (1713– 83) from *Cork followed.

The establishment of the Royal Dublin Society's Schools in 1745 improved the state of painting after a period of economic stagnation. Robert West (d. 1770) trained many important painters in his own school in *Dublin and taught figure drawing at the Dublin Society School.

James *Barry (1741–1806) won the support of Edmund *Burke with *The Baptism of the King of Cashel by St Patrick*, 1763, the earliest painting of an Irish subject, and went on to champion neoclassical ideals, history painting and *republicanism, which led eventually to his expulsion from the London Royal Academy. Nathaniel *Hone the Elder (1718–84) continued Irish rebellion against the academy in 1775 when he satirised Sir Joshua Reynolds' taste for the Old Masters.

On his return to Ireland from Florence in 1791, Dublin-born Hugh Douglas *Hamilton (1740–1808), an ex-pupil of Robert West at the Society's School, complained of having to paint portraits such as *Lieutenant Richard Mansergh St George*, 1796–98 (*National Gallery of Ireland). *Cupid and Psyche in the Nuptial Bower* (National Gallery of Ireland) is an example of the type of painting he preferred to paint. It was exhibited in Dublin in 1801 to great acclaim.

Eighteenth-century landscapes of tourist attractions by pupils of the Dublin Society Schools followed conventions of the sublime, while paintings of *Anglo-Irish estates in the nineteenth century differed little from those of English properties in their picturesque depiction of poverty and the exclusion of agrarian unrest.

In 1846, Thomas *Davis called for Irish artists to paint national historical subjects and universal themes. In response, romantic history painting such as Daniel *Maclise's *The Marriage of *Strongbow and Aoife*, 1854 (National Gallery of Ireland), made full use of decorative effects unearthed by antiquarian research.

In 1872, *Hone the Younger's (1831–1917) modern yet realist treatment of Irish landscape he learned in Paris inspired Hugh *Lane to assemble a national collection. The subject matter of Irish impressionist painting of the late nineteenth century was much simpler than that of earlier history painting with landscape painting remaining popular.

William *Orpen (1878–1931), famous for his portrait painting and his work as war artist, renounced academy conventions in the series *Sowing New Seed*, 1913 (Adelaide Art Gallery), *The Western Wedding*, 1914 (location unknown), and *The Holy Well*, 1916 (National Gallery of Ireland), with his use of marble medium and flat opaque colours. The use of unconventional nudes, political criticism and caricatures of Irish stereotypes in these three paintings acknowledged a growing awareness of national cultural identity.

Orpen's pupil Seán *Keating (1889–1977) challenged the establishment with heroic images of rebellion. Paintings such as his *Men of the West*, 1917 (Hugh Lane Municipal Gallery), reached a wider Irish audience. Keating's teaching at the Metropolitan School of Art in Dublin established a new Irish formal academic orthodoxy and Mainie *Jellett's (1897–1944) early idealist cubist paintings of the same period met with fierce opposition.

Landscape painting straddled the divide. Decoratively *avant-garde* and post-impressionist, the landscape paintings of Paul *Henry (1876–1958), seen as representations of patriotic feeling, answered demands for a national art. The emergence of Jack *Yeats' expressionist work in the 1920s perfected the combination of modern techniques and accessible subject matter. His *Communicating with Prisoners*, 1924, and *The Island Funeral*, 1923 (*Sligo County Museum and Art Gallery), portrayed the significance of historical and social events and earned Yeats the title of 'national painter'.

The *Irish Exhibition of Living Art (IELA), established in 1943 as a showcase for modernist works, opened the way for technical experimentation. Individual expression was emphasised, often at the expense of social engagement with the subject. Gradually, however, the meaning of modern works prevailed over technique as witnessed in work based on feminist subjectivity and in New Expressionism. Political unrest in *Northern Ireland has encouraged artists to interpret events and to abandon elitist objectivity but this is often dismissed as propaganda. M.C.

Paisley, Ian (1926–). Evangelical leader and *unionist politician in *Northern Ireland. Born in County *Armagh, Paisley followed his father into the clergy and was ordained a Presbyterian minister in 1946. In 1951, however, he founded his own church, the Free Presbyterian Church of Ulster. In the 1950s, he attracted notoriety by sheltering a young female convert from her Catholic parents and for his strident anti-Roman Catholicism. In the 1960s, during the liberal premiership of Terence *O'Neill, Paisley agitated against perceived unionist conciliation to *nationalism. He argued that the *Catholic church wished to see Northern Ireland subsumed into a Catholic dominated all-Ireland republic. Only a minority subscribed to Paisley's entire analysis, but he found wide and growing support as a rampart against hasty concessions. On the other hand, his relative extremism (though he consistently condemned *loyalist terrorism) embarrassed many secular unionists and confirmed nationalist and *republican prejudices regarding Protestant and unionist sectarianism.

Paisley was jailed in 1966 and again in 1969 for leading demonstrations that sparked disorder. He won Terence O'Neill's former *Stormont seat in Bannside in 1970 and the Westminster seat for North *Antrim the same year. In 1971 he merged his Unionist Party with the Ulster *Democratic Unionist Party (DUP) under the leadership of the hard-line, but secular, Desmond Boal. Paisley supported the loyalist workers' strike that brought the collapse of the *Sunningdale administration in 1974. By the late 1970s, he had outstripped rivals on the unionist right and had become the principal competitor to the *Ulster Unionist Party (UUP) for the loyalist vote. Paisley cooperated with the UUP against the *Anglo-Irish Agreement of 1985 and opposed the 1998 *Good Friday Agreement. He has won election to the European parliament several times and was elected to the Northern Ireland assembly in 1999. M.M.

Palatines. *Protestant refugees from the Rhineland. After arriving in England in 1709, 3,000 of the Palatines were sent on to Ireland. Most of them settled in counties *Limerick and *Wexford, though smaller communities were also established in counties *Cork and *Dublin. These religious refugees maintained a distinctive religious and cultural identity throughout the eighteenth century, many of them embracing early Methodism. However, their numbers declined through *emigration and the Palatines had ceased to exist as a separate group before the end of the nineteenth century. S.A.B.

Pale, the. The part of Ireland under English rule in the medieval period. Usually called the English Pale, the name is said to derive from an old word for fence or wall. The term was coined at Calais, France, an Anglo-Norman stronghold. In Ireland, the Pale stretched from *Wexford in the south to Carrickfergus in the north. For most of its existence, the Pale consisted approximately of the counties of *Dublin, *Louth, *Meath and *Kildare. The first written mention of the Pale is in a statute of 1495 by *Poynings' parliament which calls for ditches to be made around the English Pale.

The area inside the Pale was firmly under Dublin rule and the social organisation was closer to that of England. Those living 'beyond the Pale' were the native Irish, regarded as rebels, or the descendants of the original *Norman invaders who had become Gaelicised. Despite the name, it is doubtful if the Pale was enclosed by a fence. There may have been some fences and ditches, but it was a more fluid frontier marked by *castles and other fortifications. The Pale ceased to exist as a geographical entity by the seventeenth century after the defeat of the Gaelic order. T.C.

Palladius. Bishop and contemporary of St *Patrick. Palladius was sent to Ireland by Pope Celestine to minister among 'the Irish who believed in Christ' in 431. This is the first absolute date in Irish history. Starting on the east coast, his mission has been largely overshadowed by, and subsumed into, that of St Patrick, though his groundbreaking work made him equally deserving of the title *saint. P.H.

parliament, Irish (1692–1800). Introduced into Ireland in the thirteenth century by *Anglo-Norman officials, the medieval Irish parliament began as an administrative convenience for crown officers and continued to be such for the next 400 years. The activities of the Irish parliament were directed by the king's representatives in *Dublin Castle. Rarely if ever throughout its medieval and early modern history did the Irish parliament act as a check on royal authority or pretend to represent interests other than those of English colonists settled in the country. Occasionally, during periods of protracted civil strife in *England, such as the fifteenth-century Wars of the Roses, an English political faction would capture the government of Ireland and then use the Irish parliament to try and legitimise its claims to power in England.

Continuing political and religious conflict in Ireland during the sixteenth and early seventeenth century made meetings of the Irish parliament infrequent and irregular. Until the reign of *William III (1688–1702), the Irish parliament had rarely functioned as a regular working instrument of government. At that time, a group of Irish *Protestant leaders determined that the recurrent cycles of *rebellion, suppression and confiscation that had plagued the country for most of the previous two centuries had to end. They persuaded themselves that the only way the future security and prosperity of their community could be ensured was to suppress the *Catholic majority of the country and establish some form of institutionalised protection against misguided interference in their affairs by the English government. They did so by transforming a largely ineffective and occasionally meeting Irish parliament into an exclusively Protestant assembly with regularly scheduled sessions. Once in place, this new transformed Irish parliament managed the suppression, disenfranchisement and dispossession of the Catholic majority quickly and effectively, but was never able to achieve for itself the level of independence and control over its own affairs comparable to that enjoyed by the parliament of England.

The new Irish parliament, at its first meeting in 1692 and thereafter, consisted of a House of Lords and a House of Commons. Admission to the House of Lords was by hereditary right or by Episcopal appointment. In any session, there were about 140 peers and bishops called to sit in the Upper House, but less than half were regular attendees. The House of Commons consisted of 300 members elected from 32 county constituencies, 117 boroughs and the university. Though the Irish parliament professed to represent the people of Ireland, only a small fraction of the country's Protestant inhabitants (about 1,000 families) were qualified to sit in the House of Commons or even vote for its members.

The two basic laws regulating the authority of the Irish parliament were *Poynings' Law (1494) and the Dependency Act (1720). The first prevented the Irish parliament from meeting without permission from the king and his English privy council, and required approval in advance of all business to be undertaken by it. The second prohibited the Irish House of Lords from hearing appeals from Irish courts and declared the right of the English parliament to make laws that were binding in Ireland.

Thus legally constrained, Irish Protestant politicians developed techniques and a political style that succeeded until the last decade of the eighteenth century. They regularly bewildered and challenged the English noblemen sent to govern them, guided the country through the harsh realities of famine and war, while managing to keep the Catholics relatively quiescent and excluded from the political process.

Fearing that the security of Protestant property would be much diminished by the withdrawal of English troops from Ireland to fight in the *American Revolution (or War of Independence) and forced by the English government to give concessions to Catholics, Irish Protestant leaders took matters into their own hands. They responded to the military vacuum in the country by raising corps of volunteers at their own expense to defend the coasts and preserve law and order in both urban and rural areas. At the same time, under the leadership of Henry *Grattan and Henry Flood in the Irish parliament, a majority in that body pressed for greater independence from English political concerns and more control over their own affairs. In the so-called constitutional revolution of 1782, they managed to repeal the Dependency Act and obtained a renunciation of the English parliament's right to make laws for Ireland.

The *French Revolution and war with France brought great changes and political strife to Ireland, culminating in unsuccessful rebellions and a defeated small French invasion in 1798. Convinced that Ireland could be better managed through direct rule than by governing through the Irish parliament, the English Prime Minister William Pitt forced passage of the Act of *Union in 1800, which abolished the Irish parliament, gave Ireland 100 representatives in the British parliament and established a new system of governing the country that lasted for 120 years. R.B.

Parliament House. Former home of the *Irish parliament. The first purpose-built parliament building in the world, Parliament House was designed by Edward Lovett *Pearce and constructed in College Green, *Dublin, between 1729 and 1739. The original building was characterised by the huge colonnades of its central portico, graced with Edward Smyth's statues symbolising Wisdom, Justice and Liberty. After the Irish parliament acquired a greater degree of independence and control over Irish affairs, Parliament House was extended, with substantial east and west porticos being added by James *Gandon and Richard Parke between 1785 and 1797. The building continued to accommodate both houses of the Irish parliament until the Act of *Union (1800), when it was sold to its present owner, the Bank of Ireland, and subsequently modified by Francis Johnston (1760–1829). The former House of Commons is now a banking hall while Pearce's original chamber of the House of Lords remains largely intact and is open to the public. S.A.B.

Parnell, Anna (1852–1911). *Nationalist and land agitator. A sister of Charles Stewart *Parnell, Anna organised famine relief during the agricultural depression of the late 1870s and established the Ladies Land League in 1881. In 1907 she wrote *The Tale of a Great Sham*, an intensely critical account of the *Land League agitation. Anna questioned her brother's commitment to the rent strike initiated by the 'No Rent Manifesto' shortly after his arrest in October 1881. She believed that, if the strike had been strictly enforced, it would have brought benefits to the poorest and most indebted of Ireland's farmers. Anna subsequently lived in retirement in England and died in a drowning accident at Ilfracombe. S.A.B.

Parnell, Charles Stewart (1846–91). Politician, *home rule leader. One of the most important figures in modern Irish history, Parnell dominated Ireland's political landscape in the last quarter of the nineteenth century. Immortalised in the writings of James *Joyce, idealised by Irish *nationalists at home and abroad, and finally condemned and betrayed by some of his most ardent supporters and admirers, Par-

Charles Stewart Parnell

nell was known as 'the uncrowned king of Ireland'. Along with Daniel *O'Connell and Éamon *de Valera, he is considered one of the great leaders of Irish nationalism.

Parnell was born in County *Wicklow into a *landlord *Anglo-Irish family, although his mother was American. Educated at Cambridge, he was elected member of parliament for *Meath in 1875. An avid Home Rule MP from the beginning, Parnell joined Isaac *Butt's home rule coalition and embraced Joseph Biggar's tactical obstructionist policy in parliament to focus attention on Ireland's quest for a home government. Throughout the 1870s, Parnell's reputation as a leading nationalist continued to grow and in 1880 he became the *Irish Parliamentary Party leader.

While home rule was of the utmost importance, land reform had become the most pressing political issue. Land agitation and agrarian violence had been recurring problems throughout Irish history, and by the late 1870s a series of failed harvests and an almost feudal land use system had brought rural Ireland to the brink of another *famine. Michael *Davitt had mobilised tenant farmers in County *Mayo and founded the *Land League in 1879 to bring about land reform.

Parnell accepted the role of president of the league in 1880 – a shrewd tactical move. He combined in one personality the two great dreams of the overwhelming majority of the Irish people: home rule government and land reform. The *Land War that followed elevated Parnell to the pinnacle of his career. The agrarian protests – withholding of rents, boycotting and obstruction of evictions – were highly successful. Parnell walked a fine line between constitutional agitation and violent revolution, all the while maintaining a pivotal role in the balance of power between the major British political parties, Liberals and Conservatives, both of whom often needed his support to form a majority government in the 1880s.

A major source of support for Parnell came from American *Fenians and the *Clan na Gael organisation. An agreement known as the New Departure between *Irish America and the Irish Land League recognised the land issue as indispensable to the pursuit of national independence.

In 1881, the Land League was declared illegal and its leaders, including Parnell, were arrested, further inflaming the violence of the Land War. The following year, Parnell was released under the terms of the Kilmainham Treaty, in which he agreed to abandon violence and support land reform legislation.

By the mid-1880s, because of Parnell's support, the Liberals held power and home rule for Ireland and land reform made some progress in the House of Commons. However, the 1886 home rule bill was defeated when some of the Liberal Party broke from Prime Minister William *Gladstone and supported the Conservatives.

In 1887, when a series of letters linking him to the *Phoenix Park Murders of 1882 were proved to be forgeries, Parnell was elevated even further in the mainstream political world of British politics and Irish nationalism. However, the tide would soon turn as Parnell's personal life began to cloud his public achievements. In 1890, Captain William O'Shea named Parnell in a divorce action against his wife Katharine *O'Shea. Parnell offered no defence, effectively admitting Mrs O'Shea's adultery and his own part in it. The Liberal Party leader, Gladstone, whom Parnell had supported in the House of Commons, demanded Parnell's resignation as the leader of the Irish Parliamentary Party. The Irish party itself split over Parnell's leadership and, when the *Catholic church denounced Parnell on moral grounds, the great leader's career was effectively over.

Parnell died shortly after in 1891 following an excruciatingly strenuous election campaign. He was 45 years old. J.OM.

Parnell, Fanny (1849–82). Sister of Charles Stewart *Parnell. While politically less radical than her sister *Anna, she played a key role in the establishment of the New York Ladies Land League in 1880. She is particularly well known for her newspaper contributions dealing with Irish issues as well as her poetry. P.E.

partition. The division of Ireland following the 1920 *Government of Ireland Act. The act partitioned Ireland, creating the six-county state of *Northern Ireland, which remained part of the United Kingdom and led to the creation of the *Irish Free State in 1922, following the *Anglo-Irish Treaty.

In the decade prior to the outbreak of the *First World War, the partition of Ireland had gained increasing support, despite the early opposition of some *unionist leaders, like Edward *Carson, for whom abandoning the Irish *Protestants who lived outside the part of *Ulster that became Northern Ireland was unacceptable. With the seemingly imminent implementation of the *home rule bill of 1912, however, pragmatism prevailed. In Ulster (the only region in Ireland with a substantial unionist population), unionists, who were almost exclusively Protestant and believed that 'home rule was Rome rule', began to fight for the exclusion of the entire province of Ulster from home rule. However, since five of Ulster's nine counties had *nationalist majorities in 1914, some unionist leaders, such as Andrew Bonar Law, James *Craig and Lord Lansdowne, began to contemplate a political configuration that would assure Protestant ascendancy in Ulster. John *Redmond, leader of the *Irish Parliamentary Party, would not consent to partition because the home rule legislation was due to become law in 1914 and Redmond envisioned a thirty-two-county political entity. When British Prime Minister Herbert *Asquith attempted to negotiate the issue, Redmond responded with his own partition compromise.

Essentially, Redmond wanted the British government to allow the citizens of the nine Ulster counties to decide by plebiscite whether they wished to become part of a home rule Ireland. He further insisted that two Ulster cities, Newry in County *Down and Derry in County *Londonderry (both with large Catholic majorities in counties almost certain to reject home rule), would also be given the plebiscite option. Redmond also demanded that any constituency that voted for exclusion from home rule could only remain apart from the rest of Ireland for a period of six years. Unionists threatened Asquith's Liberal Government with civil war rather than agree to such terms. The crisis was resolved for the moment with the outbreak of the *First World War in Europe. Redmond responded by urging Irish nationalists to support Britain against Germany, in return for which, he believed, Ireland would surely be rewarded with home rule at the war's conclusion.

In 1916, unionists accepted Prime Minister *Lloyd George's invitation to join his coalition government. Irish nationalists, in keeping with the party's policy of abstaining from any British executive, declined cabinet positions, thereby giving the unionists the opportunity to become an uncontested lobby in the development of the British government's Irish policy. New elections were held in December 1918 when the war ended. Having unreservedly supported the war, Redmond's Irish Parliamentary Party lost the support and confidence of a majority of Irish people following the executions of the leaders of the *Easter Rising of 1916 and the government's attempt to conscript Irish citizens in 1918. The party was totally eclipsed by the *Sinn Féin republican nationalists who refused to take their seats in the Westminster parliament and, in January 1919, convened the first *Dáil and declared themselves the Provisional Government of the *Republic of Ireland.

Frustrated in its attempt to negotiate a

home rule plan satisfactory to both nationalists and unionists, the British government passed the Government of Ireland Act (1920), which established a parliament near *Belfast, for the six-county jurisdiction now sought by the unionists and a home rule parliament in Dublin for the remaining twenty-six counties. The Ulster counties of *Donegal, *Cavan and *Monaghan were excluded from the proposed new entity of Northern Ireland because of their Catholic majorities. The remaining six counties, *Antrim, *Armagh, Down, *Fermanagh, Londonderry and *Tyrone, were thought to represent a geographical region that would be sufficiently large to be economically viable and to be so selectively populated to assure unionist control. However, while unionists would comprise two-thirds of the population in this territory, nationalists would still represent a significant element. Two of the six counties, Fermanagh and Tyrone, had slight Catholic majorities, while South Down, South Armagh and West Derry were predominantly Catholic. James Craig, the first prime minister of Northern Ireland, declared that state to be a Protestant nation for a Protestant people. The *Anglo-Irish Treaty of 1921 resulted in partition and established the *Boundary Commission, which the Irish delegation hoped would eventually lead to a united Ireland.

The *oath of allegiance to the British monarch, and not partition, was the primary issue in the *Civil War (which was fought between those advocating a republic and those accepting the Free State status) because most people thought that the Boundary Commission would eventually resolve the partition issue in favour of Irish nationalists. For 50 years – from 1922 when the government of Northern Ireland was officially inaugurated, until 1972 when the British government suspended the devolved powers of the *Stormont (Northern Ireland) parliament – the six-county state functioned as a quasi-independent region of the United Kingdom. Throughout this period, there were often intense conflicts between nationalists and unionists, sometimes on the order of full-blown pogroms, which convulsed both communities. Despite the rhetorical attacks of Irish nationalists in the Dublin parliament protesting the violence against Catholics in the north during the 1920s and 1930s, partition became a grudgingly accepted reality of life in Ireland.

The Second World War had an enduring impact upon the Irish population on both sides of the border. The economically frugal but otherwise peaceful life in the south (which had remained neutral during the war) contrasted sharply with the devastating aerial bombardment that impacted nationalist and unionist communities in the north. The partition of Ireland was rendered ever more permanent by these distinctly different experiences on either side of the border. Throughout the 1950s and early 1960s, nationalists in Northern Ireland became increasingly more accepting of their separation from the Republic of Ireland because of their participation in the British welfare system. What Catholics were denied, however, was access to equal opportunities with Protestants and the culture of discrimination prompted the oppressed minority to seek greater freedom within the United Kingdom rather than pursue the forlorn hope of national unification. The civil rights movement of the late 1960s precipitated the *Troubles that would endure for the next 30 years. The *Good Friday Agreement of 1998, which established a power-sharing assembly, affirmed that there will be no change in the status of Northern Ireland without the consent of the majority of its population (which, according to the 2001 census, was approximately 53% to 44% unionists to nationalists). Meanwhile, partition remains an enduring fact of life on the island of Ireland. T.E.H.

passage-graves. Megalithic tombs of around the fourth and third millennium BC. Often located on a hilltop, the graves have a covered passage leading to a tomb at the centre of a mound. Those in the Boyne Valley – notably *Newgrange and *Knowth – and Loughcrew, County *Meath, are the most decorated. Other passage-graves are found at *Carrowmore, County Sligo, and Dowth, County *Meath. P.H.

Patrick, Saint (c.389–c.461). Patron *saint and apostle of Ireland, generally credited with bringing Christianity to the country. Since there is little or no source material from the fifth century, what we know about Patrick's life comes from two of his own writings: *The Confession*, written late in his life as a defence of his Irish mission, and the *Epistola*, a letter to the British King Coroticus denouncing the treatment of captured Irish Christians. In his writings, Patrick comes across as a humble man, well-read in Scripture, fearing and glorifying God. The rest of what we know about Saint Patrick comes from secondary sources, many contained in the early ninth-century *Book of *Armagh*, now preserved in the Library of Trinity College, Dublin. *The life of Saint Patrick* by Muirchú and the notes by Tirechan in the *Book of Armagh* originate from the late seventh century and are based on traditions, written and oral, from approximately 200 years after the saint's lifetime.

Patrick was born in Bannavem Taberniae (probably in south-western Roman Britain). His father, Calpurnius, was a deacon of the church. At the age of 16, Patrick was captured by Irish raiders and taken to Ireland where he was sold as a slave to Milchu, a chieftain in Dalriada (part of County *Antrim). Here, he tended flocks of sheep in the valley of the Braid and on the slopes of Slemish Mountain.

According to *The Confession*, during his captivity, his thoughts turned to God and he spent many solitary hours praying. After six years, he escaped and returned home, where he claims that in a dream, he heard the 'voices of the Irish' calling for his return. Patrick took this as a sign that God wanted him to become a missionary. He was ordained in circa 417 having studied in Gaul, and on the death of *Palladius, he was appointed bishop of the Irish (by Pope Celestine I, according to some writers).

In 432, Patrick began his mission in Ireland, where he preached the word of the gospel, baptising and confirming people, mostly in the north, in the area around the former capital of Ulaidh, Emhain Macha. He established his main church nearby at Ard Macha (now *Armagh) and to this day Armagh is the capital of the Irish churches – both *Catholic and *Protestant.

Some church scholars cast doubt on various legends about him (that he spent 40 days on top of *Croagh Patrick, County *Mayo, in imitation of the biblical Moses). Also, some dispute that Patrick was the first person known to have converted the Irish to Christianity, arguing that Palladius, sent by Pope Celestine in 431, preceded him.

By the start of the eighth century, Patrick had become a legendary figure. Two legends in particular are commonly known: that he drove the snakes out of Ireland and that he used the shamrock (which has become one of Ireland's symbols) to explain the concept of the Holy Trinity.

His reputation as a baptiser and wonder-worker was spread widely in Europe in the thirteenth century with the story of his life as told in *The Golden Legend* of Jacobus de Voragine. His cult was very popular in Europe in the eighteenth century and, in the nineteenth century, his renown spread with the Irish emigration to America, where his feast day, 17 March, is celebrated with huge street parades in the major cities. The first parade in America took place in Boston in 1737. Presently, the largest parade in the world takes place on New York City's Fifth Avenue, with an annual participation of over 200,000 people.

It is believed that Patrick died in County *Down and is buried at Downpatrick, where many come on pilgrimages. P.H., P.E.

Patterson, Frank (1938–2000). Tenor. Born in Clonmel, County *Tipperary, Patterson is internationally renowned for his recordings of inspirational songs and Irish ballads. He recorded 36 albums and performed at Radio City Music Hall, in New York, on the steps of the Capitol in Washington DC and in the *Phoenix Park, *Dublin, before 1.3 million people during the visit of Pope John Paul II to Ireland. P.E.

peace process, the. Negotiations to resolve the *Northern Ireland conflict (the Troubles). The 1985 *Anglo-Irish Agreement created a foundation for the peace process and by the early 1990s, a 'three strand' approach, involving three key relationships, had emerged: first, between the communities in Northern Ireland; second, between Northern Ireland and the Irish *Republic; and third, between the Irish Republic and the United Kingdom. Between 1988 and 1993, John *Hume, leader of the *Social Democratic and Labour Party (SDLP), held a series of intermittent talks with Gerry *Adams, leader of *Sinn Féin, seeking to bring the *republican movement into constitutional politics. The British government publicly confirmed in November 1993 that it had engaged in secret talks with the republican movement. In December 1993, John *Major, the British prime minister, and Albert *Reynolds, the *Taoiseach, announced the *Downing Street Declaration, whereby the British government affirmed that it had 'no selfish strategic or economic interest' in Northern Ireland and that the territory's future should be determined by its own people. US President Bill Clinton played a significant role in encouraging the peace process and in January 1994, despite considerable opposition, a visa was issued to Gerry Adams, to allow the republican leader to speak in the United States for the first time.

The *IRA announced a cease-fire on 31 August of the same year and cease-fires by *loyalist paramilitary organisations followed in October. During the next 18 months, negotiations stalled over the issue of 'decommissioning' (the term used for disarming of paramilitaries). The British government and the *unionist parties insisted that the IRA begin to disarm as a precondition to the participation of Sinn Féin in the peace talks. The republicans countered that disarmament could only occur in the context of an overall settlement. In January 1996, an international commission on decommissioning, chaired by former US Senator George Mitchell, issued the *Mitchell Report recommending that all-party peace talks and paramilitary decommissioning take place simultaneously. When the British government continued to insist on decommissioning prior to talks, the IRA ended its cease-fire with a bombing at *Canary Wharf in London on 9 February 1996. Although Sinn Féin was now excluded, talks continued between the London and *Dublin governments and the other Northern Ireland parties. In 1997, Tony *Blair, the new Labour prime minister, revived the peace process and the IRA declared a new cease-fire on 20 July 1997. Sinn Féin rejoined the ongoing multi-party talks, over which George Mitchell presided as independent chairman, in September 1997. Continuing to insist on prior decommissioning, the *Democratic Unionist Party (DUP), headed by Ian *Paisley, declined to participate. On 10 April 1998, these talks achieved a comprehensive settlement known as the *Good Friday Agreement. All signatories agreed that a united Ireland could only be created by a majority vote of the people of Northern Ireland. For its part, the Irish Republic agreed to amend the territorial claim in its *Constitution to reflect this principle of consent. The agreement mandated the establishment of a Northern Ireland assembly, in which representatives from unionist and nationalist parties would share power. In the all-Ireland referendum of 22 May 1998, the Irish people demonstrated overwhelming support for the Good Friday Agreement. In the Republic, 94.4% voted yes and only 5.6% voted no. In Northern Ireland, 71% voted yes and 29% voted no, though public opinion polls suggested that the margin of support was narrow among unionist voters.

The implementation of the Good Friday Agreement was hampered by continued acts of violence by paramilitaries, including some of those purportedly on cease-fire and intransigent positions by the political parties on the decommissioning issue. In early May 1998, a group of dissident republicans (which became known as the 'Real IRA') announced that it would continue the armed struggle. On 15 August 1998, the Real IRA claimed responsibility for the *Omagh Bombing, in County *Tyrone, which killed 29 people, the single highest death toll from any one incident during the Troubles. After a public outcry, the Real IRA announced a suspension of military action on 18 August, followed by a 'complete cessation' on 7 September. On 25 June 1998, representatives were elected to the new Northern Ireland assembly and on 1 July David *Trimble of the *Ulster Unionist Party, was chosen as first minister designate. Séamus *Mallon of the SDLP was chosen as deputy first minister designate. The Northern Ireland assembly convened for the first time on 14 September 1998, but Trimble and his party refused to form an Executive that included representatives of Sinn Féin until the IRA began to decommission its weapons. After protracted negotiations, mostly concerning the decommissioning issue and a 'review' of the agreement by George Mitchell, the parties finally agreed to institute the 10-person power-sharing Executive on 29 November 1999. At midnight on 1 December, British direct rule over Northern Ireland ended and the new institutions created by the Good Friday Agreement went into operation. The institutions have been suspended a number of times, due to distrust on both sides of the political divide, but the peace process has prevented a return to the widespread violence of the Troubles. F.B.

Peacock Theatre, the. With the *Abbey Theatre, the Peacock Theatre constitutes the National Theatre of Ireland, which is dedicated to the promotion, development and presentation of the repertoire of Irish dramatic literature. In 1924, the Irish National Theatre was granted an annual subsidy by the newly established *Irish Free State. It used the first such subsidy to establish the Peacock. The theatre is currently situated in a studio space beneath the foyer of the Abbey Theatre building on Lower Abbey Street. The Peacock presents new plays by young writers and directors and established playwrights. Plays that have premiered at the theatre include Frank *McGuinness' *Observe the Sons of Ulster Marching Towards the Somme* (1985), Sebastian *Barry's *Boss Grady's Boys* (1988) and Dermot *Bolger's *Blinded by the Light* (1990). S.A.B.

Pearce, Edward Lovett (c.1699–1733). Architect. Pearce was the first great Irish architect, responsible for introducing the Palladian style to Ireland. The *Parliament House (now Bank of Ireland) in College Green, *Dublin, is his masterpiece (1729–39). Pearce also designed notable country houses such as Bellamont Forest, in County *Cavan, and Cashel Palace, in County *Tipperary (now a hotel). He was a member of parliament and was appointed surveyor general in 1729. P.H.

Pearse, Patrick (Pádraig MacPiarais) (1879–1916). Poet, educator and revolutionary. Born at 27 Great Brunswick Street, *Dublin, Pearse was educated by the *Christian Brothers and later studied law at the Royal University. At age 17, he established the New Ireland Society to promote Irish *poetry and in 1895 he became a member of the *Gaelic League. His writings in the Irish language appeared in the league's weekly journal, **An Claidheamh Soluis*, and between 1903 and 1909, he was that journal's editor. In 1908, he founded St Enda's College, an Irish-language alternative to the state-run school system.

A supporter of *home rule, Pearse, however, believed that the British government would fail to deliver self-government in the face of *unionist opposition and that Irish autonomy could only be achieved through force. In November 1913, he joined the Irish *Volunteers and was later sworn into the *IRB. Pearse's lecture tour of the United States between February and May 1914 was a turning point. His speeches to Irish Americans, anxious for revolution in Ireland, became increasingly filled with violent rhetoric. He returned to Ireland as a radical *nationalist and in July 1914 became a member of the Supreme Council of the IRB. Following his oration at the funeral of *O'Donovan Rossa in 1915, he was admitted into the IRB Military Council.

Pearse was instrumental in planning the *Easter Rising of 1916. Even though he and the other members of the military council knew the rising was doomed, they believed in sacrificing their lives in order to ignite the cause of nationalism. Commander in chief and president of the Provisional Government, he led a column of rebels to the General Post Office, where he read aloud the *Proclamation of the Irish *Republic, which he had drafted. The rebellion was quickly crushed and Pearse was court-martialled and executed by firing squad in *Kilmainham Gaol on 3 May 1916.

Pearse's republican idealism proved enormously influential during the *War of Independence and in the early years of the *Irish Free State. He remains a controversial figure: an iconic republican hero to many, but criticised by others for his idea of martyrdom to the nationalist tradition. P.E.

Penal Laws. Series of anti-*Catholic discriminatory legislation from the late seventeenth and early eighteenth century. Also known as Popery Laws, these laws were introduced to restrict Catholic worship, exclude Catholics from political life, limit their access to *education and prohibit them from owning property. The first two statutes, an Act for the Better Securing (of) the Government and an Act to Restrain Foreign Education, were passed in 1695. Under their terms, Catholics were barred from keeping weapons, prohibited from having their children educated abroad and forbidden from teaching or running schools in Ireland. In 1697, the Banishment Act ordered all Catholic bishops and regular clergy (i.e., priests from religious orders) to leave the country by 1 May 1698, under penalty of transportation for life. Any who returned faced being hanged, drawn and quartered. Under the 1704 Registration Act, all secular (diocesan) priests had to be registered. Every parish was allowed to have one registered priest who could not be replaced upon their death. An Act to Prevent the Further Growth of Popery, passed in 1704, prevented Catholics from purchasing land and taking leases for greater than 31 years. These provisions were strengthened by a further act in 1709, which entitled *Protestants to take over land that had been purchased by Catholics in property transactions prohibited under prior penal legislation. Other laws deprived Catholics of particular rights, including barring them from public office, preventing them from practising law and excluding them from joining the army or navy. Intermarriage between Catholics and Protestants was also forbidden. In 1728, Catholics who had been excluded from parliament since 1691 lost the right to vote.

Traditionally, the Penal Laws were viewed as an attack on the entire Catholic population and its religion. Some historians suggest, however, that the Penal Laws were primarily designed to prevent Catholics from threatening the economic and political power of the Protestant ascendancy. The laws against the practice of the Catholic religion were applied only during periods of political unrest and the Catholic church (provided it was discreet) was allowed to minister to its flock in fields and in Mass houses without much difficulty. In reaction to the ban on education, a system of hedge schools (in open fields or in primitive buildings) developed where Catholic teachers, financed by the local population, taught a mixture of spelling, reading, arithmetic and religion. The laws concerning land and the professions were strictly enforced and while ordinary Catholics did suffer, it was mostly the Catholic aristocracy and landed gentry that were victimised. By 1778, less than 5% of Irish land remained in Catholic hands. In 1760, the Catholic Committee was established to exert pressure on the British government for relief and the Penal Laws were eventually nullified by the *Catholic Relief Acts (1774–93) and the *Catholic Emancipation Act (1829). P.E.

Peoples, Tommy (1948–). Musician/fiddler from East *Donegal. Peoples learned to play at age seven and eventually moved to *Dublin where he was a leading session player in the renowned O'Donoghue's bar. He moved to *Clare in 1970 and joined the *Bothy Band briefly. He has played locally in Clare for many years. His album *The Quiet Glen* won an *RTÉ Traditional Musician of the Year Award in 1998. F.V.

People's Democracy (PD). Student civil rights organisation. Formed on 9 October 1968, by students at Queen's University, *Belfast, following *RUC violence in *Derry, the organisation called for peaceful but unremitting agitation to win civil rights reform. Its most famous member was Bernadette Devlin *McAliskey, who later became a member of parliament. As traditional political allegiances asserted themselves throughout *Northern Ireland and left-wing ideologues wrested control of the People's Democracy, the movement was eclipsed. M.M.

Petrie, George (1790–1866). Artist and antiquarian, often honoured with the title of 'founder of Irish archaeology'. He worked with Eugene *O'Curry and John *O'Donovan in the Ordnance Survey during the 1830s and is best known for his work on *round towers, published by the *Royal Irish Academy in 1845. It dismissed many fanciful notions about these structures and placed the towers firmly within the Christian context of the early Irish monasteries. A talented watercolourist, tireless antiquarian and collector of ancient Irish airs, he was elected president of the *Royal Hibernian Academy of Arts in 1857. P.H.

Petty, William, Sir (1623–87). English political economist, the first to conduct detailed surveys of Ireland. Born in Hampshire, Petty studied in Europe and was appointed Oxford professor of anatomy in 1651. As physician general to *Cromwell's army in Ireland, he was enlisted to execute the 'Down Survey' (1654–59), the first largescale scientific survey of Ireland. Assisted by a team of 1,000 men, Petty supervised the production of detailed maps of land forfeited to *Cromwellian settlers, for which he was awarded an estate in *Kerry. An original member of the Royal Society (1660), Petty published numerous socio-economic studies, including *The Political Anatomy of Ireland* (1691). S.A.B.

Phoenix Park (Dublin). The world's largest enclosed urban park. Covering 1,752 acres on the north-west of Dublin, Phoenix Park was originally a royal deerpark. *Áras an Uach-*

taráin, the president's residence (formerly the Viceregal Lodge) is in the park, as well as the official residence of the US ambassador. Within the park, is the third oldest zoo in the world (after London and Paris), which was established in 1830. T.C.

Phoenix Park Murders, the (6 May 1882). Violent incident during the *Land War. W. E. Forster, in protest against British Prime Minister William *Gladstone's Kilmainham deal with Charles Stewart *Parnell, resigned as chief secretary of Ireland. His replacement, Lord Frederick Cavendish, was assassinated along with T. H. Burke, the undersecretary, while walking in the Phoenix Park, by the *Invincibles, a secret organisation. Gladstone imposed further coercive measures in Ireland and Parnell, denouncing the murders, threatened to resign from parliament. In April 1887, the *London Times* published a letter (later proved to be a forgery) implicating Parnell in the murders. P.E.

photography. Photography in Ireland began with the pioneering work of *Belfast engraver Francis Stewart Beatty in the use of 'Talbotype' and daguerreotype processes during 1840 and 1841. English businessman Richard Beard is widely believed to have established the first commercial photographic studio in Ireland at the Rotunda in *Dublin, in October 1841. With the invention of the faster and simpler 'wet plate' process in 1851, both professional and amateur photography spread throughout Ireland. Urban and rural scenes were recorded by Thomas J. Wynne and his sons, who ran thriving photographic businesses and news agencies in Castlebar, Loughrea, *Tipperary and Portarlington. Provincial life was also photographed by A. H. Poole in *Waterford and R. J. Welch in *Ulster. Commerce was clearly a driving force in the expansion of photography in Ireland. The number of portrait studios grew dramatically after the introduction of photographic calling-cards (*cartes-de-visite*) in 1861. There were more than 60 studios in Dublin's 'photographic mile' which ran through Grafton, Westmoreland and Sackville (now O'Connell) Streets. The introduction of 'dry plate' photography in the 1860s made cameras more transportable and facilitated the development of professional landscape photography. A leading entrepreneur in this field was William Lawrence, who established a shop in Sackville Street in 1865. Robert French photographed architecture, historic sites and topographical views for Lawrence's business, which sold his work as postcards and prints. Their huge catalogue of Irish landscape photography was acquired by the *National Library of Ireland in 1943. Eason & Son of Dublin and Valentine & Sons of Dundee generated similar collections (also acquired by the National Library) to cater for the postcard trade. Technical innovations made in Ireland include Thomas Grubb's experiments in stereoscopic techniques in the 1860s and the pioneering work in colour photography by Professor John Joly of Trinity College, Dublin, in the 1890s.

Recreational photography became increasingly popular among the landed gentry and aristocracy, who recorded various aspects of daily life on their estates. An early pioneer was Francis E. Curry, land agent at the Duke of Devonshire's Lismore Estate in County *Waterford. Leading exponents of the art included many women, such as the Countess of Rosse and Lady Augusta Dillon of Clonbrock, County *Galway. Technical breakthroughs made by George Eastman in the United States between 1870 and 1890, most particularly his development of roll film and the Kodak box camera, further popularised amateur photography in Ireland. Clubs and associations were formed, the most eminent being the Photographic Society of Ireland (1858–1954). Improvements to printing processes meant that photographic images were more widely used in Irish *newspapers and books. Journalistic photography captured many important documentary images. The Dublin firm Keogh Brothers recorded many incidents during pivotal events such as the *Easter Rising and the *War of Independence and their pictures constitute a valuable record of the struggle for Irish independence. Newspapers also recorded notable people, places and events associated with Irish *theatre, literature and the arts, as well as commerce and industry. The visual history of Ireland has been well preserved. The National Photographic Archive in Dublin is the largest repository of Irish photographic prints and negatives in the world. It holds 300,000 photographs in 100 discrete collections and groupings, which illustrate diverse aspects of Irish life between the 1860s and 1990s. Both amateur and professional photographers continue to advance the art of photography in contemporary Ireland, with projects such as the 'Gallery of Photography' in Dublin attracting public funding and support. S.A.B.

pilgrimage. A religious activity practised in Ireland at least as early as the seventh century. Traditional pilgrimage sites include *Glendalough, *Lough Derg, *Croagh Patrick, the *Dingle Peninsula and *Clonmacnoise. Knock, where the Virgin is said to have appeared in 1879, is one of the most popular places of pilgrimage today. P.H.

pirates. There were several pirates with Irish connections, the two most famous of them women. Anne Bonny (c.1700) was the bastard child of a Cork lawyer and the family maid, who sailed first to Carolina, where she escaped from a weak husband to take up with pirates. Disguising herself as a man, she had a brief and unusual career before being tried and sentenced to be hanged for piracy in Jamaica. Pregnant, her sentence was delayed until the delivery of the baby, after which she disappeared. Gráinne (Grace) *O'Malley (c. 1530–c. 1603) assumed control of the family domains on the Atlantic coast of *Mayo on her husband's death. Her ships harassed the British fleets on the west coast of Ireland until her arrest by Sir Richard Bingham in 1586. She was ultimately spared and even had an audience with Queen *Elizabeth I in London, where she is said to have assumed regal equality with the English monarch and insisted on speaking only in Irish. J.MD.

plantations. Sixteenth- and seventeenth-century campaign by successive English monarchs and parliament to recolonise Ireland by confiscating land from disloyal subjects and replacing (or 'planting') them with English and Scottish settlers. These settlers would provide centres of English culture (and from the 1580s *Protestantism), which would bring about the Anglicisation of the country. This in turn would prevent Ireland from being used by continental powers as a base to usurp English power.

The first plantations, one in *Laois-*Offaly in the 1550s under Queen Mary and the other in *Munster under Queen *Elizabeth I in the 1580s, failed due to a combination of bad planning and fierce Gaelic resistance. Following the *Flight of the Earls in 1607, a more ambitious and systematic era of plantation was initiated. Under the *Ulster Plantation, the *Cromwellian Settlement and the Williamite Plantation, by the 1690s over 80% of the productive land in Ireland was confiscated from the Gaelic Irish and Old English and transferred to English and Scottish settlers.

The arrival of these colonists had long-term social and political implications for the history of the country. New plantation towns such as Enniskillen, County *Fermanagh, and Bandon, County *Cork, were built and new farming methods were introduced with arable farming replacing native cattle rearing. The growing of flax also became widespread and laid the basis for the later *Ulster *linen industry. Significantly, the plantations also created the *landlord class who differed from their tenants in religion, language, culture and wealth. Ireland became a country of two separate societies, with the native Irish resentful and suspicious of the settlers, who were seen as a conquering, imperial presence. P.E.

Planxty. Musical group. Planxty was formed in 1972 from a group of musicians who had played with Christy *Moore on his classic album *Prosperous*. The original lineup reads like a who's who in Irish traditional *music, consisting of singer and guitarist Christy Moore, piper Liam Óg O'Flynn, mandolin player Andy Irvine and bouzouki player Dónal *Lunny. Moore was replaced in 1974 by Paul Brady. The group split in 1975 but re-formed three years later with the original lineup. Planxty brought an innovative approach to traditional music with Andy Irvine in particular experimenting with eastern European influences. Moore and Lunny went on to form the backbone of the traditional rock band Moving Hearts. In 2004, Planxty re-formed for a series to concerts to great acclaim. B.D.

Plunkett, Horace Curzon (1854–1932). Proponent of agricultural cooperation and politician. Born into an aristocratic family in County *Meath, Plunkett was educated at Oxford University and from 1879 to 1889 was a rancher in Wyoming, US. On his return to Ireland in 1889, he launched the cooperative Irish Agricultural Organisation Society. He was appointed first vice president of the Department of *Agriculture and Technical Instruction in 1899. Plunkett was a *unionist MP (1892–1900) who later became a supporter of *home rule. He worked unsuccessfully as chairman of the Irish Convention (1917–18), and after 1919 through his Irish Dominion League, to keep Ireland united and within the *Commonwealth. L.MB.

Plunkett, James (1920–2003). Novelist, playwright. Born in *Dublin, Plunkett (pseudonym of James Plunkett Kelly), was educated at Synge Street Secondary School and the College of Music. He worked as a clerk for the Dublin Gas Company and later became an official of the Workers' Union of Ireland. Plunkett joined the national *radio station (Radio Éireann) in the 1950s and later moved to its *television wing (*RTÉ) to work as a producer. Plunkett is probably best known for his two sweeping historical novels, *Strumpet City* (1969) and *Farewell Companions* (1977), which portray Dublin life during the first half of the twentieth century and such historical figures as James *Larkin, the *trade union leader. Other works include the plays *Homecoming* (1954), *Farewell Harper* (1956) and *Big Jim* (1955), and the collections of short stories, *The Eagles and the Trumpets* (1954), *The Trusting and the Maimed* (1955) and *Collected Stories* (1977). P.E.

Plunkett, Joseph Mary (1887–1916). Revolutionary, poet. Born in *Dublin, the son of George Noble Plunkett, Plunkett published a volume of poetry in 1911 and was one of the founders of the Irish Theatre in 1914. A prominent member of the Irish *Volunteers, Plunkett assisted Roger *Casement in importing German arms into Ireland in 1915. As a member of the Military Council of the *IRB, he was centrally involved in the planning of the *Easter Rising (1916). One of the signatories of the *Proclamation of the Irish Republic, Plunkett was executed for his part in the rising on 4 May 1916. He married Grace Gifford, his fiancée, shortly before his execution. A.S.

Plunkett, Oliver (1629–81). *Catholic archbishop. Born in County *Meath of Old English descent, Plunkett was appointed archbishop of *Armagh in 1669. Plunkett had relatively good relations with the *Dublin Castle authorities until the introduction of anti-Catholic legislation in 1673 forced him to go into hiding. In 1679, in reaction to the Popish Plot (an alleged English Catholic conspiracy to assassinate Charles II), he was arrested and accused of attempting to instigate a French invasion of Ireland. After an initial trial in Ireland collapsed, Plunkett's case was transferred to England where he was found guilty of treason even though many, including Charles II, believed him to be innocent. Plunkett was hanged, drawn and quartered in 1681. The most celebrated Irish victim of official anti-Catholicism, Plunkett was canonised in 1975. A.S.

poetry. The oldest Irish poetry was composed and transmitted orally in *Irish. It consisted of rhythmical alliterative verse, mainly in praise of kings and heroes. The word for a poet, **fili*, meant 'seer', indicating the prophetic role of the poet. The *filid* were the custodians of traditional lore and were highly trained in the metrical conventions of Irish verse. It was not until the arrival of *Christianity in the fifth century that poetry was written down. Christianity coexisted with traditional pagan practices and the *filid* continued to enjoy their privileged place in society. Christian monasteries became centres of learning and, as well as copying sacred texts, the monks compiled ancient myths and tales, which were told in a mixture of verse and prose in both Latin and Irish. These texts included tales of the gods of pagan Ireland and of heroes like *Cúchulainn and *Fionn Mac Cumhaill (Finn McCool). Poems from this period associated with the *Fenian tradition were later collected in a number of separate volumes, including *Duanaire Finn* (Lays of Finn) (1626–27) and *Leabhar na Féinne* (Book of the Fianna) (1872). Monks also composed short lyrics, which were notable for their delicacy and precision, their metrical intricacy and vivid imagery.

*Bardic schools flourished from the late sixth to the seventeenth century. The period between the *Anglo-Norman invasion in 1169 and 1600 is usually referred to as the bardic or classical period of Irish poetry, because the form changed very little during that time. Bardic poetry, emanating from schools established by learned families, chronicled the conservative society of the time. It was a highly formalised poetry, written for courtly patrons and included courtly love poetry, which was brought to Ireland by the Normans, and poems on the lore of places called *dinnseanchas*.

After the collapse of the Gaelic aristocracy under English Tudor and Jacobean colonialism, the Irish language and Gaelic culture were suppressed. The work of poets such as Dáibhí *Ó Bruadair (1625–98) and Aodhagán *Ó Rathaille (1675–1729) reflect the anguish of dispossession. Ó Rathaille's 'Gile na Gile' ('Brightness of Brightness') is a prototype of the *aisling, a political dream-vision in which a beautiful young woman personifying Ireland appears to the poet and complains of her captivity by an idiot. The blind poet/musician Anthony *Raftery (1779–1835) was a poet of the people who composed poems and songs reflecting his subversive political views, his support for rural agitation and his hatred of *Protestantism. The two most renowned Irish-language poems of the eighteenth century are Brian *Merriman's bawdy satire *Cuirt an Mheán-Oíche (The Midnight Court*; c.1780), which attacked the men of Ireland who refused to give up their freedom and accept the responsibilities of marriage, and Eibhlín Dhubh *Ní Chonaill's *Caoineadh Airt Uí Laoghaire (Lament for Art O'Leary)*, on the death of her husband, a victim of the *Penal Laws.

During the nineteenth century and especially after the *Famine, the Irish language further declined, but the English-language literature from the late eighteenth century reflected a growing sense of Irish national identity. Charlotte Brooke's anthology in English translation, *Reliques of Irish Poetry* (1789), and

Edward Bunting's *A General Collection of Ancient Irish Music* (1796) contributed to the rising *nationalism. Between 1808 and 1834, the poet Thomas *Moore (1779–1852) published 10 volumes of his *Irish Melodies*, which contain highly popular, sentimental lyrics such as 'The Harp that Once' and 'O Breathe Not His Name' (on Robert *Emmet's speech from the dock) that were set to traditional Irish airs. Two other notable nineteenth-century writers who celebrated a glorious and distinctively Irish heroic past were James Clarence *Mangan (1803–49), renowned for his versions of 'Róisín Dubh' ('My Dark Rosaleen') and 'O'Hussey's Ode to the Maguire', and Sir Samuel *Ferguson (1810–86), best known for poems such as 'The Tain-Quest' and 'The Burial of King Cormac'.

In the latter part of the nineteenth century, Irish writers continued to recapture the Gaelic past and to write a distinctively Irish literature in the English language. This interest in reviving the native tradition of Ireland was underpinned by an idea of Celticism emanating from English romanticism: the wild and imaginative Celtic temperament as opposed to Anglo-Saxon practical common sense. Matthew Arnold's *On the Study of Celtic Literature* (1867) was a formative influence on the *Irish Literary Revival (1890–1922), even though Arnold intended his contrast between *Celt and Anglo-Saxon as justification for colonialism. Other precursors of the revival were William *Allingham (1824–89), who wrote poems about local places and local lore, and Douglas *Hyde (1860–1949), who published *Love Songs of Connaught* (1893), a collection of English translations of Irish folk songs.

The major figure of the Irish Renaissance of the last decade of the nineteenth century and the first decades of the twentieth century was W. B. *Yeats (1865–1939), whose early career was greatly influenced by the work of Mangan, Ferguson and Allingham. Yeats' early poetry draws on Irish myth and *folklore and on Irish ballad forms. His collection of writings on the supernatural, *The Celtic Twilight* (1893), gave its name to a type of romantic, melancholy poetry popular among Yeats' imitators. As he became more involved in public affairs – president of the Irish National Dramatic Society (1902), director of the *Abbey Theatre (1904) – Yeats developed a more modern, less decorative style. Well-known poems from this middle period are 'The Second Coming', 'Sailing to Byzantium' and 'Leda and the Swan'. The poetry of the last phase of Yeats' career focuses defiantly on the ravages of old age, history and his own life and poetic career, which he assesses in 'The Circus Animals' Desertion'.

Other poets associated with Yeats and the revival include George *Russell, also known as AE (1867–1935), Oliver St John *Gogarty (1878–1957), Padraic *Colum (1881–1972) and James *Stephens (1882–1950). Against this group, another group of poets stressed modernity and inter-nationalism rather than Irishness: Samuel *Beckett (1906–89), Thomas MacGreevy (1893–1967), Brian Coffey (1905–95) and Denis *Devlin (1908–59).

Reacting against Yeats' revivalism and nationalism, Patrick *Kavanagh (1904–67) affirmed the value of the parochial and the way the local place can stand for the world. The rural vision of John *Montague (1929–) and Seamus *Heaney (1939–) is deeply indebted to Kavanagh's sense of place. The *Ulster Protestant planter myth of John *Hewitt (1907–87) also emphasises the value of rootedness in affirming identity. By contrast, Louis *MacNeice (1907–63) is 'an example of uprootability', a 'tourist in his own country', a celebrant of plurality and hybridity. MacNeice's poetics of displacement has had a marked influence on succeeding northern poets such as Michael *Longley (1939–), Derek *Mahon (1941–), Paul *Muldoon (1951–), Ciaran *Carson (1948–), and on southern poets such as

Brendan *Kennelly (1936–) and Paul *Durcan (1944–), who have all been involved in a radical rewriting of the sense of home and identity. Irish poetry since the 1970s has also seen the emergence of significant women's voices: from the south, Eiléan *Ní Chuilleanáin (1942–), who specialises in a disturbing realism, Eavan *Boland (1944–), who has explored the position of women in Irish national tradition, and Nuala *Ní Dhomhnaill (1952–), who combines Gaelic, feminist and modernist perspectives; and, from the north, Medbh *McGuckian (1950–), who has been hailed as an exponent of 'the woman's sentence'. E.K-A.

police. Ireland's first uniformed, professional police force was set up in *Dublin in 1786. One of its successors, the Dublin Metropolitan Police (established in 1836), was absorbed into the *Gárda Síochána (the police force of the *Irish Free State formed in 1922) in 1925. Throughout the nineteenth century, a number of police forces were created in Ireland by successive British governments. Robert Peel, chief secretary for Ireland (1812–18), established a paramilitary, cavalry constabulary, the Peace Preservation Force, which served in several Irish counties from 1814 to 1836. These were the first policemen to be nicknamed 'Peelers', a term used to this day in parts of Ireland. In 1836, the Peace Preservation Force was absorbed into the Irish Constabulary.

This force, formed in 1822 and renamed the *RIC in 1867, played an active role in monitoring and suppressing *nationalist movements and agrarian agitation. Recruited largely from the Irish small-farming class, this armed force was often unpopular in its 100-year history. Having borne the brunt of the *IRA's campaign during the *War of Independence, the RIC was disbanded in 1922 and replaced by the *RUC in *Northern Ireland and the Gárda Síochána in the Irish Free State. The armed, largely Protestant RUC was perceived as a sectarian and *unionist force by Northern Ireland *Catholics and suffered heavy casualties at the hands of *republican paramilitaries during the *Troubles. The RUC has recently been reformed as the Police Service of Northern Ireland. In contrast to the RUC's troubled history, the unarmed Gárda Síochána quickly integrated into society in the south. B.G.

political parties. The Irish political party system has shifted since independence between a multi-party system dominated by two large parties and what has been called a two and a half party system – *Fianna Fáil, *Fine Gael and a very small *Labour Party. The periods 1922–27, 1943–61 and 1987 to the present might be considered multi-party.

Characterising the major political parties in an international context has often led to a confusing use of labels. The two major parties Fianna Fáil and Fine Gael, polling between 65% and 80% collectively, are relatively conservative compared to the European social democratic tradition, but both, especially Fianna Fáil, have a populist cross-class appeal.

Since the 1990s, the party system has become more fragmented. Fianna Fáil as the largest party has captured the centre, with an average support base of around 40%, and has formed governments of the centre-left (with Labour) and centre-right (with the *Progressive Democrats).

As the traditional *Civil War divisions between Fianna Fáil and Fine Gael have diminished, Fine Gael has struggled to find an identity other than being anti–Fianna Fáil and has not won a general election since 1982.

The Labour Party has traditionally played the role of third party. Its average level of support at around 11% is very low by west European social democrat standards. The party is often divided between those who prioritise serving in government (almost inevitably with FG) and those who advocate a Labour left-leaning government.

*Sinn Féin is the only party to organise on an all-Ireland basis. The party offers a mix of militant nationalism and left of centre radicalism. Since the 1994 *IRA cease-fire, it has rapidly grown to become the largest nationalist party in *Northern Ireland and the fourth largest party in the *Republic.

The Progressive Democrats, a typically European right of centre liberal party, is the most conservative Irish party on economic matters but relatively liberal on social issues.

The Green Party, a typical European ecology-based party, is small but has developed a strong parliamentary presence both in the *Dáil and the European parliament.

The *Socialist Party has had a single deputy in the Dáil since 1997. It is well to the left of the Labour Party and, though small, has a strong campaigning presence in parts of *Dublin. J.D.

Poor Laws. Nineteenth-century poverty relief legislation. The Poor Law Act (1838) divided Ireland into 130 poor law districts (or unions), each with a *workhouse where those who required aid had to live. Entry was at the discretion of the local poor law guardians and financing came mostly from a tax levied on local landowners. During the *Famine, the Poor Law Extension Act allowed the granting of discretionary relief outside of the workhouse. The legislation was formally abolished by the *Irish Free State in the 1920s and in *Northern Ireland in 1946. P.E.

Power, Albert G. (1881–1945). Sculptor. Born in *Dublin, Power was a pupil of Oliver *Sheppard and John Hughes at the Metropolitan School, Dublin. Power produced many privately commissioned portrait busts. In 1922, he was commissioned by the government to make posthumous portrait busts of Arthur *Griffith and Michael *Collins. His work is in many public buildings and churches in Ireland, including the cathedral of Christ the King, Mullingar, and Cavan cathedral. His modelled head of the dying Terence *MacSwiney in the Cork Public Museum and the 1798 Pikeman Memorial at Tralee, County *Kerry, are among his best-known works. A regular contributor to the *Royal Hibernian Academy from 1906, Power was regarded as the major Irish sculptor by 1940. M.C.

Poynings' Law (1492). A law requiring royal approval before the Irish *parliament could be summoned. Introduced by Henry VII's Lord Deputy Edward Poynings, Poynings' Law also mandated that all legislation initiated by the Dublin parliament required the prior assent of the monarch and privy council in London. Although the original intent of the law was to curb the power of independent subjects such as the Earls of Kildare, eventually Poynings' Law subordinated the Irish parliament to its English counterpart. The statutory subservience of the Irish parliament became increasingly unacceptable to 'patriots' during the course of the eighteenth century. Poynings' Law was substantially modified in Ireland's favour by the Reform Act of 1782 and made irrelevant by the Act of *Union (1800). J.P.

Praeger, Robert Lloyd (1865–1953). Naturalist. Born in Holywood, County *Down, and educated in *Belfast, Praeger was appointed librarian of the *Royal Irish Academy in 1903. During 1909–11, he conducted an intensive and innovative survey of Clare Island, County *Mayo, and later helped to found the journal the *Irish Naturalist*. Praeger was librarian of the *National Library of Ireland (1920–24) and his works include *The Way That I Went* (1937) and *The Natural History of Ireland* (1950). S.A.B.

pre-Christian Ireland (c.7000 BC–c. AD 432). Lack of contemporaneous sources leaves us with little knowledge of the socio-political system of ancient Ireland. By analysing the legendary history as found in later sources, a tentative reconstruction can be made. The *Celtic and Celticised groups had dominance in all areas of Ireland by the second century BC. Their assimilation with earlier communities had given rise to the tribes known as Iverni ('land-people'). A strong new group from Britain, called Lagini ('spear-men'), however, extended their power in Ireland from eastern coastal areas. In succeeding generations of further migrations from Britain, culminating in refugees from the Roman legions in the first century AD, the Lagini strengthened their position. Another powerful group, the Venii ('tribesmen'), probably originating in south-western Britain and north-western Gaul, came to ascendance in the south of Ireland. The Venii, moving northward from the southern coast, pushed the Ivernian tribes to the west.

In or about the fourth century AD, the Lagini seized the ancient ritual centre of *Tara (in County *Meath) from the Ivernian tribe of Lugunii, but within a century the Lagini were driven south from Tara by the Venii. Having taken control of the rich and strategic plain of *Meath, the Venii moved northward against the strongest of the Ivernian tribes, the Uluti ('bearded men'), whose ritual centre was Isomnis (later Emhain Macha in County *Armagh). At the dawn of the fifth century AD, therefore, the most powerful groups in the country were the Uluti (by then known as Ulaidh), the Lagini (then Laighin) and two groups of the Venii (those known as *Connachta in the north midlands and those known as Eoghanacht in *Munster). Other groups of Iverni (then Érainn) still controlled some territories, especially toward the western seaboard.

The Connachta were by now the strongest group in Ireland and to gain both wealth and prestige they undertook raids on western Britain, seizing booty and captives. Their celebrated king in the fifth century, Niall Naoighiallach (Niall of the Nine Hostages), was in fact the son of a famous Connachta raider-king and of a British slave-woman. The reign of Niall saw the two most significant events in pre-Christian Ireland: the capture of the boy *Patrick (the future *saint and patron of Ireland) in a huge raid on the British coast and the taking of Emhain Macha from the Ulaidh by the Connachta.

The culture which prevailed in Ireland up to the coming of Christianity was basically *Celtic in its outlines and – just as its language reflected a quite old variant of Celtic – the customs of Ireland seem to have been more antiquated than those of neighbouring countries. Whereas the Celts abroad had developed systems that gave increased influence to the nobility in the affairs of the kings, in Ireland the kings were still holy rulers. A king was considered the intermediary between his people and otherworld powers; his inauguration reflected this with elaborate rituals and his life was circumvented by taboos. These ideas permeated all social life. There were probably well in excess of a hundred local kings in Ireland, each ruling over his own territory but linked in confederations with the over-kings who ruled the major clans and their satellites. The *druids, who played a major role in public ceremonies, were an important adjunct to royal power. D.OH.

prehistoric Ireland. *The Stone Age* was the period of man's first known appearance in Ireland as a hunter-gatherer, c. 8000 BC. Around the fourth millennium BC, farming communities emerged who lived in wooden houses and built megalithic tombs of stone. Stone was also the predominant material used for tools and weapons. The period was succeeded by the Bronze Age before 2000 BC.

The Bronze Age was a period from the late third millennium to c.500 BC, when bronze was the predominant material used for tools and weapons. At this time, however, a considerable amount of gold was used for neck ornaments such as lunulae and gorgets. Preceded by a short-lived Copper Age, the Bronze Age witnessed widespread trade along Europe's Atlantic coasts, massive production of axes and swords and, toward its end (c. 700 BC), bronze vessels and trumpets bespeaking riches. Burials were largely in single graves, often under low barrows and, to about 1200 BC, often accompanied by decorative food vessels and urns (for cremated bone). Metal extraction and agriculture were widely practised, but deteriorating weather conditions saw the development of *bogs (which were to cover one-sixth of Ireland) and the rise of *hill-forts. Cooking places known as *fulachta fiadha* also came into use at the time.

The Iron Age followed the Bronze Age around 500 BC and is named after the material favoured at the time for implements and weapons. It saw the introduction of the *La Tène art style of the continental *Celts and the widespread use of the earliest known form of the Irish language. The scattered population may have lived in *raths and *crannógs, occasionally resorting to *hill-forts. Contacts were maintained with the late Roman empire and one piratical raid on Roman Britain brought a young St *Patrick to Ireland as a slave. The Iron Age way of life continued into the medieval period. P.H.

Prendergast, Kathy (1958–). Artist. Using a wide range of media and the techniques of mapmaking, Prendergast often employs the theme of her own body's geography. Born in *Dublin, she studied at the National College of Art, Dublin, and Royal College of Art, London. In 1995, Prendergast represented Ireland at the Venice Biennale and was awarded the prize for outstanding young artist. M.C.

Presbyterians. Members of the *Protestant church of *Scotland who flooded into the north of Ireland throughout the seventeenth century. Although the *Plantation of Ulster (1609–25) is usually perceived as the key period of Presbyterian settlement in Ireland, Scottish immigration peaked in the last third of the century with as many as 10,000 arriving each year in the 1690s. Despite the prominent role Presbyterians played in preserving Protestant Ireland during the Williamite War of 1688–91, they were reduced to second-class status by the *Penal Laws of 1704. By the latter part of the eighteenth century, the rapidly expanding commercial centre of *Belfast had become the *de facto* economic and cultural capital of Irish Presbyterianism. Presbyterian radicalism and animosity toward the *Anglo-Irish ascendancy led to the founding of the Society of *United Irishmen in Belfast in 1791. The movement was brutally crushed in the *Rebellion of 1798. Yet many Presbyterians remained liberal until the Liberal Party under *Gladstone came to support *home rule in the 1880s. From this point onward, the vast majority of Presbyterians have been ardent *loyalists. Although Presbyterian numbers in the Irish *Republic are tiny, in *Northern Ireland they constitute the largest denomination in the Protestant community. J.P.

presidents of Ireland (Uachtaráin na hÉireann). Although Éamon *de Valera was formally elected 'Príomh-Aire' (chief minister) of the *Sinn Féin cabinet in the first *Dáil Éireann in 1919, it was decided for public relations reasons in connection with his trip to America in that year to refer to him generally as 'President of the Irish Republic', while seeking international recognition. It was claimed that he occupied a somewhat similar position to the president of the United States as the father of the nation. Great play was also made of de Valera's status as 'President of the Irish Republic' at the time of the *Civil War (1922–23), by the defeated *republican forces. But the term *president of Ireland*, or *Uachtarán na hÉireann*, in the modern period refers to the office established by Article Twelve of the *Constitution of 1937.

The president is elected by direct vote of the people for a seven-year term. At the end of a first term, the president may nominate him- or herself for a second seven-year term, but he or she is eligible for re-election once only. Candidates must be at least 35 years of age and Irish citizens. If only one candidate is nominated he or she can be declared elected without proceeding to a ballot in an election. The president cannot hold any other office or position and shall not be a member of either House of the *Oireachtas.

The president may not leave the state while in office, save with the consent of the government. A president may be impeached for stated misbehaviour by either House of the Oireachtas and, if the charge is sustained, may be removed by a two-thirds vote of both Houses. The president, on the nomination of Dáil Éireann, appoints the *Taoiseach and, on the nomination of the Taoiseach (with previous Dáil approval), appoints the members of the government.

Most of the president's powers and functions are symbolic but the president may 'in his absolute discretion refuse to dissolve Dáil Éireann on the advice of a Taoiseach, who has ceased to retain the support of a majority of Dáil Éireann' (Article 13.2.2). The president is empowered (in Article 26.1.1), after consultation with the Council of State, to refer a bill that has been passed by the Oireachtas to the Supreme Court for a decision on the question as to whether such bill or any part of it is unconstitutional. The supreme command of the Defence Forces is vested in the president and all commissioned officers of the Defence Forces hold their commissions from the president (Article 13).

The first president under the new Constitution of 1937 was Douglas *Hyde (Dubhghlas de hÍde) (1860–1949), who held office for the first seven-year term from 1938 to 1945 without any election being held. Hyde was succeeded in 1945 by Seán T. Ó Ceallaigh (1882–1966). Ó Ceallaigh continued for a second seven-year term as president without an election. In 1959, he was succeeded by his old mentor, Éamon de Valera (1882–1975), then aged 77 and almost blind. De Valera was re-elected for a second term in 1966. In 1973, he was succeeded by Erskine H. *Childers (1905–74), the second *Protestant to hold the office. When President Childers died of a heart attack in November 1974 – the first and only president to die in office – he was succeeded by Cearbhall Ó Dálaigh (1911–78), a former chief justice who was, at the time, a judge of the European Court. Ó Dálaigh came into conflict with the then *Fine Gael/*Labour government specifically because of his decision to refer Emergency Legislation to the Supreme Court in the autumn of 1976. He resigned in protest to protect the dignity and independence of the office in an unprecedented constitutional crisis.

Ó Dálaigh was succeeded by Patrick J. Hillery (1923–), a County *Clare career politician with Fianna Fáil who, as foreign minister, had negotiated Ireland's entry into the EEC (European Economic Community; now the *European Union) in 1972 and then became Ireland's first EEC Commissioner (for Social Affairs) in 1973. Hillery continued for a second term in 1983, by common consent. The election of Professor Mary *Robinson (1944–) in November 1990 marked a significant development in Irish presidential politics, not only because she was the first woman to hold the office but also because she was effectively the first non-Fianna Fáil nominee for the presidency to win it. Ms Robinson resigned the presidency a few weeks before her seven-year term expired in 1997, to take up a position as UN Human Rights Commissioner in Geneva. She was succeeded by another legal academic, Professor Mary *McAleese, of Queen's University in *Belfast. Ms McAleese won the election by the largest majority of any presidential winner to date. N.ÓG.

Proclamation of the Irish Republic. Formal declaration of an independent Irish *Republic at the beginning of the 1916 *Easter Rising. Drafted and read aloud outside the General Post Office by Patrick *Pearse on Easter Monday 1916, the proclamation announced the establishment of a provisional government and called the people of Ireland to arms. It explained the role of the *IRB, the *Irish Citizen Army and the Irish *Volunteers in the rebellion. British rule in Ireland was rejected as illegitimate and the Irish Republic was proclaimed as a 'Sovereign Independent State'. Expressing advanced egalitarian ideas, the document guaranteed 'religious and civil liberty, equal rights and equal opportunities' to all citizens and a future national assembly, 'elected by the suffrages of all her men and women'. The completed document was signed by all seven members of the Military Council of the IRB – Patrick Pearse, Thomas *Clarke, James *Connolly, Seán *MacDiarmada, Éamonn *Ceannt, Thomas *MacDonagh and Joseph *Plunkett – and 1,000 copies were printed in Liberty Hall on Easter Sunday. P.E.

Progressive Democrats (PD). Political party. The Progressive Democrats was founded in 1985 by Des O'Malley after his expulsion from *Fianna Fáil. O'Malley focused his initial policy programme on three key issues, neoliberal economics, liberal social policy and a less rigid stance on *Northern Ireland than Fianna Fáil. The party polled 11% in its first general election (1987) but has since struggled around 5%. The Progressive Democrats formed a coalition government with Fianna Fáil in 1989, in 1997 and in 2002. Mary Harney became leader in 1993. J.D.

Progressive Unionist Party of Northern Ireland (PUP). Political party. Formed in 1979, the PUP became prominent during the 1990s representing militant *loyalists, most notably the *UVF during the *peace process. The party attracted roughly 3% of the popular vote at the height of its popularity. M.M.

Proportional Representation (PR). Voting system. The *Republic of Ireland uses PR by means of the Single Transferable Vote (STV) with multi-member constituencies (districts) for all elections except the president. PR is used in *Northern Ireland for local council elections, European parliament elections and for the Northern Ireland assembly, but not for elections to the British House of Commons. The system allows voters to vote for every candidate contesting a specific election by marking their preferences as 1, 2, 3, etc., on their ballots. To win outright, a candidate needs a certain percentage (a quota) of first-preference votes (25% plus 1 in 3-seat constituencies, 20% plus 1 in a 4-seat, etc.). If no candidate reaches the quota after the votes are counted, then the candidate with fewest first-preference votes is eliminated and his or her first-preference votes are distributed proportionately to the other candidates who were given second preference on the eliminated candidate's ballots. This system continues until one candidate reaches the required quota of votes and is elected. If a candidate gets more votes than the quota, once they are deemed elected their 'surplus' votes are also distributed to try and ensure that no vote is 'wasted'. Despite the fact that district sizes are relatively small (between three and five seats), PR in the Irish context produces a reasonably representative parliament. The larger parties on average get about 3% more seats than they would under a purely proportional vote system, *Labour gets about 1% fewer seats and the smaller parties are much more underrepresented. J.D.

Protestant Reformation. See **Reformation in Ireland.**

Protestants. *Henry VIII's *Reformation did not initially affect Catholic worship in Ireland. By contrast with England, where there was already a large group of followers of the continental reformers Luther and Zwingli, in Ireland very few of the indigenous population were Protestants by the time Edward VI succeeded his father *Henry VIII as king of England. During Edward's short reign (1547–53), Protestantism was officially introduced in Ireland, but made little progress. Not until the *Elizabethan religious settlement of 1560 (Acts of Supremacy and Uniformity) was a stable Protestant regime established. From then on, the *Church of Ireland was Protestant, in line with the moderate reform of the English church, and the entire population was bound by law to adopt the new religion. The campaign of evangelisation was lacklustre, however, and the native Protestant coterie remained small. The majority of the Protestant community in late-sixteenth-century Ireland comprised newcomers from England who were officials, soldiers and planters. Little effort was made to communicate the Protestant doctrines through the language and culture of the majority of the Irish population.

With the foundation of Trinity College in 1592, a more systematic Protestant campaign began in Ireland, but by then the majority of the island's population was committed to the *Catholicism of the counter-Reformation. In response to their minority position, Protestants in Ireland developed their own distinctive mentality. Not only were the articles of the Church of Ireland more puritan or radical than the English counterpart, but such prominent figures as James Ussher, the Church of Ireland archbishop of *Armagh, propounded that the Protestant religion was the true successor to the pristine *Christianity of the era of St *Patrick in Ireland. The arrival of substantial numbers of Scottish Presbyterians as settlers in the *Ulster Plantation of the early seventeenth century consolidated Protestantism in Ireland.

The turmoil of the 1640s steeled the resolve of Irish Protestants to withstand challenges to their political and social position and forged greater self-identity among the *Presbyterians. After the *Cromwellian Settlement of the 1650s, a consolidated Protestant community emerged. The older and newer Protestants merged to become the politically and economically privileged class, while Catholics and dissenting Protestants, mainly Presbyterians, were excluded from power and position. After the victory of the Protestant *William of Orange over the forces of the Catholic King *James II, the *Penal Laws further consolidated and protected Protestantism.

Protestants showed little inclination to convert Catholics and dissenters. In the eighteenth century, Irish Protestants such as Jonathan *Swift, Oliver *Goldsmith, William and Thomas *Molyneux, George *Berkeley and Edmund *Burke made significant contributions to *literature, philosophy, *science and political thought. Among the Protestant political ascendancy, a strong movement for Irish legislative independence reached its climax in *Grattan's parliament of 1782.

The Presbyterian community experienced various difficulties caused by internal factionalism, but the gradual relaxing of the religious and social restrictions benefited them as well as Catholics. Methodism, which came to Ireland in the mid-eighteenth century, achieved impressive growth as an Anglican reform movement, but the following century formed its separate Protestant church.

The earlier nineteenth century was marked by a revitalisation of the Protestant churches and an attempt to convert Catholics in a movement known as 'the second Reformation'. The proselytism proved a relative failure, but heightened sectarian tensions at a time when the Catholic church itself was undergoing what has been called a 'devotional revolution'. The payment of *tithes by Catholics and Presbyterians to the Church of Ireland caused huge resentment culminating in a tithe war, which effectively ended the tithes system in the 1830s. By the mid-nineteenth century, the Protestant population had declined and the political turmoil in Ireland convinced Prime Minister William *Gladstone to introduce a bill for the disestablishment and disendowment of the Church of Ireland in 1869. Nevertheless, a more coherent Protestantism emerged into the twentieth century. The term Protestants now referred to those of the reformed faiths and not just to Anglicans. Presbyterians and Anglicans were brought closer by their shared experience of evangelical education and preaching in the nineteenth century. Politically, this heightened sense of Protestant identity was influential in the growth of *unionism. After *partition, Protestants found themselves in very different milieux, north and south. While the political force of Protestantism has been extremely significant in the north, its influence in the south has been less so. The growth of the ecumenical movement in the later twentieth century has been very important for relations within the family of Protestant faiths and between them and the Catholic church. C.L.

Q

Quakers. *Protestant sect. Quakers first arrived in Ireland during the 1650s as members of *Cromwell's armies. They had emerged in England as a radical Protestant sect during the civil war. Formerly known as the Society of Friends, the sect was reorganised by George Fox in 1669. The Quakers' pacifism and belief in social equality made them prominent in several nineteenth-century reform movements and their Central Relief Committee (1846–49) played a vital role in providing humanitarian aid during the Great *Famine. S.A.B.

R

radio. The *Irish Civil War delayed the establishment of an indigenous radio service until 1 January 1926. The Dublin Broadcasting Station (known as '2RN') was established as a state-run public service, financed by licence fees and advertising revenues and housed within the Department of Posts and Telegraphs.

Despite a chronic shortage of funds, inadequate facilities and transmission hours, 2RN's first director, Séamus Clandillon, and his small staff sought to preserve and promote Ireland's cultural heritage. Their regular programming included traditional *music performances, *Irish-language lessons, children's shows, domestic and farming instruction, as well as weather, news and other service bulletins. In August of its first year, the service broadcast live coverage of the All-Ireland *hurling final between *Galway and *Kilkenny. Later live broadcasts of sports events, especially sports commentaries by the legendary Micheál Ó Hehir, greatly increased interest in the new medium. Religious broadcasts, such as the weeklong coverage of the *Eucharistic Congress of 1932 held in *Dublin, which allowed the pope's voice to be heard in Ireland for the first time, showed radio's potential for mass communication. Efforts to make radio more widely available (i.e., to improve reception) in rural Ireland included the operation of a second station in *Cork from 1927 to 1930 and the establishment of a high-power transmitter at Athlone, County *Westmeath, in February 1933.

On the eve of the Second World War, approximately one in four families in the *Irish Free State held radio licences and for many tuning in to their favourite programmes on Radio Éireann (as the service was called from 1937 until its merger with television in 1966) was compulsive listening. The most beloved of these was the quiz show *Question Time*, hosted by popular MCs such as Joe Linnane. Its successor, *Take the Floor*, a programme on Irish *dance music with the Gárda *Céilí Band that lasted nearly 25 years, owed its popularity to the storytelling abilities of host Din Joe (Denis Fitzgibbon).

After the Second World War, *Taoiseach Éamon *de Valera, the politician who most capitalised on radio's political power, revived a plan for a shortwave service to bolster national defence and communicate with Irish *emigrants abroad. The change of government in 1948 ended construction on the new high-power station at Athlone, but Radio Éireann's resources had already been doubled. Among the most significant improvements in the service were the addition of a full-time repertory company, the Radio Éireann Players, directed by Roibeárd Ó Faracháin, and the development of new programmes aimed at reconnecting the *Republic to the outside world and stimulating intellectual debate, such as *World Affairs* and the *Thomas Davis Lectures*.

High-quality radio reception became available throughout the country in the 1960s and in the 1970s Irish radio, now part of Radio Telefís Éireann (*RTÉ), addressed social issues, including women's rights. RTÉ also set up Raidió na Gaeltachta, an Irish-language station, in 1972. The network's political scope and coverage of events in *Northern Ireland was, however, circumscribed by Section 31, a government ban against reporting on proscribed organisations such as the *IRA. On the music front, pirate radio stations such as Radio Caroline became increasingly popular among listeners, especially youth, tired of traditional radio. In the late 1970s, RTÉ responded by launching a pop music station, Radio 2, and undertaking community radio broadcasts from mobile studios, but this did not diminish interest in the pirate stations. In the late 1980s, commercial radio was legalised in the Republic and RTÉ radio now competes directly with numerous commercial and local community stations throughout the country. E.M.

Raftery, Anthony (1779–1835). Poet. Born in County *Mayo, Raftery became blind at an early age and spent most of his life in the East *Galway area. He was often described as a folk-poet, but this does not do justice to the sophistication of his best work. He wrote vicious political poetry, which gave vent to the feelings of the oppressed pre-*Famine poor. He also wrote tender love poetry and penned celebrations or laments on local events. In 'Eanach Dhúin' he recounts the drowning of nearly 20 people in Lough Corrib in 1828 when a sheep put a hole in the rotten bottom of a boat. His celebrated 'Máire Ní Eidhin' is a more conventional love song praising a local beauty. Many of these songs are still sung today. He had immense influence on the later *Literary Revival, particularly on Douglas *Hyde and Lady *Gregory. A.T.

Raleigh, Sir Walter (1552–1618). English adventurer and explorer. After organising several unsuccessful expeditions to colonise North America (1584–87), Raleigh was granted a huge estate in *Munster composed of land confiscated by the English crown following the second Desmond rebellion (1579–83). On this land, he undertook to plant English settlers, but he sold the estate in 1602. The next year, Raleigh was imprisoned on suspicion of conspiring against King James I and, following an unsuccessful expedition to South America in 1616, he was executed. Raleigh is widely credited with introducing the potato and tobacco to Europe. S.A.B.

rath. A circular area surrounded by one, two, or three circular embankments with a ditch outside – sometimes called a *lios*. Inside stood one or two houses, the home of a well-off farmer of early medieval Ireland. Built largely between AD 500 and 1000, raths once numbered between 30–50,000. While according to *folklore, the fairies – whose forts they were thought to have been – protected them for generations, modern agricultural development is destroying them at an ever-increasing rate. They are often called ring-forts, which is somewhat of a misnomer, as they would rarely if ever have been strong enough to defend. P.H.

Rathcroghan. Ancient royal site on the plains of County *Roscommon. Many prehistoric and early medieval earthen monuments (mounds and *raths) were found here. According to legend, Rathcroghan was the seat of King Ailill and Queen Maeve of *Connacht, whose pillow talk led to the old Irish epic, **Táin Bó Cuailnge (The Cattle Raid of Cooley)*. The limestone cave, Oweynagat (Cat's Cave), with two *Ogham stones, was thought to have been an entrance to the underworld. P.H.

Rea, Stephen (1948–). Actor. Born into a *Protestant family in *Belfast, Rea has worked extensively on the stage in Dublin, London and New York. In 1993, he won a Tony Award for his role in *Someone Who'll Watch Over Me* by Frank *McGuinness on Broadway. In 1980, together with playwright Brian *Friel, he founded the *Field Day Theatre Company in Ireland. Rea, who has a distinct understated acting style, has starred in many of director Neil *Jordan's films, including *Angel* (1982), *The Crying Game* (1992) – for which he earned an Oscar nomination – *Michael Collins* (1996), *The Butcher Boy* (1997) and *The End of the Affair* (1999). In 1983, he married Dolours Price, who was convicted for her part in the 1973 bombing of the Old

Bailey Court building in London. She was released after serving eight years in prison. M.E.

Rebellion of 1641. Gaelic Irish and Old English revolt (also known as the Confederate War) during the reign of King Charles I. In 1641, the native Irish in *Ulster used the conflict between Charles I and the English parliament to retake land that had been confiscated from them during the *Ulster Plantation. Under the leadership of the Irish chieftain Rory O'More, a rebellion was planned for 23 October 1641. Plans to take *Dublin Castle were betrayed, but the rebels led by Sir Phelim O'Neill succeeded in taking control of Ulster. The native Irish rebels next marched south toward Dublin. They laid siege to Drogheda in November 1641 and joined in an alliance with the Old English lords of the *Pale to form a Confederate *Catholic army. An oath was taken to defend the Catholic faith and the rights of the crown, and by the autumn of 1642, the rebels controlled all the country, except for Dublin, a handful of towns and the Scottish areas of Ulster.

An assembly known as the *Confederation of Kilkenny was organised in 1642 to govern rebel-held territory. The alliance between the Gaelic Irish and Old English was, however, marked by considerable confusion and squabbling. The Old English lords had been reluctant allies from the outset and had joined the rebellion only out of fears that a parliamentarian victory in England would usher in a new phase of plantation in Ireland. They were anxious for an early settlement to the conflict that ensured toleration for their religion and the promise that their lands would not be confiscated. The native Irish had already lost their territory and were prepared to fight to the end for the return of their land and the restoration of *Catholicism to its pre-*Reformation status. These differences in objectives widened as the war progressed. In June 1646, the Confederates under Owen Roe *O'Neill won a major battle at Benburb, but the rebels failed to take advantage of the victory. The Catholic Confederation was formally dissolved under the terms of the Second Ormond Peace in 1649. Following the execution of King Charles I in January 1649, Oliver *Cromwell led a force to Ireland to deal with what he believed was a Catholic religious uprising, and within three years all Irish resistance had been crushed. P.E.

Rebellion of 1798. Major uprising considered one of the most violent events in Irish history. By the second half of the eighteenth century, middle-class resentment among *Leinster Catholics and *Ulster *Presbyterians had reached a critical point because of their ongoing exclusion from political participation on religious grounds. This exclusion was particularly offensive in light of the middle-class' increasing numbers and wealth. Influenced by the ideals of the Enlightenment and the *American Revolution, the Irish middle-class found the political discrimination increasingly intolerable.

Inspired by the events of the *French Revolution, modern Irish *Republicanism was born in *Belfast and *Dublin in 1791 with the foundation of the Society of *United Irishmen. The organisation sought the radical reform of parliament and complete *Catholic Emancipation. Within a few years, the United Irishmen had grown to several hundred thousand members. In 1795, one of the movement's founding fathers, Wolfe *Tone, travelled to Paris to persuade the French that Ireland was ready to support an invasion. Early in 1798, the movement's leadership decided to risk an indigenous rising without French assistance. The preparations were, perhaps fatally, disrupted by the arrest of most of the Leinster leadership at Oliver Bond's house in Dublin on 12 March 1798. Nonetheless, plans for a major insurrection proceeded.

The republicans' seizure of the mail coaches

from Dublin to the provinces signalled the onset of the rebellion on 23 May 1798. The linchpin of the rebel plan was a *coup de main* directed at the capital, supported by risings in the surrounding counties. An unfortuitous leak of information quashed the planned attack on the capital, effectively dooming the insurrection. In the province of Leinster, the risings of *Carlow, *Kildare, *Meath and *Wicklow were quickly crushed. Only in *Wexford did the rebels meet with success. They managed to take most of the county, but failed to carry the rebellion north and west. On 21 June 1798, the decisive battle of the Wexford campaign was fought at *Vinegar Hill and the republican army was routed. It is at this point (the brief, if underrated, risings in *Antrim and *Down having been put down in early June) that the Rebellion of 1798 is traditionally considered to have ended. Yet, rebel armies remained in the field until mid-July (while a belated, small-scale French landing in Mayo was overwhelmed in September) and, in fact, organised resistance continued in all four provinces until 1803. Thirty thousand died in what is considered the bloodiest Irish rebellion in history. J.P.

rebellions. See **risings and rebellions**.

Redmond, John Edward (1856–1918). Politician. Born in County *Wexford, Redmond was educated at Trinity College and entered *parliament in 1881. He represented Waterford City in Westminster from 1891 until his death in 1918. After the split following the *O'Shea divorce case in 1891, Redmond led the *Parnellites. When the *Irish Parliamentary Party reunited in 1900, he became its chairman.

Redmond was a skilful political tactician. He participated in the *Land Conference (1902) which precipitated the *Land Act of 1903, effectively ending *landlordism. He also negotiated legislation that established the National University (1908). His party's votes helped to lay the foundation of the British welfare state and to reform the House of Lords. In 1912 Redmond secured the introduction of the third *home rule bill, which was suspended at the onset of the *First World War in 1914.

Redmond immediately pledged *nationalist support for the war effort. He believed that common sacrifice among Irishmen would convince *Ulster *unionists of nationalist loyalty to the empire. The threat that the British would introduce conscription in Ireland frustrated his attempts to increase voluntary recruitment among Irish nationalists, and his support for the war turned out to be a major political miscalculation. Militant *republicans worked throughout the war to subvert his leadership. The *Easter Rising of 1916 shattered Redmond's political world. He had tacitly accepted temporary *partition of some parts of Ulster, and his attempt in the Irish Convention (1917–18) to secure home rule made little headway when he suddenly died, his reputation with contemporaries seriously damaged. L.MB.

Referendum of 1998. The 1998 *Good Friday Agreement provided for referenda to be held in Ireland, North and South, on 22 May 1998, to ratify the agreement and to make the necessary changes to the Irish *Constitution. The response in the *Republic of Ireland to the agreement was very positive as both *nationalist parties in *Northern Ireland and all the major southern parties called for a 'yes' vote. The 'yes' vote of 94.4% reflected the consensus in the campaign. In Northern Ireland there were in reality two separate referendum campaigns. Within the nationalist community, the campaign, like that in the south, reflected the widespread support for the agreement. In contrast, within the *unionist community there was a bitter campaign, beginning from the moment the agreement was finalised. The 'no' lobby included not only those who had opposed the talks process but also a faction within the pro-agreement *Ulster Unionist Party. Those unionists who supported the deal promoted it in a very generalised way, as a hope for peace, and criticised those unionists who opposed the agreement of living in the past and of failing to offer a viable alternative. Unionist opponents of the deal were, however, the ones to set the agenda for the public debate. They argued that aspects of the agreement were so detrimental to their position that unionists should not support it even if it did in parts meet some unionist demands. The agreement was ultimately passed with 71% support in the north, but with a very marginal majority within the unionist community. J.D.

Reformation (Protestant) in Ireland, the. Failing to obtain a papal annulment of his marriage with Catherine of Aragon so that he could take another bride, produce a male heir and secure the continuity of the Tudor monarchy, *Henry VIII, in 1534, broke with Rome. Both the English and Irish parliaments endorsed the king's religious rebellion, declaring him head of the church in both islands. Less attached to Rome than English co-religionists, Old English feudal lords, descendants of *Normans who first arrived in twelfth-century Ireland, and Gaelic chiefs easily accepted the new state religion. Like the governing class in other parts of Europe, they believed that public acceptance of the prince's religion fostered public order and tranquillity. In addition, the transfer of spiritual leadership from pope to king did not alter the day-to-day worship of the faithful. While Henry confiscated the wealth and property of monasteries, retaining much of the spoils for the royal treasury and parcelling out the remainder to loyal followers among feudal lords and Gaelic chiefs, his rejection of papal supremacy did not replace traditional *Catholic rites and rituals.

The many cultural, political, religious and social consequences of Henry's break with Rome did not become apparent until the reigns of his son, Edward VI (1547–53), and daughter, *Elizabeth I (1558–1603), when the established church in Ireland gradually became theologically and, to a large extent, liturgically *Protestant. For the Irish majority, especially its Gaelic component, these efforts to make them truly Protestant were a more pernicious form of colonialism than previous English military and political adventures in their country. By planting Scottish *Presbyterians in *Ulster, James I (1603–25), Elizabeth's successor, diversified Irish Protestant sectarianism and intensified religious tensions. From the late fifteenth until the close of the eighteenth century, Irish rebels at various times called on Catholic powers on the continent, Spain and, later, *France, to assist their resistance to English rule. Failed seventeenth-century Irish insurrections, aspects of the English Civil Wars between parliament and Stuart kings and France's Louis XIV and his enemies, diminished Catholic political power, social influence and property. Oliver *Cromwell's brutal retaliation against the Irish Catholic *Rebellion of 1641 dispossessed many Catholics of their possessions. Anti-Catholic *Penal Laws that followed King *William III's 1688 victory over King *James II stripped Catholics of remaining civil, political and religious liberties and most of their remaining lands.

The Protestant Reformation fragmented Ireland into exclusive cultural communities, erecting impenetrable barriers against assimilation. Reacting to British imposed limitations on Irish sovereignty and trade, eighteenth-century Irish Protestants developed a local patriotism, expanded the authority of their parliament and eliminated economic restrictions. Some *Anglo-Irish Protestants and Ulster Presbyterians created the Society of *United Irishmen. Influenced by the *French Revolution, it tried but failed in 1798 to create an Irish republic. But following the Act of *Union

(1800), the vast majority of Protestants and Presbyterians abandoned an Irish for a British identity, vigorously opposing what was overwhelmingly an Irish Catholic *nationalism.

Protestant conquerors in Ireland had little respect for the 'crude and rude' natives and consequently they not only failed to convert them to their religion, Protestantism, but also alienated them socially and politically. The Old English and the native Irish became welded into one cultural nation loyal to Catholicism. In the nineteenth century, Daniel *O'Connell expanded that Catholic-rooted cultural identity into a political nationalism that eventually resulted in a twenty-six-county Irish Republic. L.J.MC.

religion in Ireland. Religion has been a powerful social and cultural force in Ireland since the earliest times. *Pre-Christian religion was strong enough to persist in many parts of the country long after the arrival of St *Patrick and other missionaries. Patrick began the campaign of conversion of the Irish in the fifth century and within 300 years a structured church was established throughout the island, with allegiance to Rome. The Irish *Catholic church's dynamism in the seventh and eighth centuries was such that it produced many missionaries who evangelised in western and central Europe, while at home there was an efflorescence of Christian art and learning. Later, the *Viking raids on Ireland may have contributed to religious dislocation in the short term, but the Scandinavian settlers eventually became Christianised and made a significant religio-cultural contribution. By the twelfth century there was an identification of the Christian church with the centres of political power at local and regional levels.

Religious reform entered late-medieval Ireland from abroad. The influence of the various orders of monks, *nuns and friars, many brought in under the auspices of the *Anglo-Normans, was significant. In return for the grant of the lordship of the island from the pope, the Norman kings beginning with *Henry II undertook to foster the interests of the Catholic church in Ireland. A system of smaller parishes based on manors developed in areas under Norman influence, while in the Gaelic regions the hereditary clerical class, very closely tied to the ruling elites, continued to dominate the more amorphous parish units. Within this framework of fractured ecclesiastical jurisdiction, a rich and variegated religious life subsisted among laity and clergy, surviving well into the post-*Reformation period.

By the seventeenth century, following the Reformation, alternative systems of worship in the Anglican and Catholic churches had developed. While relations between the denominations were equable enough, at times of turmoil such as the 1640s and the 1650s sectarian strife was inevitable. By the time of the Restoration, the consolidation of church identities, which had been evolving during the previous 100 years, was complete. Within the broad Protestant movement in Ireland, sects that were called 'dissenting' emerged. The Irish followers of Calvin became organised into worshipping units and communities, mostly in *Ulster. Their need for a separate organisation had not been as pressing in the earlier seventeenth century, because Calvinist ethos had dominated the Church of Ireland, but now that the established church had lost its puritanism, circumstances had changed. Even though *Presbyterianism was a minority religion (in comparison to the mainstream Church of Ireland and the Roman Catholic church), its strong social and community base would sustain it throughout the trials of the eighteenth century. The *Penal Laws of the eighteenth century aimed at suppressing the political and social power of the Catholics and dissenters but not necessarily their religious identities. Besides the Presbyterians and the *Quakers, other religious denominations developed in Ireland, including smaller sects such as the

*Huguenots (also Calvinist) and the *Palatines, who sought refuge from oppression on the continent. Methodism grew impressively from the mid-eighteenth century to become a major Protestant sect. The broad Protestant movement in Ireland also includes separate worshipping communities of Lutherans, Baptists and Evangelicals. *Jews have had a continuous presence in Ireland since the Middle Ages. More recently there are members of non-aligned religions such as the Baha'i faith, Jehovah's Witnesses and Mormonism in Ireland. Followers of Greek Orthodoxy and Islam have been expanding in numbers since the late twentieth century. Despite improved inter-church relations since the *Second Vatican Council, traditional religious divisions have flared up from the beginning of the *Troubles (1969) in *Northern Ireland, giving rise to ongoing sectarian violence. C.L.

Repeal. Movement to repeal the Act of *Union (1800) and restore a national *parliament in Ireland. Daniel *O'Connell saw Repeal of the union as the ultimate goal of the modern Irish *nationalism he had constructed during the *Catholic Emancipation struggle. Although he never specified what Repeal entailed, O'Connell's agenda indicated a democratic constituency, voting by secret ballot, electing an Irish parliament that would accept the British monarchy and enact legislation protecting civil liberties and the separation of church and state.

In 1843, O'Connell melded anti-*tithe fury and temperance movement enthusiasm into a massive agitation to repeal the union. Although he did not attract the same degree of support from bishops, priests and lawyers that he had for Catholic Emancipation, O'Connell did enlist the talents of *Young Ireland and their newspaper, the *Nation, an articulate voice for cultural nationalism.

Throughout the country on Sunday afternoons, hundreds of thousands listened to O'Connell's promise that by year's end, Sir Robert Peel, the British prime minister, would concede Repeal rather than face the possibility of physical force. But Peel, who had granted Catholic Emancipation to preserve the union, had no intention of dismantling it. He flooded Ireland with troops and the authorities banned O'Connell's Monster Meeting scheduled for Clontarf on 8 October 1843. To avoid violence O'Connell called off the meeting.

Repeal fervour persuaded Peel to initiate legislation to woo Irish Catholic clerical and middle-class support for the union. However, O'Connell's manoeuvring and the *Famine aborted many of his reforms. After O'Connell's death, Repeal faded in the face of physical force *republicanism and *home rule nationalism. L.J.MC.

Republic of Ireland. While the symbols of king and empire found no place in Bunreacht na hÉireann (*Constitution of Ireland) 1937, neither did the term *republic*. The term had sacrosanct connotations for Irish revolutionaries who believed that the 'Irish Republic' was baptised in the blood of the 1916 *Easter Rising martyrs and made imperishable through the sacrifices of the volunteers in the *War of Independence (1919–21) before being 'betrayed' in 1922. Éamon *de Valera had no doubt that the changes to the *Anglo-Irish Treaty his government had brought about between 1932 and 1936 had made the twenty-six-county state a 'de facto' republic. He was aware, however, that the revered term could be proclaimed only in a unified thirty-two-county context. He also naively believed that avoiding 'republic' in the constitution showed regard for *Ulster *unionist sensitivity.

Under de Valera's *External Relations Act (ERA) of 1936, the British monarch as head of the *Commonwealth was 'authorised' to act on behalf of the state in international affairs, in such matters as 'the appointment of diplomatic and consular representatives and the conclusion of international agreements ... as and when advised by the Executive Council to do so'. This ingenious, if equivocal, constitutional position exposed de Valera to the taunts of his political opponents. Challenged in the *Dáil (17 July 1945) about the status of the state, he stoutly maintained that it 'possesses every characteristic mark by which a republic can be distinguished or recognised'. He supported his argument by quoting the definition of 'republic' from various dictionaries and encyclopedias. However, this characteristically pedantic exposition did not end public confusion on the issue and provoked derisive references to 'the dictionary republic'.

In February 1948, a *Fine Gael-led coalition under John A. *Costello replaced the de Valera administration. Two parties in the coalition, *Clann na Poblachta – composed of erstwhile militant *republicans under Seán *MacBride – and *Labour, were likely to support the repeal of the ERA. But the apparently sudden conversion of Fine Gael, traditionally a strong Commonwealth party, to that view was surprising. Costello fervently hoped that a clear-cut constitutional position, ending the 'inaccuracies and infirmities' of the ERA, would satisfy national honour, placate intransigent republicans and finally 'take the gun out of politics'.

At a press conference on 7 September 1948, during a visit to Canada, Costello confirmed that his government would repeal the ERA and secede from the British Commonwealth. This seemingly arbitrary development, so far from home and without regard to diplomatic protocol, caused quite a stir. There was controversy for a long time as to whether the move reflected pre-existing cabinet policy or was an impulsive action on the part of the *Taoiseach.

The *Republic of Ireland (ROI) Bill was introduced in the Dáil in November 1948. Its purpose was to repeal the ERA, to declare that the description of the state should be the Republic of Ireland, and to enable the president to exercise the prerogatives of a head of state in the area of foreign relations. This meant that the state had a more clearly defined position, internationally.

Initially, the British government was irritated by Costello's unilateral move, but the view eventually prevailed that the Irish should remain a 'non-foreign' people. In arriving at this decision (a welcome one for the Irish community in Britain), the British were influenced by the Commonwealth voices of Australia, Canada and New Zealand. The British and Irish governments safeguarded through legislation the rights of their respective citizens in each other's countries. Existing trade preferences were maintained and Irish affairs continued to be handled by the Commonwealth Relations office.

The ROI Act served to reinforce *partition. Ulster unionists, raising the rallying cry that *Northern Ireland was in danger, gained seats in the 1949 general election. More importantly, the British parliament passed the Ireland Act of 1949 as a response to the ROI Act. It guaranteed that Northern Ireland would not cease to be part of the United Kingdom 'without the consent of the Parliament of Northern Ireland'. The Ireland Act provoked much noisy but ineffective anti-partition rhetoric in the south.

The ceremonial flourishes that marked the inauguration of the Republic of Ireland, on the symbolic date of Easter Monday 1949, were somewhat diminished by the absence of *Fianna Fáil from the celebrations. Die-hard republicans, who still did not recognise the legitimacy of the state, contemptuously dismissed the notion of a twenty-six-county republic. There were further criticisms that the ROI Act was unnecessary, fruitless and precipitate – entrenching the Ulster unionists in their position, destroying a possible bridge

(Commonwealth membership) to unity, leaving the gun in politics and resulting in a futile and frustrating anti-partition campaign.

While republics such as India regarded their status as compatible with continuing membership of an increasingly flexible Commonwealth, perhaps the painfully close relationship with Britain made Irish nationalists feel that even a tenuous constitutional link suggested subordination. Consequently, the adoption of unambiguous and formal sovereignty was imperative.

Post-1949, while the *description* of the state was the 'Republic of Ireland', the constitutionally unchanged *name* of the state remained '*Éire, or in the English language, Ireland' (Art. 4). Many northerners still referred to the defunct 'Free State'. Unionists and British politicians and journalists persisted in using the term *Éire* for the twenty-six-county state.

Irish citizens in general were slow to incorporate the description 'Republic' into everyday usage. Ideology apart, it sounded awkward or pretentious. People preferred 'the South' or 'the twenty-six counties' or simply 'the country'. Ambiguously, 'Ireland' is still commonly used to denote the twenty-six-county state, as well as the whole island. In recent years, the acronym ROI has crept into commercial usage (after the pattern of UK). For most Irish people, however, the primary connotation of the 'Republic of Ireland' is that of the state's international *soccer team. It should be noted that, prior to 1949, 'republican' was synonymous with being a separatist, whereas in subsequent decades it has come to mean a militant supporter of a united Ireland.

Thus, various issues of nomenclature have arisen from the 1949 legislation. But the enactment of the 'Republic of Ireland' was essentially cosmetic, ushering in no change in society or the economy. J.A.M.

Republic of Ireland Act (1948). Legislation by which the twenty-six-county Irish state was declared a republic, independent of the British *Commonwealth. After the 1948 general election, a group of five parties formed the first coalition (inter-party) government under *Taoiseach John A. *Costello, a member of *Fine Gael. During a formal visit to Canada by Costello in September 1948, protocol difficulties highlighted Ireland's confusing constitutional position internationally. While the 1937 *Constitution had given the country all the semblance of a republic and the *External Relations Act had associated the country with the Commonwealth, the British government held that the relationship established in the *Anglo-Irish Treaty of 1921 remained unchanged. On 7 September Costello announced his intention to clarify these issues by taking *Éire out of the British Commonwealth and declaring it a fully independent republic.

The Republic of Ireland Bill was introduced into the *Dáil in November 1948 and was passed with the support of the *Fianna Fáil opposition on 21 December. The act repealed the Executive Authority (*External Relations) Act of 1936 and declared the name of the state to be the Republic of Ireland. It also transferred to the president all the functions relating to external relations that had been carried out by the crown. The act came into force on Easter Monday, 18 April 1949. P.E.

Republicanism. Dominant political philosophy underlying militant Irish *nationalism. Irish republicans traditionally trace the origins of their political philosophy to the era of the *French Revolution and, in particular, to the *United Irish movement and its leader Wolfe *Tone. The United Irish movement, under the influence of the revolutionary ideas coming from *France and with some minimal French assistance, sought to organise an armed uprising in 1798. The *Rebellion of 1798 was unsuccessful but was historically important in establishing a nonsectarian radical current in Irish nationalism, which sought to unite *Catholic, *Protestant and Dissenter around a programme of Irish independence from Britain. The term *Irish republican*, also originating from this date, has suggested a willingness to use force to achieve an independent united Irish republic.

There was always a more conservative and often exclusively Catholic current in Irish nationalism, and republican organisations have used Catholic imagery and symbolism in their writing. However, Irish republicanism had also had a more radical and secular current. During the first half of the nineteenth century, in the aftermath of the failed Rebellion of 1798 and the passing of the Act of *Union (1800), Catholic nationalism was the stronger force in Ireland, focused in particular on Daniel *O'Connell's campaign for *Catholic Emancipation. After the Great *Famine of the 1840s, the *IRB (also known as the *Fenians) was formed in 1858 as a secret organisation. It launched an ineffective rising in 1867 and a bombing campaign in England. The IRB also worked by infiltrating other nationalist organisations such as the *Gaelic Athletic Association (GAA) and the *Gaelic League. As Ireland moved into a more radical era in the early twentieth century, with the Irish and nationalist *Literary Revival, the new labour movement and the *women's suffrage campaign, the IRB became more active particularly within *Sinn Féin and the *Volunteer movement. It was instrumental in launching the *Easter Rising of 1916 and the *War of Independence in 1919.

Even though the split in Sinn Féin and the *IRA over the *Anglo-Irish Treaty in 1921 is often analysed as a split within the republican strand of politics, it can be more accurately seen as a return to the long-term division between republicanism and more conservative nationalism – a split which had been briefly hidden by the unique Sinn Féin alliance from 1917 to 1921.

After *partition, these two strands of conservative nationalism and radical (and often armed) republicanism were the key competitors for nationalist support in *Northern Ireland. In the south, the lines were less clear. *Fianna Fáil split from anti-treaty Sinn Féin, leaving a largely marginalised party behind. Fianna Fáil used the subtitle 'The Republican Party', and initially pursued a radical programme. They also, however, reflected and absorbed the conservative Catholic ethos of the new state – abandoning the traditional commitment to secularism.

The modern meaning of republicanism in Irish society entered public debate to a limited extent in the 1980s when some politicians used the term to justify the introduction of a series of socially liberal and occasionally controversial laws, on contraception, gay rights, *divorce and abortion information. In this instance, the term republicanism was used in a purely secular sense, to emphasise the separation of church and state within the Republic of Ireland, and was not focused on the question of partition. However, this ideological use was largely rhetorical and disappeared when the liberalising agenda (apart from abortion) was largely achieved in the 1990s.

The most significant contemporary debate on republicanism revolves around the conflict and *peace process in Northern Ireland. Sinn Féin has, following the IRA cease-fire of 1994, sought to re-establish republicanism as the dominant strand of Irish nationalism, but without the use of force to achieve its aims. The party's vote in Northern Ireland increased dramatically after the IRA cease-fire and, for the first time, in June 2001 Sinn Féin won the support of a majority of nationalists in Northern Ireland. In the Republic of Ireland, Sinn Féin has increased its support from a very small base, and offers a more left-wing, more strongly nationalist and more secular policy package than the mainstream parties. J.D.

Restoration, the. The re-establishment of the monarchy in Britain and Ireland, in 1660. The term is often used to refer to the reign of the restored king, Charles II (1660– 85), and the first three years of the reign of *James II (1685–89). Irish Catholics hoped that the Restoration would lead to the reversal of many aspects of *Cromwell's rule, especially the *Cromwellian Land Settlement, which had greatly reduced the amount of property Catholics controlled. Charles II could not afford to alienate *Protestant opinion in Britain or Ireland, however, and thus under the Irish Acts of Settlement (1662) and Explanation (1665), this settlement was left, with some exceptions, as it was. By 1685, Catholics owned only about 20% of the land, compared with the approximately 60% in 1641. Other features of Cromwell's administration that were retained in the Restoration era in Ireland included a large military establishment, taxation innovations (e.g., the introduction of customs and excise) and the discontinuation of outmoded feudal courts, such as the Court of Wards and Liveries. Generally, Charles II's reign was a peaceful, reasonably prosperous period, with the only notable period of religious persecution occurring at the end of the 1670s. By 1685 the population of Ireland was close to two million. J.C.

Reynolds, Albert (1932–). Politician, leader of *Fianna Fáil and *Taoiseach, 1992–94. Born in County *Roscommon, Reynolds had a successful entrepreneurial career and in 1974 he became involved in electoral politics, winning a seat on *Longford County Council. In 1977, he was elected Fianna Fáil TD for Longford. In the *Dáil, he became a supporter of Charles J. *Haughey. When Haughey became Fianna Fáil leader and Taoiseach in 1979, Reynolds was appointed minister for posts and telegraphs and for transport and power. In later Haughey cabinets, he would serve as minister for industry and commerce (1987–88) and for finance (1988–91).

Albert Reynolds

Reynolds resigned as finance minister in November 1991, following a break with Haughey over revelations of questionable business deals in which the latter had been implicated. When Haughey resigned due to those scandals in February 1992, Reynolds took over as leader of Fianna Fáil and as Taoiseach in the Fianna Fáil–*Progressive Democrat coalition government. In his early days as Taoiseach, Reynolds' image as a simple, decent man helped him restore the country's faith in government. In November, however, political wrangling between the coalition partners led to the collapse of the government and Reynolds called a general election. That election resulted in the loss of several Dáil seats for Fianna Fáil while the *Labour Party doubled its representation. After long negotiations, those two parties formed a new coalition government and Reynolds continued as Taoiseach.

The coalition faced difficulties in getting its domestic policies passed into law. However, Reynolds and his Tánaiste Dick Spring, the leader of the Labour Party, were instrumental in furthering the *Northern Ireland *peace process. Some of the most dramatic steps in the process took place during his tenure as

Taoiseach, and his active involvement in the peace process is Reynolds' greatest contribution to the course of Irish history. Most notably, Reynolds' good working relationship with British Prime Minister John *Major resulted in the two leaders' *Downing Street Declaration of December 1993, which opened the way for *Sinn Féin to join the Northern Ireland peace talks. The declaration led to the historic *republican and *loyalist cease-fires of 1994.

In November 1994, tensions surrounding a controversial appointment to the high court forced Reynolds to resign his position, but he continued to serve as acting Taoiseach until December. Many worried that, without his leadership, the peace process might falter, but his successor, *Fine Gael leader John *Bruton, kept the process on track. T.D.

RIC (Royal Irish Constabulary). The main Irish *police force in the nineteenth and early twentieth centuries. In 1822, the chief secretary of Ireland, Henry Goulburn, established a paramilitary police force which was responsible for preventing and detecting crime throughout most of Ireland. Originally known as the County Constabulary, it was organised on a provincial basis and constituted the first professional, national police in the United Kingdom. In 1836, the force was reorganised as the Irish Constabulary. Housed in hundreds of barracks throughout the country, the constabulary became the 'eyes and ears' of the *Dublin Castle authorities, providing them with an intimate knowledge of the state of law and order, including the activities of illegal secret societies. In 1867, the Irish Constabulary was the main body responsible for the suppression of the *Fenian rebellion, for which it received the epithet 'Royal'. Its loyalty was further demonstrated during the *Land War, when the RIC constituted the authorities' main weapon against the *Land League and the National League. During the *War of Independence, the *IRA killed hundreds of members of the force in its campaign against British rule. The RIC was disbanded in 1922 and replaced by the *Gárda Síochána in the *Irish Free State and the *RUC in *Northern Ireland. B.G.

Rice, Edmund Ignatius (1762–1844). Founder of the Irish *Christian Brothers. Born near Callan, County *Kilkenny, Rice became a merchant in *Waterford in 1779. Following his wife's death, he was drawn to religious life. From his own resources he founded a free school for poor boys in Waterford and soon a network of these schools was set up in Ireland and England. In 1820, the pope formally approved Rice's religious community as an order of *Christian Brothers. Rice devoted the rest of his life to developing the schools in which a Catholic ethos pervaded the whole teaching programme. He was beatified by the Catholic church in 1996. C.L.

risings and rebellions. Perhaps in no other country has the role of rebellion played so central a part in the development of a national identity. Often distorted by myth, the persistent theme has been that of the native Irish resisting Anglo-Saxon invasion and conquest. Modern examples date from the failed Geraldine Rising (1534–35), which featured a formidable alliance of Gaelic and *Anglo-Norman lords headed by 'Silken Thomas' Fitzgerald resisting *Henry VIII's efforts to impose direct rule on Ireland. Other doomed rebellions against London's centralising efforts were led by the Desmond branch of the Fitzgeralds in *Munster 1569–73 and 1579–83. The rising of the *Ulster lords under Hugh *O'Neill resulted in the *Nine Years War (1593–1603), and the later *Flight of the Earls 1607, which effectively ended Gaelic resistance to English direct rule. Subsequently, large numbers of English and Scottish *Protestants were 'planted' on the lands confiscated from the defeated northern lords. A new era of resistance in which *religion merged with politics was ushered in with the *Rebellion of 1641 and the subsequent *Confederate War (1641–53). An alliance of *Anglo-Irish and Gaelic Catholics nominally supporting Charles I against a Puritan parliament succeeded in controlling much of Ireland before being brutally suppressed by *Cromwell between 1650 and 1653. Widespread confiscations and the further settlement of Protestant tenants followed. Modern Irish *republicanism was born in the 1790s with the formation of the Society of *United Irishmen. The group, which was influenced by the enlightenment and advocated secular and democratic *nationalism, organised the *Rebellion of 1798, the single bloodiest event in Irish history (30,000 dead). Smaller-scale republican risings by Robert *Emmet in 1803, *Young Ireland in 1848 and the *Fenians in 1867 were easily quashed. The linear descendants of the Fenians, the *IRB, took advantage of Britain's distraction with the *First World War to rise in *Dublin on Easter Monday, 1916 (the *Easter Rising). Although the republicans were compelled to surrender within a week, the execution of the principal leaders, including Patrick *Pearse and James *Connolly, dramatically swung public opinion in favour of revolutionary separatism. The final act came in the *Anglo-Irish War for independence (1919–21), in which Michael *Collins' genius for unorthodox warfare convinced the British that a negotiated peace was preferable to continued fighting, despite their superiority in numbers and firepower. J.P.

Riverdance. Internationally renowned show of traditional Irish *music and *dance. *Riverdance* integrated traditional and modern music, choral singing and Irish dancing in a spectacular manner. With music and lyrics written by Bill Whelan, and produced by Moya Doherty and directed by John McColgan, the show was originally an interval act for the 1994 Eurovision Song Contest. The initial piece was expanded and opened as a two-hour show at the Point Theatre in *Dublin in February 1995 and made international stars of step-dancers Michael *Flatley and Jean Butler. The show has since divided into several touring groups and has played to millions of people worldwide. P.E.

Roberts, Thomas Sautelle (1760–1826). Painter. Born in *Waterford, Roberts studied at the Dublin Society Schools. In 1778, he took up the name and profession of his dead brother Thomas, probably completed his brother's unfinished paintings, and went on to become the best-known Irish romantic landscape painter of the period. He was a founding member of the *Royal Hibernian Academy. M.C.

Robinson, Lennox (1886–1958). Playwright and theatre director. Robinson was born in Douglas, County *Cork. His first play, *The Clancy Name*, appeared at the *Abbey Theatre in 1908. As the Abbey's producer and manager (1909–14 and 1919–23), Robinson was responsible for opening the *Peacock Theatre. His trendsetting plays, such as *The Round Table* (1922) and *Portrait* (1926), influenced other early-twentieth-century Irish dramatists. In the 1930s, Robinson worked in the United States and later edited *Lady Gregory's Journals 1916–1930* (1946) and *The Oxford Book of Irish Verse* (1956). S.A.B.

Robinson, Mary (1944–). President of Ireland, constitutional lawyer, UN High Commissioner for Human Rights. Between 1969 and 1975, Robinson was a professor of law in Trinity College, *Dublin, and was involved in many high-profile constitutional cases in the area of human rights, especially on women's rights. She was also a member of *Seanad Éireann representing Trinity College from 1969 to 1989. Robinson campaigned unsuccessfully as a *Labour Party candidate for the *Dáil in the 1977 and 1981 general elections. She resigned

Mary Robinson

from the party in 1985 in protest against *unionist exclusion from negotiations on the *Anglo-Irish Agreement (1985). Although she never rejoined the Labour Party, she was Labour's nominee in the Irish presidential election of 1990. Robinson, elected as the country's first woman president, greatly increased the profile of the presidency. Her controversial visits to *Northern Ireland, including a brief meeting with *Sinn Féin leader Gerry *Adams in 1993 (at a time when the Irish government would not meet him), created tension with Labour Party leader Dick Spring. She resigned from the presidency 11 weeks early to become the UN High Commissioner for Human Rights (UNHCHR). Robinson developed a very high international profile for the UN's work on human rights but felt frustrated at the limited funds available to her office. She withdrew a threat to resign only when the UN secretary general promised to improve funding and staffing at the UNHCHR. In September 2002, Robinson relinquished her UN post to work with another human rights organisation. J.D.

Roche, Kevin (1922–). Architect. Born in *Dublin and educated at University College, Dublin, Roche is considered Ireland's most famous ex-patriot architect. After graduation, he entered Michael *Scott's growing practice, which promoted international-style architecture. Roche left Dublin, went to London and then to Chicago, where he earned a postgraduate degree in architecture at the Illinois Institute of Technology. Working in Eero Saarinen's firm (noted for the TWA terminal at Kennedy Airport and the Gateway Arch in St Louis), Roche designed such sleek, modern, commercial premises as the Ford Foundation headquarters, New York (1968); the Knights of Columbus Building, New Haven (1968); United Nations Plaza, New York (1969–75); and the Oakland Museum, California (1961–68). A.K.

Roche, Stephen (1959–). Cyclist. Born in *Dublin, Roche won cycling's three biggest races in 1987 – the Tour de France, the World Championship and the Giro d'Italia. Roche excelled as an amateur, winning the Rás Tailtean, Ireland's premier cycling event, in 1979. He also won the coveted Paris-Nice race in his first year as a professional in 1981. B.D.

ROSC. Exhibition society. Founded in 1967, ROSC showed contemporary international work alongside new and old Irish works of art every four years until 1988. Organised by the architect Michael *Scott with the advice of American curator James Johnson Sweeney, the first two shows were hung by painter Cecil King. Difficulties in choosing the 1984 Irish selection signalled a growing tension between international modernism and a more localised expressionism. This, plus limited funding and the establishment of the *Irish Museum of Modern Art, led to its dissolution. M.C.

Roscommon, County. Inland county in the province of *Connacht. Comprising 983 square miles, the county has a population of 53,803 (2002 census). The economy of the county is *agriculture, primarily cattle. Its many market towns include Boyle, Strokestown, Castlerea, Elphin and the largest, the county capital, Roscommon town. Roscommon is the Anglicised form of *Ros Comain*, 'the wood of Coman', referring to the site of the monastery of the early *saint, Coman. Enclosed on the south, west and north by counties *Galway, *Mayo and *Sligo, County Roscommon forms an extensive, low and rather flat plateau, broken at its northern end by the Curlew Mountains that rise to 863 feet. Its eastern border is Lough Ree, one of the River *Shannon's largest lakes.

The plains of Roscommon were the heart of ancient Ireland. Here lies *Rathcroghan, where the legendary Queen Maeve lived with her consort Ailill and from where she launched her cattle raid on Cooley in County *Louth, as told in the great Irish epic **Táin Bó Cuailnge (The Cattle Raid of Cooley)*. The nearby Carnfree was the inauguration place of the ancient kings of Connacht, including Ireland's last high king, Rory *O'Connor. Clonalis House, near Castlerea, displays the O'Connor family heirlooms. The *Normans built significant *castles at Rinndoon on Lough Ree, Ballintober and Roscommon town. The county's finest ecclesiastical monument is the great Cistercian abbey in Boyle, built between 1161 and 1220. The abbey lies beside a small river, which drains into Lough Key, one of Ireland's most beautiful lakes. Roscommon was badly affected by the *Famine of the 1840s and a Famine Museum in Strokestown dramatically tells the story of the county's plight. Distinguished natives of Roscommon include Sir William *Wilde, great polymath and father of Oscar; Dr Douglas *Hyde, poet and first president of Ireland; and Percy *French, a poet and songwriter. Kilronan is the burial place of Turloch *Carolan (1670–1738), blind *harpist and reputed composer of the melody to which 'The Star-Spangled Banner' is sung. P.H.

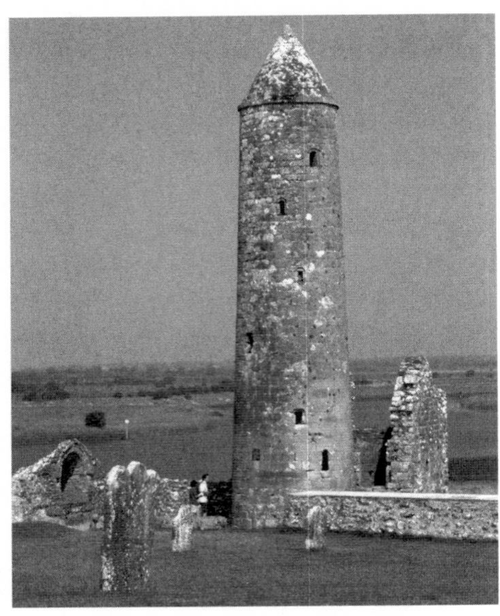

Round Tower, Clonmacnoise, County Offaly

Rosenstock, Gabriel (1949–). Poet in the *Irish language and translator. Rosenstock is author of more than 80 books, including original poetry, translations, children's literature, haikus, plays, novels and short stories. His original poetry is marked by a sympathy for the marginalised and the unusual. The best of these are selected in *Rogha Rosenstock* (1994). He has translated from German, Spanish and Flemish and has added the smell of the earth and the taste of what might have been in his translations into Irish of the poetry of Seamus *Heaney. A.T.

round towers. Pencil-like towers with conical caps, reaching up to 100 feet. Built between 950 and 1238, 65 are known from early monastic sites, their Old Irish name *cloigtheach* suggesting their use as bell towers. But the normal positioning of the door about ten feet above ground has led to much speculation about their use as refuges, hermits' towers, beacons, or monastic treasuries. P.H.

Rowsome, Leo (1903–70). Musician. Rowsome was an *uilleann piper, pipemaker and *music revivalist. The third generation of pipers (his own father was a pipemaker), Rowsome formed one of the earliest **céilí* bands in 1922, revived the Dublin Pipers' Club in 1936 and was a founder of *Comhaltas Ceoltóirí Éireann in 1951. An award-winning piper, he played internationally and taught at the Dublin School of Music. His 1936 textbook on piping is still in use today and his recordings, now on CD, remain classics. F.V.

Royal Dublin Society (RDS). Organisation for the promotion of arts and sciences. One of the oldest bodies of its kind in the world, this organisation originated in 1731 and became the Royal Dublin Society in 1820. It aimed to improve agricultural and manufacturing techniques by carrying out research, encouraging industries and promoting the arts and sciences. In 1877, parliament transferred responsibility for several of the society's activities to the state and several Irish cultural institutions owe their origins to the RDS, including the *National Botanic Gardens, the *National Library and the *National Museum. The society received a special grant with which it purchased land at Ballsbridge for equestrian and social events. The RDS complex presently comprises 10 multipurpose exhibition halls which host sporting events, concerts and conferences. (Address: Merrion Road, Ballsbridge, Dublin 4. Web site: *www.rds.ie*.) S.A.B.

Royal Hibernian Academy of Arts. Founded in *Dublin in 1823, the academy holds an annual exhibition of carefully selected artists' works, which is one of the highlights of the Dublin social scene. It also holds separate artists' exhibitions throughout the year. Its premises were destroyed by fire in 1916, but its new home in the Gallagher Gallery (Ely Place) enhances any work it displays. (Address: 15 Ely Place, Dublin 2. Web site: *www.royalhibernianacademy.com*.) P.H.

Royal Irish Academy (RIA). The premier learned institution in Ireland. Founded in *Dublin in 1785, the RIA houses an important collection of Irish *manuscripts, including the **Cathach*, and publishes proceedings in the natural sciences and humanities, as well as other journals and monographs. (Address: 19 Dawson Street, Dublin 2. Web site: *www.ria.ie*.) P.H.

Royal Irish Academy of Music. From its beginnings in *Dublin in 1848, the academy has strived to improve and develop musical performance and teaching in Ireland. It also played a role in founding the Municipal School of Music, which it administered from 1895 to 1910. Since 1898 the academy has operated a nationwide examination system, which now examines 30,000 students annually. In December 1998, a new Traditional Irish Music Examination syllabus was officially launched by the president of Ireland, Mary *McAleese. (Address: 36–39 Westland Row, Dublin 2. Web site: *www.riam.ie*.) S.A.B.

RTÉ. Irish National Public Service Broadcasting Organisation. Radio Telefís Éireann is a statutory corporation that provides a comprehensive service on *radio (since 1926) and on *television (since 1961), as well as a large range of ancillary services. Under the terms of the Broadcasting Act, 1960, and subsequent legislation, RTÉ policy is guided by a government-appointed committee (the RTÉ Authority). The day-to-day running of RTÉ is the responsibility of the Executive Board, which reports to the RTÉ Authority. S.A.B.

RUC (Royal Ulster Constabulary). The *Northern Ireland *police force from 1922 to 2001. Approximately 93% of the officers of the RUC were *Protestant. Since the recent *Northern Ireland conflict (the Troubles), the force has been continually criticised by the *nationalist community. During the period

1969 to 1975, the British army had primacy in security matters and the RUC was relegated to a relatively minor role in combating the *IRA. The force was extremely unpopular with nationalists and, due to reforms following the Hunt Report of 1969, considerably weakened by the stress of reorganisation. Beginning in 1975, a greatly expanded (from about 3,000 to about 8,500 with nearly 5,000 'reserves') and heavily militarised RUC gradually resumed the main responsibility for security. The force was criticised for its brutal interrogations of IRA suspects, especially in the late 1970s, and for operating a *shoot-to-kill policy in the early 1980s. In the early 1990s, collusion with *loyalist paramilitaries – which some explained as the result of rank-and-file indiscipline and secret intelligence operations – came to light. The RUC lost 301 members during the Troubles since 1969 and were responsible for the deaths of (approximately) 52 people; of these, 30 were civilians, mostly *Catholics. Following the signing of the *Good Friday Agreement in 1998, a commission was established to make recommendations on the future of the RUC. The Report of the Commission, the Patten Report, was published on 9 September 1999 and made 175 recommendations, including a total overhaul of the force. In 2001, the RUC was disbanded and replaced by the Police Service of Northern Ireland (PSNI). M.M.

rugby. A popular outdoor field game that originated in England. Students from English public schools introduced rugby football (from which American football evolved) to Ireland and set up the first club at Dublin University in 1854. The game consists of two teams of 15 players. Rugby grew in popularity and various organisations merged in 1879 to form the Irish Rugby Football Union (IRFU), which administers the game nationally. The club game is popular around Dublin and throughout mid-*Ulster, but many regard *Limerick as rugby's spiritual home in Ireland.

Ireland competes annually in a Six Nations Championship, along with England, Scotland, Wales, France and Italy. A World Cup tournament takes place every four years. Rugby was traditionally played as an amateur sport, but the game in Ireland, following the trend in other countries, has become more commercialised with top international players now turning professional. Some of the great names of Irish rugby include Jackie Kyle, Jack McCarthy, Tom Kiernan, Willie John MacBride and Ollie Campbell. Even with many extra matches being played today, Mike Gibson's record of 69 international appearances for Ireland still stands. F.S.

Russell, George (William); AE (1867–1935). Writer, mystic and social reformer. Russell was born in County *Armagh and educated at the Metropolitan School of Art, Dublin. A member of the Irish Theosophical movement and the Hermeneutic Society, he also supported the cooperative movement and edited its journal, *The Irish Homestead*, and later, *The Irish Statesman*. Vice president of the Irish National Theatre Society, he resigned having clashed with its president, W. B. *Yeats. In 1916 he published essays and editorials outlining his spiritualism and pacifist *nationalism in *The National Being* (1916). His visions are described in the essays of *The Candle of Vision* (1918), and his novel *The Avatars* (1932) evokes the excitement of theosophists awaiting a new deity.

AE supported young writers generously and enjoyed modest success as a watercolourist. He refused a nomination to the *Irish Free State *senate and in 1932 settled in England, disillusioned with Ireland. M.S.T.

S

saints. People of outstanding holiness venerated by the *Catholic church. The early Christian era produced outstanding exemplars of sanctity, most notably St *Patrick, the apostle of Ireland, St *Brigid, the foundress of *Kildare, St *Colm Cille, the founder of monasteries in Ireland and at Iona in Scotland, and St *Columbanus, the great missionary to continental Europe. In addition, substantial numbers of holy people were popularly acclaimed as saints. Medieval hagiographies celebrated both the lives of the famous and the locally venerated who were the subject of devotion and dedications.

A fallow period for outstanding sanctity seems to have coincided with (though not necessarily caused by) the *Viking raids on Ireland. Significantly, the first Irish saints to be proclaimed by official papal canonisation, Saints Malachy and Lawrence O'Toole, both twelfth-century figures, were closely associated with reform of decayed ecclesiastical institutions. During the Irish counter-*Reformation, there was a new vogue for hagiography in which the lives of early Irish saints were presented as models of devotion and fortitude. Contemporaneously there emerged the cults of dozens of men and women who were regarded as having died for their Catholic beliefs in the *rebellions of the period and their lives were written up in the seventeenth-century martyrologies. In 1975, Oliver *Plunkett, archbishop of *Armagh, who was executed in 1681, was the first Irish saint to be canonised in modern times, and more recently, 17 Irish martyrs of the sixteenth and seventeenth centuries were beatified in 1992. Currently, many are promoting the causes for the canonisation of other martyrs, as well as more modern Irish exemplars of charity and piety such as Edmund *Rice and Matt *Talbot. C.L.

Samhain. *Celtic festival of the dead. The Irish word for November or winter, and literally meaning 'summer's end', Samhain marked the beginning of winter. Originally, the year was divided into two halves, the dark half beginning at Samhain and the bright half at Bealtaine. The November feast Samhain was when the otherworld was thought to intervene in this world. In *Christianity (which has appropriated much pagan *mythology), this pagan Celtic festival of the dead, celebrated on November eve, became the feast days of All Saints (All Hallows) and All Souls. *Samhain* was the title of an occasional journal associated with the Irish Literary Theatre in the first decade of the twentieth century. W. B. *Yeats launched *Samhain* in October 1901 to coincide with the third and final season of the Irish Literary Theatre. It contained the text of Douglas *Hyde's *Irish-language play *Casadh an t-Súgáin (The Twisting of the Rope)*, as well as reflective essays by Yeats, George *Moore and Lady *Gregory on the future of *theatre in Ireland. Subsequent issues reveal the tension between Yeats' aesthetic mission to create a poetic, avant-garde drama rooted in Irish mythology and many of his colleagues' desire for a realist, thoroughly national, drama celebrating the virtues of the native peasantry. E.S.M.

Saor Éire. Left-wing republican group. Formed in the 1930s, as a breakaway group from the *IRA, Saor Éire emerged in the 1960s after the IRA had ended its border campaign in 1962. It has had a shadowy existence and played little part in the *Northern Ireland conflict, despite claims to the contrary. T.C.

Sarsfield, Patrick (1655–93). *Jacobite military leader. Born into a gentry family in County *Kildare of both *Norman and Gaelic descent, Sarsfield served in France from 1675-1677. When James II adopted a policy of promoting Catholics in his army, Sarsfield became a leading commander in Ireland, and captured *Connacht for the Jacobite cause. An excellent cavalry commander, Sarsfield was, however, not fully appreciated by the French commanders who came to Ireland with James II. His omission from the command structure at the Battle of *Aughrim is generally seen as contributing to the Jacobite defeat. He came to prominence following Aughrim and his capture of the Williamite gun train at Ballyneety, County *Limerick, led to the defeat of the first siege of *Limerick. Sarsfield played a key role in defending the city and later in negotiating the Treaty of *Limerick. In exile, he became a *maréchal de camp* in French service and was killed at the Battle of Landen (in Flanders) in 1693. T.C.

Saunderson, Edward (1837–1906). *Unionist politician. Saunderson was the Liberal Party's MP at Westminster for his home county of *Cavan, between 1865 and 1874. Disillusioned with William *Gladstone, he gravitated toward the *Orange Order and the Tory Party. As MP for North *Armagh (1885–1906), he led the *Ulster unionist faction of the Tory Party and saw the defeat of two *home rule bills. In time, his loyalty to *landlordism came to be seen as an anachronism, but he is still remembered as one of the founders of Ulster unionism. M.M.

Sayers, Peig (1873–1958). Storyteller. Sayers was born in Dunquin, County Kerry, and married a Blasket. Islander. Celebrated for her autobiography *Peig* (1936), which begins by saying she has one leg in the grave, Sayers presents a life that is hard but in which the people are happy in their closeness to God. Her autobiography is a valuable social document describing the life of island women at the time. Its principal beauty is in its language, which is clear, precise and poetic, exactly mirroring the speech of its author. Her stories were collected by folklorists and are an excellent example of the kinds of narrative common to women. A.T.

science and technology. Ireland is more noted for its letters, which represent a distinctively Irish culture, than it is for its sciences, which developed in tandem with the evolution of modern science throughout Europe. Nevertheless, the list of prominent scientists who were either born or pursued careers in Ireland is impressive, as are the scientific contributions they made. In the seventeenth century, the list includes William *Molyneux (1656–98) and Robert *Boyle (1627–91), founder of the Royal Society, father of chemistry, discoverer of Boyle's Law and principal proponent of the new mechanical, corpuscular science based on the experimental method.

Unlike their Anglican-educated, amateur and theoretically inclined precursors, the most prominent Irish scientists of the eighteenth century were Dissenters or *Catholics educated on the continent (because of the *Penal Laws), professional and inclined toward the practical sciences, especially chemistry with its rich applications to the *brewing, *distilling, mining, pharmaceutical, *textile and vintage industries. Joseph Black (1782–99), the son of Belfast Scottish Dissenters and professor of chemistry at Edinburgh, discovered 'fixed air' (carbon dioxide), the specific heat of substances and the latent heat of fusion. Richard Kirwan (1733–1812) was the discoverer of chlorine bleaching and principal defender of phlogiston theory against Lavoisier's new oxygen theory. Bryan Higgins (1737–1818) founded a school of practical chemistry in fashionable Soho, where his lectures were attended by such luminaries as Benjamin Franklin, Edward Gibbon, Samuel Johnson and Joseph Priestley. He spent time in Russia (as chemist at the court of Catherine the Great) and Jamaica (as consultant to sugar and rum manufacturers). His patents included cement, oil lamp fuel, soda and mineral water, beer and a warm-air heating system. His nephew, William Higgins (1762–1825), had an acrimonious priority dispute with John Dalton, each claiming credit for the discovery of the atomic theory of chemistry.

As in the rest of Europe throughout the eighteenth and nineteenth centuries, science in Ireland became professionalised and institutionalised. Scientific bodies like the Dublin Philosophical Society (1684), the *Royal Dublin Society (1731) and the *Royal Irish Academy (1785) provided forums for scientists to meet and journals to disseminate their ideas. Trinity College's curriculum in mathematics and natural philosophy, modelled on the French methods of Laplace and Lagrange, was one of the most progressive in Europe. New professorships in engineering and other applied sciences were established. The newly formed Queen's Colleges at *Belfast, *Cork and *Galway attracted top scientists and mathematicians to Ireland. Ten of the top 30 Victorian physicists were Irish-born, including: George Francis Fitzgerald (1851–1901), who independently invented the Lorentz-Fitzgerald contraction, subsequently incorporated by Einstein into his theory of Special Relativity; George Gabriel Stokes (1819– 1903), the foremost Victorian theorist of hydrodynamics and elasticity; William Rowan *Hamilton (1805– 65), the best mathematician of the era; and Lord Kelvin (1824–1907), the pre-eminent Victorian physicist who pioneered the mechanical theory of heat, masterminded the laying of the first transatlantic telegraph cable and invented a host of scientific instruments.

The Victorian period in Ireland also produced remarkable technological innovations: Nicholas Callan (1799–1864) invented the induction coil (1836); Charles Parsons (1854–1931) invented the steam turbine (1884) and designed the first steam turbine powered ship, the *Turbinia* (1897), whose blueprint was quickly adopted for all major shipping. Thomas Grubb (1800–78) and his son, Howard (1844–1931), were the premier designers and builders of large telescopes in the world. Most remarkable, however, was the *Birr telescope, designed and built in Ireland in 1845 by William Parsons (1800–67), the father of Charles. With its mammoth 72-inch reflecting mirror, it was the largest telescope in the world until the Mt Wilson telescope was constructed in 1917 in the United States. With it, Parsons was the first to observe the spiral structure of nebulae and identify them as distinct galaxies.

The most prominent Irish scientist of the twentieth century was the physicist E. T. S. *Walton (1903–95), who won the Nobel Prize for his pioneering work in nuclear physics. John Joly (1857–1933) pioneered radiation treatment for cancer. Erwin Schroedinger, the founder of quantum wave mechanics, became a naturalised citizen having fled Nazi-occupied Austria and spent the years 1940 to 1956 at the Dublin Institute for Advanced Studies (DIAS) founded by Éamon *de Valera in 1940. John L. Synge (1897–1995), the nephew of J. M. *Synge and world-renowned relativity theorist and mathematician, was also at DIAS. The engineer Harry *Ferguson (1864–1960) revolutionised *agriculture with his redesign of the lightweight tractor. In 1945, Kathleen Lonsdale (1903–71), who worked on X-ray crystallography and showed that the benzene ring was flat, became the first woman fellow of the Royal Society, the society her compatriot Boyle helped found in 1660.

In the twenty-first century, Ireland continues to be an international centre of scientific and technological research and development. Most of the foremost global giants in the computer industry (including Adobe, Compaq, Dell, IBM, Intel and Microsoft) have major operations there. In 2000, Ireland became the largest net exporter of software in the world. M.L.

Scotland. Constituent part of the United Kingdom. A tremendous cross-fertilisation of people, culture and ideas has continued between Ireland and Scotland from the early *Christian era to the present. In fact, the name Scotland is derived from the Scots, a northern Irish tribal grouping, who expanded into the west of Caledonia from their kingdom of Dál Riata by the fifth century. Under the Gaelic-speaking Scots Mac Alpin dynasty, *Celtic Picts, Britons and Scots merged with the Germanic Angles of the south-east to form the Kingdom of Scotland between the ninth and eleventh centuries. Irish missionaries, most prominently *Colm Cille (St Columba), converted much of Scotland to Christianity in the sixth century from their monastic centre on the isle of Iona.

Scottish migration has played a prominent role in the development of Ireland. Edward *Bruce, the brother of the famed Scottish King Robert Bruce, invaded Ireland in 1315 and nearly established a unified Scottish-Irish state at the expense of the *Anglo-Norman Plantagenets. Scottish mercenaries (Gallowglasses) were the backbone of the military structures maintained by many northern Irish lords throughout the late medieval and early modern periods. Ultimately, the greatest Scottish impact on Ireland came in the form of long-term migration during the seventeenth century. This heavy influx of Scottish, largely *Presbyterian, settlers in *Ulster radically altered the religious composition of the northern province. The notorious, officially sanctioned *Ulster Plantation (1609–25) displaced many native Irish landholders, but peaceful Scottish immigration had both preceded and continued long after these dates. In counties *Antrim and *Down, Scots came to constitute the population's absolute majority. There were also major settlements in *Derry, *Armagh, *Tyrone and *Donegal. Although Presbyterians were at the forefront of secular republican nationalism in the 1790s, by the mid- to late nineteenth century, they had largely become loyalists. In the present day, the descendants of Scottish settlers comprise the majority of the northern Irish *Protestant community. J.P.

Scots-Irish. A term describing *Ulster *Presbyterians who migrated to the British North American colonies in the seventeenth and eighteenth centuries. By 1775, they constituted the largest white ethnic minority in the colonies. Politically radical, the Scots-Irish played a major role in the *American Revolution. Known for their fierce independence, this group settled mostly on the frontiers. Thirteen American presidents, including Andrew Jackson and Woodrow Wilson, were descended from the Ulster Scots. In the nineteenth century, the term was adopted by many *Protestant Irish Americans to differentiate themselves from the new waves of *Catholic *immigrants arriving from Ireland. J.P.

Scott, Michael (1905–88). Architect. Born in Drogheda, County *Louth, Scott is considered by many the most important architect of twentieth-century Ireland. He studied at the Dublin Metropolitan School of Art and was an architect's apprentice before joining the Office of Public Works. In 1927, he started his own practice, initially designing several modern structures for the *Irish Free State, including hospitals at Tullamore (1934–37) and Portlaoise (1933–36). In 1937, Scott brought Walter Gropius to *Dublin and, from then on, concentrated on promoting modernism in Ireland. Scott's buildings include his own home, 'Geragh', at Sandycove, Dublin (1937– 38), the Irish Pavilion for the New York World's Fair (1939), Donnybrook Bus Garage (1952), Busáras (1944–53) and the *Abbey Theatre (1958–66). Scott's modernist style is now considered controversial (some say inhumane and cold), but his work is still highly regarded internationally and at home. A.K.

Scott, Patrick (1921–). Painter, designer and graphic artist. Born in Kilbrittain, County *Cork, Scott was a member of the modernist White Stag Group in the 1940s. His painting, under the influence of architectural training and Japanese art, has evolved into formal geometric images using white and gold leaf on linen. He also works in tapestry, carpets, mosaics and furniture. He represented Ireland at the Venice Biennale in 1960 and was involved with *ROSC and *Kilkenny Design Workshops. M.C.

Scott, William (1913–89). Painter. Born in Scotland, Scott grew up in County *Fermanagh and studied art in *Belfast and London. His flat modernist treatment of still-life borders on an abstract formalism, softened and made more accessible by its painterly qualities. M.C.

Scully, Seán (1945–). Painter. A native of *Dublin, Scully was influenced by the work of Mark Rothko and Bridget Riley. He now works in Barcelona, London and New York. Since the late 1960s, horizontal and vertical stripes arranged to create monumental structures have been the sole formal motif of his painting. A member of *Aosdána, he has been a visiting lecturer at National College of Art and Design, Dublin. M.C.

sculpture. A tradition of sculpture has existed in Ireland since earliest times, mostly in connection with *architecture, tombs and free-standing crosses of the early *Christian period. Church building declined with the coming of the Black Death in the mid-thirteenth century, but the fifteenth century saw a revival in the use of stone carving, mainly for the sides of box tombs.

The Dublin Society Schools, set up in 1740, facilitated the training of sculptors. During the relative political stability of the Georgian period, many superb buildings were constructed. Sculptors were employed to add decorative features to exteriors and interiors. Some of the best work is by Edward Smyth (1749–1812) on the façade of the Custom House in *Dublin (1781). His carvings are richly animated with a variety of textures. John Henry Foley (1818–74), one of a number of sculptors who sought work in England, established himself as a leading portrait sculptor and was one of eight artists chosen to work on the Memorial to Prince Albert. John *Hogan (1800–58), who lived in Rome for a few years, is renowned for the quality of his religious sculpture and his classical subject matter.

In the first half of the twentieth century, sculptors like Albert *Power (1881–1945) continued in the artistic tradition of the late nineteenth century. His near contemporary Oliver *Sheppard (1865–1941) was much influenced by art nouveau, while the public monuments of Andrew O'Connor (1874–1941) recall the artistic expression of Rodin. In the building boom that began in the 1960s, minimalist sculpture was commissioned for public buildings. Since then, the use of geometric shapes in wood, steel, or aluminum has created exciting visual effects. Many of these works are by talented women artists including Gerda Fromel (1931–75) and Eilis O'Connell (1953–). Today sculpture has broadened to include performance art and body sculpture, and the traditional means of expression are being left behind. S.B-L.

Seanad Éireann (senate). Upper House of the *Oireachtas, Ireland's legislature. When the British government partitioned Ireland under the *Government of Ireland Act (1920), provision was made for a second consultative chamber in both *Dublin and *Belfast. When, following the *Anglo-Irish Treaty (1921), a twenty-six-county *Free State was established within the British empire in 1922, provision was made for a similar senate. The Northern senate together with the *Stormont assembly in Belfast made up the government of *Northern Ireland. It was finally abolished in 1972, when the British government instituted direct rule of Northern Ireland from Westminster. The senate of Northern Ireland has not been restored.

The powers of the Irish Free State senate were limited, though it gained a reputation for lively debate throughout the 1920s. However, after Éamon *de Valera came to power as head of the new *Fianna Fáil government in 1932, his attempt to abolish the *oath of allegiance which all elected members of the Irish legislature were required to take, was frustrated by the senate. After a sudden Dáil election in January 1933, where the oath was a major issue, de Valera, who gained an overall majority for the first time, abolished the senate. However, when de Valera then proposed the *Constitution of 1937, he included a senate, Seanad Éireann, as an Upper House of the Oireachtas.

Today's senate (Seanad Éireann) consists of 60 members. Forty-three are elected from five vocational panels (representing culture and education, agriculture, labour, industry and commerce, and public administration), by the members of the main local authorities, along with members of the incoming Dáil and the outgoing senate. Six are elected by graduates of the two older universities, three from the National University (NUI) and three from Dublin University (Trinity College), while the remaining 11 are nominated by the new *Taoiseach. In theory, the senate does not recognise party political affiliations, but the nature of the electorate that votes for the 43 senators and the fact that the Taoiseach can nominate 11 members in a house of 60 seats usually means that the government has a comfortable majority. The senate's main business is to review legislation sent to it by the Dáil. But it can also initiate nonfinancial legislation and, on occasions, has played a significant role in delaying controversial legislation that the Dáil has passed. N.ÓG.

***seán-nós* singing.** *Seán-nós* (or 'old style') is used to denote the unaccompanied song tradition in Irish or Scots Gaelic. The style is most prevalent in the *Gaeltacht areas (particularly *Connemara) and there are distinct regional differences. The compressed vocal range of the Connemara singers, for instance, contrasts with the less ornamented style of *Donegal.

Theories vary as to the origins of *seán-nós*. Professor Seán *Ó Tuama traces a connection with *amour courtois* and speculates that the models for popular Irish folk songs were established after the *Norman invasion. Filmmaker Bob Quinn believes that Ireland's maritime culture may have exposed it to stylistic influences from Spain and North Africa, which were under Islamic rule for 700 years. *Seán-nós* singing is currently experiencing something of a revival, the yearly highlight being the Corn Uí Riada competition which takes place during the Oireachtas festival. Organised by the *Gaelic League, the festival is a celebration of the arts among the Irish-speaking communities and includes musical, singing and literary competitions. B.D.

Second Vatican Council (1962). Ecumenical Council of the Roman Catholic church. Pope John XXIII convened the Second Vatican Council in 1962 to reform church teaching, discipline and liturgical practice in order to bring the church into dialogue with the modern world. The council was a triumph for Irish *Catholicism in the sense that many of the bishops attending, not only from Ireland but from the United States, Australia and other parts of the world, were either Irish or of Irish descent. However, the council's implementation in Ireland led many Irish Catholics away from traditional devotions and practices. A new model of Catholicism developed that emphasised religious freedom, ecumenism and liturgical renewal in lieu of popular devotions. The reforms renewed the religious commitment of many Catholics, but caused controversy among those who still embraced a more traditional Catholicism. M.P.C.

set-dancing. A social *dance form (literally a set of quadrilles) involving nineteenth-century French choreography using Irish 'steps' – and performed to Irish traditional music (jig, reel, polka and hornpipe). An earlier version, the cotillion, was hugely popular in Ireland since the 1770s. The quadrille form spread from Europe as a dance fashion after 1816. 'Sets' of quadrilles had different names and foot patterning, often connected to place. They are grouped according to type, the 'first set' typified by the Plain (Clare) Set and the Fermanagh Quadrille set. The 'second set' is the Lancer Quadrilles and the 'third set' of quadrilles is known as the Caledonian. Set-dance was condemned by the *Gaelic League as un-Irish, but was revived to huge popularity after the 1970s by pioneering independent dance teachers as well as by *Comhaltas Ceoltóirí Éireann and the *Gaelic Athletic Association. F.V.

Shannon, Sharon (1968–). Musician. Born in County *Clare, Shannon plays the accordion and fiddle and is considered one of Ireland's most dynamic young traditional musicians. Taught by Frank Custy of Toonagh, she began playing at an early age. While at college in *Cork, she started playing professionally. Shannon was part of the band Arcady, but it was with the popular Waterboys that she gained an international reputation. In the 1990s, she embarked on a solo career and played internationally with her own support bands. Her taste in music includes the broader Irish/Celtic world, with Cajun, Cape Breton, American country and other such influences. F.V.

Shannon, River. The longest river in Ireland or Britain. The Shannon rises in the Shannon Pot in County *Cavan, forms an estuary west of Limerick City and flows into the Atlantic at Loop Head, County *Clare. Its total length is 214 miles. Formerly an important north-south traffic artery, it is now used mainly for pleasure cruising and is linked with the Erne system through the Ballinamore-Ballyconnell Canal. In its course, the Shannon feeds three important lakes (Allen, Ree and Derg). In 1926–30, water was diverted from the river to create the country's first major hydroelectric scheme at Ardnacrusha, County Clare. P.H.

Shaw, Fiona (1958–). Actress. Born in *Cork, Shaw graduated with a BA in philosophy from University College, Cork, before entering the Royal Academy of Dramatic Art (RADA) in London. Her rapid rise in the London theatre world and the rarity of her appearances on the Irish stage, led many to describe her incorrectly as a British, rather than Irish, actress. Shaw is widely acclaimed as one of the most talented and intellectually rigorous actors of her generation. Her theatre credits at the Royal National Theatre include: Julia in Richard Brinsley *Sheridan's *The Rivals*, Shen Te Shui Ta in Bertolt Brecht's *The Good Person of Szechuan*, the title role in *Richard II*, the stage version of Muriel Spark's *The Prime of Miss Jean Brodie* and Euripides' *Electra*, and Rosalind in *As You Like It*. She has won a number of awards, including three Laurence Olivier Awards for best actress and two London Critics Awards. She received a New York Critics

Award for her performance in the BBC film version of T. S. Eliot's *The Waste Land*. Notable film credits include roles in two important Irish films, *My Left Foot* (1987) and *The Butcher Boy* (1997). She has also taken lighter roles in such big-budget films as *Three Men and a Little Lady* (1990) and *Harry Potter and the Sorcerer's Stone* (2001). In 2002, she played Medea in the *Abbey Theatre production of Euripides' classic, which received rave reviews in London and New York. H.L.

Shaw, George Bernard (1856–1950). Playwright and man of letters, Nobel laureate. Born in *Dublin, Shaw was the son of an unsuccessful grain merchant with a drinking problem and an artistic mother. Early on, Shaw developed an interest in literature, music and art, influenced by his mother and her friend George Vandeleur Lee, a singing teacher with whom the Shaws shared a house. After leaving school at age 15, Shaw worked for a number of years as a clerk and unsuccessfully submitted short articles to newspapers and magazines.

In 1876 Shaw joined his mother in London, where, unemployed, he wrote five novels in an outmoded style, none of which were successful. In 1884 he joined the Fabian Society, a utopian movement designed to achieve a socialist society by peaceful means. For the Fabians, Shaw wrote political and economic treatises, edited *Fabian Essays* (1889), and was one of their most popular speakers.

Between 1885 and 1898, Shaw established a reputation as an art and music critic (he championed Wagner and published *The Perfect Wagnerite* in 1898). He also wrote incisive theatre criticism for the *Saturday Review*. At the suggestion of William Archer, the first English translator of Henrik Ibsen, Shaw began writing plays inspired by Ibsen's social criticism. An expanded version of a lecture on Ibsen, *The Quintessence of Ibsenism*, appeared in 1891. Shaw's play *Widowers' Houses*, in which

George Bernard Shaw

he addresses middle-class hypocrisy and economic exploitation, was produced in 1892. Other plays of this early period, including *Mrs Warren's Profession* (1894), on the theme of prostitution, and *Arms and the Man* (1894), a satirical look at the military establishment, were published in two volumes as *Plays Pleasant and Plays Unpleasant* (1898). Shaw married Charlotte Payne-Townshend in 1898.

Shaw's plays – invariably accompanied by extensive and argumentative introductions – indicted the institutions of society rather than the questionable actions of individuals, which he saw as the effect rather than the cause of social ills. His work is characterised by provocative wit and by the polemical nature of his dramatic dialogues. Shaw's reputation as a dramatist was established internationally with *Man and Superman* (1903), in which he developed his 'religion' of Creative Evolution, a belief in a force that seeks to elevate mankind to a more evolved existence. *Pygmalion* (1912), the story of flower girl Eliza Doolittle's transformation into a society lady under the tutelage of professor Henry Higgins, illustrates Shaw's lifelong interest in the spelling and pronunciation of the English language. The play was the basis for the musical *My Fair Lady* (1956), later made into a popular film.

Shaw was horrified at Britain's involvement in the *First World War, a sentiment expressed in *Heartbreak House* (1917). A prolific writer (he wrote 53 plays), Shaw increasingly experimented with form and subject matter. The five-part science-fiction cycle *Back to Methuselah* (1921) further developed his theories about the 'Life Force'. *Saint Joan* (1924), often considered Shaw's masterpiece, depicts the trial of Joan of Arc as a struggle between honest forthrightness and hypocritical opportunism. Shaw received the Nobel Prize for literature in 1925. (He is one of four Irish writers to have won the prize.) His last full-length play, *In Good King Charles' Golden Days*, appeared in 1939. Shaw died at 94, at his home in Ayot St Lawrence, Hertfordshire. J.C.E.L.

Sheehy Skeffington, Francis (1878–1916). *Socialist, pacifist, journalist and writer. Sheehy Skeffington (husband of *Hanna Sheehy Skeffington) was a committed suffragist and a supporter of *women's emancipation. He was active as a campaigner for women's suffrage and edited the suffrage paper the *Irish Citizen*. He joined the *Irish Citizen Army, but left as it moved from being a workers' defence organisation to being an armed revolutionary group. Sheehy Skeffington opposed the use of force in the *Easter Rising of 1916, but went on the streets to prevent looting, so that it would not be used as 'black propaganda' against the *Volunteer movement. He was arrested by a British army patrol and summarily executed. Following public outrage, the British officer who ordered Sheehy Skeffington's execution was later court-martialled. E.C.

Sheehy Skeffington, Hanna (1877–1946). Feminist, suffragist and *nationalist. Hanna Sheehy Skeffington (wife of Francis *Sheehy Skeffington) was a prominent feminist campaigner who founded the Irish Women's Franchise League in 1908. In 1904, she joined the United Irish League (a support group for the *Irish Parliamentary Party) and the newly formed Socialist Party of Ireland. She broke with the Irish Party in 1912 on the issue of votes for *women. Sheehy Skeffington lectured extensively in the United States in support of the *republican cause after the 1916 *Easter Rising. She joined *Sinn Féin in 1918 as a member of the party executive. She took the anti-treaty side in the *Civil War and joined *Fianna Fáil on its formation in 1926 as a member of its first Executive. Sheehy Skeffington left Fianna Fáil when its TDs took the *oath of allegiance to enter the *Dáil in 1927 but remained active in republican and feminist politics until her death. E.C.

Sheela na Gig. A stone carving of a nude female exposing her vulva. Allegedly from the Irish *Síle na gCíoch* (Sheela of the breasts), or *Síle ina Giob* (Sheela on her Hunkers), such carvings have been interpreted variously as fertility figures, Celtic goddesses, or as objects to ward off evil. Generally of poor quality, these carvings are found on churches and *castles between AD 1200 and 1600. P.H.

Sheppard, Oliver (1865–1941). Sculptor. Born in County *Tyrone, Sheppard studied in *Dublin and London and taught at the Dublin Metropolitan School of Art. Influenced by Rodin, he used traditional modelling technique to achieve a naturalistic effect. He is best known for his 1798 memorials at *Wexford and Enniscorthy and his *Death of Cuchulainn* (1911), which later served as a 1916 *Easter Rising commemoration in the General Post Office, Dublin. M.C.

Sheridan, Jim (1949–). Filmmaker. One of Ireland's leading directors, Sheridan grew up on *Dublin's northside in a working-class family (described in his brother Peter Sheridan's 1999 memoir, *44: Dublin Made Me*). Sheridan was educated at University College, Dublin, and the Abbey School of Acting. In 1977, the two brothers founded Dublin's Project Theatre Company, an alternative to Ireland's National Theatre, and supported the early work of actors such as Gabriel *Byrne and Liam *Neeson. Artistic director for New York's Irish Arts Center theatre from 1982 to 1987, Sheridan returned to Ireland in 1988 to work on the film version of Christy *Brown's autobiographical *My Left Foot* (1989). Sheridan co-wrote the script with Shane Connaughton and directed the film, which won the first Oscars ever (Daniel *Day-Lewis, best actor, and Brenda Fricker, best actress) for an Irish film. Sheridan's adaptation of John B. *Keane's classic Irish drama *The Field* (1990), featuring Richard *Harris as a small farmer fighting for land against a wealthy Irish American, was followed by a trio of films about the *Troubles. The seven-times Oscar nominated *In the Name of the Father* (1993), co-scripted by Terry George, is based on Gerry Conlon's autobiographical narrative of his 1974 arrest, trial and, wrongful imprisonment as one of the so-called *Guildford Four. Sheridan and George later co-wrote *Some Mother's Son* (1996), a story about the 1981 *hunger strikes in Long Kesh (Maze) prison that stars Helen Mirren and Fionnula Flanagan. *The Boxer* (1997), starring Daniel Day-Lewis and Emily Watson, melodramatically examines love across the barricades in a divided *Belfast. Sheridan acted in Mary McGuckian's 1994 film *Words Upon the Window Pane*, wrote the screenplay for Mike Newell's mystical story about the Irish *travellers, *Into the West* (1992) and co-produced Anjelica Huston's *Agnes Brown* (1999). In 1993, with Arthur Lappin, Sheridan created Hell's Kitchen, a Dublin-based production company that continues to develop both indigenous talent and a wide range of international commercial collaborations. His film *In America* (2002) describes Irish life in the United States. C.H.

Sheridan, Richard Brinsley (1751–1816). Playwright and politician. Born in *Dublin, Sheridan first won fame with his comic play *The Rivals* (1775), which features the enduring character of Mrs Malaprop, whose misuse of words inspired the term malapropism. Subsequent plays such as *The School for Scandal* (1777) and *The Critic* (1779) enhanced his reputation as a writer of comedy and a brilliant wit. In 1778, Sheridan purchased the Drury Lane Theatre, which he subsequently managed until it was destroyed by fire in 1809. Sheridan was first elected MP for Stafford in 1780. One of the most brilliant orators in the House of Commons, Sheridan was a close friend of Charles James Fox and a consistent supporter of the radical element within the Whig Party. He held a number of government offices, including the post of undersecretary for foreign affairs (1782) and treasurer of the navy (1806–7). Sheridan's later years were marked by financial problems, culminating in his arrest for debt in 1813. A.S.

shoot-to-kill. Controversial anti-terrorist policy of the security forces in *Northern Ireland. On 11 November 1982, three unarmed men were shot dead by members of a special *RUC anti-terrorist unit just outside Lurgan, County *Armagh. Less than two weeks later, on 24 November 1982, two youths were shot – one killed and the other seriously wounded – by the same unit in a hay shed also just outside Lurgan. Three weeks after that, on 12 December 1982, two more unarmed men were shot dead, yet again by a member of the same special unit, this time in Armagh City. Initially the shootings were investigated by the RUC. However, suspicions of a cover-up led, in May 1984, to an independent inquiry conducted by John Stalker, Deputy Chief Constable of Greater Manchester. In September 1985, Stalker delivered a highly critical interim report, recommending the prosecution of 11 RUC officers.

He alleged that there was an RUC shoot-to-kill policy and an attempt to cover it up. The RUC became increasingly truculent and refused to hand over the tapes of an MI5 bug hidden at the site of one of the killings. On 28 May 1986, Stalker was relieved of his duties when rumours were raised about his association with criminal elements in Manchester. Colin Sampson, chief constable of West Yorkshire, was asked to conduct an inquiry into all allegations concerning Stalker. Sampson also took over the shoot-to-kill inquiry. Sampson exonerated Stalker, but after reinstatement to his post in the Greater Manchester Police, Stalker retired in March 1987. In early 1988, the British government acknowledged that the Stalker/Sampson inquiry in Northern Ireland had produced *prima facie* evidence of a conspiracy to pervert the course of justice by RUC men, but announced that, for reasons of national security, no criminal proceedings would take place. M.M.

Siamsa Tíre. The national folk theatre of Ireland based in Tralee, County *Kerry. Started by Father Pat Ahern in 1974, the theatre combines drama with traditional *music. In association with Tralee Institute of Technology, it offers a degree programme in drama teaching and traditional music performance courses. F.V.

Sinn Féin. *Political party. Founded in 1905 by Arthur *Griffith as a *nationalist party, Sinn Féin remained marginal to the growing *Volunteer movement until after the 1916 *Easter Rising. In 1917, it was effectively reformed as a *republican party and quickly became the militant nationalist opposition to the moderate nationalist (*home rule) *Irish Parliamentary Party. In the 1918 British general election, Sinn Féin won 73 of the 105 seats and in the territory of what would become the *Free State, 70 out of 75. The elected Sinn Féin candidates refused to take their seats in Westminster and instead established their own parliament in *Dublin – the first *Dáil Éireann – on 21 January 1919. Sinn Féin split on the issue of the *Anglo-Irish Treaty in 1922, with pro-treaty Sinn Féin renaming itself *Cumann na nGaedheal. Anti-treaty Sinn Féin split in 1926 with the majority joining Éamon *de Valera's newly formed *Fianna Fáil. Sinn Féin remained largely in the political margins until 1968, though they did win four seats in the Irish general election of 1957, at the start of the *IRA 'Border Campaign'.

As the civil rights campaign in *Northern Ireland heightened expectations of change and brought a repressive response from the *unionist government, Sinn Féin saw a new opportunity for growth. The party, however, split on the issue of whether to recognise and take seats in the parliaments in Dublin, Belfast and London. The majority, labelled 'official' Sinn Féin, moved to a more reformist position, supported a cease-fire by the 'official IRA', and eventually renamed themselves the Workers Party, abandoning nationalism altogether. The minority faction in 1969, 'Provisional Sinn Féin', grew rapidly as a grassroots political force and was eventually the only party to use the name Sinn Féin.

Sinn Féin was a minor part of the republican campaign against British rule in Northern Ireland in the 1970s, with the IRA clearly the dominant organisation. After the *hunger strikes of 1981, with the election of IRA hunger striker Bobby Sands to the British parliament, Sinn Féin was drawn into serious electoral politics, receiving, on average, the support of 40% of the nationalist community. Gerry *Adams was elected to the British parliament (but did not take his seat) in 1983 and became president of the party that autumn. Fearful that Sinn Féin, with its close links to the IRA, would become the dominant nationalist party in Northern Ireland, the British and Irish governments signed the *Anglo-Irish Agreement of 1985, to demonstrate the capacity of constitutional politics to deliver reform and to marginalise Sinn Féin.

In the late 1980s, the Sinn Féin leadership recognised that the combination of its electoral support and an IRA campaign (largely though not fully contained by the British army and *RUC) could not break the political stalemate. Neither was any progress being made in talks between moderate nationalists, unionists and the two governments. A series of secret talks, initially between Gerry Adams and the *Social Democratic and Labour Party (SDLP) leader John *Hume, and later involving representatives of the Irish government, eventually led to an IRA cease-fire in August 1994. In the post-cease-fire period, and especially after the *Good Friday Agreement (1998) (which Sinn Féin endorsed), Sinn Féin made considerable political progress, increasing support at each election until it had become the main nationalist party in Northern Ireland by June 2001. The party's support is built on a continuing radical republican position, combined with a left-wing economic programme and a very serious commitment to community politics. Sinn Féin also began to build a significant level of support in the *Republic, having their first TD in many years elected to the Dáil in 1997 and increasing their number of TDs to five in 2002. In 2004, the party won two seats (one in the Republic and one in Northern Ireland) in the European Parliament. J.D.

Skellig Michael. Island in the Atlantic, seven miles off the *Kerry coast. Skellig Michael was a monastery and place of *pilgrimage first mentioned in 823. Difficult to land on, it has six *beehive huts with square interiors, two oratories (all built in the corbel technique), a cemetery, a hermitage and a lighthouse. P.H.

Sligo, County. Maritime county in the province of *Connacht in the west of Ireland. Sligo, covering an area of 709 square miles, has a population of 58,178 (2002 census). Bordered on the east by *Leitrim, on the west and south by *Mayo and on the south-east by *Roscommon, Sligo is famous for its natural beauty. The county's most celebrated natural sites include the mountains Ben Bulben, at the foot of which the poet William Butler *Yeats is buried in Drumcliff churchyard, and Knocknarea, which is claimed to be the burial place of the mythic Queen Maeve of the legend **Táin Bó Cuailnge (The Cattle Raid of Cooley)*. In the west of the county lie the Ox Mountains and in the south-east the Curlews. Principal rivers are the Sligo, the Arrow, the Owenmore and the Esk, and lakes include Lough Gill, Lough Arrow and Lough Colt. The name Sligo itself is derived from the Irish *Sligeach*, meaning river of shells. It is believed to refer to the large number of shellfish in Sligo Bay.

Until the seventeenth century, the county was dominated by the O'Connor family. The poet W. B. Yeats, who spent part of his childhood in his grandfather's substantial home in Sligo, was greatly influenced by the county's stunning landscape and its *folklore. Important archaeological sites include the *passage-graves at *Carrowmore and Carrowkeel and a monastic site at Inishmurray, which was founded in the sixth century. Rosses Point, just outside Sligo town, has a famous *golf links course. The main towns in the county are Sligo town, the county capital, Collooney, Ballymote and Tubbercurry. The county enjoys a reputation for traditional Irish *music and the distinct Sligo style is exemplified in the recordings of Michael *Coleman. Coney Island lies in the bay off Sligo town; the name was also given to a a famous section of Brooklyn in New York City. A.S.

Smith de Bruin, Michelle (1969–). Swimmer. Born in Rathcoole, County *Dublin, she made sporting history when she won one bronze and three gold medals at the Atlanta Olympics in 1996. She received a four-year competitive ban in 1998 for tampering with the results of a random drug test. She has always protested her innocence. B.D.

soccer. An immensely popular sport both nationally and internationally. The Irish Football Association (IFA) was formed in *Belfast in 1880. Following the *partition of Ireland, the game's organising body was divided into two administrations, the IFA for *Northern Ireland and the *Dublin-based Football Association of Ireland (FAI) for the *Irish Free State. Ireland's first international game was a 1926 friendly, non-competitive appearance against Italy in Turin.

Despite a smaller population to choose from, Northern Ireland enjoyed greater success abroad, qualifying for three World Cups (Sweden, 1958; Spain, 1982; and Mexico, 1986). The *Republic of Ireland finally reached the World Cup in Italy in 1990, in the United States in 1994 and in Japan/South Korea in 2002.

The IFA and FAI each run semi-professional leagues for Irish soccer clubs. Linfield is the most successful northern club while Shamrock Rovers leads the honours list in the Republic. However, both leagues have declined in popularity since the 1960s and the vast majority of top Irish soccer players now pursue their professional careers in England.

Belfast's George *Best is Ireland's best-known soccer player. Pat Jennings from Newry, County *Down, is internationally recognised as one of the most outstanding goalkeepers. Other major players include Liam Brady, Paul McGrath, John Giles, Noel Cantwell, Charlie Hurley and Roy Keane. F.S.

Social Democratic and Labour Party (SDLP). Until recently, the largest of the *nationalist parties in *Northern Ireland. The SDLP was formed on 21 August 1970, from a coalition of nationalists, *socialists and anti-*unionists at a time of escalating violence. Its first leader was the socialist Belfast politician Gerry Fitt. The party initially absorbed much of the traditional *Nationalist Party support. It claimed to focus on social and economic issues and advocated eventual Irish unity by agreement. In 1971, under pressure from *Sinn Féin, the SDLP withdrew from the local *Stormont parliament in protest at British army repression and later *internment without trial. In September 1972, the party proposed a form of joint sovereignty by the British and Irish governments for Northern Ireland. After constitutional negotiations, the SDLP became part of the historic power-sharing Executive, which lasted from January to May 1974. The party was gravely disappointed when the power-sharing Executive collapsed because of a loyalist strike. The SDLP hardened its nationalist position, and its socialist founders, including Gerry Fitt, drifted away disillusioned.

In 1979, John *Hume replaced Fitt as party leader. Despite Sinn Féin's increased involvement in electoral politics during the 1981 *hunger strikes, the SDLP retained its position as the leading nationalist party in Northern Ireland. Newly confident, the SDLP took part in the New Ireland Forum in the 1980s, which sought to reconsider nationalist grievances and attitudes. The party's candidates Séamus *Mallon and Eddie McGrady won seats in the British parliament in 1986 and 1987, respectively. Beginning in 1988, John Hume initiated a secret and controversial series of talks with Gerry *Adams, president of Sinn Féin and MP for West *Belfast, in an attempt to persuade the republican movement that politics could prove more fruitful than violence. Despite initial failure, dialogue was resumed in 1993 following the *Downing Street Declaration (December 1993). These talks would prove essential to the success of the *peace process and the *Good Friday Agreement.

Of all the political parties, the SDLP was probably most pleased with the 1998 Good Friday Agreement. The agreement's emphasis on power-sharing and north-south cooperation were particularly satisfying to the party because they reflected the long-held aspirations of its nationalist constituency. Ironically, however, by drawing republicanism from violence, the SDLP helped make Sinn Féin a potent threat to its domination of the nationalist electorate. In 2001, Sinn Féin outstripped the SDLP in electoral support and John Hume resigned as leader. The party receives about 22% of the Northern Ireland vote in elections and its support comes predominantly from middle-class and working-class Catholics. M.M.

socialism. For over a century, socialism has been a minority force on the fringe of Irish politics. In 1896, James *Connolly formed the Irish Socialist Republican Party and later he organised the Socialist Party of Ireland. Although the Socialists Connolly and James *Larkin were prominent in the labour movement before the *First World War, socialism did not emerge as a significant political force.

Socialists took part in strikes and *soviets between 1918 and 1922, but even then remained marginal. The *Labour Party soon dropped its early socialist rhetoric. In the 1920s and 1930s, the *Communist Party gained little support. In 1934, left-wing *IRA members, led by the Socialist Peadar *O'Donnell, joined with Communists in the short-lived Republican Congress. Increasing *Catholic church hostility toward socialism (from the 1930s) and cold war propaganda (from the 1950s) created a hostile climate for such politics.

The Workers' Party, adhering to Stalinism, emerged from the 1970 IRA split and won some *Dáil seats in the 1980s. With the collapse of the Soviet Union, leading Workers' Party members formed a social democratic party, Democratic Left, and then merged with the Labour Party. The Labour Party, despite its 1969 slogan 'the 1970s will be socialist', has never adhered to ideological socialism. Today, a Trotskyist party, the Socialist Party, has one TD in the Dáil, Joe Higgins.

Ireland has one of Europe's weakest socialist movements. In *Northern Ireland, which was the industrial base of the island, socialists faced the obstacles of sectarianism and the ongoing *nationalist/*unionist conflict. Until recently, the *Republic of Ireland had a weak industrial proletariat; but more significantly, workers felt no need for socialism. They supported populist nationalist parties – first *Sinn Féin and then *Fianna Fáil – which absorbed working-class protest by offering reforms and waving the green flag. P.D.

Somerville and Ross. (Pen names for Edith Somerville, 1858–1949 and Violet Martin, 1862–1915). Novelists. Cousins and members of an Anglo-Irish family, Somerville and Ross co-authored many popular novels which portrayed the life of the rural gentry in Ireland. Their best-known works include *The Real Charlotte* (1894) and *Some Experiences of an Irish R.M.* (1899). S.A.B.

song, English-language. Introduced to Ireland after the twelfth century, it became particularly popular from the seventeenth century onward. After the demise of the *Irish language following the Great *Famine in the mid-nineteenth century, English-language song became widespread. Ancient English ballads still survived up to the 1960s in the mouths of travelling singers such as John Reilly. Other forms of English-language song include: the interface macaronic song (with mixed Irish and English-language lyrics); the political-allegorical *Jacobite song; the florid, Gaelic-idiom 'hedge-schoolmaster' song; the *Ulster ballad city-specific or 'street' styles; regional traditions (particularly distinctive in *Wexford and *Clare); political song; emigration song; Napoleonic song; sporting songs; place-praise song; satirical and comic song; popular nineteenth-century music-hall song; and Irish American song. Modern ballad styles have been created by the *Clancy Brothers, the *Dubliners and others who combine theatrical performance with traditional type melody. F.V.

soviets. Term applied in Ireland to workers' councils, workplace seizures and local general strikes in the years 1918–22. Most soviets involved the Irish Transport and General Workers' Union (ITGWU). During a wave of strikes for wage increases, the Irish labour movement widely employed Bolshevik rhetoric and symbols, including the red flag. While workers' socialist intentions should not be exaggerated, labour's awareness of its own strength peaked in these years.

In May 1920, workers seized 13 creameries in County *Limerick and raised the red flag over the central factory at Knocklong where *Socialist ITGWU organisers directed the 'Knocklong soviet'. At Arigna, County *Roscommon, coal miners seized mines and operated them for two months. Elsewhere, flour mills, gasworks and factories were taken over. Workers also took direct action in support of the national cause during the *War of Independence (1919–21). For example, the 'Limerick soviet' of April 1919 was a nine-day general strike in the city against British militarism. During a national strike for the release of *republican prisoners in April 1920, *trade union councils, often calling themselves soviets, took over the administration of many towns. From 1921, an economic slump led employers to reduce wages, forcing workers on the defensive. About 80 soviets occurred in 1922, mostly in *Munster. But the labour movement was weakening and the *Free State army assisted employers and farmers in ending the occupations. P.D.

Spanish Armada (Sept.–Oct. 1588). Failed naval expedition of Philip II of Spain to conquer England. It turned to disaster through bad weather and English counter-attack. Possibly more than 20 ships foundered on Irish coasts from *Antrim to *Kerry. The treasures from one – the *Girona* – are displayed in the *Ulster Museum in *Belfast. Only in rare instances did the Irish offer help or refuge to the Spanish survivors. Some places are particularly identified with the Spanish Armada, such as the village of Spanish Point in County *Clare, near which several of the Armada's ships were wrecked during a fierce storm. P.H.

Spanish Civil War (1936–39). Ireland's political left and right saw the Civil War in Spain as an opportunity to revive their political fortunes. Left-wing and *republican activists followed Frank Ryan to serve with the International Brigades. Eoin *O'Duffy, hoping to regain his popularity by defending *Catholicism, took 600 *Blueshirts to fight for Franco. T.C.

Spenser, Edmund (1552–99). English poet and administrator. Born in London, Spenser was secretary to the Lord Deputy Grey in Ireland in 1580. In 1588, he acquired an estate at Kilcolman Castle, County *Cork, where he wrote most of his poetic works, notably the allegorical epic *The Faerie Queene* (1590–96). Spenser's writing is profoundly influenced by his Irish experience. He depicts the mountains and rivers around Kilcolman as an Edenic pastoral landscape in *Colin Clouts Come Home Againe* (1591), in Book 6 of *The Faerie Queene*, and in *Cantos of Mutabilitie* (published posthumously in 1609). In contrast, he repeatedly attacks Irish culture and society as inimical to law, civility and love of goodness, and espouses the view that the Irish 'must be altogether subdued ... by the sword, for all [their] evils must first be cut away with a strong hand before any good can be planted'. He argues this view at length in *A View of the Present State of Ireland* (written 1596, printed 1633) and gives it vehement poetic expression in *The Faerie Queene*, Book 5. Kilcolman was destroyed during the *O'Neill rebellion in 1598 and Spenser fled to London where he died in poverty. J.MD.

sport. Sport has always been an essential part of Irish life. *Hurling has been played since *pre-Christian *Celtic times and as far back as 1272 BC. Since its inception in 1884, the *Gaelic Athletic Association (GAA) has built an infrastructure for the indigenous sports, hurling and *Gaelic football, and provided recreation and leisure facilities for vast numbers of the population. International sporting events, such as the World Cup tournaments in *soccer and *rugby, the Olympic Games and the Tour de France cycling race, have become for Irish people a means of expressing national identity. Levels of public funding for sport, however, have traditionally been low. This has been countered by the GAA's organisational success and the voluntary efforts of countless coaches across a wide range of sports. Established in 1987, the National Lottery, which funds sports and the arts, and the economic prosperity of the 1990s have given sport a much needed financial boost.

Although inevitably influenced by the evolution of organised sport in Britain, sport in Ireland hasn't been as thoroughly reliant on elite education. This is largely because one of the GAA's original missions was to wrest control of sport and athletics from the existing socially elite administration as part of its revival of the national games of hurling and Gaelic football. Soccer and rugby have traditionally based their seasons on the academic year, reflecting the importance of universities and secondary schools to those sports. The GAA promoted Gaelic football and hurling as summer pursuits. While Gaelic games were stronger in rural areas, soccer was associated with British garrisons, generally in cities or big towns, where it was played by soldiers and gradually developed a base in these urban areas. Until it became a professional sport in the 1990s, rugby was largely based in the universities and private, middle-class schools. Because it was played overwhelmingly by the professional classes, rugby was a reluctant convert to professionalism.

The *partition of Ireland in the 1920s created difficulties for soccer and athletics. Eventually soccer administration was split between the Football Association of Ireland (FAI) in the *Republic and Irish Football Association (IFA) in *Northern Ireland. The refusal of the National Athletic and Cycling Association of Ireland (NACAI) to cede control of athletics in Northern Ireland led to recognition disputes at the Olympic Games in 1936 and 1948.

Young Irish athletes have traditionally relied on US college scholarships. Many of the top Irish track and field performers of the past 50 years, including Eamonn Coughlan, Ronnie *Delaney, Marcus O'Sullivan, Niall Cusack, Sonia *O'Sullivan and John Treacy, have benefited from training in the United States.

Water sports of all kinds are found throughout Ireland. Sailing is popular in coastal areas, particularly *Dublin and *Cork, and the rivers and lakes are home to Irish rowing. The Irish Amateur Rowing Union celebrated its centenary in 1999, but the sport has been established for much longer with Irish clubs competing at the Henley regatta in England since the 1870s. Swimming became popular, especially since the success of Michelle *Smith de Bruin at the Atlanta Olympics of 1996. (In 1998, Smith de Bruin was accused of tampering with a drug test and banned from competition for four years. She has always protested her innocence.)

Field hockey, especially women's hockey, is a favourite sport played in many schools. The 1994 Women's World Cup of field hockey was held in Dublin. Similarly, basketball, with a semi-professional league in both the men's and women's game, has been an established sport in Ireland since the 1950s. Women's Gaelic football is the fastest-growing sport in the country, with crowds of over 20,000 attending its All-Ireland senior finals. The longer-established sport of *camogie (women's hurling) is also widely played. Regional sports include road bowling, played principally in County Cork in the south and County *Armagh in the north, and rounders – a little-known version of baseball that is actually one of the GAA's four national games, along with Gaelic football, hurling and handball. *Golf is one of the most popular leisure sports in the country. Boxing, especially at the amateur level, has had a big following in contemporary Ireland.

Ireland as an independent nation, represented by Dr Pat O'Callaghan in hammer-throwing, won its first Olympic gold medal in 1928, at the Amsterdam Olympic Games. O'Callaghan won another gold medal in hammer-throwing in Los Angeles, in 1932, the same year that Robert Tisdall won the gold medal in the 400-metres hurdles. Other Irish Olympic medalists include: John McNally (silver medal, 1952, boxing), Ronnie Delaney (gold medal, 1956, 1,500 metres), Fred Tiedt (silver medal, 1956, boxing), Tony Byrne, Freddie Gilroy and John Caldwell (bronze medals, 1956, boxing), Jim McCourt (bronze medal, 1964, boxing), Hugh Russell (bronze medal, 1980, boxing), David Wilkins and Jamie Wilkinson (silver medals, 1980, yachting), John Treacy (silver medal, 1984, marathon), Michael Carruth (gold medal, 1992, boxing), Michelle Smith de Bruin (three gold medals, 1996, swimming) and Cian O'Connor (gold medal, 2004, individual showjumping) S.M.

St Patrick's cathedral. One of Dublin's two *Protestant cathedrals and the national cathedral of the *Church of Ireland. St Patrick's, built on a site where St *Patrick is said to have baptised the pagan Irish, began as a college of priests and became a cathedral around 1220. The largest church in medieval Ireland, it was built in a harmonious early English Gothic style and consecrated in 1254. Between 1832 and 1904, the *Guinness family financed its extensive restoration, which succeeded in leaving much of the medieval fabric intact. Its most famous dean from 1713 to 1745 was Jonathan *Swift, author of *Gulliver's Travels*, who is buried in the cathedral. P.H.

Stalker affair. See **shoot-to-kill.**

Stanford, Sir Charles Villiers (1852–1924). Composer, academic, conductor. Born into a distinguished *Dublin legal family, Stanford wrote the first of his seven symphonies at the age of 24, was appointed professor of composition at the Royal College of Music in London at 31, and professor of music at Cambridge four years later. His operas and orchestral works were performed in Europe and the United States by leading musicians (including Richter, Bülow, Kreisler, Mahler and Mengelberg) and he was one of the most influential teachers in Britain. His nine operas are now neglected, but his choral music is highly prized – his Anglican church music is still in use – and his six *Irish Rhapsodies* (1902–23) and *Irish Symphony* (1887) show his traditional orchestral mastery at its best. M.D.

step-dancing. A performance genre of *dance by males and females largely focused on foot and leg movements. Its aesthetics and features make it distinct from such forms as the English 'clog' dance. Step-dancing is performed either solo or in groups, mostly to set tunes of the reel, jig and hornpipe variety. It also uses the treble reel, slip jig, single jig and light jig. Generally, step-dancing takes place within a competition or display framework. It has been taught in seasonal and weekend 'schools' since the 1920s using a code of rules set mostly by An Coimisiún le Rincí Gaelacha (Commission on Irish Dancing). Older forms of step-dancing, known as *seán-nós dance, have survived mostly in the Irish-speaking *Connemara area of County *Galway. F.V.

Stephens, James (1882–1950). Writer. Born in a *Dublin slum, Stephens published his first poems in Arthur *Griffith's *Sinn Féin*. With the encouragement of George W. *Russell and W. B. *Yeats, he published his first volume of poetry, *Insurrections* (1909), and the highly coloured and lyrical novels *The Charwoman's Daughter* and *The Crock of Gold* (1912). While registrar of the National Gallery, Stephens wrote a *nationalist account of the *Easter Rising, *The Insurrection in Dublin* (1916), and a collection of poems celebrating Irish themes, *Reincarnations* (1918). He subsequently lived in Paris and London, where he broadcast verse and stories for the BBC. S.A.B.

Sterne, Laurence (1713–68). Novelist. Born in Clonmel, County *Tipperary, Sterne spent part of his childhood in Ireland. His mother was Irish, his father an English soldier. Sterne is best known for his novel *Tristram Shandy* (published in a series of volumes between 1759 and 1767). Its loose narrative structure influenced many later writers, including James *Joyce. The novel also reflected Sterne's comic gifts and delight in wordplay. The best-known of his other writings is *A Sentimental Journey* (1768), an episodic and impressionistic account of a tour of France and Italy that he made in 1765. A.S.

Stoker, Bram (Abraham) (1847–1911). Novelist. Born in *Dublin and educated at Trinity College, Dublin, Stoker married Florence Balcombe, one-time fiancée of Oscar *Wilde. He entered the civil service in Dublin and wrote a standard reference book, *Duties of Clerks of Petty Sessions in Ireland*. He managed the career of his close friend, successful actor Henry Irving, until Irving's death in 1905, recording the experience in *Personal Reminiscences of Henry Irving* (1906). His first novel, *The Snake's Pass* (1891), is set in Ireland. His reputation stands on *Dracula* (1897), a complex vampiric novel, which has enjoyed popular and cult success and has spawned several films, including Murnau's *Nosferatu* (1922) and Coppola's *Dracula Love Never Dies* (1992). M.S.T.

Stormont. Parliament building of *Northern Ireland. The term is widely used to describe the *unionist government of Northern Ireland from 1921 to 1972. During this period only one party – the *Ulster Unionist Party – ever served in government. In a sharply divided society and with *nationalists in a clear minority, unionists were guaranteed that they would win every election. Despite their local majority, unionist policy was framed in an atmosphere of insecurity, often referred to as a siege mentality. Unionists look back on this period with nostalgia. In comparison with the period of recent conflict, the Stormont era was, for unionists, a period of relative peace, when they had at least apparent control over their destiny. For nationalists, however, the period was characterised as intensely discriminatory, often summed up by the phrase that Stormont was a 'Protestant Parliament for a Protestant people', although the nationalist community made up more than one-third of the population.

The scale of nationalist alienation can perhaps best be summarised by the demands of the *Northern Ireland Civil Rights Association in the late 1960s – universal franchise, the end of gerrymandering and an end to discrimination in employment practices, housing and policing. The unionist government initially refused to consider any reform, banned civil rights protests and used the *police to harass marchers. Reform was ultimately forced upon the unionist government by the scale of the protests, but when it did come it was 'too little and too late'. It was also combined with a continuing highly repressive security policy, culminating in the introduction of *internment without trial of alleged *IRA members (many of whom were civil rights protestors or innocent nationalists) in August 1971. The unionist government had lost control of the situation by early 1972 and, when they refused to allow the British government to take direct responsibility for security matters, the British government suspended the parliament and government in Northern Ireland and transferred all its powers to London, thus ending the Stormont period. J.D.

Strongbow (c.1130–76). Colloquial name for Richard fitzGilbert de Clare, the Cambro-Norman nobleman whose arrival in Ireland in 1170 marks the beginning of the *Anglo-Norman Conquest. Strongbow succeeded his father as earl of Pembroke in 1148, but his support of the pretender Stephen led to his estates being confiscated by *Henry II, the Norman king of England. In 1168, Dermot *MacMurrough, the exiled king of *Leinster, recruited Strongbow (with Henry II's consent) to fight for him in Ireland. In return, MacMurrough offered the earl his daughter Aoife (Eva) in marriage and succession to the kingship of Leinster.

Strongbow arrived in Ireland in August 1170 with about 1,000 foot soldiers and 200 knights. This force quickly took *Waterford, and on 23 August 1170, Strongbow married Dermot's daughter. After a series of battles, much of the eastern part of the country, including *Dublin, was under Norman control. Following Dermot's death in May 1171, Strongbow became lord of Leinster.

On the surface, the Normans were acting on behalf of Henry II, but there were suspicions that Strongbow was planning to establish an independent kingdom. Henry, concerned, travelled to Ireland in 1171 and landed in Waterford on 17 October with a formidable force of 4,000 men, including 500 knights. He placed his own men in charge of the coastal cities, but having received Strongbow's declarations of loyalty, Henry confirmed him as ruler of Leinster.

Strongbow in a further attempt to prove his loyalty to the king, fought for Henry in Normandy in 1173–74, and when he returned to Ireland as the king's governor was rewarded with the restoration of Waterford, *Wexford and Dublin. He was, however, to be engaged in almost continuous fighting against the native Irish until his death in 1176. P.E.

Stuart, Francis (1908–2000). Novelist. Born in Townsville, Australia, Stuart was reared in County *Antrim. While still a teenager, he married Iseult, daughter of Maud *Gonne. He was interned for his participation in the *Irish Civil War. Stuart's first book was a collection of poems, *We Have Kept the Faith* (1924). Numerous pre-war novels, notably *Pigeon Irish* (1932) and *Try the Sky* (1933), project the revolutionary romanticism of his formative years. In 1939, he accepted a position lecturing in Berlin and made radio broadcasts to Ireland from there on behalf of the axis powers. Post-war experiences of dislocation and rejection inspired later novels such as *Redemption* (1949) and *Black List Section H* (1971). Stuart returned to Ireland in 1957, where he became a controversial and influential presence. G.OB.

Sunningdale Agreement (1973). Agreement to implement the first power-sharing government in *Northern Ireland. In November 1973, three parties, the *Ulster Unionist Party (UUP), the *Social Democratic and Labour Party (SDLP) and the Alliance Party, agreed to form a power-sharing Executive to govern Northern

Ireland. The 'Irish Dimension' – i.e., north-south links – had yet to be sorted out and to this end, in December 1973, the parties met at Sunningdale, a civil service training centre in Britain. A 'Council of Ireland' to regulate the north-south links was agreed upon. This was to include a council of ministers, in which both the Irish government and the Belfast Executive would be represented equally and which would have an 'executive and harmonising' function. The new coalition took office on 1 January 1974. The power-sharing experiment worked well enough, but the Sunningdale Agreement proved altogether contentious. In February 1974, a United Kingdom general election was called and unionist anti-Sunningdale parties won 11 of the 12 Northern Ireland seats, gaining 51.1% of the votes. In May 1974, loyalist violence and a general strike in protest against the power-sharing Executive toppled the entire arrangement. Direct rule from London was re-introduced. The *Good Friday Agreement of 1998, reinstituting power-sharing and the Irish dimension, has been called 'Sunningdale for slow learners'. M.M.

Swift, Jonathan (1667–1745). Writer. Born in *Dublin, Swift attended Kilkenny School, along with future playwright William *Congreve. When the Catholic King *James II invaded Ireland, political uncertainty drove Swift to England, where he worked as secretary to retired diplomat Sir William Temple. A year after his return to Ireland in 1694, he was ordained in the Anglican church, and in 1702 he received a doctorate in divinity from Trinity College, Dublin. An outspoken and witty man, he had little time for Deists, Freemasons, Catholics, or nonconformists and, due in part to his formidable intelligence, was subsequently given the prestigious deanship of *St Patrick's cathedral in 1713. Swift never married, but had long friendships with two women. One was Esther Johnson, whom he met in England and referred to as 'Stella'. She was younger than Swift and little is known about their relationship except that he educated her, they wrote to each other often and clearly enjoyed each other's company. Swift also had a friendship with Esther Vanhomrigh, whom he later named 'Vanessa'.

Widely regarded for such satiric works as *A Tale of a Tub*, *The Battle of the Books* and *The Mechanical Operation of the Spirit* – all of which were published in 1704 – Swift is most familiar as the author of *Gulliver's Travels*. First printed anonymously in 1726, this fictional travelogue, consisting of four parts that chronicle the adventures of Lemuel Gulliver, caused a sensation. A radical and daring narrative, the first printing became a best-seller. To protect Swift from potential political backlash, the publisher altered the original manuscript. Unhappy with these changes, Swift eventually had it reprinted nine years later the way it was originally written. *Gulliver's Travels* is considered a masterpiece. In this ingenious critique of society, Swift delivers subtle attacks against such institutions as government and church, and against the savagery of humankind. The voyage to Lilliput (where Gulliver is perceived as a giant and tied down by a swarm of tiny Lilliputians) has become part of popular culture.

Swift was also a gifted satirist who wrote numerous political articles. Many of these, written anonymously, inflamed local politicians. Under the pseudonym of 'Marcus Brutus, Drapier', Swift repeatedly called for a *boycott of British goods and, although many readers knew the real identity of the famous rabble-rouser, Swift was never reported to the authorities. His most famous satiric tract is *A Modest Proposal*, which appeared in 1729 and advocated that eating babies would solve not only problems of overpopulation, but would also solve chronic malnutrition among the poor.

At the end of his life, Swift suffered from what was thought to be bouts of madness but was in fact Ménière's syndrome, which affects the inner ear, causes deafness, nausea and a sense of dizziness. Swift contracted this disorder in his early twenties and, as he aged, the symptoms worsened. In 1742, his friends declared him of unsound mind. He died three years later and was buried next to Stella in the graveyard of St Patrick's cathedral. His entire fortune was used to establish a mental institution. An immensely complicated and dynamic figure, Jonathan Swift remains one of the most important writers in the English language. P.J.H.

Swift, Patrick (1927–83). Neo-realist portrait and landscape painter. Swift studied in *Dublin and Paris, and in the 1960s in London he founded *X: A Literary Magazine* with Anthony *Cronin. He wrote criticism under the pseudonym of James Mahon. M.C.

Synge, John Millington (1871–1909). Playwright. J. M. Synge is considered the most significant playwright of the *Irish Revival and one of the most important Irish playwrights of the twentieth century. Born in *Dublin, Synge, like many of the leading figures of the Irish Revival, came from a comfortable *Anglo-Irish ascendancy background. He became increasingly alienated from his class while developing an interest in Irish national culture. Having read Darwin at an early age, the young Synge renounced the evangelical *Protestantism of his family and became interested in the wonders of the natural world. He was educated at Trinity College, Dublin, and his study there of *Irish language and *literature would have a profound effect on his subsequent literary development. After graduation, he was drawn to mainland Europe, where he spent several years studying and writing. In 1896, he met W. B. *Yeats in Paris who advised him to go to the *Aran Islands to seek artistic inspiration. Synge's time on Aran constituted a turning point for the budding writer. Here he chose to live among the people and to learn to speak Irish as the islanders spoke it. Attracted to the unconventional lifestyle that he encountered on Aran, Synge also developed an interest in the lore and folktales of local storytellers. Many of these tales are collected in his fascinating account of his time on the islands, *The Aran Islands* (1907), which blends autobiography, travel writing and folklore.

By 1902, Synge had turned to writing plays for the emerging Irish *theatre movement. He created a folk drama that was based on the stories he had gathered in his travels around Ireland and that was beholden to the rhythms and cadences of Gaelic speech. His plays are distinctive for their exuberant use of the English language as it is spoken in Ireland. His discovery of the literary potential of *Hiberno-English stands as one of his lasting achievements. Although it was fashionable for *nationalist writers to idealise the Irish peasantry at this time, Synge pledged that he would reflect the realities of rural Ireland 'warts and all'. Consequently, his plays caused controversy when they were first produced. The first play to be performed, *The Shadow of the Glen* (1903), which explores the subject of a loveless marriage, caused a heated row because the play's heroine leaves her husband to run away with a vagrant. *The Playboy of the Western World* (1907) caused even more outrage. This play, in which the hero is acclaimed for telling a story of how he murdered his father, caused a fullscale riot in the *Abbey Theatre when it was first produced. Audience members who had come to expect idealised versions of Irishness blamed Synge for defaming the image of the nation. Other plays include: *Riders to the Sea* (1904) – widely regarded as an almost perfect one-act tragedy – *The Well of the Saints* (1905), *The Tinker's Wedding* (1907) and the posthumously produced *Deirdre of the Sorrows* (1910). Synge was struck down by Hodgkin's disease in 1909. P.J.M.

Tailtinn Games. Annual festival of athletic contests in Old Ireland. The *rath of Tailtinn is situated near the Blackwater River, midway between Navan and Kells in County *Meath. One of the residences of the high king, Tailtinn takes its name from the ancient form of the placename *Tailtiu* (meaning 'valuable site'). It was the chief cultic site of the god Lugh, patron of the harvest, who was said to have introduced ball games, chess and *horse racing to Ireland. A great assembly was held in autumn each year at Tailtinn, with games and athletic contests as the major attraction. This assembly continued until the Middle Ages. D.OH.

Táin Bó Cuailnge (The Cattle Raid of Cooley). The most celebrated hero-tale of Ireland. The tale seems to have grown out of the dim memory of a war between the Ulaidh people of Emhain Macha (in County *Armagh) and the Connachta clan of *Tara (in County *Meath). Legends of this and related matters were strung together by the poets for the Gaelic chieftains of east *Ulster in the seventh century AD, but in its full form the story was the compilation of authors some centuries later. The principal versions are in **Leabhar na hUidhre (The Book of the Dun Cow)*, *The Yellow Book of Lecan* and *The *Book of Leinster*. The *Táin* tells of how Maeve (or Meadhbh), queen of the province of *Connacht in the west, wished to have a bull equal to the great white bull owned by her husband. She therefore invaded Ulster to seize the brown bull of Cooley (on the south-eastern boundary of Ulster). The Ulstermen were stricken by an old curse in this hour of need, debilitating them, and only the young champion *Cúchulainn could take the field on their behalf. Cúchulainn performed prodigious feats, keeping Maeve's army at bay and when the curse wore off the Ulster warriors routed Maeve's forces. A melodramatic high point has Cúchulainn killing his best friend, Fear Diadh, in single combat. The epic ends with the clash of the two bulls, the brown bull of Cooley rending asunder his opponent, the white bull, in a frightful contest. D.OH.

Talbot, Matt (1856–1925). Ascetic. Talbot, a *Dublin labourer and alcoholic, resolved upon a life of abstinence and piety after reading the works of St Augustine in 1884. Considered highly eccentric even by the standards of Irish Catholic asceticism, he practised strict penitential exercises in which he wore chains around his body and slept on a plank bed. Talbot led a campaign against alcohol and its vices mostly aimed at the poor working-class of inner-city Dublin. A bridge on the River Liffey was dedicated to Talbot in 1978 and his cause for beatification is now well advanced. S.A.B.

Tandy, James Napper (1740–1803). Revolutionary *nationalist. Born in *Dublin, Tandy was prominent in radical circles from the late 1770s onward. One of the founding members of the *United Irishmen, he was the first secretary of its Dublin branch. Fearing arrest, he went to America in 1793 and then in 1797 to France. A year later, Tandy led an unsuccessful expedition of French troops, which landed on the Donegal coast. After this failure, he fled Ireland and was captured in Hamburg. Although sentenced to death at a trial held in Lifford, County *Donegal, he was not executed (due to intervention by Napoleon), but instead deported to France in 1802, where he died a year later. A.S.

Taoiseach. Prime minister of Ireland. The term *Taoiseach* (an Irish word that means 'chief' or 'head of the clan') originates from the 1937 *Constitution. The Taoiseach has considerable political power compared with other European prime ministers. The Taoiseach appoints other cabinet members, the attorney general and junior ministers. The Taoiseach also nominates 11 members of the *Seanad. Most importantly, the Taoiseach can call a general election at any time (provided he or she has not lost the confidence of the *Dáil). In addition to constitutional powers, the Taoiseach chairs government meetings and controls the cabinet agenda. Irish prime ministers before 1937 were known as the president of the executive council. The following is a list of Taoisigh:

William T. *Cosgrave (*Cumann na nGaedheal), President of Executive Council, 1922–32
Éamon *de Valera (*Fianna Fáil), President of Executive Council, 1932–37, Taoiseach, 1937–48; 1951–54; 1957–59
John A. *Costello (*Fine Gael), 1948–51; 1954–57
Seán *Lemass (Fianna Fáil), 1959–66
Jack *Lynch (Fianna Fáil), 1966–73; 1977–79
Liam *Cosgrave (Fine Gael), 1973–77
Charles J. *Haughey (Fianna Fáil), 1979–81; March–December 1982; 1987–92
Garret *FitzGerald (Fine Gael), 1981–February 1982; 1982–87
Albert *Reynolds (Fianna Fáil), 1992–94
John *Bruton (Fine Gael), 1994–97
Bertie *Ahern (Fianna Fáil), 1997–present
J.D.

Tara. The symbolic seat and coronation site of early medieval Ireland's high kings (though not their permanent residence). Located in County *Meath, this site includes a stone pillar – the

Three Taoisigh: Seán Lemass, Jack Lynch, Charles J. Haughey

Lia Fáil, or Stone of Destiny – and an earthen mound known as the Mound of the Hostages, together with many other earthworks. Many generations of the royal *O'Neill (Uí Néill) dynasty fought over this seat of power in their quest to restore the old Irish monarchy. In the nineteenth century, Tara was used to invoke the glories of ancient Ireland by Daniel *O'Connell, who held a Monster Meeting here in 1843 during the campaign to *Repeal the Act of *Union. P.H.

Tara Brooch. Ireland's most superbly crafted piece of jewellery, dating from the eighth century. The brooch was found at Bettystown, County *Meath, and given the name Tara by a commercially minded jeweller. It is now in the *National Museum in Dublin. The brooch's exquisite minuscule spiral, animal and interlace designs are made of bronze, gold, amber, glass, silver and copper. P.H.

television. The *Republic of Ireland's indigenous television service began on 31 December 1961 and developed in competition with the British Broadcasting Corporation and Ulster Television, whose signals had for several years reached parts of Ireland. Telefís

Éireann, renamed Radio Telefís Éireann (*RTÉ) in 1966 after it merged with Radio Éireann, was set up as a government-controlled network, funded by licence fees and advertising revenues.

Beginning in the early 1960s, television quickly became a major catalyst of social change. By importing programmes from other cultures, Telefís Éireann familiarised Irish citizens with foreign values and images and encouraged them to scrutinise their own assumptions and convictions. The service also employed foreigners and returned émigrés because, in the early 1960s, there were very few resident Irish citizens with training in television broadcasting.

Gay *Byrne's talk show *The Late Late Show*, launched in 1962, pioneered what might be termed 'confrontational television'. It regularly challenged the views of conservative politicians and church leaders and greatly liberalised public discourse on such taboo topics as sex and contraception. Byrne's studio audience often participated and the unpredictable and spontaneous nature of the show attracted viewers throughout the nation.

RTÉ's drama serials also addressed social problems. Although not subversive, the network's first hit, *Tolka Row* (1964–68), dealt with crises such as alcoholism and unemployment in a working-class *Dublin family. Uniquely Irish in content, such serials modelled their formats on Anglo-American shows. The long-running soap opera *The Riordans* (1965–79) took the serial drama out of the studio, making unprecedented use of outdoor location work.

Whereas foreign television broadcasts successfully alerted the international community to the escalation of violence in *Northern Ireland in the late 1960s and early 1970s, RTÉ was not able to cover, let alone illuminate, the conflict for its viewers. In 1971, Gerry Collins, then minister of posts and telegraphs, reissued Section 31 of the 1960 Broadcasting Act, which prohibited the broadcast of any matter engaging 'the aims or activities' of paramilitary organisations. (This ban was lifted in 1994.) In 1972, when RTÉ tried to circumvent this blatant form of censorship by showing mute footage of *IRA members, the government dismissed the entire RTÉ governing body.

RTÉ has nevertheless maintained a high-quality national service, especially in serial drama, news and current affairs. Recently, it has been criticised for its dearth of serious dramas – single plays, mini-series and serials. By 1980, the percentage of Irish programmes had fallen to 30% because importing programmes was often cheaper than making them in Ireland. Some media critics have urged greater state financial support for indigenous television.

While there is no privatised alternative to the national network in the Republic, RTÉ has never enjoyed a monopoly due to competition from foreign broadcasting companies. In addition to RTÉ's three channels (RTÉ 1, Network 2, Teilifís na Gaeilge) and the independent TV3 station (launched in 1998), most people watch on cable and satellite channels programmes from the United States, Great Britain and, increasingly in the past decade, from Australia. E.M.

textiles. Woollen and linen textiles have been manufactured in Ireland from *pre-Christian times, while Irish lace became famous in the 1800s.

Sheep rearing is one of Ireland's main *economies, especially in the mountainous areas of the country and in places with poorer soil. After the *Anglo-Norman invasion, large-scale wool production began, particularly within abbeys. The south-east was the most important area of production and much of the output was exported. Cloaks of coarse cloth and frieze were the most widely produced woollen commodities, and England was a major market. During the 1600s, regulations to ensure that Irish wool went exclusively to England were passed, culminating in the 1699 Woollen Act, which effectively ended Ireland's export trade to any other country.

Contemporaneously, flax, the raw material for linen, was grown extensively. Fibres from this plant are woven into linen cloth, bleached and dyed to produce the finished textile. In the 1700s, an influx of skilled settlers, strong British demand and encouragement from *landlords and government, combined to make linen Ireland's major industry. The area of heaviest linen production – both coarse and fine – was *Ulster, though coarse-linen manufacture was common throughout Ireland until the 1840s. At this time linen weaving took place mainly within individual cottages, with bleaching and dying in specialised bleach yards. From the 1820s onward, English competition and falling domestic demand caused both coarse-linen manufacturing and cottage-based weaving to decline. In nineteenth-century Ulster, however, due to a lack of foreign competition, continuing international demand and the mechanisation of production within factories, fine-linen manufacture continued to expand, making a major contribution to the province's industrialisation. By the mid-1800s, *Belfast was the fine-linen capital of the world, with a global reputation for quality. In the face of growing competition from artificial textiles, however, the fine-linen industry declined from the early 1900s onward, though it did not die out.

Despite the impact of the 1699 Woollen Act, domestic demand ensured that the wool industry remained important in the 1700s, with coarse woollen cloth also being manufactured on a cottage industry basis. Likewise, fine woollen cloth manufacturing developed in major towns in the 1700s, especially *Dublin. Competition from British exports caused this industry to die away from the late 1700s. The same pressures began to affect cottage-based coarse woollen cloth manufacturing in the nineteenth century, though it still managed to survive in many parts into the late 1800s, notably on the west coast. The latter half of this century also saw major developments in factory-based woollen cloth manufacturing. This sector grew significantly, due to concentration on niche products, such as blarney tweed.

Meanwhile, lacemaking, brought from France in the 1700s, became an important craft in many parts of the country in the mid-1800s. Limerick lace, the most famous style of Irish lace, was first produced at Mount Kennet, County *Limerick, in 1829. Strictly speaking, this is not true lace, but rather an embroidered machine-made net, which was first introduced into Ireland by an English entrepreneur.

Lace production as a whole grew greatly in the mid-1800s, mainly because a number of individuals and groups, particularly *nuns, wished to provide some measure of *Famine relief. Lacemaking also helped to offset the financial losses of some households after the decline of the coarse-linen industry. *Women were central to this handicraft and their earnings were important to their standing within Irish society. At the end of the nineteenth century, the Congested Districts Board and the Department of Agriculture established classes to improve the quality of Irish lace.

The production of lace, wool and fine-linen goods continues today and these Irish textiles have become world-renowned. J.C.

Thatcher, Margaret (1925–). British Conservative prime minister, 1979–90. Known as the 'Iron Lady' because of her intransigent conservative politics, Thatcher continually clashed with *republicans, nationalists and unionists in *Northern Ireland. She refused to recognise the H-Block prisoners' political status during their 1980 *hunger strike. However, the same year, she held a high-level meeting with *Taoiseach Charles *Haughey at *Dublin Castle that seemingly acknowledged the Irish government's place in Northern Ireland affairs. When the hunger strikes resumed in 1981, Thatcher remained opposed to the strikers' demands, even after Bobby Sands' election to parliament and the death of Sands and nine other hunger strikers. In October 1984, Thatcher barely survived a Provisional *IRA assassination attempt during the Conservative Party's annual conference in Brighton. A month later, she firmly rejected the New Ireland Forum's (a meeting of constitutional nationalists) solutions to the Northern Ireland crisis in her infamous 'out, out, out' speech: a united Ireland, a federal structure consisting of the Irish *Republic and Northern Ireland, and joint rule by Dublin and London – were all out of the question. Pressed by US President Ronald Reagan to maintain dialogue with constitutional nationalists, however, Thatcher signed the *Anglo-Irish Agreement in November 1985. The agreement, which gave the Irish government a direct consultative role in Northern Ireland for the first time, infuriated unionists. Ultimately, Thatcher was reviled by republicans, resented by nationalists and distrusted by unionists. R.D.

theatre. The Irish dramatic tradition goes back to at least the fourteenth century, with the performance of miracle plays and pageants. During the Renaissance, most plays were produced privately in great houses, but around 1635, a theatre was built in Werburgh Street, *Dublin. It closed in 1640. In 1662, English dramatist John Fletcher's *Wit Without Money* was the first play to be performed at the newly opened Smock Alley Theatre. Shakespeare was a favourite, but there were few productions of contemporary plays. The Smock Alley Theatre closed in 1689, during *William of Orange's campaign in Ireland, but it reopened in 1692.

A theatre opened in Aungier Street in 1734. Around this time, Dublin theatres introduced changes in performance, including more elaborate stage machinery. Thomas Sheridan became manager of Smock Alley in 1745 and made reforms that professionalised the theatre business and curtailed rowdy audience behaviour. A former Smock Alley actor, Spranger Barry opened a theatre in Crowe Street, Dublin, in 1760, for which *Donegal-born Charles Macklin, who was already successful in London, wrote his first Irish play, *The True-Born Irishman*. Dublin theatre companies began touring other cities on a more frequent basis. In *Cork, the Theatre Royal had opened its doors in 1736, followed in 1770 by similar venues in *Belfast and *Limerick.

In 1784, Robert Owenson (Lady *Morgan's father) opened the Fishamble Street Theatre in Dublin. Dedicated to staging patriotic plays, he gave theatre a more Irish flavour. The Crowe Street Theatre was demolished and replaced in 1821 by the Theatre Royal in Hawkins Street. The Queen's Royal Theatre opened in 1844. Thus far, the Irish theatre world produced few Irish playwrights, but this changed with the arrival in Dublin in 1861 of Dion *Boucicault, who by then had already had a successful career in London and New York. Boucicault added an Irish setting and characters to traditional sentimental comedy. His play *The Colleen Bawn* received its Irish premiere at Hawkins Street in 1861. In 1884 the Queen's Royal Theatre declared itself the 'home of Irish drama' with productions of political melodramas like Hubert O'Grady's *The Fenian* (1888) and J. W. Whitbread's *Wolfe Tone* (1898). In Dublin, the *Gaiety Theatre opened in 1871, followed by the Star of Erin Music Hall (now the Olympia Theatre) in 1879. In 1880, the Theatre Royal burned down. In Belfast, the magnificent Grand Opera House opened in 1895. At the turn of the twentieth century, the Irish drama scene became increasingly international, with visiting performances by the likes of Sarah Bernhardt and touring productions of Maeterlinck, Ibsen and Sudermann.

In 1897 W. B. *Yeats, Lady *Gregory and Edward *Martyn established a national theatre, the Irish Literary Theatre, dedicated to staging Irish plays. Its first performance, in 1899, was Yeats' *The Countess Cathleen*. In 1903, the Irish Literary Theatre joined forces with Frank and William *Fay to form the National Dramatic Society. Annie Horniman sponsored the purchase of buildings for the National Dramatic Society in Abbey Street and the *Abbey Theatre opened on 27 December 1904, with performances of plays by Yeats and Lady Gregory. The Fay brothers, who had previous experience as actors and directors, would significantly influence the development of the Abbey Company's understated acting style. Also in 1904, Bulmer Hobson and Lewis Purcell founded the *Ulster Literary Theatre, which would develop plays that reflected the defining characteristics of northern Irish society. The Abbey's staging of J. M. *Synge's *The Playboy of the Western World* in 1907 caused a riot when the audience objected to what it perceived as the play's disparaging depiction of the west of Ireland. In 1910, Miss Horniman withdrew her support and from then on the Abbey increasingly staged rural comedies, much to Yeats' chagrin. In 1925 the Abbey was granted an annual government subsidy, establishing its position as the national theatre.

Also in 1925, at a time when travelling companies were fast disappearing, Anew *McMaster set up his own touring company to bring Shakespeare to the Irish provinces. Two of its members, Micheál *MacLiammóir and Hilton *Edwards, became the directors of the first Irish-language theatre, An Taibhdhearc, which opened in *Galway in 1928. In the same year, the partners started the *Gate Theatre company, which staged a groundbreaking production of Oscar *Wilde's *Salomé*. The Gate Theatre, which acquired a venue in the Rotunda Buildings on Parnell Square, Dublin, in 1930, was dedicated to a modern, international repertoire. Early productions included Eugene O'Neill's *The Hairy Ape* and Strindberg's *Simoom*.

Seán *O'Casey's politicised social melodrama dominated the Abbey stage in the early 1920s, including *The Shadow of a Gunman* (1923), *Juno and the Paycock* (1924) and *The Plough and the Stars* (1926). The depiction of the heroes of the *Easter Rising in the latter play led to protests during its opening run. Yeats wrote some of his best dramas in his later years, including *Purgatory* (1938), but he was troubled by the mainstream direction taken by the Abbey, an approach furthered by Ernest *Blythe, the Abbey's managing director from 1941 to 1967. The Abbey Theatre burned down in 1951 and was rebuilt in 1966.

The Amateur Dramatic Association (founded in 1932) and its many member organisations became a rich breeding ground for local talent, many of whom became professional actors. Amateur standards were high and the first competitive All-Ireland Drama Festival was held in Athlone in 1953. Professional theatre, which had become less exciting, did have some notable moments, especially when Samuel *Beckett's *Waiting for Godot* received its English-language premiere at the Pike Theatre, Dublin, in 1955. In 1957 Pike's director, Alan Simpson, was arrested when a production of Tennessee Williams' *The Rose Tattoo* led to charges of obscenity. The following year, the fledgling Dublin Theatre Festival was cancelled when O'Casey withdrew his play *The Drums of Father Ned*, because the archbishop of Dublin refused to sanction the staging of Alan McClelland's *Bloomsday*, an adaptation of James *Joyce's *Ulysses*.

The 1960s, an era of economic and social renewal, also heralded a new era in the theatre, which saw a plethora of new talent, including playwrights like John B. *Keane, Brian *Friel, Tom *Murphy and Thomas *Kilroy. Memorable Dublin premieres include Friel's *Philadelphia, Here I Come!* at the Gaiety Theatre in 1964 and Kilroy's *The Death and Resurrection of Mr Roche* (1968). The innovative Druid Theatre was founded in *Galway in 1975 by

Garry *Hynes, Marie Mullen and Mick Lally. In 1980, Brian Friel and actor Stephen *Rea staged the first play of their *Field Day Theatre Company, which was dedicated to creating a 'fifth province of the imagination' that would overcome set ways of political and sectarian thinking. The play, Friel's *Translations*, was performed, to universal acclaim, in the Guildhall in Derry, with a cast including Ray McAnally and Liam *Neeson. Over the years, Irish theatre has produced many celebrated, often internationally acclaimed actors, including Barry *Fitzgerald, F. J. *McCormick, Siobhán *McKenna, Cyril *Cusack and Dónal *McCann. Since the 1980s, established playwrights such as Friel and Murphy have been joined by younger talent, including Frank *McGuinness, Sebastian *Barry, Marina *Carr, Conor *McPherson and Martin *McDonagh. Irish theatre since the 1980s has been characterised by increasing diversification and fragmentation, with numerous new theatre groups and small theatres being founded all over the country. J.C.E.L.

Tipperary, County. Inland county in the province of *Munster. The county, divided for administrative purposes into North and South Ridings, covers 1,662 square miles and has a population of 140,281 (2002 census). Tipperary became known worldwide through the *First World War song 'It's a Long Way to Tipperary'. The county has a varied and beautiful landscape, ranging from the Golden Vale, to the Knockmealdown and Galtee Mountains. The legendary peaks Galtymore (3,018 feet) and Slievenamon (2,364 feet) are immortalised in song and story. Tipperary is agriculturally one of the richest counties, with an active dairy industry centred in the fertile plain known as the Golden Vale. Rising dramatically out of this rich landscape, the Rock of *Cashel consists of a *round tower, Cormac's Chapel (twelfth century) and a Gothic cathedral, all perched on what was once the seat of the MacCarthy (MacCarthaigh) kings of Munster. The county has a wealth of important historic monuments, with *castles at Cahir, Nenagh, Roscrea and Carrick-on-Suir, and the abbeys of Holy Cross and Lorrha. In 1980, the Derrynaflan hoard, a treasure of early medieval metalwork, was discovered. Medieval *high crosses can be seen at Ahenny, near the *Kilkenny border.

Tipperary consists of a number of small to medium-sized prosperous towns, including Clonmel, the county capital, Thurles, where the *Gaelic Athletic Association (GAA) was established in 1884, and Tipperary town – from the Irish name *Tiobraid Árann*, 'well of Ara'. Natives of Tipperary include the *Fenian John *O'Leary; Gaelic poet Geoffrey *Keating; Laurence *Sterne, author of *Tristram Shandy* (who was born in Clonmel); and the novelist and Fenian Charles *Kickham. P.H.

Titanic. White Star liner built by Harland and Wolff in *Belfast, which sank in the most famous maritime disaster. On 10 April 1912, the ship embarked on its maiden voyage from Southampton, England, bound for Cherbourg, France, Queenstown (Cobh), Ireland, and New York. At Queenstown, 123 Irish passengers boarded the *Titanic*. Of these, 113 were third-class passengers, aged between 17 and 25, from poor rural backgrounds, intent on beginning a new life in the United States. Just before midnight on 14 April, the *Titanic* struck an iceberg about 95 miles south of the Grand Banks of Newfoundland. Between 1,503 and 1,517 of the 2,224 people on board perished. Of the passengers who boarded at Queenstown, only 44 survived. The wreck of the liner was located by a joint French–United States expedition in 1985. P.E.

tithes. A traditional medieval payment (10% of the produce of the land) levied on farmers for the support of the clergy. Tithes were first imposed in the twelfth century. After the establishment of the *Protestant *Church of Ireland in 1537, such payments were used by the new church. From the seventeenth century, members of the *Catholic majority, as well as *Presbyterians, were required to support the minority clergy. This taxation bred tremendous animosity among the roughly 90% of the population who were not members of the established church. By the second half of the eighteenth century, pasture lands were no longer tithable because of a resolution passed by the Irish *parliament. The change in policy placed the tithe burden entirely on tillage lands. Compounding the problem was the fact that the clergy increasingly leased their rights of collection to brutally efficient 'tithe farmers'. Coupled with a rapidly growing population and corresponding increase in rents, the situation became intolerable for much of the peasantry. Resentment over tithes and other agrarian issues resulted in the appearance of secret societies in the 1760s. Overt resistance to such payments crested in the Tithe War (1830–33). In 1838, tithes were directly incorporated into rents ending the worst of the hostilities. The final removal of tithe payments came with the disestablishment of the Church of Ireland in 1869. J.P.

Titley, Alan (1947–). Writer in the Irish language. Born in *Cork, Titley has written several novels and collections of short stories in Irish, as well as a play, *Tagann Godot* (Godot Comes). *An Fear Dána* (The Daring Man; 1993), which is based on the ramblings of medieval poet Muireadhach Albanach Ó Dálaigh, is one of the finest historical novels written in Irish. He also published a definitive critique of the Gaelic novel (*An tÚrscéal Gaeilge*; 1991) and two collections of fables. A comic fabulist, Titley's prose is notable for his prodigious punning and word-play. B.D.

Tóibín, Colm (1955–). Novelist and journalist. Born in Enniscorthy, County *Wexford, Tóibín gives a resonant depiction of a changing Ireland in such novels as *The Heather Blazing* (1992). Subsequent novels, notably *The Blackwater Lightship* (1999), focus on homosexuality, making Tóibín Ireland's leading gay novelist. *The Master* (2004), a novel based on the life of Henry James, received critical acclaim. A prominent cultural commentator, he has written nonfiction books, including *The Sign of the Cross* (1994). G.OB.

Tone, Theobald Wolfe (1763–98). Founder of the *United Irishmen. Born in *Dublin and educated at Trinity College, Dublin, and the Middle Temple, London, Tone was called to the Irish Bar in 1789. A talented polemicist, he began examining the status of his native country in the British empire. His 1790 anti-government pamphlet 'A review of the conduct of administration addressed to the electors and free people of Ireland' brought him to the attention of the Whig Club, a pro-reform association of intellectuals and politicians who admired Henry *Grattan. Although he disapproved of the moderation of the Whig Club, Tone participated in their activities and came under the influence of the radical MP Sir Lawrence Parsons. The latter helped Tone refine his theories about the negative role of Westminster in Irish affairs, even though the repeal of *Poynings' Law in 1782 had somewhat ameliorated the situation. Having parted with the Whig Club, Tone gravitated toward a group that included Thomas Russell, an ex-army officer, Dr William *Drennan, a *Belfast medical practitioner based in Dublin, and barrister Thomas Addis Emmet, who were anxious to exploit the opportunity for political reform in the aftermath of the *French Revolution.

Political debates sparked by the publication of Thomas *Paine's *Rights of Man* in February 1791 convinced Tone that Ireland required total separation from Britain in order to democratise the country. In 1791, Tone wrote an address to celebrants of the anniversary of the French Revolution in which he claimed it was necessary 'to break the connection with England, the never-failing source of all our political evils' by 'substituting the common name of Irishman, in place of the denominations of Protestant, Catholic and Dissenter'. Tone reassured a sceptical element within *Presbyterian radicalism in 1791 with a brilliant polemic, 'An argument on behalf of the Catholics of Ireland', in which he argued that *Catholicism was waning and that Irish Catholics were open to political alliances with other groups. This vision distinguished Tone as the key figure in the creation of the Irish *republican tradition.

Tone's organisational and propaganda skills were essential to the founding of the Society of United Irishmen in Belfast and Dublin in October/November 1791, a legal and largely middle-class association pledged to bring about an independent Irish republic. The United Irishmen sought out and ultimately absorbed kindred political societies and in early 1792 Tone accepted the secretaryship of the Catholic Committee (a national organisation that sent delegates to a Catholic Convention in Dublin in December 1792). The disappointing *Catholic Relief Act of 1793 and the harsh tenor of the accompanying debates indicated to Tone that parliament was incapable of implementing *Catholic Emancipation. The declaration of war on *France made it extremely difficult for the United Irishmen to advance their perspective. Prohibitions on public assemblies, armed bodies and seditious publications effectively ruled out any repeat of the successes enjoyed by the *Volunteers in the early 1780s. In April 1794, Tone was offered French military assistance and from that time the United Irishmen were an avowedly revolutionary organisation. However, the government discovered the overture and the subsequent arrest of French emissary Reverend William Jackson implicated Tone in treason. The Jackson case offered the pretext of proscribing the United Irishmen and those members who continued to meet did so under threat of *transportation. Tone was permitted to exile himself in America and, before departing for Philadelphia from Belfast in June 1795, he and his leading associates in Dublin and Belfast remodelled the United Irishmen as a paramilitary organisation. The *Defenders, a violent and sprawling anti-government movement, which drew inspiration from France, were merged with the United Irishmen.

Tone sailed to France on 1 January 1796 and successfully petitioned the French government to invade Ireland. A large army reached Bantry Bay, *Cork, in December but was unable to land because of severe weather. Tone had accompanied the French and, while bitterly disappointed, did not give up hope that his allies would try again. A small expeditionary force under General *Humbert landed in Killala, County *Mayo, in late August 1798 when the premature uprising of the United Irishmen was waning. They were contained within a month. Tone participated in another unsuccessful French effort off the Derry coast on 12 October 1798. He was placed under arrest in Buncrana, County *Donegal, and tried for treason in the Royal Barracks, Dublin, on 10 November. It is believed that Tone inflicted a mortal throat wound in Newgate prison the following day to protest the decision to hang him as a traitor rather than execute him as a uniformed officer in the French army. He died from this wound on 19 November and was buried in Bodenstown, County *Kildare, where his life and legacy is annually commemorated by various Irish republican parties. R.OD.

tower houses. Tall, often four- or five-storey, *castles erected in the fifteenth, sixteenth and early seventeenth centuries. Affluent Irish landowners built these tower houses as defences, status symbols and homes for their families and retainers. Sparsely furnished within, the houses sometimes had an outer protective wall. P.H.

trade unions. Irish trade unions originated in guilds and illegal workmen's associations in the eighteenth and early nineteenth centuries. Each skilled trade formed its own society and many then joined British-based unions. In the 1890s, Irish railway workers and dockers also joined British unions. Later, Irish-based national unions emerged. James *Larkin's Irish Transport and General Workers' Union (ITGWU), founded in 1909, organised labourers, dockers and transport workers and launched several major strikes, culminating in the great Dublin Lock-out of 1913.

In 1894, an Irish Trade Union Congress (ITUC) was formed and Larkin and other radicals dominated the leadership from 1911. Larkin and James *Connolly hoped to build one big union as a step toward *socialism. In 1914, after the Dublin workers' defeat, Larkin left for America and Connolly was executed as a leader of the 1916 *Easter Rising.

Wartime conditions caused unions to expand dramatically between 1917 and 1921. The ITGWU, now led by William O'Brien, increased from 5,000 members in 1916 to over 120,000 in 1920, with hundreds of branches all over the country. The southern unions supported the national struggle and there were countless wage strikes and short-lived *soviets. White-collar unions also expanded and joined the mainstream labour movement.

Economic depression and unemployment caused union membership to fall steeply in the 1920s. When Larkin returned from America in 1923, he clashed with the ITGWU's new leaders; from 1924 he led a breakaway Workers' Union of Ireland (WUI). The feud between Larkin and O'Brien continued through the 1930s and 1940s, sapping the labour movement's energies. Rivalry also occurred as British and Irish unions competed for the diminishing membership.

During the Second World War, the *Fianna Fáil government's policy of dealing only with the larger Irish unions and continuing rivalry between O'Brien and Larkin, caused the ITUC to split, but the unions reunited in 1959 in the Irish Congress of Trade Unions (ICTU). In 1945, the ITUC had established its *Northern Ireland Committee, which campaigned in defence of jobs and, since the 1970s, organised public demonstrations against sectarian violence.

In 1990, the ITGWU and the WUI merged to form the Services Industrial Professional and Technical Union (SIPTU), now Ireland's largest union, with over 200,000 members. It has branches throughout the south and in Northern Ireland, where British-based unions are strong. Today, in the island as a whole, 65 unions are attached to the ICTU, with over 680,000 members. Since the 1980s, southern unions have entered a series of national pay deals with governments and employers.

In the *Republic, union membership (as a proportion of employees) fell in the 1990s. This happened as jobs in technology and services increased, employers' attitudes toward unions hardened and the state no longer encouraged companies to recognise or bargain with unions. The decline was mainly in the private sector. While unions face many challenges today, actual membership in the Republic is at its highest ever, at 561,800, and the Irish union movement remains one of the strongest in Europe. P.D.

transportation. The transport of convicted criminals overseas to British colonies. Transportation became a regular punishment in Ireland after the Transportation Act of 1717 was used to send some convicted criminals (for whom neither execution nor imprisonment was deemed appropriate) overseas. By 1789, approximately 15,000 Irish men, women and children had been dispatched to plantations in the 13 continental North American colonies. Most went to Virginia, Maryland and Pennsylvania, but some ended up in the Carolinas, Connecticut and Massachusetts, either as plantation workers or as indentured servants. Convicts were required to serve their employers for set periods before being emancipated and free to either settle in the colonies or return home.

The outbreak of the *American War of Independence in 1775 closed colonial ports to British and Irish shipping for eight years, and created a crisis in the criminal justice system as convicts filled prisons and hulks. During this time, the illegal transportation of Irish felons to Maryland, *Newfoundland and the Bahamas precipitated a series of diplomatic incidents which compelled the British government to include the Irish in the Botany Bay scheme, the first use of *Australia as a penal colony. The penal colony founded in Port Jackson, New South Wales (Australia), in January 1788, was initially intended for the sole use of convicts sentenced in Britain, but in 1791 Irish convicts were also sent to Australia (on the *Queen*) as part of the Third Fleet. At least 48,000 Irish convicts were transported to Australian penal colonies by 1853, and small numbers of political prisoners were sent to Western Australia in 1868.

From 1840, when transportation to New South Wales ceased, Van Diemen's Land (Tasmania) was the destination of virtually all Irish convicts until 1853. Many of them had been tried during the *Famine years and were not regarded by the authorities as hardened recidivists. *United Irishmen and *Defenders, who comprised a sizable number of Irish transportees between 1793 and 1806, mounted a series of armed challenges to the colonial administration in 1800 and 1804. Members of the revolutionary *Young Ireland and *Fenian movements were also exiled to Australia. Some of them integrated into colonial society while others, such as John Boyle *O'Reilly and Thomas Francis *Meagher, escaped to America. R.OD.

travellers. Irish gypsies. There are an estimated 25,000 travellers living in Ireland. It is commonly believed that they are the descendants of *Famine victims or of those dispossessed during *Cromwellian times. Though their ranks may well have swollen during these upheavals, neither theory is now thought to hold much weight. There is plenty of historical evidence to show that travellers existed in Ireland prior to these events. The surnames Tynkler and Tynker began to appear in the twelfth century and the Acte for Tynkers and Peddlars was issued in 1551. In 1834, the Royal Commission on the *Poor Laws made a clear distinction between 'ordinary beggars' and 'wandering tynkers'. (The word 'tinker' was used inter-changeably with 'traveller' or 'gypsy'.) It would appear therefore that Ireland, in common with most other European countries, had an indigenous community of travelling tradesmen and tinsmiths from medieval times.

Though Irish travellers have a similar lifestyle to European gypsies or Romanies and share a history of persecution, they are not believed to belong to the same ethnic group. Some historians believe that there were commercial nomads in Europe – independent of the Romanies – who migrated from India through Persia between the fifth and thirteenth centuries and that they have survived today as distinct ethnic groups. Irish travellers are thought to belong to this group.

One of the defining characteristics of Irish traveller culture is nomadism. Though some travellers have settled in houses, many still take to the road. With the advent of social welfare payments in the 1950s, travellers started to gravitate toward the large urban areas. This led to efforts by the state to assimilate them into mainstream Irish settled society. Though well intentioned, the state considered 'nomadism' as a deviancy rather than an integral part of traveller culture. The Commission on Itinerancy (1963), for example, suggested that all efforts directed at improving the lot of travellers 'must always have as their aim the eventual absorption of the itinerants into the general community'.

The 1995 *Report of the Task Force on the Travelling Community* put much emphasis on the accommodation issue, recommending the construction of 3,100 living units, ranging from halting bays, transient sites and group housing schemes. All local authorities have subsequently adopted a five-year traveller accommodation plan.

In his book *The Secret Languages of Ireland* (Cambridge University Press: 1937), R. A. S. Macalister compiled hundreds of words of the travellers' language, known as 'Travellers' Cant'. Much of the vocabulary consisted of inverted Irish words and Macalister concluded that Cant was like a secret code designed to exclude members of the settled community. Although its syntactic structure is solidly based on English, a lot of the vocabulary clearly stems from Irish. This has led scholars to believe that it may have developed about 350 years ago when its original speakers would have been bilingual.

Successive studies have shown that the Irish traveller community is still among the most marginalised and disadvantaged in the country. Infant mortality among travellers is more than twice the national average and only 1% reach the age of 65. Only a handful have graduated from third-level institutions and fewer than 1,000 transfer to post-primary schools. More than 24% of travellers live on unofficial halting sites and on the side of the road, and often have no access to running water, toilets, refuse collection, or electricity.

The most common surnames among travellers are Connors, Ward, Maugham, O'Brien and McDonagh. B.D.

Trevor, William (1928–). Novelist and short story writer. Born William Trevor Cox in Mitchelstown, County *Cork, Trevor was educated at Trinity College, Dublin. He has lived in England since 1953 and a good deal of his work addresses his experiences there. His early novels, notably *The Old Boys* (1965), highlight the foibles, cruelties and delusions of the English middle-classes. He continues to revisit the eccentric domestic interiors of the Home Counties in such novels as *Elizabeth Alone* (1973) and *Death in Summer* (1998), but he has increasingly focused on Irish themes, particularly in his short stories. The novel *Fools of Fortune* (1983) is his most substantial statement on the violence of Irish history. Trevor uses the family to portray Irish history's destructiveness. He elaborately delineates the devastating effects of politics on personal lives. Decline is another recurring Trevor subject, whether it is the dwindling of the *Protestant minority in the *Republic of Ireland, as in 'Reading Turgenev' (in *Two Lives*, 1991), or a more general air of private loss and lack of emotional fulfilment, as in the title story of his collection, *The Ballroom of Romance* (1972). Trevor has adapted his overall sense of the misfit and the incompatible to represent Anglo-Irish relations in such works as the title story of his collection *The News from Ireland* (1986), the novels *Felicia's Journey* (1994) and *The Story of Lucy Gault* (2002). He has also written two works of nonfiction, *A Writer's Ireland* (1984) and *Excursions in the* Real World (1993). Trevor's many awards include that of Honourary Commander of the British Empire for services to literature. G.OB.

Trimble, David (1944–). Politician. Born on 15 October 1944, Trimble was educated at Bangor Grammar School and at Queen's University, *Belfast, where he read law and later lectured. In the early 1970s, Trimble was associated with the Vanguard, an organisation that straddled constitutional *unionist politics and paramilitary *loyalism. Though Trimble repudiated violence, he worked to develop populist agitation against the temporising unionist

David Trimble and George Mitchell

leadership and played an important role in the successful loyalist strike against *Sunningdale in 1974. He did much to provide intellectual ballast for intransigent unionism.

After the Sunningdale Executive fell, Trimble was expelled from the United Ulster Unionist Council, a coalition of parties opposed to Sunningdale, because he favoured 'voluntary coalition' with the *Social Democratic and Labour Party (SDLP). Even in his militant phase, Trimble was not averse to dialogue.

Trimble helped fellow loyalists on the fringe produce a policy document – *Ulster can Survive Unfettered* – advocating an independent *Northern Ireland. Such a state would seek cross-border cooperation as an equal with the *Republic and, an idea Trimble resurrected (in diluted form) in the *Good Friday Agreement, a Community of the British Isles. In 1987 he presented to the Ulster Clubs (a movement established in 1987 to oppose the *Anglo-Irish Agreement) a document advocating dominion status for 'Ulster'.

Trimble had joined the *Ulster Unionist Party in 1978, though his application was approved by only 103 votes to 100. Nevertheless, by trading upon his hardline reputation, he won the leadership of the UUP in 1995, after the 75-year-old James *Molyneaux had resigned. The same year he had notoriously marched in triumph with Ian *Paisley in an *Orange parade through the predominantly Catholic Garvaghy Road in Portadown.

Throughout the *peace process negotiations, Trimble believed that the *republican movement intended to place such pressure on the unionists that they would walk away from the talks. Determined to avoid a 'green settlement' (favouring the *nationalists) imposed by the British and Irish governments, he trenchantly criticised nationalist manoeuvres, but stayed in the all-party talks. The result was the *Good Friday Agreement of 1998. Though he lost votes to anti-agreement unionists, Trimble, as leader of the single largest party, became first minister of the new devolved government in the *Northern Ireland assembly. Determined to push on with unfinished business, principally forcing the *IRA to decommission weapons, in November 2000, he banned *Sinn Féin ministers from participating in the north-south bodies until the IRA gave up arms. In the summer of 2001, he resigned as first minister in protest at the IRA's failure to act. The agreement was saved and Trimble re-elected, when the IRA conceded a token decommissioning in the autumn of 2001. However, in 2002–

2003, the Northern Ireland assembly was again suspended.

Trimble is a pragmatist with considerable intellect and vision. His unionism draws upon an impressively eclectic range of intellectual influences, including Edmund *Burke and modern constitutional concepts of sovereignty borrowed from Canada, Australia and New Zealand. He envisages the development of an 'Ulster patriotism' no longer based upon religious cleavages, but rather grounded in a pluralist conception of a devolved United Kingdom. M.M.

Troubles, the. See **Northern Ireland conflict.**

Tuatha. Term for approximately 150 small independent kingdoms within Gaelic Ireland, each ruled by a local king, or *Rí. Tuatha* were populated by four classes of people: the king and royal family, or derbfine, the nobles, the freemen and the unfree. Under *brehon law, the *Rí* was elected by the freemen. Since claimants could include sons, grandsons and great-grandsons of kings, wars of succession were common. To prevent such wars, a successor or *Tánaiste* was often chosen during the king's lifetime. P.E.

Tuohy, Patrick (1894–1930). Painter. Born in *Dublin, Tuohy studied art at St Enda's under William Pearse and at Dublin Metropolitan School of Art under William *Orpen. He was an accomplished portrait painter of such celebrated figures as James *Joyce, Richard *Mulcahy, James *Stephens and George *Russell. He taught at the Dublin Metropolitan School of Art from 1920 and exhibited regularly at the *Royal Hibernian Academy until his departure to New York in 1927. He exhibited there in 1929. M.C.

Tyrone, County. Inland county in the province of *Ulster, one of the six counties of *Northern Ireland. Covering an area of 1,260 square miles, Tyrone has a population of est. 152,827 (1996). The county's economy is mainly agricultural with some *textile production. Tyrone comes from the Irish *Tír Eoghain*, the land of Eoin, who was a son of Niall of the Nine Hostages, the fifth-century ancestor of the Uí Néill (*O'Neill) dynasty. One of their great scions was Owen Roe *O'Neill, who defeated the English General Monroe at the Battle of Benburb, in County Tyrone, in 1646. A little farther to the north, a famous convention took place at Dungannon in February of 1782, at which *Protestant *Volunteers asserted Ireland's claim to independence and free trade and demanded the relaxation of the *Penal Laws.

A reconstruction of Tyrone's past can be seen in both the Heritage Park, at Gortin Glen, and in the Ulster-American Folk Park outside Omagh. Important urban centres include Dungannon, Omagh, the scene of a horrific dissident *IRA bombing in 1998 (known as the *Omagh Bombing), Cookstown and Strabane, birthplace of Brian O'Nolan (1912–66), known also as Flann *O'Brien and Myles na Gopaleen. Strabane was also the birthplace of John Dunlop (1747–1812), who printed the first copies of the American Declaration of Independence, and Dergalt, nearby, was the birthplace of American President Woodrow Wilson's grandfather. Tyrone's landscape varies from the 2,000-foot-high Sperrin Mountains (where gold may have been panned 4,000 years ago), to the lowlands around Lough Neagh, Ireland's largest lake. On its shores stands the 'Old Cross of Ardboe' (ninth/tenth century), one of Ireland's most venerable monuments. Famous natives include William *Carleton, author of *Traits and Stories of the Irish Peasantry*; man of letters Benedict *Kiely; sculptor Oliver *Sheppard; and Bernadette Devlin *McAliskey, the youngest ever member of the House of Commons. P.H.

U

UDA (Ulster Defence Association). *Loyalist paramilitary group. Formed in September 1971 from a number of loyalist vigilante groups (principally the Shankill Defence Association), the UDA was, and remains, the largest loyalist paramilitary group in *Northern Ireland. From the imposition of direct rule in March 1972, the UDA participated in an assassination campaign against Catholic civilians. The UDA sought to 'punish' support for the *IRA in Catholic areas and to warn the British government of the loyalist capacity for atrocity in the event of a 'sell-out to *nationalism'. The association reached a peak in 1974, when it played an important role in the strike that brought down the *Sunningdale Agreement. With fluctuating degrees of intensity, UDA violence continued throughout the *Troubles, killing hundreds. At first the UDA backed the *Good Friday Agreement, particularly as it led to the release of its prisoners. However, support for the agreement gradually dissipated as the UDA witnessed apparent *republican political gains. M.M.

UDR (Ulster Defence Regiment). British army unit. A locally recruited regiment of the British army, the UDR was formed on 1 April 1970, to replace the *B-Specials (Ulster Special Constabulary). The UDR was merged with the Royal Irish Rangers in July 1992. The UDR initially attracted *Catholic membership of 18%, but this figure fell to 3%. There has been collusion between loyalist paramilitaries and some UDR members. During its existence, the UDR lost 197 serving members and 47 former members, killed mainly by the *IRA. The UDR killed two members of the IRA and six Catholic civilians. M.M.

UVF (Ulster Volunteer Force). *Loyalist paramilitary organisation. Originally formed in 1912 to resist *home rule, the Ulster Volunteer Force was revived in 1966 by loyalists to oppose attempts by the *Belfast and *Dublin governments to improve north-south relations. As the recent *Northern Ireland conflict erupted in the early 1970s, the UVF embarked on an intensive campaign of assassination of *nationalists and was responsible for some of the most infamous killings of the Troubles, including the *Dublin and *Monaghan Bombings. In the Miami Showband killings, three members of a southern music group were killed in a gun and bomb attack by a UVF gang which included two *UDR soldiers. The Shankill Butchers, an infamously violent UVF gang, brutally attacked innocent Catholic civilians in the 1970s and were convicted of 19 murders and over 100 other offences.

The UVF has made a number of attempts to organise a political party (the Volunteer Political Party in 1974), but there were long periods when the organisation saw its role as purely military and left politics to the mainstream *unionist parties. The formation of the *Progressive Unionist Party (PUP) in 1979 was a re-emergence of open political activity for the UVF, but that party remained marginal until after the 1994 cease-fires.

As a paramilitary organisation, the UVF was always smaller, more disciplined and more centrally controlled than its main rival the *UDA, which had a reputation for drug dealing, extortion and personal enrichment. In later years, the UVF has been involved in some of the most brutal attacks on nationalist civilians in Northern Ireland, such as the pub shootings in Loughinisland in 1994, when six people were killed while watching a World Cup *soccer match on television. Following the 1994 cease-fire, the Portadown-based organisation led by Billy Wright opposed the UVF leadership. Wright was eventually expelled from the UVF and ordered to leave Northern Ireland. (He was killed by the Irish National Liberation Army in the Maze prison on 27 December 1997.) While there have been breaches of the UVF cease-fire, the organisation has been much more disciplined than the UDA. The PUP have made some political inroads, having two members elected to the assembly in 1998 and maintaining a reasonably high media profile. Consequently, the UVF has remained positive toward the *peace process, despite the ultimate rejection of the process by the UDA. J.D.

uilleann pipes. A bellows-blown bagpipe peculiar to Ireland, which evolved from earlier Irish pipes most likely in the mid-seventeenth or early eighteenth century. A key feature is a versatile melody-producing chanter which covers two full octaves. It also has three accompanying drones tuned to the chanter's lowest note (tenor, baritone and bass) and, also a unique feature, additional melody pipes (usually three – tenor, baritone and bass), which extend the lower range of the instrument to G below middle C. Called 'regulators', these additional pipes are used in harmonic, melodic, or vamping ways and use double (oboe-style) reeds. The pipe's chanter also has a double reed which, with the dry air that the bellows supplies, can be easily 'overblown' to yield the second octave; the drones use 'single' reeds. Its modern, popular concert form was evolved in Philadelphia during the 1870s to 1890s by the Drogheda-born Taylor brothers. F.V.

Ulster. Northern province, which is divided between the *Republic of Ireland and *Northern Ireland. Six of Ulster's nine counties – *Antrim, *Armagh, *Down, *Derry, *Fermanagh and *Tyrone – have made up Northern Ireland since the *Government of Ireland Act (1920). The other three counties – *Cavan, *Donegal and *Monaghan – are part of the Republic of Ireland. The name derives from the Uluti, a tribe in *pre-Christian Ireland. The term Ulster is often used inter-changeably with Northern Ireland, even though the province includes the three counties of the Republic of Ireland. In the fifteenth and sixteenth centuries, Ulster was a stronghold of Irish resistance (mostly by the *O'Neill and O'Donnell clans) to the spread of English power. *Belfast, the capital of Northern Ireland, is located in the southern part of County Antrim. The province has the island's largest lake – Lough Neagh – and the unique rock formation known as the *Giant's Causeway. J.OM.

Ulster Democratic Party (UDP). Political party. The UDP was formed in 1989 from the Ulster Loyalist Democratic Party, which had been set up by the *UDA in 1981. The UDP seeks to present itself as a distinct and separate organisation from the UDA, much in the same fashion as *Sinn Féin sees its relationship with the *IRA. The poor electoral showing of the party has reduced its political leverage on the loyalist paramilitants. M.M.

Ulster Museum. *Northern Ireland's principal museum. Located in *Belfast, the museum displays artifacts relating to the history and heritage of *Ulster. The collection of the Belfast Natural History Society (which was first displayed in 1831) was incorporated into the Belfast Museum and Art Gallery in the 1890s. The museum came to its present location in the city's *Botanic Gardens in 1929 and was later renamed the Ulster Museum. A major extension was opened in 1972. (Address: Botanic Gardens, Belfast BT9 5AB. Web site: *www.ulstermuseum.org.uk*.) S.A.B.

Ulster Plantation, the. Seventeenth-century colonisation of *Ulster by English and Scottish settlers. In March 1603, the Treaty of *Mellifont ended the *Nine Years War against England. To avoid the confiscation of their lands, the rebels had to renounce their Gaelic titles and ancestral rights and live by English law. However, in what is known as the *Flight of the Earls, *O'Neill and over 90 other Ulster chieftains sailed for the continent in September 1607. This flight was considered treason and the British government confiscated all their lands. Approximately four million acres in six counties (*Donegal, *Derry, *Tyrone, *Fermanagh, *Armagh and *Cavan) mapped out in a survey were to be colonised. The confiscated territory was divided into estates of 1,000, 1,500 and 2,000 acres. The estates were distributed to three groups: English and Scottish Undertakers, who undertook to bring settlers to Ireland; Servitors, who were being rewarded for service to the crown; and Irish 'of good merit', whom the British trusted. Any remaining land was to be set aside for the established church, Trinity College and the building of towns and six free schools. Rents for the English and Scottish planters were low, but settlers were expected to build fortified enclosures or bawns.

Despite extensive planning, problems with the *plantation quickly developed. Not enough Undertakers arrived, while some began taking Irish tenants illegally. The scheme did not succeed in establishing purely English-Scottish settlements because the native population was never fully removed. Despite these setbacks, by 1640, over 40,000 English and mostly Scottish settlers had arrived. Even though the *Rebellion of 1641 showed that the Ulster Irish still had the capacity to wage war, the plantation by that stage was too well developed to be totally overthrown. The arrival of these colonists led to a social and political revolution that was to have long-term implications for the history of Ulster. P.E.

Ulster Unionist Party, the (UUP). Political party. The Ulster Unionist Party grew out of the Irish and British *unionism of the nineteenth century. In 1904/05, the Ulster Unionist Council (UUC) was set up in protest against British Prime Minster Arthur J. Balfour's perceived *home rule policies in Ireland. When the UUP emerged as a semi-independent party after *partition, the UUC became and remained its ruling body. The UUC consists of delegates from all the constituent parts of the party (e.g., women, *Orange men and women, youths, students, the actual local constituency organisations, etc.). These delegates elect the leadership of the UUP and determine its policies. (In this they are probably the most democratically organised party.) The party's main rationale had been the prevention of home rule, but after the *Government of Ireland Act (1920) and the *Anglo-Irish Treaty of 1921 had ironically bestowed a version of home rule on *Northern Ireland, the UUP felt compelled to defend the union with Great Britain not only against a perceived hostile southern state, but also against Irish *nationalism within its own jurisdiction. It was, and remained, the largest party in Northern Ireland, which it governed from 1921 to 1972. Until the 1960s, the UUP was led by a landed social elite distant from its rank and file, but its policies comprised a populist agenda that addressed the attitudes, prejudices and expectations of its constituency. In the tradition of nineteenth-century British parties, it was a coalition of interests embracing left-to-right policies with the common aim of maintaining the union with Britain and its parliament at *Stormont.

The relative prosperity of the 1960s allowed the liberal wing within the party to grow and Prime Minister Terence *O'Neill used Catholic-friendly rhetoric in the hope of encouraging nationalist acceptance of the state. This, combined with the growing self-confidence of the Catholic middle-classes and the civil rights movement, alienated the conservative wing of the party. With O'Neill's fall and the subsequent imposition of direct rule from London in 1972, the UUP found itself weakened and removed from government. Unless willing to engage in some form of power sharing with the constitutional nationalists, the *Social Democratic and Labour Party (SDLP), the UUP was bound to stay in the wilderness. A first attempt, Brian *Faulkner's power-sharing Executive of 1974 failed, however, under pressure from a constituency not willing to compromise with nationalists.

Throughout the following 25 years, the major policy issue for the party was whether or not a compromise with constitutional nationalism was possible. Its opposition to the *Anglo-Irish Agreement of 1985 showed the difficulties the party faced, which were increased when subsequent British governments changed their policy in Northern Ireland by encouraging *republican political participation. It was only in 1997, under its new leader (from 1995), David *Trimble, that the party was willing to enter negotiations with *Sinn Féin. A year later, the UUC endorsed the *Good Friday Agreement and the UUP joined a power-sharing government that included constitutional as well as republican nationalists. Over the coming years the party remained split as to the benefits of the new arrangements, which appeared to many to offer political benefits to nationalists at the expense of unionists. In the early years of the new century, it was becoming clear that the *Democratic Unionist Party (DUP), a much more radical unionist party, could overtake Trimble's unionism. S.W.

Union, Act of (1800). The law that created the United Kingdom of Great Britain and Ireland. After the *Rebellion of 1798, the British Prime Minister William Pitt decided to abolish the Dublin *parliament and introduce direct rule from London. The act, which was passed by both the Irish and British parliaments, came into effect on 1 January 1801. Under the union, Ireland was represented at Westminster by 100 members of parliament and in the House of Lords by four bishops and 28 lords chosen from the Irish peerage. The union meant common citizenship for the two islands, the same legal, tax and trading systems, and a new state Church of England and Ireland. Ireland would have to contribute two-seventeenths of United Kingdom Expenditure.

Initially many opposed the union: merchants who feared English competition, patriots loyal to the national parliament and the *Orange Order that believed the union would end Protestant ascendancy because Pitt had promised full *Catholic Emancipation in order to win Catholic support. Catholic bishops and others welcomed the union and the new era of stability it promised.

The bill was first introduced in January 1799 and was rejected in the Irish parliament by 111 votes to 106. Following this defeat, anti-union office-holders were replaced with supporters. The government won over MPs and peers with promotions and titles, and compensated corrupt borough patrons who would lose influence under the union. When the bill was re-introduced a year later, there was a large pro-union majority.

Protestants did well under the union and, in time, became its strongest supporters. However, the British government's failure to deliver Catholic Emancipation and continuing social problems led Irish Catholics to seek the act's *repeal. But all attempts to gain even a modest measure of *home rule failed for over a century and the Act of Union remained in effect until the *Government of Ireland Act (1920) and the *Anglo-Irish Treaty (1921). T.C.

unionism. Political philosophy that advocates the union of *Northern Ireland with

Great Britain. Founded in 1886, unionism was initially a loose collection of unionist associations spread throughout Ireland, united in opposition against *home rule, or self-government for the island of Ireland. The unionist movement changed British politics, which until then mainly consisted of rivalry between the Conservative and Liberal Parties. Unionists allied themselves with the Conservatives in opposition to the pro-home rule Liberals and their combined strength in the House of Commons kept the Liberals out of power from 1886 to 1906. To this day, the formal title of the British Conservative Party remains the 'Conservative and Unionist Party'.

In the north, where it was concentrated, unionism had roots going back to the late eighteenth century. One of unionism's most important constituent elements, the *Orange Order (which still nominates a substantial part of the Unionist Party's ruling council) had been founded in 1795 following an attack by a *Catholic group on a *Protestant inn in County *Armagh.

After 1906, home rule was back on the political agenda, and as Britain moved inexorably toward granting a measure of self-government to the rebellious island, unionism became, in effect, a rebellion within a rebellion. Unionists were determined to resist home rule by force of arms if necessary, even if this meant military opposition to the government of the state with which it wished to remain united. By 1912, a total of some 447,000 people (Northern Ireland had approximately 500,000 adult Protestants) signed the so-called *Ulster Covenant, by which they swore, among other things, to use 'all means which may be found necessary to defeat the present conspiracy to set up a home rule parliament in Ireland'.

Under unionist pressure, Prime Minister *Lloyd George passed the *Government of Ireland Act (1920), thereby establishing the state of Northern Ireland. In 1921, under the *Anglo-Irish Treaty, the *Irish Free State, was created consisting of twenty-six counties. The largely autonomous region of Northern Ireland as provided in the Government of Ireland Act continued to remain an integral part of the United Kingdom. This statelet (which had its own parliament) embodied six of the nine counties of the province of Ulster and was specifically constructed to ensure that unionists would have a guaranteed electoral majority for the indefinite future.

Political unionism was now confined to Northern Ireland, where it had an effective monopoly of state power, including control over security. For the following half a century, it exercised this power under the shadow, as unionism saw it, of two distinct threats: one from Northern Ireland's dissident *nationalist minority, the other from the irredentism (rarely if ever backed up by practical action) ritually displayed by successive governments of the new state in Dublin. This, in turn, produced a regime in Northern Ireland characterised by subtle and not-so-subtle erosion of the civil rights of the nationalist minority, harsh security policies and by an endemically sectarian administration.

Unionism united Protestants of all social classes in opposition to the perceived threat of rule by the island's overwhelming Catholic majority. This outward unity, however, concealed rather than eradicated class tensions. Working-class Protestants, in particular, were tempted by *socialist solutions to political problems, leading to the emergence of splinter groups among unionism in the 1920s. The Northern Ireland government's abolition of the proportional voting system in 1929 checked this trend. Another threat to the hegemony of unionism arose in the mid-1930s, when harsh economic conditions provoked anti-government joint hunger marches by Catholic and Protestant working-class men. Unionist leaders, however, deflected this political threat with well-worn anti-nationalist rhetoric.

From 1940 to 1963, unionism was an implacable, immovable political force, both to the nationalist minority and to the British parliament, which had effectively washed its hands of responsibility for the gerrymandering and discrimination which had become hallmarks of the *Stormont administration. The *IRA heightened unionists' fears by mounting a sporadic and largely ineffective campaign of attacks on Northern Ireland security installations between 1956 and 1962. In the latter year, however, Captain Terence *O'Neill became prime minister of Northern Ireland with a mildly reformist agenda and, in 1965, made well-intentioned but sometimes gauche attempts to create better relationships with nationalists within Northern Ireland and, across the border, with the Republic. O'Neill was prompted partly by a desire to attract industrial entrepreneurs to the region, especially from the United States. These moves, however, created fresh tensions within unionism. Liberal unionism, most firmly entrenched among the middle-classes, embraced the idea, albeit with some initial hesitation and caution. The emergence of the Ian *Paisley's brand of independent unionism provoked ungovernable tensions within unionism generally, and contributed to O'Neill's loss of office in 1969. Paisley's creation of the *Democratic Unionist Party (DUP) in 1971 was a religiously inspired, formal rejection of mainstream unionism. Since then, the DUP has become a powerful force within unionism, continually threatening its older parent and influencing its political agenda. Extreme unionism, or loyalism as it is more generally described, is characterised by its willingness to resort to armed force and has spawned a number of paramilitary organisations. Other factions, such as the *Progressive Unionist Party (PUP) and the Ulster Popular Unionist Party, are left-leaning working-class splinter groups. These parties' relationship with paramilitaries mirrors the relationship between *Sinn Féin and the IRA, the major difference being that loyalist paramilitaries have been less susceptible to political influence or control than their republican contemporaries.

This process of splintering within unionism, aided by the re-introduction of a proportional electoral system, has allowed for the representation of most of the variegated forms of unionism within the *peace process and, more importantly, within the new legislative assembly. These groups, with their strong social bases, distrust the traditional middle-class leadership of unionism to the point that, without relinquishing their traditional constitutional allegiance to Britain, on occasion they find themselves sharing at least part of a political agenda with working-class nationalists in Sinn Féin and similar organisations. In this, as in some other respects, the future of unionism may be markedly different from its past. J.H.

United Irishmen, the Society of. Organisation that pioneered the politics and agenda of Irish *republicanism from its inception in October 1791. The United Irishmen were a product of the political environment in Ireland in the years following the *American War of Independence and the *French Revolution of 1789. Many Irish liberals argued that the democratic rights effected by force of arms in America and France should be extended to the people of Ireland where an elite comprising less than 3% of the population had total control of the government. An exceptionally narrow franchise, weighted toward large property owners and from which Catholics and *Presbyterians were all but excluded, was increasingly regarded in progressive Irish circles as unjust. The pioneering republican coterie of Theobald Wolfe *Tone, William *Drennan, Thomas Addis Emmet, Thomas Russell and Samuel Neilson, whose political ideas drew on the most promising international precedents and the diffused legacy of the Enlightenment, founded the Society of United Irishmen in *Belfast and *Dublin in October/November 1791. Using the *Northern*

Star and other radical organs, the United Irishmen sought to mobilise popular opinion through print and thereby exert pressure on government to instigate far-reaching reforms.

After the outbreak of war with France in February 1793, the organisation was banned in April 1794 when proof of seditious contact with the French government was uncovered in Dublin. On 10 May 1795, the United Irishmen were effectively revived using a model constitution for an organisationally sophisticated paramilitary organisation intended to function as auxiliaries to their invading French allies. The Jacobin and violent *Defenders were quickly subsumed into the United Irishmen's superstructure, and a major recruitment drive was mounted after December 1796 when a French army came within sight of the *Cork coast but did not disembark. Refinements were made to the *modus operandi* of the United Irishmen in August 1797, but it proved necessary to mount a unilateral *Rebellion on 23–24 May 1798, owing to severe losses of personnel and equipment under martial law. Early setbacks in Dublin and unexpected communications problems turned a potentially decisive revolution of up to 300,000 United Irishmen into a partial and *ad hoc* effort in various zones. Lack of coordination between the provinces, inadequate leadership and the chronic imbalance of firepower between the insurgents and crown forces produced a string of heavy defeats and Pyrrhic victories for the rebels. Nonetheless, several important wins by the rebels, most notably in *Wexford, contributed to the extreme seriousness with which the rebellion was regarded in Dublin and then in London. It required the transfer of the bulk of available military forces in Britain and the extension of a liberal amnesty programme to contain and then demobilise the rebel armies. Rebels held out in several sectors until the end of 1803 and the chronic disaffection of the Irish population was a critical consideration in effecting legislative union with Britain in 1800. R.OD.

United Nations (UN). Ireland joined the UN in 1955 as part of an agreement between the United States and the Soviet Union on new members. Ireland has served three times on the UN Security Council, in 1962, 1981–82 and from 2001 to 2003. The Nuclear Non-Proliferation Treaty originated in an Irish initiative at the UN general assembly in 1958 and Ireland was the first to ratify the treaty. The Irish Defence Forces have been a major contributor to UN peacekeeping and peacemaking missions, with a significant proportion of the forces deployed on UN missions at any time. J.D.

universities. Following two failed attempts to found a native university in the fourteenth century, Trinity College, the sole college of the University of *Dublin, was established with the city's assistance in 1592. Trinity was modelled on the residential colleges of the universities of Oxford and Cambridge. In spite of an early effort to encourage the teaching of the *Irish language, Trinity remained a bastion of the New English *Protestant establishment in Ireland and much of the college's revenues came from its extensive landholdings. The Anglican constitution of the university was firmly established by Chancellor William Laud during the 1630s. Roman *Catholics and Protestant Dissenters were formally excluded from the University of Dublin until 1793 and religious tests for some fellowships survived until 1873.

The academic reputation of the University of Dublin fluctuated during the seventeenth and eighteenth centuries. However, the 'Debating Club' founded at Trinity by Edmund *Burke in 1747 provided a forum for undergraduates to discuss political issues. The club proved to be a seedbed for radical ideas and its members included the revolutionary leaders Wolfe *Tone and Robert *Emmet, who was expelled from the college in 1798. The number of Catholic students attending Trinity rose steadily during the early nineteenth

Trinity College, Long Room, Old Library

century. Catholics accounted for almost one in ten of the student body in 1830, but their numbers declined thereafter. Both Protestant and Catholic students of Trinity College, such as Thomas *Davis and John *O'Leary, became prominent Irish *nationalists during the nineteenth century. However, the university remained a stronghold of the *Anglo-Irish establishment and elected *unionist MPs to parliament until 1922. Trinity College acquired a reputation as an important centre for the study of medicine and produced many leading scholars in the fields of classics and history, including J. P. Mahaffy (1839–1919) and J. B. Bury (1861– 1927).

Because of Trinity's discrimination against Catholics and Protestant Dissenters, several *Presbyterian academies were established in the north, including the Belfast Academical Institution (1814) and Magee College in *Derry (1865). During the seventeenth and eighteenth centuries, Roman Catholic students were forced to attend seminaries known as 'Irish colleges' in *France and Spain. After a number of these colleges were closed by the revolutionary regime in France, William Pitt encouraged the Irish parliament to establish a seminary. St Patrick's College, founded in *Maynooth in 1795, was state-funded until 1871. It served primarily as a seminary for clerical students, but also provided higher education for lay students until 1817. Its creation stimulated the foundation of diocesan seminaries throughout Ireland.

After *Catholic Emancipation in 1829, the 'Irish university question' became a highly charged political issue as middle-class Catholics sought equal access to university education. Sir Robert Peel's decision to substantially increase the annual grant to Maynooth in 1845 aroused considerable anti-Catholic sentiment in Great Britain and Ireland. That same year, parliament created three 'Queen's Colleges' in *Belfast, *Cork and *Galway. They opened to students in 1849 and were linked together in 1850 to form the Queen's University of Ireland. The university offered students low fees and vocationally orientated curricula and was designed to meet the Catholic demand for higher education. However, the institution's secular constitution was criticised by both Daniel *O'Connell and the Catholic church. A papal rescript issued in 1847 condemned the Queen's Colleges and proposed the foundation of an autonomous Catholic university modelled on Louvain. In 1851, John Henry *Newman was appointed first rector of the Catholic University, which opened in Dublin in 1854. The new institution was, however, underfunded and failed largely because it was not empowered to award its own degrees.

In 1873, Prime Minister William *Gladstone's ambitious scheme to create a single university for Ireland consisting of the Dublin, Queen's and Catholic universities was decisively rejected by all sides. Nevertheless, in 1879 the University Education (Ireland) Act established an examining body, the Royal University (1882), which was empowered to grant degrees to any students who passed its examinations. This scheme allowed Catholic students, whose attendance at Trinity College was later restricted by a ban imposed by the Catholic church (1944), to graduate from their own colleges. The government made a further concession to Catholic students in 1908 when it established two new universities. The National University of Ireland (NUI) was a federal institution consisting of the Catholic University, known since 1883 as University College, Dublin (UCD), and the Queen's Colleges in Cork and Galway. Maynooth was recognised by the NUI in 1910 and became a full constituent college in 1967. The remaining Queen's College was re-established as the Queen's University of Belfast. While the NUI was in theory a nondenominational body, the Catholic hierarchy was given a major role in governing its colleges. The NUI played an important part in educating a Catholic professional class and the staff and students of UCD, such as Thomas Kettle, Francis *Sheehy Skeffington and James *Joyce, were particularly influential in Irish cultural and political life. The early twentieth century also saw Irish *women establish themselves within the universities. Since 1882, the Royal University had awarded degrees to female students including Hanna *Sheehy Skeffington. Women were first admitted to Trinity College in 1904 and the vibrant atmosphere at UCD encouraged the emergence of a new generation of feminist campaigners.

After *partition, university education in *Northern Ireland centred upon the Queen's University of Belfast. After the Second World War, improved funding enabled increasing numbers of Catholic students to attend the university and by the 1960s, Queen's had become an important centre of the civil rights movement. During 1965 to 1968, the New University of *Ulster was created. Controversy ensued when *Stormont decided to situate the campus in the *unionist stronghold of Coleraine rather than in the more populous and largely nationalist city of Derry. Public protest at this decision was mobilised by a new generation of national figures including John *Hume. In 1984, the multicampus University of Ulster was created by merging the New University with the Ulster Polytechnic and the Ulster College of Art.

As higher education expanded in the *Republic of Ireland during the 1960s, the rivalry between and perception of, Trinity College and UCD as Protestant and Catholic colleges declined significantly. The Catholic church lifted its ban on Catholics attending Trinity in 1970 and most of the students currently attending Trinity, Queen's and the New University of Ulster are Roman Catholics. Nevertheless, government schemes to merge the two institutions were unsuccessful. As the number of fulltime students in the Republic rose from 19,000 in 1966 to 115,000 in 2001, reform of the university system became necessary. National Institutes of Higher Education were established in *Limerick (1970) and Dublin (1976) and both became universities in 1989. In 1997, the Universities Act redefined the constitution of the NUI and gave its four constituent colleges in Dublin, Cork, Galway and Maynooth a greater degree of administrative independence. S.A.B.

urbanisation. Ireland has been a predominantly rural society. The original inhabitants of the island and, later, the *Celts were nomadic. Monastic sites became important population centres in the age of *Christianity, but they were not cities as presently defined. The origin of towns begins with the arrival of the *Vikings in the late eighth century, who founded the cities of *Limerick, *Dublin and *Waterford. The original towns were trading centres for the Norse. After the *Anglo-Norman Conquest in 1169, the Normans built *castles. The church, which up to then had been monastic-centred, became diocesan-based and controlled by bishops. Whereas the church organised people in parishes or small villages, the commercialisation of *agriculture under British dominance led to the establishment of towns as trading centres. Towns, however, remained small with a few notable exceptions because the agrarian-based *economy did not need large urban centres for industrial production. In the nineteenth century population growth continued to be concentrated in rural areas until the *Famine. After the Famine, the population stabilised based on high levels of *emigration, decreasing the demographic pressure for urban growth. By the time of independence in 1922, less than a third of the population lived in urban areas. Throughout the twentieth century, the mechanisation of agriculture production caused the rural population to decline, so that by the 1990s only about 40% of the population lived in rural areas. This is a remarkably high number, considering Ireland's recent dramatic economic growth. Because of Ireland's small size, the urbanisation has resulted in almost 40% of the population living in and around Dublin, making it one of the most capital-concentrated countries in the *EU, with the exception of Greece.

There are several reasons for the slow pace of urbanisation. First, Ireland never experienced the industrial revolution and the majority of its workforce did not work in industry. In most other European countries, the industrialisation of the workforce in the nineteenth century propelled urbanisation. Ireland has made a transition from an agrarian economy to a service-oriented economy in the latter half of the twentieth century. Today, approximately two-thirds of the Irish workforce is in the service sector and less than 6% is engaged in agriculture and related activities. Secondly, the Irish people generally prefer living in the countryside rather than in Dublin and other cities. The pace of life, county and local loyalties, as well as a lower cost of living, make life in small towns and villages much more attractive. Thirdly, the Irish government actively promotes economic growth and job creation in non-urban areas and subsidises agriculture. While urbanisation has been comparatively slow, recent projections by the Central Statistics Office in Dublin suggest a continuing decline in the rural population, especially in the midlands, while the major cities of Dublin, Cork, Limerick and Galway will continue to grow rapidly. Urbanisation is accelerating and changing the character of Irish society. T.W.

Ussher, James (1581–1656). Anglican archbishop of *Armagh, scholar and theologian. Born in *Dublin, he was ordained in 1601 and was professor of theological controversies and twice vice chancellor at Trinity College, Dublin, between 1607 and 1621. He became bishop of *Meath in 1621 and archbishop of Armagh in 1625. His most famous work, *Annals of the World* (published between 1650 and 1654), used his chronology of the Old Testament to date the creation of the universe to 4004 BC. His extensive library is now in the possession of Trinity College, Dublin. P.E.

U2. Rock band. Consisting of Bono (Paul Hewson, b. 1960), The Edge (David Evans, b. 1961), Adam Clayton (b. 1960) and Larry Mullen, Jr (b. 1961), U2 is one of the most successful rock bands of all time. Formed in 1976 while its original five then-teenage members were students at Mount Temple Comprehensive School in *Dublin, the band was initially known as Feedback and then as the Hype. The current lineup became known as U2 in 1978. Their first full-length album, *Boy*, was released on Island Records in 1980, to critical acclaim. What distinguishes U2 are the intelligent, spiritual, politically and socially aware lyrics and the band's unique sound. Since the early 1980s, the band has attracted a huge following and in 1985 *Rolling Stone* magazine branded them 'Band of the '80s'. Stellar performances at the 1985 Live Aid concert and Amnesty International's 1986 Conspiracy of Hope tour were followed by the album *The Joshua Tree* (1987), which became an international hit. In 1988, the band released *Rattle and Hum*, a concert film and album, to mixed reviews. The 1990s were a time of musical experimentation for U2, to varying degrees of success in terms of sales, critics and fans. Their 2000 release *All That You Can't Leave Behind* was hailed as a critical success, winning seven Grammy Awards. Bono continues to work tirelessly for humanitarian causes such as the cancellation of Third World countries' debt and the elimination of land mines. N.H.

Bono, lead singer with U2

Victoria, Queen (1819–1901). Queen of Great Britain and Ireland (1837–1901), Empress of India (1876–1901). Queen Victoria made the first of four visits to Ireland in May 1849, bestowing the name of Queenstown upon Cobh, County *Cork. She was criticised for ignoring the plight of her Irish subjects during the Great *Famine. The queen supported the public funding of the Roman *Catholic seminary at *Maynooth (1845) and disapproved of the violent public reaction against the Vatican's revival of territorial titles for Roman Catholic bishops in England (1851). After the death of her husband, Prince Albert, in 1861, she played a significant role in domestic politics. She disapproved of the disestablishment of the *Church of Ireland (1871), but recognised its inevitability and endeavoured to minimise opposition to the measure in the House of Lords. She was strongly opposed to *Gladstone's Irish *home rule bills (1886 and 1893). In April 1900, Victoria visited Ireland for the last time to encourage army recruitment for the *Boer War. S.A.B.

Vikings. Norsemen, largely from western Norway, who made raids on Ireland from 795 onward. The Vikings founded the first Irish cities, such as *Dublin, *Limerick, *Wexford and *Waterford, after 840. Their frequent raids on Irish monasteries gave them a reputation of being uncivilised barbarians. However, by bringing home looted treasures and later burying them in graves in Scandinavia, they preserved important Irish metalwork fragments that might otherwise have perished and which are now preserved in museums in Bergen, Oslo, Stockholm and elsewhere. Recent research suggests that the Vikings had a complex and dynamic culture.

The Vikings often made strategic alliances with Irish kings, intermarried with the native population and many became Christian by the year 1000. Great traders, they taught the Irish much about commerce and boat building, at which they excelled. Contrary to popular tradition, the Viking influence began to decline before the Battle of *Clontarf in 1014. P.H.

Vinegar Hill, Battle of (County *Wexford; 21 June 1798). One of the turning points of the *Rebellion of 1798 in which the *United Irishmen attempted to establish an Irish republic with French military assistance. By mid-May 1798, the United Irishmen decided to mount an insurrection on 23 May without awaiting the French. A string of victories in Wexford marked that county as the most successful rebel sector and led to the mobilisation of large insurgent armies. At Vinegar Hill camp, which towered over the town of Enniscorthy, Reverend Philip Roche ordered all Wexford rebel groups to mass there on 21 June but only a proportion came before the government forces attacked. The military focused their counter-attack on Enniscorthy and used almost 10,000 men backed by artillery to drive the rebels from Vinegar Hill. While losses were comparatively slight owing to a gap in the army's cordon through which the vast majority of rebels escaped, the strategic initiative passed decisively to the government. Wexford quickly became untenable as a theatre for the rebels and the rebellion waned in the eastern counties outside the Wicklow mountains. R.OD.

Volunteers, the. Militia force organised in Ireland during the *American War of Independence to protect Ireland from an opportunist attack from *France. Uniformed units of infantry, cavalry and artillery, frequently formed by lesser gentry and magistrates at their own expense, offered nominal service to the Irish *parliament at College Green, *Dublin, for the duration of the war. While predominantly *Protestant in membership and overwhelmingly so at officer level, many units made ostentatious overtures to Catholic recruits in 1777–78 to signal their support for the 'Patriot' reform agenda of Henry Flood and Henry *Grattan, which sought to free Irish legislation from the Westminster system. A series of conventions or rallies, most notably that held at Dungannon, Tyrone, in 1782, issued pro-reform resolutions which identified the Volunteers as a *de facto* armed wing of the Grattanites. It rapidly became apparent that the Irish Patriots and the Volunteers in particular were perhaps not only capable, but possibly willing, to emulate the achievements of the rebellious American colonists with whom they sympathised. Veiled threats of violence by the Volunteers obliged Westminster to concede a measure of legislative independence to the Dublin parliament in 1782. After Ireland had a largely sovereign parliament, Grattan rejected violent coercion pressures and the Volunteers faded away. But later the Society of *United Irishmen posed a serious threat of revolution. Alarmed, *Dublin Castle imposed tight control of the *Yeomanry raised in 1796. At the same time, army headquarters strictly supervised the fulltime Irish militia, which had enlisted for the duration of the French War and served as infantry alongside the regular army mustered in 1793.

The term was also used for the Irish Volunteers, which was formed in 1913 and later became the *Irish Republican Army. R.OD.

W

Wall, Mervyn (pseudonym for Eugene Welply) (1908–97). Writer, playwright. Born in *Dublin, Wall presents in his novels and plays a sardonic view of the alliance of priests, shopkeepers and farmers dominating post-treaty (*Anglo-Irish Treaty) Irish life. In the novels *The Unfortunate Fursey* (1946) and *The Return of Fursey* (1948), he uses the adventures and misfortunes of a speech-impaired early medieval monk to satirise twentieth-century puritan, *Catholic Ireland. Wall's beautifully crafted 1952 novel, *Leaves for the Burning*, is a most insightful literary look at 1940s and early 1950s. After many years in the civil service, Wall became secretary (1957–73) and director (1973–75) of the Irish Arts Council, where he championed Irish *literature, *theatre and the visual and *musical arts. L.J.MC.

Walton, E[rnest] T. S. (1903–95). Physicist and Nobel laureate. Born in Dungarvan, County *Waterford, Walton spent most of his life at Trinity College, Dublin, as student, fellow and physics professor. From 1927 to 1934, he was a member of Rutherford's nuclear physics research group at the Cavendish Laboratory. In 1932, he and John Cockcroft bombarded lithium nuclei with protons accelerated to high energies, caused the nuclei to disintegrate, and identified the products as helium nuclei. They thus achieved the alchemists' dream of transforming one substance into another and launched accelerator-based experimental nuclear physics. In 1951, they received the Nobel Prize for physics. M.L.

War of Independence. See **Anglo-Irish War, the.**

Waterford, County. Maritime county in the province of *Munster. Covering 716 square miles, Waterford has a population of 101,518 (2002 census). The county is bounded on the north by the River Suir, on the east by Waterford Harbour and on the south by the Celtic Sea. The Knockmealdown (2,609 feet) and the Comeragh/Monavallagh mountains on its western boundary provide dramatic scenery. Waterford has many megalithic tombs, including Harristown near the fishing port of Dunmore East. Tramore (with one of the longest beaches in Ireland) and Dunmore East are the county's most popular summer resorts. Ardmore has an elegant twelfth-century *round tower and cathedral, built on a site founded by St Declan, one of the four *saints reputed to have been in Ireland before St *Patrick. Waterford was the ancient territory known as the Decies (Déise), some of whose people crossed the Irish Sea and settled in Wales in the fifth century. The area around Ring (An Rinn) is an Irish-speaking, or *Gaeltacht, area. The name Waterford derives from the ninth-century *Viking name for the harbour – *Vethrafjörthr* in old Norse. Its Irish name is *Port Láirge*. The city's most prominent monument is Reginald's Tower on the Quays, which local tradition dates to 1003.

Since 1783, Waterford has been a centre for glassmaking and its handcrafted *Waterford Crystal ranks among the most famous in the world. Other industries in the county are dairy farming and crop production, electronics and pharmaceuticals. Although Waterford City's population of 44,564 makes up almost half of the county's total, the county capital is the much smaller town of Dungarvan. Waterford City has an annual Light

*Opera Festival. Natives of the county include the great actor Tyrone Power (1797–1841), great-grandfather of the Hollywood swashbuckling actor of the same name; the theatrical producer Sir Tyrone *Guthrie; and Robert *Boyle, father of modern chemistry. P.H.

Waterford Crystal. World-famous crystal. The Waterford Glasshouse was founded by George and William Penrose in 1783. Over several generations, this family perfected the art of mixing minerals and glass to produce brilliant yet durable crystal ware. In 1851, the Penroses' crystal won several prizes at the Great Exhibition in London, but heavy export taxes forced their factory to close. The production of Waterford Crystal was revived in 1947 and it was relaunched on the world market in 1951. In the early 1960s a larger glassworks was built and by 1980 Waterford Crystal was the world's largest producer of handcrafted crystal. S.A.B.

wedge tombs. The last type of megalithic tomb. These wedge-shaped graves were erected largely during the early Bronze Age, before and after 2000 BC. Some, particularly in West *Cork (Altar and Lahardane Mór), may have been associated with early copper miners. Consisting of a long, gallery-like burial chamber facing westward and sometimes preceded by a portico, many were probably originally covered by a mound. P.H.

Wellesley, Arthur; Duke of Wellington (1769–1852). Politician and military leader. Born in *Dublin, Wellington always denied his Irishness and is reputed to have said: 'If one is born in a stable, one is not necessarily a horse'. He began his military career in India and became Britain's leading general against Napoleon, finally defeating him at Waterloo, in Belgium, in 1815. He was chief secretary for Ireland from 1807 to 1809. A hero after the Napoleonic War, Wellington became prime minister and in 1829 he oversaw the passing of *Catholic Emancipation. T.C.

Wentworth, Thomas (1593–1641). English statesman and lord deputy of Ireland (1632–40). Wentworth re-established royal authority and reformed the system of government, building for himself a large official residence in Jigginstown, County *Kildare. Wentworth's despotic style of government alienated both Old and New English landowners. As chief advisor to King Charles I, Wentworth (made the earl of Strafford in January 1640) raised funds from the Irish *parliament for the king's wars against the Scottish Covenanters (1639 and 1640). However, Wentworth's ruthless and unpopular use of the law to confiscate lands from English settlers coincided with a widespread belief that he intended to use an Irish army to crush parliamentary opposition to the king. Consequently, he was impeached by the English parliament and put on trial in March 1641. Wentworth mounted a sturdy defence against these charges but he was found guilty and was executed on 12 May 1641. Portraits of Wentworth include *Thomas Wentworth and his Secretary, Sir Phillip Mainwaring* by Anthony van Dyck (c.1634). S.A.B.

Wesley, John (1703–91). Evangelist who established Methodism in Ireland. Born in Epworth, Lincolnshire, John Wesley was educated in Oxford, where he and his brother Charles founded a 'methodist' society in 1729. In 1739, he began 'field preaching' in Bristol and formally established Methodism. Wesley first visited Ireland in 1747 and by the time of his death, 15,000 Irish members had joined Methodist societies. By 1901 there were 62,000 Methodists in Ireland, making them the country's third-largest *Protestant denomination. S.A.B.

Westmeath, County. Inland county in the province of *Leinster. The county has an area of 710 square miles and a population of 72,027 (2002 census). The old royal kingdom of Mide became part of the de Lacy earldom of Meath during the twelfth- and thirteenth-century *Anglo-Norman Conquest. In the sixteenth century, Meath was subdivided into East Meath and West Meath, the latter retaining its name, while the former is now simply County *Meath. Westmeath is a gentle, pastoral county with livestock and dairy farming the principal economy. The county capital, Mullingar, has a population of around 12,000. Athlone, on the River *Shannon, is a larger town with an urban district council and a rich history. It was besieged more than three times during the course of the seventeenth century, most famously in June 1690 when Williamite forces overcame the *Jacobites in what was the largest bombardment in Irish history. Athlone is the birthplace of renowned tenor John *McCormack and the novelist John Broderick (1927– 89). To the north-west of the town lies Lissoy, where Oliver *Goldsmith went to school and which is normally identified with the 'Sweet Auburn' of his famous poem *The Deserted Village*.

The centre of ancient Ireland was at Uisneach, east of Ballymore. The county is now bisected by the early-nineteenth century Royal Canal, which connects the Shannon with *Dublin City. Eskers, wormlike earthworks formed by glaciers millions of years ago, are found throughout the county. Fore is famous for its Seven Wonders (1. monastery in a *bog; 2. the mill without a race; 3. the water that flows uphill; 4. the tree that won't burn; 5. the water that won't boil; 6. the anchorite in a stone; 7. the stone raised by St Feichin's prayer), some associated with St Feichin who founded a monastery here in the seventh century. Other attractions in the county include Belvedere House, a mansion dating from the mid-eighteenth century, and Ballinlough Gardens. Tullynally *Castle is the home of the Pakenham family, earls of Longford. (Edward Pakenham, Lord Longford, was a playwright and director of the *Gate Theatre.) The novelist J. P. *Donleavy has lived in the county for many years. P.H.

Wexford, County. Maritime county in the province of *Leinster. Often referred to as 'the sunny south-east', Wexford (913 square miles) has a population of 116, 543 (2002 census). Its terrain falls gradually south-eastward from the Blackstairs Mountains (2,409 feet) to the low-lying countryside around the county's capital, also called Wexford. The origin of its name is Norse, as the town was founded by the *Vikings in the ninth century. But the agriculturally rich county had been settled thousands of years before that. Beg Eire, on the opposite bank of Wexford harbour, was founded by St Ibar, who may have been in Ireland before St *Patrick. Close by are the Wexford Slobs, an extensive wildfowl reserve. The Normans first landed at Baginbun in Wexford in 1169, initiating the *Anglo-Norman Conquest. South Wexford has fine *tower houses, built by the Norman invaders. In the baronies of Bargy and Forth, the most ancient English speech was preserved in a dialect known as Yola, until around 1850. County Wexford was one of the few places where the *Rebellion of 1798 actually took place under the leadership of Father John Murphy. The disastrous battle on *Vinegar Hill outside Enniscorthy ended the rebellion in Wexford.

The county is well endowed with historic monuments, including the great medieval Cistercian abbeys of Dunbrody and Tintern, the Norman church in New Ross and the *castle, *churches and high *crosses at Ferns, seat of Dermot *MacMurrough, who first invited the Normans to Ireland. Wexford's past is imaginatively re-created at the National Heritage Park at Ferrycarrig on the Slaney estuary. Kilmore Quay, with its picturesque thatched houses, looks out onto Saltee Islands, one of the great gannet colonies of north-western Europe. The port of Rosslare offers links with Wales and France by car ferries, which ply routes that have brought people and ideas to Ireland since the Stone Age. In Wexford town, a fine statue by the American sculptor Wheeler Williams commemorates Wexford-born Commodore John Barry (1745–1803), father of the American navy. The internationally renowned *Wexford Opera Festival, held annually since 1951 in October/November, is devoted to the staging of rarely heard *operas. Notable natives of the county include the painter Francis Danby (1793–1861) and the novelist John *Banville. The famous English architect A. W. Pugin (1812–52) designed a number of churches in county Wexford, including the cathedral at Enniscorthy. The John F. *Kennedy Arboretum near New Ross commemorates the American president, whose ancestors came from nearby Dunganstown. P.H.

Wexford Festival. *Opera festival. Since it was founded by Dr Thomas Walsh in 1951, the annual Wexford Festival has presented productions of rare opera at the tiny, atmospheric Theatre Royal. The festival now includes 40 daytime events and 18 evening performances of three major opera productions, each of them unique to the festival. Over the years, Wexford has displayed the talents of many young singers who went on to achieve international success, such as Dame Janet Baker, Sir Geraint Evans and Fiorenza Cossotto. (Web site: *www.wexfordopera.com.*) S.A.B.

Whelan, Leo (1892–1956). Portrait and genre painter. Born in *Dublin, Whelan was considered one of William *Orpen's finest pupils at the Dublin Metropolitan School of Art. He exhibited regularly at the *Royal Hibernian Academy from 1911. Whelan taught at the Royal Hibernian Academy schools and was elected to the academy in 1924. Reproductions of his portraits of *saints were widely circulated. His portraits of leading statesmen and dignitaries can be viewed at the *Ulster, *Cork and *Hugh Lane galleries. M.C.

whiskey. The whiskey that most of the world drinks is spelled without the e, as in Scotch whisky. But Irish whiskey once dominated the world market. Besides the spelling of the word, the main difference between Scotch and Irish is that Scotch features malted, or germinated, barley, and Irish uses a wide variety of grains including both malted and unmalted barleys. Other crucial differences include the tendency for the Scottish product to blend various whiskeys and for the Irish to distil multiple times. We do not know when or where the first whiskey was distilled, although it seems to have been a *Celt who did it. The earliest written references are a 1494 record from *Scotland and a 1556 Irish law. Whiskey, however, was drunk far earlier than this. English soldiers under *Henry II allegedly brought whiskey back home with them from Ireland in 1174. Legend further has it that in the early Middle Ages, travelling Catholic clerics imported *distilling technology directly or indirectly from the Middle East. The etymology of the word *whiskey* (from the Irish language *uisce beatha*, meaning 'water of life') indicates a Celtic origin.

The golden age of whiskey-making in Ireland lasted from the 1600s, when massive amounts of the liquour were consumed on both sides of the Irish Sea (Queen *Elizabeth I was a great fan) through the middle of the nineteenth century, when the world fell in love with Scotland's new, smoother, blended whiskies. Previously, Irish whiskey had been favoured over Scotch and was the main beneficiary of the phylloxera epidemic that devastated French vineyards in 1872. With brandy unavailable, the drinking nations adopted whiskey and soda as their evening drink. The 1600s saw the first tax on Irish whiskey and, consequently, the first poitín (pronounced 'potcheen'), or moonshine, whiskey. Poitín is still made today.

After a long fallow period, the 1980s and 1990s have seen a tremendous upsurge in both quality and variety in Irish whiskies. Principal brands of Irish whiskey today include Bushmills, Jameson, Power, Paddy, Connemara, Locke's, Tullamore Dew and Midleton Reserve. T.G.

Whitaker, T[homas] K[enneth] (1916–). Economist, public servant. Born in 1916, T. K. Whitaker was the pre-eminent economist of the *Republic of Ireland. As secretary of the Department of Finance (1956–69), he was pivotal in charting a new economic course, which he outlined in a government document, *Economic Development* (1958). Whitaker advocated abandonment of protectionism in favour of competitive participation in world trade. He was instrumental in arranging the historic meeting between *Taoiseach Seán *Lemass and Prime Minister of Northern Ireland Terence *O'Neill in 1965. Whitaker was governor of the Central Bank between 1969 and 1976 and subsequently served in the Irish senate. His public service continued after his retirement from the Central Bank: as chairman of the Constitution Review Group in the 1990s, chancellor of the National University of Ireland from 1976 to 1996, and chairman of Bord na Gaeilge, the Irish Folklore Council and the Salmon Research Agency. F.OM.

Whiteboys. Agrarian secret society. Active in *Munster in the mid-eighteenth century, the Whiteboys protested against evictions, high rents and *tithes. The name comes from the white smocks they wore as a uniform. Seen as a major threat to the social order, 'Whiteboys' became a term used to describe any group of agrarian protestors. T.C.

Wicklow, County. Maritime county in the province of *Leinster. The county, covering an area of 782 square miles, has a population of 114,719 (2002 census). Bordered to the north by County *Dublin, Wicklow is divided by a central range of mountains, the highest of which is Lugnaquilla at 3,070 feet above sea level, Ireland's second-highest mountain after *Carrantuohill (3,414 feet) in County *Kerry. The Wicklow mountains were used as refuge points by rebels from the time of the O'Byrnes in the late sixteenth century to the time of Michael Dwyer and Joseph Holt after the *Rebellion of 1798. These mountains impeded communications between the various regions of the county. This isolation was the main reason why the county was not formed as an administrative unit until 1606.

The principal rivers in the county are the Liffey and the Slaney. Wicklow, known as the garden of Ireland, has been a centre for regional tourism since the early nineteenth century, principally for attractions like the monastic site at *Glendalough and the impressive gardens and waterfall at Powerscourt. Charles Stewart *Parnell, the most important Irish *nationalist leader in the second half of the nineteenth century, was born at Avondale House, near Rathdrum. His family owned an estate there of 3,800 acres. The celebrated art collection of Sir Alfred Beit is housed at Russborough House, near Bray. The principal towns in the county are Arklow, Bray, Greystones and Wicklow, the county capital. A.S.

Wild Geese (Irish Brigades). Popular name given to those who left Ireland after the Treaty of *Limerick. Under the treaty, Irish regiments were allowed to enter French service. The Irish Brigade of the French army is the most famous, but there were also Irish regiments in the Hapsburg empire and Spain. It is estimated that up to 300,000 Irishmen served in European armies in the eighteenth century. To the *Protestant ascendancy, the

Irish Brigades were a *Catholic army in exile, proof of the *Jacobite threat. Their exploits were followed eagerly at home. The brigade in *France fought together only once as a unit in 1745, at the Battle of Fontenoy, during the War of the Austrian Succession. The brigade played a decisive part in France's victory over the British and their allies. In the nineteenth century, various units of Irishmen in foreign armies were known – usually unofficially – as Irish brigades. These units fought for Napoleon, in the South American wars of liberation, for the papacy and in the *American Civil War. In the twentieth century, the name was applied to those who fought in the *Boer War and to Eoin *O'Duffy's Catholic volunteers in Spain. T.C.

Wilde, Lady Jane Francesca (1826–96). Poet and folklorist; mother of Oscar *Wilde. A native of County *Wexford, Jane Elgee was influenced by the *nationalist poetry of Richard D'Alton Williams, which was published in the **Nation*. She also contributed to the *Nation* under the pen name 'Speranza'. Elgee married renowned physician Sir William *Wilde in 1851. Her works include the poem 'The Famine Year' (1871) and the nationalist-inspired prose collection *Ancient Legends of Ireland* (1887). S.A.B.

Wilde, Oscar (1854–1900). Playwright. Wit, raconteur, poet and brilliant speaker, Wilde is one of the great dramatists of the English language. He was born in *Dublin, the son of Sir William *Wilde, a famous surgeon, and Lady *Wilde, an eccentric, *nationalist poet. As a student at Trinity College, Dublin, and Magdalen College, Oxford, where he excelled in classics, Wilde was strongly influenced by the aestheticism of Ruskin and Pater. He moved to London in 1879 and embarked on a career as a writer, lecturer and critic. His publications from this period include *The Happy Prince and Other Tales* (1888) and *Lord Arthur Savile's Crime and Other Stories* (1891), which includes 'The Canterville Ghost', often considered his best story.

Oscar Wilde

Wilde cultivated his reputation as a dandy and wit. The satirical magazine *Punch* caricatured him as the adorer of white lilies, while Gilbert and Sullivan's *opera *Patience* made fun of him in the figure of Bunthorne. Arriving in New York for his very successful lecture tour of the United States in 1882, he quipped to a customs' officer, 'I have nothing to declare but my genius'. An outrageous and extravagant aesthete, Wilde confessed in one of his witticisms, 'I can resist everything, except temptation'. He married Constance Lloyd in 1884. They had two sons, Cyril (1885) and Vyvyan (1886). The latter, under the adopted name of Vyvyan Holland, wrote the history of his family in *Son of Oscar Wilde* (1954). In 1887 (until 1889), Wilde became editor of a women's magazine in London, *The Woman's World*, for which he wrote literary notes and articles on fashion.

Wilde is known chiefly for his plays, masterpieces in the genre of the comedy of manners: *Lady Windermere's Fan* (1891), *The Importance of Being Earnest* (1895) and *An Ideal Husband* (1895). Never before had the hypocrisy of London's high society been satirised with such hilarity. A planned London production of Wilde's biblical play *Salomé* (with Sarah Bernhardt) was censored in 1893, but the play was performed in Paris in 1896. Published in 1891, Wilde's controversial novel *The Picture of Dorian Grey*, whose beautiful, hedonistic protagonist miraculously retains his youth while his portrait increasingly exhibits signs of decay, was described as 'filthy', 'dangerous' and 'brilliant'.

At the height of his fame in the mid-1890s, Wilde's public affair with Lord Alfred Douglas, the son of the Marquess of Queensberry (who invented the rules of modern boxing), created a scandal and led to Wilde's ill-fated decision to sue the Marquess for libel. The legal proceedings that followed would become legendary and lead to Wilde's downfall. Prosecuted for, and convicted of, homosexuality, he was sentenced to prison in 1898 and served two years in Reading Gaol. A modified version of a letter written to Douglas during the final months of his incarceration was published in 1905 under the title *De Profundis*. Wilde's final work is the moving if uneven poem *The Ballad of Reading Gaol* (1898). After his release, Wilde moved to France and died in Paris in 1900, a broken and lonely man. J.OM., L.R., J.C.E.L.

Wilde, Sir William (1815–76). Surgeon, father of Oscar *Wilde. Wilde was also an archaeologist, ethnologist, antiquarian, biographer, statistician, naturalist, topographer, historian and folklorist. From 1855 to 1876, this remarkable nineteenth-century polymath lived at No.1 Merrion Square, *Dublin, where a plaque commemorates him. His wife, Lady *Wilde, was a *nationalist and a poet, who wrote under the name Speranza. P.H.

William III, Prince of Orange (1650– 1702). King of England (1688–1702), leader of the Netherlands. William of Orange invaded England in 1688 and deposed *James II, his uncle and father-in-law, in order to secure naval and financial resources for his ongoing war (the War of the Grand Alliance, 1689– 97) with Louis XIV, the 'Sun King' of France. He also sought to pre-empt any Anglo-French alliance. This so-called 'Glorious Revolution' shifted the balance of constitutional power decisively from the monarch toward parliament, but for William III it was a necessary means to a larger end – defeating France. James II fled to France and, in March 1689, landed in Ireland with a view to using it as a stepping-stone to regain his other two kingdoms, Scotland and England. Later that year, a Williamite army of 14,000 men landed in *Ulster, led by the elderly Duke of Schomberg. His instructions were to march on *Dublin without delay and destroy the Jacobite forces opposing him. However, Schomberg failed dismally to end the Irish campaign in the autumn of 1689 thereby forcing William to intervene in person. Having to go to Ireland was, as he explained apologetically to one of his allies, 'a terrible mortification', but '... If I can reduce that kingdom quickly, I shall then have my hands free to act with so much more vigour against the common enemy'.

However, William did not 'reduce that kingdom quickly': he failed to encircle and prevent the retreat of the much smaller Franco-Irish army at the Battle of the *Boyne (12 July 1690), though James II's flight made it a propaganda triumph which counteracted simultaneous defeats on land (Fleurus) and sea (Beachy Head). Deluded, perhaps, by his own propaganda, William of Orange demanded more-or-less unconditional surrender after the Battle of the Boyne. The Finglas Declaration promised pardon to 'the meaner sort' but did not offer guarantees of property and religious freedom. This severity was mistaken because it stiffened Irish resistance and ensured that the Boyne would not be a decisive victory.

After an unduly long delay, William of Orange decided to attack *Limerick. This was a key to the Irish defensive line along the *Shannon River. His assault (27 August, 1690) was repulsed and his forces suffered heavy losses. William was forced to call off the siege because of increasingly wet weather and a shortage of gunpowder. He returned to England shortly afterward. The war would not end until October 1691, when the Treaty of *Limerick offered improved peace terms to the Irish and the Finglas Declaration was disregarded.

William of Orange's commemoration as an Irish *Protestant folk hero in the eighteenth century owes much to the simple fact that he personified definitive Irish Protestant victory after the uncertainty of the seventeenth century. Moreover, his repeated and unflinching exposure to danger at the Boyne, notably when struck on the shoulder by an artillery shot, conspicuously exemplified the forbearance in battle that contemporaries most admired. 'He may not have always won' admitted a *Huguenot biographer, 'but he always deserved to win'. The *Orange Order, founded in 1795, revived and popularised the cult of William III. The annual Battle of the Boyne parades on 'the twelfth' of July affirm its continuing potency and appeal to *Northern Ireland's Protestants. P.L.

witchcraft. The belief in magic was common in ancient Ireland as in other countries, but Gaelic Ireland was little influenced by the demonisation of magic, which was widespread in medieval Europe. In Irish tradition, the devil remained a mischievous character who could be outwitted by clever individuals. Accusations of sinister collusion with the devil, leading to witchcraft trials, seem to have occurred only in *Norman and English settlements. One such case concerned Dame Alice Kyteler, a wealthy lady who was accused of witchcraft in *Kilkenny in 1324 by the Norman Bishop Richard de Ledrede. Her maidservant was burned at the stake, but Dame Alice herself escaped to England. Another celebrated case occurred at a puritan colony in Youghal, County *Cork, in 1661, when an old woman called Florence Newton was accused of bewitching several of the local residents. The verdict is unknown, but the evidence offered was of a standard nature – that of inveigling people into her power by pretensions of affection and causing them to vomit up many kinds of strange objects. In another case, at Island Magee in Country *Antrim in 1710, seven women were accused of causing the death of a widow and of bewitching a young girl. They were found guilty in court after quite selective evidence was offered by the prosecution, and they were jailed for a year and pilloried.

In more recent generations, some old festival rituals have become confused with malicious practices. This is particularly so in the case of the May Festival. It was customary to collect the dew from the fields and to sprinkle the crops after sundown on May Eve for good luck. Such practices, especially when carried out surreptitiously, have attracted suspicion and certain individuals are thought to magically steal the good fortune of their neighbours. The practice is usually known as pishoguery, from the Irish word *piseog* meaning 'superstition'. It is based on the notion that only a limited amount of prosperity is available and that for one person to gain another must lose. Abstract feelings tend to be given physical form in traditional belief; thus, it is often held that people can be magically harmed by the envious feelings of others or by malicious comments.

Other beliefs and practices, sometimes confused with witchcraft by outsiders, reflect concerns about the relationship between human society and the fairies and between the world of the living and the world of the dead. It was thought, for instance, that the fairies could inflict sickness on people and even 'abduct' individuals and replace them with fairy beings. Various means were employed to banish such 'changelings' and recover the 'real' person, sometimes with tragic results. As late as 1895, this happened to a young woman called Bridget Cleary, whose husband caused her death by submitting her to such ordeals, including burning. People who were noted for healing and who used arcane practices in this regard, were regarded as being 'wise' and their influence was generally beneficial. The most famous such 'wise woman' was Biddy Early from Feakle in County *Clare in the nineteenth century. D.OH.

women. Under *brehon law, women had certain property and marital rights and women were accepted, though not often, as heads of lordships. Irish abbesses, like their European counterparts, had extensive ecclesiastical authority. However, this power and independence applied mainly to rich and powerful women. Little is known about the lives of women at the humbler levels of society. The political and religious changes of the sixteenth and seventeenth centuries, brought about by English law, removed women's property rights. The *Reformation suppressed religious houses and the counter-Reformation brought in new and stricter regulations for *nuns. Eighteenth-century middle- and upper-class women were expected to take an interest in politics and many did, particularly in the revolutionary generation of the 1780s and 1790s.Women often ran commercial and craft enterprises. Working-class and small-farming women's home-based *textile and garment work gave them a measure of economic independence from the 1790s, though the poverty and vulnerability of this class is illustrated by the dramatic decline in their number in the calamitous decade of the 1840s.

Home-based textile and manufacture, however, continued to be important in some areas up to the early twentieth century. The farm woman, involved in all aspects of farm work, controlled poultry and dairying up to the mid-twentieth century. Most shopkeepers' womenfolk would have had hands-on involvement with the family business, and the widowed female shopkeeper, like the widowed female farmer, was a familiar and authoritative figure. Paid work for unskilled or uneducated women was, however, quite scarce. In the north the textile and garment industry employed females in factories and mills from the mid-nineteenth century. In other parts of Ireland, however, apart from some factory work in the major cities, the only work these women could hope to find was in domestic or institutional service. *Emigration to North America or *Australia was, therefore, an attractive option for Irish women. Not only was the number of women who emigrated roughly equal to that of men (unusual for Europe at the time), but almost all Irish women who emigrated did so with friends, or peers, rather than under family/male protection.

For women from lower, middle and skilled working-class backgrounds whose parents could afford to let them stay on at school into their teens, the mid-nineteenth century was a time of economic opportunity. They could work as national (primary) teachers, prison officers, nurses, trained midwives, or, by the end of the century, post office clerks or telegraphists/telephonists.

There were no bars to hiring married women, though informal ones might have operated in some offices. Upper-middle-class girls who attended fee-paying superior schools could take the Intermediate Certificate School-Leaving Examination from 1878, when it was established on a basis of strict gender equality. Women were admitted to most Irish *universities in the 1880s.

In the opening decade of the twentieth century, women became involved in *nationalism, *unionism, the labour movement and the suffrage movement. The *Proclamation of the *Easter Rising of 1916 addressed men and women as equal citizens and promised equal citizenship. Women participated in the rising and were particularly important in the propaganda and support work thereafter. *Ulster unionism, while it had a much bigger women's auxiliary movement than nationalism, had no commitment to gender equality and no high-profile women. Irish women voted for the first time in 1918 when the Representation of the People Act in the UK granted the vote for the first time to all men over 21 and all women of certain property qualifications over 30. The first woman elected to the House of Commons was Constance *Markievicz; as a *Sinn Féin member, she did not take her seat, but became minister for Labour in the First *Dáil, in Dublin in 1919. Women played a strong administrative role in the new state set up by the first Dáil during the *War of Independence, 1919–21. After the *Anglo-Irish Treaty (1921), most of the high-profile women – Markievicz, Mary MacSwiney, Hanna *Sheehy Skeffington – took the anti-treaty side. An exception among the famous women was Jennie Wyse Power, veteran of the Ladies Land League (1879–82) and of all the struggles since then, who took the pro-treaty side and was a strong defender of women's rights in the *Free State senate. The 1922 Constitution of the Irish Free State granted equal citizenship to women and men, without qualifications of any kind.

Once granted, political equality was never rescinded and women sat in both houses of the *Oireachtas. Women's citizenship came under attack in a number of ways, however. They were 'exempted' from jury duty in 1927 and the 1937 *Constitution seemed to imply a synonymity between women and motherhood – ironic, in view of the falling marriage rate. Employment bars against married women in teaching and the public service were introduced 1928–32 and the number of women in industrial employment was cut down in 1936. Sex-specific labour legislation affected lower-middle and working-class women, leaving the wealthier women professionals – doctors, solicitors, barristers, accountants and public representatives – untouched. Birth control was totally banned by 1936. *Divorce was unconstitutional.

From 1940 until about 1960, tens of thousands of Irish women and girls emigrated, this time to Britain, to plentiful, well-paid work and training. Thousands of women deserted domestic service, to the oft-expressed chagrin of upper-middle-class women. Life was also changing for women who did not emigrate. Many women chose financial independence over marriage, prompting alarm at population decline. The employment bar on married women as national teachers was lifted in 1958 partly to encourage marriage. Women who stayed on the land began to demand electricity and indoor plumbing, and membership of the Irish Countrywomen's Association soared in the 1950s and 1960s. Meanwhile a free-for-all maternity *health care system, introduced in Northern Ireland in 1948 and in the *Republic in 1953, caused an already-declining maternal mortality rate to fall even further. Family allowances, introduced in both administrations in the mid-1940s, improved women's nutrition. The economic recovery of the 1960s saw industrial work opening up for women, while the introduction of free secondary education in 1966 in the Republic (it had been introduced in Northern Ireland with the Butler Act in 1948) gave opportunities to a new generation of Irish girls. Female participation in every area of economic life rose significantly from the 1970s, keeping pace with their higher profile in public life. The feminist movement of the early 1970s led to the establishment of a Council for the Status of Women in 1973. Groups such as Irishwomen United, AIM, Cherish, the Women's Political Association and other organisations improved women's legal, occupational, economic and social position. Reforms such as the removal of the marriage bar on public servants, the introduction of paid maternity leave, improvement of women's family law status, support for unmarried mothers and deserted wives, access to contraception and other reforms – all came in the 1970s and 1980s. C.C.

Wood's Half-Pence Controversy (1722–25). Political scandal. This controversy arose over the granting of a patent to produce copper coin for Ireland to William Wood, an English manufacturer. The patent had been issued without the consent of the Irish *parliament, which passed resolutions condemning the measure. It was rumoured in Ireland that Wood had acquired the patent through King *George I's mistress, the Duchess of Kendal. The controversy inspired the famous series of pamphlets, *Drapier's Letters* (1724–25), by Jonathan *Swift. Ultimately, a combined campaign of political and popular protest led to the rescinding of the patent in 1725. While much of the hostility to the new coinage was based on the fear that it would debase the Irish currency, it also served to highlight popular hostility to what was perceived as English misgovernment of Ireland. A.S.

wool. See **textiles**.

Workers' Party. Political party. The Workers' Party evolved from the left-wing Official *IRA, which declared a unilateral cease-fire in 1972. The party suffered a serious split in 1992 when leading members set up a rival organisation, Democratic Left, which has since merged with the *Labour Party. The Workers' Party support in *Northern Ireland has also withered away. M.M.

workhouse. Institutions established to provide poor relief. The *Poor Law Act, 1838, divided Ireland into 130 poor law districts (unions), each with a workhouse. Entry for those who required aid was at the discretion of the local poor law guardians and financing came mostly from a poor-rate collected from local landowners. The buildings were of a standardised design, drawn up by George Wilkinson, an English architect. In general, conditions were deliberately harsh and degrading in order to discourage the poor from using them. During the *Famine, thousands of destitute people flocked to these institutions, causing an accommodation crisis. In reaction, the government established temporary soup kitchens and introduced a system of out-relief under the 1847 Poor Law Extension Act. The workhouse system was formally abolished by the *Free State government in the 1920s and in *Northern Ireland in 1946. P.E.

World War, First. The Great War, which claimed ten million lives in Europe, played a pivotal role in the creation of an independent Ireland. Some 200,000 Irishmen served in the British army during the war, with tens of thousands of casualties. The list of Irish regiments that fought in France includes the largely Catholic Connaught Rangers, Dublin Fusiliers and Munster Fusiliers. Similarly, the Thirty-sixth Division, which enlisted in block form from the loyalist *UVF, was decimated on the first day of the Battle of the Somme (1 July 1916) having advanced, in the face of withering German fire, farther than any other British army unit.

At the onset of hostilities, John *Redmond and his *Irish Parliamentary Party successfully traded their support for the imperial war effort in exchange for parliament's passage of the *Home Rule Act (September 1914). However, home rule was suspended for the duration of the conflict and the war ultimately doomed constitutional *nationalism. The radical *republicans of the *IRB took advantage of Britain's distraction with the First World War to rise in Dublin on Easter Monday, 1916, in what is known as the *Easter Rising. Although the rebels were compelled to surrender within a week, the execution of the principal leaders, including Patrick *Pearse and James *Connolly, dramatically swung public opinion in favour of independence. By 1918, *Sinn Féin, partially as a result of London's attempts to extend conscription to Ireland, had supplanted Redmond's Irish Parliamentary Party as the largest single party in the country. In fact, for Ireland, the *Anglo-Irish War (1919–21) was the final act of the First World War. J.P.

wren-boys. Midwinter revellers in traditional Ireland. It is customary throughout most of Ireland for groups to travel in disguise from house to house on St Stephen's Day, 26 December, playing music and singing songs. They chant a verse claiming to have killed a wren and seeking money for its funeral. In former times, the dead body of a wren was carried on top of a little pole or branch of holly. There is evidence for such a 'wren-hunt' from the Middle Ages in Ireland and in parts of Britain and France, and it may be that the custom originated in prehistoric times with a ritual to banish the spirit of winter, envisaged as the tiny bird. D.OH.

Y

Yeats, Anne (1919–2001). Painter and lithographer. A committee member and regular exhibitor of the *Irish Exhibition of Living Art (IELA), Anne Yeats was the daughter of the poet and niece of the painter Jack Butler *Yeats. Born in *Dublin, she studied at the *Royal Hibernian Academy school and worked as a designer and painter of sets at various theatres, including the *Abbey Theatre. She eventually took up painting fulltime and later moved on to lithography and monotypes. She helped revive the Cuala Press in 1969. M.C.

Yeats, Jack B. (1871–1957). Painter. The best-known Irish painter of the twentieth century, Jack B. Yeats was born in London and influenced greatly by his childhood years spent with maternal grandparents in County *Sligo. He was the younger brother of the poet William Butler *Yeats. Jack B. Yeats attended art schools in London and worked as a magazine, book and poster illustrator in England before producing watercolours of Devon and the west of Ireland. Yeats also edited and illustrated traditional ballads and wrote prose, novels and plays. He travelled with John *Synge around *Connemara in 1904, providing illustrations for the writer's articles for the *Guardian* newspaper, and in 1907 advised Synge on costumes for *The Playboy of the Western World.* In 1910, he moved to *Dublin and painted in oils for the first time. His landscapes, dominated by dramatic characters, were often used as book illustrations. American John Quinn collected his work and helped Yeats exhibit his paintings at the Armory Show in New York in 1913 and many times after in America. Elected to the *Royal Hibernian Academy in 1917, he began to use colour in the 1920s as an emotional form of expression often in work that was based on memory. He captured the subjective world of individuals and their natural dignity in relation to each other and their environment. His sensitive portrayal of national events such as *The Funeral of Harry Boland*, 1922 (Sligo County Museum and Art Gallery) and *Death for Only One*, 1927 (private collection), captured the new note of intensity in Irish life and earned him the title of Ireland's first national painter. *Going to Wolfe Tone's Grave*, 1929, demonstrates his ability to capture memory directly with passionate authority. He published three plays in 1933, as well as reminiscences and articles and wrote four novels: *Sailing, Sailing Swiftly* (1933), *The Amaranthers* (1936), *The Charmed Life* (1938) and *The Careless Flower* (1947). The National Gallery in London hosted a retrospective exhibition of his paintings in 1942. A loan exhibition was held in Dublin in 1945 and at the Tate Gallery London in 1948, and a retrospective exhibition travelled to American cities in 1951–52. M.C.

Yeats, John Butler (1839–1922). Portrait painter and writer. Father of the famous painter Jack and the poet William, Yeats was born in County *Down and studied law at Trinity College, Dublin. His determination to be a painter prevented him from practising law and kept the family impoverished, but provided them with an appreciation of intellectual independence. Seeking portrait commissions, he and his family moved back and forth from London to Dublin. He was elected to the *Royal Hibernian Academy in 1892 and at his exhibition with Nathaniel *Hone in 1901 he came to the attention of American collector John Quinn. Before settling in New York in 1909, he painted many portraits of leading figures in the Irish artistic and literary world, some of which were commissioned by Hugh *Lane. In America he lectured on art, wrote magazine articles and memoirs, painted and sketched portraits and gave public readings of the poetry of his son William. A selection of his letters made by Ezra Pound (*Passages from the Letters of J. B. Yeats*) was published in 1917 and Cuala Press published his *Early Memoirs* in 1923. M.C.

Yeats, William Butler (1865–1939). Poet, playwright, Nobel laureate. Widely reckoned the greatest English-language poet of the twentieth century, Yeats was born in *Dublin on 13 June 1865, the first child of John Butler *Yeats and Susan Pollexfen Yeats. His childhood and youth were spent in London, Dublin and in *Sligo, where his mother's family, originally from Devonshire, had settled and prospered in the nineteenth century. John Butler Yeats, scion of a *Protestant family that came to Ireland in the seventeenth century, was heir to lands in County *Kildare that made him an *Anglo-Irish gentleman but did not supply an adequate income. He had abandoned a promising career in the law for the insecure profession of artist and portrait painter in which he never achieved financial success. The poet grew up in an atmosphere of bohemian indifference to money values and of genteel poverty alleviated by sojourns in his grandfather's substantial home in Sligo, where he developed his profound love of the Irish countryside and its folk.

Yeats' young manhood in London, where his family took up residence in 1887, was marked by an urgent need to establish himself as poet and man of letters and by his burgeoning interest in magic and occult knowledge. Around this time, he became increasingly committed to Irish *republican *nationalism to which he had been introduced by the old *Fenian John *O'Leary in 1885. He was also hopelessly in love with his poetic muse, the nationalist firebrand and beauty Maud *Gonne, who spurned his romantic and marital advances.

William Butler Yeats

Yeats' early reputation as a romantic and symbolist poet who exploited Irish mythic and national material was established by *The Wanderings of Oisin* (1889), *Poems* (1895) and *The Wind among the Reeds* (1899).

In 1899, along with Lady Augusta *Gregory and others, Yeats started the Irish Literary Theatre, the precursor of the *Abbey Theatre that opened in 1904. He gave much of his energy to the theatre in the first decade of the twentieth century, escaping each summer from his home in London and the theatre in Dublin, to the comforts of Lady Gregory's Galway home, *Coole Park. It was not until the publication of *Responsibilities* (1914) that he moved away from the romantic poetry of dreams and mythology and established his reputation as a poet of modernity. In this austere and harsh volume, Yeats registered his bitter alienation from an Ireland whose philistine reaction to John Millington *Synge's *The Playboy of the Western World* had hastened, Yeats believed, its author's premature death, and from the city of Dublin whose citizens scorned great art.

Yeats spent the *First World War years of 1914–18 in Sussex and London. He was deeply distressed and moved – in a way that he was not by the vast slaughter of the Great War –

by the *Easter Rising in Dublin in April 1916, which drew from him the troubled elegy and peroration 'Easter 1916', with its memorable refrain 'A terrible beauty is born'. From the war years came many of the poems gathered in the most ample collection he had published since 1899, *The Wild Swans at Coole* (1917, 1919). It was also during the war years that he began his dramatic experiments with the Japanese Noh theatre.

Yeats married in 1917. His young bride Georgie Hyde-Lees brought him domestic security and her talents as a medium made the first five years of their marriage an extraordinary spiritualist experiment. From her spirit communications, Yeats assembled a body of psychological and historical doctrine published as *A Vision* (1925, 1937). This material stimulated the poet to address a disturbed period of revolution and civil war in Europe and Ireland in highly charged dramatic verse. The collaboration of poet and medium bore particular fruit in what is regarded by many as Yeats' finest single volume of poetry, *The Tower* (1928).

Yeats served as a senator in the *parliament of the *Irish Free State from 1922 until 1928. He was awarded the Nobel Prize for literature in 1923. Yet honours and advancing years did not diminish his creativity or his imaginative engagement with the destiny of his country. In the 1930s he blamed the crude democracy of a levelling age ('the filthy modern tide') for the puritan zeal with which the new Irish state sought to impose Catholic social values, and he increasingly represented himself as a self-consciously *Anglo-Irish poet, a poet of Swiftian, savage indignation. He also allowed himself moments of bawdy sexuality in his verse and struck wildly intemperate social attitudes. *The Winding Stair and Other Poems* (1933) combined Anglo-Irish hauteur and distaste for modernity with lyric celebration of bodily experience.

A tragic note is struck in Yeats' late poetry, when ill health and impending death made him seek the warmer climes of southern Europe for extended periods. As the continent was riven by extreme social philosophies, Yeats reacted with a mixture of rage, dark premonition and the 'tragic joy' he sought to express in his most ambitious late work. His posthumously published *Last Poems and Plays* (1939) is a chilling testament of a poet *in extremis*. Yeats died in the south of France on 28 January 1939, where he was buried. He was reinterred in Drumcliff churchyard, County Sligo, in 1948, the resting place he had chosen for himself in his poem 'Under Ben Bulben'.

Yeats' oeuvre includes experimental drama, fiction, autobiography and criticism, but it is in the indisputable power of his poetry that he makes his claim on posterity. T.B.

Yeomanry, the. Volunteer civilian militia. Formed in September/October 1796 to assist the authorities in the event of French invasion, the Yeomanry was responsible with policing local areas if the regular military forces were called away to repel invaders. In regions where martial law was declared between 1797 and 1803, the uniformed yeomen were placed on 'permanent duty', housed at government expense in barracks, subjected to military command and given patrolling and guard duties. Yeomen proved useful auxiliaries to the military during the *Rebellion of 1798, when they participated in several pitched battles with insurgents. R.OD.

Young Ireland. *Nationalist group of the 1840s. In October 1842, several idealistic young Irishmen, including Thomas *Davis, Charles Gavan *Duffy and John Blake *Dillon, founded a newspaper in *Dublin, the **Nation*, which advocated both political autonomy and cultural revival for a nonsectarian Ireland. This circle became known as 'Young Ireland' by reference to Giuseppi Mazzini's 'Young Italy' organisation. Davis, who died at

30 in 1845, emphasised the need to preserve the *Irish language and create a new national literature. Initially, the 'Young Irelanders' allied themselves with Daniel *O'Connell's *Repeal movement. As some Young Ireland leaders were *Protestants firmly committed to a non-sectarian national identity, however, the group objected to the close ties that O'Connell's movement had developed with the *Catholic church. Even more serious differences emerged over O'Connell's pragmatic and nonviolent strategy and, in July 1846, 'Young Ireland' withdrew from the Repeal movement. In January 1847, two of the most influential Young Ireland personalities, John *Mitchel and Thomas Francis *Meagher, founded the Irish Confederation in opposition to O'Connell's Repeal Association. The confederation, which soon established clubs throughout Ireland and Britain, formed a militantly revolutionary and *republican rival to O'Connell's constitutional movement. In July 1848 during the Great *Famine, William Smith *O'Brien led an unsuccessful *rebellion in County *Tipperary. In its aftermath, most leaders of Young Ireland fled abroad or were *transported to penal colonies in *Australia. The movement's legacy for later nationalists included a willingness to use physical force to achieve its goals and an emphasis on cultural revival as a vital aspect of nationalism. F.B.

Z

Zozimus (1794–1846). Nickname for Michael Moran, a blind *Dublin storyteller. Born in the Liberties section of Dublin, Zozimus lost his sight as a child following a short illness. Described by some as Ireland's nineteenth-century Homer, he had an exceptional memory for stories and songs and a prodigious talent for composition and recitation. His nickname came about because of his fondness for reciting the story of Zozimus, a bishop who administered the Holy Sacraments to St Mary of Egypt in the fifth century. P.E.

Chronology of Irish History

BC.

c. 7000	Evidence of Ireland's earliest people, Mesolithic hunter-gatherers, at Mount Sandel, County *Derry.
3500–3000	Arrival of Neolithic farmers. Construction of megalithic tombs.
2500	Construction of the *passage-grave at *Newgrange, County *Meath.
2000–1800	Bronze Age begins.
c. 500–150	The *Celts (iron-using farmers and warriors from central and western mainland Europe) arrive.

AD.

c. 130–80	Ptolemy's Geography contains a map of Ireland and a list of Irish rivers, settlements and tribes.
300–450	Irish raiders plunder Roman Britain.
c. 377–405	Niall of the Nine Hostages, high king of Ireland.
431	Pope Celestine I (422–32) appoints *Palladius as the first bishop to Ireland.
432	St *Patrick begins his mission in Ireland.
c. 490	St Enda sets up the first Irish monastery on the *Aran Islands.
493	Traditional date for the death of St Patrick (17 March).
Sixth century	Start of the Golden Age of Irish Monasticism.
547	Monastery of *Clonmacnoise founded by St Ciarán.
563	St *Colm Cille establishes a monastery on Iona.
795	*Viking raids on Ireland begin with an attack on the monastery on Lambay Island.
841	The future city of *Dublin is established by Vikings on the River Liffey.
914–22	Viking settlements established at *Waterford, *Wexford and *Limerick.
1002	Brian *Boru becomes high king.
1014	Battle of *Clontarf. Brian Boru defeats the Vikings of Dublin and their *Leinster allies. After the battle, Boru is slain by a fleeing Norseman.
1152	Synod of Kells. Diocesan organisation of the Irish church.
1155	A proposed invasion of Ireland by the Norman King *Henry II is sanctioned by Pope Adrian IV in the papal bull Laudabiliter.
1166	Rory *O'Connor becomes the last high king of Ireland. Dermot *MacMurrough, king of Leinster, is defeated in battle by O'Connor and goes to England and France to seek assistance from Henry II. Dermot obtains permission from Henry II to enlist the services of Norman knights in Wales and England.
1167	MacMurrough returns to Ireland with Norman, Flemish and Welsh mercenaries.
1169	The *Norman invasion begins when a large force arrives at Bannow Bay, County *Wexford.
1170	*Strongbow (Richard fitzGilbert de Clare) lands with an army near *Waterford and takes the city. He marries Aoife, daughter of Dermot MacMurrough.
1171	Dermot MacMurrough dies and is succeeded by Strongbow. Henry II lands in Ireland near Waterford with 400 ships and a large army. He receives submission from his Norman lords, native kings and the entire Irish clergy at Cashel.
1175	Treaty of Windsor: in return for a declaration of loyalty to Henry II, Rory O'Connor is recognised as king of *Connacht.
1177	Prince John (Henry II's son) becomes Lord of Ireland.

1210	King John arrives in Ireland, establishes English common law and government.
1250	Normans control most of the south, as well as parts of eastern *Ulster.
Fourteenth century	Gaelic resurgence throughout Ireland
1315–18	Edward *Bruce, the brother of Robert Bruce, King of *Scotland, invades Ireland and attempts unsuccessfully to overthrow the Anglo-Normans.
1348	The first Irish cases of Black Death in Howth and Balbriggan, near Dublin.
1366	A parliament in *Kilkenny passes the *Statute of Kilkenny, forbidding English settlers from adopting native customs.
Fifteenth century	Area under English control shrinks to the *Pale – counties Dublin, *Meath, *Kildare century and *Louth
1494	*Poynings' Law enacted at Drogheda. Irish *parliament to convene only with the permission of the king of England. All legislation needs royal approval.
1535	Rebellion of Silken Thomas is crushed by Lord Grey's army.
1536–37	Protestant *Reformation begins with the establishment of the *Church of Ireland and the dissolution of Irish monasteries.
1540	*Henry VIII begins his policy of Surrender and Regrant. Native and Old English lords are granted titles in return for submission to the king's sovereignty and English law.
1541	Henry VIII declared king of Ireland by the Irish parliament.
1550–57	*Plantation of *Offaly and *Laois.
1561–67	*Rebellion of Shane O'Neill.
1569–83	Two Desmond rebellions are crushed.
1586	Plantation of *Munster.
1588	Spanish Armada is destroyed in storms off the west coast
1592	Trinity College, Dublin, is established.
1593–1603	The *Nine Years War rebellion by Hugh *O'Neill and Red Hugh *O'Donnell against the crown.
1601	The Battle of *Kinsale. O'Neill, O'Donnell and their Spanish allies are defeated by Lord Deputy Mountjoy.
1603	The Treaty of *Mellifont brings the Nine Years War to an end.
1607	The *Flight of the Earls. Hugh O'Neill, Earl of Tyrone and Red Hugh O'Donnell, Earl of Tyrconnell, along with 90 other Irish chiefs flee to the continent.
1609	The *Plantation of Ulster.
1641–49	The *Rebellion of 1641 begins the Confederate Wars – Rebellion of Ulster Irish and Old English Lords of the Pale against the crown.
1649	Oliver *Cromwell arrives in Ireland.
1652	*Cromwellian land settlement commences.
1685	*James II accedes to the English throne.
1688	James II deposed as king of England.
1689	*William of Orange becomes king of England and the Williamite campaign in Ireland begins. James II lands at Kinsale.
	The Siege of *Derry.
1690	Battle of the *Boyne. James II and Irish forces defeated by William of Orange. First siege of *Limerick.
1691	Battle of *Aughrim. The bloodiest battle in Irish History – Irish and French allies of James II defeated by William of Orange.
	Second siege of Limerick.
	The Treaty of Limerick ends the Williamite war in Ireland.
	Williamite land confiscations.
1695–1709	*Penal Laws enacted against *Catholics.

1713 Jonathan *Swift becomes Dean of *St Patrick's cathedral.
1742 World premiere of Handel's *Messiah* in Dublin.
1791 Society of *United Irishmen founded in *Belfast and Dublin.
1795 *Orange Order formed.
1796 French invading fleet arrives at Bantry Bay with Wolfe *Tone.
1798 United Irishmen rebellion in Wexford, *Antrim and *Down crushed. French fleet which arrives in Mayo is defeated at Ballinamuck (8 Sept.), County *Longford. Wolfe Tone is arrested and commits suicide in prison.
1800 The Act of *Union passed, creating the United Kingdom of Great Britain and Ireland.
1803 Attempted rebellion in Dublin by Robert *Emmet.
1823 Catholic Association founded to campaign for *Catholic Emancipation.
1828 Daniel *O'Connell elected to the Westminster House of Commons for County *Clare.
1829 Catholic Emancipation Act allows Catholics to enter parliament and hold civil and military office.
1840 Repeal Association founded to campaign against the Act of Union.
1842 The **Nation* *newspaper founded by Thomas *Davis, John Blake *Dillon and Charles Gavan *Duffy.
1843 Mass Repeal Association meeting at *Clontarf, County Dublin, cancelled by O'Connell following government ban.
1845–49 The Great *Famine. Potato blight causes starvation and mass *emigration.
1847 Daniel O'Connell dies in Genoa, Italy.
1848 Rebellion led by the radical wing of the *Young Ireland movement fails.
1854 Catholic University of Ireland founded in Dublin.
1858 *Irish Republican Brotherhood (IRB) founded in Dublin by James *Stephens.
1859 *Fenian Brotherhood founded in *New York by John O'Mahony.
1867 Fenian Rebellion fails.
*Clan na Gael founded in New York.
1868 William *Gladstone elected British prime minister.
1869 Gladstone disestablishes the Church of Ireland.
1870 *Home Government Association started by Isaac *Butt.
Gladstone's First *Land Act is passed.
1873 Isaac Butt founds the Home Rule League.
1874 Fifty-nine Home Rule candidates elected to parliament in general election.
1875 Charles Stewart *Parnell elected MP for Meath.
1876–78 Obstructionism used by some Home Rule MPs led by Joseph Biggar in parliament.
1878 New Departure – parliamentarians, agrarian reformers and *nationalist revolutionaries agree to seek land reform and a settlement of the national question.
1879–82 The Land War.
1879 Irish National Land League founded in Dublin.
1881 Gladstone's Second Land Act passed.
The Land League is suppressed and Parnell imprisoned in *Kilmainham Gaol.
1882 Parnell released under the terms of the Kilmainham Treaty.
Land War ends.
*Phoenix Park Murders.
1884 *Gaelic Athletic Association (GAA) established in Thurles, County *Tipperary.
1885 Ashbourne Land Act is passed.
1886 First home rule bill defeated in the House of Commons.

1889	Parnell named as co-respondent in *O'Shea divorce case.
1890	Home Rule party splits over Parnell's involvement in O'Shea divorce case.
1891	Death of Parnell.
	Balfour Land Act is passed.
1893	Gladstone's Second home rule bill defeated in the House of Lords.
	The *Gaelic League founded by Douglas *Hyde.
1898	Local Government Act establishes County and Urban councils.
1899	Irish Literary Theatre (precursor to the *Abbey Theatre) established in Dublin.
1900	Home Rule party reunited under the leadership of John *Redmond.
1903	Wyndham Land Act passed.
1904	The Abbey Theatre is founded in Dublin.
1905	*Sinn Féin founded by Arthur *Griffith.
1909	Birrell Land Act enacted.
1912	Third home rule bill introduced into parliament.
	Ulster Solemn League and Covenant pledges resistance to home rule by *unionists.
	Irish *Labour Party founded.
	**Titanic*, which was built in Belfast, sinks.
1913	*Ulster Volunteer Force (UVF),
	*Irish Citizen Army and Irish *Volunteers founded.
	Lockout of workers under James *Larkin in Dublin.
1914	Outbreak of the *First World War.
	John Redmond supports British war effort.
1915	*Lusitania* sunk by German U-boat off the Irish coast.
1916	*Easter Rising, on Easter Monday, 24 April.
	Executions of 15 leaders, 3–12 May.
1918	Sinn Féin wins a majority of seats in the general election.
1919	Sinn Féin MPs abstain from British parliament and form first *Dáil in Dublin.
1919–21	*Anglo-Irish War.
1920	*Government of Ireland Act establishes two Irish parliaments (in Dublin and Belfast).
	*Black and Tans arrive.
	*Bloody Sunday (21 November): British forces open fire on crowd in *Croke Park in retaliation for assassinations of British agents.
1921	*Anglo-Irish Treaty signed in London.
1922	The *Irish Free State is created.
	Ulysses, by James *Joyce, is published in Paris.
1922–23	*Civil War between Free State forces and anti-treaty Republicans.
1922	Arthur Griffith dies on 12 August.
	Michael *Collins killed on 22 August.
	Erskine *Childers executed.
1922–32	William T. *Cosgrave becomes the first head of government (President of the Executive Council) of the Irish Free State.
1923	W. B. *Yeats awarded the Nobel Prize for literature.
1925	*Boundary Commission disbanded. Border between the Irish Free State and *Northern Ireland remains as set out in the Anglo-Irish Treaty.
1926	*Fianna Fáil party founded by Éamon *de Valera.
	George Bernard *Shaw is awarded the Nobel Prize for literature.
1931	The Statute of Westminster passed.
1932–48	Éamon de Valera serves as President of the Executive Council and (after the 1937 constitution) *Taoiseach.
1933	*Fine Gael founded.

1937 A new *Constitution (Bunreacht na hÉireann) approved by referendum. Name of country changes from the Irish Free State to *Éire (in Irish), or Ireland.
1938 Economic War with Britain (begun in 1932) ends.
1938–45 Douglas Hyde is the first president.
1939 Outbreak of the Second World War (known as the Emergency). Ireland remains neutral.
1941 Dublin and Belfast bombed by the German air force.
1945–59 Seán T. Ó Ceallaigh is president.
1948–51 John A. *Costello is Taoiseach.
1948 Ireland declared a Republic (*Republic of Ireland Act).
1949 Ireland Act passed at Westminster.
1951 E. T. S. *Walton shares Nobel Prize for physics.
1951–54 Éamon de Valera is Taoiseach.
1954–57 John A. Costello is Taoiseach.
1955 Ireland becomes a member of the *United Nations.
1957–59 Éamon de Valera is Taoiseach.
1959–66 Seán *Lemass is Taoiseach.
1959–73 Éamon de Valera is president.
1961 *Television service is established in the Republic.
1963 John F. *Kennedy visits Ireland.
1966–73 Jack *Lynch is Taoiseach.
1967 Civil Rights Association established in Northern Ireland (*NICRA) to campaign for equal rights for the Catholic Community.
1968 Civil rights demonstrators clash with police in Northern Ireland.
1969 Commencement of the *Troubles in Northern Ireland – British troops sent to Northern Ireland.
Samuel *Beckett awarded Nobel Prize for literature.
1970 The IRA splits into Provisional and Official wings.
1971 *Internment without trial introduced in Northern Ireland.
1972 *Bloody Sunday: 13 unarmed civilians are shot dead by the British army in Derry.
Northern Ireland *Stormont parliament abolished. Direct rule of Northern Ireland from London.
1973–77 Liam *Cosgrave is Taoiseach.
1973 Ireland becomes a member of the European Economic Community (EEC).
Erskine *Childers is president; he dies in office in November 1974.
1974 *Dublin-*Monaghan bombings.
Seán *MacBride is awarded the Nobel Peace Prize.
1974–76 Cearbhall Ó Dálaigh is the fifth president.
1976–90 Patrick Hillery is the sixth president.
1976 Máiréad Maguire *Corrigan and Betty Williams are awarded the Nobel Peace Prize.
1977–79 Jack Lynch is Taoiseach.
1979 The IRA assassinate Lord Mountbatten and three relatives at Mullaghmore, County *Sligo. On the same day (27 August), 18 British soldiers are ambushed and killed at Warrenpoint, County Down.
Pope John Paul II visits Ireland.
1979–81 Charles J. *Haughey is Taoiseach. He holds the office again briefly between February and November 1982.
1981 *Hunger strikes by republican prisoners in Long Kesh (Maze), including Bobby *Sands, MP.

1981–Feb. 1982	Garret *FitzGerald is Taoiseach, also Nov. 1982–87
1985	*Anglo-Irish Agreement signed.
1987	IRA bombing in Enniskillen kills 11 civilians.
1987–92	Charles J. Haughey is Taoiseach.
1990s	Decade of the Celtic Tiger economy.
1990–97	Mary *Robinson is first woman president.
1992–94	Albert *Reynolds is Taoiseach.
1993	Single European Act binds Ireland closer to the European Union.
	*Downing Street Declaration begins the Northern Ireland *peace process.
1994	The IRA announce a complete cessation of military operations. Loyalist paramilitaries follow suit. In December the British government holds its first public talks with Sinn Féin.
1995	Framework document for all-party negotiations launched by Dublin and London governments. David *Trimble elected leader of the *Ulster Unionist party.
	Seamus *Heaney is awarded the Nobel Prize for literature.
1994–97	John *Bruton is Taoiseach.
1996	IRA cease-fire ends but resumes a year later.
	*Mitchell Report published.
1997–2002	Bertie *Ahern is Taoiseach. He continues as Taoiseach for a second term following general elections in May 2002.
1997	Mary *McAleese becomes the eighth president.
1998	The *Good Friday Agreement is signed.
	Northern Ireland assembly established.
	David Trimble and John *Hume awarded Nobel Peace Prize.
	Bombing in *Omagh by dissident IRA group kills 29.
2000	Northern assembly suspended in February over the issue of weapons decommissioning by the IRA. It reconvenes in May 2000.
2001	Irish voters reject the Treaty of Nice.
2002	The Republic of Ireland adopts the euro as its currency.
	Treaty of Nice ratified in a second referendum.
	Northern Ireland Executive suspended.
2004 Jan.–June	Ireland held the presidency of the EU.

Acknowledgments

We are deeply indebted to our General Editorial Advisor Lawrence J. McCaffrey and our Editorial Consultant José Lanters for their extraordinary help. Their immense knowledge and patience were invaluable. Special thanks for editorial suggestions and fact checking to Nollaig Ó Gadhra and for editorial assistance in the art category to Sighle Breathnach-Lynch. For helping to shape the list of entries, we want to thank: Terence Brown, Sighle Breathnach-Lynch, Peter Harbison, Declan Kiberd, José Lanters, Joe Lee, Lawrence J. McCaffrey and Kevin Whelan. We are very grateful for their comments to Patrick J. Egan, Troy Davis, Frank Biletz, Jody AllenRandolph and Hugh Linehan. Our thanks to all our contributors.

A special thanks to David Mattingly for technical computer assistance.

We also want to thank photographer B. P. Fallon, Catherine Gale at Tourism Ireland, Debbie McGoldrick at the *Irish Voice*, Peter Thursfield at the *Irish Times*, Ciaran O'Reilly and Charlotte Moore of the Irish Repertory Theatre (New York) and Niall Rynne for their generous help with photographs.

Photo Credits

We gratefully acknowledge the following for permission to reproduce photographs listed on the pages below:

Áras an Uachtaráin: 230
BP Fallon/bpFallon.com: 241, 269
©BP Fallon/bpFallon.com, from BP Fallon's book *U2 Faraway So Close*: 374
Christy Moore ©Jill Furmanovsky: 239
The Irish Times: 44, 173, 233, 272, 279, 310, 322, 351,
The Irish Voice: 12, 36, 80, 141, 163, 171, 192, 252, 264, 325, 362,
Lelia Ruckenstein: 246
Tourism Ireland: 2, 25, 34, 108, 193, 197, 213, 216, 253, 326, 371

Every effort has been made to establish the sources of all the photographs used and acknowledgement given – should a source not have been acknowledged, we take this opportunity of apologising for such an oversight and will make the necessary correction at the first opportunity.

Cover Illustrations

Front Cover
First row, from left: Bunratty Castle, Co. Clare; Charles Stewart Parnell; Adare Village detail, Co. Limerick; Ennis Abbey, Co. Clare

Second row, from left: Maud Gonne; River Liffey, Dublin; Fenit Strand, Co. Kerry; Jerpoint Abbey, Co. Kilkenny

Third row, from left: the Olympia Theatre, Dublin; Puffin Island, Co. Kerry; Oscar Wilde; Traditional Irish fishing boat, the Curragh

Fourth row, from left: Samuel Beckett; Crag Caves, Co. Kerry; Cross of Clogher, Monaghan County Museum; Hurling match

Fifth row, from left: Kilkenny Castle and River Nore, Kilkenny; Mary Robinson; Ratoo Round Tower, Co. Kerry; Sinéad O'Connor

Sixth row, from left: Bewley's Oriental Cafe, Grafton St.; Traditional cottage, Aran Islands; Edna O'Brien; Detail in Newgrange, neolithic passage grave, Co. Meath

Spine
From top: Government Buildings, Co. Dublin; Cove Coastline, Co. Kerry; Cliffs of Moher, Co. Clare; Muiredach's Cross, Monasterboice, Co. Louth; Holy Trinity Church, Co. Cork; Blarney Castle, Co. Cork

Back Cover
Top row, from left: Morrissey's pub in Abbeyleix, Co. Laois; Interior of St Columb's cathedral; Drombeg Stone Circle, Glandore, Co. Cork; Ayesha Castle and garden, Killiney, Co. Dublin

Bottom row, from left: Evening light on lake near Killarney, Co. Kerry; The Geraldine Experience, Tralee, Co. Kerry; Birr Castle Gardens, Co. Offaly; The Liberties, Co. Dublin

Jacket photos courtesy of Tourism Ireland and Stockbyte except for: Edna O'Brien and Mary Robinson, courtesy of the Irish Voice*; and Sinéad O'Connor © BPFallon/bpfallon.com.*

CELEBRATE THE EXPERIENCE

By GEORGE LUCAS

S WE NEAR THE 20TH ANNIVERSARY *of the theatrical release of* STAR WARS: A New Hope, *I am now intimate- involved in creating a new* STAR WARS *trilogy of "prequel" films. When* STAR WARS *opened in 1977, I hoped that it would enough business to allow me to tell more of the story with further films in the saga. To my surprise,* STAR WARS, The npire Strikes Back *and* Return of the Jedi *were bigger hits than I ever could have expected. But success didn't mean e films were everything I wanted them to be. In truth, each of the films in their own way fell short of my ideal creative vi- n. We ran out of time and money, which is inevitable in making movies, and I had to compromise to meet schedules and dgets. I was also frustrated because the technology of the time did not allow the full realization of all the special effects quences that I had in mind. Today, with the digital-imaging technology that Industrial Light & Magic has pioneered, I ve had the rare opportunity to go back and complete the first trilogy the way that I originally intended. Working on e* STAR WARS Trilogy Special Edition *has helped me to get back into the world of* STAR WARS *and begin work on the pre- els. After* Return of the Jedi *was released in 1983, I refocused my life away from* STAR WARS. *There were three areas at became most important to me: raising a family; getting my company to be self-sufficient; and advancing the technol- y to enable me to make films the way I envisioned them, without the many compromises of the past. I've now spent years addressing those areas, and today they are no longer holding me back but instead are push- g me forward. At the 20-year mark in* STAR WARS' *history, it is a time to look forward, t back, and celebrate the experience that I hope will live for generations to come.*

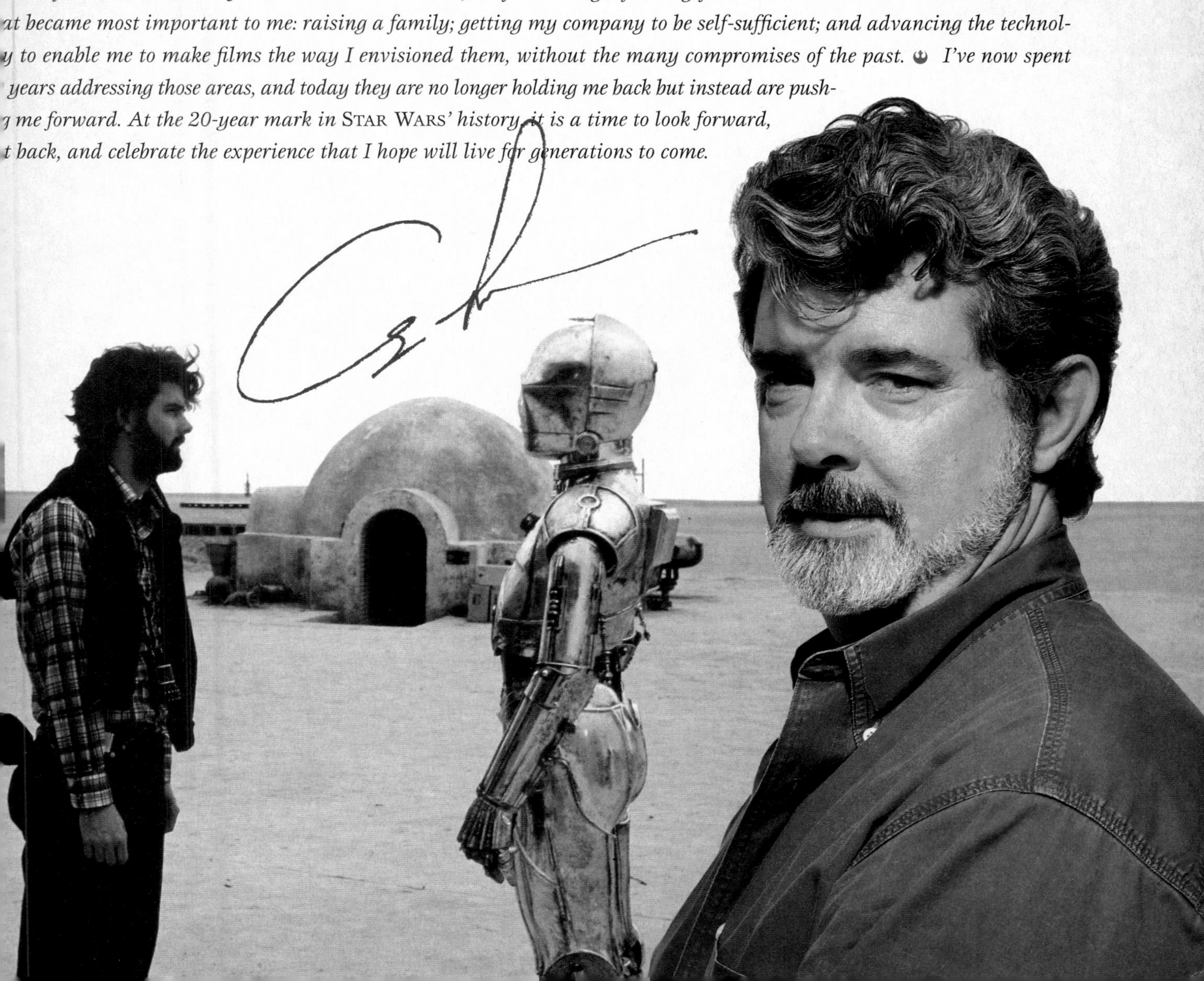

OFFICIAL 20TH ANNIVERSARY COMMEMORATIVE SOUVENIR

STAR WARS

CONTENTS

The Creation Of STAR WARS *20 Years Ago Incited A Revolution In Moviemaking*

BY MARK COTTA VAZ

Launching The REB

On a gigantic sound stage built at England's Elstree Studios, actors Peter Mayhew, Mark Hamill, Alec Guinness and Harrison Ford portrayed Chewbacca, Luke Skywalker, Obi-Wan Kenobi and Han Solo aboard Han's Corellian freighter, the **Millennium Falcon.**

ELLION

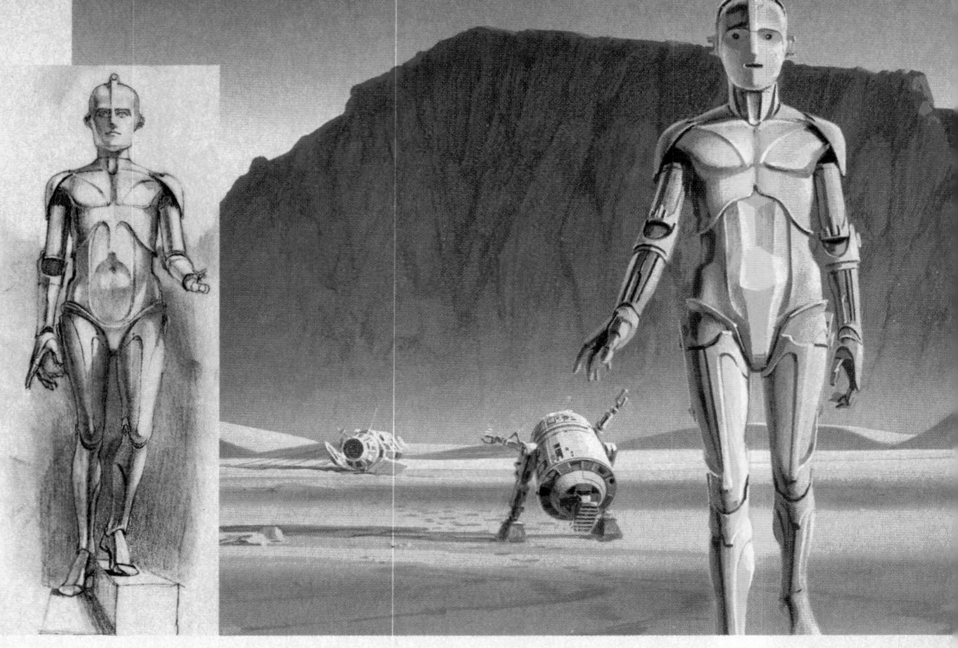

"...it took the paintings OF CONCEPT ARTIST RALPH McQUARR

and other FOX executives to Sta

North of San Francisco, on a country road that winds through groves of redwood trees and rolling hills, mountain lions roam, deer abound and dreams are made.

Along that road is a place, nestled in a valley that for a century was a cattle and dairy farm, called Skywalker Ranch, named for the young hero of George Lucas' famed *STAR WARS* trilogy. Skywalker Ranch is home to the offices of Lucasfilm Ltd., including its production facilities and archives. A short drive to the east, in the town of San Rafael, are LucasArts Entertainment Company, the company's best-selling computer games division, and Industrial Light & Magic (ILM), Lucasfilm's award-winning visual effects house.

Although Lucas has attained power and prestige, it's ironic that he's sometimes referred to as a movie mogul. The very concept was anathema to him when he was fresh out of the University of Southern California film school. For his budding career Lucas aimed for creative independence from Hollywood, and his natural business savvy led to a short-lived partnership in Francis Ford Coppola's fledgling American Zoetrope Studios. In those days all the world was a stage as Lucas filmed his first feature, *THX 1138*, a 1971 movie about a futuristic police state, shot in locations around the San Francisco Bay area (including the subterranean Bay Area Rapid Transit tunnels then under construction and the elegant Marin County Civic Center designed by architect Frank Lloyd Wright).

Those were funky, freewheeling days. When *THX* was entered in a special program at the renowned Cannes Film Festival, the young director, his bank account down to his last $2,000, strapped on his backpack and headed off for the French Riviera resort town. While he was hardly greeted as a conquering hero—Lucas had to sneak intc a screening of his own film because he didn't have a festival pass—the scrappy filmmaker did strike a $10,000 deal with a United Artists studio representative tc develop his script for *American Graffiti*

In the immediate post-Cannes period, with the studio rejecting several early drafts of his script and his finances further dwindling, Lucas was tempted by an offer to abandon his *Graffiti* dreams to direct *Lady Ice*, a heist film for which he was offered an up-front $100,000 check and profit percentage. Lucas stuck to his plans and saw *Graffiti* through to its 1973 release by Universal. The film's success paved the way for a certain space opera movie. And *Lady Ice*? Although it starred Donald Sutherland and Robert Duvall, the 1973

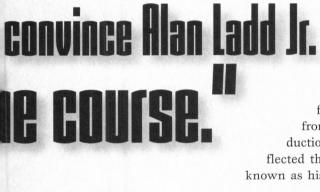

Wanting to provide Fox with art to supplement his fanciful script and win their financial backing, Lucas hired former NASA illustrator Ralph McQuarrie. In McQuarrie's initial concepts, droid R2-D2 traveled on a large ball bearing which Lucas later changed to three sturdy legs. An early version of C-3PO was feminine-looking, reminiscent of the "robotrix" in Fritz Lang's 1926 **Metropolis.**

release suffered a swift box-office death and left Lucas with the suspicion that his promising career could have ended up on ice as well.

Everything in Lucas' career to date had been a prelude to the making of STAR WARS. In rosy retrospect, it was the film that built an entertainment empire and kicked off a mythic saga that has enthralled fans worldwide for the past 20 years. But during the nearly two-year production period, the project always seemed to be skating on the razor's edge of disaster. After United Artists and Universal passed, 20th Century-Fox decided to gamble on the film but was often in a fret about what seemed an out-of-control production with questionable prospects. At one point, it took the paintings of concept artist Ralph McQuarrie—including a rendition of the droids R2-D2 and C-3PO on the twin-sun desert world of Tatooine—to convince Alan Ladd Jr. and other Fox executives to stay the course.

convince Alan Ladd Jr. ...he course."

Looking back, the consternation in the halls of Fox was understandable. For one, the science fiction genre in those days didn't automatically mean blockbuster success. On the technical side, Lucas was planning to conjure up an entire universe with a scope and complexity never before attempted. The spacecraft alone were a radical departure from the traditionally shiny disk spaceships of classic sci-fi productions. Lucas envisioned scratched and battered vessels that reflected the rigors and wear of space travel and war—what became known as his "used universe" concept. He also imagined massive Star

McQuarrie's take on Darth Vader evolved from a sort of medieval samurai to the screen version. The artist initially depicted the character wearing a breathing mask so he could pass from ship to ship in space. However, Lucas liked the sinister-looking mask so much, it became a permanent fixture.

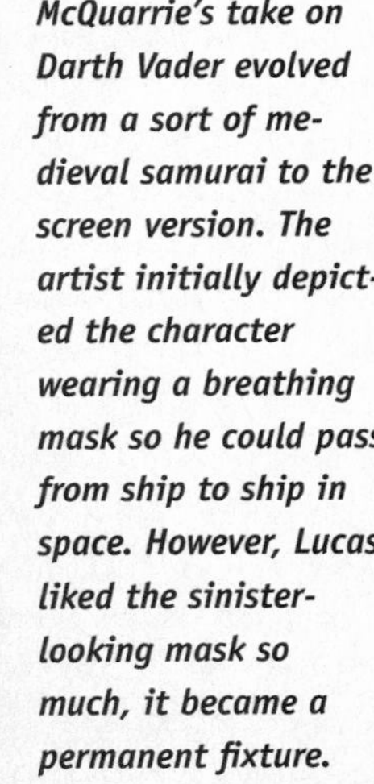

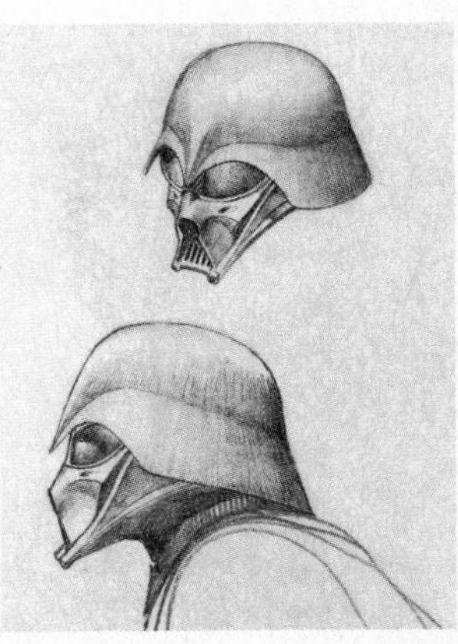

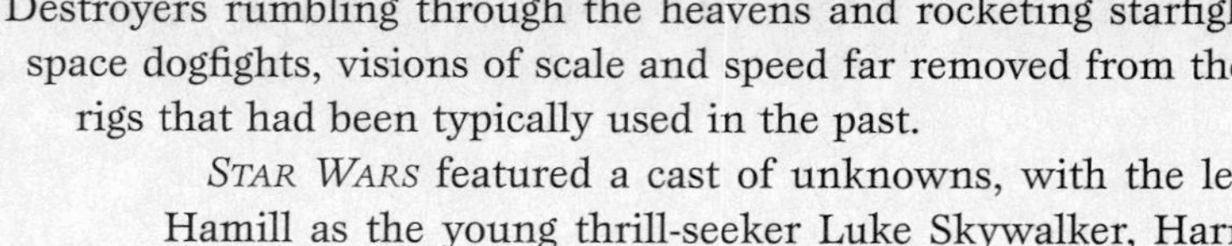

Destroyers rumbling through the heavens and rocketing starfighters engaging in oute space dogfights, visions of scale and speed far removed from the models flown on wir rigs that had been typically used in the past.

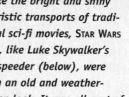

Unlike the bright and shiny futuristic transports of traditional sci-fi movies, ***Star Wars*** *craft, like Luke Skywalker's landspeeder (below), were given an old and weather-beaten look. It was all part of Lucas' idea to create a "used universe" which gave the film more realism.*

STAR WARS featured a cast of unknowns, with the lead roles going to Mar Hamill as the young thrill-seeker Luke Skywalker, Harrison Ford as the cage smuggler Han Solo and Carrie Fisher as the headstrong Princess Leia Organa The novice nature of the actors was underscored by Ford, who worked at od carpentry jobs in between stray TV roles and bit parts in Lucas' own *Amer ican Graffiti* and Coppola's *The Conversation*. Anchoring the productio would be the esteemed, Oscar-winning British actor Sir Alec Guinnes (knighted by Her Majesty in 1959) in the role of the sage Jedi Knigh Ben "Obi-Wan" Kenobi, and Peter Cushing, a veteran of Great Britain' celebrated Hammer horror films, as Grand Moff Tarkin, the grim-face Imperial governor.

Other cast members were transformed into virtual walking ef fects: the muscular David Prowse, who had a small role in Stanle Kubrick's 1971 *A Clockwork Orange*, was encased in the armore helmet and suit of Lord Darth Vader (whose ominous voice, though was supplied by James Earl Jones); the 7'3" Peter Mayhew, wh had played the Minotaur in *Sinbad and the Eye of the Tiger* befor being called to audition for *STAR WARS*, found himself fitted int the hot and sweaty knitted mohair and yak hair body suit o the Wookiee Chewbacca; while Anthony Daniels and Kenn Baker would be transformed into the mechanical droids C-3P and R2-D2, respectively.

"Except for Harrison, Mark and Carrie, the actors proba

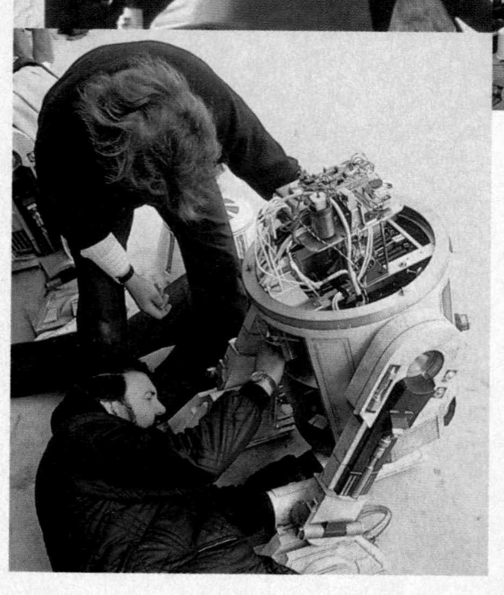

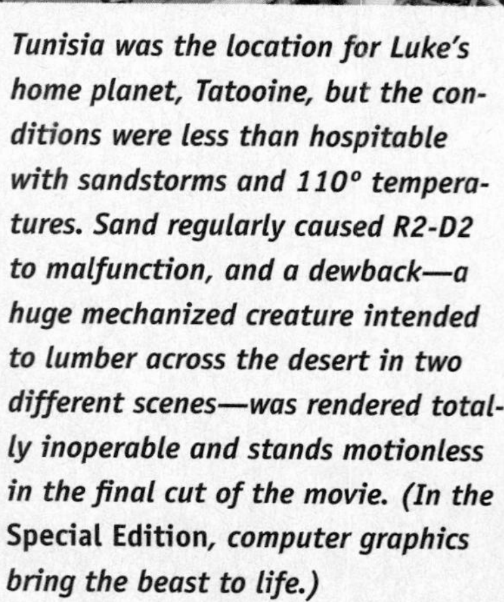

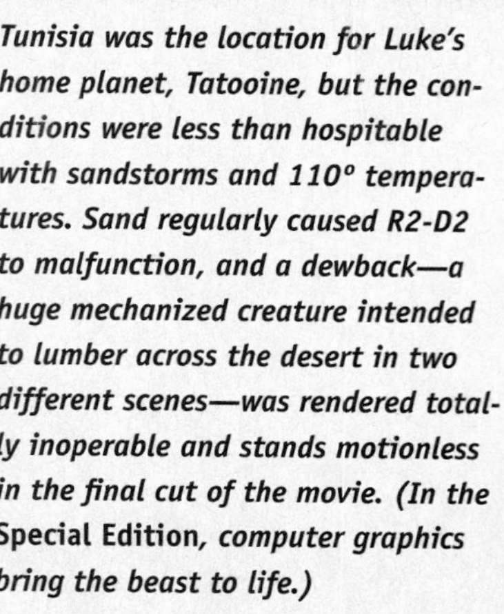

Tunisia was the location for Luke's home planet, Tatooine, but the conditions were less than hospitable with sandstorms and 110° temperatures. Sand regularly caused R2-D2 to malfunction, and a dewback—a huge mechanized creature intended to lumber across the desert in two different scenes—was rendered totally inoperable and stands motionless in the final cut of the movie. (In the ***Special Edition****, computer graphics bring the beast to life.)*

ly didn't have a clue as to what the film was about," ommiserates Rick McCallum, producer for the upcoming *STAR WARS* prequels. "It must have been extraordinarily difficult to be Darth Vader with your oice being dubbed, or to have to perform in a ır suit in a movie where the principle photography was staged at Elstree Studios in England, a country not used to doing science fiction movies let alone something as visually omplex and difficult as *STAR WARS*."

The $10-million production was contentious from the start. Lucas shot the rinciple photography in England with a rew that was both suspicious and resentful of the then 32-year-old whiz kid moviemaker from the United States. 'here were also constant problems getıng things to work while pushing the ımits of special effects. For example, a ocation shoot evoking Tatooine in the esert wastes of Tunisia had a scene vith an Imperial stormtrooper mountd atop a giant "dewback," a planned hysical animation creature effect that idn't work and in the final film sits motionless on the horizon.

Mardji, an Asian elephant, was dressed up as a bantha, a pack animal used by violent Tatooine Sand People, also known as Tusken Raiders.

"Lucas was planning to conjure up an entire universe with a scope and complexity never before attempted."

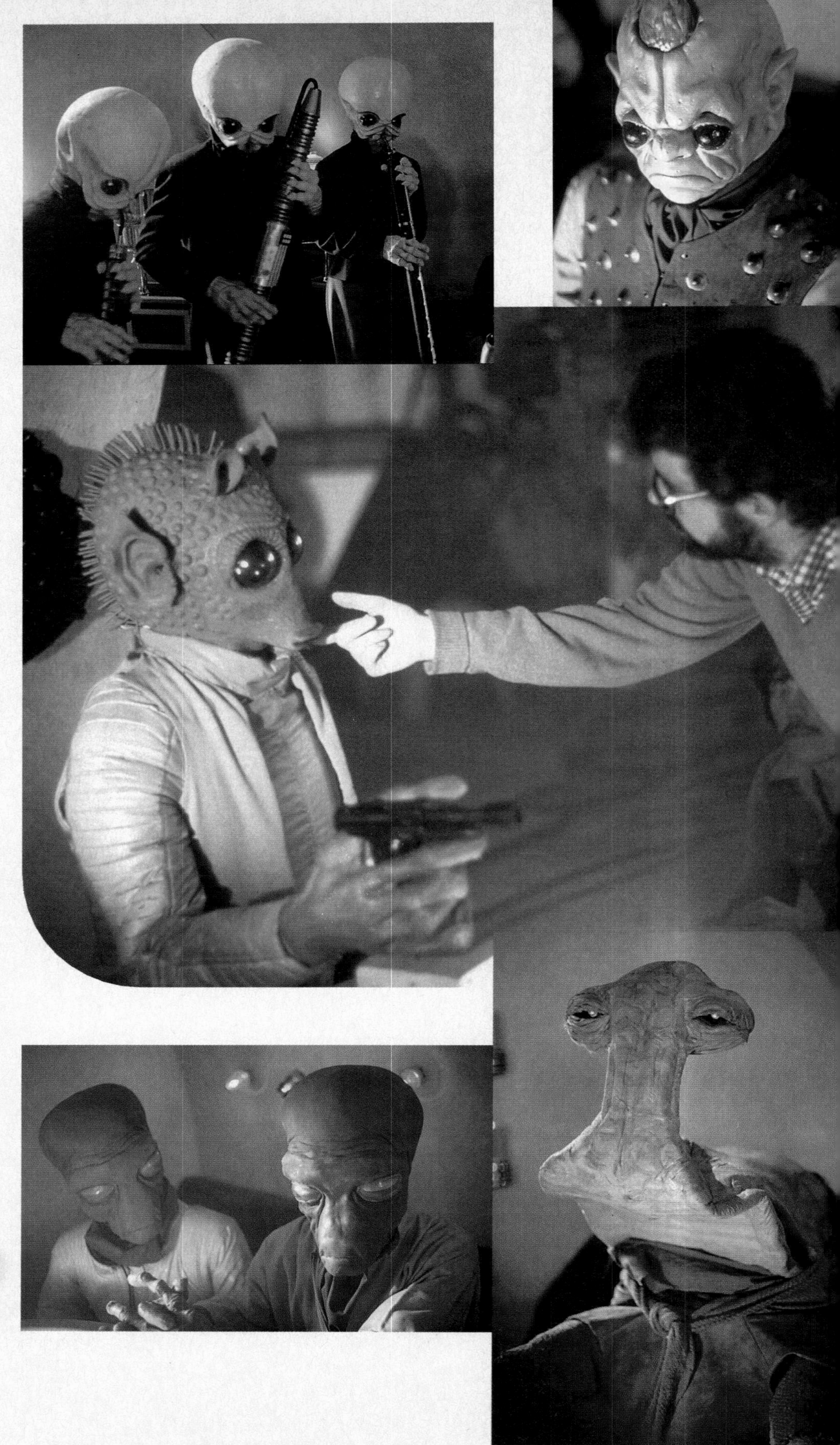

"There were always problems with the physical effects," notes McCallum. "There were things like trying to get R2-D2 to move, and the radio controls wouldn't work, or sparks and flames would suddenly come out and nothing would happen. And then you're taking physical effects from England to Tunisia, where it's 110 degrees and you're working in the sand. This isn't to be disparaging against any of the physical effects guys. I can't even imagine a typical English filmmaker who's been in the business for 25 to 30 years putting down the script which says, 'We see a dewback in the horizon move from right to left.' First, he doesn't know what a dewback is, and then you add in the shipping [of a giant animatronic puppet] and desert conditions."

While Lucas was wrestling with first-unit pressures and the limits of physical effects in England, his stateside visual effects unit was experiencing its own travails. To them had fallen the challenge of crafting such visions as the majestic Star Destroyer, starfighters blasting through the galaxy in the faster-than-light currents of hyperspace, planets spinning in space, the vistas of unknown worlds and a space battle finale above the massive Imperial Death Star. With the exception of such off-world adventures as Kubrick's *2001: A Space Odyssey* (1968), visual effects was not exactly a growth industry. The technology did not exist for much of Lucas' flights of fancy, and the traditional studio effects shops had long since vanished. The buzz from Hollywood was that Lucas was out of his depth, over his head, asking for the impossible.

To create the *Star Wars* visual effects, Lucas' "Miniature and Optical Effects Unit" (as the future ILM was so designated in the film's credits) had set up shop in a 30,000-square-foot industrial warehouse in Van Nuys, Calif. For harried Fox executives it wasn't so much the several million dollars they were investing in literally building an effects shop from scratch, but the volatile makeup of the crew that dismayed them. Like Lucas, that seminal ILM group was young (average age in their late 20s) and disdainful of Hollywood ways (in choosing up sides in the galactic struggle, those first ILMers felt kinship with the Rebel Alliance). As model shop veteran Lorne Peterson once said, "We had this feeling of man against machine."

It probably didn't allay concerns that the Van Nuys facility, which operated without a time clock or dress code, had been nicknamed the "Country Club." It wasn't only the hang-loose groove that rankled traditionalists. Many on the lot had never worked in movies, much less a major studio release. Past and present ILMer Paul Huston, for example, was in the University of Colorado's architectural school when one of his teachers recommended him to the production. Huston heeded the call and went to southern California not with stars in his eyes, but with the prospect of gluing plastic parts on spaceship models.

ne of the most talked-about Star Wars enes takes place in the Mos Eisley aceport cantina, where Luke and Ben ok up with Han. They stand out like re thumbs in this den of iniquity, here the dregs of the universe—pirates, nugglers, bounty hunters and other efarious types—take refuge. As the odal Nodes Band plays, aliens, some ith stories as elaborate as their make-, eye the humans suspiciously. At left, cas instructs the actor dressed as reedo, a Rodian gunning for Han. Near ft, an Ithorian, or Hammerhead, a eace-loving alien, keeps his distance om the fracas Luke steps into, while devilish Devaronian (above) looks on.

Unlike the slick, well-oiled machinery of today's studio blockbuster, the *Star Wars* model and opticals set-up often conducted business on the cheap. Model department supplies were often pennies-to-the-dollar purchases made at a nearby government supply store. The facility had a screening room that was later recalled as being furnished in "early Goodwill," with a screen, projector, old furniture and a mattress with springs poking out.

Like the film crew shooting overseas, the *Star Wars* effects squad had to deal with its share of adversity, as well. There were the constant rumors swirling

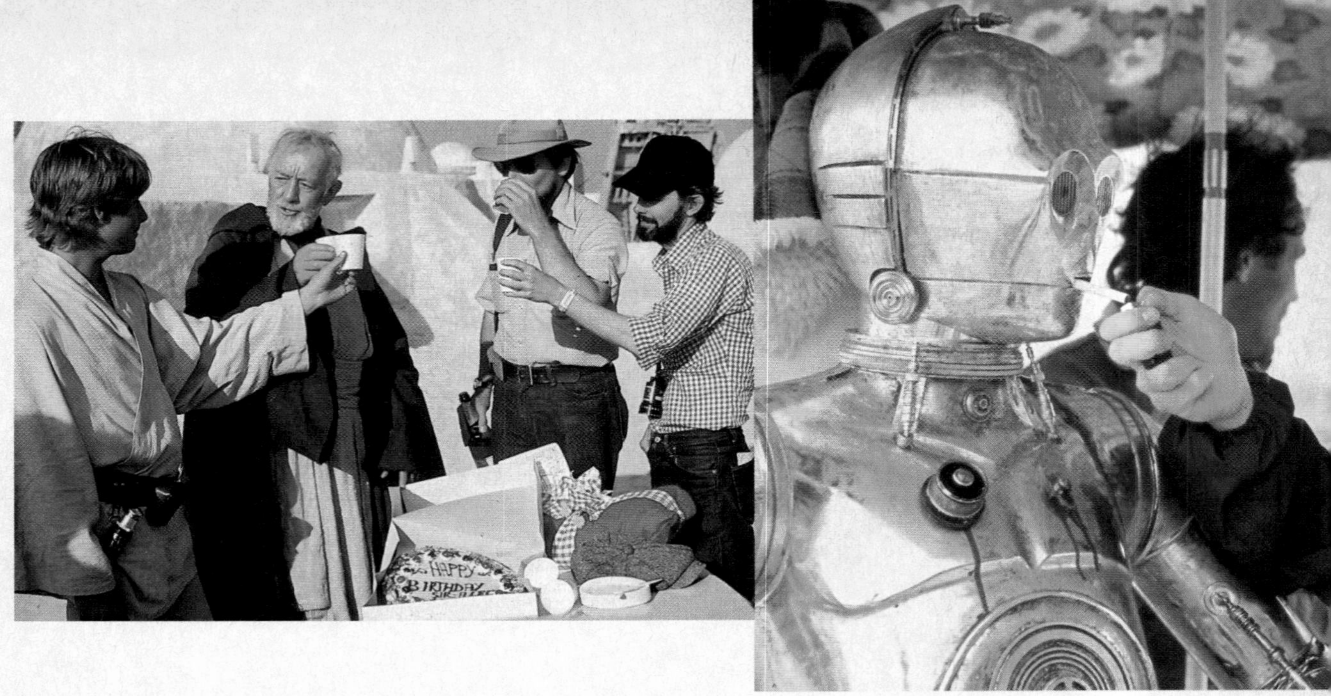

around the Van Nuys facility, usually predicting the production's imminent shutdown by the studio. The unit, which had begun as a non-union shop, was also operating in a heated political climate that even engendered rumors of a firebomb threat. (Once the studio and unions came to an agreement, and ILM went union, there was no more scuttlebutt about firebomb threats.)

Of monumental concern to the entire production, and the grim scenario that greeted an exhausted George Lucas when he came home from England, was that the visual effects group—that had been running for more than a year and gone through an estimated million dollars—had only three shots out of hundreds to show for itself. Distraught at the lack of progress, Lucas soon after felt the telltale chest pains of a heart attack. He was taken to a hospital, where he was diagnosed as being in the throes of hypertension and exhaustion. Reduce the stress in your life, he was told. It was while staring in a hospital mirror at his pale, fatigued countenance that Lucas decided he wasn't going to direct another film. (And he hasn't, until now. In September, Lucas announced he would direct the first of the much-anticipated *STAR WARS* prequels, scheduled for release in 1999.)

But once you hit bottom, you either crash and burn or rise back to the top. And so it was with the *STAR WARS* effects unit. A night shift was headed up by Dennis Muren and Ken Ralston. The studio brought in an old Hollywood pro named George Mather, whose duties included seeing that the lab processing the daily production footage did so in a timely manner. Most importantly, the young visual effects artists—who had seemed all long hair and shortsighted to many observers—turned out to be as resourceful and hardworking as any ve eran Hollywood unit. In retrospect, it was clear th no one had anticipated the implications of startir up a full-service effects shop, particularly one as i novative as that *STAR WARS* team.

Members of the original *STAR WARS* crew woul later recall the time as a kind of Golden Age, wit everyone contributing without regard to status or o ganizational hierarchy. Paul Huston, for instanc went to Van Nuys to glue parts on models but ende up drawing storyboards and not only making model but even assisting in shooting them.

There was a sense of adventure, as well. At o point, ILMers Lorne Peterson, Richard Edlund an Dick Alexander were sent down to Tikal, Guatemal to film ancient pyramids, a shot that would represe the Rebels' secret base. (Peterson would later obser that the same scene shot today would probably i volve a 20-to-30 person crew.) After flying in t Guatemala, the threesome drove with their film equi ment in a battered old Volkswagen bus to the ancie pyramids. The site was so overrun by jungle that n tive hirelings had to help drag the equipment to th top of the pyramid from which they'd be shootin hacking a path with machetes to the 300-foot summi

Once up there—at the spot where priests onc cut out the hearts of human sacrifices and tossed th bloodied victims down the precipitous stone steps- the trio waited for the steamy sky to clear so the could film a jungle vista broken by the peaks of crum bling pyramids. In the final shot, which features composited element of Han Solo's *Millennium Fa con*, a Rebel guard surveys the horizon with field glas es; that's actually Peterson in costume, chosen to stan

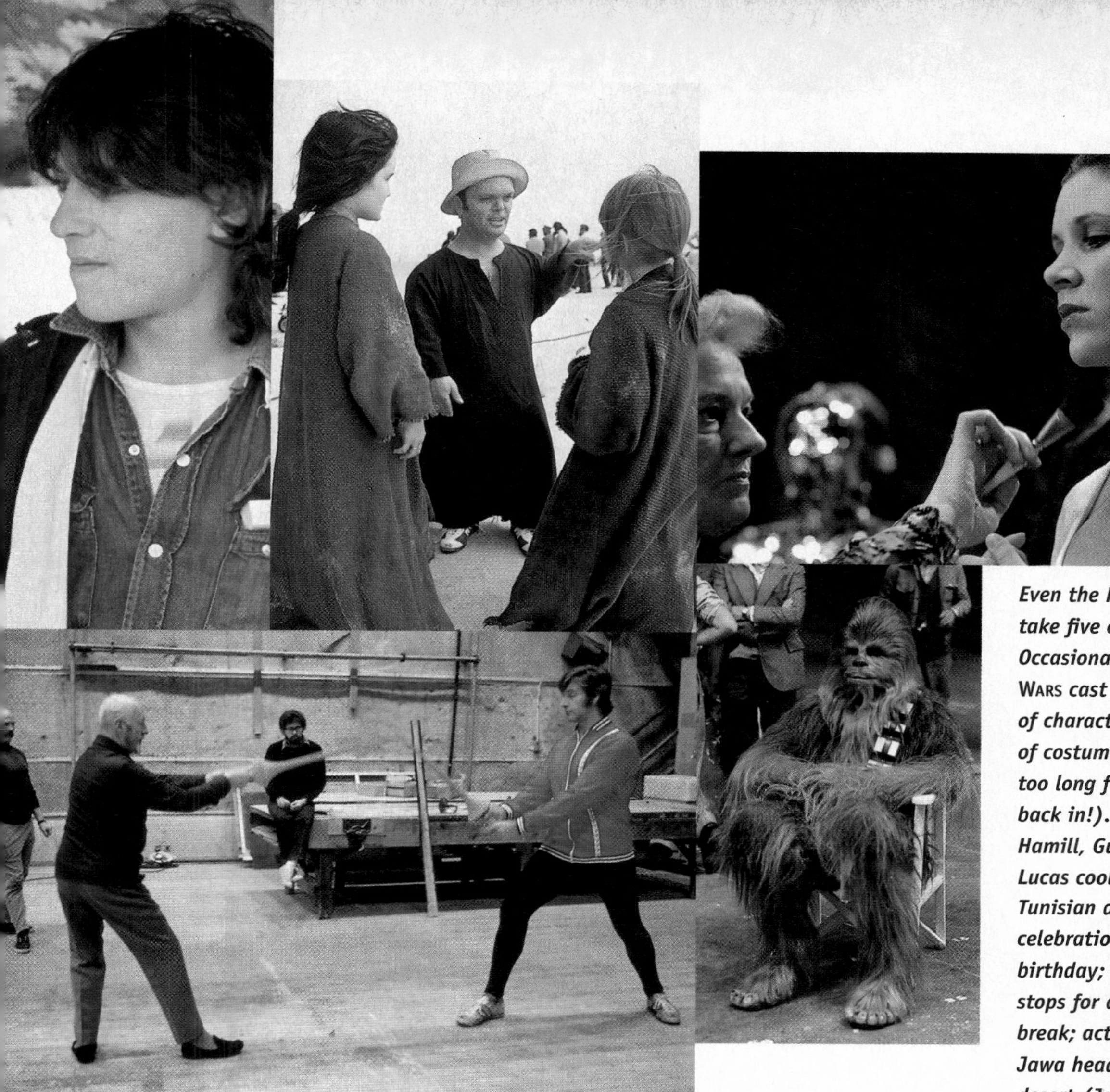

Even the Force had to take five once in a while. Occasionally, the STAR WARS cast would step out of character, but not out of costume (it would take too long for them to get back in!). From left: Hamill, Guinness and Lucas cool off in the Tunisian desert during a celebration for Sir Alec's birthday; Anthony Daniels stops for a cigarette break; actors shed their Jawa head gear in the desert (Jawas are the Tatooine scavengers who sell R2-D2 and C-3PO to Luke's uncle, Owen Lars); Carrie Fisher is dabbed with a little make-up before filming the final sequence; actor Mayhew, relaxing in his yak and mohair Chewbacca costume, found the suit more of a sauna ("The heat was incredible," he remembers); Guinness and David Prowse (sans his Darth Vader regalia) rehearse their pivotal lightsaber duel scene with the help of a fencing instructor and director Lucas.

"The novice nature of the actors was underscored by Harrison Ford, who worked at odd carpentry jobs in between stray TV roles and bit movie parts."

at the pyramid's dangerous precipice because h was the only one of the three without kids. Becau they hadn't brought appropriate props, "actor" P terson was festooned with a couple of photogr pher's light meters tied together with gaffer's tap

That original effects team was also in th vanguard of developing new ways of makin movies. Part of the earlier union problem cou even be traced to the fact that the unit wasn working exclusively in the traditional materia of wood, plaster and steel. The model make alone were experimenting with different kin of plastics, silicon, epoxies, machined aluminu and other innovations.

Most importantly, to create the film's co plex multi-element composite shots, a new tec nology had to be invented. The driving force of th work was still the traditional optical compositi techniques, in which a device called an optic printer combined separately filmed elements on new film. But ILM's wrinkle would be compl menting optical compositing with "motion co trol," a breakthrough process by which camera models and other hardware could be prepr grammed to make specific, repeatable moves. Thu separately filmed elements could be programm to synch-up with each other and look like a si gle filmed image when optically composited. Lea ing the charge on that front would be Photograph Effects Supervisor John Dykstra, whose team d veloped a motion-control track camera for *St Wars* that was dubbed the Dykstraflex.

The *Star Wars* unit also resurrected old, aba doned technology to work in tandem with their t ditional tools and space-age innovations. Such w the use of VistaVision, a wide-screen process Pa mount had developed in the 1950s and used f such big-screen spectacles as *The Ten Comman ments* and *North By Northwest*. But the format,

From drawing table to sound stage, the crew realized the main hangar deck of the secret Rebel base on Yavin Four, where Luke and Rogue Squadron prepare for the assault on the Death Star. From top: A McQuarrie production painting sets the scene; the original storyboard of the Rebel fleet by Gary Meyers, Paul Huston, Steve Gawley and Ronnie Shepherd, under the direction of Joe Johnston; Lucas, at ILM, eyes a model of the X-wing fleet; the completed set as actors ready the "real" starfighters for battle.

which standard 35-millimeter film ran vertically instead of horizontally through the gate of a camera or projection system, required new theatrical projection systems which theater owners did not want to buy. Although the format soon fell by the wayside, its advantage to Lucas and ILM some 20 years later was that VistaVision allowed the filmmakers to double each film frame's exposure area, resulting in a clearer, sharper picture—"motion picture high-fidelity," as Paramount had proclaimed in the heady, hopeful days of the format's release.

The format was vital to ILM's composite-shot effects. Because the approach of rephotographing separate elements inevitably built up film grain and degraded the final image, VistaVision's doubled frame area allowed the creation of composite shots closer to the "first generation" quality achievable when a live-action scene is filmed and cut into the final film without resorting to any kind of optical trickery. After completing their composites in the VistaVision format, the final shots could then be printed out to standard 35-millimeter stock and cut in with the rest of the film.

Another bonus for the filmmakers was that abandoned but available VistaVision cameras and optical printers were available at fire sale prices. (The workhorse printer secured during that period, known as the Anderson Optical Printer, was purchased from Paramount for some $11,000. The same printer, still in perfect working order, has a current market value of about $300,000.)

Even as the production progressed and the movie took shape, it was

Several scale models of Han's beat-up pirate ship—and unlikely hero—the* Millennium Falcon*, were built for the film shoot. A life-size version, complete with realistic-looking dents and scars, was used for ground scenes. ILMers built smaller models for blue-screen shots of intergalactic travel and space battles.

"Members of the original *Star W*

crew would later recall the time as a kind of **Golden Age,** with everyone contributing without regard to status…"

TAR WARS *spurred refinements of composite hotography. Here, the crew builds the scene of the dogfight between Imperial TIE fighters and Rebel X-wings in the Death Star trenches: an X-wing is prepared for a shot; pyrotechnicians shoot an exploding fighter in front of a bluescreen ; a camera films the trench background; the Anderson optical printer combines all the footage.*

difficult to tell whether *STAR WARS* was a classic or a disaster in the making. There were a few inklings of success along the way, such as an advance look at theatrical trailers in the unit's funky screening room, which seemed to portend exciting things. On a hunch, a few confident effects crew members literally invested in the film's potential success by purchasing some 20th Century-Fox stock (which would end up doubling).

But no one was prepared for the phenomenal impact when *STAR WARS* opened in 32 theaters nationwide on May 25, 1977. Lucas himself was on the way to a hamburger joint in Hollywood when he noticed long lines and a general commotion at the venerable Mann's Chinese Theater. He was astounded when he saw the words *STAR WARS* emblazoned on the theater marquee and realized those long lines were filing in to experience the work for which he'd personally suffered.

As reports of record box-office numbers daily poured into the studio and roduction offices, Lucas retreated to Hawaii for a much needed vacation. here, while relaxing on a beach with his friend and fellow director Steven pielberg, the two built a sand castle to celebrate the *STAR WARS* success. It vas during that seaside respite that the duo began to swap ideas for a new ind of movie hero. Spielberg was eager to do an action film in the James Bond tradition, while Lucas shared another of his dreams—a concept about n adventuring archaeologist whose thirst for fortune and glory leads him n a quest for the legendary Ark of the Covenant. The two made a handshake eal, a friendship pact to bring such a hero—later to be dubbed Indiana ones—to life on the silver screen… but that's a story for another time.

Today Lucasfilm greets the 20th anniversary of *STAR WARS*—the film

Lucas wanted a classical score to accompany his good-versus-evil saga. He'd used well-known music as placeholders in the rough soundtrack, and then asked John Williams (below), who scored Steven Spielberg's Jaws, *to compose new music that had the same emotional thrust.*

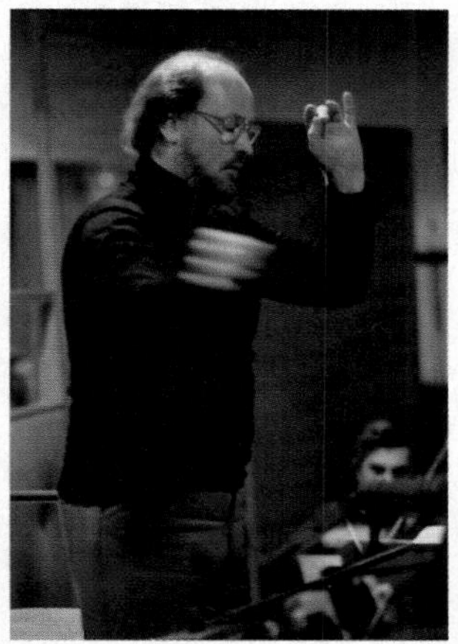

NO ONE WAS PREPARED FOR THE PHENOMENAL IMPACT WHEN *STAR WARS* OPENED IN 32 THEATERS NATIONWIDE ON MAY 25, 1977.

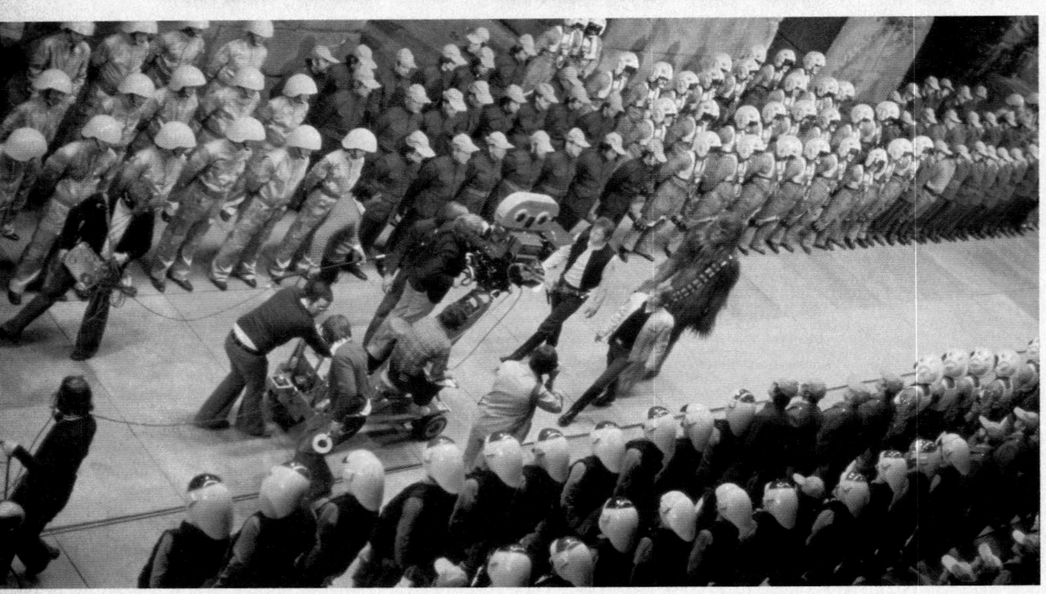

The finale was filmed in the Great Assembly Hall of the Rebel base, where Princess Leia presented Luke and Han (but why not the Wookiee?) medals for their bravery. The cast and crew of* STAR WARS *was honored too with unprecedented box-office sales and seven Academy Awards.

that started it all—with not only a *Spe cial Edition* release, but with ambi tious plans for a new trilogy of pre quel chapters. The prequels wil be produced in a moviemakin environment completely dif ferent from the days when Lu cas was struggling with non functioning dewbacks in th Tunisian desert and a rag tag band of visual effect artists working out of warehouse. This over heated moviemaking cli mate has, in fact, bee directly traced back t the breakthrough visua effects and successfu merchandising tie-ins o *STAR WARS* itself.

The launching o the *STAR WARS* prequel is already underway with Lucasfilm havin inked a $2-billion pro motional agreement wit PepsiCo in May of 199 that will cover at least th first of the upcoming pre quels. On the creative sid the bar couldn't be set high er: to entrance today's audi ences with the same kind o awesome, other-worldly expe rience that greeted moviegoer back in 1977. One current ILMe describes the prequels as being lik the distant rumbling of a yet unsee locomotive.

For the man who laid the original track and engineered the *STAR WARS* train, 199 should be a monumental year. Not only wi the world celebrate the film's 20th anniversar with enhanced versions of the entire *STAR WAR* trilogy in theaters, but the dawn of a long-awaited ne threesome of films will come when full-scale production on th first prequel begins. Last year George Lucas was rarely seen at Skywalker Ranch, opting t spend months at home working on the prequel scripts. More than 20 years ago, the strug gling filmmaker had similarly devoted his time to crafting a grand story with compellin characters that ultimately captivated the world. Now he's taking his time creating new ad ventures, laying out another mythic voyage into the *STAR WARS* universe. As Lucas know all too well, you just don't take shortcuts on a dream.

Mark Cotta Vaz is a senior writer for Cinefex *and author of* Industrial Light & Magic: Into th Digital Realm *(Virgin Books, 1996), a history of the last 10 years of ILM.*

Where Are

For many members of the cast ar
or the culmination—of a long

ACTOR: **Mark Hamill**
CHARACTER: **LUKE SKYWALKER**

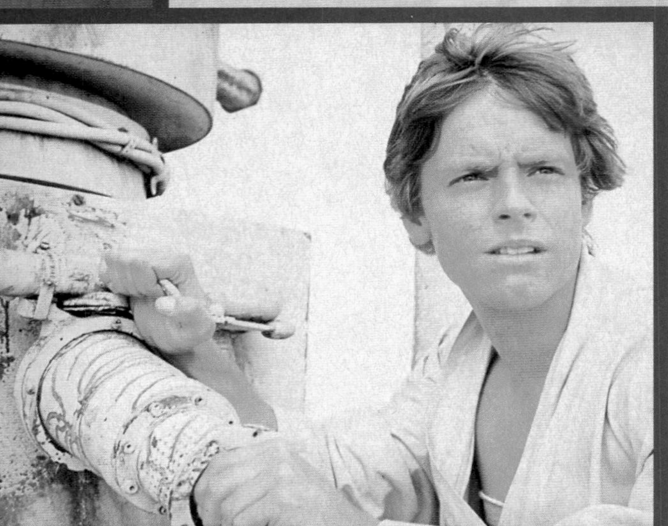

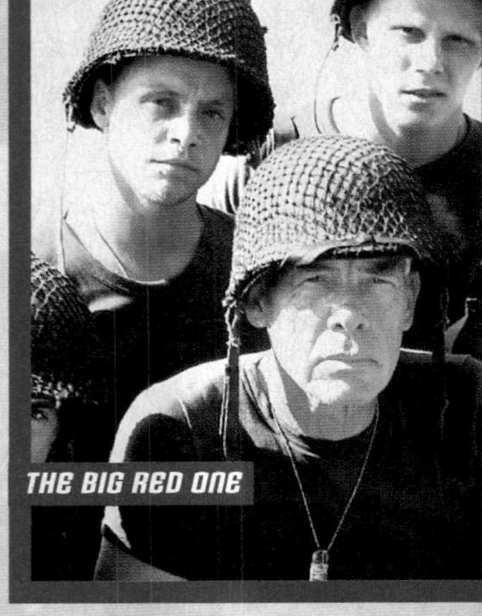

THE BIG RED ONE

SINCE *STAR WARS*: Hamill has enjoyed success in a variety of mediums. In the two decades since the trilogy he's starred in eight Broadway productions, including *The Elephant Man*, *Room Service*, *The Nerd* and *Amadeus*, for which he won a Best Actor Award from the New York Drama Critics. His films include *Sleepwalkers*, *The Big Red One*, *Corvette Summer*, *Silk Degrees*, *Time Runner*, *Black Magic Woman* and *Body Bags* (TV). He's developed a major career as a voice talent, playing Joker in *Batman*, the animated movie, and the *Batman* TV cartoon series. In the last two years, in fact, he's done more than 400 cartoons, including a Saturday-morning animated version of the two Wing Commander CD-ROM games he's starred in, called *Wing Commander Academy*, on USA Network.

WHERE IS HE NOW?: Hamill lives in Los Angeles with his wife of 17 years, Mary Lou, and their three kids. He's working on the big-screen version of his *Black Pearl* Dark Horse comic book and a prime-time animated series for USA Network called *The Blues Brothers*.

IN HIS OWN WORDS: "*STAR WARS* was one of the most amazing experiences of my life. I hear [the *Special Edition*] is fabulous. I understand that the special effects have withstood the test of time very well, and they've actually redigitized my hairdo because that was the only thing that really dated the film."

BODY BAGS

187 CORP/SHOWTIME

CORVETTE SUMMER

MGM-UA

They Now?

ew, STAR WARS was the beginning—er in films

BY MONIKA GUTTMAN

ACTOR: **Harrison Ford**

CHARACTER: **HAN SOLO**

SINCE *STAR WARS*: **The former carpenter's career hit lightspeed after the trilogy, and the success of the (on average) one film per year he's made since—notably Lucasfilm's Indiana Jones series—has put him atop the list of international top-grossing talents, eclipsing even Sylvester Stallone and Arnold Schwarzenegger. Among the 28 films he's made since '77: *Devil's Own, Sabrina, Clear and Present Danger, The Fugitive, Patriot Games, Regarding Henry, Presumed Innocent, Indiana Jones and the Last Crusade, Indiana Jones and the***

***Temple of Doom*, *Raiders of the Lost Ark*, *Working Girl*, *Witness*, *Blade Runner*. He was nominated for the Best Actor Oscar for *Witness* and for Golden Globe Awards for *Sabrina*, *The Fugitive*, *The Mosquito Coast* and *Witness*.**

LUCASFILM/PARAMOUNT (COURTESY KOBAL)

BLADE RUNNER

WARNER BROS.

INDIANA JONES AND THE LAST CRUSADE

ACTOR: Carrie Fisher

CHARACTER: PRINCESS LEIA ORGANA

SINCE *STAR WARS*: Both Fisher's personal and professional lives have been tied into the big screen since she took that famous swing with Luke Skywalker. In addition to such films as *The Blues Brothers*, *Under the Rainbow*, *The Man with One Red Shoe*, *Hannah and Her Sisters*, *The 'burbs*, *When Harry Met Sally*, *Drop Dead Fred*, *Soapdish* and *This is My Life*, her own struggle with

UNDER THE RAINBOW

WARNER BROS./ORION PICTURES

WHERE IS HE NOW?: Ford lives in Los Angeles; he replaced Kevin Costner as the President in the soon-to-be-released *Air Force One*, and will star in Ivan Reitman's *African Queen* remake, *Six Days, Seven Nights*.

IN HIS OWN WORDS: "The job of an actor is to help tell a story. That's one reason *STAR WARS* worked as well as it did. The characters' relationships were real and interesting and couched in an ingenious telling of a familiar tale about good and evil."

THE FUGITIVE

WARNER BROS. (COURTESY KOBAL)

WITNESS

PARAMOUNT

CLEAR AND PRESENT DANGER

PARAMOUNT (COURTESY KOBAL)

IMAGE ENTERTAINMENT

WHEN HARRY MET SALLY

COLUMBIA PICTURES/NELSON ENTERTAINMENT

THE 'BURBS

THIS IS MY LIFE

TWENTIETH CENTURY FOX (COURTESY KOBAL)

drug addiction became a book (*Postcards from the Edge*) and a movie. In fact, Fisher's writing career is equal to her acting career—her other best-selling books include *Surrender the Pink* and *Delusions of Grandma*. She's also one of Hollywood's most sought-after script doctors, having performed surgery on *Hook*, *Sister Act* and *Lethal Weapon 3*.

WHERE IS SHE NOW?: Fisher lives in Los Angeles.

IN HER OWN WORDS: "As far as most people are concerned, I'll go to my grave as Princess Leia. In the street they call out, 'Hi, Princess,' which makes me feel like a poodle. See, my grandmother had a dog named Princess."

ACTOR: Sir Alec Guinness
CHARACTER: BEN "OBI-WAN" KENOBI

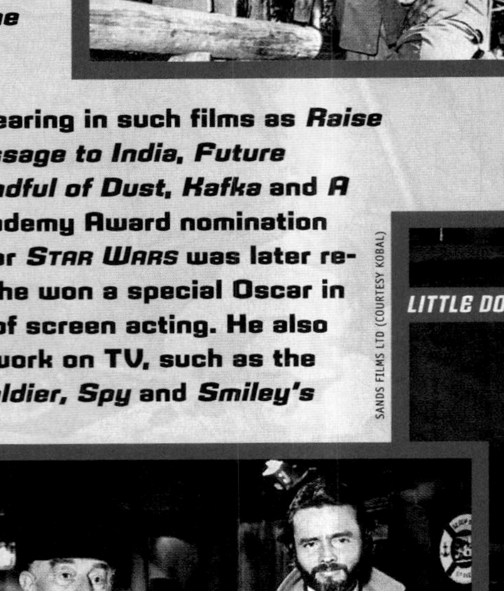

THE BRIDGE ON THE RIVER KWAI

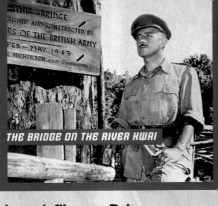

SINCE *STAR WARS*: A veteran actor whose credits span seven decades (1957 Oscar for *The Bridge on the River Kwai*), Guinness has continued to work since STAR WARS, appearing in such films as *Raise the Titanic, Lovesick, A Passage to India, Future Schlock, Little Dorrit, A Handful of Dust, Kafka* and *A Foreign Field*. His 1977 Academy Award nomination for Best Supporting Actor for STAR WARS was later repeated for *Little Dorrit*, and he won a special Oscar in 1979 for advancing the art of screen acting. He also has been acclaimed for his work on TV, such as the miniseries *Tinker, Tailor, Soldier, Spy* and *Smiley's People*. His biography, *Blessings in Disguise*, was published in 1985.

LITTLE DORRI

SANDS FILMS LTD (COURTESY KOBAL)

WHERE IS HE NOW?: He lives outside London and, contrary to some reports, has *not* retired.

IN HIS OWN WORDS: "When we were making [STAR WARS] in England, some of the set people didn't understand George Lucas at all. They would come up to me and say, 'What's with this American chap?' I'd tell them, 'I think he's rather marvelous, and I can promise you that the film may never be heard of, but it's rather good.'"

RAISE THE TITANIC

COURTESY KOBAL

ACTOR: Peter Mayhew
CHARACTER: CHEWBACCA

SINCE *STAR WARS*: Immediately after STAR WARS, the 7'2" Mayhew went back to the work he'd been doing for the previous 10 years, as a hospital porter at Mayday Hospital in suburban London. In '77, he also appeared in *Sinbad and the Eye of the Tiger*. After starring in the STAR WARS sequels, he had a little more financial security and bought a house south of London.

WHERE IS HE NOW?: Mayhew still lives in England.

IN HIS OWN WORDS: "When we began, STAR WARS was just another film, and by the time the negative was in the can, we thought we'd been in a pretty good film."

SINBAD AND THE EYE OF THE TIGER

COLUMBIA PICTURES

DOCTOR ZHIVAGO

ACTOR: **Anthony Daniels**

CHARACTER: **C-3PO**

SINCE *STAR WARS*: **Besides starring in all three *Star Wars* movies, Daniels' career has included roles on both sides of the camera. He has recorded audio-book versions of several recent *Star Wars* novels and reprised his C-3PO role for the National Public Radio dramatizations of the *Star Wars* film trilogy. He did voice-over work for *The Lord of the Rings* and the *Droids* TV series (in which he played Threepio, of course); he appeared in *I Bought a Vampire Motorcycle*, the British TV drama *Prime Suspect* and in George Lucas' TV series, *The Young Indiana Jones Chronicles*. He's done theater work in London, including *Forget Me Not Lane* and such Shakespearean productions as *Much Ado About Nothing* and *Macbeth*. Daniels also produces interactive, special effects shows for conventions, museums and other events. He's currently authoring a column in *Star Wars: The Official Magazine*.**

WHERE IS HE NOW?: **Daniels currently lives in London.**

IN HIS OWN WORDS: **In his inaugural column for the US magazine *Star Wars Insider*, Daniels wrote: "When I first went to George Lucas, I was a serious actor, and I didn't want to be a robot. But he had the painting of Threepio by Ralph McQuarrie, and I fell in love with the look of the character. We spent several months trying to make the costume around my body—although people are often surprised to find that I was actually inside the suit and not just the character's voice. Eventually Threepio took on his own life without me meaning for it to happen, and I was a bit surprised by how he came out. He was almost a doppelganger."**

RETURN OF THE JEDI RADIO PLAY

ACTOR: Kenny Baker
CHARACTER: R2-D2

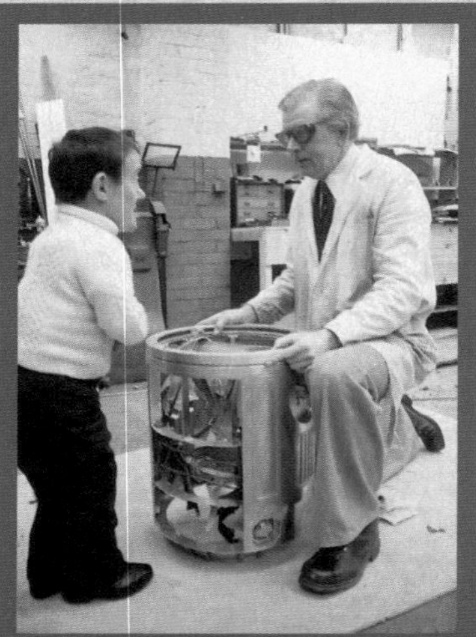

TIME BANDITS (BAKER, RIGHT)

SINCE *STAR WARS*: The diminutive (3') Baker has been busy performing in stage plays—he tours annually in a pantomime stage play of *Snow White and the Seven Dwarfs*, in which he plays Dopey. He was partnered for 30 years with Jack Purvis (Chief Jawa) in a musical/comedy act called the Mini-Tones, and appeared in several features, including *Amadeus* and *Time Bandits*.

WHERE IS HE NOW?: He lives north of London in Ashton and tours with a one-man stand-up comedy show aptly entitled "Kenny Baker."

IN HIS OWN WORDS: "I didn't have a clue about how popular this film would be. Everybody thought the first film was unbelievably incomprehensible at first. It was all funny and weird, with wonderful names like Obi-Wan Kenobi that we can say now but at the time were quite a mouthful. I thought, if Sir Alec Guinness is in it, there must be something to it."

HAMMER FILMS

ACTOR: David Prowse
CHARACTER: DARTH VADER

SINCE *STAR WARS*: Besides the *STAR WARS* trilogy, Prowse's filmography includes the feature films *The People that Time Forgot* and *Jabberwocky*, as well as the *Hitchhikers Guide to the Galaxy* TV series. He was a technical adviser on *Superman* and still appears at *STAR WARS* conventions.

WHERE IS HE NOW?: The former professional weightlifter lives in London and runs the Dave Prowse Fitness Centre, a body-building training center, in south London. He also does fund-raising for arthritis research.

IN HIS OWN WORDS: "Given the choice of playing Darth Vader or Chewbacca, I chose Darth Vader. I wanted to be a villain, and I didn't want to get stuck in a costume where no one could see my face." [Of course, Prowse's face *was* hidden by Vader's helmet and mask. Moviegoers didn't hear Prowse's voice, either, as veteran actor James Earl Jones supplied the vocals for the Dark Lord of the Sith.]

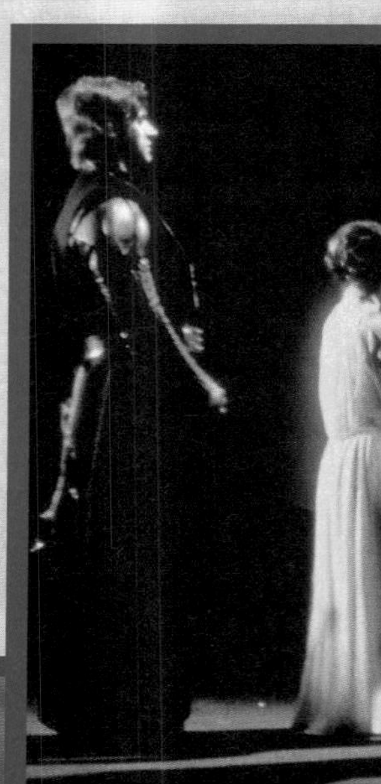

HAMLET

RANK

THE VAMPIRE LOVERS

AIP/HAMMER FILMS

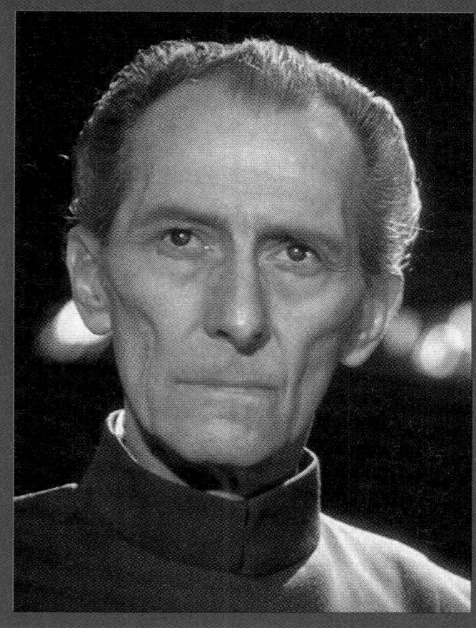

ACTOR: **Peter Cushing**

CHARACTER: **GRAND MOFF TARKIN**

SINCE *STAR WARS*: Cushing died in August 1994 at age 81. A prolific actor who appeared in almost 100 films, Cushing was well known long before *STAR WARS*, mostly for his roles in horror, fantasy and thriller films including *The Curse of Frankenstein* and *Dracula*, as well as his portrayal of Sherlock Holmes in *The Hound of the Baskervilles*. After *STAR WARS*, the thespian made a number of US and British features including *Arabian Adventure*, *A Tale of Two Cities*, *Monster Island*, *Black Jack*, *The House of the Long Shadows*, *Biggles* and *Helen and the Teacher*. He also appeared with Val Kilmer in *Top Secret*. Cushing was dubbed an officer in the Order of the British Empire by Queen Elizabeth in 1989.

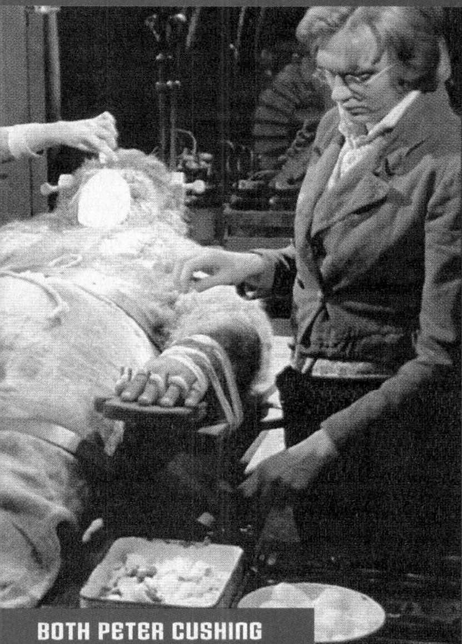
BOTH PETER CUSHING (LEFT) AND DAVID PROWSE (ON TABLE) WERE FEATURED IN THIS SCENE FROM *FRANKENSTEIN AND THE MONSTER FROM HELL* ('74)

Ben Burtt
SPECIAL DIALOGUE & SOUND FX

SINCE *STAR WARS*: After winning an Oscar for *STAR WARS*, Burtt worked on *E.T.*, the Indiana Jones series, *Alien*, *Dark Crystal* and *Willow*. In '95 he directed the made-for-IMAX documentary *Special Effects*.
WHERE IS HE NOW?: Since reworking the sound for the *STAR WARS Trilogy Special Edition*, he's busy on the prequels in California.
IN HIS OWN WORDS: "There are things wrong with *Star Wars* that I was able to fix—bigger explosions, more dynamic sound effects—but nothing that will change the overall movie."

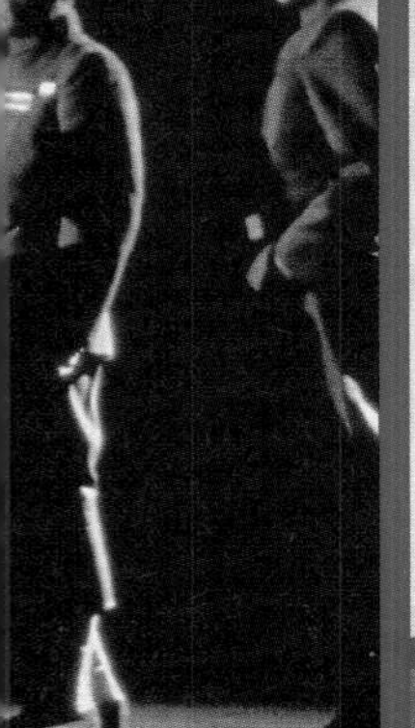

ACTOR: Shelagh Fraser
CHARACTER: AUNT BERU

SINCE *STAR WARS*: *Hope and Glory* was Fraser's most visible film role, although she's appeared in more than 500 radio dramas and TV productions, including *Frankie and Johnnie, A Woman of Substance, Absolute Hell, The Old Men at the Zoo* and *The Last Train Through the Hardcastle Tunnel*.

WHERE IS SHE NOW?: She is currently living in London, recovering from hip surgery.

IN HER OWN WORDS: "Actually, when we were doing STAR WARS, it all seemed rather straightforward, as far as I was concerned."

ACTOR: Garrick Hagon
CHARACTER: BIGGS

SINCE *STAR WARS*: Hagon has mixed character roles in feature films, such as *Mission: Impossible, Bor to Ride, La Grieta, Batman, Cry Fr dom, Nowhere to Hide* and *A Bridg Too Far*, with TV work. Among his TV credits: *Dalziel and Pascoe: A Autumn Shroud, Lie Down with*

ACTOR: Denis Lawson
CHARACTER: WEDGE

SINCE *STAR WARS*: The former mime artist became a star after his appearing in the West End production of the musical *Pal Joey* in 1981, and went from there to star in the international hit film *Local Hero* in 1983. Between STAR WARS and those successes, he appeared in some TV productions (*The Girl Who Walked Quickly, Fearless Frank, Diary of a Nobody* and *If Winter Comes*). Since *Local Hero*, he's worked in several more West End musicals, including *Lend Me a Tenor*, David Mamet's *Olleana*, the STAR WARS sequels and the TV movie *The Man in the Iron Mask*.

WHERE IS HE NOW?: Lawson currently lives in England.

IN HIS OWN WORDS: "It's extraordinary. STAR WARS, as an acting job, was by no means the most important thing I've ever done. But it has generated more mail than anything else I've ever done."

Ralph McQuarrie
PRODUCTION ILLUSTRATOR

…ions, Revolver, Red Knight, White Knight, The Great Escape II: The Untold Story and *…ace II*. His other TV work includes the miniseries *Scarlett, The Nightmare Years* and *London Embassy*. Hagon is also a prolific voice-over artist, and he won an ACTRA award for best supporting actor in 1985.

WHERE IS HE NOW?: Living in London, he's working on radio plays and the feature film *Opium War*.

THIS SCENE OF LUKE AND BIGGS WAS FILMED 20 YEARS AGO BUT DIDN'T MAKE INTO THE FINAL CUT – OR THE SPECIAL EDITION.

SINCE *STAR WARS*: The prolific McQuarrie has worked on some of the biggest sci-fi films of all time: He designed E.T.'s personal spaceship in *E.T.: The Extra-Terrestrial*; contributed to the design of the mother ship in *Close Encounters of the Third Kind*; worked on the two *STAR WARS* sequels and contributed to such other films as *Batteries Not Included* and *Cocoon*. His work also includes amusement park adventures, such as the *Back to the Future* ride at Universal Studios. He did illustration for TV's *Battlestar Galactica*. In addition, he designs book covers (mostly science fiction) and has worked on some interactive CD-ROM games, including Isaac Asimov's Robot Dreams and Robot Visions.

WHERE IS HE NOW?: He's living in northern California, working on multimedia cover illustrations for Ballantine Books and Byron Price.

IN HIS OWN WORDS: "*STAR WARS* was the most interesting and happiest project I've ever worked on. I liked it so much when I saw the film, but still the fact that it has this kind of staying power amazes me. I'm still signing prints for people. It's astounding."

ACTOR: Jack Purvis

CHARACTER: CHIEF JAWA

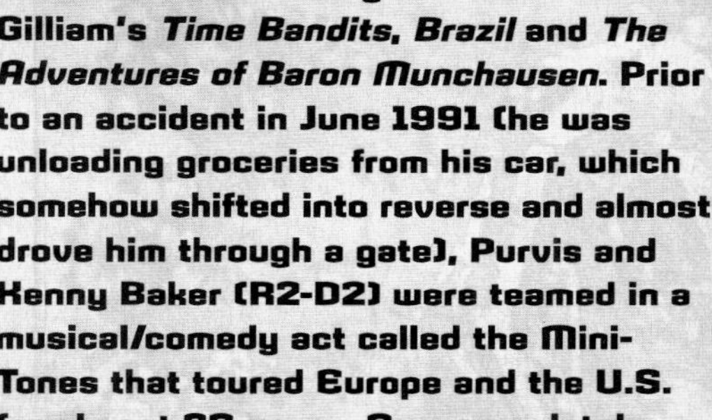

SINCE *STAR WARS*: In addition to the *STAR WARS* sequels, Purvis appeared in TV comedies, miniseries like the Chronicles of Narnia's *Prince Caspian and the Voyage of the Dawn Treader* and *The Silver Chair*, commercials and several feature films, including *Flash Gordon, The Dark Crystal, Mona Lisa, Willow* and Terry Gilliam's *Time Bandits, Brazil* and *The Adventures of Baron Munchausen*. Prior to an accident in June 1991 (he was unloading groceries from his car, which somehow shifted into reverse and almost drove him through a gate), Purvis and Kenny Baker (R2-D2) were teamed in a musical/comedy act called the Mini-Tones that toured Europe and the U.S. for almost 20 years. Now completely paralyzed, Purvis gets around with the help of his wife and a specially adjusted van. For the most part, he stays close to his home north of London, where he remains on a breathing machine. "He still laughs and giggles," his friend Baker reports. "Luckily he was always a TV freak, and that keeps him entertained."

TIME BANDITS

HANDMADE FILMS (COURTEAY KOBAL)

John Williams
MUSICAL SCORE

SINCE *STAR WARS*: Williams, who was named 19th conductor of the Boston Pops Orchestra in 1980 and retired as a Laureate Conductor in 1993, is considered by many to be one of the most successful composers of our day. He has composed music and served as music director for more than 75 films, including *Sleepers*, *Nixon*, *Sabrina*, *Schindler's List*, *Jurassic Park*, *Far and Away*, *Presumed Innocent*, *Home Alone*, *Home Alone 2*, *Empire of the Sun*, *E.T.*, *Superman* and the Indiana Jones movies. Williams has been nominated for 33 Academy Awards—he's won five—16 Grammies and four British Academy Awards. In addition to concert pieces and symphonies, he composed the NBC News theme "The Mission," as well as themes for the broadcasts of the 1984, 1988 and 1996 Summer Olympic Games. Williams has served as guest conductor of such prestigious ensembles as the London Symphony, the Chicago Symphony and the Los Angeles Philharmonic.

WHERE IS HE NOW?: Williams resides in Los Angeles, where his latest project is scoring the upcoming feature *Rosewood*.

IN HIS OWN WORDS: "The music in [*STAR WARS*] relates to the characters and to the human problems—even for non-humans. I think the film is wildly romantic and fanciful. George and I both felt that the music should be full of high adventure and the soaring spirits of the characters in the film."

John Dykstra
SPECIAL PHOTOGRAPHIC EFFECTS SUPERVISOR

SINCE *STAR WARS*: Dykstra followed *STAR WARS* with a turn as supervisor for effects on *Star Trek: The Motion Picture*, *Firefox*, *Lifeforce* and *Spontaneous Combustion*. He had a parallel career as a director of commercials, and turned almost entirely to that arena in the late 1980s and early 1990s before returning to movie effects with *Batman Forever* in 1995, which he says "renewed my enthusiasm for making films."

WHERE IS HE NOW?: Dykstra lives in Los Angeles, where he's working on the fourth installment of the Batman features, *Batman and Robin*.

IN HIS OWN WORDS: "From a professional point of view, *STAR WARS* was the most intense educational experience. I learned more in less time than on any experience prior to or subsequent to that film. Personally, it was a labor of love, a labor of obsession, one of those deals where you get to do what you do well because you enjoy it. I can't believe it's been 20 years. I think it had a profound effect on everybody who worked on it."

John Barry
PRODUCTION DESIGNER

SINCE *STAR WARS*: Barry worked on two feature films following *STAR WARS*—*Superman* and *Superman II*—before he succumbed to infectious meningitis in May of 1979.

Richard Edlund

MINIATURE AND OPTICAL EFFECTS, FIRST CAMERAMAN

SINCE *STAR WARS*: Edlund continued to work for ILM through the two *STAR WARS* sequels and *Raiders of the Lost Ark*, earning four Oscars. He moved to Los Angeles in 1983, took over a 65mm motion picture effects facility in Marina Del Rey and created his own effects firm called Boss Film Studios. His subsequent film credits include *Multiplicity*, *2010*, *Ghostbusters*, *Die Hard*, *Alien 3*, *Poltergeist* and *Poltergeist 2*, which have earned him an additional six Oscar nominations. He was named chairman of the Academy of Motion Picture Arts and Sciences Visual Effects branch.

WHERE IS HE NOW?: Edlund remains in L.A. as president of Boss Film Studios; he oversees effects work for feature films, theme park attractions, video games and CD-ROM titles.

IN HIS OWN WORDS: "*STAR WARS* meant a great deal, personally and professionally. It was what I dreamed about doing. It had a lot of things that had been missing from movies—moral values, respect for your elders—all those things were built into it. I used to tell the guys I was working with, Remember these days, guys, because these are the good old days. And here we are, looking back 20 years, and those *were* the good old days. *STAR WARS* created the renaissance in visual effects. I meet young people now in the digital era—which is the new renaissance in effects—and many of them tell me that *STAR WARS* is what spurred them to follow a career in the business. So it had a very wide-ranging effect on America and the world."

Dennis Muren

MINIATURE AND OPTICAL EFFECTS, SECOND CAMERAMAN

SINCE *STAR WARS*: Muren has won eight Oscars for visual effects for his work on such films as *Jurassic Park*, *Terminator 2: Judgment Day*, *The Abyss*, *Innerspace*, *Indiana Jones and the Temple of Doom*, *Return of the Jedi*, *E.T.* and *The Empire Strikes Back*. He won a special Oscar for Technical Achievement for his creation of an apparatus called the Go-Motion Figure Mover. Among his other film credits are *Twister*, *Mission: Impossible*, *Casper*, *Ghostbusters II*, *Willow*, *Empire of the Sun* and *Dragonslayer*.

WHERE IS HE NOW?: Muren lives in northern California and works as Senior Visual Effects Supervisor at ILM, where he is currently supervising visual effects for the *Jurassic Park* sequel, *The Lost World*, and developing new effects techniques and equipment.

IN HIS OWN WORDS: "Without George Lucas and *STAR WARS*, I'd still be animating bathroom tissue for TV commercials. Instead, I have a great time working with hundreds of creative people making cool images for really big movies. With each show I try to top myself, and that's my favorite part: figuring out what's next and how to make it amazing. I began doing effects when I was seven, and I'm still trying to do it better than the last time."

BLAS

The STAR WARS **Trilogy Special Edition** *dazzles with new scenes, characters and creatures, treating moviegoers to a fresh look at all three classic films*

BY MARK COTTA VAZ

T To The Past

The **Special Edition** *of* **Star Wars** *features a completely computer-generated scene of Rebel X-wing fighters attacking the Death Star. The difference from the original is subtle, though remarkable.*

The final, all-digital composite (below) of this scene from A New Hope, *which replaces a 20-year-old optical composite (left), includes a CG starfield background, Death Star and X-wings. To recreate the starfighters, ILM artists made digital renderings from the original models. The computer was also able to continuously track the X-wings, from front view to rear view.*

Among the scenes that George Lucas could not complete 20 years ago—for lack of time, money and technology—was a confrontation between Jabba the Hutt and Han Solo. The shot was filmed with actor Declan Mulholland standing in as Jabba (below), to be replaced with a mechanized puppet, but the effect failed. Now, ILM has finally harnessed the computer and added a CG Jabba.

ovie lore is full of tales of bitter control battles between film directors and studio executives. For whatever reasons—censorship, too-lengthy running time or sheer back-stabbing spite—much footage has fallen on the cutting-room floor over the years, even at the expense of characters and story continuity. But the growing interest in film preservation, as well as video and laser disc reissues of classic movies have brought about a new trend: directors' cuts that restore films to the form their creators originally intended.

Lucasfilm gave a new spin to that revisionism with the 1995 announcement that the 20th anniversary of *Star Wars: A New Hope* would be celebrated with a theatrical rerelease—dubbed the *Special Edition*—featuring four and a half minutes of new shots and seamless fixes to enhance the original film. The effort would range from adding characters and graphic elements that did not appear in the 1977 release (and were never shot or created) to restoring a badly deteriorated negative from which new theatrical prints would have to be struck.

The legions of *Star Wars* fans caught up in the film's story and spectacle might not have noticed anything amiss in the original, but for creator George Lucas, flaws and missed opportunities abounded and had rankled him for years. As a young filmmaker heading up the project originally known as *The Star Wars*, Lucas had to face limits on time, technology and budget. Not surprisingly, he had to make compromises. For instance, Mos Eisley, the dusty frontier town on Luke Skywalker's home planet of Tatooine, was originally conceived as a bustling spaceport city. Some starfighter model shots did not look nearly as realistic as the filmmaker would have liked. And nightmarish mechanical effects problems had resulted in such snafus as giant dewback creatures, domesticated reptiles native to Tatooine, that didn't move and therefore couldn't be used.

"...FOR CREATOR GEORGE LUCAS, flaws and missed opportunities abounded and had RANKLED HIM for years."

Another sequence from STAR WARS *that has vexed Lucas for the past two decades is Mos Eisley. Thanks to the digital technology that his special effects company, ILM, has since developed, the city is now the bustling spaceport he originally conceived. To do so, a 3-D model of Mos Eisley was built and scanned into a computer as the basis of a digital matte background (left). To add bustle to the streets, additional stormtroopers and assorted citizens were filmed and composited to the original scene.*

Perhaps the biggest modification to the original script was the removal of an entire sequence in which actor Harrison Ford's character, Han Solo, was confronted in a Mos Eisley hangar by the gargantuan crime lord Jabba the Hutt (who didn't show up in person until *Return of the Jedi*, the third movie in the trilogy). The planned creature effect simply failed to achieve the degree of realism Lucas was looking for and was cut out.

But movie technologies have caught up with Lucas' vision—in great part because of his vision—and so *STAR WARS* marks its 20th anniversary in a new moviemaking world. Digital image-processing techniques and computer-generated (CG) imagery, pioneered by Lucas' own Industrial Light & Magic (ILM) effects unit, provided facile new tools with which Lucas could finally redress his wish list for *STAR WARS*.

For example, with computer graphics, ILM has created a realistic, animated Jabba (based on the full-scale animatronic puppet that had been created for *Jedi*). Digital compositing tools allowed ILM to seamlessly insert Jabba into the 20-year-old Mos Eisley hangar footage using computers. Because Jabba's feud with Solo is a dramatic thread that runs through the trilogy, the sequence adds a crucial—and up to now missing—piece of continuity.

The Jabba sequence was an exception to the main objective of the *Special Edition*. Instead of restoring discarded footage, Lucas' initial goal was to enhance specific scenes and shots. That included replacing certain shots with computer graphics recreations (such as a scene of Rebel X-wing starfighters lining up to attack the Death Star), inserting CG elements into existing footage, doing image processing clean-ups and subtle digital fixes of shots and even filming new cuts or live-action elements to expand specific sequences.

Helping to realize Lucas' specific wishes for the *Special Edition* of *A New Hope* were producer Rick McCallum, who headed up the project, film editor Tom Christopher, film restoration expert Leon Briggs, Phil Feiner of Pac Title, Peter Comandini of YCM Labs, visual effects producer Tom Kennedy, ILM veteran Dennis Muren and other ILM stalwarts. By early 1996, Lucasfilm was so satisfied with the results of the project that the decision was made to give the *Special Edition* treatment to *The Empire Strikes Back* and *Return of the Jedi* as well and to celebra the *STARS WARS* anniversary by releasi the entire trilogy one after the other i quick succession. (The original, *A Ne Hope*, will return to theaters on Janua 31, 1997, followed by *Empire* on Febr ary 21 and *Jedi* on March 7.)

"It's interesting that ILM was cr ated to do *STAR WARS*, and after all th amazing pictures the company ha worked on since, the new technology. is being folded back into the original pi ture," says TyRuben Ellingson, an a director for the *New Hope Special Ed tion* (along with Mark Moore).

Ironically, the *Special Editions* als entailed traditional technologies, suc as optical printing. Ultimately, the pro ject would be a time-traveling exper ence, with the high-tech wizards of th digital age confronting decades-old fil made during the vanished age whe optical processes ruled the movies.

It was vital that any new CG en hancements perfectly blend with th original footage. At ILM that meant new generation of computer-savvy v sual effects artists had to emulate in the virtual creations the look and aestheti of a universe designed and produce with props and old-fashioned camer tricks. At one point, art director Elling

son brought in a box full of shower heads and threaded pipe to show to the digital artists, making the point that of such stuff was the *Star Wars* universe made.

The new computer-made elements had their own camera moves (the so-called "virtual camera"), which had to match the original physical camera moves in a scene. In one *Special Edition* shot, Lucas wanted an original Mos Eisley scene of worried droids Artoo and Threepio watching stormtroopers search for Obi-Wan and Luke enlivened with the addition of a synthetic stormtrooper dismounting one of several computer-generated dewbacks. The shot had been filmed live-action in Tunisia and was never intended for processing with optical effects, much less synthetic, photorealistic creations. ILM's CG crew had access to the original production notes, which indicated the camera move had been made from a truck platform. After matching the virtual camera to the original camera move—no mean trick, considering that today's physical cameras are steadier than the cameras used for the original shoot—the *Special Edition* team then had to coordinate the new elements to match the original footage.

In addition to CG dewbacks and flying ships, Mos Eisley itself has been built up and expanded with layers of structures to transform the frontier village into a busy, albeit dusty, spaceport. For instance, now when Luke, Ben, R2-D2 and C-3PO enter the city in Luke's landspeeder, moviegoers will witness a new cityscape—actually a digital matte painting created by ILM's Yusei Uesugi, who computer-built the vista in 3-D and colored it with painting software.

"Just a few years ago Yusei was working with brushes and oil paints, and now he's rebuilt Mos Eisley completely in CG," notes John Berton, the project's CG supervisor. "Pulling off that shot gave us an interactive digital set in which we could put real actors. The shot really stretches our creative muscles."

Mos Eisley wasn't the only galactic city to experience a computerized makeover. In the *Special Edition* of *The Empire Strikes Back*, vistas of Cloud City, the floating metropolis high above the planet Bespin and watched over by Han Solo's friend and sometime-rival Lando Calrissian, has been digitally renewed. Originally, Lucas had conceived Cloud City as a fantastic, Flash Gordon-ish vision, but the effect was limited by the use of glass matte paintings, a two-dimensional effect that restricted camera movement. Matte paintings have been the classic recourse for filmmakers who need to expand a set or establish an entire environment in one shot (with the illusion often heightened by integrating live-action film into the painted environment). But the limits of paint and photographed elements restricted any possible interactivity with those environments.

New digital technology has broken the limitations. Now painters like Yusei Uesugi can create an image that once required not only matte painters, but model makers, camera operators and optical compositors, too. Digital painting gives artists the ability to construct in virtual space three-dimensional, wire-frame objects and cover them with surface textures and details. They can create environments that combine digitized elements and digitally painted effects, and even allow them to design virtual camera views on a synthetic scene. The *Special Edition* Cloud City scenes show just such a completely synthetic environment, for which ILM artists utilized Viewpaint, in-house software that allows textures to be painted directly onto 3-D building constructions. Moviegoers will now see Han's ship, the *Millennium Falcon*, zoom in from space and fly past Cloud City CG skyscrapers.

Not all the *Special Edition* reconstruction required cutting-edge technology. An original scene early in *A New Hope* of stormtroopers scanning the Tatooine sand dunes has been augmented with new live-action footage shot last year in the desert outside Yuma, Ariz. In *Empire*, an updated cut of Darth Vader walking along a Cloud City platform to board his shuttle necessitated new blue-screen photography of an actor in Vader's suit. And while the mechanized puppets that composed the Max Rebo Band (Jabba the Hutt's palace "jizz-wailer" aliens) in *Jedi* have been replaced with CG figures, new *Empire Special Edition* cuts of the wampa ice creature that attacks Luke were recreated with the tried-and-true, actor-in-a-suit method.

Classic photochemical-based optical printing technology was also resurrected for the *Special Editions*. Whereas digital technology was used to clean up tell-tale "matte lines" around optically composited elements—notably in *Empire*'s opening Battle of Hoth scenes where flying Rebel snowspeeders stand out against the icy planet's bright white snowfields—time and expense dictated that modern optical printers address the many "wipes" scattered throughout the trilogy. (A wipe is a storytelling device in which an image is replaced by another in a sweeping move across the frame.)

"We went back to the original elements from Lucasfilm and recomposited with 1990s optical effects technology, which features new lenses and film stock," explains Phillip Feiner, vice president for Pacific Title, the vendor hired to rework the tradition-

"Inside Lucasfilm, the *Spe*

ARE SEEN AS A TUNE-UP FOR THE LONG-A

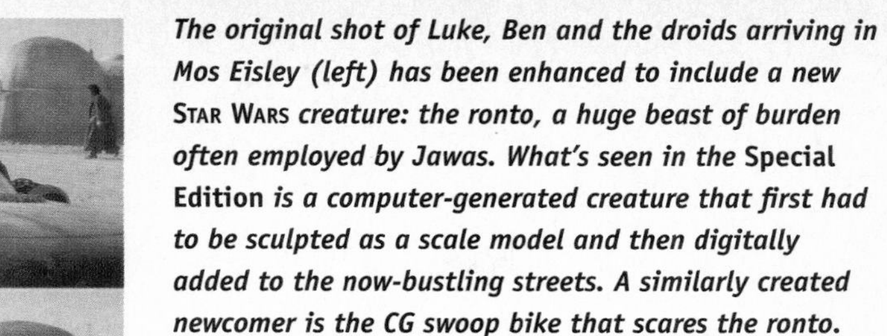

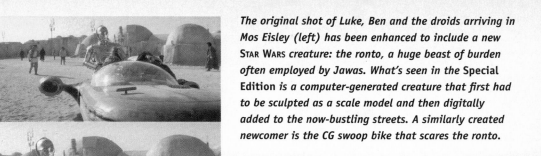

The original shot of Luke, Ben and the droids arriving in Mos Eisley (left) has been enhanced to include a new STAR WARS *creature: the ronto, a huge beast of burden often employed by Jawas. What's seen in the* **Special Edition** *is a computer-generated creature that first had to be sculpted as a scale model and then digitally added to the now-bustling streets. A similarly created newcomer is the CG swoop bike that scares the ronto.*

al Editions

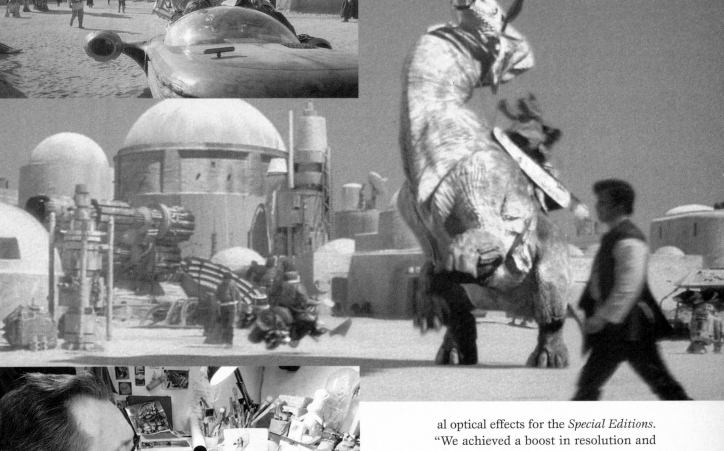

TED PREQUELS."

al optical effects for the *Special Editions.* "We achieved a boost in resolution and color saturation."

Feiner notes that in the years since the *STAR WARS* movies were first filmed, not only has the computer replaced a whole range of traditional techniques, but most of the photochemical houses have gone out of business, including outside vendors that assisted ILM with its original optical compositing. Even ILM's once-vaunted optical department has been replaced by the scanners and workstations of the digital age.

Before Pacific Title did its *Special Edition* chores, the original elements had to be given a chemical bath to literally wash away years of accumulated dirt. "We were able to get rid of a lot of stuff and improve the quality and consistency of each optical," explains Ted Gagliano, 20th Century-Fox's senior vice-president for feature post-production, who

What To WATCH FOR

More than 300 new and enhanced shots are included in the* STAR WARS Trilogy Special Edition, *most of them added to* A New Hope. *Here is a guide to the key changes.

A NEW HOPE

• TATOOINE: Look for new live-action footage of Imperial stormtroopers milling about the desert in front of the half-buried lifepod that brought C-3PO and R2-D2 to the planet. CG stormtroopers ride CG dewbacks *(above)*. An Imperial heavy shuttle transport lifts off in the background, wings unfolding as it flies off.

• TATOOINE: An enhanced scene shows a sandcrawler *(right)*, the monstrous vehicles of the scavenging Jawas, slowly motoring over rocky terrain. The original sandcrawler model was refurbished.

• MOS EISLEY: Luke's landspeeder zooms into the spaceport of Mos Eisley, scattering small "scurriers" that jump to get out of the way. The cityscape is a new digitally created matte painting; the scurriers are CG creatures. As the landspeeder heads for the cantina, it now passes new structures and an Asp droid that argues with a probe droid. Also added to the street scene, via computer graphics, are two Jawas atop a huge, dinosaur-ish "ronto" that rears back and throws its riders when a "swoop bike" veers in front of it. As Luke pilots his vehicle to the center of the spaceport, various CG rontos appear, and a starship, the *Outrider*, takes off overhead. (The *Outrider* is a relatively new addition to the *STAR WARS* armada, flown by one Dash Rendar, a Han Solo-esque character introduced last year in *STAR WARS: Shadows of the Empire*, a multimedia Lucasfilm project including a novel, comic book series, video game, trading cards and other ancillary products.)

• THE CANTINA: To the barroom scene in which Han Solo is confronted by Greedo, the green bounty hunter attempting to deliver Han to Jabba the Hutt, there's an added blast from Greedo's weapon

hitting the wall behind Han before Han fires back and Greedo disappears.

• DOCKING BAY 94: This is the most heralded addition, finally placing a CG Jabba the Hutt *(left)* in front of the *Millennium Falcon* to confront Han about illicit money owed the rotund slug.

• MOS EISLEY: Now when the *Falcon* flies safely away from the docking bay *(below)*, escaping from Imperial troops, it lifts off into the sky, revealing another the matte painting of the cityscape.

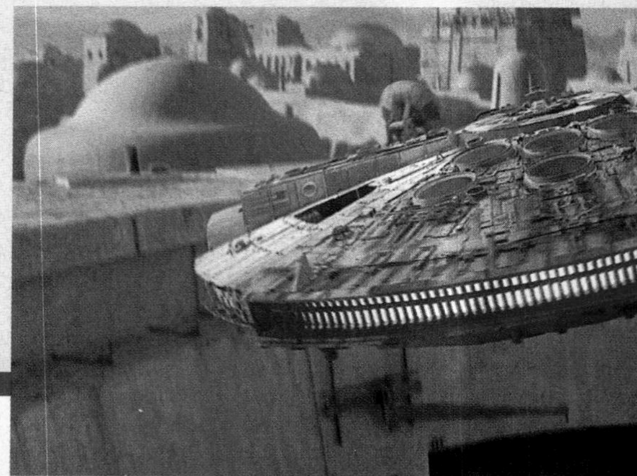

THE EMPIRE STRIKES BACK

• HOTH ICE CAVE: Thanks largely to an actor in a suit *(right)*, new live-action has been added to the scene inside the lair of the wampa, the abominable creature that attacks Luke while he's on patrol aboard a tauntaun. The wampa is now seen eating carrion when Luke, hanging feet-first from the cave ceiling, awakens. New action shows the wampa approaching Luke as he retrieves his lightsaber and attempts to free himself.

• BESPIN/CLOUD CITY: Digitally added to the scene in which the Rebels aboard the *Millennium Falcon* first approach Cloud City are shots of the *Falcon* and intercepting cloud cars banking around a large structure and flying toward a landing platform. Also inserted is originally filmed footage of the *Falcon*'s door dropping down after the ship lands. Additional shots of twin-pod cloud cars flying around Cloud City buildings are now included, as is a crowd shot of Cloud City citizens listening to a public announcement by Lando Calrissian. Following Vader's appearance and confrontation with the Rebels, there's a new live-action scene of the Dark Lord walking to his shuttle. A later CG enhancement shows Vader's shuttle as it approaches his Star Destroyer. Finally, as the *Falcon* escapes from Bespin, a new shot of Vader's shuttle landing in his Star Destroyer's hangar bay has been inserted, with Vader exiting and walking toward stormtroopers.

RETURN OF THE JEDI

• JABBA'S THRONE ROOM: New live-action shots have repopulated Jabba's sanctum with a number of new aliens partaking in the raucous party, culminating in the feeding of the dancer Oola *(above)* to the rancor. There's also new footage of the musicians in Max Rebo's jizz-wailing band.

• The film's final scene, in which the Rebels celebrate their defeat of the Emperor and his evil Empire on Endor, has been digitally expanded to include galas at three new locations, with fireworks exploding over Cloud City as a cloud car zooms by, a skyhopper weaving around buildings as confetti falls over Mos Eisley and a similar scene over Coruscant as citizens revel under full moons.

represented the studio in the *Special Edition* effort.

Many of the problems and challenges faced during the making of the first film were avoided in *Empire* and *Jedi*. The historic success of STAR WARS had not only allowed Lucas the grace of studio cooperation and a bigger budget for the sequels, but all the opticals could be done in-house at ILM. For the *Special Editions*, *Empire* only required CG enhancements to augment the limited palette of 2-D paintings used to create Cloud City and an ambitious slate of image-processing fixes (notably removing the snowspeeder black matte outlines visible against snow backgrounds). For *Jedi*, even less work was needed, most of it involving the CG recreation of the Max Rebo Band.

The extensive *Special Edition* work required for *A New Hope* was exacerbated by a crisis that threatened to derail the rosy prospects of its planned nationwide 20th anniversary rerelease. Both Lucasfilm and Fox discovered early in the process that the original negative, from which pristine new theatrical prints were to be struck, was in disastrous shape. The color values had deteriorated an estimated 10-15% and there was an unusual amount of embedded dirt which had produced pits and scratches that would appear larger than life if projected on today's theater screens. Available prints had their own wear and tear and certainly couldn't be used in screenings befitting a special celebration for a classic film.

STAR WARS video and laser disc releases recently had been produced, in 1994 and 1993, respectively, but those duplications had been taken from a "master interpositive" (or IP, a positive made from the original negative), which had been prepared in 1985. For the high-resolution medium of big-screen projected film, striking prints off an IP wouldn't produce the high-generation prints needed. Fox's Gagliano—who was in high school when he first saw *STAR WARS* and credits the experience with his decision to seek a film career—explains that viewing a print made from the original negative was like seeing an old, damaged

movie. It was all up there on the big screen, but much of the magic had gone out of the experience.

The *Special Edition* effort, undertaken to fix shots that had long vexed Lucas, suddenly had to wage a creative battle on a totally unexpected front: saving the film itself. Eventually, the restoration unit included representatives from Lucasfilm (led by Tom Christopher), Fox, Pacific Title, YCM Labs (to provide color timings) and film restoration consultant Leon Briggs.

It was a shock to discover that *Star Wars* was in need of a life-saving restoration. That fate was supposed to be the domain of badly preserved negatives and nitrate-based silent reeler celluloid, not a 20-year-old film that represented a technological breakthrough in its day.

Ironically, *Star Wars* had been preserved under optimum conditions, stored for years in the subterranean cool of man-made caverns in Kansas. In those underground chambers, wherein salt miners once toiled, the major Hollywood studios stored their film libraries, the constant 50-53 degrees considered ideal for arresting the inevitable fading of color film. But one of the problems with *A New Hope* was that some 62 shots had been made with a Kodak film stock later discovered t be so prone to fading, it was discontir ued in the early 1980s. In addition, was determined that the dirt on the ne ative had probably come from backin that had never been properly washed o in the developing process. Fortunatel the original negatives of *Empire* and *Je* did not suffer the same fate.

The goal of the *Special Edition Tri ogy* team was, of course, to provide theatrical experience true to the aud ence's memories of the originals, not t mention enthrall a new generation c fans accustomed to effects-laden specta cles. To do so meant restoring the *Sta Wars* negative to its original luster. A

ne of the most significant enhance-
ents in the *Special Edition* of *Return
f the Jedi* is to the scene inside Jabba
he Hutt's throne room. A bevy of exotic
ancers—one that caught the eye of
oba Fett (right)—were filmed enjoying
he music of the Max Rebo Band, which
ow includes some new musicians. While
omputers aided much of the *Special
dition* work, traditional model makers
ade valuable contributions, too.

"Many of the PROBLEMS AND CHALLENGES faced during the making of the first film were avoided in *Empire* and *Jedi*."

ucasfilm's Rick McCallum puts it, "The original egative is the only life-force we have."

The success of the *STAR WARS* restoration can e ultimately credited to Lucas' amazing prescience 1 saving everything connected with the making f his films. The old opticals could be recomposed because all the elements have been safely tored in the Lucasfilm Archives. Even though the olor has faded, the *Special Editions* have been colr timed to match the originals because Lucas had e foresight to keep unique Technicolor process rints (basically a non-photochemical color record ot prone to fade-outs) stored in the basement of is home. The sound for the entire *Special Edition Trilogy*—dialogue, John Williams' music, sound ffects—could be remastered because every piece nd layer were recorded on hundreds of reels of faithfully preserved magnetic tape.

Lucas had even saved the films' production art, storyboards and model and creature mock-ups that went into dreaming up the *STAR WARS* universe. Most importantly, Lucas had held onto the actual production artifacts themselves—matte paintings, model ships, creature suits and puppets, costumes, full-scale props. Those items from the Lucasfilm Archives represent not only the talismanic icons from a celebrated movie series, but the historic remains of a vanished moviemaking era. (A portion of the archives were honored for their historical and artistic values in a rare series of public displays that began with a 1993 tour of Japan, a 1994 show at San Francisco's Center for the Arts and an exhibit at Washington's Smithsonian Institution that will open later this year.)

But those *STAR WARS* props are more than museum pieces. Some were actually reused in the *Special Editions*. The enhanced recreation of Rebel X-wings descending upon the Death Star in *A New Hope* features CG starfighters produced with data directly taken from 20-year-old X-wing models. While the physical reference allowed ILM computer graphics artists to faithfully replicate the Rebel ships, the digital medium allowed the CG X-wings to be animated with subtle movements impossible two decades ago, when models were mounted against blue screen backing and shot on sound stages with track cameras.

It may indeed be a fortuitous turn that Lucas had a sense of history and an urge to preserve. The restoration side of the production should serve as a wake-up call to Hollywood studios and filmmakers to check their own libraries and consider methods of preserving their film heritage. The *Special Editions* also brought back into play traditional photochemical techniques and technology, at least for one more shining moment. And in reworking the classic *STAR WARS* films—an enterprise in which wholesale changes could easily have been made—the *Special Edition* team used their new digital capabilities with laser-like precision to subtly enhance the original, producing the trilogy as Lucas had always intended.

The discoveries being pioneered in the digital realm not only allowed for seamless *Special Edition* enhancements of the *STAR WARS* trilogy, but for the continued unfolding of Lucas' inimitable universe. Practically from the moment the initial trilogy was sealed with the 1983 release of *Jedi*, fans have clamored for a return to that galaxy far, far away. Since then, many have also asked why Lucas had seemingly abandoned that fantastic world. The fact is, Lucas had maxed out on traditional effects technologies, the limits of the photochemical medium and physical materials. Thus one of the main objectives of the *Special Editions* is to improve on those specific instances where the limited technology had affected the final visuals and the story.

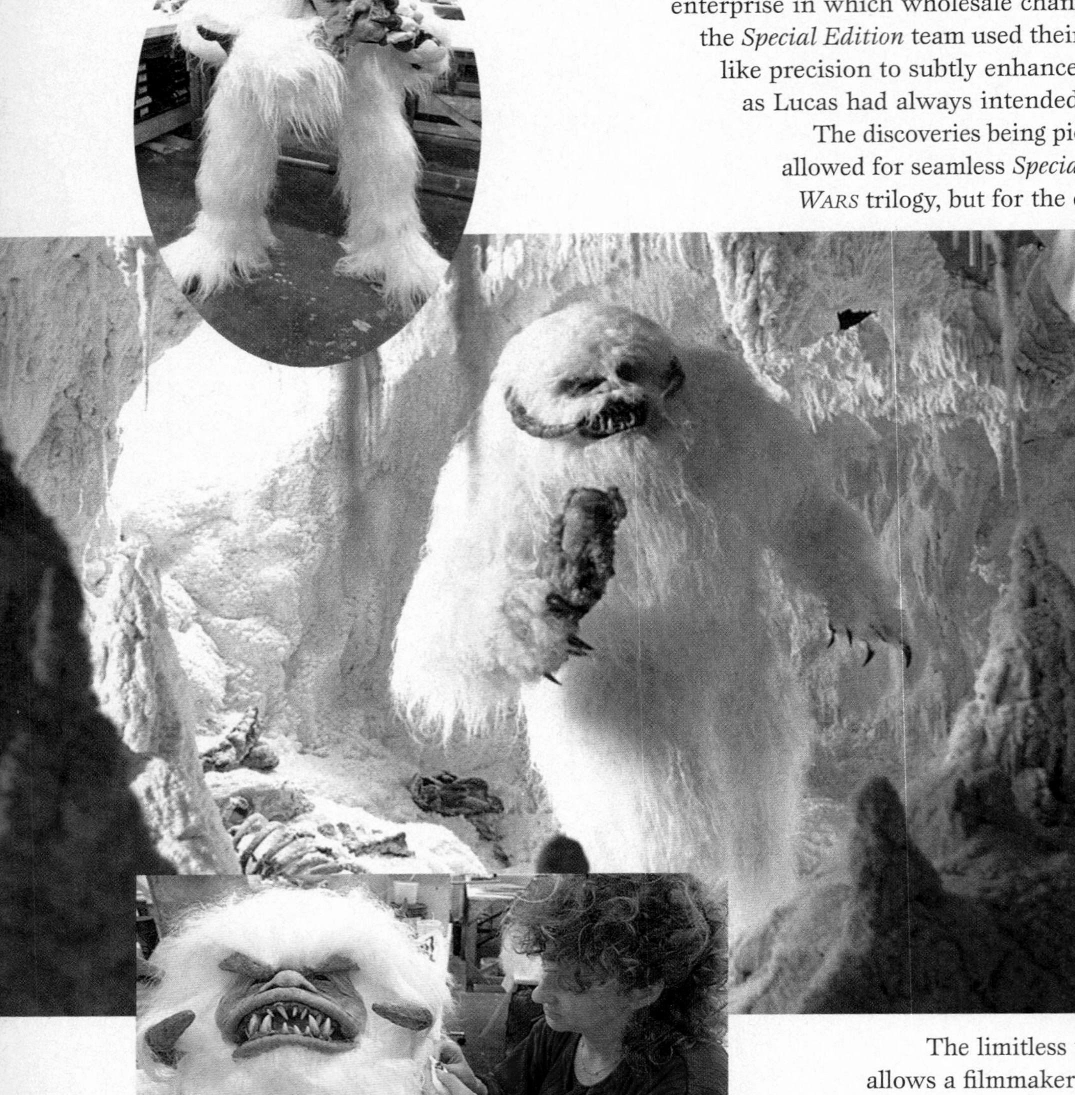

A hair-raising addition to* The Empire Strikes Back *was the live-action filming of new scenes featuring the wampa ice creature. Eschewing digital tools, Lucas deemed the old man-in-a-suit route best to portray the carnivorous behavior of Luke's furry attacker.

The limitless virtual space of the computer finally allows a filmmaker's imagination to fly free, unencumbered by physical limits. Even as the finishing touches were being put on the *Special Editions*, Lucasfilm was deep into the preproduction of the "prequels," an all-new *STAR WARS* trilogy set 40 years before the original, during the glory days of the Jedi Knights and featuring a young Obi-Wan Kenobi and his disciple Anakin Skywalker, before his turn to the dark side and the persona of Darth Vader.

Inside Lucasfilm, the *Special Editions* are seen as a tune-up for the long-awaited prequels. Assembling them was a blast to the past, immersing the team in the alchemy of the film process, the very textures of the *STAR WARS* universe. So fortified, with sophisticated digital magic at their command, Lucas and company now look to the future and make ready for their triumphant return to the universe.

THE FORCE IS STRONG WITH THESE...

STAR WARS®

THE OFFICIAL 20TH ANNIVERSARY POSTER MAGAZINES FROM TITAN

TITAN

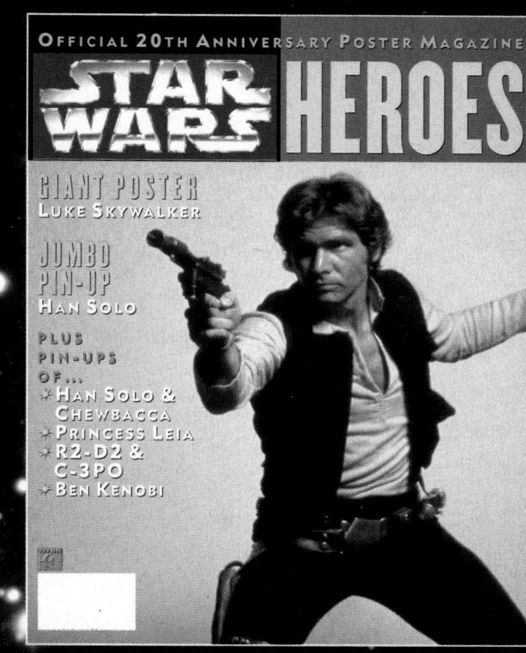

OFFICIAL 20TH ANNIVERSARY POSTER MAGAZINE
STAR WARS HEROES
GIANT POSTER
LUKE SKYWALKER
JUMBO PIN-UP
HAN SOLO
PLUS PIN-UPS OF...
HAN SOLO & CHEWBACCA
PRINCESS LEIA
R2-D2 & C-3PO
BEN KENOBI

ON SALE NOW!

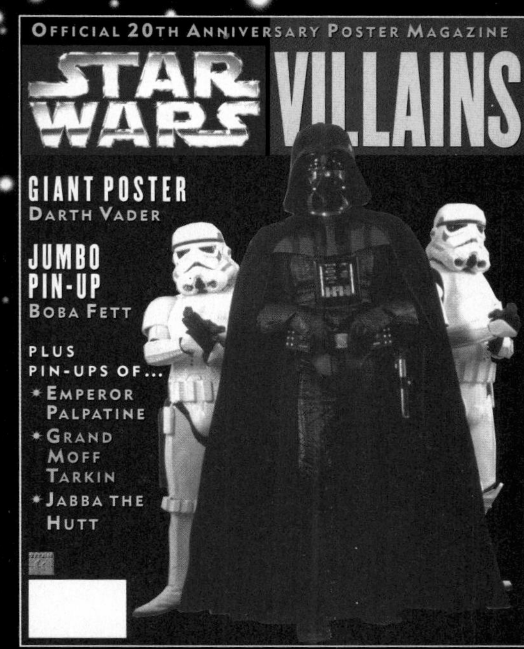

OFFICIAL 20TH ANNIVERSARY POSTER MAGAZINE
STAR WARS VILLAINS
GIANT POSTER
DARTH VADER
JUMBO PIN-UP
BOBA FETT
PLUS PIN-UPS OF...
EMPEROR PALPATINE
GRAND MOFF TARKIN
JABBA THE HUTT

ON SALE 3 APRIL

EACH PRICED £2.50

FROM ALL GOOD NEWSAGENTS AND SPECIALIST STORES

It Took The

More than forever changing moviemaking and marketing,* STAR WARS *remains a phenomenal part of our culture

BY BOB WOODS

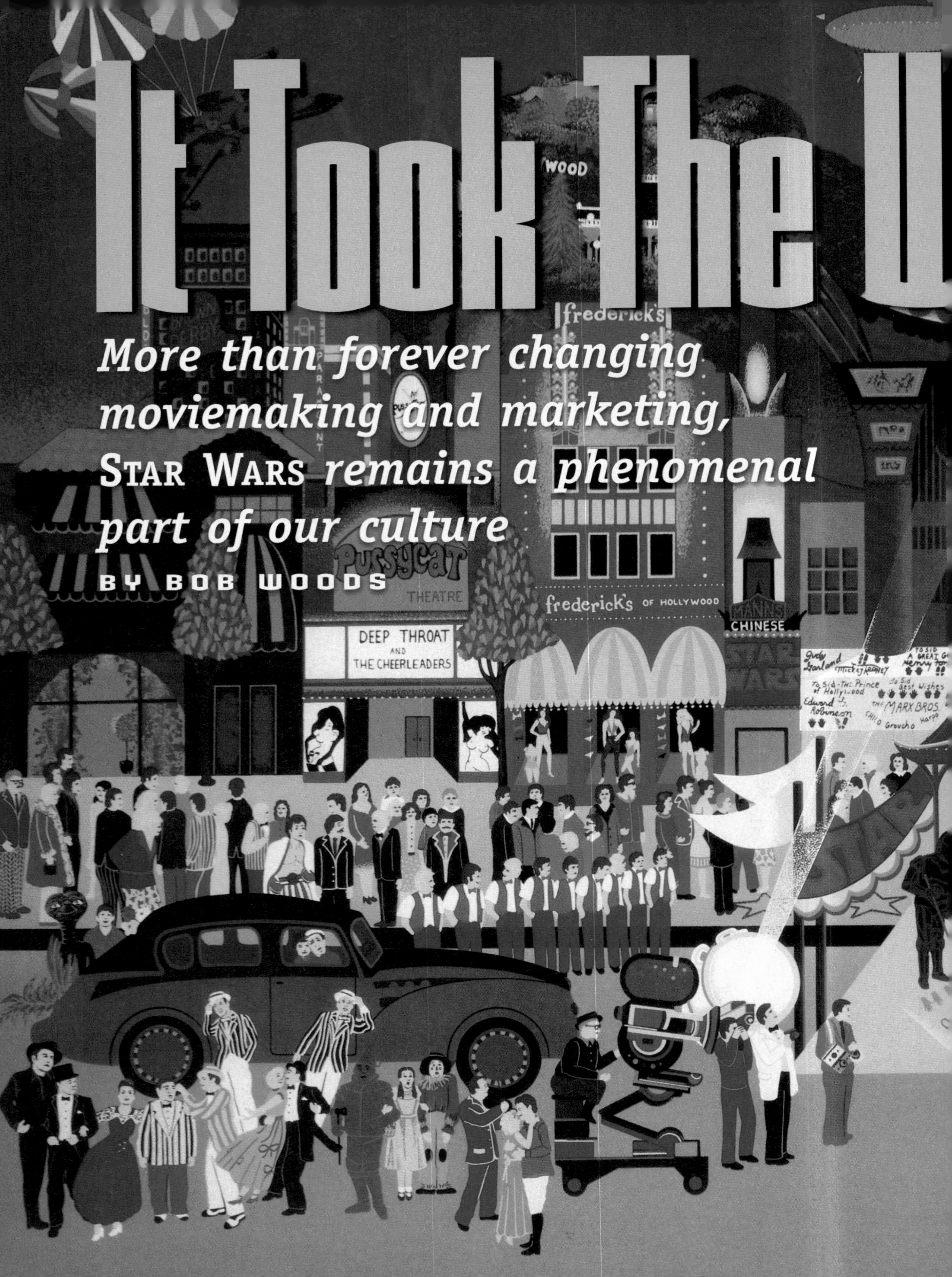

rld By Force

This L.A. street scene by Melanie Taylor Kent, entitled "Hollywood Boulevard," is a folksy homage to the celebrity status that Star Wars has long enjoyed.

"The first time I saw *Star Wars*..."

It's safe to assume that millions of people are completing that sentence these days as George Lucas' landmark 1977 movie storms back into theaters in celebration of its 20th anniversary. They're recalling how old they were, where they saw it, who they went with and their favorite scenes and characters. While *Star Wars* may not rank among the most Earth-shattering events of the 20th century—up there with world wars, political assassinations or lunar landings—it undoubtedly is among its top cultural movers and shakers.

"There was only one topic of conversation in the film industry yesterday—the smash openings of *Star Wars*." That's how *Daily Variety* described the film's debut, on Wednesday, May 25, 1977, at 32 theaters across the nation. The space fantasy that almost never got made went on to blow away every previous box-office record and foster an unprecedented merchandising program that is still paying dividends on the relatively paltry $10 million invested to create *Star Wars*. To date, the movie, along with the galaxy of ancillary products based on *Star Wars* and its sequels, *The Empire Strikes Back* and *Return of the Jedi*, have garnered more than $4 billion.

COMING TO YOUR GALAXY THIS SUMMER.
STAR WARS
GEORGE LUCAS, THE MAN WHO BROUGHT YOU AMERICAN GRAFFITI, NOW BRINGS YOU AN ADVENTURE AS BIG AS THE COSMOS ITSELF: STAR WARS, THE STORY OF A BOY, A GIRL, AND A UNIVERSE. IT'S A SPECTACLE LIGHT YEARS AHEAD OF ITS TIME. FROM 20TH CENTURY-FOX.

Who knew, back in the spring of 1977, that "the story of a boy, a girl, and a universe" was about to become a cultural phenomenon

As that summer of '77 unfolded, *Star Wars* gave a whole new meaning to the term "blockbuster." Endless lines of moviegoers clogged the sidewalks and streets outside theaters everywhere. Inside, "oohs" and "aahs" reverberated every time John Williams' opening music blared and that gigantic Star Destroyer rumbled across the screen. The entire nation—kids and adults, males and females, sci-fi lovers and haters—were swept up in *Star Wars* fever overnight.

In its first week of limited release (it didn't go wide until July), the box-office gross was an unheard-of $2.8 million; by summer's end it had out-earned the summer's number-two movie, *Smokey and the Bandit*, fourfold. Stock in 20th Century-Fox, the studio that bankrolled and released *Star Wars*, more than doubled. By mid-summer there were stories of other studios clamoring to ride the science-fiction coattails of *Star Wars*. "Having crunched its way through disaster movies, animal terror movies and Satan movies, Hollywood now is putting its chips on sci-fi and space epics," reported the *Washington Star*. "The star-struck studios are feverishly developing feature films, TV programs and remakes of previous movies in the genre."

Headlines heralded "The *Star Wars* Craze" and "*Star Wars* Mania—New Cult!" One local paper after another marveled at the steady flood of wide-eyed fans, especially those who came back time after time, such as the

INSPIRED BY *STAR WARS*

Rather than finding interest in film-making, sound scoring, art, writing or special effects, I found my keenness in geology—seeing Luke, Ben, the Jawas and Artoo and Threepio in the sandstone of the Tunisian desert. In the many years since seeing *A New Hope* I have gone through school, got my degree and launched into a professional career, not once leaving geology behind or forgetting *Star Wars*.

JEREMY BECKETT, arw93el@soton.ac.uk

paperboy who saw it 40 times, and the bleary-eyed theater projectionist who sat through 600 showings. Plenty of theaters—welcoming not just historic ticket sales, but record popcorn, candy and soda business, too—were still screening the movie a year later.

The previously unknown Mark Hamill (Luke Skywalker), Harrison Ford (Han Solo) and Carrie Fisher (Princess Leia) were catapulted into superstardom, their faces and interviews popping up all over the place. George Lucas, already lauded for his two earlier features, *THX 1138* and *American Graffiti*, was now elevated to genius status in cinematic circles. Secrets surrounding STAR WARS were revealed (Lucas' first script was based solely on the droids' adventures), and trivia quizzes abounded (Q: In how many parsecs did Han Solo make the Kessel Run in his starship, the *Millennium Falcon*? A: 12). Special effects artists were finally recognized for their magical contributions to moviemaking.

INSPIRED BY *STAR WARS*

I was seven when the movie came out, and became so intrigued by X-wings that I began a nearly 20-year quest to get my hands on the Earth equivalent. Last May I finished initial training in the F/A-18 Hornet and am now based in Lemoore, CA, and fly with the Blue Diamonds of Strike Fighter Squadron 146. LT. TODD NELSON, TNELSO@aol.com

In August of '77, the droids C-3PO and R2-D2—roundly hailed as the hottest comedy duo since Laurel and Hardy—had their footprints immortalized in the sidewalk outside Los Angeles' famed Manns Chinese Theater. In September, a "Making of STAR WARS" special aired on national television. The following April, the movie garnered seven of the 10 Academy Awards for which it was nominated.

Reasons for the mania were debated in TV news reports, newspaper and magazine articles, and at office water coolers, on street corners and in living rooms everywhere for months. Was it the special effects, or the timeless story of good triumphing over evil, or the escapist fantasy pulling the populace out of its post-Watergate/Vietnam War doldrums? Indeed, stalwart fans are still arguing, two

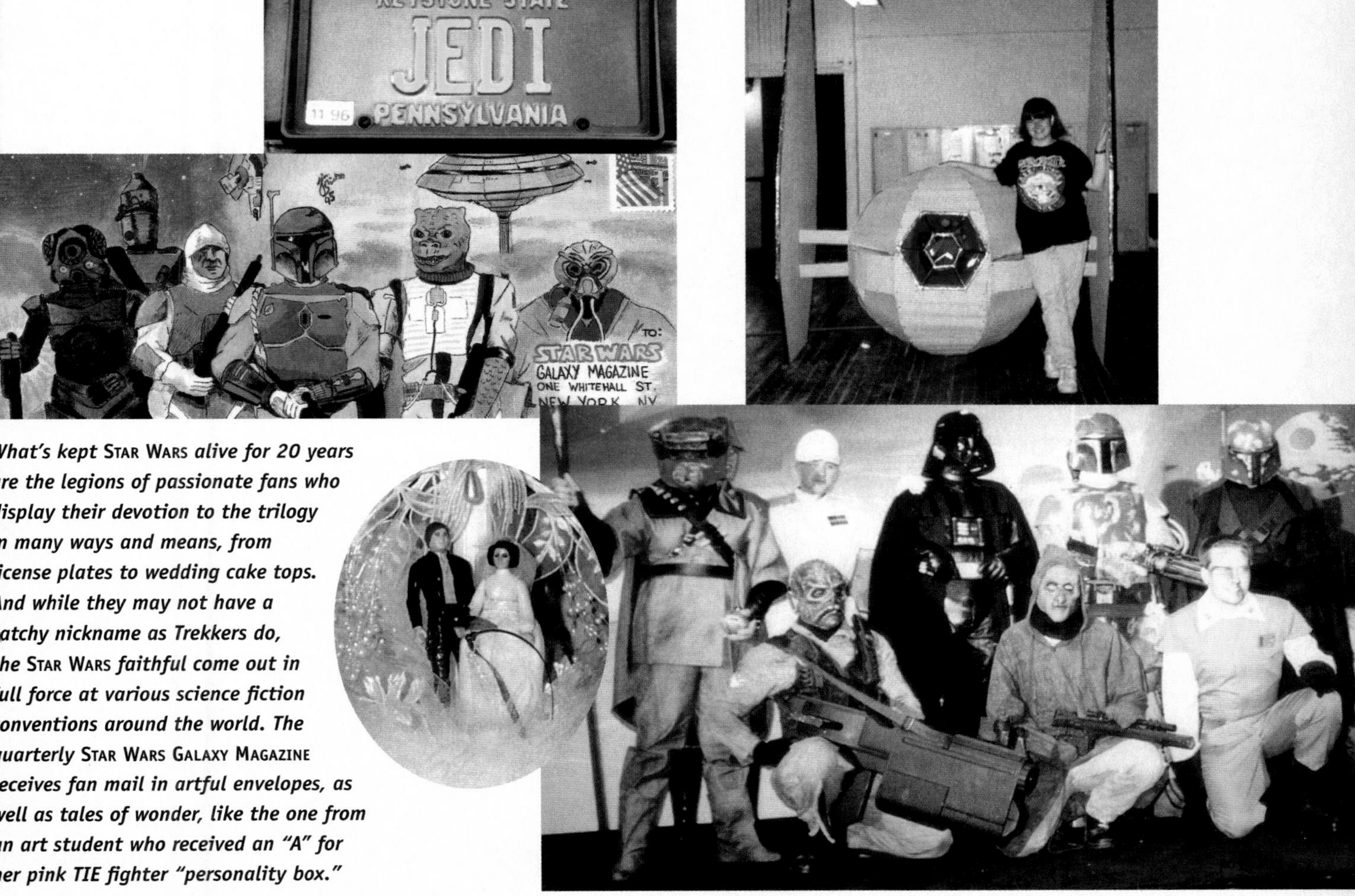

What's kept STAR WARS *alive for 20 years are the legions of passionate fans who display their devotion to the trilogy in many ways and means, from license plates to wedding cake tops. And while they may not have a catchy nickname as Trekkers do, the* STAR WARS *faithful come out in full force at various science fiction conventions around the world. The quarterly* STAR WARS GALAXY MAGAZINE *receives fan mail in artful envelopes, as well as tales of wonder, like the one from an art student who received an "A" for her pink TIE fighter "personality box."*

INSPIRED BY *STAR WARS*

The cantina bar inspired me to become a cocktail slinger in a town that would clone the fictional interstellar bar, Las Vegas, where every life form on this planet eventually visits. TONY THOMAS, LAS VEGAS, NV

decades later, and micro-analyzing each and every facet of the movie.

Looking back at the initial reactions, one fact is undeniable when assessing its universal popularity: There had never been a movie like *STAR WARS*.

Any good movie will find its audience, but *STAR WARS* was generally met with unbridled praise from the critics. Revisiting the reviews is an insightful, sometimes prescient, even ironic time trip.

"The Year's Best Movie," blared *Time* in its May 30, 1977 story. "A grand and glorious film that may well be the smash hit of 1977," the article declared, citing in particular "the two manned robots, the Laurel and Hardy of the cybernetic world... a menagerie of monsters and grotesques... and

DREAM TEAM

Before the Kenner account came along, they were just three ordinary guys working for Grey Advertising in New York City. Now they're the *STAR WARS* team.

Adam Seely, Rob Travalino and Doug Fallon were happy enough creating TV ads for Batman, Nerf and other properties. Little did each of them know, however, that all three harbored one very common passion—*STAR WARS*. Now in their mid 20s, they'd been ardent fans since childhood, into their teen years and right through college. None of them dreamed that *STAR WARS* would someday become a major part of their careers.

Assisting Grey's STAR WARS *trio of Travalino (center), Seely (2nd from right) and Fallon (right) are copywriter Ben Lippel (left) and art director Greg Daly.*

Then about two years ago Travalino, a creative director whose nickname in high school had been Han Solo, had a brainstorm. Let's make a pitch for the *STAR WARS* account with Kenner, he thought. His idea was to produce what in the trade is called a "sizzle film," which would include not just Grey's attributes, but also clips, sound effects and music from the trilogy to demonstrate an intimate knowledge and devotion to *STAR WARS*.

It was after he proposed the notion to Seely, a producer, and Fallon, an art director, that Travalino discovered their shared bond. "I had to 'twist' Adam's arm to go along with it," Travalino recalls.

They ended up making their presentation to Kenner twice, wowing the toy maker both times and ultimately winning the account. And to date, the trio has produced eight different *STAR WARS* TV spots for a variety of Kenner action figures, vehicles and playsets, as well as a stunning *Shadows of the Empire* ad that brings Luke, Xizor and Dash Rendar to life through 3-D computer animation.

Beyond their creative duties, these guys remain unabashed *STAR WARS* fanatics. "I've never stopped watching the movies," says Seely, who also still has his original *STAR WARS* toys. Fallon's weakness are the many *STAR WARS* video games. "My wife is a game widow," he confesses. Travalino admits that *STAR WARS* directly influenced his decision to study broadcasting. "It taught me to believe in myself."

So even as they toil away on upcoming Kenner *STAR WARS* ads, anticipation of seeing the trilogy on the big screen for the first time has them on the edge of their seats. "I'll be camped outside the theater in my C-3PO sleeping bag," says Fallon.

he wizardly special effects." Even compared to Stanley <ubrick's *2001: A Space Odyssey*, the benchmark in science fiction films at the time, *Time* opined, "*STAR WARS* is tops."

"The year's most razzle-dazzling family novie," wrote Charles Champlin in the *Los Angeles Times*. His upstate counterpart, John Wasserman of the *San Francisco Examiner*, called *STAR WARS* "the most exciting picture o be released this year—exciting as theater and exciting as cinema." The *Boston Herald*'s David Rosenbaum called it "one of the greatest adventure stories ever told," while *Newsweek*'s Jack Kroll dubbed it "pure sweet fun all the way."

Many seasoned pundits, especially those who grew up—as did George Lucas—with movie serials, radio dramas and comic books, enthusiastically compared *STAR WARS* o the futuristic tales of Buck Rogers and Flash Gordon. Vincent Canby, in *The New York Times*, defined *STAR WARS* as "the movie that's going to entertain a lot of contemporary folk who have a soft spot for the virtually ritualized manners of comic-book adventure." Champlin declared it "Buck Rogers with a doctoral degree." In *The Boston Phoenix*, David Denby wrote that "*STAR WARS* is undoubtedly something new n the history of popular culture: an homage o the cheesy space-ship-and-ray-gun serials of the '30s, it's both a loving parody and an awesomely beautiful work of imagination."

The more erudite of critics, whether they liked the film or not, couldn't resist attaching deeper sociological, philosophical or theological meanings to Lucas' intent. "It is soothing to find a funny film imagining something a great deal worse than South Africa's possessing nuclear weapons," wrote Penelope Gilliatt in *The New Yorker*, later concluding, "There is something dazzling about a sci-fi film that manages to call upon the energies of both futurism and long-held faith." Pete Hamill,

BROOKSFILMS/MGM-UA

NBC

THE MUPPET SHOW

The characters in STAR WARS *are among the most memorable in movie history. So of course they've been parodied. Mel Brooks, the sultan of send-ups, gave us* Spaceballs *(top), complete with Ham Salad and Barf, Lord Helmet and a power called the Schwartz, presided over by just plain Yogurt. Carrie Fisher appeared on* Saturday Night Live *as a teen alien in a skit that also poked fun at Frankie and Annette beach movies. And even Miss Piggy got to ham it up with Mark Hamill on* The Muppet Show.

INSPIRED BY *STAR WARS*

It was a scorching hot day in Oklahoma when my parents took us to see the premiere of *STAR WARS*. I left that theater forever changed. I knew that I had to be part of that high-tech future, and today I am. I spent the remainder of my teenage years constantly tinkering with computers and moving on to my engineering degree before joining Intel, where I now manage part of a design team developing the next generation of Intel microprocessors. Who knows? The latest product we just finished might even be used at some point in the computer-generated portion of the upcoming prequels! **ROBERT STEAR, rstear@mipos2.intel.com**

INSPIRED BY *STAR WARS*

In 1977, I became friends with Chris and Oliver. The night *STAR WARS* came out, my mother went to the 7 o'clock showing. She was so impressed, she brought us back for the later show. We were instant converts. Chris' folks were artists, and we took advantage of their facilities. Days were spent hunched over drawings. Often they were *STAR WARS*-related. Our friendship endures to this day. Oliver became a painter. Chris moved to L.A. and found work building models for Hollywood. I kept illustrating into college, and picked up editing skills. Eventually, I wound up in Oregon, at Dark Horse Comics. My aptitude for *STAR WARS* made me a natural for editing Dark Horse Comics' line of *STAR WARS* titles, and here I am. I love my job. PEET JANES, PORTLAND, OR

writing in the *Chicago Tribune*, after assuring readers he wasn't related to Luke's portrayer, termed *STAR WARS* a Big Dumb Flick ("it's just entertainment") before declaring, "It is a perfect film for a time when no Americans are dying anywhere in a war, when no American bombs are landing on anyone, when no President is facing indictment or impeachment." In *The Village Voice*, reviewer Molly Haskell, referring to the war between the Rebels and "Imperialists," wrote: "Between these two factions, the ideological differences are hardly more striking than those that separate the Greens and Golds in prep-school athletics."

And then there were those who simply didn't get it. With a flip-flopping thumb, Gene Siskel, in the *Chicago Tribune*, follows up praise for "striking visual trick[s]... Lucas' scriptwriting... [and] weird-looking creatures" with this: "On the debit side are the film's human performances. Save for Alec Guiness [sic], the cast is unmemorable." In *New York*, John Simon exclaimed, "O dull new world! ... It is all as exciting as last year's weather reports. ... What you ultimately have is a set of giant baubles manipulated by an infant mind." Cross-country, in sister publication *New West*, Stephen Farber offered: "*STAR WARS* is an entertaining crowd-pleaser and a monumental technical achievement, but it's a long way from being a classic."

"Who knew?" Farber might say today. The fact is, though, that even as those first reviews were being written, *STAR WARS* was penetrating our culture. Sure, there was the extraordinary merchandising and licensing program, bombarding our senses and kids with *STAR WARS* T-shirts, posters, lunchboxes, games, action figures,

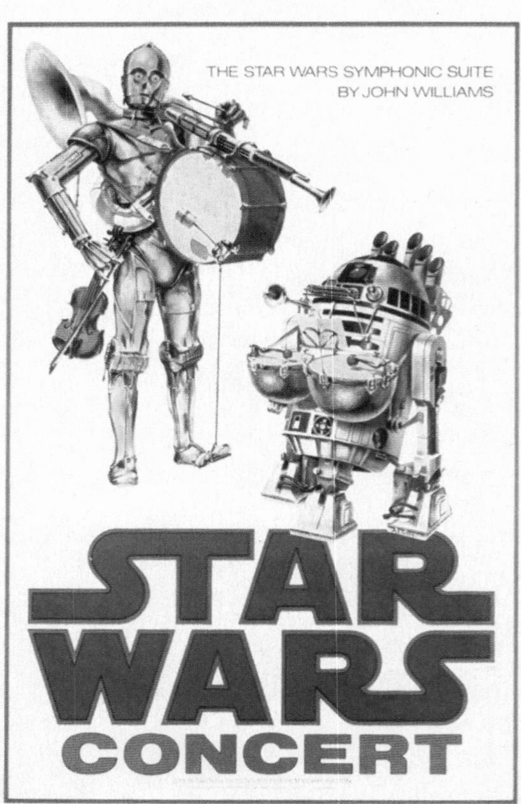

From the beginning, the droids C-3PO and R2-D2 were a large part of what made STAR WARS *work. They were instantly compared to such revered comic twosomes as Abbott and Costello and Laurel and Hardy. They played well away from* STAR WARS, *too, making guest appearances in all sorts of places, whether promoting a one-night John Williams concert or as a cartoon punch line by Bill Plympton in the* Soho Weekly News.

DER SPIEGEL
C 7007 C
Nr. 46
38. Jahrgang · DM 4,–
12. November 1984
REAGAN
NACH DER WAHL
Waffen für den
Krieg der Sterne?

When former President Ronald Reagan proposed a space-based missile defense system for the U.S., his political opponents dubbed the program "Star Wars," and the name immediately stuck. It went so far as the November 12, 1984 cover of the German newsmagazine Der Spiegel. *In picturing Reagan as Darth Vader and borrowing spaceships directly from the movie, the cover wondered, "Reagan After the Election. Weapons for Star Wars?"*

masks, costumes, soundtrack albums (the single, "*STAR WARS*: Cantina Band," by Meco, rode atop the pop charts all that summer), model kits... and more. A lot more.

Part of that "more" was the language and imagery of *STAR WARS*. "May the Force be with you" became a buzz-phrase, uttered in place of "good luck" or "Godspeed." Cartoons and parodies were ubiquitous. Darth Vader was installed as the new poster boy for "the bad guy." The robots—though in Lucas-ese they are always referred to as droids—became not only matinee idols but also symbolic of our society's turning the corner in finally accepting anthropomorphic technology. (Also, the personal computer revolution, marked by the founding of Apple Computer in 1976, was just underway.)

Observers liked to call it a cult, though that sometimes sinister connotation was lost on the millions of grade schoolers who gleefully idled away hours with Luke and Leia action figures, or innocently carried a *STAR WARS* lunchbox to school. Or the members of the hundreds of unofficial fan clubs that sprang up around the country. It wasn't uncommon to hear of grooms and brides dressed as Han Solo and Princess Leia for their wedding ceremonies.

And, of course, the boffo sequels, *Empire* in 1981 and *Jedi* in 1983, kept *STAR WARS* fever high well into the mid 1980s. Yoda became a sort of celluloid Confucius, espousing philosophical soundbites ("You must unlearn what you have learned." "Try not. Do. Or do not. There is no try.") that became inspirations for the Pepsi Generation. On the more practical side, careers in filmmaking, special effects, computer technology, art and other creative and technological arenas were launched as a result of *STAR WARS* "mania."

INSPIRED BY *STAR WARS*

I first saw *STAR WARS* at the age of five. It tempted me to pick up a pencil and draw, and I drew it all. I decided to attend art school. After graduation I was given a chance to work at LucasArts Entertainment Co. I've been with the company two years and recently worked on Jedi Knight, the sequel to Dark Forces. It has been the chance of a lifetime, and I owe it all to a little movie called *STAR WARS*. CLINT YOUNG, Cyoung@LucasArts.com

The news media paid a sort of homage to the films in the early '80s when it referred to former U.S. President Ronald Reagan's controversial space-based missile defense system as "*STAR WARS*." The term had first been used by Reagan's opponents to the plan. Lucas wasn't particularly thrilled with the infringement, yet it proved, however perversely, just how much the movie had become an icon.

Americans weren't the only ones caught up, either. As *STAR WARS* was released around the world, foreign audiences were similarly captivated.

"May the Force be with you" became a colloquialism in France (Que la Force sout avec toi), Italy (Che la Forza sia con te), Spain (Que la Fuerza te acompane), Germany (Die Macht sei mit dir) and Holland (Moge de Kracht met u zijn).

While much of the incredible effect that *STAR WARS* had on so many individuals was hardly by design, it didn't happen by accident, either. Lucas was, and is, an astute filmmaker and student of pop culture. But he also had a genuine creative intent when he concocted his *STAR WARS* universe. He wanted more than simply to evoke bygone comic books and serials. He studied mythology and classic storytelling, especially that aimed at children, from Ulysses' *Odyssey* to Robert Louis Stevenson's *Treasure Island*.

STAR WARS was immediately branded "science fiction," yet Lucas preferred a less rigid definition. "I just wanted to forget science," he said soon after the film's release. "I wanted to make a space fantasy, more in the genre of Edgar Rice Burroughs," the creator of Tarzan.

"Most civilizations, whole cultures and religions were built on the 'science fiction' of their day," Lucas said. "It is just that. Now we call it science fiction. Before, they called it religion or myths or whatever they wanted to call it."

Also a proponent then of space exploration, Lucas espoused a hope that *STAR WARS* would infect the younger generation with a combination of romanticism and thirst for knowledge. "I'm hoping if the film accomplishes anything, it takes some 10-year-old kid and turns him on so much to outer space and the possibilities of romance and adventure... I would feel very good if someday they colonize Mars, when I am 93, and the leader of the first colony says: 'I did it because I was hoping there would be a Wookiee up there.'"

Those 10 year olds have grown up and are now 30, though none has gone to Mars. Still, many of the kids who were turned on to *STAR WARS* 20 years ago have remained faithful to Wookiees and the rest of the movie's fantastic characters and environments over the years. At first, holding their interest was easy; the production and release of the sequels, exhaustively followed by a slew of science fiction "fanzines" and other media, kept devotees fervently in the fold until the mid 1980s, when the major merchandising sizzle began to fizzle.

Home video releases and occasional TV airings of the trilogy sated the faithful and brought new fans to the table, mostly kids too young to have caught the initial fever. Then, in 1991, Lucasfilm—which had been flourishing with non-*STAR WARS* films and busi-

INSPIRED BY *STAR WARS*

It is clear that *STAR WARS* affected me on many levels. The idea of heroism was lost on post-Vietnam America. Even so, I began to dream about becoming a Naval officer and experiencing valor first-hand. I also began to build a lifelong love for science. Today I am an ex-Naval officer teaching junior high science. You wouldn't believe how many difficult or listless topics have seemed clearer and easier when prefaced with "Remember that scene in Star Wars when...?" MATT FLEMING, ESCONDIDO, CA, CaberTssr@aol.com

Languages and alphabets may be different in countries around the world, but STAR WARS is spoken everywhere, as graphically displayed on movie posters in (from left) England, Hong Kong, Italy, Israel and France.

nesses, including the Indiana Jones series, Industrial Light & Magic and its sound-technology divisions—launched a new *STAR WARS* licensing program. Primarily fueled by books, comics and trading cards, a *STAR WARS* resurgence again kindled the original fan flames and, more importantly, ignited interest among the members of Generation X. From there, a new generation of toys, action figures, games, collectibles, artwork and other merchandise have brought *STAR WARS* squarely back into the cultural limelight. The theatrical release of the *STAR WARS Trilogy Special Edition*, coupled with news that an all-new *STAR WARS* trio of prequels is in the works, fairly guarantees that George Lucas' space fantasy will remain an icon well into the next millennium.

Given that Lucas will turn 53 this year, and considering that today's 10 year olds will be 50 when he celebrates his 93rd birthday, it's still within the realm of possibility that a *STAR WARS* loyalist will help colonize Mars in 2037. So don't be surprised if he or she invokes the name Chewbacca when the spaceship hatch opens and the first human sets foot on the Red Planet.

"Que la Force sout avec toi"

"Che la Forza sia con te"

"QUE LA FUERZA TE ACOMPANE"

"Die Macht sei mit dir"

"MAY THE FORCE BE WITH YOU"

The Stuff Of Legends

STAR WARS *launched a whole new generation of movie licensing and merchandising*

BY STEVE SANSWEET

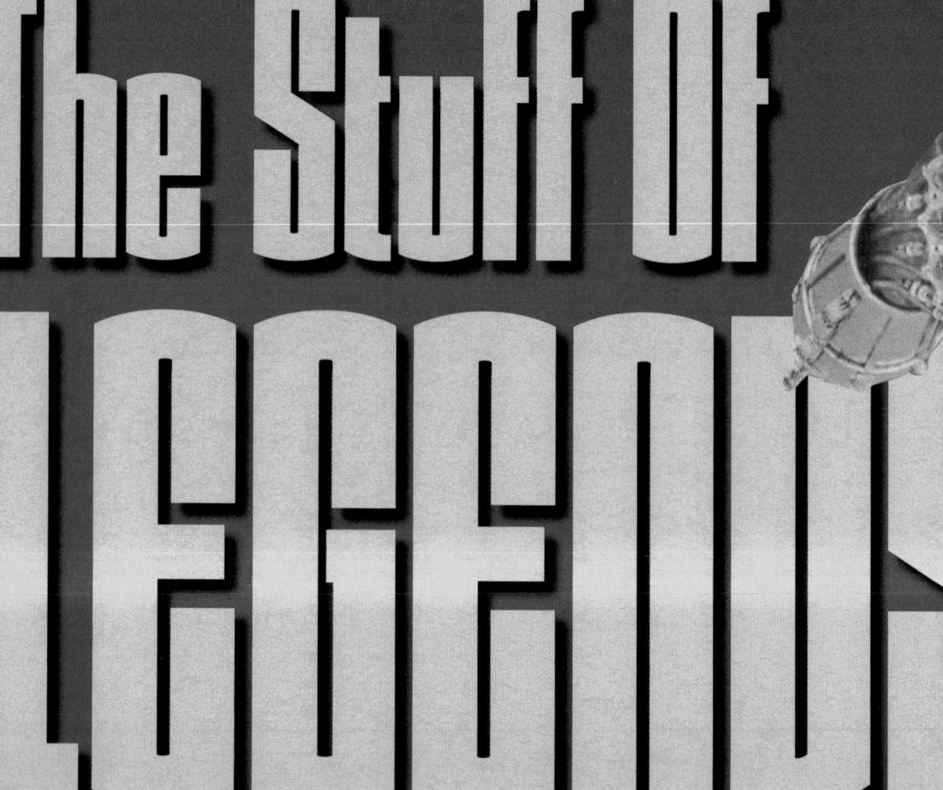

From Fruit Loops to Franken Berry, cereal boxes and premiums helped make STAR WARS a household staple. While C-3PO's didn't blow away taste buds, collectors feast on the packaging and in-store displays like this one.

In the beginning, there was the film.

Well, actually, that's not quite true. For even before the first notes of John Williams' heroic score or the now-familiar opening crawl ("A long time ago..."), there was "the stuff," the merchandise that helped propel the *Star Wars* trilogy from three exciting films into a worldwide pop-culture phenomenon that still resonates 20 years later. There wasn't much of it at first, to be sure. And while George Lucas thought it would be fun to have a sculpted Wookiee coffee mug or to turn the cracker-barrel-shaped R2-D2 into a cookie jar, there had never been a really successful licensed movie property, and no indication that this film would be any different.

Well, actually, that's not quite true either. The way Charles Lippincott tells it, an unhappy incident actually seemed to augur well for the film's future reception. One of the first full-time Lucasfilm Ltd. employees, Lippincott originally was hired to generate publicity for *Star Wars*. He had gone to film school at the University of Southern California with Lucas, had become a film publicist and was approached by producer Gary Kurtz about Lucas' new space fantasy film.

"I'm a science-fiction fan, so I asked to read the script and was fascinated by it," Lippincott recalls. "I told George I really wanted to work on it, and we ended up in the lobby of the office tower at Universal Studios, where he had his office, and we spent three hours just standing there talking about *Star Wars* as people passed by. It was also the first time we talked about merchandising."

Lucas told Lippincott that he wasn't sure there would be many products tied to the film, but what he especially wanted—and what got written into Lucas' contract with 20th Century-Fox—were three *Star Wars* boutiques, of all things. The stores would sell limited-edition merchandise, but neither director nor publicist had much of an idea what kind of products might work, and the idea of boutiques got lost in the overwhelming aftermath of the film's opening.

The impact of *Star Wars* can be measured in many ways. On strictly a bottom-line basis, the three films themselves collected a total of about $1.3 billion worldwide at the box office—before this year's release of the *Star Wars Trilogy Special Edition*—and tens of millions more through video sales and rentals. Mer-

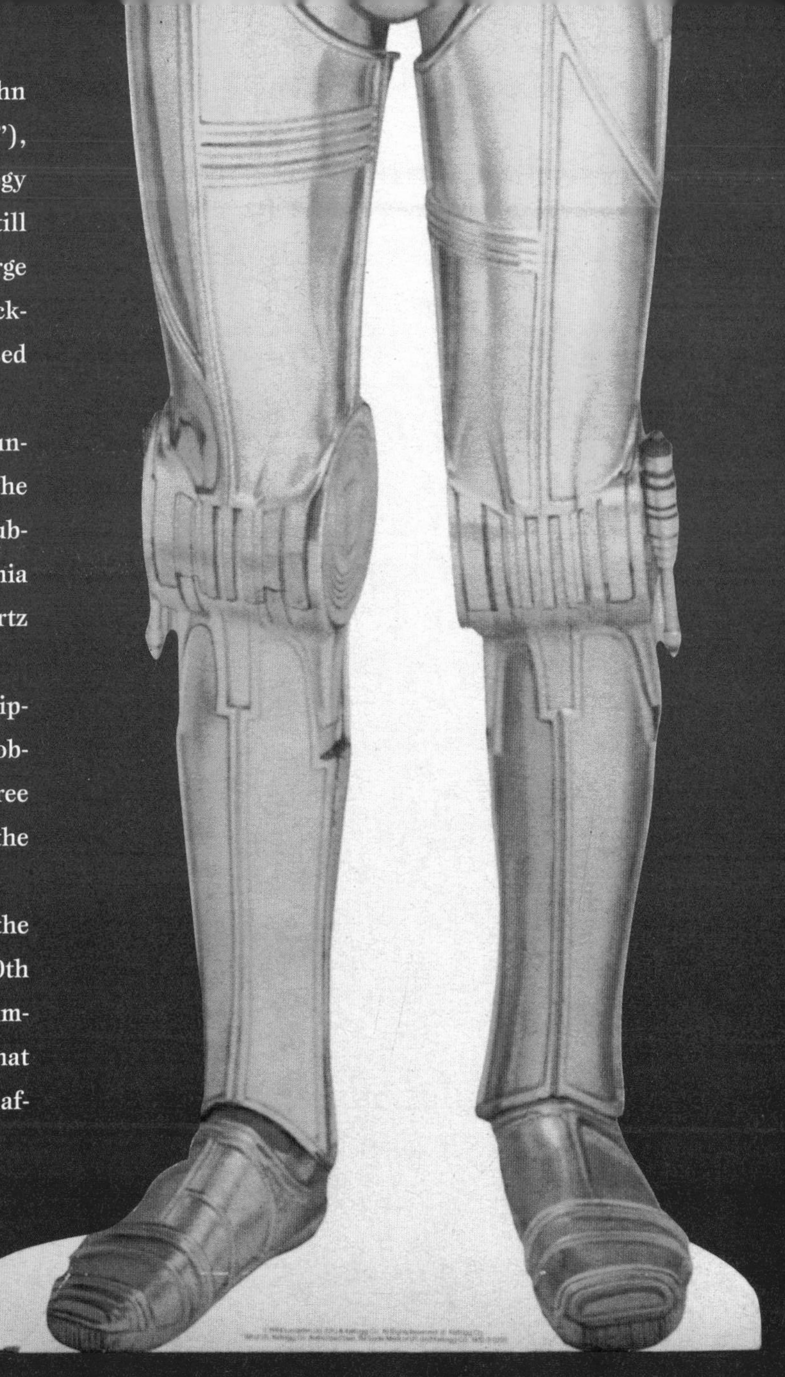

chandise sales, even before the current STAR WARS revival, added up to more than another $2.5 billion. In today's dollars, the films' footprints might translate into as much as $7 billion.

STAR WARS jump-started the slow-growing licensing business in the late 1970s and was responsible for the now taken-for-granted mega-marketing of major movies for products ranging from novels and trading cards to toys and clothing. In fact, according to *The Licensing Letter*, prior to the release of STAR WARS in 1977, globally consumers spent less than $5 billion a year for licensed merchandise. By 1990 that figure had topped $66 billion.

Charlie Lippincott joined Lucasfilm in November 1975 as Vice President for Advertising, Publicity, Promotion and Merchandising. Within a few weeks, the first merchandising deal had been struck. Lucas' lawyer, Tom Pollock, signed an agreement with science fiction publishing guru Judy-Lynn del Rey at Ballantine Books to publish the STAR WARS novelization, Lucas' script and a book about the making of the film. Nothing else came quite so easily. After Lippincott got an initial turndown at Marvel Comics, he used a back-door route to get Marvel contributing editor Roy Thomas excited about writing an adaptation for comic books.

Kenner was the first toy manufacturer to ride STAR WARS' coattails. To take advantage of Christmas '77 (even without a product), it shipped certificate packages with a mail-in coupon for four action figures. Kenner's original vinyl-caped Jawa (below) was replaced with a cloth version, and though the taller of two Snaggletooth aliens (far right) is less accurate, it is valued more by collectors.

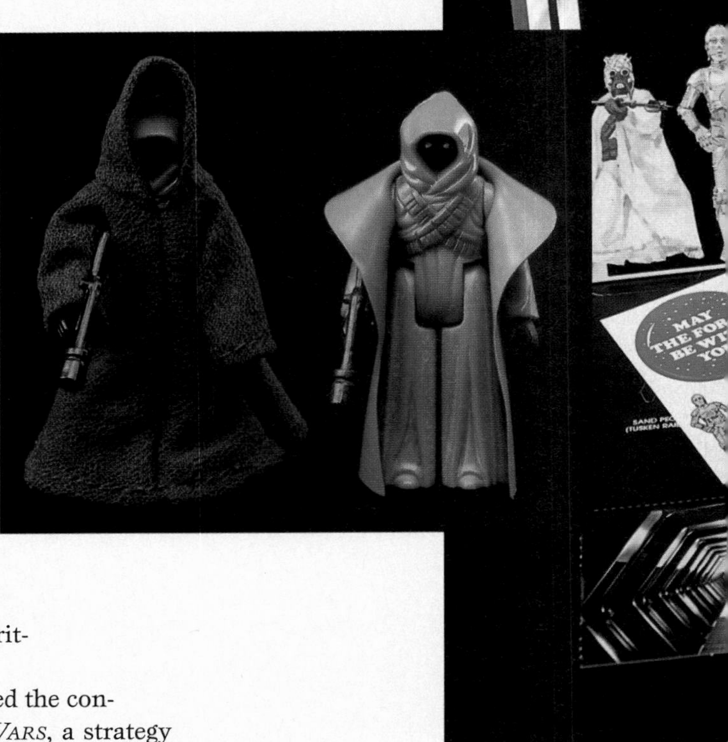

Wearing his promotional hat, Lippincott developed the concept of attending fan conventions to talk up STAR WARS, a strategy that was partly responsible for the huge opening-day crowds. The first and biggest gathering was the San Diego Comic Convention in the summer of 1976, an annual affair that draws fans and comics professionals from all over the world. Artist Howard Chaykin and writer Thomas spoke about the upcoming comic series, and Lippincott asked con-goers what kinds of merchandise they'd like to see.

The first limited STAR WARS collectibles were available in San Diego. There were T-shirts with the movie's initial triangular logo, badges with the film's name and a special poster drawn by Chaykin, marked "STAR WARS Corporation Poster #1." Only 1,000 were printed and offered at $1 each. Today, this early STAR WARS collectible brings $400 or more.

Lippincott also attended that year's World Science Fiction Convention in Kansas City. This time he brought along art, costumes and props. Meanwhile, he was providing a new science fiction magazine, *Starlog*, with tantalizing tidbits about the film. In essence, Lippincott was priming the target audience for the most successful movie merchandising campaign in history.

There was one unfortunate result. The Lucasfilm production office at Universal (ironically, although the film was produced by Fox, Lucas remained at his old base) was burglarized and photographic copies of some of the original Ralph McQuarrie artwork, storyboards and other sketches were taken. "We were angry, of course," Lippincott says. "But in a perverse sort of way it told us that the buzz about STAR WARS was getting out there."

While the film was an overnigh box-office and media sensation, the me chandise only trickled out at first fro surprised manufacturers. They had nev er heard of a movie spawning successfu licensed products, much less one wit weird-sounding character names suc as Princess Leia Organa of Alderaan o Obi-Wan Kenobi. The paperback nove ization of the screenplay, released si months before the film, had sold out; th first issues of the Marvel comics also ap peared prior to the film's opening an did quite well. There were a couple of ad vance theatrical posters—one notabl because it was printed on silvery "my lar" stock—a couple of cast and crev promotional items, and that was it.

But after May 25, 1977 things wer never quite the same. Moviegoers, caugh up in this new universe, wanted to tak

A galaxy of goodies: Mask maker Don Post produced a friendly Chewbacca mask and discontinued the first—and fiercer—version; Lucas considered an R2-D2 cookie jar (produced later by Roman Ceramics) when he saw Ralph McQuarrie's sketches of the droid; Topps bubble gum cards and STAR WARS *pillow cases by Bibb were must-haves for young fans.*

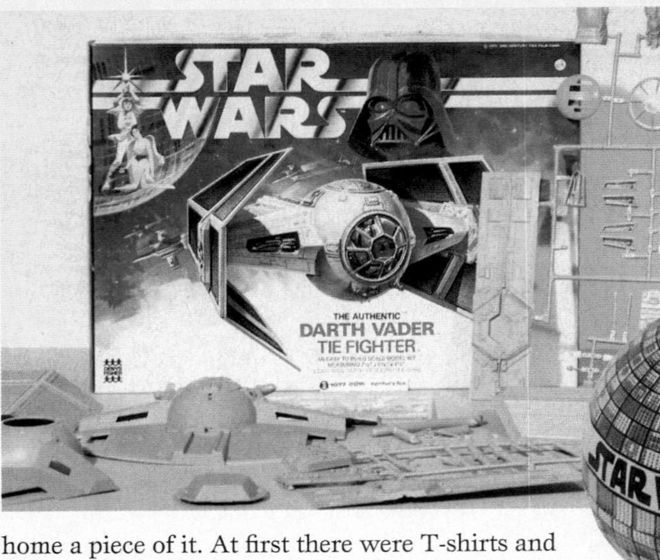

home a piece of it. At first there were T-shirts and iron-on transfers, jewelry and badges that spelled the arch-villain's name wrong (Darth Vadar). Those posters that fantasy and comics conventioneers had bought for a buck started commanding $10, and there were other, commercially produced posters to buy. Some sheets and pillow cases, the first of many sets of stickers and trading cards, sheet music, a couple of books… but no toys.

If ever there had been a "toyetic" movie, in the words of one toy industry visionary, this was it. And four months before STAR WARS opened, Kenner Products, now a unit of Hasbro, decided to give it a shot. Kenner didn't know if the film would be a big hit, but that didn't matter. Space toys had been sort of moribund since the early 1950s, yet this one film had enough action, adventure and neat ships and gadgets to make a natural toy line.

Bernie Loomis, then president of Kenner, assumed that the film would come and go quickly, and that when the toys arrived a year later they would have to stand on their own. Kenner's contract called only for one "all-family action board game" in 1977 and perhaps three different playsets with figures the following year. But the sci-fi-obsessed design department worked overtime to come up with ideas and prototypes to present to Fox and Lucas, who had the right of final approval.

The central decision in the launch of the STAR WARS line—one that not only assured its success but affected the entire toy industry—was made in Loomis' office one morning in March 1977. Loomis called head designer David Okada a little after 7 a.m. and asked him to come upstairs to help figure out "what we're going to do with these STAR WARS figures." Kenner had been successful with 12-inch-tall *Six Million Dollar Man* dolls, as Hasbro had been with G.I. Joe. But if the only Han Solo figure was going to be 12 inches tall, his spaceship, the *Millennium Falcon*, would have to be fiv feet in diameter and cost several hundred dollar

"We were hashing it around, trying to decid what to do, when Bernie held up his right han the thumb and forefinger apart, and asked, 'Ho about *that* big, Dave?'" Okada recounts. The d signer took a six-inch steel ruler from his shi pocket, measured the open space at 3 3/4", an both men decided that would be as good height as any for Luke Skywalker, wit the other figures scaled to size.

While Kenner thought that kid would pick and choose among the favorite characters, it turned out th at the initial price of around $2 a fi ure, they wanted them all (the lin grew to 115 figures by '85), plus eve kind of packaging and other variation The size of the figures also led to re sonable prices for vehicles and playset

The initial plan was to turn o three vehicles and six small action fi ures, but after STAR WARS premiere more than 30 products were put into d velopment overnight. Kenner managed get out some boxed puzzles, paint-b number sets and even a board game b late fall, but it just couldn't produce a tion figures or vehicles in time for Chris mas. So the toy maker sold a promise. F about $10, fans could buy a tightly seale certificate package containing a thin car

Darth Vader's TIE fighter was a popular model kit—and ILMers found some models so real, they could use them in making* Empire. *Helix, in England, made a 3-D Death Star pencil sharpener. And you could collect* STAR WARS *plastic cups from Coke via fast-food chains.

In between movies, STAR WARS *fans have been glued to a galaxy of adventures in print* BY DON CHARLES

PUBLISHING EMPIRE

The last we saw of our *STAR WARS* heroes on the silver screen, they were celebrating the destruction of the second Death Star and the fall of the Empire. But by no means was that the end of the *STAR WARS* story. In the nearly 14 years since the *Return of the Jedi*—and especially during the '90s—Lucasfilm has worked with a select group of publishing partners to weave an ever thicker and richer *STAR WARS* tapestry with new exploits and revelations of Jedi history in the form of novels, non-fiction books, comics, trading cards and roleplaying games.

NOVELS

While the occasional *STAR WARS* book tickled the public's fancy in the '70s—notably *Splinter of the Mind's Eye* by Alan Dean Foster in '78—it wasn't until 1991 that the *STAR WARS* universe took on a life of its own in hardcover, adult novel form. That's when Bantam Books and Lucasfilm teamed up with best-selling science fiction author Timothy Zahn to expand the *STAR WARS* universe in *Heir to the Empire*, the first of a Zahn trilogy.

The initial story is set five years after the events in *Jedi*, when the Empire is in shambles. A new villain, Grand Admiral Thrawn, has plans to overthrow the New Republic while Leia, Han and Luke are caught in political turmoil. The book hit number one on the *New York Times* best-seller list and effectively kicked off a renaissance of *STAR WARS* interest.

Other novels, written by top science fiction authors, followed. The events they cover include the marriage of Han and Leia and the birth of their three children, who all exhibit Jedi powers; the gradual evolution of a new galactic government, under constant threat from the feisty Empire; and Luke's revival of ancient Jedi skills.

Among more than 20 best-selling titles:

- *The Courtship of Princess Leia* by Dave Wolverton. Four years after *Jedi*, Leia is offered a new home for Alderaan's refugees if she marries Prince Isoldar.
- The Jedi Academy trilogy by Kevin J. Anderson. Luke starts a training academy for young Jedi Knights.
- *Children of the Jedi* by Barbara Hambly. The Rebels search for the long-lost children of the Jedi.
- The Corellian trilogy by Roger MacBride Allen. Han Solo returns to his home planet where he faces off against an evil cousin.
- *The Crystal Star* by Vonda McIntyre. Leia's children are kidnapped.
- *Darksaber* by Kevin J. Anderson. A group of Hutt crime lords attempt to build a weapon, the Darksaber, and take over the galaxy.
- *Shadows of the Empire* by Steve Perry, a multimedia venture also including comics, cards, video game and soundtrack. In plotting to assassinate Luke, evil Prince Xizor pits Darth Vader against the Emperor.

Bantam continues to publish several original hardcover titles annually, as well as paperback and audiobook editions.

Over the years, Random House's Del Rey division has produced novelizations of the movies and two original trilogies, The Lando Calrissian Adventures and The Han Solo Adventures.

For younger readers, Berkley Books produces Young Jedi Knights and Junior Jedi Knights series. The Young Jedi follows the adventures of Han and Leia's twins, Jacen and Jaina (age 14), while Junior Jedi centers on their third son, Anakin, as he trains to be a Jedi at his uncle's academy. Bantam also publishes a series of books geared for 8-to-12 year olds, while Little, Brown offers a line of juvenile pop-up books.

NONFICTION BOOKS

Del Rey has examined the saga in a variety of projects. Among more than two dozen titles are an "art-of" trilogy that reproduces storyboards, sketches and other art from all three films; guides to characters, vehicles, weapons and planets; technical journals (with Starlog Press) featuring blueprints; trivia books; annotated script books for the original movies;

companions for the NPR radio dramatizations of the movies and an upcoming ultimate encyclopedia.

STAR WARS non-fiction titles also include:

- A guide to STAR WARS collectibles (toys, games, posters, cards, etc.) published by Tomart.
- *The Illustrated STAR WARS Universe*, a coffee-table compendium featuring art by Ralph McQuarrie and text by Kevin J. Anderson, from Bantam.
- Behind-the-scenes books, with rare photos from the films and Lucasfilm Archives, from Chronicle Books.
- Two books documenting the first and second decades of Industrial Light & Magic, from Ballantine.
- Strategy guides to the STAR WARS PC and video games from LucasArts Entertainment, from Prima Publishing and Brady Games.

COMIC BOOKS

One of the first STAR WARS-related items to hit the shelves in 1977 was the adaptation of the movie by Marvel Comics. Marvel also produced a monthly series, annuals and a black-and-white magazine.

Marvel adapted *Empire* and *Jedi*, too, often exploring some then-minor characters and cultures, such as bounty hunters Zuckuss, IG-88 and Boba Fett, Luke's childhood friend and fellow Rebel pilot Biggs and Chewbacca's homeworld of Kashyyyk.

Dark Horse Comics acquired the license in 1991 and began publishing new STAR WARS adventures beginning with *Dark Empire*. The series, created by writer Tom Veitch and artist Cam Kennedy, was set six years after the events in *Jedi* and introduced readers to another malevolent Emperor, a clone of the deceased Palpatine; it was followed by *Dark Empire II* in 1994-95.

Dark Horse has pursued other STAR WARS stories, such as Jabba's nefarious business dealings, Boba Fett's bounty hunting, the droids' pre-Luke background and centuries-old Jedi history. Dark Horse has compiled several anthologies, including collections of the old Marvel titles and the newspaper strip.

TRADING CARDS

During the 1970s, science fiction-themed cards were not in high demand. But Topps executives had a hunch STAR WARS might be different. When the movie opened to huge business, they contracted with Lucasfilm to produce the original STAR WARS movie trading cards, followed by *Empire* and *Jedi* series.

Topps wasn't the only producer of STAR WARS-related cards. General Mills and Wonder Bread each produced sets in 1978, as promotional tie-ins, and the trend continued with *Empire* and *Jedi*.

In 1993, Topps introduced the first of three STAR WARS Galaxy card sets that showcase various artists' interpretations of the STAR WARS mythos. The series features preliminary sketches and production art by Ralph McQuarrie as well as visions by top comics and book-cover illustrators. Companion trade paperback books were produced for the first two series.

Two years ago, Topps debuted its three-part STAR WARS Widevision series—extra-wide images taken directly from laser disks of the entire trilogy; a *Special Edition* set is about to be released. Topps latest innovation is a STAR WARS Widevision series in 3-D.

ROLEPLAYING GAMES

Roleplaying games, in which two or more players take on the persona of STAR WARS characters and act out adventures, have added a wealth of background to the STAR WARS legend. Since the late '80s, West End Games has produced a wide series of STAR WARS roleplaying game sourcebooks and game adventures.

The company provides gamers with detailed skill descriptions of all aspects of the STAR WARS universe: backstories for existing and newly created characters; technical information about ships, vehicles and weapons; characteristics of environments and planets; and history and cultural references.

MAGAZINES

Currently, Lucasfilm has licensed two quarterly American magazines, *STAR WARS Galaxy Magazine* (Topps) and *STAR WARS Insider* (The Fan Club, Inc). Last year, British Publishers Titan launched *Star Wars: The Official Magazine* in the UK. There are also licensed STAR WARS magazines in France, Germany and Australia.

oard "stage" for the first 12 action figures, a few assorted pieces f paper and a certificate redeemable by mail for the first four acion figures. About 600,000 were shipped, although many weren't old. But those who mailed in their coupons got a set of four *STAR VARS* figures early in 1978—the first of some 250 million small acion figures that would be sold worldwide over the next eight years. A so-called Early Bird Certificate Package still sealed now rings about $150 in the collectors' market.)

There were many figure variations. The first Luke, 'ader and Obi-Wan figures had a hard plastic lightsaber hat telescoped twice, but it was complicated and ostly, so it was quickly replaced with a lightsaber hat telescoped once. The tiny Jawa went from vearing a vinyl cape to a somewhat richer-lookng cloth cape. Today, the "cheap-looking" vinylaped Jawa sells for $1,400 or so mint and sealed n a card—more than 20 times the cost of its clothaped counterpart.

Mistakes were made. Kenner's Cantina Advenure Set, a Sears exclusive for Christmas 1978, inluded four new action figures. One was Snaggletooth, 3 3/4″ figure dressed in royal blue with beige gloves nd silver boots. The only reference Kenner had showed the reature cut off at the waist, so its designers had to guess. ctually, Snaggletooth was short, with hairy hands nd large, ugly paws for feet. The revised naggletooth released later on a card was nly 3″ tall and wore a red uniform nd no boots or gloves.

While *STAR WARS* collectng has always been toyriven, there were hundreds f other kinds of products vorldwide. More than 00 manufacturers sold nillions of individual tems tied to *STAR VARS*, *The Empire trikes Back*, *Return f the Jedi* and all f their offshoots hrough the middle 980s. Among the arly major licensees for he first trilogy was the Bibb o. with a line of *STAR WARS* sheets, illow cases, blankets, bedspreads, sleeping bags, curtains, beach ads, beach towels, bathroom towels and washcloths. Bibb had diferent designs—Galaxy, Space Fantasy, Lord Vader and Jedi Knight, nd special designs for Sears, J. C. Penney, Montgomery Ward and atcliffe Bros. in England. And that was just for the first film.

Don Post Studios, a small California mask maker, saw its busiess soar as it produced authentic-looking overhead masks of six ifferent characters, and then added more for the next two films. he current *STAR WARS* revival finds new Don Post masks—as well as the earlier ones—hot all over again. While the home Super 8-millimeter film business was giving way to home video in the late 1970s, Ken Films did its best business ever by selling a few minutes of *STAR WARS* excerpts.

By 1979 there were *STAR WARS* Halloween costumes and masks, overalls and jackets, digital and analog wristwatches, T-shirts, socks, shoes, sneakers and sandals, plastic tableware, greeting cards, gift wrap, a syndicated newspaper comic strip, flying rockets, plastic model kits, wallpaper, buttons and patches, lunch boxes, belts and buckles, jewelry, school supplies, ceramic mugs, banks and cookie jars, posters, trading cards, records and tapes, books and comics, pajamas and robes, sheets and towels—and, of course, lots of toys.

One of the more prized* STAR WARS *toys among collectors is the chipboard Death Star playset distributed by Palitoy in England, Kenner Canada and Toltoys in Australia—and worth up to $650 in mint condition. Japanese companies made a number of Jedi-worthy toys, including one of Lucas' favorites, a 2″ walking R2-D2 wind-up by Takara.

Right: Passports to the set of* Empire *were few and far between and are now highly prized collectibles. Below: Rarities Mint issued sets of gold and silver coins, sculpted by artist Karen Worth, to commemorate* Star Wars' *10th anniversary. Far right: A Yoda statuette from Killian Industries sculpted by Larry Noble.

The U.S. merchandising success was repeated around the world. In the United Kingdom alone there were 36 manufacturers with 136 products. England's Helix International made one of the few three-dimensional representations of the Death Star: a round metal pencil sharpener for 35 pence. In Spain, Ediciones Manantial made an R2-D2 rotating calendar and a C-3PO mobile. Italy's Edizioni Panini produced a stamp album story book. You could eat *Star Wars* in Europe and Asia—and eventually in the U.S.—with C-3PO's, a breakfast cereal from Kellogg. In England, there were ice lollies, lemon chew bars and molded marshmallows in the shapes of C-3PO, R2-D2 and Darth Vader. Italy had licorice twists. There were ice cream bars in Australia and Malaysia. And in Japan, those with a hankering could buy chocolate or caramel candy, rice snacks and dry bread sticks—all with small *Star Wars* premiums like Cracker Jack prizes. For *Jedi*, England's Bridge Farm Dairies offered *Star Wars* low-fat yogurt in eight varieties, including Jabba the Hutt Peach Melba.

There were promotional tie-ins galore. *Star Wars* trading cards were stuffed with 65 million loaves of Wonder Bread. General Mills ran cereal promotions with plastic tumblers, kites, cards, stickers and miniature cardboard vehicles. The cereal boxes themselves are quite collectible, as are the hundreds of different in-store point-of-purchase displays that manufacturers used to attract buyers. There were collectors' cards on six-pack trays of Hershey candy bars; and hats, placemats and even a sweepstakes to win an in-home appearance by Darth Vader from the maker of Dixie Cups.

R2-D2 and C-3PO promoted childhood immunization campaigns in the U.S. and Australia and a savings campaign for the German Post Office and a bank in Australia. The biggest beverage tie-in was with the Coca-Cola Co. In the U.S., there were dozens of different plastic cups and glasses to collect from fast food outlets and convenience stores. Coke also offered a flying disc collectors' cards and a stamp album. In Asia and Canada, many of the offers were tied to collecting bottle caps with photos of characters or vehicles inside. In Japan, there were 50 assorted caps and an R2-D2 radio with a Coca-Cola logo as a premium. Twenty years later, it is Coke's chief rival, PepsiCo, that has become Lucasfilm's major partner for the launch of the *Star Wars Trilogy Special Edition* and the first of the new prequels.

While the foreign toy market was dominated by Kenner replicas, there were some notable exceptions. In England, Palitoy sold a brightly colored chipboard Death Star playset that is highly prized by collectors. In Japan, Takara's line of toys included a sonic-controlled R2-D2 that "spits" plastic discs and another with a viewer in its stomach showing seven various scenes from *Star Wars*. Takara also produced one of George Lucas' favorite toys—a two-inch-tall wind-up, walking R2-D2.

Besides the licensed products, there are other, non-mass produced items that *Star Wars* fans seek for their collections. These include various size posters and lobby cards made for movie theaters, along with press books and press kits. In the U.S. alone, the trilogy produced an amazing 23 different one-sheets, the standard 27" x 41" posters that theaters hang in outdoor and lobby frames. Distinctive foreign posters from countries like Israel, Hong Kong nd Poland and advertising sheets for international products well the number of posters to well over 1,000.

There are also limited-edition promotional items, including a Lucite star that was given at early *Star Wars* fund-raising screenings, brass paperweights with the films' names and even a "passport" used to admit VIPs to the set of *The Empire Strikes Back* in England. Some collectors seek original art from the posters or books, and there are some props and costumes that have made it into the collecting world.

Lucasfilm has occasionally given away such things as a piece of the Death Star in a fan club sweepstakes. And sometimes it has donated items for charity auctions. These have included an original script autographed by Lucas ($3,500), a C-3PO hand ($5,000) and a mounted Darth Vader helmet, mask and shoulder plate from *Empire* ($20,000). But unlike nearly every other filmmaker, Lucas has kept most of the props and costumes in the company's archives. So most allegedly authentic props and costumes offered by dealers and even usually reputable auction houses have turned out to be bogus.

Left: Detailed 11″ vinyl figurines, including this one of Luke and Yoda, are produced by Applause, as are multipacks of* Star Wars *action figures (right). Below: Prototypes for Kenner's 2″-3″ metal figures show tiny details and can be fit together in a variety of scenes. Below right: Don Post appeals to legions of Boba Fett fans with this replica of the bounty hunters' helmet.

By 1985 the *Star Wars* line was fading despite the best efforts of Kenner and other licensees. There were no more films in the series—at least for the foreseeable future. Attempts to do lines based on the short-lived *Droids* and *Ewoks* TV cartoon series were more popular in some European countries than the U.S.

Still, there were events such as the 10th anniversary celebration of *Star Wars*, a 1987 fan convention that got lots of media coverage. There are now Star Tours rides—and merchandise—at four Disney theme parks on three continents. Collectors' silver and gold coins released in 1988 have zoomed through the stratosphere; coin dealers say there were only 14 complete sets of all 24 coins minted, and they are now quoted at $20,000-$25,000 for the full set.

Star Wars collecting has gone through several phases. At first, diehard collectors were a source of amusement for some. "You collect *that*? But isn't that stuff still in the stores?" some would ask. Trekkers would smirk. Toy show promoters had to be cajoled into letting any *Star Wars* merchandise be put out on dealers' tables. "There seems to be so much of it around; are people really buying those things?" the promoters asked. Yes, they were. They still are. Only more so.

At first, the original 12″ dolls took off in price, a crossover for *Star Wars* and doll collectors. A few of

in with a small line of *Star Wars* metal figures in its Action Masters line, its plastic action figures, with sculpting and "attitude" for the play patterns of the '90s, have been such a hit that demand often has outrun supply. The toys have been at or near the top of toy trade industry best-seller lists ever since their introduction. Lewis Galoob Toys has also won over buyers' hearts with an extensive line of *Star Wars* Micro Machines and playsets, and a new and larger line called the *Star Wars* Action Fleet.

Applause has scored with meticulously sculptured vinyl figures, Hallmark with Christmas ornaments, Illusive Concepts with movie maquettes and Icons with the first-ever authorized prop replicas. And there are costumes, masks, calendars, greeting cards, model kits, new and reissued posters, keychains, refrigerator magnets, postage stamps, framed clips of actual 70mm film prints, chromium art and more to come.

All of that precedes the first of the *Star Wars* prequels, targeted for the summer of 1999. In the late 1970s, a Kenner advertising agency came up with a marketing slogan that the toy company used for years. It is even truer today: *Star Wars* is forever!

the rarer ones were bid up to $400 or so in mint boxes. Then the vehicles became popular. And the posters. And finally the action figures, which have been red-hot since about 1991.

What's driven the current round of *Star Wars* mania? For one thing, an entire generation of youngsters has grown up with the trilogy. The merchandise evokes childhood memories. Now that many of those fans are entering the work force, they have the money to try to recreate those warm feelings. And an even newer generation of kids who were born after 1977 has watched the films over and over on video.

But the renaissance really kicked in with the publication starting in June 1991 of Timothy Zahn's trilogy of new *Star Wars* novels, the first of which, *Heir to the Empire*, zoomed to first place on the all-important *New York Times* best-seller list. Other novels, nonfiction and comics started appearing, and after years of being suspended in carbonite, the *Star Wars* license became hot again.

Lucasfilm has carefully nurtured the *Star Wars* property, never pushing products out before there was a demand for them. "There's a natural life cycle to properties with strong kid appeal," notes Howard Roffman, Lucasfilm's Vice President of Licensing. "Even classics like Mickey Mouse go through cycles. The kids who were enamored of *Star Wars*, and their younger brothers and sisters, started to grow out of it in the mid '80s, and there weren't any new films to attract the next group."

Even so, four years ago, Roffman said he was convinced the phenomenon was far from dead; it was just resting in the public's subconscious. "When the public is ready for *Star Wars* again, you can be sure we'll be there to provide what they want."

Those were prophetic words. Although Kenner tiptoed back

Star Wars *collectibles run the gamut from the basic to the outrageous. Walnut-sized helmet playsets from Galoob open to reveal tiny figures in an action scene. But a full-size replica of a Rebel X-wing, while too big for the toy chest, packs a lot more punch. This fiberglass-over-steel starfighter was auctioned off by Neiman Marcus last Christmas.*

Steve Sansweet is the author of Star Wars: From Concept to Screen to Collectible *and* Tomart's Price Guide to Worldwide Star Wars Collectibles.

THE
ART
OF
STAR

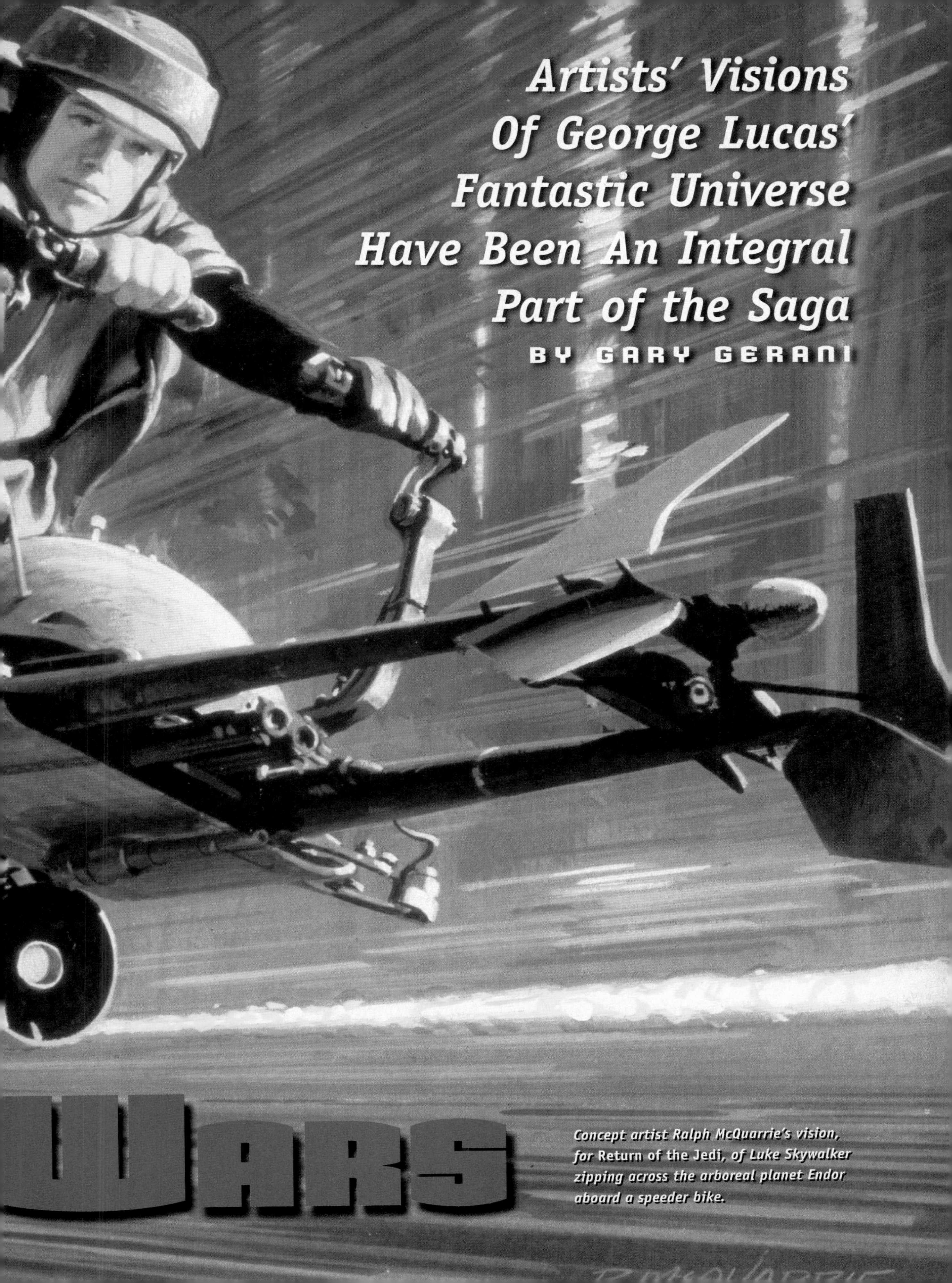

Artists' Visions Of George Lucas' Fantastic Universe Have Been An Integral Part of the Saga

BY GARY GERANI

WARS

Concept artist Ralph McQuarrie's vision, for Return of the Jedi, *of Luke Skywalker zipping across the arboreal planet Endor aboard a speeder bike.*

Art From The Archives

Art that's now part of the Lucasfilm Archives played a pivotal role throughout the production of the trilogy, from concept sketches of creatures and costumes to matte paintings used as backgrounds during filming. Clockwise from top left: Harrison Ellenshaw's matte painting of Boba Fett's Slave I at Cloud City; early sketches of the wampa ice creature and Yoda by Joe Johnston; miniature AT-AT models against an airbrushed background; development sketches by Nilo Rodis-Jamero of snouted aliens, Ree-Yees, Oola and the Emperor.

WONDERFUL!

ASSORTED ALIENS
©LFL

Three Eyes ©LFL 1981

Ralph McQuarrie

Imagine an artist having to create an entire universe based on another man's vision. So it was for illustrator Ralph McQuarrie. Here are several of his interpretations for the STAR WARS *trilogy. Clockwise from far left: production painting of an Imperial TIE fighter closing in on a Rebel X-wing in* STAR WARS*; approaching heavenly Cloud City in* The Empire Strikes Back*;* Empire's *motley crew of Han-seeking bounty hunters; in* Return of the Jedi *Luke defeated a rancor beast; Max Rebo's "jizz-wailer" band from* Jedi.

It was the summer of 1977. We'd been hearing for months about George Lucas' new movie, a grand space adventure boasting dueling spacecraft, exotic droids and a myriad of bizarre alien creatures. We couldn't wait to experience it first-hand. In those days, movie posters were often our first visual encounter with a motion picture. And those early *STAR WARS* posters did much to fuel our expectations.

Before we entered the theater, we were confronted not by a pretentious photo collage of superstar faces—the norm in today's marketing mentality—but rather by a breathtaking, classical-style painting by artist Tommy Jung, who specializes in heroic fantasy illustration. That was the tip-off: *STAR WARS* embraced the swashbuckling romance of the past without apology, updating it with a storyline that was fresh and vital for a receptive new audience.

Art and creative design had played integral roles at every stage of *STAR WARS*' existence—from the initial pitches to Hollywood executives to the posters advertising the release to comic books and other collectibles that the movie's fans craved—and did so with unprecedented success.

"Today, more than 15 years since the release of *STAR WARS*, fantasy art continues to play a dynamic role in the history of the saga," George Lucas said in 1992. "For me, it's been a gratifying creative journey that is not even halfway completed."

That journey began in the mid-1970s. Lucas had completed his screenplay and was looking for ways to turn his script into a motion picture. At the time, Hollywood's attitude toward science fiction was lukewarm, at best. Films such as *Westworld*, *Soylent Green* and *Logan's Run* had been expensive productions that were short on box-office returns. Lucas knew he had to find a way to convince studio heads that his story was different—and, in the process, help them "see" the final product. He realized the best way to convey his exotic vision to no-nonsense movie execs was through a series of illustrations.

"I never really thought *STAR WARS* would become a film when I was working on those original paintings," admits concept designer Ralph McQuarrie, the artist Lucas selected to help create those studio presentations. "It seemed so funky at the time, so vast a project."

Nevertheless, it was McQuarrie's breathtaking vistas that helped convince 20th Century-Fox executives that *STAR WARS* was a worthwhile gamble. His compelling alien landscapes, vehicles and life forms set the style of the film, and when Fox gave the project the green light, McQuarrie stayed on to develop those concepts in greater detail.

He was joined by other accomplished artists. Joe Johnston, Phil Tippett, Ron Cobb and Rick Baker all contributed astonishing alien and vehicle designs. Aggie Guerard Rodgers and Nilo Rodis-Jamero conceived the imaginative costumes. And, of course, a new age of computer-controlled special effects was inaugurated by the film's Special Photographic Effects Supervisor, John Dykstra, who won an Academy Award for his efforts.

"To make [the *STAR WARS* films], a team of amazingly talented artists and designers had to create creatures, vehicles and environments that began only as words on a page," says Lucas. "Art also became a significant factor in the advertising for the trilogy because each movie poster had to convey the complex moods of the film in a single painting."

One of the very first *STAR WARS* posters was never intended for display in movie theater lobbies. Unlike most '70s film producers, Lucas was a huge fan of science fiction, and recognized the importance of sci-fi conventions as a forum for promoting upcoming film projects. He wanted his movie to have a presence at those events. (Now it's standard practice to preview such movies at conventions.) Comic book illustrator Howard Chaykin rendered a now-classic poster of an intense, almost Marvel-esque Luke Skywalker brandishing his lightsaber. The image dazzled convention patrons, who had never heard of the

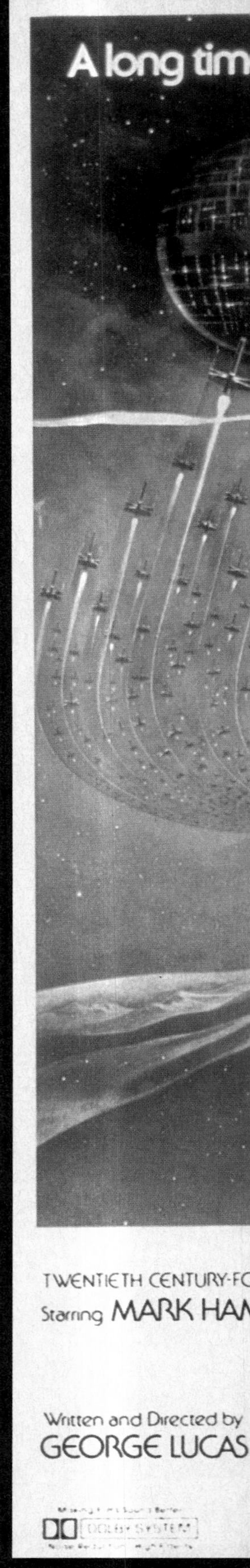

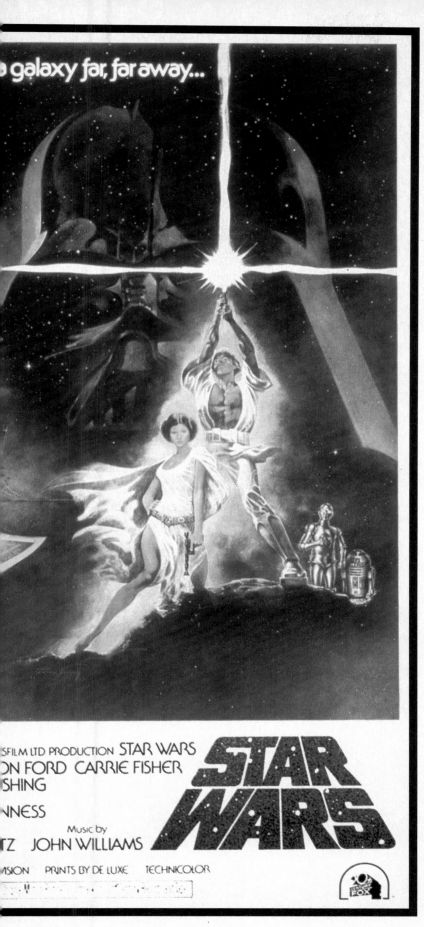

a galaxy far, far away...

SFILM LTD PRODUCTION STAR WARS
ON FORD CARRIE FISHER
SHING
NNESS
Music by
TZ JOHN WILLIAMS
VISION PRINTS BY DE LUXE TECHNICOLOR

STAR WARS

Poster Art

Tommy Jung's romantic movie poster style (left), emphasizing good-versus-evil, was a departure from the usual science fiction poster fare. A 1976 STAR WARS *comic poster by Howard Chaykin (above) is in keeping with comics art popular in the 1970s. A lithograph by Witold Dybowski (below) for the Polish release of* Return of the Jedi, *shows Darth Vader's exploding head and is considered one of the most unusual of all foreign posters.*

Comic Art

The space fantasy has continued in Star Wars *comics from Marvel and Dark Horse. Enlisted to help tell the stories are some of the best comics illustrators in the business. Clockwise from right: Hug Fleming's painting of Luke and Leia from Dark Horse's* Splinter of the Mind's Eye *cover; Fleming's chilling portrait for a cover from the* Dark Lords of the Sith *series; a page from* Dark Empire II *by Cam Kennedy; a page from Marvel's* Empire *adaptation, by Al Williamson and Carlos Garzon; Rebel heroes on Hoth, by Terry Austin, a bonus pin-up in Marvel's* Empire *series; another Marvel pin-up, of Luke and Vader, by Frank Miller.*

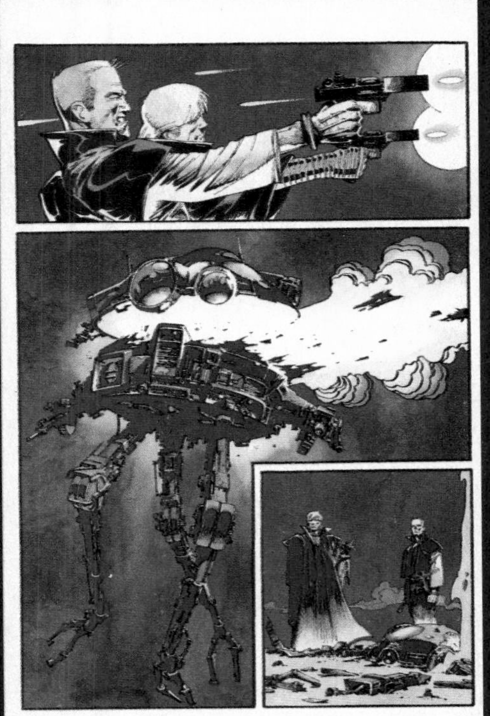

Hugh Fleming

character but now anxiously awaited his premiere appearance in the soon-to-be-released film.

That poster was so impressive that Lucas asked Chaykin to illustrate the official Marvel Comics adaptation of *STAR WARS* a short time later. The concept was ideally suited to the wildly fantastic comics medium. The original *STAR WARS* comic books, based on Lucas' screenplay and scripted by Marvel veteran Roy Thomas, were enormously successful and inspired an ongoing series of new tales, this time illustrated by Carmin Infantino. Later, young hotshot artists such as Arthur Adams and Walter Simonson brought their own visions to the series, which continued at Marvel until 1986, following comics versions of *The Empire Strikes Back* and *Return of the Jedi* .

In a related venture, comics legend Al Williamson illustrated the *STAR WARS* comic strip, which was syndicated in newspapers across the country from 1981-84. Williamson, a veteran of EC Comics' classic science fiction titles from the 1950s, was heavily influenced by Alex Raymond, Flash Gordon's creator, and had previously rendered the Flash Gordon newspaper strip. Williamson's elegant line and natural flair for swashbuckling space fantasy were well-suited to Lucas' characters.

Since the late 1980s, Dark Horse Comics has been publishing the ongoing adventures of Luke and his companions, opening up new directions for the characters and allowing artists such as Dave Dorman and Hugh Fleming the freedom to experiment with luminous, breathtaking cover paintings. Just as impressive is the interior line work by Cam Kennedy who, like Williamson, captures the soul of *STAR WARS* with his sensitive approach.

Of course, the international film promotion of *STAR WARS* enabled artists from different countries to interpret Lucas' flamboyant brainchild. Al-

Drew Struzan

at the saga continues in written form ves fans enormous satisfaction. Struzan, guably the best movie poster artist of our y, has also illustrated covers for many STAR ARS *novels. Left: The Bithian band, Figrin an and the Modal Nodes, depicted for the ver of the audio book* **We Don't Do Wed-ngs** *by Kathy Tyers. Right: Cover art for* **owdown at Centerpoint,** *whose action curs 14 years after the events in* **Return the Jedi.** *Below: Cover art for Barbara mbly's* **Children of the Jedi.**

though many foreign posters adhered to the Jung-style heroic composition, including a Spanish poster by twin artists Tim and Greg Hildebrandt, there were some notable exceptions. In Japan, artist Noriyoshi Ohrai played with extravagant, almost surreal color schemes. A Polish illustration for *Return of the Jedi* by Witold Dybowski features the startling image of Darth Vader's exploding head, a nice piece of pop symbolism.

Arguably the greatest movie poster painter of our time, Drew Struzan, began his association with *STAR WARS* back in 1978. For the summer rerelease of the film, Struzan worked with designer Charlie White III on what is commonly referred to as the "circus" poster, an imaginative simulation of a poster seemingly torn from a billboard display. Struzan would later illustrate Lucasfilm's campaigns for *Indiana Jones and the Temple of Doom* and the *Ewoks* TV movies; more recently, he's rendered covers for a series of Bantam hardcover novels based on the *STAR WARS* saga and its characters.

Assembling the various artistic creations into one collection was the goal of 1992's *STAR WARS* Galaxy, a trading-card set issued by The Topps Company that inspired two additional sets of cards, a pair of trade paperbacks

New Visions

New art inspired by the movies has helped build renewed interest in STAR WARS. *Clockwise from right: Salacious Crumb by comics artist Mike Zeck; Greedo, the bounty hunter, by painter Mike Lemos; Luke and Vader by the king of comics, Jack Kirby; an Ewok by motion picture and comics designer William Stout; R2-D2 and C-3PO by Peruvian painter Boris Vallejo; an Imperial stormtrooper aboard a dewback by veteran illustrator Al Williamson; bounty hunter Boba Fett by comic book artist Rick Buckler; Princess Leia by commercial artist-turned-comic illustrator Brian Stelfreeze; Ben Kenobi and Yoda by Russell Walks.*

LEMOS

Merchandising A

From lunch boxes to trading cards, Star Wars *art has been hot for 20 years. Clockwise from above: a 15-y anniversary commemorative plate by Morgan Weistli a scene from* Empire, *by Gene Lemery, appeared on lunch boxes; overseas video packaging showcased mo poster artist John Alvin; Michael Whelan's portrait o Yoda illustrated the cover of a journal; box art for th CD-ROM game Rebel Assault by Greg Winters; and* Famous Monsters *magazine featured this cover portr of a Tusken Raider by sci-fi artist Basil Gogos.*

and a quarterly magazine. For the first time, fans could revel in original production art, poster and promotion art and art developed for merchandising tie-ins and brand-new interpretations—called "New Visions"—by top illustrators inspired by the movies themselves.

Although the first collection of New Visions was created mostly by comic book illustrators—a veritable who's who of the industry—Series 2 and 3 of Galaxy boasted original work by mainstream artists (Gahan Wilson, Will Vinton, Joann Daley), as well as artists currently designing for motion pictures (Mark "Crash" McCreery, Mike Smithson, John Eaves, among many others). Veteran movie poster painter Joe Smith (*Ben Hur*, *Dr. Zhivago*, *The Birds*) was coaxed out of retirement to illustrate a series of portraits of the main characters, paintings that eventually wound up in the personal collection of George Lucas.

Not surprisingly, licensed products and promotions gave birth to a plethora of memorable *Star Wars* art. Samples of it are featured in the Galaxy sets, ranging from collectors' plates (Thom Blackshear, Morgan Weistling) to lunch boxes (Gene Lemery) to exquisite Coca-Cola painted posters (Boris Vallejo). Computer games and related graphics soon provided even more directions for the saga's imagery.

Star Wars art is ongoing, just as *Star Wars* the movie lives on, inspiring new generations of fans and future illustrators. George Lucas let the genie out of the bottle when he invited fellow artists to partake in Luke Skywalker's fantastic adventures. Now, we can all sit back and enjoy their breathtaking interpretations in every medium they appear. Like the Force itself, the excitement, romance and imagination of *Star Wars*—on film or in graphic art form—will be with us... always.

Gary Gerani is Topps' West Coast editor, based in Los Angeles.

Expanding Galaxy

As the galaxy of heroes and villains expands, so does the gallery of artistic interpretations of the Star Wars *phenomenon. At right, the Hildebrandts' take on Prince Xizor, the evildoer from Topps'* Shadows of the Empire *card set; Han Solo and Chewbacca as illustrated by Ray Lago for the Topps' card set* Star Wars *Finest; an explosive portrait by Chris Moeller of Boba Fett, the bounty hunter, cover art for issue 6 of* Star Wars Galaxy Magazine.

Special Edition-*inspired illustration of a ronto and scurriers by Jeff Rebner, color by Robert Ro, inking by Mark Irwin.*

In Good Compan

With Star Wars *as the cornerstone, George Lucas has built an impressive and cutting-edge galaxy of businesses*

BY STEVE SANSWEET

Of all the *Star Wars* legacies, few are more concrete than the group of companies that grew out o George Lucas' need to put on film things that had never been seen before, and that nay-sayers swor couldn't be done. Today, the Lucas companies are still pushing the boundaries of technology and cre ativity. And as they gear up for the *Star Wars* prequels, there's an even greater sense of excitemen and purpose than before. It's as if their mission statement was written by Yoda himself: "Try not. Do Or do not. There is no try."

Three Lucas companies have long been leaders in their fields. Lucasfilm Ltd., the parent compa ny, includes all of George Lucas' feature film and television activities, as well as the business activities of the THX Group and Lucasfilm Licensing. As one of the most successful independent production companies in the world, its feature films have garnered 44 Academy Award nominations and 17 Oscars. It has produced six of the top 20 box-office hits of all time.

In television, *The Young Indiana Jones Chronicles* received 25 Emmy nominations and 11 awards. THX which first set the standards for quality film presentation in theaters, is now having a major impact in the home And Lucasfilm Licensing, which carefully nurtured the *Star Wars* property during the commercially "quie years"—from about 1985-91—today represents one of the hottest licensed properties in the marketplace.

Digital Illustration By Slim Films, Photo of George Lucas By Eric Millette

SKYWALKER SOUND
INDUSTRIAL LIGHT + MAGIC
THX

The LucasArts Entertainment Company is one of the world's leading developers and publishers of interactive entertainment. Its *Star Wars*-based CD-ROM and video games consistently top the best-seller lists, and many of its originally created games are not far behind with their challenging play and creative sense of humor. LucasArts' titles have won more than 100 industry awards.

Lucas Digital Ltd. incorporates two divisions—Industrial Light & Magic (ILM) and Skywalker Sound. Beginning with its pioneering work on *Star Wars*, ILM virtually created the modern visual effects industry, and 20 years later is still the undeniable leader in an ever-changing field. In the past 17 years, ILM has won 14 Academy Awards for Best Visual Effects and nine technical achievement awards. It has worked on well over 100 films and played a key role in six of the top 10 box-office hits of all time, including the Indiana Jones series, *Terminator 2: Judgment Day*, *Forrest Gump* and *Jurassic Park*. Skywalker Sound is one of the largest and most versatile audio post-production facilities in the entertainment industry, and has received 10 Academy Awards for Outstanding Achievement in Sound and sound effects editing.

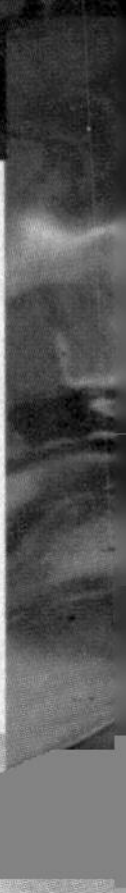

Lucasfilm itself has gone through a series of transformations over the years. Between 1977 and 1985, it concentrated on making the *Star Wars* and Indiana Jones films and started up ILM, Licensing, THX and a computer division. "Even back then, George was investing to bring digital technology into the filmmaking process," says Lucasfilm president Gordon Radley. "Out of the first computer division sprang a number of businesses and technologies: interactivity in the form of games from LucasArts; ILM's computer-graphics department; Pixar, which we later sold [and which then produced *Toy Story*]; and our Droid picture- and sound-editing technologies, which were acquired by Avid."

The period from 1985-89 was one of professionalization, Radley says. "We set up separate operating units for accountability and management responsibility." By 1989 there were 10-12 divisions all under one corporate umbrella, so film production was retained in Lucasfilm and everything else was put into a subsidiary called LucasArts. The divisions were then grouped according to their commonality, but there was still a tug when it came to strategic and capital needs. Another reorganization in 1993 led to the current three-company structure.

"During that period, the digital advances that George had pioneered were finally coming to fruition and creating a revolution in the entertainment industry," Radley says. "We expected turbulence and chaos in the industry, and we wanted to be nimble and able to address the future without being tied to any particular platform or hardware." Since 1993 the company has been more successful than at any point in its history, from a revenue and profit standpoint.

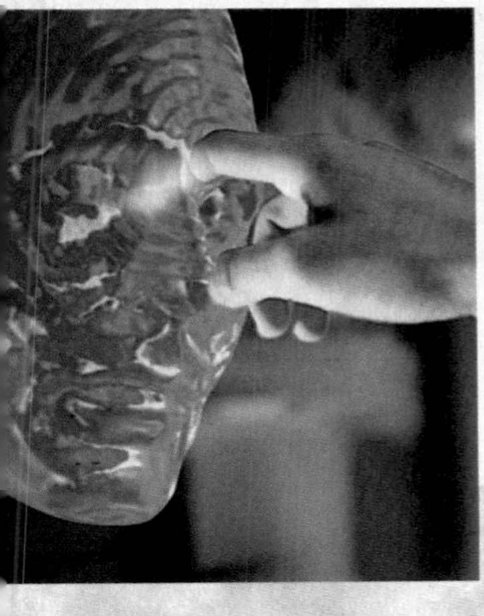

While George Lucas is chairman of his companies, he leaves the day-to-day operations to his top managers. "George is very good at being the chairman of the board," Radley notes. "He's sees the big picture, he's a company builder as well as a filmmaker, someone interested in education, and a person who creates unique work environments."

But having an owner who is also a client is a fairly rare situation. "If George needs special effects from ILM, he negotiates with them," Radley says. "The next day, he may make decisions about investing millions in new technology for ILM. But rather than seeing this as purely a numbers game, he'll look at how he and other filmmaker clients could take advantage of that new technology."

The emergence of Industrial Light & Magic has been one of the most enduring aspects of STAR WARS. *The company that revolutionized the special effects business has recently tapped the creative powers of the computer and forged into digital moviemaking with such films as (from top)* **Willow, The Abyss, Death Becomes Her** *and* **Jurassic Park.** *Left: ILM stalwarts at work.*

The next STAR WARS trilogy, Radley believes, is an opportunity, not a necessity. "These companies have been more successful than ever; the prequels just kicks it all to a different level."

At LucasArts' new headquarters near Skywalker Ranch, president Jack Sorensen is equally optimistic about the future of his business. In an industry where well-known players have been bought up, gone out of business or seen their lines shrivel, LucasArts is more successful than ever, with a library of 26 titles—17 based on STAR WARS or Indiana Jones—not including add-on programs or games ported to different systems. Its games are distributed in more than 30 countries and translated into seven languages.

What accounts for LucasArts' success? "From the beginning, the strategy hasn't changed," Sorensen says. "We have George Lucas as an example. He's creative, quality-oriented and story-oriented, but also aims at a very large audience. We've tried to avoid the fads in the industry and build good quality products—not a lot of them—but each one getting attention and each one an event when it hits the marketplace."

Lucasfilm's games operation—which became LucasArts—was launched in the early 1980s as a small group of about a dozen developers and has slowly evolved. "I view LucasArts as being no different from film or television or music, where you're really taking a gamble on every project based on its creative content and whether it's interesting and attractive and what people want," Sorensen says. "No one is successful every single time, and you have the technological uncertainty layered on top, but LucasArts does have a reputation as one of the most highly regarded developers in the world."

Risk is involved at every turn. "Two years ago when we said we were developing a Shadows of the Empire game for a new cartridge platform, the Nintendo 64, a lot of people thought we were nuts, but it will be one of our most successful titles," Sorensen says, referring to the recently released video game tied into *Shadows*, the STAR WARS multimedia project launched last year. The game is likely to join such LucasArts best-sellers as Rebel Assault, X-Wing and Dark Forces.

Around the same time LucasArts released Shadows for the Nintendo 64 last December, the company also came out with versions of the CD-ROM games Dark Forces and Rebel Assault II for Sony's Play Station.

The first quarter of '97 will see the introduction of X-Wing vs. TIE Fighter, Rebellion, a strategy game, and Jedi Knight, to coincide with the theatrical release of the *STAR WARS Trilogy Special Edition*.

"That body of products, across multiple genres and multiple platforms, just hasn't been done before," Sorensen says, "and that in many ways is only a warm-up for what we expect to be doing for the prequels. As the prequels come together, I think all the companies will be working very closely with one another. We'll continue our tradition of taking hints from what's in the film and extrapolating on them."

"We have George Lucas as an example. He's creative, quality-oriented and story-oriented, but also aims at a VERY large audience."

South on Route 101 from LucasArts is ILM, housed in a nondescript industrial park in San Rafael, Calif. The company logo—a magician pulling a rabbit out of his top hat—has long symbolized what its 700 employees do practically every day. "Our mission is to provide the best state-of-the-art visual effects and computer animation for motion pictures and to produce the best visual effects for television commercials, which now makes up about 25 percent of our business," says Jim Morris, president of Lucas Digital and general manager of ILM.

The addition of advertising work allows a cross-fertilization between the feature and commercial sides, and gives ILMers the chance to do projects of varied lengths and to play different creative roles, Morris notes. "When some of those people who produce or direct commercials come back to the feature side, they're better able to get into the heads of feature directors and get on the screen what they want. Conversely, in features, there's a longer period of time to do research and development, and that technology can then be applied to the commercial group."

What's truly amazing is that ILM has managed to stay on the cutting edge of the industry that it created 20 years ago, despite constant and revolutionary technological changes. "One of the main reasons ILM is what it is, is because of George [Lucas]," Morris says. "He started it to figure out a way to do the kinds of images he wanted in the STAR WARS films. Despite the fact that he never comes across as a techie, he has a high level of comfort and interest in [high technology]. There have been times when ILM wasn't exactly a profitable operation, but George kept it going to support his work and that of other filmmakers." Lucas' commitment and the happy convergence of a large number of creative and technical people over the years have created the kind of esprit de corps and culture that has served ILM well in the face of increasing competition.

Good projects breed more good projects, and ILM has had a large number of top-notch director clients who have constantly sought more and better visual effects. "All of our best innovations have resulted from the need to solve specific problems on projects," Morris says. Thus, among many other breakthroughs, ILM can boast:

* The first "morphing" or on-screen transformation sequence, in *Willow*.

* The first creation of a wholly computer-generated (CG), three-dimensional character, the "pseudopod" in *The Abyss*.

* The first main character "built" from computer graphics, the liquid-metal cyborg in *Terminator 2: Judgment Day*.

* The first CG human skin texture, in *Death Becomes Her*.

* The first use of digital technology to create realistic characters—dinosaurs—with skin, muscle and texture, in *Jurassic Park*.

* The first 3-D photo-real cartoon character, in *The Mask*.

* The first fully synthetic speaking characters with distinct personalities and emotions, the ghosts in *Casper*.

* The first CG hair and fur, in *Jumanji*.

For the coming years, ILM has already set a number of lofty goals. "Technologically, we want to create tools that are easier for ıe artists to use in order to create the kinds of images that directors ant," Morris explains. "We're also seeking faster processing of ıta in order to get more on screen in shorter periods of time, ıd to bring the cost of that imagery down."

And for those fans who pine about the "death" of tra-ıtional prop and model-making for the movies, Morris ɔtes that the demise has been much exaggerated. "A w years back, people thought we had seen the end f stage shots with miniatures," he says. "But ıite often the traditional solutions are the best, specially with things like pyrotechnics. Our odel shop and motion-control photography ɔerations are still going strong."

Another part of Lucas Digital is Sky-alker Sound. Its vice president and ɜneral manager, Gloria Borders, has ɜrsonally supervised sound editing on ɔme of the biggest films of the last 10 ɜars, including *Terminator 2*, for hich she won an Academy Award. he unit is headquartered in the 45,000 square-foot Technical Build-ıg at Skywalker Ranch. Borders versees a facility that has five mix-ıg rooms, numerous edit bays, ansfer rooms and a large scoring age that's been used by everyone om country singers to symphony rchestras. There's also a Foley ound effects) stage and a commer-al sound unit.

George Lucas has asked Borders redefine the state of post-produc-on on films when it comes to ɔund, and to make Skywalker ɔund ready for the all-digital future, ot only for the *Star Wars* prequels ut for the multitude of outside pro-cts that Skywalker Sound services. esides state-of-the-art technical facili-es, Skywalker Sound also offers on-anch accommodations and overall top uality at "prices that are beyond competi-ve," Borders says. "We have turned around ıe perception that we are too far away, too xpensive or that we only work on George's rojects," Borders says. "Plus, we have a talent ool that definitely is the best in the world."

Besides its own logo and that of *Star Wars*, erhaps the next most recognizable, if sometimes mis-nderstood part of Lucasfilm is its THX Group, which rives to provide the finest in film presentation, whether ı a movie theater or at home. "The impetus [for its creation] vas George Lucas' desire to improve film standards in exhibition ı the early 1980s," says Monica L. Dashwood, the division's general

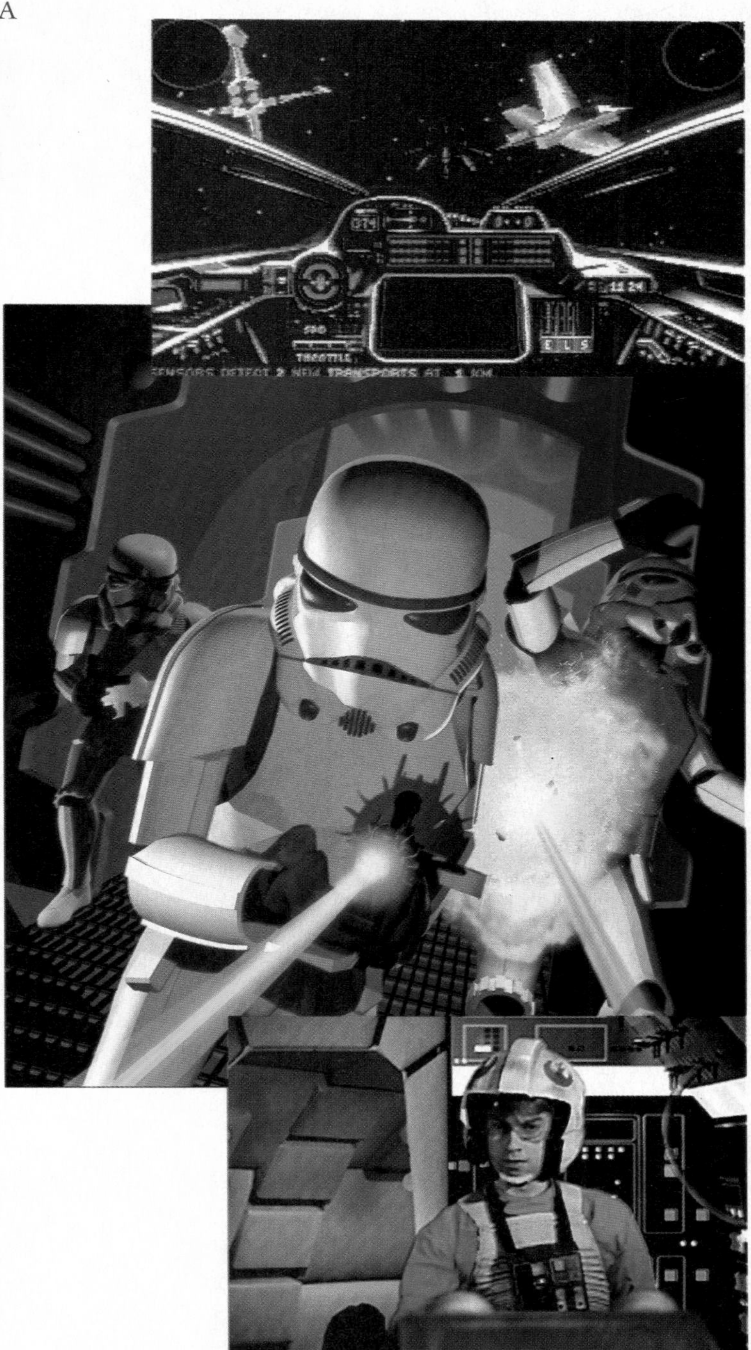

LucasArts Entertainment Company has emerged from the Lucasfilm business empire to become a pioneering leader in the video and PC game industry. Among the best-selling titles from LucasArts are X-Wing (top), Dark Forces (center) and Rebel Assault II, the sequel to the popular original.

manager. "He was frustrated when he went to theaters to see *Return of the Jedi* and found that some of the special effects and sounds they had worked so hard to create were lost in the presentation."

With a small group of engineers, Lucasfilm found the most effective way to duplicate the designs of the mixing room and translate them to the theater setting. Today THX is known for establishing standards in theaters and in homes. THX isn't a film format or the encoded sound information on a film, but rather the

What appears to be a grand Victorian manse is actually the main office building at Lucas' Skywalker Ranch.

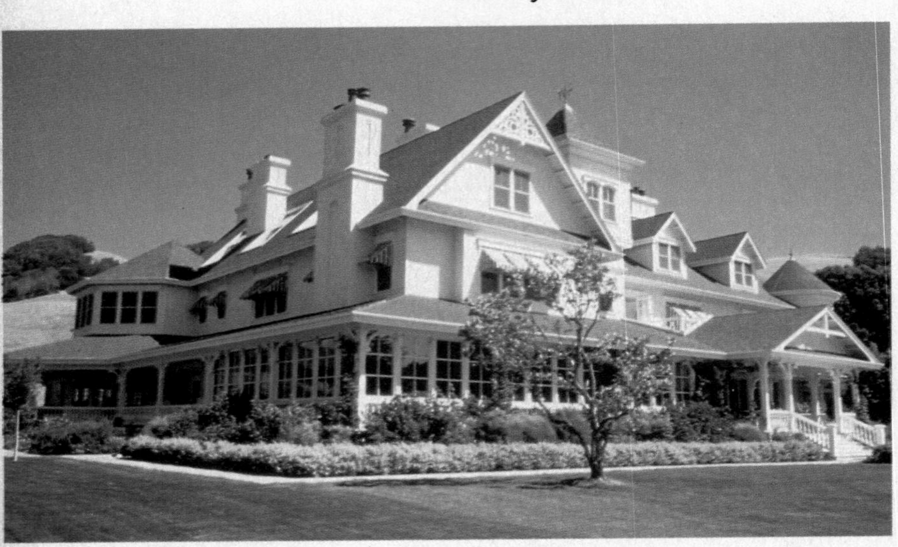

design of the playback environment. There are specific criteria that hardware manufacturers have to meet in order to get the THX trademark.

THX is now used on 1,400 theater screens, 35 percent of them outside the United States. The division works with more than 55 equipment manufacturers on the home-theater side. On the software side, through its THX Digital Mastering operation, the division certifies the quality of the transfer of a film to laser disk or videotape, the latter pioneered with the release of the STAR WARS trilogy in late 1995. "We make sure that the colors and sound are as close to the original master film as possible," Dashwood says. There are now well over 100 tape and disk titles that have received the THX mark.

Another THX unit, the Theater Alignment Program, works with studios to review prints of films when they come from labs and before they go to theaters. Later, a freelance staff of up to 400 people goes to selected films to evaluate how they are being presented in theaters across the country.

For some fans, Lucasfilm means three-inch STAR WARS action figures or trading cards or a new novel. The man behind all that is Howard Roffman, vice president of licensing. How does he explain the huge revival of interest in the original trilogy years before the next trilogy is scheduled to be released?

"One reason is that STAR WARS made such an impact on people's lives the first time around," Roffman says. "It wasn't something that you forgot after you left the theater; it stayed with you in so many different ways. As the original audience grew older, STAR WARS not only retained its relevance, but became a reminder of a lot of things for people as they went through different phases of their lives. STAR WARS is a timeless saga. It speaks as much to this generation as to the prior generation."

STAR WARS as a licensed property is stronger and broader today than ever before, Roffman explains. "That's because it's not only small kids buying products, but also grown-ups. Our philosophy is that we're not trying to drum up demand, we're satisfying demand. STAR WARS is too important, even 'sacred' to people, because it means something very personal to them. Everything we've done has been out of a belief that this is a product that has some integrity which will bring added enjoyment to people who are into STAR WARS. In virtually every case, the demand was there beyond our wildest expectations, and people just came back hungry for more."

The rerelease of the trilogy on video in late 1995, spurred by better technology, also fed demand. In fact, 20th Century-Fox Home Video sold three times more tapes than it had expected—nearly 30 million worldwide.

Lucasfilm Licensing tries to stay in touch with its audience to see what fans want, and has been aiming its products and promotions at older children and adults. But now the division sees younger children as part of the mix. In seeking licensees, Roffman says, it looks for companies with size and clout, but also those with a passion for STAR WARS. He points out that all six episodes, including the upcoming prequels, are all one story, and that "classic" STAR WARS, the original trilogy, will always remain one focus of licensed products.

"There can definitely be too much of a good thing, and it's our responsibility to keep STAR WARS enjoyable for the millions who love it," Roffman says. "We're not perfect, and it's possible we'll make some missteps along the way. But I don't think we'll ever again have the perception that existed after *Return of the Jedi*, that STAR WARS was dead, was over. I think we've learned 20 years after the original that it's never going to be over. The task now is to produce the new trilogy, see where that takes us and keep STAR WARS interesting and meaningful for many generations to come."